The College World		The Working World
Research Papers	Essay Examinations	Critical Papers	Reports
225–229	300	326–331	368–371
230–256	302–307	331–341	372–377
256–259	309	342–343	377–380
228, 259–262	301–302	326, 343–345	380–383
266–270	311–315	348	384–385
224			367–368
223–225	300	325–326	367–368
262–266	309–311	345–348	384–386
263		345–347	
263–264			
		347	384–386
264		347	
	316	348	
	316		
254–255, 267–273	318–319	349–352	386–388
272		349, 352	386–387
272		349–350	387–388
278–284	316–318	353–357	393–397
284–287	319	357–360	397–400

Four Worlds of Writing

Four Worlds

Second Edition

of Writing

Janice M. Lauer
Purdue University

Gene Montague
University of Detroit

Andrea Lunsford
The University of British Columbia

Janet Emig
Rutgers University

1817

Harper & Row, Publishers, New York
Cambridge, Philadelphia, San Francisco,
London, Mexico City, São Paulo, Singapore, Sydney

Sponsoring Editor: Phillip Leininger
Project Editor: Susan Goldfarb
Text Design: Betty L. Sokol
Text Art: Fineline Illustrations, Inc.
Production: Delia Tedoff
Compositor: York Graphic Services, Inc.
Printer and Binder: The Murray Printing Company

Credits

Four Worlds of Writing, Second Edition

Library of Congress Cataloging in Publication Data

Main entry under title:

Four worlds of writing.

Includes index.
1. English language—Rhetoric.   2. English language—Grammar—1950–   .   I. Lauer, Janice M.
PE1408.F547   1985   808′.042   84-25248
Regular edition ISBN: 0-06-043857-6
Special instructor's edition ISBN: 0-06-043859-2

85 86 87 88 9 8 7 6 5 4 3 2 1

BRIEF CONTENTS

Preface xv

Introduction 1

ONE Guide to Composing 19

1 **Writing with an Expressive Aim**
In the Private World / Places 20

2 **Writing with an Expressive Aim**
In the Private World / Persons 73

3 **Writing with a Persuasive Aim**
In the Public World / Issues 123

v

4   **Writing with a Persuasive Aim**
In the Public World / The Media   175

5   **Writing with an Expository Aim**
In the College World / Research Papers   223

6   **Writing with an Expository Aim**
In the College World / Essay Examinations   299

7   **Writing with an Expository Aim**
In the College World / Critical Papers   325

8   **Writing with a Dual Aim: Expository and Persuasive**
In the World of Work / Reports   367

TWO   Guide to Editing and Sentence-Combining   407

9   Editing   408

10   Sentence-Combining: Imitating and Generating Sentences   449

Appendix: Exploratory Guide   510

Glossary   517

Index   533

Front Endpaper: Table of Writing Acts and Strategies

Back Endpaper: Editing Symbols

DETAILED CONTENTS

Preface   **xv**

Introduction   **1**

The Processes of Writing   2
This Text and Your Writing Class   4
Four Worlds of Writing   5
    The Private World: Places and Persons   6
    The Public World: Shared Issues and the Media   8
    The College World   9

The Working World   11
Writing as Learning   12
Writing as a Multimodal Process   13
    Writing as a Record of Meaning   13
    Writing as a Whole-Brained Activity   15
Conclusion   16
    Notes   17

Guide to Composing   19

1 **Writing with an Expressive Aim   20**
In the Private World / Places

    Composing Processes   21
    Factors That Influence Writing   22
The Guiding Question and Potential Situations   23
    The Subject   23
    The Guiding Question   24
    Potential Situations   27
    Class Exercises   28
    Assignments   29
Exploration   30
Focus and Situation   41
    Incubation   41
    The Focus: Subject and Point of Significance   41
    The Situation: Audience and Medium   42
    Focus and Drafting   42
    The Focus in the Paper   43
    The Focus and the Expressive Aim   43
Audience and Modes of Organization   45
    Audience Roles   46
    Audience Analysis   47
    Modes of Organization   50
    Modes as Organization Versus Modes as Content   51
The First Version   53
Writing a Paper with an Expressive Aim   53
Reader Responses   56
Revising and Editing   61
    Problems of Focus   62
    Problems of Development   62
    Problems of Organization   63
    Problems of Style   63

Problems with Conventions   63
A Writer's Process   65

2   Writing with an Expressive Aim   73
In the Private World / Persons

The Guiding Question and Potential Situations   74
      The Subject   74
      The Guiding Question   74
      Potential Situations   76
Exploration   78
      Alternative Exploratory Guides   81
Focus and Situation   84
      From Exploration to Focus   84
Audience and Modes of Organization   86
      Setting the Role for the Audience   86
      Modes of Organization   89
The First Version   94
      Unity and Coherence   94
      Transitions   95
      Paragraphs   96
      The Expressive Style   103
Reader Responses   111
      A Writer's Process   117

3   Writing with a Persuasive Aim   123
In the Public World / Issues

The Guiding Question and Potential Situations   124
      The Subject   124
      The Guiding Question   125
      Potential Situations   127
Exploration   130
Focus and Situation   139
      Incubation   139
      A Persuasive Focus   139
Audience, Appeals, and Modes of Organization   142
      Setting the Role for the Audience   142
      Persuasive Appeals   145
      Misuse of the Appeals   146
      Strategies for Persuasive Appeals   146
      Organizing a Persuasive Paper   151
      Persuasive Plans   152
The First Version   156

Diction   156
Sentence Patterns   157
Reader Responses   162
Revising and Editing   166
A Writer's Process   170

4 Writing with a Persuasive Aim   175
In the Public World / The Media

The Guiding Question and Potential Situations   175
The Subject Context   175
Potential Situations   178
Exploration   180
Evaluation   181
Focus and Situation   187
Incubation   187
Formulating a Persuasive Focus   187
Choosing an Audience   187
Audience, Appeals, and Modes of Organization   190
Setting the Role for the Audience   190
Credibility and Affective Appeals   193
Rational Appeals   195
Organization   199
Organization Plans   201
The First Version   204
Refutation   206
The Persuasive Style   209
Reader Responses   211
Revising and Editing   214
A Writer's Process   217

5 Writing with an Expository Aim   223
In the College World / Research Papers

Aims for Research Writing   223
The Guiding Question and Potential Situations   225
The Subject   225
The Guiding Question   226
Potential Situations   228
The Audience   228
Exploration   231
Compiling a Working Bibliography   232
Annotating   236
Notetaking   241
Focus and Situation   256

Incubation   256
The Informative Focus   257
Audience and Modes of Organization   259
Organizing a Research Paper   262
The First Version   266
Citation   267
Quotation   268
The Informative Aim   269
Conventions in Research Papers   270
The Expository Style   272
Reader Responses   278
Revising and Editing   284
A Writer's Process   287

6   Writing with an Expository Aim   299
In the College World / Essay Examinations

The Expository Aim   300
Guiding Questions   300
Audience   301
Exploration: Preparing for the Examination   302
Incubation   307
Planning During the Examination   308
Time Plans   308
Focuses   309
Organization   309
Define   310
Explain   310
Compare and Contrast   311
Evaluate   311
The Examination   311
Reader Responses   315
Revising and Editing   318
The Expository Style   318
A Writer's Process   319

7   Writing with an Expository Aim   325
In the College World / Critical Papers

The Guiding Question   326
Audience and Situation   326
Poetry   327
Essays   328
Exploration   331
Exploring a Poem   331

Focus   342
    The Critical Focus   342
Audience and Modes of Organization   343
    Analyzing the Audience   343
    Modes of Organization   345
The First Version   348
    Refining the Expository Style   349
Reader Responses   353
Revising and Editing   357
    A Writer's Process   360

---

8 Writing with a Dual Aim: Expository and Persuasive 367
In the World of Work / Reports

    Expository and Persuasive Aims   368
The Guiding Question and Situation   368
Exploration   371
    Static View   371
    Dynamic View   371
    Relative View   372
Focus and Situation   377
    Incubation   377
    Recommendations (Focuses)   377
Audience, Appeals, and Mode of Organization   380
    Audience   380
    Audience Analysis   381
    Mode of Organization: The Format of a Report   384
    Appeals   385
The First Version   386
    Expository Style   386
Reader Responses   393
Revising and Editing   397
    A Writer's Process   401

TWO Guide to Editing and Sentence-Combining 407

---

9 Editing 408

Grammatical Conventions   410
    A. Number   410

B. Tense   411

C. Agreement Between Subject and Verbs   411

D. Agreement Between Pronouns and Their Antecedents   412

E. Pronoun Reference   413

F. Case (Subjective, Objective, Possessive)   414

G. 1. Sentence Faults: Fragments   417

   2. Sentence Faults: Fused Sentences   419

   3. Sentence Faults: Comma Splices   419

H. Dangling and Misplaced Modifiers   420

I. Parallel or Grammatically Equal Structures   421

Punctuation Conventions   424

A. Periods, Question Marks, and Exclamation Points   424

B. Commas   425

C. Semicolons   426

D. Colons   428

E. Dashes   428

F. Parentheses and Brackets   429

G. Apostrophes   430

Spelling Conventions   433

A. *IE/EI*   433

B. Unpronounced *E*   434

C. Doubling Consonants   435

D. *Sede, Ceed, Cede*   436

E. Words That Sound Alike but Have Different Spellings   436

F. Miscellaneous Suffix and Prefix Patterns   437

G. Spelling Inventory   437

Mechanical Conventions   440

A. Preparing Final Copy   440

B. Capitalizing   441

C. Quoting   442

D. Italicizing (Underlining)   443

E. Numbering   443

F. Abbreviating   444

G. Hyphenating   445

10 Sentence-Combining: Imitating and Generating Sentences   449

I. Simple Expansion Combinations   450

II. Clausal Expansion Combinations   455

III. Phrasal Expansion Combinations   465

IV. Combined Patterns   492

V. Free Paragraph Combinations   502

VI. Recombining and Revising Exercises   504

Appendix: Exploratory Guides   510

Informal Exploratory Guides   511
   A. Brainstorming   511
   B. Speed Writing   511
   C. Looping   511
   D. Meditating   512
Formal Exploratory Guides   512
   A. The Journalistic Formula: Who, What, When, Where, Why, How?   513
   B. Kenneth Burke's Pentad: Action, Agent, Means, Purpose, Scene   513
   C. The Classical Topics of "Places"   513
   D. Larson's Topic Questions   514
   E. Toulmin's System of Analysis   515

Glossary   517

Index   533

Front Endpaper: Table of Writing Acts and Strategies

Back Endpaper: Editing Symbols

PREFACE

This second edition represents a major revision, not of the central conceptions of writing that informed the first edition, but of the explanations, examples, and exercises provided to help students develop their writing skills and powers. We base these revisions on our experience and other users' experience with the first edition. The following list identifies some of the major changes.

1. Each writing experience is contextualized. Students begin each writing experience identifying not only a compelling question but also several potential situations (audiences and media) in which they would like to write. These situations are intended to help students

realize that every assignment should lead to genuine writing, not just the fulfillment of academic requirements.

2. Each chapter also provides and exemplifies the use of organization plans (based on the modes of organization) to help students move from planning to drafting.

3. A revised audience guide gives more explicit help in setting audience roles and adapting writing to those roles.

4. A new type of sentence-combining exercise and new cumulative exercises on editing and sentence-combining help students develop syntactic fluency and control over conventions.

5. More detailed advice on reader responses and revision is available to guide revising and editing.

6. The second edition continues to stress the importance of a workshop atmosphere in the class. Most of the exercises are still designed to engage students in discussing real student writing and to encourage practice with composing strategies. The second edition introduces more of these types of exercises, especially in the areas of question formation, organization, diction, and revising.

7. We have extensively revised Chapters 3 and 4 on persuasive writing to include
   • checklists of credibility, affective, and rational appeals, with examples from student writing and discussions of the use of the appeals;
   • new work on persuasive organization and deductive appeals; and
   • more advice on persuasive styles, reader responses, and editing.

8. There are new student examples, and the entire writing process of one student appears at the end of each chapter.

9. A new teacher's manual, written by two instructors who have worked with the text, offers many practical ideas for implementation:
   • ways of presenting each writing strategy
   • suggestions for using the Class Exercises
   • checklists to guide responses to assignments
   • a bibliography
   • planning examples for new contexts
   • a glossary of terms

This second edition reaffirms its premises derived from rhetorical theory of the last decade:
• that writing is a unique way of learning
• that meaningful writing grows from a writer's own pressing questions
• that the composing process is a series of acts that can vary in sequence and are often recursive, even though they must be ordered in certain ways in a text
• that primary to meaningful writing is the discovery and communica-

tion of a significant focus to which aims and modes are subordinate

- that an appropriate and actual writing situation (audience and medium) is central to every writing experience
- that choices of organization and style vary with different audiences and aims
- that specific skills such as sentence-combining, paragraph-building, and conventions of usage are best developed within the framework of the whole composing process

Throughout, we have merged theory with the practical experience of college instructors who have developed, tested, and refined that theory in their classrooms. Numerous samples of student work exemplify the composing process and present the struggles and achievements of many kinds of students attempting many different types of writing.

In developing this approach, we have been aware always of the difference between *acts* of writing and *strategies* that guide writers through stages. Alternative strategies can be helpful at a given stage. For example, the exploratory guide alluded to in each chapter does not preclude the use of others (see the Appendix). We adopted this model, however, because it is easily understood, easily remembered, and applicable to all writing situations.

Our general approach in each chapter has been this:

1. To identify for the student the writing context the chapter poses and to differentiate it from the context in the preceding chapter or chapters.
2. To explain the acts of the writing process as they bear on the unique writing context.
3. To explain strategies a writer can use to engage well in these acts.
4. To exemplify, by copious display and analysis of student work, the movement from questions to finished text.
5. To supply class exercises on students' own work and examples presented in the text that will encourage a writing workshop atmosphere.

Taken in sequence, the chapters move the student from the expressive paper to the expository, from the inward to the outward, both in subject matter and audience. The order in one sense is arbitrary, in another logical and desirable. But the instructor who wishes to change the sequence can do so easily by using the Table of Writing Acts and Strategies on the front endpaper, which permits the use of sections of chapters the instructor may not wish to deal with as wholes. Thus *Four Worlds of Writing* can be adapted for either a one- or two-term course; our arrangement permits the instructor to limit the course by aim, by type of writing, or by subject matter.

The Table of Writing Acts and Strategies also allows the instructor to choose the emphasis to be placed on developing editing skills. Part II of the book deals with the conventions and includes editing checklists, assignments in sentence-combining, and a convenient glossary of terms. The chapters contain introductions to choosing appropriate diction and syntax and appropriate paragraphing, at points where instruction in these matters is most profitable. All of these sections are cross-referenced.

Our concern for producing a book that is "adjustable" grows out of a practical, unavoidable fact: a book that can be used by all students must be flexible enough to provide practice materials for students who need a good deal of work in the conventions, but it must not burden all students with the same work. On the other hand, there are limits to flexibility. This book is deliberately arranged to discourage the notion that students must wait to write until they have eliminated their problems with the conventions of language. Fundamentally, this book directs the attention of the student and the instructor to the composing process and puts the acquisition of conventional skills in perspective as only one part of that process.

That view manifests itself in the organization of the book. Janet Emig's introduction emphasizes the necessity of some conscious control of the writing process at the college level, the importance of understanding what the writer is doing and why he or she is doing it. The center of the book—the eight chapters by Janice M. Lauer and Gene Montague—stresses the pedagogical importance of the repetition of the process and the pedagogical advisability of mastering one aim at a time. The final section, by Andrea Lunsford, addresses self-instruction in self-editing skills. Among other things, the book attempts to reduce the confusion between matters rhetorical and matters grammatical and to put the emphasis where it belongs.

We wish to acknowledge the aid we received from Harper & Row and a corps of editors. It was not easy to coordinate the work of four people, especially when one lives on the west coast of Canada, another on the east coast of the United States, and the remaining two in the American Midwest. We are indebted to the students whose work runs through our pages; to Richard E. Young and James Kinneavy, whose rhetorical work underlies several key features of our text; to Virginia Patek, whose help in the chapters on the research paper and the essay exam was invaluable. We are grateful to the writing instructors who have been working with the first edition of *Four Worlds of Writing;* their advice has been invaluable in creating this second edition. We wish to thank Michael Carter and Nancy Coy, who have prepared a fine teacher's manual for the text. We also wish to thank the following teachers who commented on the revised manuscript: Bonnie Barthold, Western Washington University; Mary K. Wallum, North Dakota State University; Suzanne K. Webb, Texas Woman's University; Richard Tuerk, East Texas State University; and

John A. Perron, St. Edward's University. We are grateful to our families and friends, whose support sustained us through a prolonged effort. Finally, we wish to express our particular (if somewhat peculiar) gratitude to and for our obedient servants, the Apple II Plus and KAYPRO II computers on which the manuscript of this second edition was written.

JANICE M. LAUER
GENE MONTAGUE
ANDREA LUNSFORD
JANET EMIG

Four Worlds of Writing

INTRODUCTION

Writing is one way of making meaning from experience for ourselves and for others. For many of us, writing serves as the most available and the most compelling way because its outcome as visible language is satisfying as a permanent record of thought and feeling. We are consequently willing to engage in processes that are often long and complex in order to render meaning as sequences of words on a page. Can others help us as we move through these processes of writing? Can others strengthen our abilities to write effectively and well?

The authors of *Four Worlds of Writing* believe that the answer to both these questions is *yes* and that this text offers direct help to writers of all ages. We have spent many years investigating how writers work. We have analyzed statements made over the centuries by many of the world's noted writers. We have asked student writers about their practices and have observed them as they write. Most importantly, we have asked ourselves how we write.

● THE PROCESSES OF WRITING

In this text we stress points about the processes of writing. These points are generalizations based on research by ourselves and others, as well as on our experience as teachers and writers.

In the text, we will examine each of the following statements about writing:

1. Writing represents a way of making meaning from experience. Generally defined, the process by which we make meaning from experience is called *learning*. Writing provides us with a unique way of learning.
2. Writing occurs as a chain of processes in an individual's interactions with words and ideas that develop and change over time.
3. These interactions may sometimes be complicated and difficult to describe. They are complicated because writers engage in so many activities almost at the same time. Writers try to remember past or ongoing experiences. They plan what they intend to write, from the next word, phrase, or concept to the shape that the entire piece of writing will take. They put down on paper the selections they have made from the range of available possibilities. They read and reread what they have written. They change and revise parts or even the whole. They try to convey large concepts and themes, while at the same time supplying supporting evidence and detail. They consider who their audiences will be, how each audience will respond to what has been written, and how they can direct words effectively to the audience.
4. The processes of writing can differ from text to text. For example, most writers require different lengths of time for writing an original story or a poem and for writing a letter to a friend. Usually, however, when they have written regularly over a period of time, writers tend to develop somewhat consistent patterns and strategies of working.
5. External factors affect writers. These factors include what aspect of

experience they are dealing with, how much time they have for doing the writing, who it is they are writing for, and how much the writing will count.

6. Internal factors also affect writers. These factors include how deeply writers care about the writing they are doing and how certain they are of their abilities to do it well.

7. Many students write differently for their college classes and independent of classes. Independent of classes, they tend not to be so limited by deadlines; and their readers usually concentrate on the message conveyed, rather than on the way it is conveyed. When writers do not have deadlines or grades or teachers' comments to worry about, many of them are willing to spend more time writing, rather than less. Often (perhaps consequently), writers do higher-quality writing on their own than they do for classes.

8. Another reason that writing done independent of classes is different from writing done for classes is that writers discover that the descriptions some teachers have given them about how people write are too simple, or even downright inaccurate. Planning what one wants to write, for example, is much more complicated than making any kind of outline, even a sentence outline. Writers also find that they do not plan only when they begin: they plan and replan as they write.

9. Perhaps another reason for differences in writing in and out of classes is that some students may have had negative experiences in learning to write in school—especially if they wrote exclusively for teachers who did not concentrate on the meaning they were trying to make, but instead were distracted by a forgotten comma or a misspelled word. Part of the problem may have been that teachers did not share in the writing process from the outset, but waited until students handed in papers before commenting on what should have been done differently during the writing of those papers. Those methods are neither helpful nor efficient for teachers or for writers.

10. There is no doubt, however, that teachers can help writers learn to write. In fact, a *variety* of persons can help them write more skillfully and successfully; friends and other students, as well as teachers, can make useful response to their writing. Teachers and peers tend to make different contributions. Writers can learn to balance what each group gives, and thus profit from both.

Obviously, as these descriptions and generalizations make clear, the authors and editors of this book believe that writing can be taught. What do we mean when we make this statement? We believe that teachers and peers can provide students with helpful and even powerful methods for dealing with the processes of writing, processes that can begin with a telling phrase or a pressing question and end with a satisfied reading of one's own writing and even the sense that one has made memorable meaning of some experience.

● THIS TEXT AND YOUR WRITING CLASS

What do these findings about writing mean to you in your writing class? How will they translate into action as you write? What will it mean that you follow the process approach to writing presented in *Four Worlds of Writing?*

Your instructor will

- lead a full discussion of your assignment.
- give you a choice of topics.
- encourage you to set your own writing question.
- show you how to explore your topic.
- help you find your focus—its subject and its point of significance.
- show you how to make an audience analysis.
- help you decide on the appropriate role for your audience.
- show you options for organizing your essay.
- show you ways to reshape your first and early drafts.
- read these early versions, making suggestions for how best to continue.
- help you revise (resee) your work.
- allow you to revise after the first advice.

You will

- begin looking for subjects about which you have strong feelings, puzzlement, and unanswered questions; sometimes found in a journal if one is kept.
- identify your writing question.
- learn many ways of invention and exploration.
- discover strategies for deciding on your focus and your writing situation.
- learn how to analyze your audience.
- learn how to set specific and relational roles for your reader.
- learn to find your voice, your role in relation to your reader.
- learn how to persist.
- learn how to come unblocked.
- learn how to revise.
- reread creatively.
- make effective use of your classmates' comments.

- read papers on the same topic by student writers like yourselves.
- understand some key acts in the processes of writing.
- practice strategies with different aims and audiences and in different worlds of writing.

The difference between an approach that emphasizes processes in learning how to write and approaches that emphasize only your finished paper is not unlike the difference between taking a nonstop flight between New York and San Francisco and driving across the country. It is the difference between being interested exclusively in reaching a destination swiftly and being interested not only in reaching that destination, but also, at times far more, in the journey itself, with its surprises, delights, even disappointments.

In the process approach, we are, of course, interested in the destination—a theme that tellingly and vividly sets forth your thoughts, feelings, and responses. We are more interested in helping you to learn how to become a skillful traveler who can find insight and pleasure in any journey through any of our four worlds of experience.

CLASS EXERCISES

Compare or contrast the process described above with ways in which your previous writing classes have been taught.

FOUR WORLDS OF WRITING

What are those worlds? We live in at least four:

1. *The private world:* the world of meaningful places and environments, peopled with families, friends, and others we care about;
2. *The public world:* the world of the media—television, radio, magazines, books, newspapers, and films—and of shared issues that connect us with our society and with others in the world;
3. *The college world:* the world of classes, courses, and diplomas—of class notes, laboratory reports, research papers, and essay examinations; and
4. *The working world:* the world of jobs, careers, and professions—of memos, reports, applications, evaluations, and studies.

We respond to experience in all of these worlds. In fact, it could be said that the more we respond to all of the worlds, the more we are alive.

THE PRIVATE WORLD: PLACES AND PERSONS

To describe in detail here the private worlds in which we live is, of course, impossible. They are too diverse and too individual. But individual and diverse as these worlds are, they are also alike in major and important ways. Perhaps the most important is that, in our private worlds, if we are at all thoughtful, we try to understand ourselves and our connections with others, particularly those closest to us. We also try to understand our connections with places that are parts of our past and present.

Places can shape experiences for us as significantly as persons can. In fact, as we scan our pasts, we realize that persons and places are often closely connected in our memories. We think of certain people in given settings that affect the ways they act and respond and the ways we respond in turn.

Places do not serve merely as backgrounds, however. They can become the foreground of interest, as happens when we travel. In some cases, places even become central characters, as they have for great travel writers: Greece for Henry Miller, the Hebrides for James Boswell, Alaska for John McPhee.

New places are inherently intriguing for many of us. They have the value of providing a contrast to settings that have become so overfamiliar that we no longer experience them. New places can help us see, hear, taste, and smell the worlds in which we lead our daily lives; they often make familiar places grow fresh and alive once more. "Coming to our senses" is not a trite saying where writing is concerned: it is solid advice to observe when experiencing and writing about places and persons.

Some people as they get older lament that life seems to have passed them by, that they have been caught up in the superficial. Most of us at some time experience this sense of having missed something in the past, of having lived so fast that we don't remember or understand what happened to us. But writers sense this loss less than most. Why? Because each piece of writing has given them the chance to catch those swiftly passing moments of loving, encountering, wondering, and fearing and to hold them long enough to find personal meaning. Writers save the meaning of their lives by dealing with that meaning in writing. They *act* on experiences and events through their writing. Writing is one of the most active ways we can engage in and with the world.

When we write in our private worlds, we may find what is unique in our personal experiences. We may also find patterns and structures in our own lives similar to those we have heard or read about from others. Most likely, we will find a mix of what is unique and what is shared: what makes us unlike anyone else who has ever lived, as well as what makes us like all others who have ever lived. Writing about the private world can even prove a form of preservation and renewal. The philosopher George Gusdorf puts these values eloquently:

> To speak, to write, to express is to act, to survive crisis, to begin living again, even when one thinks it is only to relive one's sorrow.[1]

What forms does writing about the private world take? To discover these forms for yourself, over a given period of, say, one or two weeks, collect all private writing that you do. Forget nothing. Include every fragment, every piece of writing. Into what categories do these writings fall? Compare what you wrote with what other members of your class wrote, and make a master list.

Did you find what we found? Although the writings within our private worlds were divided into writing produced exclusively for ourselves and writing directed toward intimates, the forms were common to both audiences:

autobiographies	diaries
journals	letters
lists	memoirs
notes	personal essays
poems	stories

Who is it, again, that we write for in the private world? Chiefly, we write for ourselves and for those close to us. If there is a reader outside this intimate group, it is someone we have decided to treat as an intimate. What this usually means is that we establish an unspoken contract with the outside reader to respond as an intimate would: to focus upon message and meaning above form. Such a contract may apply to teachers as well as to peers. It requires the outside reader to behave like a listener in an intimate conversation. We know that when we listen to someone close to us, we usually pay close attention to what is being said. We are generous, often supplying what is not yet stated, since the speaker may be expressing certain feelings and thoughts for the very first time. We are understanding, since we know from our own experience that sharing our feelings and thoughts is one of the most difficult forms of expression. We try not to judge the message prematurely or recast the experience in terms that have meaning only to *us*. Nor do we initially criticize the language in which the speaker casts the experience.

Examine again all the writing you did for your private world over that two-week period. Recall now how you wrote; how much time you spent on various forms of writing; how you divided your time among phases of the process. Is is not true that

- your starting point was often a puzzle, an enigma in your private life that you wanted to solve?
- you spent little time planning what you wanted to say?

- your central concern was to convey as exactly as you could how you felt and thought about your subject?
- you did not worry at first about any audience but yourself?

THE PUBLIC WORLD: SHARED ISSUES AND THE MEDIA

The private world is not, of course, the only world in which we move and have our being; we live in larger, more public worlds as well. We experience these larger worlds in two ways: (1) what we know directly because things happen to us and to those we know; and (2) what we perceive through the media—radio, television, tapes, newspapers, magazines. We respond to events that come to us vicariously as well as directly. One powerful and effective way to respond to events as well as to affect them is through writing about them.

If you consider the kinds of writing you do in order to respond to and to affect your immediate world, your block, your neighborhood, or your country, you probably will find that the forms of writing include posters, signs, notices, petitions, and handouts. The purpose of these is probably to correct a wrong or to get action on an issue.

As you attempt to affect or influence an audience farther away, someone you do not know and are unlikely to have encountered personally, you probably add other forms of writing, as the following list suggests:

- posters, signs, and notices
- petitions and handouts
- letters to individuals and groups with particular responsibility and power:

> directors and administrators of social, civic, and religious groups
> editors of newspapers and magazines
> announcers, producers, and sponsors of radio and television programs
> political representatives and spokespersons
> consumer advocates and agencies
> individual businesses and corporations

An important form of writing that we found through our own search in the world of shared issues is what could be called *consumer writing*. Why? The reason is not difficult to discover. In our society, we often find that the products we use are as unsatisfactory as they are expensive. What are we to do, for example, about a $7000 car with a $7 part that cannot be obtained for three weeks, three months, or at all? Beyond citing warranties and guarantees, is there any written action we can take?

When we looked into the effect we could have as consumer writers, we were heartened by what we found. We had long known that certain consumer advocate writers like Ralph Nader had affected policies and products in our society. For example, as a result of Nader's being bumped from an airline, there is now a law to recompense us for the inconvenience if the same thing happens to us. But we did not know the power of just one well-written and well-directed letter until we had interviewed people in consumer affairs, radio and TV station managers, and executives of some large corporations. The president of a large manufacturer of automobile parts, for example, told us that when a consumer writes to complain about a specific product or problem, every person with any major responsibility for that product must write an explanatory memo detailing a response and a solution. The president or a member of his staff then combines these memos into a personal letter of response, which is sent to the consumer. Such a system of memo writing and accountability is common practice in many individual businesses and corporations. In other words, through skillful letter writing, we may be able to affect the products, programs, and policies that touch on our daily lives.

Consumer writing affects our lives in the economic realm. Another form of writing, which might be called *citizen writing,* can affect our lives in the political realm. A well-written and well-directed letter or campaign of letters can affect and even change political events, as well as the laws under which we live. Examples are frequent and easy to cite. A well-known recent example is the letter Allan Bakke wrote to the Regents of the University of California, a letter which led to a Supreme Court decision that resulted in the reformulation of affirmative action programs for colleges and universities.

THE COLLEGE WORLD

The world in which you now write most frequently is the college world—the world of courses, classes, and seminars, of papers, research reports, and essay examinations.

Like other bureaucracies, schools also require the filling out of forms and more forms. The way you present yourself in writing on an application form, for example, is the first encounter a college has with you. The most significant portion of that application can be the writing of an autobiography and a statement of your academic intentions and ambitions. Admissions counselors, committees, and deans often regard these presentations as the most revealing portion of the admissions packet and the most predictive of college and postcollege success.

School may also be the world in which you will be expected to observe the most fixed and formal sets of writing conventions that you will ever experience. In what other world, for example, are you asked to describe to others in elaborate written essays what you and they already know and have demonstrated through other forms of expression (such as class discussion)? Unless you become an editor, critic, or professor, you will not again be asked to respond to a book with an analysis of its stone or bird symbolism, or with a discussion of how the minor characters develop in contrast to the major characters. We are not suggesting that the writing you are asked to do in your English, psychology, history, music appreciation, or chemistry classes should not be appropriate, even unique, to the discipline. One way a discipline is distinguished from others is in the writing conventions it observes.

One virtue of this text is that such kinds of special responses are not stressed. The writing assignments in this book stress, instead, your making meaning in many kinds of texts in all four worlds of writing. The book shows how engaging in the full writing process, which starts with a question significant to you, can turn outside assignments, which may seem artificial, into genuine learning experiences. The forms of writing that you will encounter in the world of school include:

CLASS-RELATED FORMS	**COLLEGE-RELATED FORMS**
bibliographies	applications
essay examinations	continuations
journals	registrations
lecture notes and outlines	
lists	
précis	
prospectuses and proposals	
reports	
research and critical papers	
reviews	

There is now some research about the processes of writing in and for school that is interesting, if not necessarily surprising. When college students are given the opportunity to participate in the selection of their subjects, they tend to write pieces of higher quality, according to evaluations of both their instructors and outside judges. This generalization also holds true if students participate in choosing writing topics for entrance or placement examinations. In other words, your involvement or engagement with what is to be written enhances the quality of your writing.

Whether or not you can choose or help choose your own topics can also affect the amount you write, at least if you are like your younger counterparts. Donald Graves, now of the University of New Hampshire, contrasted two groups of second graders.[2] Those who wrote whenever they wanted to wrote *four times* as much as did children whose teachers assigned all the writing they did. High school seniors, when interviewed by Janet Emig, revealed that they did much more writing outside of school because there they did not have deadlines to worry about and because their friends and families, unlike their teachers, focused on what they were trying to say, not on how they were saying it.[3]

Other research suggests that the abler the college writer, the more time that writer spends on a given piece of writing. As Sharon Pianko has shown, college writers who are deeply engaged in their writing processes spend more time planning, more time writing, and far more time revising and reformulating. Also, when they finish, they spend time contemplating what they have written—that is, they like what they have done.[4]

Which comes first? Does lengthening and intensifying your processes of writing increase your abilities as a writer? Or do your abilities lengthen and intensify your processes? We don't know. We do know, however, that length and complexity of your writing process are correlated with establishing the quality and success of what is written.

THE WORKING WORLD

"You do not need to write in order to survive and to succeed in the working world." Such is the curious, if powerful, student myth that has grown up over the last decade or two in North America. According to this myth, a person can engage in most kinds of work, even the most significant and high-salaried work, without even writing a sentence. Students believe that secretaries, clerks, and other kinds of assistants are hired to do most of the writing within businesses and corporations. Only a handful of professions, like law, teaching, the ministry, publishing, and journalism, require that their members write with any regularity and seriousness.

Recently, large-scale studies have begun to assess the amount of writing done in government offices and labor unions. Such a study describing and analyzing who writes what to whom, when, and why in a given social group is called an *ethnograph*. This term, which comes from the field of anthropology, refers to a detailed descriptive examination of the customary behaviors and beliefs of a particular social group. Their initial findings indicate that almost all Americans write on the job.

Writing in the world of work takes a wide variety of forms:

- résumés and applications
- personnel records:
    personal (i.e., job performance valuations)
    medical
    insurance, pension, and other benefits
- expense and travel requests and reports
- diaries, logs, and journals

- letters
- memos
- outlines
- presentations and evaluations of concepts, products, and programs, within and outside the company:
    - studies
    - reports
- in-house journals, newspapers, magazines, and summary sheets
- professional, career, and business journals
- media releases

The audiences for writing in the working world are perhaps more diverse than those in the other three worlds. In-house audiences include peers, superiors, and special offices. Outside, they include work affiliates, work rivals, the public as individuals, the public en masse, and the media.

Much writing in the working world consists of record keeping. Even when computers keep the records, programs must be written. Particularly in smaller businesses and units other than data processing units, a very large number of records are written by individuals. Much writing in the working world also consists of justification: explanations to a range of audiences as to why an individual or group has taken a particular course of action or made a certain decision; why a unit did not show a profit; or why management should promote or abandon existing policies or programs of action.

Research suggests that, despite the student myth that secretaries and other kinds of scribes write the memos and letters in the working world, the person whose name appears on that memo or letter usually composes it, no matter who types and transcribes it. Quite soon, the working world will use voice-activated typewriters that will type letter-perfect copy directly from dictation. Whether or not such technology eliminates the role of secretary, it will assuredly eliminate the myth that people do not do their own writing in the working world.

WRITING AS LEARNING

We said earlier that writing is unique as a way of learning. The very nature of the writing processes requires that you perform several activities almost simultaneously: for instance, you observe even as you write, or you revise even as you plan.

WRITING AS A MULTIMODAL PROCESS

Psychologists who study *cognition*—the process of learning—have found that we learn best when we learn in several ways, or *modes,* at the same time. Psychologists like Jerome Bruner and Jean Piaget point out that we learn in three basic ways: (1) "on the muscle" (*motoric*); (2) "by the image" (*iconic*); and (3) "by restatement in words" (*representational* or *symbolic*). What is unusual, if not unique, about writing is that the process requires that we make use of all three modes at once. Literally putting words on paper—writing or typing them—is a physical act (motoric). The piece of writing represents an image (iconic). This image is composed of words that represent verbal symbols (symbolic). In other words, when we write, all three modes are involved and, very likely, reinforce one another.[5]

Using words as symbols to describe experience has certain special features. It requires that we assign an order to experiences and set them out as linear sequences, one word (one graphic symbol) after another. In this process, we make explicit to ourselves and others the relationships we find among words, meanings, and concepts. We indicate, through the verbal symbols we use, when one event causes another; the words *because* and *since* are signals that we use when we believe a causal connection exists. We must also make clear whether one element is larger than another, whether it is a generalization of which the second element is an example; the phrases *for example* and *that is* are common signals of this relationship between thoughts. As the psychologist Lev Vygotsky put it, we are required to structure "the webs of meaning."[6]

WRITING AS A RECORD OF MEANING

What we write can obviously provide evidence to others that we have learned. Written examinations represent one of the oldest records of meaning. In China the tradition of the Imperial Examination, by which aspirants achieved the highly respected status of scholar, can be traced back thousands of years. Even today written examinations, quizzes, and tests represent far more than half of all writing college students do. We regard such written examinations as only one form of writing as learning. The writing of examinations has as its audience only one person, the instructor. Sometimes making this kind of record comes after the process of learning has been completed and serves only as evidence that certain facts and concepts have been acquired. Other examinations foster learning by the way they are designed.

But in a broader sense, writing as learning concerns the values writing can have for you as an ongoing process. What are these values? We need writing to offset the severe limits of our working memory. Since a single paragraph in a textbook or a five-minute portion of an instructor's lecture may contain many more pieces of information than we can readily store, think of our losses if we could not take notes to help us remember. Taking notes is a personal, even idiosyncratic, process of record keeping. If you have ever asked a friend to take notes on a lecture you were unable to attend, you are aware that what someone else elects to record may have no value for you at all: your interests, your emphases, your ways of remembering are different.

The value of setting out one's understanding fully and graphically is immense. We have a visual and readily available record of our thinking, one that can be shared with others. It can be rescanned, reread, reviewed, revised. Such a record shows, in graphic form, the evolution of our thinking and feeling, from the first few words we tentatively jot on a page to a final finished version that sets out the shape and scope of our comprehension.

Many of us have kept diaries and journals as records of meaning in our private lives. In a recent essay about the British novelist Virginia Woolf, Cynthia Ozick makes an important distinction between genuine diaries and a kind of record keeping she describes as "a hound padding after life: . . . a diary is a shoring-up of the ephemeral, evidence that the writer takes up real space in the world." She notes of Virginia Woolf's diaries:

> As these incandescent streams of language show, the life she lived and the people she knew did not become real until they were written down.[7]

Or as the writer Anaïs Nin notes,

> When I don't write I feel my world shrinking. . . . I feel I lose my fire, my color.[8]

The record of meaning that we keep through journals and diaries may become, then, our lives themselves in the only form in which we can truly preserve them. Photographs, home movies, and tapes may evoke what we saw and heard; but only the words of our diaries can fully record how we felt.

Journals and writing in general can also serve us well in the world of school and college, representing our responses to tests and lectures. Michael Polanyi, a philosopher of science, states that we learn only when there is a "fusion of the personal and the objective": when we achieve what he calls *personal knowledge*.[9] The value of diaries and journals for learning is that they sponsor the integration of the personal with the objective, that they sponsor personal knowledge.

Do we have evidence that writing aids learning? Do we master concepts in courses where we are required, or where we require ourselves, to write? Recent studies suggest that writing about the major concepts in a course or seminar expands, clarifies, and solidifies our understanding of those concepts. Robert Weiss and Susan Walters contrasted the comprehension of college students who wrote frequently about key concepts in their classes with the comprehension of students who wrote infrequently. They found that students who kept learning logs and journals revealed a far firmer grasp of the principles and concepts of their courses than students who did not.[10]

WRITING AS A WHOLE-BRAINED ACTIVITY

The process of writing engages hand, eye, and brain. Scientists have found that as we mature, the two hemispheres of our brain develop certain special functions. The dominant hemisphere (for those who are strongly right-handed, the left hemisphere) deals with what is linear, logical, sequential. The nondominant hemisphere (for right-handers, the right hemisphere) receives and interprets wholes, such as the visual and spatial. The process of writing requires integration of the functions of both hemispheres of the brain. In the process of writing, experiences that come to our right hemisphere as wholes must be rendered by our left hemisphere into linear sequences of verbal symbols with explicit logical and psychological connections.

Here are a few of the ways in which our two hemispheres differ:

DOMINANT HEMISPHERE	NONDOMINANT HEMISPHERE
evaluates, revises, judges	creates, originates
makes propositions	makes associations
analyzes	synthesizes
renders experience as parts, as verbal sequences	treats experiences as wholes; as images, shapes, forms
acknowledges denotations, public meanings	forms private connotations

How do these two halves of the brain work together as we write? The following description is of course a hypothesis, or a series of hypotheses. We have, however, some evidence to support this description.[11] In the following chapters we suggest that as we write we follow certain sequences of feelings, thoughts, and actions. These can originate in the left or in the right hemisphere.

Identification of a subject and its exploration are for most of us right-brained activities that follow a shared sequence. When we decide what we want to write, or when someone suggests or assigns a topic, what often happens first? An image comes before the mind's eye: we *see* a person or object or place. Many professional writers tell us that their stories and novels begin with such an image. Virginia Woolf's novel *The Waves* began with the image of a fin turning in the water; Joan Didion's novel *The Book of Common Prayer* with the image of a woman in an airport making a telephone call; William Faulkner's *The Sound and The Fury* with the image of a little girl's drawers as she sat in a tree watching her grandmother's funeral.

Making an audience analysis, on the other hand, is a rational and logical way of gathering information about our readers so that we can consciously try to persuade them of a given point of view. Systematically using well-known methods of persuasion from classical rhetoric is another activity of our dominant hemisphere.

Two of our higher-learning processes are analysis and synthesis. *Analysis* is the process of breaking or dividing wholes into coherent parts; *synthesis* is the process of combining parts to form coherent and, often, fresh wholes. The dominant hemisphere of the brain proceeds by analysis, the nondominant hemisphere by synthesis. The act of writing requires the double action of analysis and synthesis. The process seems to work this way: Experience comes to us as a whole; the outcome of even what seems a linear experience such as reading a book still results in our having a whole response. A way to comprehend an experience and then to communicate its meanings to ourselves and to others is to write—that is, to organize a response or account in a linear sequence that, in its turn, becomes a whole. The cycle seems to be:

WHOLE $\longrightarrow$ **Analysis** $\longrightarrow$ **PARTS** $\longrightarrow$ **Synthesis** $\longrightarrow$ **WHOLE**
Experience,   Linear   Account, such
direct or   rendering   as a letter,
vicarious   theme, or essay

Writing and learning, then, are integrative processes. For the purposes of understanding and communicating, they translate wholes into parts. These parts are then reformed into new wholes, the finished written accounts.

Since writing is so powerful, it is understandable that we want it to be a part of all the worlds of experience in which we live.

● CONCLUSION

In a powerful essay, Marjorie Kirrie, a professor of writing from Oregon, makes the argument that all of us live in a world that writing built:

> Once we had writing, we could exploit the hitherto unattainable possibilities of language, and that exploitation led to an acceleration of change—we usually call it progress—undreamed of in the purely oral millenia of our ascent to dominance. Writing made possible

science and technology; it made possible educational systems, bureaucracy, corporate structures, complex philosophies, and even the fine arts as we know them. Writing made possible our forms of government, space exploration, and today's struggle for human rights. Writing is ultimately responsible for nearly all of the man-created aspects of our rapidly changing world.[12]

Richard Rodriguez speaks of another value of writing:

> By rendering feelings in words that a stranger can understand—words that belong to the public, this Other—the young diarist no longer need feel all alone or eccentric. His feelings are capable of public intelligibility. In turn, the act of revelation helps the writer better understand his own feelings. Such is the benefit of language: By finding public words to describe one's feelings, one can describe oneself to oneself. One names what was previously only darkly felt.[13]

In this text the authors suggest that all of us live in four worlds that writing can help to shape and to make understandable, since writing either serves or actually represents so many of the functions that make us human, that make us civilized. Through writing we can record, describe, explain, justify, codify, discover, create, reflect, and destroy; we can build our own lives in the four worlds in which we live.

NOTES

1. George Gusdorf, *Speaking* (Evanston, Ill.: Northwestern University Press, 1965), p. 59.
2. Donald Graves, "An Examination of the Writing Processes of Seven Year Old Children," *Research in the Teaching of English* (Winter 1975), pp. 227–241.
3. Janet Emig, *The Composing Processes of Twelfth Graders* (Champaign, Ill.: National Council of Teachers of English, 1971).
4. Sharon Pianko, "Reflection: A Critical Component of the Composing Process," *College Composition and Communication* (October 1979), pp. 275–278.
5. Janet Emig, "Writing as a Mode of Learning," *College Composition and Communication* 28 (1977), pp. 122–128.
6. Lev Vygotsky, *Thought and Language,* trans. Eugenia Haufmann and Gertrude Vakor (Cambridge: Harvard University Press, 1978), p. 100.
7. Cynthia Ozick, "Diary-Keeping," *Art and Ardor* (New York: Alfred A. Knopf, 1983), p. 60.
8. Anaïs Nin, *Diary of Anaïs Nin,* vol. 5, ed. Gunther Stuhlmann (San Diego: Harcourt Brace Jovanovich, 1974), pp. 149–150.

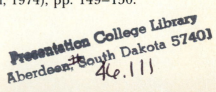

9. Michael Polanyi, *Personal Knowledge* (New York: Harper & Row, 1958).

10. Robert H. Weiss and Susan A. Walters, "Writing to Learn." Paper presented at the Annual Meeting of the American Educational Research Association (Boston, April 7–11, 1980).

11. J. E. Bogen, "Some Educational Implications of Hemispheric Specialization," *The Human Brain,* ed. M. C. Whittrock (Englewood Cliffs, N.J.: Prentice-Hall, 1977).

12. Marjorie Kirrie, "Writing in the World That Writing Built," *The College Board Review,* Spring 1978, p. 23.

13. Richard Rodriguez, *The Hunger of Memory* (Boston: David R. Godine, 1982), p. 187.

ONE

Guide to Composing

WRITING WITH AN EXPRESSIVE AIM

In the Private World/Places

The power to write is like an extra eye that can see things you would otherwise fail to see. One of the major directions it can turn is inward, helping you to create and share meanings in your life that might otherwise escape you.

When you turn your writing eye inward, you are writing with an *expressive aim*. Your private world, the center around which all the other worlds develop, remains something of a mystery both to you and others. It is a unique set of pieces made up of the places, relationships, and experiences that have formed your life so far, pieces that you may not have fully assembled into a meaningful whole. Writing allows you to withdraw from the whirl of your activities to the quiet center of yourself where you can spend time pondering the major influences in your life, the places, people, events, and ideas that have subtly shaped your out-look and values. When you turn your eye inward to examine these im-portant parts of your life through writing, you can begin to solve more fully some of the mysteries that puzzle you about yourself.

Writing with an expressive aim emphasizes *the writer*, focusing on dis-covered meanings and attitudes. At the same time, expressive writing also offers a special way of sharing your deepest self with others. The writer's purpose is to share important personal insights and feelings with readers. The word *aim* means *purpose* or *emphasis*. What other purposes and emphases does writing have? A good way of answering that is to look at the communication triangle, which includes elements found in all written discourse: writer, audience or reader(s), subject, and language/ form.

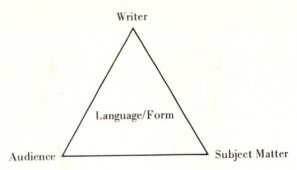

Every piece of written communication has all four elements but emphasizes one or another, thus creating different aims:

1. Writing that emphasizes *the writer* has an *expressive aim.*
2. Writing that emphasizes *the audience* has a *persuasive aim.*
3. Writing that emphasizes *the subject* has an *expository aim.*
4. Writing that emphasizes the *language/form* has a *literacy aim.**

Each type of writing includes all the elements; its aim is a matter of *emphasis*. Chapters 1 and 2 of this book will examine writing with an expressive aim; Chapters 3 and 4 will deal with the persuasive aim; Chapters 5 through 8 will treat the expository aim. This book does not treat literary discourse like short stories or poetry because these are usu-ally studied in a separate course.

COMPOSING PROCESSES

Knowing the aim of your writing does not, however, fully enable you to engage well in the composing process. You also need to understand the

* This discussion is adapted from James Kinneavy's book *A Theory of Discourse* (Englewood Cliffs, N.J.: Prentice-Hall, 1971).

kinds of powers and skills that good writers exercise when composing. And, more important, you need some useful strategies to enable you to develop those powers and skills. The rest of this chapter will discuss these powers and strategies, suggesting that you practice using them when you write each of your papers. To build writing powers, you need to practice these strategies, eventually adapting them to your own style of thinking and composing. Strategies are tools that writers should make their own.

Each chapter of the book offers you three ways of improving your writing ability:

1. *understanding* some key *acts* of the writing process
2. *using* helpful *strategies* during these acts
3. *practicing* these *strategies* with different aims and in different worlds of writing

Each of these strategies is essential for the development of a competent writer. Understanding without practice does not work; practice without understanding freezes you at an elementary level of development. Writing without powerful strategies is like building a house without carpenter's tools.

FACTORS THAT INFLUENCE WRITING

But no book can offer advice on every facet of writing. Furthermore, you alone can assess some of the important factors that affect your writing performance—those acts and attitudes that are not conscious. It is important for you to recognize the way these influences operate on your composing process. For example, you may have fears of writing because past instructors often bloodied your work with red pencil marks. You may be afflicted with a "correctness" paralysis that inhibits you from composing fluently. Your environment may influence your success: you may work better in a quiet place than with a stereo or television playing. Your writing time may influence your effectiveness: you may stretch your composing over a period of days or weeks to allow time for planning, writing, and revising, or you may dive into a paper the night before it is due. Even your composing style may affect your outcome: you may write fluently and later cross out a great deal or you may revise each sentence as you go along. It would be wise to examine these writing factors and perhaps discuss them with your instructor in conference. This book will not deal with such attitudes and habits but will instead concentrate on the *conscious* activities, helping you to build better habits of thinking, imagining, inquiring, and symbolizing.

The writing process will be clustered into several acts:

1. The Guiding Question and Potential Situations
2. Exploration

3. Focus and Situation
4. Audience and Modes of Organization
5. The First Version
6. Reader Responses
7. Revising and Editing

Although the chapters must follow an order in discussing these acts, *they do not provide a mechanical formula for writing a paper.* As you engage in these activities, you must bring to bear your own knowledge, imagination, and sentence and editing skills. You may find yourself moving back and forth among these acts as the writing process of any given paper proceeds. Allow yourself to follow your own leads. For example, when you are exploring, you may discover a better question. When drafting, you may feel the need for further exploring or may wish to change your audience. But while you are learning the proposed strategies, it might be helpful to follow the general progression outlined in the chapters until you feel more comfortable and able to experiment.

In learning any complex process, deliberate practice of separate skills is useful so that these skills can be orchestrated eventually into the whole process. If you recall how you learned skills like playing a musical instrument or engaging in an athletic activity, you may be able to see the importance of practicing key moves and useful strategies.

THE GUIDING QUESTION AND POTENTIAL SITUATIONS

THE SUBJECT

As we discussed above, your first writing assignment, with an expressive aim, will allow you to examine some facet of your private world in order to understand its influence on you. One of the most subtle but powerful influences on your life has been the *places,* the environments in which you have found yourself, either for long stretches of time or for brief but striking periods. Many places have become a part of you. Even though you may think you "just" live in Chicago or Birmingham or Seattle, these places have changed you. The houses, neighborhoods, and job locations that you have spent time in have crept into a part of yourself so quietly that you may never have puzzled over their influence. Your first writing experience will give you a chance to investigate the impact of one of these places on your development.

But because each writing experience is precious and time-consuming, it is important that you not waste it by selecting either a place with only minor influence or a place whose meaning you already know. Writing is not only communication of something you already know, but much more important, it is a chance to figure out something you do not yet understand. How, then, can you determine what subject, what place is worth spending your time investigating and writing about?

THE GUIDING QUESTION

The way to begin is by trying to set a *guiding question.* Good writing begins with questions, not answers—with puzzlement, wonder, curiosity. A writer is basically a questioner. However, you may have been discouraged from questioning by a world that rewards right answers rather than uneasy questions. Even if you have been educated to be an answerer, you can learn to be a questioner. Questions begin with a sense of discomfort or with feelings of exhilaration that arise when your expectations are either not met or are exceeded, when your values are challenged by some situation, event, or experience, when the image of the world in which you grew up does not fit with the world in which you find yourself. Such a state, known as *dissonance,* is one of the best frames of mind for creativity, because it sets the climate for making discoveries, for learning.

To decide on the place you wish to investigate, therefore, one way to begin is by making a list of places that elicit strong attitudes in you—places that you would or did regret leaving, places you despise, fear, or have nightmares about, places that puzzle or amaze you. To test which one provokes the most pressing question you want to answer, apply to each the following two-part strategy.

STARTING GUIDE

1. State your subject.
2. Identify the expectations or values you hold that seem to conflict with the place. Are there aspects of the place that do not meet your expectations or that exceed your expectations? Are there aspects of the place that clash with your values?
3. Formulate a question that (*a*) captures that clash or dissonance; (*b*) poses what you need to know to eliminate your puzzlement.
4. Identify potential writing situations.

The first two parts of this strategy interact. A meaningful question comes from a sense of challenge, of incongruity about the place, not directly from the place itself. What is puzzling to you about a place may not be puzzling to someone else. This is *your* question. If you cannot ask a meaningful question (not a question that could be answered by merely *yes* or *no*), perhaps the subject is not the best one to pursue. If you ask a question to which you already know the answer, the subject is not worth investigating in this writing experience. Choosing the subject that poses the most important question for you will make your writing process worth pursuing. Posing a well-formulated question is crucial if a writer wishes to begin well, to use writing to reach new understanding. Here are some guidelines to follow in formulating your questions:

1. Study the dissonances you have noticed between aspects of your subject and your values or expectations.
2. Determine which dissonance seems most pressing, which you would most like to pursue.
3. Formulate several questions that, if answered, would help you resolve your puzzlement or unease. Try different types of questions: who, what, why, and so on. Ask yourself which type best represents what you want to answer through your writing investigation. Rule out any questions whose answers you already know or that could be answered by yes or no. These do not initiate genuine writing investigations.
4. Check your questions to see if they express elements of your dissonance.
5. Choose one question as a starting guide, but realize that your question may and often does change as you begin to investigate your subject.

Below are some choices that other students made to begin their writing.* Some analyzed their dissonances and posed their questions in more helpful ways than others. Study the examples to determine which students set useful writing questions.

GUIDING QUESTIONS

WRITER 1

Subject: My summer job as a bank teller—I took the job because it was all I could find. I was not looking forward to it at all; little did I know that I would stay a year and a half and hate to leave.

My Values and Expectations	My Subject
—complicated transactions	—constant flow of money
—stuffy, all-business coworkers	—tellers pulled for one another
—strict regulations and security checks	—responsibility and trust in each teller

* The student writing displayed throughout the book is the work of the following students: J. Ambrose, S. Anderson, J. Ballew, K. Braun, B. Buchanan, J. Clark, J. DuBose, J. Hassell, A. Humbert, G. Hungerman, L. Kleinrichert, J. Linn, M. Massaron, M. Mosiman, B. Nichols, M. Rabaut, D. Rutherford, B. Shields, K. Sovine, M. Spriggs, W. Tigchelaar, J. Tully, J. Walker, R. Webber, M. Wheatley, and R. Wheatley.

—pressure of accurately counting money

—never had a business class and knew very little about banks

—didn't even have my own money in this bank

—suspicious customers

—realize everyone makes mistakes

—training program which proved challenging and gets teller involved in all aspects of banking

—friendly, dependable customers

Question: What aspects of working at a bank appealed to me and altered my attitudes enough for me to really enjoy the work and hate leaving it behind?

WRITER 2

Subject: My stay in a clinical institution

My Values and Expectations	**My Subject**
—freedom	—sense of confinement
—pleasant surroundings	—the smell and artificiality of the place

Question: What impact has a stay in a clinical institution had on me?

WRITER 3

Subject: My visit to Rio in Brazil

My Values and Expectations	**My Subject**
—natural beauty	—the ugliness of the surrounding huts
—excitement of a jet set city	—the richness and glamour of the city

Question: Why did Rio disappoint me, somehow change me?

WRITER 4

Subject: My childhood in Grand Rapids

My Values and Expectations	**My Subject**
—culture and nightlife of a big city	—small-city limitations
—memories of childhood security in G.R.	—reality of present-day Grand Rapids

Question: Why do I dream of going back to Grand Rapids to live when I like a big city?

WRITER 5

Subject: My uncle's farm in Wisconsin

My Values or Expectations	**My Subject**
—a quiet, pleasant place	—very slow pace, more than usual restlessness
—nice, even beautiful, spot	—very beautiful spot, special beauty
—few people	—few of the opportunities a metropolitan area has for entertainment
—opportunities for outdoor recreation close by and without crowds	—no decent Chinese or Mexican restaurants

Question: How do I resolve the conflict between the introverted me and the type of life I grew up with and my appreciation for it?

● **COMMENTARY**

Writer 2 chose a very good subject—a psychiatric clinic that had long haunted her but that she had never ventured to investigate before. She selected two strong values that clashed with her experience of the place—her need for freedom and her need for pleasant surroundings. Her question, however, could more explicitly reflect that dissonance. She revised it to read: "What impact on my need for freedom has a stay in the institution had?"

Writer 5's farm exceeded his expectations on the whole, although he expressed some dissatisfaction with the lack of entertainment. But his question had nothing to do with the farm. Nor is it clear what type of life he grew up with that forms a contrast with the farm. He revised his question to read: "What impact have the visits to my uncle's farm had on me?" This second question, however, still does not capture the dissonance. His second revision was better:

What impact have my visits to my uncle's farm in Wisconsin had on the conflict between the introverted me and my upbringing in the Bay Area of California?

POTENTIAL SITUATIONS

To test your question, select some alternative situations in which to set your investigation. The *writing situation* includes such elements as an audience or readers and a medium of communication—letter, essay, diary entry, and so on. Expressive writing, which emphasizes the writer, often is written for friends, family, or oneself. Sometimes, though, writers like to share their insights with a larger audience such as magazine readers. To guide your writing, therefore, make a list of potential situations in which you see yourself writing about your subject. Here are some that the writers above considered.

POTENTIAL SITUATIONS

WRITER 1
—an essay or letter for my best friend, Anne
—an essay to share with those working at the bank
—a letter to my dad

WRITER 2
—an entry in my diary
—an essay I'd send back to those in the institution
—an essay I'd write for myself to keep
—a letter to my older sister
—an article for a magazine (which ?) that has featured the subject of institutions for teenagers

WRITER 3 —an essay I'd send to my mother, who is interested not only in my reaction
  to the trip but also in my writing—she's a writer
—a letter to my dad
—an essay sent to the tourist bureau of Rio? too ambitious

WRITER 4 —a letter to my friend Joyce
—an article for a corporate magazine read by employees who are transferred
  often
—a long diary entry?
—an essay for my classmates and instructor

WRITER 5 —a letter to my best friend, Joe, who has always lived on the West Coast
—an essay I would send to my oldest sister, who appreciates good writing
—an essay for my classmates
—an article in farming magazine—about rural life? (not yet ready for this)

Primary and Secondary Situations

Even though each piece you write for a class has as its secondary audience the instructor and the other students (if the class is conducted as a
workshop), you can set a primary situation other than the classroom. If
you choose to do so, then the class can help you shape your writing for
the audience and medium you select. Later in this chapter, you will be
given advice on how to adapt your writing to different situations. As part
of your first assignment, however, you will only need to identify alternative situations in which you could work.

CLASS EXERCISES

Before you begin the first writing assignment, take time to try out the
strategies in class. To help you understand the strategies for each stage
of composing, this book suggests two kinds of class exercises to give you
guided practice with these strategies before you try them on your own.
These exercises encourage a *workshop* atmosphere in the classroom, stimulating discussion of student examples and group practice of strategies.

1. The first kind of exercise involves *discussion* of the student examples
   in the text. This kind of exercise is useful not only for getting a grip
   on how the strategies work for different writers but also for illustrating that *the student examples are not included as perfect models,* but rather
   as examples of actual student work with strengths and weaknesses.
2. The second kind of exercise offers suggestions for *classroom practice
   sessions* using sample subjects. Even though this kind of exercise is
   artificial because you are not working on your own subject, it gives
   you a chance to try out the strategies under guidance.

CLASS EXERCISES

1. Discuss the subjects and questions of Writers 1, 3, and 4.
   - How carefully did they analyze their dissonances?
   - What kinds of investigations will their questions direct: searches for what, how, why, and so on?
   - Have they asked questions that, if answered, will resolve their puzzlement?
2. Discuss types of places that might be puzzling to members of the class.
3. Select a place familiar to the entire class.
   - Share the attitudes and feelings it triggers.
   - Discuss the values and expectations that individuals have in relation to it.
   - Write down or discuss ways in which the place either exceeds or falls short of those expectations.
   - Formulate different types of questions that could be asked to lead to new understanding.
4. Discuss varieties of writing situations in which members of the class already write expressive discourse or in which they can envision themselves doing so. Select several that would fit the place examined in Exercise 3.
5. Consider the following case.

   Cameron had grown up in a small town in the South where he had many friends. When he was sixteen, his family moved to Chicago where he enrolled in an inner-city school. The first person that befriended him was someone from another race. He wanted to take this new friend home to meet his family, but had misgivings because in the small town he came from the races did not mix socially.

   What kinds of dissonances did Cameron experience? What values and expectations were clashing with his new situation? If he wanted to understand this situation better through writing, what kinds of questions could he ask?

ASSIGNMENTS

The out-of-class assignments constitute the most important parts of each chapter because they engage you in some phase of writing that leads to a finished paper. In contrast to the exercises, the assignments are parts of a genuine writing experience in which you investigate a subject you have selected and then share your understanding with a reader. If you can obtain advice on your work in each assignment before going on to the next, your writing process, carried out under the guidance of your instructor and perhaps your classmates, will benefit immensely.

● ASSIGNMENT: The Guiding Question and Potential Situations

1. From a list of places about which you have strong feelings, select one that continues to puzzle you.
2. Identify your values or expectations and the aspects of the place that challenge them.
3. Write a question to guide your search for answers.
4. List several actual situations in which you could write on the subject.
5. Seek advice on this early phase of your planning.

● EXPLORATION

After you have set your guiding question and potential situations, you need to explore your subject, seeking a broad view of it. You already have many memories stored, but you must retrieve them. The exploratory guide will help you *recall* and also *discover* ideas about your place; it will increase your flexibility of mind, prompting you to examine your subject from several points of view to prepare for the understanding you seek. The exploratory guide will direct you to take three views of your subject.*

1. The *static view* directs you to recall those relatively unchanging features, details, definitions of your subject that differentiate it from similar subjects. The static features of a place, for example, might include distinguishing elements (aspects it shares with no other place), sensory impressions it evokes (sights, sounds, scents, tastes), and its parts, or layout.

2. The *dynamic view* directs you to see your place as a *process*, noting its movements and its physical and historical changes. The dynamic features of a place, for example, would include the activities that occur there, the changes that you recall during different periods of

---

* These three views are adapted from a writing theory of Young, Becker, and Pike, based on a linguistic theory called *tagmemics*. See Richard E. Young, Alton Becker, and Kenneth Pike, *Rhetoric: Discovery and Change* (New York: Harcourt Brace Jovanovich, 1970).

time: morning to evening, one week or month or year to the next, or even through history.

3. The *relative view* prompts you to create relationships between your subject and other things. *Classifying* relates your subject to larger groups in which it fits and to other members of the same group. *Comparing and contrasting* relate your subject to other subjects of like order. *Analogizing* relates your subject to apparently unlike subjects. This relative view is the most freewheeling, stimulating you to create rich associations that often reveal your deepest feelings and lead to new understanding.

Here is the exploratory guide that includes the directives discussed above.

EXPLORATORY GUIDE

● **Static View**
- Recall and record as many features as you can about your subject: aspects of it that describe and identify your place so that anyone can distinguish it from other places.
- Note down as many of your attitudes toward the place as you can.
- Identify the parts that make up the whole of your place.
- Record in specific detail the sights, sounds, smells, and tastes that characterize your experience with the place.

● **Dynamic View**
- Record the activities (physical movements, events) that you recall about the place.
- List the changes it has undergone during different time periods: days, weeks, months, years.
- Trace your involvement with the place.
- Trace its larger surrounding history.

● **Relative View**
- Classify your place, locating it in different kinds of groups, and put other members in that group or class.

Example: larger group or class (places where you learn)

| your subject | other member | other member |
| (Midwestern University) | (your high school) | (your church) |

| other member | other member |
| (your sports team) | (your 4H club) |

- Compare and contrast your place with other places, noting the similarities and differences.

Example: your subject   other subject
          (Midwestern University) (your high school)

Likenesses: X, Y, Z
Differences: A, B, C, D, E

- Create analogies for your place, relating it to something of an entirely different order.

  Example: <u>your subject</u>   <u>other subject</u>
         (Midwestern University)   (supermarket)
  Likeness: A, B, C

Writing down the ideas that each view generates helps you to find specific words for your experiences and to remember your ideas so that you can arrange, organize, and play with them. This exploratory activity is freer than drafting or even freewriting because you are not trapped within sentence or paragraph boundaries. During planning you need as much leeway and flexibility as possible as you search for answers to the question you asked.

The two student explorations below will illustrate the different ways in which writers use the exploratory guide. Although these explorations may suggest that the writers discovered all their static features first and then went on to look at the dynamic and relative aspects of their subjects, the process of exploring is not always that neat. You should feel free to move back and forth among the perspectives as you investigate your subject. Keeping separate lists may be a good idea. The three ways of looking are, after all, *means* of recalling and creating ideas; they are not ends in themselves. Taking more than one perspective on a subject keeps you from getting trapped in a mental or imaginative rut. What is important to you as a writer is the quality and number of ideas you gather by changing perspectives.

Notice that the writers below generated ideas without concern for conventions and without worry that some of their ideas might eventually prove to be inaccurate or irrelevant. Exploring is not the time for being critical.

EXPLORATION

WRITER 3   RIO

STATIC VIEW

The Beach
—harsh, white sand
—brown, lean bodies
—the smell of gasoline mixed with the salty air
—the ocean salty clear
—soccer games on the beaches   men yelling & the sand crunching underfoot

—old cars and horns that are never quiet
—Volkswagen taxis
—long beaches lined with hotels
—the hotels casting shadows on Copacabana beach, leaving small spaces of sunlight between them, looking out of the window & seeing sunbathers arrange themselves into those irregular rectangles
—hot oppressive heat
—greasy suntan lotion, sticky sand
—young men and their soccer games
—different schools of fish visit the beaches, sharks & jellyfish
—kite and cake vendors
—little black boys & girls from the apartment buildings

The City
—mosaic sidewalks, the Moors & the Portuguese
—the vendors, kites & coconuts
—the Brazilian people and their rhythm
—hundreds of caterpillar buses, new, proud drivers, weary passengers

The Hotel
—busy, frantic, disorganized
—people lifting luggage and arranging packages
—uniformed men
—brown, sweating bodies
—baths with sand in the bottom, wet bathing suits, soggy towels
—the slap of the keys on the wood dock

DYNAMIC VIEW

Movements in Early Morning
—digging a hole in the sand, wriggling into it & watching people arrive
—the vendors getting set up
—buses, traffic jams, honking
—people eating rolls & fruit, looking out of their hotel windows onto the beach
—mountains crowding in on the city, appearing to move in the night and pushing the city slowly ahead of them into the ocean

Movements in Later Afternoon
—squinting to find the right windows & waving to my parents
—hot, sweating office workers, shedding clothes & cares, relaxing
—tourists sunning & protecting themselves from the fierce sun with lotion

Movements in Night
—car doors slamming, people talking, laughing
—walking on the beach sidewalk
—laughing young men shouting at pretty girls
—people holding hands

—beggars returning from a day's foraging in the city

—new surfers, some drowned today, some will die tomorrow

Inner Change—The City

—the mountains temperamentally shedding the favelas that hug them

—feeling sad when the stricken jumble of tin and paper cartons slides down and leaves them uncovered and cold

—poverty-ridden shacks are redecorated with a new piece of cardboard to shield the owners from the rain

—tiny corners in parks & empty lots are settled by destitute mountain people

—new shacks go up

—huge, dreary concrete apartment buildings are being constructed in the little space left in the city

—a beggar stakes out a corner—territory once belonging to different emaciated face

—new advertisements come with the arrival of a new import—Japanese radios—American Coke

—eager young men & brown-eyed girls meeting in bars & leaving together

—street markets: farmers & their little boys arriving 4 a.m. Saturday and leaving 9 p.m. Sunday

—flowers and fruit change hands

—young, unskilled men, maybe drought-stricken farmers from the North flock to Rio to help in the construction of the concrete dominos

—government changes: coup d'etat last night—generals & newspaper censorship this morning

—rich Brazilians & their families leaving their hot city apartments for their houses in the country

—poor families leaving their shacks to visit their relatives in the mountain forests

—taxis scuttle between the airport & the hotels

The Beach

—new, translucent, multicolored shells are daily washed onto the beaches, little boys & girls redistribute them with their toes & new shells come tomorrow to replace the old

—the sand—unshifting, still in the morning, at the end of the day marked & hilly, after a rain—brown, damp, cold with tiny little craters

—people shifting between beaches: Copacabana today, Ipanema tomorrow

—scalding in the afternoon, covered by towels & mats

—bums awakening

Outer Change

Past:

—Cabral—discovered, rich clothes, Portuguese settlers

—years of Portuguese rule & exploitation

—Rio, once capital of Brazil: kings, queens, slaves

—agricultural marketplace surrounded by coffee fazendas, rubber plantations

—primitive tribes

—wealthy Europeans, poor Cariocas

—remote, isolated

Today:

—Brazil—the sleeping giant stirs & yawns

—effect on cities like Rio is tremendous

—foreign enterprise & industry booming

—international tourist playground

—Rio will continue in exactly the same fashion, unchangeable

—character of the Brazilians, particularly the Cariocas, works against progress

—poor will get poorer, favelas will continue to be washed off the mountainsides

Future:

—rich will remain rich, their grandchildren will inherit millions & be sent to Europe for their education

RELATIVE VIEW

Classification

1. places that remain suspended in time — the industrial & political events of the rest of the world have little effect on the people & their strong cultures

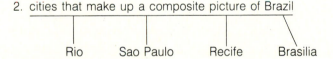

Rio

tiny villages in Iraq & Lebanon

India—the caste system

small cities in Africa starting to emerge industrially like Rio

2. cities that make up a composite picture of Brazil

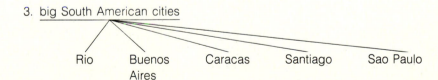

Rio   Sao Paulo   Recife   Brasilia

3. big South American cities

Rio   Buenos Aires   Caracas   Santiago   Sao Paulo

4. countries where people love and enjoy children, reflecting their own love of life

Brazil (Rio)   Mexico   Italy

5. one of the international jet set cities

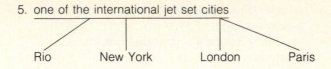

| Rio | New York | London | Paris |

6. places that have been settled by Europeans and still demonstrate signs of European influence

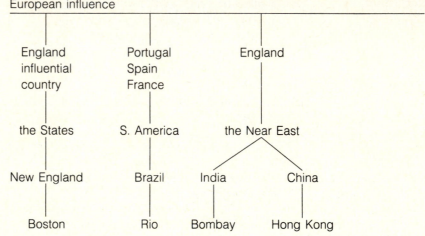

England
influential
country

Portugal
Spain
France

England

the States

S. America

the Near East

New England

Brazil

India

China

Boston

Rio

Bombay

Hong Kong

Comparison/Contrast

São Paulo	*Rio*
—Brazil's largest city—huge population	—not too many people
—flat on a plateau, can devour more land from the jungle as it needs it	—naturally bounded by the mountains on one side and the Atlantic on the other
—fast, energetic people	—slower pace of life
—the sea—one main difference	
—the sea helps to slow people down; they stop to look, smell & hear the roar	
—S.P. is a few miles from the Atlantic	—Rio is a coastal city
—architectural beauty created by man	—natural beauty
—not too many tourists	—a shifting population of tourists
—few cultural events	—a cultural center (for Brazil)
—industrial city	—not much industry—tourism
—no Carnival	—Carnival!

Analogy

—Rio is like a zebra

—the zebra's stripes remind me of the black & white mosaic sidewalks of Rio

—a zebra can graze slowly, resting often just like the Cariocas—they take their time & stop to rest often in the day

—a sleek animal—the wealthy men & women of Rio are smooth & polished

—an unusual animal—Rio is unique

—an animal of hot climates—Rio is hot, Brazil is hot

—a zebra gallops at night—a part of Rio, silent in the day, comes alive at night—the city gallops like the zebra

—zebras can move fast—Rio's beat can speed up to fever pitch at Carnival time

—zebras are wild animals—Cariocas are free-spirited people—uninhibited

—Rio is alive & moving constantly

● **COMMENTARY**

In the static view, Writer 3 has recorded some good sensory details from memories of her visit. She has clustered them under her own headings: beach, city, hotel. The only distinctive features she notes, however, are such details as "Copacabana," "mosaic sidewalks, the Moors and the Portuguese." Her static perspective would have been better if she had added more of such features to distinguish Rio from other resort places. Her dynamic view, tracing movements in a day and inner and outer changes, helped her to recall and symbolize many vivid aspects of her experience. Finally, in the relative perspective, she generated several classifications, some more fascinating than others, a fine comparison of Rio and São Paulo, and a zebra analogy that expressed some of the variety and vitality that Rio represented. This exploration was fruitful for Writer 3 not only in guiding her to a deeper understanding of her experience there, but also in providing her with good material for eventually writing her paper.

EXPLORATION

WRITER 2   A STATE HOME

STATIC VIEW

Sensory Impressions of the Home

—a loud clatter . . . unknown, distant voices, mingling, a low hum

—a gray clock set into the cement block wall . . . it lingers over endless minutes, then pulled reluctantly, jerks ahead with a loud flat click

—a hoarse female whine: "please miz wells"

—arid smell . . . disinfectant

—dirty socks

—faded tile, ceiling and floor . . . walls green—dull institutional green

—fluorescent lights, cruel . . . a harsh whitish glare

—bathroom: darker green door with half-legible obscenities scratched into it, always locked

—"Keep your hands to yourself. There are some girls who *like* to touch other girls."

—green plastic and metal chairs

—girls in faded jumpers sit, tipped back against the wall

—gray underwear . . . grayish tennis shoes . . . gray oatmeal

—"I wouldn't if I were you. They pulled a rat out of the tureen once."

—brown mats pulled out at night, lined up along the floor

—a gray tennis shoe tapping, tapping behind the girls . . . brilliant yellow and pink seclusion rooms, pure unscarred, unscratched paint

—hoarse female cry rising from behind the yellow door, heavy, weighted down in the air . . . "Miz wells. . . . Please. . . . Oh, God help me!"

—the hands of the clock jump forward—a click

DYNAMIC VIEW

Public Attitudes (Fortas) Versus Present Reality

—Fortas' opinion attached firmly the prevailing view that because juvenile courts were virtually therapy clinics, children who came before them did not need the protection of the Bill of Rights of the American Constitution (case of *Gault* vs *US,* from *The Throwaway Children,* by Lisa Richette).

—a huge brick structure with long steel screens over its windows and a high brick wall which ran in waves down Fort Street and turned the block—a castle, a fortress we would pass on the way to school and laugh. "WASPS: There's the Youth Home!"

—"Witness Gerald Gault's sentence of six years for a crime which for adults carried a five-to-fifty dollar fine and a maximum sentence of two months." *The Throwaway Children.*

—By standing close to the mesh screen and craning my neck, I could see the snow falling outside. I pushed my fingers into the metal screen and pressed against it. A child pulled his sled across the snow, and two school-girls, in plaid skirts, hurried down the street. I could just make out the letter-ing on the brown metal sign facing me a hundred miles below—Wayne County Youth Home. Established 19–.

—"How many Gerald Gaults had been here? How many Croziers" *Ibid.*

—putting my own wrinkled clothes on again, throwing the faded jumper and the old socks into a hamper, I was led back up to the ward to wait for re-lease. I went back into the room not seeing or feeling the buzz of excite-ment that surrounded me. "You're going home? Karen's going home! I'll miss you kid. You're going home . . . "

—"There is nothing worse than the smell of a dirty female. You will take a shower every day and clean yourselves thoroughly." God, yes, let me get the sound of you out of my pores.

—"you're going home Karen? I hope I do too soon."

—"What kind of hearing should a child receive in a juvenile court." *Ibid.*

—Waiting on a wooden bench, pink and blue jumpers, scared, tapping feet. Braids, Afros half picked out, stringy dyed hair; slept-in curls. "Don't cry, they don't feel sorry for you and it only goes worse on you."
—moving . . . but not all stagnant . . . trapped in their small circular environment going through the motions like the hands of the clock on the wall

Contrast

do not pity   cindy . . . throws
mehitabel   back her head
she is having   her breasts, too
her own kind of   large for a 14 yr
a good time   old rest on her
in her own way   protruding stomach
she would not   "God: you lost your
understand any other   navel kid—
sort of life   a bitter cry—
but the life   You're all whores.
she has chosen   just because I'm
to lead   the only one who
she was predestined   got caught."
to it as the   poor mehitabel . . .
sparks fly upward   "all marriage is
chacun a son gout   is one damn
as they say in france   kitten after
start her in   another," (archy)
as a kitten   spotted
and she would   mulatis kitten
repeat the same story   another litter
and do not overlook   for grandma
the fact that   to look after
mehitabel is really   poor baby.
proud of herself
she enjoys
*her own sufferings**

RELATIVE VIEW

Analogy

—the children move about as the hands of the gray metal clock
  steady . . . numbly . . . sluggishly
  crawling about routine tasks
    routine which cannot vary
  dragging their chairs behind them down the hall
  tipped back against the wall . . . fingers drumming against the metal legs of the chairs . . . feet tapping . . . tennis-clad . . . muffled . . . like the toneless noisy clicks of the clock

* From *Archys Life of Mehitabel* by Don Marquis (New York: Doubleday, 1927).

—day is highlighted by feedings everyone awaits eyes glancing up pushing
  the hands of the clock forward from breakfast . . . waiting for lunch from
  lunch waiting for dinner . . . after dinner waiting until the garish lights are
  turned off and fanciful dreams begin
—time . . . clicking . . . an endless, toneless whisper of a scream inside
  heads of the girls
  muffled by dirty cotton tennis shoes that muffle the angry
  pounding of feet against the floor
—the muted anguish of the clock . . . black hands jerking forward caught
  suspended in its black cage
    some frightened black insect trapped under the glass face
  impaled on a slender rod . . . its legs kicking in the air . . . its antennae jerk
    convulsively while the rod moves slowly in its cycle
  unable to escape—impaled and waiting for death—oblivion blackness
    which hides in the corner of the brains of all the girls
—the soft whispered screams . . . watching the quiet anguish of the clock
—cockroach under glass

CLASS EXERCISES

1. Compare Writer 2's exploration with that of Writer 3 (pp. 32–37) on
   the following points:
   a. Static view:
      • the inclusion of distinctive features
      • the use of sensory detail to express the remembrances of the
        place
      • the amount of information
   b. Dynamic view:
      • their different uses of history (one speaks of past views of institu-
        tions and the other of inner and outer changes)
      • their identification of changes
   c. Relative view:
      • the use of contrast and classification
      • the analogies created
   (If you wish to see a third exploration, you will find Writer 4's at the
   end of this chapter, where an entire writing process is presented.)
2. As a class, practice creating classifications, comparisons and contrasts,
   and analogies for the following subjects:
   a. your college cafeteria
   b. one of your local social spots
   c. the building in which your composition class is held
   Discuss the kinds of attitudes toward these subjects that are revealed
   by those classifications, comparisons, and contrasts.

3. As a class, use the exploratory guide to explore the place you selected in the last class exercises.

● **ASSIGNMENT: Exploration**

1. Using the exploratory guide, explore the question you formulated in the first assignment, discovering as many ideas under each view as you can.
2. Record these ideas in the most vivid words you can find.
3. Seek advice on your work.

● **FOCUS AND SITUATION**

INCUBATION

After you explore as thoroughly as time permits, allow your ideas time to settle, at least for a day and night. During writing, more than your conscious mind is at work. You also operate in ways that are not conscious. This second kind of activity, called incubating, plays a critical role in your efforts to reach new understanding.

1. It uses what your conscious explorations supply.
2. It is the wellspring of your insights and answers.
3. It requires time and relaxation from deliberate effort.

Sometimes without realizing it you may block its functioning by trying to complete your writing in one evening. Sometimes you may fail to nourish this source of insight by not exploring well. But if you prepare yourself with a rich stock of ideas during your exploration, your chances of finding the answer to your starting question increase. You need time (at least a good night's sleep) after your conscious searching. Even though you are pressured, you can still pace yourself by starting the writing process early enough to give yourself time for incubating.

THE FOCUS: SUBJECT AND POINT OF SIGNIFICANCE

Your next task is to reexamine your exploration, looking for any potential insights that recur or any important connections. You are looking for *insight* into your starting question or into any new question that may have emerged during exploration. To find a satisfying answer, you will probably have to write down many tentative ones.

To test these alternative answers, these tentative insights, you need to formulate them into two-part statements that will reveal more clearly what you have discovered. When an insight has been expressed in a two-part statement, we call it a *focus*. It can be distinguished from an insight in that insights are the potential answers that the mind creates during incubation. Some of these under scrutiny appear less useful responses to a writer's original question or inconsistent with a writer's sense of experience. They are discarded. The insights that sound most promising, however, have to be tested by putting them into words and eventually by shaping them into a whole discourse.

A well-stated focus has the following two parts: *subject* and *point of significance*. The subject can be the entire subject or that part of it which you have found to be most important in answering your question. The point of significance is your best answer to your original question, the new meaning you have tentatively discovered. For example, Writer 4's focus is:

Subject

Point of Significance

The Grand Rapids of my childhood——is not so much a place I want to return to as a lifestyle with more security and sense of permanence.

THE SITUATION: AUDIENCE AND MEDIUM

A focus also helps you to select the situation in which you want to communicate that insight. With your focus in mind, you can take better stock of the potential situations which you posed at the beginning. What audience and what medium will you select? Your focus offers a basis for choice. Try applying this principle: *The best audience is the one that will find your focus most helpful.* Ask yourself who will profit most from the focus you will share. That's your audience. The same principle will guide your selection of medium. *Ask yourself what medium will best allow you to share that focus with your reader.*

FOCUS AND DRAFTING

Expressing your insights as focuses not only helps you to clarify them for yourself, to test them, but also to choose one as a guide for drafting your paper. During drafting, a focus acts as a compass, guiding you to select relevant material from your exploration and to reject other material. It tells you whether you need to do more exploring. A focus gives you clues about organizing your paper. But a focus at this stage of your writing is not cast in bronze. As you engage in the process of drafting, your writing may lead you to a more qualified or sometimes a quite different answer. If that happens, then a new focus can be articulated.

THE FOCUS IN THE PAPER

Your focus not only acts as a guide during drafting; in your paper itself, the focus expresses a commitment you make to your reader. Whether explicit or implicit, your focus becomes for the reader the thread that ties your paper together, the radar that directs your audience's reading. A focus acts as a unifying force for your paper, indicating what you will discuss and avoid.

THE FOCUS AND THE EXPRESSIVE AIM

In a piece of writing with an expressive aim, the focus generally is stated in the first person and has a point of significance that expresses an attitude, an insight into the writer's private world. In expressive papers, the focus is often implicit, not expressed in a sentence, but present invisibly tying the paper together. In a well-focused paper, even though the focus is not expressed, a careful reader can reconstruct it, can identify the writer's focus. Writer 2's focus is:

Subject	**Point of Significance**
Being confined in a state home————	oppressed me but could not wipe out my sense of inner freedom.

Notice that the writer's point of significance is a personal one, explaining the ambivalent answer she discovered. Her point of significance is written in the first person; it does not express an insight into the nature of state homes in general. Moreover, when she writes her paper, this focus, this sentence, does not appear explicitly in the paper. It does, however, act as the paper's unifying thread.

Notice the expressive qualities in the insights given below, formulated into focuses. Beneath each focus the writer's original question or a revision is in parentheses to help you compare the focus with the question.

FOCUSES AND SITUATIONS

WRITER 1

Subject	**Point of Significance**
Working at F.W. bank————	was a learning experience for me because it challenged my ability to adapt to different situations as they arose and I discovered liking the responsibility that came with the job.

(**Question:** What aspects of working at a bank appealed to me and altered my attitudes enough for me to really enjoy the work and hate leaving it behind?)
Situation: I will write a letter to my best friend, Anne, who cannot understand why I like working in a bank.

WRITER 2

Subject	**Point of Significance**
Being confined in a state home———	oppressed me but could not wipe out my sense of inner freedom.

(**Revised Question:** What impact on my need for freedom and beauty did a stay in a clinical institution have?)
Situation: I want to write an essay for myself to keep because I would profit most from the focus.

WRITER 3

Subject	**Point of Significance**
Rio, with its extremes of poverty and wealth,———	will remain oblivious to the suffering of the poor, a horror I had never experienced before.

(**Question:** Why did Rio disappoint me, somehow change me?)
Situation: I will write an essay to my mother because she would like to know my reactions and because she likes to read what I write.

WRITER 4

Subject	**Point of Significance**
The Grand Rapids of my childhood———	is not so much a place I want to return to as a lifestyle with more security and sense of permanence.

(**Question:** Why do I dream of going back to Grand Rapids to live when I like a big city?)
Situation: I would like to try writing an article for a corporate magazine that has readers who often have to move.

WRITER 5

Subject	**Point of Significance**
My visit to my uncle's farm———	caused me to give up nine years of steady work, a good-paying job, all my friends and much of my family, to come to this strange place to school.

(**Revised Question:** What impact have my visits to my uncle's farm in Wisconsin had on the conflict between the introverted me and my upbringing in the Bay Area of California?)
Situation: I will write a letter to my sister.

● **COMMENTARY**

Notice that Writer 2's focus ends up with an ambivalent point of significance— she admits the oppression but concludes that inner freedom was not destroyed. Her paper must develop both ideas in some way. Notice also that this focus will proba-

bly exclude most of the material she generated under the dynamic view in her exploratory guide.

At first glance, you might be tempted to say that Writer 3 did not learn much beyond her early perceptions of the contrast between rich and poor in Rio. If you look closely, however, at her point of significance you will see that she does discover two new insights: first, that this contrast seems to be accepted and will therefore continue inevitably, and second, that this very inevitability is the horror her suburban life had never exposed her to.

CLASS EXERCISES

1. Examine the focuses of Writers 1, 4, and 5.
   Have these writers answered their questions?
   What kind of commitment to readers does each focus entail?
2. Discuss the following alternative focuses. Are they well stated?
   a. "I liked working at the bank."
   b. "Clinical institutions are poor places in which to live."
   c. "My vacation to Rio."
   d. "The history of Grand Rapids."
   e. "My experience at my uncle's farm had a good impact on me."
3. Using the ideas from the sample exploration done by the class, formulate alternative focuses.

● ASSIGNMENT: Focus and Situation

1. After allowing time for incubation, formulate your insight into a focus. (If you have alternative focuses, formulate all of them so that you can decide which best answers your question.)
2. Select a situation that best suits your focus.
3. Seek advice on your work.

● AUDIENCE AND MODES OF ORGANIZATION

Selecting an audience is only the beginning of the important task of shaping your writing for a reader. More crucial and difficult is the task of creating the *role* you want the reader to play. The role you select will determine your own *voice* as a writer. What do the notions of role and voice entail? The section below will explain these concepts.

AUDIENCE ROLES

In expressive writing, the writer usually has a choice of audience, as you saw earlier. But after you have made your choice, you still have another decision to make: What role will you ask that audience to play? Take one of Writer 2's possible audiences—her older sister. What roles does she play? First of all, she is obviously a sister, a family member. But she may also be a homemaker and mother, a taxpayer, a Republican, Democrat, or independent, a student, a jazz buff, a jogger, a confidante or rival—and so on. When you write, you ask the reader to assume a role. For example, when Writer 2's sister reads *Parents Magazine,* she is playing the role of mother; when she reads *Runner's World* she is playing a different role. Writer 2 could set one of a number of roles for her sister to play: as a mother, a Democratic voter, a confidante, or a rival. Notice that readers not only can play a variety of roles, but they have the option of refusing to play a role. The sister who refuses to read *Runner's World* refuses to play the role of a *Runner's World* reader—and hence rejects the attitudes and values that underlie *Runner's World.* It is important that you choose a role that your audience can play.

● Specific and Relational Roles

The role the audience will play is both specific and relational—*specific* in that the audience is asked to act as if one part of its total character were the whole: for example, Writer 2's sister can be asked to read as if she were only (or at least primarily) a mother, a runner, a Democrat, and so on. Its role is *relational* in that the audience is asked to accept a certain relationship to the writer: equal, subordinate, or superior, opponent, rival, friend, or disinterested observer. The writer must set and control both aspects of the reader's role.

● Writer's Voice

The *voice* a writer chooses may encourage the reader to adopt one relational role rather than another. If the writer's voice is reasoned and polite, the reader may adopt a relational role radically different from that adopted if the writer's voice is angry and belligerent. Voice in writing is much like tone in a verbal exchange. If you are approached by someone who blurts out loudly, "What the heck do you think you're doing?" you may respond differently—you may adopt a different relational role—than you might if that person had inquired, "May I help you?" In writing, your choice of voice rests on two considerations: what you know of the audience in itself and what you know of the audience in relation to your subject matter.

Tone of voice emerges in writing when you choose to be, for example: (1) serious about the subject and therefore rather formal in your attitude toward the reader; (2) humorous about the subject and therefore informal, even familiar with the audience; or (3) both serious and humorous and therefore ironic. Some audiences and some subjects invite one tone, others another. Following is a guide to help you set role and voice.

AUDIENCE ANALYSIS

After you have identified which of your possible audiences would best profit from your focus, you need to get to know this audience better. Most writers know more about their audience than they are consciously aware of. The task is to bring the knowledge to the surface by asking yourself a series of pertinent questions. Pertinent to what? Remember that you want to establish a role the audience can play. That means that the questions must pertain to the knowledge, values, and attitudes that the audience possesses or professes. It is important to answer these questions realistically because to fantasize an audience may be disastrous. We'd all like to write for the audience that mirrors our own knowledge, values, and attitudes, but audiences like that are rare.

The following audience guide and student examples will help you set the role for the audience.

AUDIENCE GUIDE

1. State your audience and the reasons for choosing it.
2. Analyze the audience in itself.
   a. Identify the levels and types of experiences that your audience has had (cultural, recreational, educational, and so on).
      • What is the median level of education in your audience?
      • Are most of your audience males or females?
      • What is the median age of your audience?
      • Is there anything special about your audience that will affect their image of you and themselves (racial, cultural, recreational, occupational, etc.)?
   b. Identify the hierarchy of values that your audience holds (money, power, friendship, security, intellectual growth).
3. Analyze the audience in relation to the subject.
   a. Identify the knowledge and opinion your audience holds on the subject.
   b. Determine how strongly your audience holds those views.
   c. Assess how willing your audience is to act on its opinion—if acting is appropriate.
4. In light of the information you gained above, determine the specific role your audience will play.

5. Repeat steps 2 and 3, but this time analyze only the *specific* role you want the audience to play.
   a. Determine what levels and types of experience fit the role your audience will play.
   b. Identify the values that fit that role.
   c. Determine what opinion you want your audience to hold in that role, how strongly you want the audience to hold it, and whether you want the audience to act on it.
6. Determine your voice and the *relational* role you want your audience to play. State why you have chosen that relationship.

SPECIFIC AND RELATIONAL ROLES

WRITER 1

1. My audience is my best friend, Anne, who just turned 21. We like sharing whatever we have discovered about ourselves. Numbers bore her so she could never quite see any more than I could why I liked my bank job so much.
2. a. Background: Anne is the oldest of seven children. Her family is typical middle class and she regularly attends family affairs. She attended a Catholic grade school, high school, and college for two years. Presently she is going to school at a local university. She is most intelligent in matters dealing with common sense, but textbooks bore her. For leisure activities, Anne loves to curl up with a good love story, listen to her favorite pop singers, go shopping, and especially go swimming. Socially she prefers a close group of friends to big loud parties.
   b. Values: High atop her hierarchy of values is her responsibility to her family and friends. She values family ties highly and some day she wants a big family of her own. Anne's friends are extremely important to her and she sees that each one knows her feelings. Anne's religion is also important to her; she puts a lot of time into trying to understand it better. Other things she values are health, useful education, and everyone getting a fair chance. Matters of little importance to her are money and social standing.
3. Attitude toward the subject: Anne knows what an average person knows about banking—what she sees. She has never had any bad experiences with a bank, so she has neutral feelings toward them. Action doesn't seem to fit here.
4. Specific role: A curious practical-minded job seeker. She will want to understand the joys of my work even though it may not seem like her kind of job.
5. Analysis of the role:
   a. Background: The role presupposes that she doesn't know much about banks. But as a job seeker she will know the kinds of rewards one looks for in a good job.
   b. Values: She will value a straightforward, honest, sincere explanation of what gives me satisfaction in my work.

    c. Attitude toward the Subject: I want her to accept my account and to accept my happiness in my new position; I want her to understand and so not argue about my attitude anymore.

6. Relational role: We have been friends for over six years and regard each other as equals, yet we do realize that there are subjects where the other has more knowledge and experience. Ever since the beginning we have been very close and have turned to each other as confidantes.

WRITER 2

1. I have selected myself as audience because although someone else might profit from it, I know that it will be most helpful to me. I am exorcising demons, trying to rid my present self of the dread and fear that hellhole imprinted on me. I'm the one who needs to understand the experience so that I can grow beyond it.

2. a. Background:
   —lower middle class, white neighborhood
   —experience of being in a psychiatric clinic
   —my father deserted my family
   —private city high school
   b. Values:
   —I value security, concern for others, ability to write, freedom from fear and confinement
   —I have a difficult time relating well to my mother but I value my relationship with my sister

3. Attitude toward subject: My two selves—the demon-tormented, fearful self versus the free, loved, secure self
   a. My fearful self hates the institution and dreads remembering it
   b. My fearful self clings to that dread.
   c. Doesn't apply.

4. Specific role: A learner, one being counseled, eager to learn.

5. Analysis of the role:
   a. Background: A learner has an interest in the subject but can't know all about it as there would be nothing to learn. A learner here would be someone familiar with my general situation but who needs detailed explanations of the time in the home.
   b. Values: A learner values the truth no matter how unpleasant or painful it may be.
   c. Attitude toward the subject: A good learner will have a strong interest but will refrain from judgment and action until all the facts are in. I want her to see that although my/our actual time in the home was terrible it didn't cripple me/us. I want her to see strength and victory in the outcome.

6. Relational role: My fearful self feels estranged from my free self; the two selves are both strangers and intimates, but I can't write as if that were true. It will be best to treat the audience as a stranger and to speak to her from a distance but as an equal. My voice should be calm and reflective and friendly.

● **COMMENTARY**

With Writer 2, the answers to question 2 are limited and even occasionally hesitant, understandable in light of the focus. The answers to 3 are more definite, and the answer to 6 is very perceptive. One has to read between the lines in dealing with a sensitive subject like this, but it appears that the writer is trying to solve the problem of self as audience by putting some distance between the two, while at the same time maintaining an even, balanced relationship. The writer is struggling with a very complicated situation. Writing for oneself in this fashion is an ambitious, challenging task, since the writer must write as if the audience—one's own self—is a different person.

MODES OF ORGANIZATION

Writing your paper requires having not only an aim but also a pattern of organization. *Modes* are patterns of organization, ways of putting together material. Choosing your mode before writing saves you endless meandering drafts that grope for organization. To make your choices feasible, this book will deal with four large organizational options that include many of the minor forms of organization you probably have used in your writing. These four modes are description, narration, classification, and evaluation. This chapter will discuss the descriptive and narrative modes because they are often used in expressive writing.

Most important to understand about modes is that they are just what the word indicates—*means* that help writers share their insights, their focuses. Modes become ends when assignments require that you write descriptive papers or narrative papers, often making writing an artificial act that emphasizes writing for its own sake rather than for communication. As a developing writer, you may need to practice using these four modes during your writing course, but you need never do so at the expense of what you're trying to communicate.

● **The Descriptive Mode**

The *descriptive mode* organizes your paper by moving from part to whole or whole to part. If your subject is physical, like a place, the model entails a sequence in space: left to right, far to near, up to down, clockwise or counterclockwise. You can start with the parts and conclude with the whole or vice versa. Writer 5 could communicate his sense of peace on the farm, for example, by opening with a sentence or two about the farm as a whole and then presenting a series of sections or paragraphs (depending on the amount of detail he wished to offer) devoted to the parts of the farm: the smells, the sounds, the sights; or the animals, the woods, the sky, the yard. If he chose the latter set of parts, his organizational plan might look like this:

¶ 1   The farm as a whole—quiet
¶ 2   The quietness of the animals
¶ 3   The peacefulness of the woods and sky
¶ 4   The serenity of the yard

This plan would then guide his drafting. If as he begins to write he wants to shift order or add other paragraphs, his plan can be set aside or modified. A plan is only the writer's own guide. Notice that this plan does not call for a general opening paragraph or a formal conclusion. That so-called five-paragraph form, while useful in research and other kinds of expository prose, does not govern expressive discourse.

The descriptive mode is also useful for subjects other than physical things. A writer can use it to organize a paper about ideas, political issues, or any kind of subject. In later chapters, we will illustrate how this whole/part structure works for other topics and aims of discourse.

● The Narrative Mode

The *narrative mode* implies a sequence in time, basically chronological, as one o'clock is followed by two o'clock. The sequence can be altered by rearranging significant units of time (i.e., incidents, events, and happenings) so that they fit more closely with other units. A "flashback," a unit from the past, may be suddenly inserted in order to help the audience understand the unit in the present sequence. Audiences expect certain sequences. But a writer may wish to break that expectation and thus achieve emphasis.

Two particular forms of narrative mode are (1) *cause and effect,* which emphasizes the causal relationship between one part of the chronology and another; and (2) *process,* which emphasizes repeated and repeatable chronological sequences. In expressive discourse, the straight narrative often works best.

Writer 5 could also have planned a narrative organization to communicate the sense of peace that influenced him. His plan might have looked something like this:

¶ 1   Early morning peace on the farm
¶ 2   Day's quiet activities
¶ 3   Evening leisure
¶ 4   Night stillness
¶ 5   The farm in retrospect

MODES AS ORGANIZATION VERSUS MODES AS CONTENT

The overall organizational plan a writer follows does not, however, limit the kind of material that can be used to develop each section or paragraph. If Writer 5 decides to organize using narration, he does not have to limit his material in each paragraph to narration. In his discussion of early morning, for example, he may wish to use many descriptive parts— sights, sounds, and smells—to help the reader experience the peace of the morning. Or he may wish to tell a story about one morning at the farm or to use a comparison or analogy to communicate the sense of peace. (These materials are from the classification mode, which is discussed in Chapter 2.) In other words, he can use any of the materials from his exploration or any new material he generates *within* his overall narrative structure.

Writer 2's previous choice of audience indicates that she wants to show that a "demon" has "been exorcised"; that her present self understands the past self, that the fearful self is understood and accepted by the free self. Narration is a distinct possibility; she could show the deadly round of a day in the prison of a state home. Description is also a distinct possibility; her exploratory list is crammed with details—parts of the institution. Writer 2 chose to use the descriptive mode of organization.

CLASS EXERCISES

1. Examine the audience analyses and situations of Writers 1 and 4 (Writer 4's appears at the end of this chapter).
   - How well have they analyzed their audiences?
   - What will the roles they have set entail in writing the paper?
   - What other specific roles could have been set? What writing changes would they entail?
   - Were their choices of situation good in the light of their focuses?
2. For the place you chose to investigate as a class, select an audience and do an analysis, setting the specific and relational roles. On the basis of the exploration, work out several organizational plans.

● ASSIGNMENT: Audience and Mode of Organization

1. Analyze your audience in order to set the specific and relational roles.
2. Create a plan of organization, using either description or narration.
3. Seek advice on your work.

● THE FIRST VERSION

At this point you move from planning to writing the paper. Even though you have given yourself a good running start, you have considerable work ahead. If you are like most writers, you will probably work though several drafts to a first version you wish to share with your instructor and classmates. But your planning work has given you several advantages. Effective writers write from abundance; they do not use everything they generate as raw material. Instead they tuck it away for future use. Developing a paper is a matter of (1) selecting material generated in earlier steps in the process and (2) adding useful material as it occurs to you during drafting. You now have several bases for selecting the material you will use.

1. Your *focus* will eliminate anything that does not relate to it. Writer 3 must eliminate from her paper any details about Rio that do not underscore the inevitability of the gap between the rich and poor. Even though she has striking details about the beach, they probably do not pertain.
2. Your *audience* will guide your selection. You should not present information or details as new and fresh if the audience is already familiar with them. If you wish to use an analogy or a comparison for some part of your paper, select the one that would work best for your audience.
3. Your *mode of organization* also offers some help even though, as explained above, each paragraph or section of your paper can be developed in several ways. Writer 3, for example, if she chooses a descriptive organization—the poor on the city streets, the poor huts on the hillside, and the rich city dwellers—may not find a use for her zebra analogy.
4. Your expressive aim also offers guidelines in writing your first version.

WRITING A PAPER WITH AN EXPRESSIVE AIM

The expressive aim requires that the writer select material on the basis of these principles:

1. Exclude material that is not personal, except on very good grounds. Appealing to books, other people's experiences or popular truths tends to shift the emphasis to either the expository or the persuasive. You will seem to be trying to justify your perceptions or feelings. The expressive aim does not require the writer to be absolutely

right, but only open, honest, and sincere about private feelings and understandings.

2. Include, as much as possible, the language of feeling; avoid the language of flat statement. The language of feeling abounds in images, metaphors, and concrete diction (see the Glossary). Emotion is not conveyed by abstract statements like "I feel sad," but rather by sharing the circumstances in as vivid a language as possible in order to allow the readers to recreate the scene for themselves.

For example, the exploratory list that Writer 2 will work from looks promising (see pp. 37–40). She has amassed a good many descriptive details that don't state but imply an emotional attitude. The use of "arid [acrid] smell," "disinfectant," and "dirty socks" in conjunction with "dirty cotton tennis shoes that muffle the angry pounding of feet against the floor" conveys an emotional attitude that would be very hard to state directly. Suppose we tried to paraphrase those perceptions. To say that the place was dirty and it smelled bad is expository rather than expressive, but misses the point as well. So we would say something like, "We felt that we were dirt, something to be disinfected (but without much care or enthusiasm) and it made us feel dirty and angry and frustrated." But the statement still doesn't convey the feeling; it only summarizes inaccurately and turns the feeling into information. The items on the list, however, are useful and appropriate because they invite the reader to recreate and share the perceptions and the feeling.

On the other hand, there are other items, particularly in the dynamic view, that probably should not be used. The writer has researched her own case, so to speak; she has read Lisa Richette's *The Throwaway Children*, probably in an effort to understand better her own difficulties. It's doubtful that the material can be used because the issue here is not one of convincing an audience by appeal to external authority, as it might be in expository or persuasive writing. Introducing Lisa Richette's study might break the focus.

That is not to say that reading *The Throwaway Children* and noting its contents were not useful to the writer. Richette may have helped the writer understand her own plight. But there is a difference between what a writer has available and what a writer uses in a paper. Although this principle is common to all the aims, it is particularly important to the writer of expressive discourse because of the temptation to turn away from the painful exploration of feelings to other things, external, objective, and neutral.

Chapter 2 will give you more advice on how to use concrete diction to develop your paper.

3. Feel free to use first person. Expressive papers are often written in the first person—*I* or *we*. Although you may have been told always to use third person—*he, she, it, they, them,* or *one*—that advice applies primarily to expository writing. Sometimes, however, an expressive

writer decides to use third person to gain distance—a practice useful when the audience is oneself. This holds true for Writer 2, whose first version appears below.

FIRST VERSION

WRITER 2

THE CAVERN

The room draws itself into a triangle. It spreads out from the wide glass-enclosed booth that holds the guards, and runs into a long narrowing corridor, walls tucking themselves under, past the rows of bright pink and yellow doors until they meet together, in a brief green corner. The low ceiling, as well as the floor is tiled, in a dull beige. It traps the odors that rise out of the floor and holds them in the air, the disinfectant from the mop pail mingling with the sweat from graying tennis shoes. The walls are dull green concrete blocks, broken by the lines of steel doors in the corridor. Painted by a sure, hard hand, their enamel coats are smooth and shiny, unmarred by graffiti scratches and usage. They have a gaiety inappropriate to the room. A small, high window in each door looks out into the hall; so many eyes watching over the children.

The girls, in loose jumpers sit, tipped back in green plastic and metal chairs lined up along the hall. Muffled in cotton tennis shoes, feet bang against the concrete, the girls watch the gray metal clock set into the wall above the guards' station. He holds back, languidly, hoarding over precious minutes, until pulled, against his will, he jerks forward with a loud click. A clattering, followed by distant shouting rises promisingly in the air, then dies down. Music from a local radio station, piped into the room, settles, mixing with the dirty disinfectant smell. Fingers drumming against the seat of the chairs, the girls watch the miser clock give up his minutes.

Behind the steel doors, in the dark, there is life still. There is no need of paint on this side of the door. The close walls are green-tiled and bare. It has a thick, dark odor all its own. In the corner, on the cement floor, a young girl sits in a white nightgown, rocking back and forth. She is far away, riding her horse through an English meadow, sweet yellow-green dotted with flowers.

CLASS EXERCISES

1. Compare Writer 2's first version with her exploration. What material from her exploration has been used?
2. Is there any other material in the exploration that could have been used? If so, what?

● ASSIGNMENT: The First Version

1. Write a first version of your paper that communicates your focus to your audience. Use either the descriptive or the narrative mode of organization.
2. Submit your first version for reader responses.

● READER RESPONSES

Effective writers are rewriters. A first version is never as good as a second version, a second version is rarely as good as a third, and so on. But changes should be introduced for good reasons—that is, reasons that lead to an increase in clarity, coherence, and credibility. How do you arrive at good reasons?

Professional writers give three opinions:

1. There is no substitute for advice from another professional (editor, teacher, publisher, successful writer, and so on).
2. There is no substitute for advice from your audience.
3. There is no substitute for self-criticism.

All three are true. If you can obtain all three, your writing has a greater chance of improving.

You also need to be able to sort out the major areas in which your strengths and weaknesses occur in your first version. It is sometimes difficult to separate major from minor problems by reviewing comments in the margins or at the end of your paper. The following reader guide will allow you to pinpoint the areas where you are succeeding and where readers are having trouble following you. Using the reader guide, your classmates can let you know whether:

1. your *focus* is coming across,
2. you have *developed* your focus enough for your audience to recreate it,
3. you have *organized* coherently,
4. your choices of *style*—sentence patterns and words—are working for your aim and focus,
5. you have control over the *conventions of standard written English.*

READER GUIDE

1. Focus:
    * What is the writer's focus?
    * Are there any sections of the paper that seem to be out of focus, i.e., seem unrelated to the total focus?
    (Chapter 2 will discuss this matter of unity.)
2. Development:
    * What specific and relational roles seem to be at work in the paper?
    * What material has the writer used effectively to help the reader *experience* the focus.
    * What sections of the paper need more development for the reader?
3. Organization:
    * What mode of organization has the writer used?
    * Are there any sections that break that structure?
    * Does the paper maintain consistency of person, number, and tense?
    * Does the paper have internal coherence between the paragraphs? Between the sentences?
    (Chapter 2 will discuss coherence.)
4. Style:
    * Does the writer use diction (word choices) that works for the audience, aim, and focus?
    * Does the writer use effective sentence patterns?
    (Chapter 2 will discuss sentence patterns and diction.)
5. Conventions:
    * Are there any places in which the writer has failed to use the conventions of standard written English—grammar, spelling, and punctuation?

Each of the three types of readers discussed above can use this reader guide to give you advice on your paper.

1. Instructors can provide you with either oral or written responses, using the guide. They may delay grading your paper until revision.
2. Your classmates, playing the roles you set for your audience, can also give you valuable advice. Often their advice is more useful if they have had time to read your paper and prepare written responses before group discussions. The reader guide can direct their attention to the important points on which you need advice. If time does not permit a discussion of every aspect of your paper, your classmates should be encouraged to give you advice on focus, development, and organization.
3. Although it is often difficult for you to get enough distance from your work for effective self-criticism, you can improve that power by responding to others' papers. Another useful practice is to read your work aloud.

A suggested format for a reader guide in written form is shown below.

```
┌─────────────────────────────────────────────────┐
│                                                  │
│  READER GUIDE        NAME_____          │
│                                  (Writer)        │
│                                                  │
│                      NAME_____          │
│                                  (Reader)        │
│                                                  │
│  1. Focus                                        │
│                                                  │
│                                                  │
│  2. Development: Aim and Audience                │
│                                                  │
│                                                  │
│  3. Organization: Coherence                      │
│                                                  │
│                                                  │
│  4. Style: Diction and Sentence Patterns         │
│                                                  │
│                                                  │
│  5. Conventions: Grammar, Spelling, Punctuation  │
│                                                  │
│                                                  │
└─────────────────────────────────────────────────┘
```

INSTRUCTOR'S RESPONSE TO WRITER 2

FOCUS

The title "The Cavern" helps your audience find the focus because it suggests a carved-out passage with a dead end. The whole essay seems to be saying at first that the experience of being in the room was oppressive, but at the end you turn that around nicely by showing your audience how the girl escaped in her own mind. Thus your essay is communicating that the imprisonment was oppressive but could not completely wipe out your inner freedom. Every part of your paper seems to support either one or the other of these parts of your focus.

DEVELOPMENT

Two perhaps surprising things work well here. First is the amount of material you have discarded from your exploration. All those impressions have come down to a short essay—but an essay with a punch. Second, the use of the third person also works well to give you the distance you need.

In the first paragraph, you powerfully recall for your other self some of the key dismal details of her "prison." Because your reader was there, you don't need to include every aspect but only highly suggestive reminders. But even your secondary audience (your classmates and I) can experience the horrible sense of confinement. In the second paragraph, you also do a good job of reminding your audience of the sense of waiting—to be free. But the clock cannot release you, nor can the guards. You imply the question: If people are not free in time or space, in what way can they be free? That question sets you up well for the final paragraph, which answers the question by showing that in her imagination the girl can ride a horse through an English meadow. I am impressed with the way you transmute the yellow of the imprisoning doors and the deadly institutional green into the colors of sunlight, sweetness, and growth—the colors of a meadow. You have thus enabled both your audiences to understand and *experience* how you could and did escape, transcending time and space.

ORGANIZATION

Your choice of descriptive mode works well as it moves from the whole to the parts—from the total floor plan of the room to the ceiling, to the walls with their windows, to the girls, and finally to the inner room behind the steel doors. But in the first paragraph you confuse the reader with the description of the room as a triangle which runs into a long narrow corridor. Where is the observer? What are the spatial relationships between the booth, room, and hall corridor? You need work here. You might also try making your paragraphing correspond to the descriptive mode by separating description of the ceiling and the walls, as separate parts, into paragraphs.

STYLE

Your use of understatement is remarkable here.* The sense of something imprisoning everyone in the home, something almost suprahuman or subhuman, is conveyed in a series of dependent sentence constructions. The guards themselves are imprisoned in the "booth that holds the guards"; the doors have been "painted by a sure, hard, hand"; the windows suggest "so many eyes watching over the children"; "the girls watch the miser clock give up his minutes." Your concrete diction puts the readers on the scene, allowing them to see, smell, and hear the oppression, the depression—and finally the escape to the yellow-green meadow.

* See the Glossary for a definition of *understatement*.

CONVENTIONS

The only problems you have here are with punctuation—but punctuation is important for your audience because the movement and syntax of your paper are complex. Examine your essay carefully for mistakes.*

STUDENT RESPONSE TO WRITER 2

FOCUS

I found it hard to detect the focus at first reading, maybe because I expected something else. Anyway, the focus was clear when I finished reading. There's a kind of suspense in the essay. I didn't understand until I was all the way through that it was an essay about survival.

DEVELOPMENT

The details are very good. The essay is mostly detail. Some of it confused me, like at first when I thought you were talking about a drug experience. But pretty soon I saw that the development is a piling up of things that tried to beat you down and destroy you. There is enough to make that point.

ORGANIZATION

I'm not sure I understand the organization. It seems that there is a kind of descriptive organization. The first paragraph deals with the big room. The second paragraph talks about the girls. The third talks about one girl in one room. It works OK so I can't criticize it.

STYLE

The best part of the essay. It's like the prison (state home) is more alive than the people in it, and that's done by your choice of words. Every paragraph is loaded with great detail. And then the ending. Instead of stating the focus, you use descriptive details to imply it.

CONVENTIONS

You don't have any problems.

---

*Consult the section on punctuation in Part Two of this book, pp. 424–430.

CLASS EXERCISES

1. Give written responses to Writer 4's essay (at the end of this chapter).
2. Discuss your responses with your classmates and instructor.

● ASSIGNMENT: Reader Response

1. Using the reader guide, give a written response to several of your classmates' first versions.
2. Discuss these responses with your classmates.

● REVISING AND EDITING

As a rewriter, you always benefit from getting as many reactions as possible to your first version, but that is not to say that you must take every suggestion. However, if several readers see the same flaw in the paper, it's a good bet that the flaw exists. And there's another benefit: if you are able to collect four or five reactions to three or four of your papers and the same flaws keep popping up in the reactions, you know that you have an ingrained problem.

Assuming, then, that you have accumulated some useful responses, you are ready to start rewriting your paper. Rewriting involves two kinds of work: revising and editing.

Revising concerns improving any aspects of your focus, development, organization, or style that need reworking. This kind of revising can sometimes involve major changes. If major flaws rest in focus or development you might have to junk the paper and begin again, because the problems may lie so far back in the writing process that repairing would take more work than starting over. Flaws in organization call for a large repair job—as if your car had thrown a rod or dropped its transmission. But repairs can be made.

Editing involves cleaning up mistakes in grammar, spelling, and punctuation (essentially a proofreading activity) and stylistic improvement, which involves reconsidering your choices of diction and sentence structure.

Let us examine these two kinds of rewriting more closely.

PROBLEMS OF FOCUS

Problems of focus must be solved before any other revision can fruitfully take place. You will waste time adding more development or better organization to an unfocused paper. You will waste even more time polishing your sentence structure and your diction and cleaning up problems of convention in an unfocused paper.

If your reader cannot find your focus, it may be because you yourself are hazy about it. Your problems may go back to earlier stages in your writing, when you were unclear about what point of significance had emerged. If so, you will have to return to that point. Your paper may have helped you grope your way toward a clearer focus, but you will still have to recast the writing to reflect that understanding. If you were writing only on a subject with no clear point of significance, your paper also needs major repair because it has no guide, no center yet.

But sometimes your problems with focus come from the fact that some of your material does not fit and hence confuses your reader about what point you're trying to communicate. If so, then you need to remove the irrelevant section or sentence or paragraph. This revision is easier.

PROBLEMS OF DEVELOPMENT

If you have a focused but undeveloped paper, your problems may stem from several sources.

First, you may not have given your readers enough specific material to enable them to understand or experience your focus. Your ideas and information may be too general or too limited. Your paper may be lopsided, heavily developing one paragraph and leaving another undernourished.

A second kind of problem may stem from the fact that you insult your readers by giving information they already have, signaling that you have not considered the audience's background when writing the paper. Or you may use examples and details that are inappropriate, choosing material that is either above or below the level of your audience or examples that your readers find boring or unclear. Problems of development, therefore, involve careful reconsideration of your material and your audience roles. If your paper has been judged undeveloped, you may profit from rescanning your exploration to see if you can find unused ideas, information, analogies or comparisons that work to communicate your focus to your audience. If you do not find what you need there, you will have to generate more material.

Third, you may have difficulty maintaining the roles you set for your audience. You may introduce material that is unrelated to the specific role you established, or you may shift the voice—the relationship you set with your audience. Examine your information, your examples, and your language for any of these problems.

PROBLEMS OF ORGANIZATION

Problems of organization are most evident at the paragraph level. Paragraphs are the large way you signal the kind of movement and order you want your paper to follow. Usually the opening words of each paragraph point out to the reader the direction the paper is going. In descriptive organization, each paragraph normally treats one part of the whole. But sometimes the reader has to wade through to the middle of the paragraph to find out which part is being treated. That problem of organization can be remedied by letting the reader know at the beginning of each paragraph which part or which segment of time (in the case of narrative mode) is about to be discussed. In Writer 2's revision, she starts each paragraph with the parts: the room, the ceiling, the walls, the girls, the steel door.

Sometimes the problem stems from a mixture of modes. The writer starts out using description, taking up one part after another, and then switches to narrative mode, organizing by time segments. That problem can often be solved by shifting the framework to one or the other. But remember that the *contents* of paragraphs can come from any mode. In a long discourse like a fifty-page essay or a dissertation, of course, a writer may shift from one mode to another, but in a shorter piece such shifts may disorient the reader.

Other problems of organization may stem from lack of cohesion—the failure of sentences to stick together and follow one another easily. Chapter 2 will examine some causes of this problem and offer suggestions for revision.

PROBLEMS OF STYLE

Chapter 2 will concentrate on problems of style in expressive writing. In revising this paper, turn your attention, therefore, to the other difficulties.

PROBLEMS WITH CONVENTIONS

If you have problems with conventions, consult Chapter 9. If the examples, explanations, and exercises there are insufficient to help you, consult your instructor or your writing center.

REVISION

WRITER 2

THE CAVERN

The room draws itself into a triangle From the wide, glass-enclosed booth that holds the guards, it narrows into a long corridor, walls tucking themselves under, past the rows of bright pink and yellow doors until they meet sharply in a dead end.

The low ceiling, like the floor, is tiled a dull beige. It traps the odors that rise out of the floor and holds them in the air, the disinfectant from the mop pail mingling with the sweat from graying tennis shoes.

The walls are dull green concrete blocks, broken by the lines of steel doors. Painted by a sure, hard hand, their enamel coats, smooth and shiny, are unmarred by graffiti scratches. They have a gaiety inappropriate to the room. A small, high window in each door looks into the hall: so many eyes watching over the children.

The girls in loose jumpers sit, tipped back in green plastic and metal chairs lined up along the hall. Muffled in cotton tennis shoes, feet thump against the concrete. The girls watch the gray metal clock set into the wall above the guards' station. He holds back languidly, hoarding precious minutes, until, pulled against his will, he jerks forward with a loud click. A clattering, followed by distant shouting, rises promisingly in the air, then dies down. Music from a local radio station, piped into the room, settles, mixing with the dirty disinfectant smell. Fingers drumming against the seats of the chairs, the girls watch the miser clock give up his minutes.

Behind the steel door, in the dark, there is life still. No need of paint on this side of the door; the close walls are green-tiled and bare. The room has a thick, dark odor all its own. In the corner, on the cement floor, a young girl in a white nightgown sits rocking back and forth. She is far away, riding her horse through an English meadow, sweet yellow-green dotted with flowers.

CLASS EXERCISES

1. Compare Writer 2's revision (above) with her first version (p. 55). What advice has she followed? Has it improved her paper?
2. Examine Writer 4's planning, writing, and rewriting efforts at the end of this chapter. As a class, discuss the relationship between his work at different stages.
3. Either alone or in a small group, work on the exercises in Chapter 9, "Editing," that address the kinds of mistakes present in your first version.

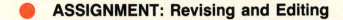

● ASSIGNMENT: Revising and Editing

> 1. Guided by the advice you received on your first version, rewrite your paper, revising its major problems.
> 2. Edit it for correctness of conventions.

A WRITER'S PROCESS

To illustrate more clearly the way in which different writing acts contribute to a finished product, we present at the end of every chapter a single writer's efforts from guiding question through revising and editing. Below is the work of Writer 4.

THE GUIDING QUESTION AND POTENTIAL SITUATIONS

WRITER 4

Subject: My childhood in Grand Rapids

My Values and Expectations
—culture and nightlife of a big city
—memories of childhood security

My Subject
—small-city limitations
—reality of present-day Grand Rapids

Question: Why do I dream of going back to Grand Rapids to live when I like a big city?

Situations
—a letter to my friend Joyce
—an article for a corporate magazine read by employees that are transferred often
—a long diary entry?
—an essay for my classmates and instructors

EXPLORATION

GRAND RAPIDS

STATIC VIEW
—old-fashioned green frame house with a big front porch
—a tree-lined street filled with children playing
—an attic filled with treasures hidden in boxes, books which had been my

mother's, like *Little Women* and *Black Beauty,* old dolls with a broken leg or arm that someone had carefully packed away to be fixed and never did, clothes, pictures

—our backyard—large lawn with an overgrown rock garden and an empty goldfish pool at the back

—a mammoth fallen tree which stretched from end to end behind our lot blocking the view of the field beyond—filled with crevices for hiding in or making into secret mailboxes

—The "Field," about five acres of undeveloped land in the middle of the city

—wild grass which grew as tall as I was

—weather-beaten tree stumps with branches still protruding here and there (we used for riding on)

—a swamp with its musty smell, green moss, mud, snakes and pollywogs

—a steep hill over which children swung from ropes tied to tree branches like Tarzan and in winter sledding.

—the library, an old stone building with the smell of bookbindings and cool quiet aisles filled with books of every kind—a park across the street that had a fountain with cool splashing water

—stores with names like Herpelsheimer's and Steketee's and hospitals named Sunshine, Mary Freebed, and Butterworth

—the museum—small and not intimidating, its exhibits seen so often they became like old friends—the doll collection, china dolls and rag dolls—the room filled with rocks and gems which had a little booth you could go into like a photo booth to see certain stones which lit up in the dark, a history exhibit with an Indian hunter crouched near the ground, camouflaged in an animal skin, arrow poised, his unsuspecting prey nearby

—the art gallery—at Christmas a tree for every country, each with its own decoration

DYNAMIC VIEW

Activities

—walking to Booth's Dairy on summer evenings—real old-fashioned ice cream and spinning on stools by the soda fountain

—children laughing and playing on front porches during summer rain storms

—public parks where families had picnics—hot dogs and marshmallows roasting on sticks, lovers holding hands strolling through the formal rose gardens while children raced in and out on the paths playing tag, a stream, dark and cool in the woods, wading pools where children played "Sally sitting in the water" and other games

—sparklers, parades, picnics, and fireworks on the fourth of July with flags neatly hanging on nearly every house

—grown-ups raking leaves into piles by the curbs and watching them burn while children played mother may I and tag until the last embers burned out

Going Back to Grand Rapids

—my old house, now smaller and less impressive—the front porch gone and a garage stood where the goldfish pond was once
—the swamp, used as a landfill by the city, was gone
—the field, its grass all neatly cut, fallen trees sawed up and cleared away, stood empty now
—park—a victim of city budget cuts—unkempt now, grass filled with bare dirt patches, overgrown roses, and a wading pool with cracked cement and not a drop of water
—articles written in newspapers about urban problems, slums, and crime, followed by optimistic reports of rebuilding efforts
—staying at the Pantlind, a downtown hotel, its graceful elegance now faded into peeling paint and threadbare carpets
—a once grand downtown movie house now showing pornography

RELATIVE VIEW

Classifying

—medium-sized Midwestern city
—city with strong religious influence, Dutch Reform and German Catholic
—hometown—place of roots and family

Compare/Contrast with Detroit

—slower pace to life of a smaller town
—friendlier, more neighborly people
—more homogeneous population
—both towns (although Detroit's image may be changing) where people seem to enjoy living more than out-of-towners want to visit
—both towns where most people want to live in single-family homes with their own lots
—both have had suburban malls and other things which led to deteriorating downtowns which are being rebuilt

Analogy

—like a snapshot taken in black and white—when looked at by the people in it, it calls to mind the feelings of that moment, long since gone in time and yet still there in memory
—to a stranger the photo seems drab and poorly taken
—when I see Grand Rapids now, I don't see the physical reality as much as I recall the happy, carefree days of childhood when I was surrounded by people who loved me and were convinced that nothing bad or hurtful could ever happen to me
—to a stranger Grand Rapids seems like an industrial town of medium size with most of the big city problems and few of the advantages

FOCUS AND SITUATION

Subject	*Point of Significance*
The Grand Rapids of my childhood ——	is not so much a place I want to return to as a lifestyle with more security and sense of permanence.

Situation: An article for a corporate magazine with readers that are transferred often.

AUDIENCE AND MODE OF ORGANIZATION

AUDIENCE ANALYSIS

1. Audience: I will write for an audience of mature people who have participated in corporate moves, because they are likely to have had a nostalgia similar to mine, with or without understanding its roots.
2. Audience in itself:
   a. Background: Most of these people are well educated and middle class and have lived in large urban areas. They often live in middle-class suburbs which are usually quite transient.
   b. Values: These people often believe that America's history is one of almost uninterrupted progress. Corporate families place a high value on intellectual growth, position and influence, and material well-being. Families, while important, are often secondary to the corporation.
3. Audience in relation to the subject:
   a. I believe that most corporate families feel the conflict between permanence, security, and family ties and adventure, new people and places, and ever-upward mobility.
   b. They have made a choice and are living with it, but I think they sometimes regret some of the things they've given up.
   c. No action is appropriate.
4. Specific role: The readers should play the role of reflective corporate nomads.
5. Analysis of role:
   a. Background: They will have gone through repeated uprootings. They will have had to cope with loneliness, insecurity as a result. They will have thought through the problem to construct defenses.
   b. Values: In that role, one values permanence and tradition even while forced into rootlessness.
   c. Attitude toward subject: They doubtless feel strongly about the ways in which they handle their own feelings.
6. Relational role: I think the audience should be peers of mine. My story is a reflection on and remembrance of a place and time which I left. Many of them have had similar feelings. My voice, therefore, will be that of an equal.

MODE OF ORGANIZATION: NARRATIVE

1. Grand Rapids then—Looking back
2. Summer in G.R.—Joy of family activities
3. Autumn—Games
4. Winter—Fun of inside games
5. Grand Rapids now—A snapshot

FIRST VERSION

LOOKING BACK

My family became corporate nomads when I was eight. Each year in the spring as other people looked forward to new flowers blooming in their gardens, we looked forward to a new house, new school, new people in a new and different city. It was, we assured each other in later years, a "broadening upbringing." It made us tolerant of other life-styles.

Still I often think back to Grand Rapids, the city where I was born, the city of my parents and of their parents before them. I dream of returning, of experiencing again the sense of belonging that I knew there, but the Grand Rapids of my childhood no longer exists except in my memory.

We lived in an old-fashioned green frame house with a big front porch. In the back of our house was a large lawn, an overgrown rock garden, and an empty goldfish pool at the back. A mammoth fallen tree which stretched from end to end behind our lot blocked the view of the field beyond which consisted of about five acres of undeveloped land right there in the middle of the city.

The seasons seemed more vivid then, each with its own sights, sounds, smells, and activities.

In summer we would go exploring in the field, wandering through the wild grass which grew as tall as me. Some days we found weather-beaten tree stumps with branches still protruding here and there. These became horses and we would ride. Some days we spent at the swamp with its musty smell, green moss, mud, snakes, and pollywogs. There was a steep hill nearby and sometimes we swung off it from ropes tied to tree branches like Tarzan. On summer evenings my father walked with us to Booth's Dairy where we would spin on stools by the soda fountain licking our ice cream cones. Or sometimes he and my mother took us to the library. My father watched the younger ones at a park across the street. They played by the fountain with its cool splashing water while we older ones were allowed to accompany my mother across to the old stone library building with its smells of bookbindings. We tiptoed up and down the quiet aisles filled with books of every kind, carefully choosing one book from the children's room to take home. My grandparents lived no more than a mile away, as did most of my dad's seven brothers and sisters. Frequently we met at the public park in our neighborhood for a picnic. We roasted hot dogs and marshmallows on sticks. The children would then race off to play tag, or change into bathing suits and play "Sally sitting in the water" at the wading pool. Lovers, holding hands, strolled through the formal rose gardens or down cool dark paths in the woods. On the fourth of July we celebrated with sparklers, parades, picnics, and fireworks. There was a flag neatly hanging from nearly every house. In autumn the grown-ups raked leaves into piles by the curb and stood watching them burn while we children played "mother may I" or tag until the last embers burned out.

When winter came there were other things to do. We would climb the stairs to the attic filled with treasures hidden in boxes. We never knew what we might find. There were books which had been my mother's, like *Little Women* or *Black Beauty,* old dolls with a broken leg or arm that someone had packed carefully away to be fixed and never did, strangely styled clothes we dressed up in playing grown-up, and faded pictures of people posed stiffly in front of a camera. Sometimes we visited the museum, its exhibits seen so often they became like old friends. There was a doll collection with china dolls, rag dolls, dolls filled with sawdust and dolls made of wood. One room, filled with rocks and gems, had a little booth you could go into like a photo booth to see certain stones which lit up in the dark. There was a history exhibit with an Indian hunter crouched near the ground, camouflaged in an animal skin, arrow poised, his unsuspecting prey nearby. At Christmastime, we trudged through the snow to the art gallery to see the Christmas trees each decorated in a different country's style. There were also trips downtown to stores named Herpelsheimer's (which I pronounced purple-shiners and thought of black eyes) and Steketee's.

There were many out-of-the-ordinary names there, a part of what made the city unique. No Grand Rapids Municipal or Kent County General to name their hospitals. Instead they were called Mary Freebed, which I was sure meant no charge, and Butterworth and Sunshine, which is still the most cheerful name for a hospital I've ever heard.

I went on my own tour of Grand Rapids not long ago. I stayed at the Pantlind, a downtown hotel, its graceful elegance now faded into peeling paint and threadbare carpets. Across the street was a once grand downtown movie house now showing pornography. My old house seemed smaller, less impressive now. The front porch was gone and a garage stood where the goldfish pond was once. The swamp, used as a landfill by the city, was gone now. The field, its grass neatly cut, fallen trees sawed up and cleared away, stood empty. The park, a victim of city budget cuts, looked unkempt. The grass was filled with bare dirt patches, the roses overgrown, and the wading pool had cracked cement and not a drop of water.

For me Grand Rapids is like a snapshot taken in black and white. To someone who was there when the picture was taken it calls to mind all the colors, sounds, smells, and emotions of that moment even though the picture may be faded and poorly taken. What I see in Grand Rapids is a life-style of permanence where families lived and died in close proximity and life seemed somehow simpler and roles more easily defined.

REVISION

LOOKING BACK

My family became corporate nomads when I was eight. Each year in the spring as other people looked forward to new flowers blooming in their gardens, we looked forward to a new house, new school, new people in a new and different city. It was, we assured each other in later years, a "broadening upbringing." It made us tolerant of other life-styles. But, as I realize now, it cost us something too.

I often think back to Grand Rapids, the city where I was born, the city of my parents and of their parents before them. I dream of returning, of experiencing again the sense of belonging that I knew there, even though the Grand Rapids of my childhood no longer exists except in my memory. We lived in an old-fashioned green frame house with a big front porch. In the back of our house was a large lawn, an overgrown rock garden, and an empty goldfish pool. A mammoth fallen tree which stretched from end to end behind our lot blocked the view of the field beyond, which consisted of about five acres of undeveloped land right there in the middle of the city.

The seasons seemed more vivid then, each with its own sights, sounds, smells, and activities.

In summer we would go exploring in the field, wandering through the wild grass which grew as tall as me. Some days we found weather-beaten tree stumps with branches still protruding here and there. These became horses and we would ride. Some days we spent at the swamp with its musty smell, green moss, mud, snakes, and pollywogs. There was a steep hill nearby and sometimes we swung off it from ropes tied to tree branches like Tarzan. On summer evenings my father walked with us to Booth's Dairy where we would spin on stools by the soda fountain, licking our ice cream cones. Or sometimes he and my mother took us to the library. My father watched the younger ones at a park across the street. They played by the fountain with its cool splashing water while we older ones were allowed to accompany my mother across to the old stone library building with its smells of bookbindings. We tiptoed up and down the quiet aisles filled with books of every kind, carefully choosing one book from the children's room to take home. My grandparents lived no more than a mile away as did most of my dad's seven brothers and sisters. Frequently we met at the public park in our neighborhood for a picnic. We roasted hot dogs and marshmallows on sticks. The children would then race off to play tag, or change into bathing suits and play "Sally sitting in the water" at the wading pool. On the Fourth of July we celebrated with sparklers, parades, picnics, and fireworks. There was a flag neatly hanging from nearly every house.

In the brief Michigan autumn the grown-ups raked leaves into piles by the curb and stood watching them burn while we children played "mother-may-I" or tag until the last embers burned out.

When winter came there were other things to do. We would climb the stairs to the attic filled with treasures hidden in boxes. We never knew what we might find.

There were books which had been my mother's, like *Little Women* or *Black Beauty,* old dolls with broken legs, or strangely styled clothes we dressed up in playing grown-up, and faded pictures of people posed stiffly in front of a camera. Sometimes we visited the museum, its exhibits seen so often they became like old friends. There was a doll collection with china dolls, rag dolls, dolls filled with sawdust, and dolls made of wood. One room, filled with rocks and gems, had a little booth you could go into like a photo booth to see certain stones which lit up in the dark. There was a history exhibit with an Indian hunter crouched near the ground, camouflaged in an animal skin, arrow poised, his unsuspecting prey nearby. At Christmastime, we trudged through the snow to the art gallery to see the Christmas trees, each decorated in a different country's style. There were also trips downtown to stores named Herpelsheimer's (which I pronounced purple-shiners and thought of black eyes) and Steketee's. There were many out-of-the-ordinary names there, a part of what made the city unique. No Grand Rapids Municipal or Kent County General to name their hospitals. Instead they were called Mary Freebed, which I was sure meant no charge, and Butterworth and Sunshine, which is still the most cheerful name for a hospital I've ever heard.

I went on my own tour of Grand Rapids not long ago. I stayed at the Pantline, a downtown hotel, its graceful elegance now faded into peeling paint and threadbare carpets. Across the street was a once grand downtown movie house now showing pornography. My old house seemed smaller, less impressive now. The front porch was gone and a garage stood where the goldfish pond was once. The swamp, used as a landfill by the city, was gone now. The field, its grass neatly cut, fallen trees sawed up and cleared away, stood empty. The park, a victim of city budget cuts, looked unkempt. The grass was filled with bare dirt patches, the roses were overgrown, and the wading pool had lost its water down a deep crack in the cement.

For me today's Grand Rapids is like a badly focused snapshot. To someone who was there when the picture was taken it calls to mind all the colors, sounds, smells, and emotions of that moment, even though the picture may be faded and poorly taken. What I see in that fuller Grand Rapids is a life-style of permanence, where families lived and died in close proximity and life seemed somehow simpler and roles more easily defined.

2

WRITING WITH AN EXPRESSIVE AIM

In the Private World/Persons

This second chapter, also devoted to writing in your private world with an expressive aim, has a threefold purpose: (1) to provide a new context, persons or relationships, about which you can create new understandings, using again the powerful strategies introduced in Chapter 1; (2) to add the classification mode to your repertoire of organizations; and (3) to offer advice to help you improve your style. In order to gain benefit from the powerful guides, you need repeated practice using them in your own individual way so that they become what they are intended to be: means, not ends.

Later in this chapter you will receive extensive advice on what constitutes good expressive style—a discussion postponed in the last chapter while you were learning how to plan, focus, organize, and develop a paper for a specific audience.

THE GUIDING QUESTION AND POTENTIAL SITUATIONS

THE SUBJECT

In the last chapter, you examined a place that had a significant influence on your life. The subject context for this chapter will be another major influence, a relationship you have had or still have with someone whom you suspect has contributed to your way of thinking, your attitudes toward life, your character development, and so on.

By investigating the meaning of an important relationship in your life, you can learn a great deal about yourself. You can come to know yourself in the mirror of other people. In their reactions, you can see reflected your own way of behaving, your personality, your aspirations. Your relationships with members of your family, your friends, some of your teachers, employers, or neighbors have struck deep roots in you and turned your life in new directions, quickening your deepest emotions. But often such influences remain unexamined.

Writing offers you a chance to understand the significance of those relationships. Because your writing opportunities in this class are limited, choose an important relationship whose meaning for your life you do not yet understand. Setting a guiding question and several potential situations will help you get started.

THE GUIDING QUESTION

A good way to begin is by making a list of important relationships about which you have strong feelings. Ask yourself questions like: Does a past relationship still cause me to tingle or shudder? Does some current relationship puzzle, excite, challenge, or irritate me? To test which relationship is most compelling, use the same strategy discussed in Chapter 1: Identify the expectations or values you hold that seem in conflict with the relationship. Are there aspects of it that do/did not meet your expectations or that exceed them? Are there aspects of the relationship that clash with your values? Below are subjects that five student writers chose:

GUIDING QUESTIONS

WRITER 1

Subject: My relationship with my brother

My Values and Expectations	**My Subject**
—love of my family, esp. my brother	—the news of my brother's impending death
—my sense that life was secure	

Question: How did the news of my brother's impending death influence my outlook on life and my sense of security?

WRITER 2

Subject: My relationship with Julia, my high school rival

My Values and Expectations	**My Subject**
—the two of us to be good friends	—didn't get along at all
—her to win *everything*	—I won something "big"

Question: Why couldn't my competitor Julia and I be friends and what changed our attitudes toward each other?

WRITER 3

Subject: My relationship with my father

My Values and Expectations	**My Subject**
—a Dad that I could respect	—my Dad had talents I didn't realize at first
—I expected my Dad to be from another generation that didn't understand mine	—my Dad understood my problems
—someone that had high expectations (too high sometimes) for me	—my Dad's goals for me were very high

Question: Why do I now have a respect for my Dad that I didn't always feel or show when I was in high school?

WRITER 4

Subject: My relationship with my grandmother

My Values and Expectations	**My Subject**
—love and concern from my family	—my grandmother gave me a special love
—never expected anyone close to me to die	—my grandmother's death but I didn't realize what had happened, or didn't want to

Question: To this day, why can't I believe or come to the reality that my grandmother has passed away? Or: Why was my grandmother so special to me, and why can't I accept her death?

WRITER 5   **Subject:** My relationship with my eighth grade teacher

My Values and Expectations   **My Subject**
—a teacher who respects students   —his belligerence and humiliation of
and helps them   members of the class

Question: How did my eighth grade teacher help or hinder my growth?

● **COMMENTARY**

Writer 1 has identified two deeply rooted values that are challenged by the news of her brother's impending death. Her question incorporates this challenge and seeks to understand the extent of its impact. The writer already senses that her brother's death did influence her feeling of security. What she wants to discover through writing is the precise nature of that influence.

Writer 4 asks two questions. Each will result in a different answer. The second question is better because it allows the writer to investigate his grandmother's influence while at the same time dealing with his lack of acceptance. The first question might turn him away from his relationship with his grandmother toward an analysis of his own personality.

POTENTIAL SITUATIONS

While asking your question, it is important to list several *actual* situations in which you can write about the subject. Doing so will help free you from the artificiality of classroom writing. While it is true that the class, your instructor, and fellow students act as a secondary audience, you can still use your writing assignments as opportunities to communicate with whatever readers you wish. Here are the situations chosen by the five writers above.

POTENTIAL SITUATIONS

WRITER 1   —a letter to my family, sharing my feelings and whatever understanding I
come to
—an essay for the class
—an article in a magazine that publishes human interest stories

WRITER 2   —an essay that I'd send to my mother, who feels much competition with one
certain woman in her church choir
—an essay for the class
—an entry in my journal

WRITER 3   —a letter to my dad to thank him for all he's meant to me
—an essay for my older brother, who never thought that I respected my father like I should have and never listened to my father's advice or looked to him for guidance as I should have
—an article for the campus paper

WRITER 4   —an essay for my girlfriend Lana, who would like to have known my grandmother
—a letter to my parents
—an essay for the class

WRITER 5   —an article for my hometown paper
—an essay that I would send back to some of my friends who were in the class
—an essay for this class

CLASS EXERCISES

1. Examine the guiding questions and potential situations of Writers 2, 3, and 5.
   • What kinds of investigations will each stimulate?
   • How well do the questions flow from the dissonances expressed?
   • What other questions could be asked?
   • What differences will result from the kinds of writing posed for each question?
2. Choose a relationship known by the class (e.g., famous dramatic characters like Romeo and Juliet, a relationship on one of the soap operas, a historic relationship).
   • Identify in the two people the values or expectations that are in conflict or that are exceeded.
   • Formulate several questions that could be investigated.
3. Study the following case:

   David had a great relationship with his dad. They had gone camping together and participated in many scouting events. David had always worked hard in school and sports to live up to the high expectations his father held for him. When he was thirteen his parents divorced, leaving David with his mother, who blamed his father for the divorce. For several years, David had very mixed feelings about his father. He stopped trying hard in school and dropped out of basketball. By the time he got to college, he seldom saw his father but wanted to understand him better and create a new relationship.

   • What kinds of dissonance does David experience?

• What kinds of questions could he ask to set his investigation of this relationship?

● ASSIGNMENT: The Guiding Question and Potential Situations

1. Make a list of relationships about which you are puzzled and select one that you find compelling and worth investigating.
2. Identify your values and expectations and the aspects of the relationship that challenge them.
3. Write a question to guide your search for answers.
4. List several potential situations in which you could write on this subject.
5. Seek advice on your work before proceeding.

● EXPLORATION

The following exploratory guide suggests questions to help you examine your relationship from more than one point of view.

EXPLORATORY GUIDE

● **Static View**
  • Recall and record the nature of your relationship: what makes it different from all others.
  • Describe the other person's physical and personality traits that play a special role in the relationship.

● **Dynamic View**
  • Trace the stages of your relationship from its beginning to its current state and then speculate on its future potential.
  • Analyze the changes that have occurred in both of you as the relationship has developed.

● **Relative View**
  - Determine in what classification (personality type, role player) the other person fits as an individual and in relation to you (nurturer, competitor, and so on). Note down your reasons for these classifications.
  - Compare and contrast this person with others, or this relationship with other relationships, analyzing the likenesses and differences.
  - Create at least one analogy for your relationship (something other than another person) with which you can connect your person or your relationship.
  - Probe the basis for the analogy.

  Writer 1 followed the directions to explore her relationship with her brother.

EXPLORATION

MY BROTHER

STATIC VIEW

—details of learning about my brother's illness
—increasingly frequent visits with my 17-year-old brother, Paul, to Children's Hospital
—a worn expression on my father's face
—my mother, at time, seemed depressed and preoccupied
—a gathering of the family in the basement, 5:30 in the evening
  —hesitance
  —my mother's trembling voice—"Paul has leukemia."
  —shock
  —bewilderment
  —a McDonald's hamburger turning to dust in my mouth
  —spontaneous racking, sobbing
  —a sense of disbelief and unreality
  —the stern facade melting from my father's face, being replaced by a soft, vulnerable expression
  —pressing queries filling our minds
  —"Does Paul know what he has?"
  —"What are the doctors doing to alleviate progression of the disease?"
  —all medication has been exhausted
  —a fresh effusion of tears
  —anger and bitterness

—helplessness

—a realization of the loss at stake—the preciousness and rarity of our relationship

—numbness

—an attempt to regain lost composure

—soothing hands comforting exhausted bodies and spent minds

—an acceptance of our fate

—a swelling of strength and determination within each of us

—a release of tension

DYNAMIC VIEW

Changes

—a release as family progresses from tension to relief

—a concerted family will to rise above our burden

—a whole new perspective on life around me—an aligning of my values and priorities

—a desire to revert back to the "way we were"

—a strong, overwhelming desire to live each day to the fullest

—a reluctant sense of acceptance

RELATIVE VIEW

Comparison: The stages we went through to accept the illness were similar to the stages my brother experienced. He, also, had to cope with denial, anger and frustration, severe depression, and finally, acceptance, after learning of the nature of his illness.

● **COMMENTARY**

In the static view, the writer concentrates on the details of the family's gathering to confront her brother's death. In this act of recalling, she has indirectly expressed some of her feelings about Paul and noted her family's closeness. She needs to explore her own relationship with her brother, as well as his personality and appearance. Although the dynamic view lists general changes in the family's attitude, it makes little note of changes in the writer's, lacking examples of "aligning my values and priorities." What values? What priorities? The relative view makes a short comparison between the family's and Paul's stages of acceptance. In what ways did these stages manifest themselves in behavior? Because analogies *(see the Glossary) reveal strong feelings, Writer 1 should try to create some for her brother (Paul was like X), for her relationship with him (my brother was like X to me), or for her process of acceptance (learning to live with my brother's death was like X). Writer 1's additions to her exploration are shown next.*

STATIC VIEW

Relationship with my brother
—one year apart
—common interests, friends, experiences
—no petty rivalries
—would seek him out for counsel, friendship, pass the time of day
—shared fears and anxieties
—liked introducing him as my brother

Paul's attitude toward death
—took pleasure in a sunny day
—never complained
—relished talking with friends
—worked to improve his mind & body

DYNAMIC VIEW

Changes in priorities & values
—spent more time with my family
—worried less about boyfriends or dates
—concerned more about compassionate aspect to personality

RELATIVE VIEW
—Paul was like a bridge between me and what I valued

ALTERNATIVE EXPLORATORY GUIDES

You use an exploratory guide for at least two reasons: to encourage you to investigate broadly before trying to answer your question and to direct you to take more than one perspective on your subject. The ability to withhold judgment, to refrain from jumping to early and often superficial answers, is an important one for the writer who wants to find good answers to pressing questions. The ability to take more than one perspective is also critical if a writer wants to avoid mental ruts. The exploratory guide described in Chapter 1 is not the only way of developing these abilities. In the Appendix we present several other guides. Below we illustrate a visual strategy called *clustering* which you can use alone or with the exploratory guide introduced in Chapter 1. Writer 4 uses clustering to help him generate static and dynamic information. Notice that this strategy shows the connections between ideas. Because the relative perspective identifies relationships between ideas—member with group (classification), subject with other like subject (comparison), subject with unlike other subject (analogy)—Writer 4 did not use clustering in conjunction with this perspective.

EXPLORATION

WRITER 4 **STATIC VIEW**

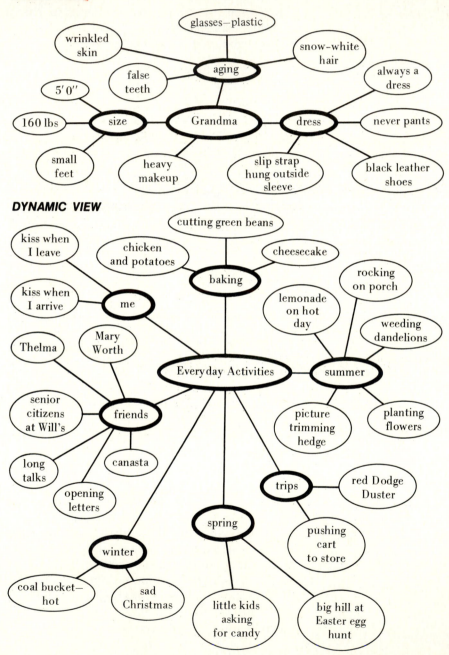

DYNAMIC VIEW

RELATIVE VIEW

Classification
—optimist, loving, low-tempered
—never flies off the handle about small things
—always feels I can accomplish anything (college)
—always has a kiss for me

Compare: to death of Grandpa

Death of Grandpa	**Death of Grandma**
—too young to realize	—old enough to realize
—wasn't close (love)	—very close (lot of love)
—in funeral home I didn't stay by him very much, I would talk to my friends	—was always by the casket

Analogy: My grandma was like a good song. During the prime of a good song, it is always good every time you listen to it. After the song is no longer a hit, one tends to listen to other songs. Just as people die, one tends to turn to other people. But every time you hear that song, you remember how good it was. The same is true with my grandma. Every time I see a picture of her I remember her.

CLASS EXERCISES

1. Examine the exploration of Writer 4.
   • How fully and specifically has he identified the features of his relationship?
   • What sections need further exploration?
2. As a class, explore the relationship you chose to investigate in the previous class exercise.

● ASSIGNMENT: Exploration

1. Using an exploratory guide, explore the question you formulated in the first assignment.
2. Seek advice on your work.

FOCUS AND SITUATION

FROM EXPLORATION TO FOCUS

After you explore as thoroughly as time permits, allow your ideas time to settle, at least through a day and a good night's rest. Then reexamine the ideas you have generated, noting any recurrent ones or any connections. Review your starting question, making sure that this question is still what you find important to answer. If so, write down any answers that seem to have emerged. If your question has changed during exploration, write down the new question and any answers that suggest themselves. Review these alternative answers and phrase them in the form of focuses so that you can clearly separate your subject from the point of significance. Examine these statements in terms of your potential writing situations. Then decide which focus and situation you wish to pursue. Although this phase of writing is not lengthy, it is one of the most important tasks of your process.

Remember that your focus should reflect your expressive aim. You will be sharing an insight into your private world, emphasizing yourself as writer.

FOCUSES AND SITUATIONS

WRITER 1

Subject
My family's sharing of grief over my brother's death ————

Point of Significance
— helped me to accept it and caused me to realign my values.

(**Revised question:** What happened to my outlook on life and my sense of security as a result of my brother's illness and death?)

Situation: I will write an article for a magazine that publishes human interest stories. My audience will be those who face the death of loved ones.

WRITER 2

Subject
Our different attitudes toward success ————

Point of Significance
— made friendship between Julia and me impossible for a long time but eventually we became friends.

(**Question:** Why couldn't my competitor Julia and I be friends, and what changed our attitudes toward each other?)

Situation: I want to write a letter to my mother, who has a strong competition with a woman in her church choir.

WRITER 3   **Subject**   **Point of Significance**

My father————————————was the best coach, teacher, and
                                                    counselor anyone could have.

(**Question:** Why do I now have a respect for my Dad that I didn't always feel or
show when I was in high school?)

Situation: I will write an essay for my older brother, who never thought I appreci-
ated my father enough.

WRITER 4   **Subject**   **Point of Significance**

My grandmother's relationship with   ┌—led me to realize what love was all
me and her death————————┘   about.

(**Question:** Why was my grandmother so special to me, and why can't I accept
her death?)

Situation: I want to write an essay for my girlfriend Lana because I want her to
know my grandma.

WRITER 5   **Subject**   **Point of Significance**

My eighth grade teacher's unusual   ┌—eventually caused us to learn a great
style————————————┘   deal.

(**Question:** How did my eighth grade teacher help or hinder my growth?)

Situation: I'll write an essay to send back to some friends who also had this
teacher.

● **COMMENTARY**

*Writer 1's excellent dual focus is not an answer to her original question but an
answer to a more profound question that must have suggested itself to her as she
was working through her material. The question she answers is: "What happened
to my outlook on life and my sense of security as a result of my brother's illness and
death?" Although the two questions look alike, they are significantly different.
Her choice of a magazine article format is ambitious but realizable. There are
"inspirational" magazines that specialize in first-person narratives dealing with
overcoming personal tragedies.*

*Writer 2, like Writer 1, has created a dual focus, in response to a dual question.
As her choice of format—a letter to her mother—suggests, her experience may be
of immediate help to someone in similar circumstances. Notice the difference between the audience chosen by Writer 2 (one person well known to the writer) and
that chosen by Writer 1 (a large, faceless group united by one common problem).
Yet in both cases the writers intend that readers in similar emotional straits shall
profit from hearing of their safe passage through those straits. The difference
illustrates that there is often no inevitable audience for any focus.*

CLASS EXERCISES

1. Review the focuses and situations of Writers 3, 4, and 5. How well do the writers answer their starting questions? What boundaries will these focuses set for the writers?
2. Examine the following alternative statements of focus. Which will (or won't) work for the writers? Why (or why not)?
   a. "The news of my brother's impending death was troubling."
   b. "My father's good qualities."
   c. "One of my teachers was great."
   d. "I valued my relationship with my grandmother."
3. From your class exploration of a relationship, formulate alternative focuses and situations.

● ASSIGNMENT: Focus and Situation

1. Allow time after exploring; then review your exploration for recurrent or connected ideas.
2. Write down several possible answers to your original or revised question.
3. Formulate your focus, differentiating between subject and point of significance.
4. Select the situation that best suits your focus.
5. Seek advice on your work.

● AUDIENCE AND MODES OF ORGANIZATION

SETTING THE ROLE FOR THE AUDIENCE

Analyzing your audience will be easier this time because you have been through it once. You probably learned from your audience analysis in Chapter 1 that the most important parts of the audience guide are determining the specific and relational roles for your audience and determining your own voice.

- ### Specific and Relational Roles

  Review here the terms *specific* and *relational*. The *specific* role is the part of an audience's total character that it is asked to assume. The *relational* role is the relationship that you want to establish between the audience and the writer. The writer must set and control both roles.

- ### Writer's Voice

  Recall that your voice as a writer is the role you play in relation to the readers and subject matter. Are you equals or superior or inferior? Are they knowledgeable or ignorant on a subject? Do you share with your readers a serious, ironic, or humorous attitude toward the subject? To guide your analysis, use the audience guide provided in Chapter 1 (pp. 47–48). Below are the analyses of Writers 1 and 4. By discussing their strong and weak points you can learn some useful pointers about what to look for and what to avoid in analyzing your own audience.

AUDIENCE ANALYSIS

WRITER 1

1. Readers of *Guideposts,* an inspirational magazine, because they may be able to profit from my experience.
2. Audience in itself:
   a. Adult readers of both sexes who are facing the death of a loved one for the first time.
   b. They put a high value on human life and they don't want to lose loved ones.
3. Audience in relation to the subject:
   a. They are frightened by the prospect of death and loss; they want to feel secure and to be happy, and neither of those seems possible when death is near.
   b. They hold these views with the strength of desperation.
   c. They would be willing to do almost anything to feel secure.
4. Specific role: Victims of family tragedies. People who have difficulty coping with family tragedy.
5. Analysis of role:
   a. Background: They will know the fear and desperation that comes from feeling helpless in the face of family tragedy. They will not know any workable solution.
   b. Values: They will value stability, escape from grief.
   c. Attitude toward subject: They will be receptive to any suggestion I have because of their own predicaments. But their strength of conviction and willingness to act will depend on how convincing my account is.

6. Relational role: They will play the role of the inexperienced to my role as the knowledgeable one.

● COMMENTARY

Writer 1 has created a useful analysis. She has chosen as the specific role of the audience the chief role most readers of Guideposts *may play: they seek solutions to personal problems and find comfort in others' triumphs over adversity. As Writer 1 observes, she will be writing to a receptive audience. Her challenge will be to write convincingly of her own experience.*

AUDIENCE ANALYSIS

WRITER 4

1. My Audience will be my girlfriend Lana.
2. Audience in itself:
   a. Background: Lana is my age and goes to college. Her background is similar to mine.
   b. Values: She is a good listener and very considerate of others. She is also an emotional person.
3. Audience in relation to the subject:
   a. Knowledge and opinion: She hasn't yet experienced the death of anyone close. She has had a close friend in the hospital. She can sympathize with me but can't tell me how she would feel if someone close to her were to die.
   b. Strength of opinion: She can postulate how she will feel, but something inside her tells her she just really doesn't ever want to experience it.
   c. Willingness to act: She's not very willing to act on her opinion because she's afraid if she did lose someone she loved she would probably not do as she thought she would.
4. Specific role: A grandchild who is fond of grandparents
5. Analysis of the role:
   a. Background: A happy grandchild will know the special things a grandparent can do for you that a parent can't. She will know how the differences in age affect the relationship. She will know what grandparents can teach you about love and death.
   b. Values: She will value expressions of sympathy, respect, and love, especially since the relationship between grandparents and grandchildren is usually short.
   c. Attitude toward the subject: She will be prepared to like my grandma.
6. Relational role: She will be a peer.

MODES OF ORGANIZATION

The descriptive and narrative modes of organization were explained in Chapter 1. By now you should have used one in your own writing and seen the other used by your classmates in their papers. But the only way to gain control over these modes is to practice them in your own writing. Being able to recognize them in someone else's writing can help you understand how they work, but it is no substitute for trying them out.

The Classification Mode

This chapter will introduce another mode, *classification,* which offers flexible ways of organizing your paper. Classification involves several things:

1. putting a subject into a larger group
2. defining the group
3. showing how the subject shares the features defined for the group
4. comparing or contrasting members of the group
5. creating analogies—showing the similarity between the subject and something of a different nature

For example, Writer 4 classified his grandmother in a group entitled *optimist,* defining this group as people who don't get angry easily, who feel things can be accomplished, and who have loving relations with others. He then related his grandmother to these three features of the definition, saying that she never flew off the handle, that she felt he could accomplish things, and that she always had a kiss for him.

Writer 2 put Julia in the category of competitor, along with her sister Mandi and her best friend Christy. She then contrasted the type of competition between Julia and the other two. Julia made her insecure, but Mandi didn't because their parents praised both and never compared them. Julia usually excelled whereas the opposite was true with Christy.

Writer 4 created an analogy showing the similarity between his grandmother and a good song: both have primes; both make a person feel good; both pass their prime, causing us to turn to others; and both trigger good memories. A woman and a song have different natures; the task of the writer is to point out the similarities.

You can use any of the material from the classification mode anywhere in your paper. You can classify your subject, compare or contrast it, or use an analogy wherever you need it to help support your focus. But you can also use classification as an *organizing* principle for your entire paper.

Organizational Plans

Using classification as a mode of organization can be done in many ways. Here are some of the major plans that a writer can use. The first plan uses all the options in the classification mode. Most short papers do not use the full array of possibilities.

PLAN 1: Full Use of Classification

¶ 1   Indicate the group into which your subject falls and define the group.

¶ 2   Show how your subject shares feature 1 of the definition.

¶ 3   Show how your subject shares feature 2 of the definition.

¶ 4   Show how your subject shares feature 3 of the definition.

¶ 5   Compare/contrast your subject with one other member of the group.

¶ 6   Create an analogy for the subject and explain it.

If Writer 4 wanted to use this plan to communicate his focus, his plan might look something like this:

¶ 1   Place my grandma in the class of optimist and define *optimist*.

¶ 2   Show how my grandmother has the first feature of an optimist.

¶ 3   Show how my grandma has the second feature of an optimist.

¶ 4   Show how my grandma has the third feature of optimist.

¶ 5   Contrast my grandma with an older person Lana knows.

¶ 6   Explain my analogy of my grandmother as a good song.

You can also organize a paper using as a framework only paragraphs 1–4.

PLAN 2: Use Only of Comparison or Contrast

¶ 1   Indicate the group to which subjects belong and the bases of comparison or contrast—e.g., two similarities and one difference

¶ 2   Compare subjects on the first point of similarity.

¶ 3   Compare subjects on the second point of similarity.

¶ 4   Contrast subjects on the point of difference.

PLAN 3: Use of Analogy

¶ 1   Identify the analogy and the bases of similarity—e.g., three likenesses.

¶ 2   Explain and exemplify the first likeness.

¶ 3   Explain and exemplify the second likeness.

¶ 4   Explain and exemplify the third likeness.

● **Choice of Classification Mode**

How do you know when you should use the classification mode? Or what version of it to use? Your decision depends on at least three factors:

1. Your focus: Will classification best help you to communicate your focus?

2. Your audience: Will classification best organize for your audience?

3. Your exploration: Have you created useful classifications, comparisons, and analogies?

Writer 3 used the classification mode to organize his paper. Here is his plan of organization:

¶ 1 Show how my father fits in the class of coach.
¶ 2 Show how he fits in the class of teacher.
¶ 3 Show how he fits in the class of counselor when I was in Junior High.
¶ 4 Show how he was a counselor when I was in high school.
¶ 5 Show how he remains a counselor now that I am in college.

Here is Writer 3's first version, which develops the plan above.

MY FATHER: THE COACH, THE TEACHER, THE COUNSELOR

"We'll get 'em next time," my father told me. "Don't worry about it, you gave it your best." I could not believe what I heard. I had just pitched one of my poorest Little League games as we lost the county championship by a score of 12–0. I knew he was disappointed as he had coached us to an undefeated season until that evening. I waited for his criticism, but it never came. While many fathers criticized their sons until they cried and felt about a foot tall, my father took me over to the bench where he sat down beside of me and told me that winning wasn't everything and that losing one game was not the end of the world.

My father, a blue-collar railroad worker, doesn't look much like your average coach or teacher or counselor, but he's been all three to me.

My final year in Little League proved him right. We went undefeated that year and won the county championship. But there was something more important to us than that championship trophy: the sportsmanship and effort trophy which I received from the league officials. A coach is someone who gets the best out of the people he works with. That was certainly true of my father. For the two of us, it produced a relationship that was not, as with so many coaches, built around a win-at-all-costs philosophy, but one that was built around the idea that one should always give their best effort and keep giving their best effort whether one is successful or unsuccessful at what one is trying to accomplish.

He taught this important lesson, as well as many others, in his Sunday school class. As I entered junior high school, I was looking for direction in my life, and my father, as Sunday school teacher, provided me with guidance and leadership just as he had done as a coach. He was not a preacher and never claimed to be, but what he said to the Sunday school class was more important than any sermon I heard as a youth. He taught me that all the material things in the world meant nothing if I was not at peace with myself. He taught me something more important than the basic, traditional church values. To live my own life cleanly and uprightly was not enough. He taught me a philosophy that has shaped my view of social issues and politics. This philosophy is one of the main reasons I decided to study political science and become involved in politics and social matters. He told me that "as long as somebody in the world is hungry, as long as somebody in the world is homeless, and as long as somebody in the world is oppressed, then we have failed our Christian duty of making a better life for all." Going to church and praying at every meal was not enough. He told me that we should try our hardest in everything that we did so that others could be as fortunate as we were.

As I entered high school I had an important decision to make, and I needed a good counselor. My high school guidance counselor gave me little direction in what I should pursue as far as career opportunities and my education were concerned. I expected that my father, the blue-collar worker, would be content if I graduated from high school and got any job that I could. That was not the case. My father insisted that I work hard at my studies and go on to college and make something of myself. He told me not to waste my brains or talent. He told me that things would be difficult no matter what route I chose, but that anything that is worthy in life is never too hard to reach. While my guidance counselor and teachers looked on from the sidelines, it was my father who helped me plan a curriculum in high school and it was my father who helped me decide where I should go to college and what I should pursue as a career.

This wasn't the only time that he helped me as a counselor during my high school years. I decided to quit the basketball team in order to have more time to study and to take a part-time job in a grocery store. I thought that this might separate us because it looked as though I was giving up at sports and not giving it my best. It did just the opposite as it brought us closer together as my father respected my decision and respected my courage for making it while so many of my classmates were angered at me and resented what I did. Many of my high school relationships ended at this point, but my relationship with my father became stronger as he respected my intellect, my independence from conformity (the unwritten rule that no one is supposed to quit playing sports at my high school), and my decision to plan for my future education by getting a job on my own and not asking him for money all the time.

During my college years our relationship has remained close despite being far apart and not seeing much of each other. Nothing lifts my spirits more than just getting a letter from him telling me to be optimistic about job opportunities although there are not too many for political science majors. One particular instance earlier in my college career sticks out in my mind. Two years ago was one of my biggest disappointments as I had applied for a congressional internship and was turned down. The next year I was not sure about reapplying as I was afraid of being rejected again. Some of my friends and professors told me to reapply, but I was still afraid of being turned down again. I talked to my father about it and he told me that I was old enough to make my own decisions about this type of matter, but he told me that whatever is worth anything in life is worth trying. I remembered what he told me when I was in high school: "Never give up, just keep working and giving your best and the opportunities will come." I reapplied for the internship and received it. Had I forgot what my father told me when I was younger, I probably would have never reapplied. "Anything that is worthy is never too hard to achieve" continues to keep me going.

My father has been the person whom I have looked to for guidance, teaching, and counseling for all of my life. Our relationship and the experiences that have evolved from it have helped shaped my outlook of life and has provided me with the will to pursue my dreams and has given me a course of direction in my life.

CLASS EXERCISES

1. Review the audience analysis of Writer 4.
   What roles has he set for the audience?
   Have these roles been adequately analyzed?
   What further information can be added to the analysis?
   What alternative roles can be set? What writing changes would these roles entail?
2. From the explorations of Writers 1 (pp. 79–81) and 4 (pp. 82–83), create different organizational plans the writers could have used.
3. Examine the organizational plans below.
   What modes of organization have been forecast?
   Identify any problems with these plans.

PLAN 1

¶ 1   Show Carol when we first met in the seventh grade.
¶ 2   Show seventh grade competition with Carol for cheerleader.
¶ 3   Show sophomore year competition with Carol for choir slot.
¶ 4   Show junior year competition with Carol for beauty queen.
¶ 5   Show senior year relationship.

PLAN 2

¶ 1   Set up situation: I could take only one friend with me to Florida and I chose Elizabeth.
¶ 2   Show how both Barbara and Elizabeth are fun to be with.
¶ 3   Show how Elizabeth and I are compatible in sports and recreation, Barbara and I in cultural and career interests.
¶ 4   Show that fairness made me choose Elizabeth because Barbara travels with her family a lot, even to the Orient, and Elizabeth has never been anywhere.

● ASSIGNMENT: Audience and Mode of Organization

1. Using the audience guide, analyze your audience in order to set their specific and relational roles.

2. Devise a plan of organization for your paper, using either description, narration, or classification. Try a mode that you have not used yet if it fits your focus and audience.
3. Get advice on your analysis and plan.

● **THE FIRST VERSION**

Writing the first version usually entails doing several drafts until you are satisfied that you have developed and organized your paper so that the audience can experience or comprehend the focus you wish to share. Before submitting the first version for responses, be sure that you examine it for *unity* and *coherence*.

UNITY AND COHERENCE

Any mode of organization requires unity and coherence, virtues that manifest themselves in orderly sentences and paragraphs that connect to one another. Let's examine how ideas of unity and coherence appear in sentences and paragraphs.

Crucial to both unity and coherence is the focus that you have worked toward. A focus is a planned route on which your sentences and paragraphs will travel: the focus sets direction and boundaries for the selection of ideas and examples. A focus is also a commitment you make to your readers; it sets up their expectations. When you maintain that commitment, satisfy their expectations, the paper has *unity*.

Whenever an idea, example, or fact wanders beyond the boundaries of the first or second half of your focus, unity vanishes. Writer 5, for example, has pledged himself to discuss the positive influence of his teacher's unusual style. The reader therefore expects to learn about that style and the ways in which it had a positive influence. If Writer 5 speaks about his teacher's family tree, he could wander beyond the focus. If he includes a discussion of the teacher's influence on local politics, his paper could also drift out of focus, losing its unity. If he dwells on physical details of the classroom or the appearance of his classmates, his paper will also lack focus. As you develop your paper, therefore, ask of any example, detail, or fact whether it supports *your entire focus*.

Coherence is a matter of putting the selected material in the right order with the right connectives. If you follow the mode of organization you chose, your paper will have a coherent framework. But coherence must also be maintained on a smaller scale. Coherence literally means "to stick together." The basic elements of the written piece must be so clearly related that (1) the reader is never confused and (2) the paper moves forward smoothly. Thus the total paper is like a chain, each unit interlinking with the one before it.

When readers attempt to read an incoherent paper, they suddenly come to a part that doesn't connect, because the bridge has crumbled. They fall through the holes between ideas or sentences. It is your responsibility to make sure the bridges from one section or idea to another are strong and smooth. But such bridge building is not a feat of magic. Tools are available. Practice helps.

TRANSITIONS

We spoke in the previous paragraph of using "the right connectives" to achieve coherence. These connectives are called *transitions*—literally, a means of "getting across." They are the bridges across which the reader moves.

The simplest device for building a transition is repetition: something in the preceding sentence or paragraph is repeated in the following sentence or paragraph. The thing repeated can be a word, a phrase, a clause, or the total statement of an idea. And, within obvious limits, it can be repeated exactly or approximately. For example, if the repeated element is a single word, you can repeat it by

1. repeating it exactly,
2. substituting a pronoun for it, or
3. using a synonym for it.

Writer 3's second paragraph says, "My father, a blue-collar railroad worker, doesn't look much like your average coach or teacher or counselor, but he's been all three to me." In that sentence, *he* is a pronoun substituting for *my father,* and *all three* is a synonym for *coach, teacher,* and *counselor.* The sixth paragraph begins, "This wasn't the only time that he helped me as a counselor during my high school years." *This* is a pronoun referring to the entire anecdote in the preceding paragraph; *he,* of course, is a pronoun substituting for *my father.*

Consistency is itself a kind of repetition and therefore adds to coherence. Maintaining the same relational role, for example, helps to hold a discourse together. Grammatical consistency serves the same purpose. A discourse flows smoothly and coherently when there are no abrupt shifts in number, person, or tense to confuse the reader.

There are only two grammatical numbers in English—singular and plural. Coherence breaks down when, for example, pronouns and their antecedents don't agree in person and number. (Person distinguishes the person speaking (first person— *I, we*); the person spoken to (second person—*you*); and the person or thing spoken of (third person—all other pronouns and all nouns).) Writer 3, for example, writes, "one should always give their best effort and keep giving their best effort whether one is successful or unsuccessful at what one is trying to accomplish." The subject, *one,* is third person singular, but then it reappears twice as the third person plural *their* before dropping back again into the singular *one* in the last five words.

There are six tenses in English: present, present perfect, past, past perfect, future, and future perfect. Fortunately, they are usually easy to keep consistent. Discourse that begins in the past tense, for example, should continue in that tense except when a reference to another time requires a shift, as in this sentence from Writer 3: "As I entered junior high school, I was looking for direction in my life, and my father, as Sunday school teacher, provided me with guidance and leadership just as he had done as a coach." In this sentence, the writer reflects the time changes by shifting tenses: *entered* is in the past tense, as are *was looking* (although it shows what is called "progressive aspect," that is, continuing action rather than completed action) and *provided; had done* is past perfect; *provided* is simple past; and *had done* is past perfect.

But repetition is only one transitional device. We often use specialized words as transitions to signal to the reader any of several relationships:

1. Contrast: *but, although, yet, however,* etc.
2. Coordination: *similarly, likewise, just as,* etc.
3. Consequence: *consequently, therefore, thus, so, as a result,* etc.
4. Causation: *because, for, since,* etc.
5. Accumulation: *moreover, furthermore, in addition, for example,* etc.
6. Alternation: *or, either,* etc.
7. Sequence: *first, second, next, finally,* etc.*

Writer 3 says, "Many of my high school relationships ended at this point, but my relationship with my father became stronger as he respected my decision . . ."; *but* is a contrast signal; *as* (that is, because) is a causation signal. Consider the reader's difficulty if those transitions were not there: "Many of my high school relationships ended at this point. My relationship with my father became stronger. He respected my intellect. . . ."

PARAGRAPHS

So far we've been using the term *paragraph* without defining it. A paragraph is a series of statements dealing with a central idea. Structurally, it

* Adapted from W. Ross Winterowd, "The Grammar of Coherence," in *Contemporary Rhetoric: A Conceptual Background with Readings,* ed. W. Ross Winterowd (New York: Harcourt Brace Jovanovich, Inc., 1975), pp. 229–231.

is usually composed of a core sentence of greater generality than any other sentence in the group and a number of sentences of lesser generality supporting the core sentence. A good paragraph, like a whole discourse, will adhere to a focus and therefore will show unity. To the unity it will add coherence. Let's take those points one at a time.

● **Unity of Paragraphs**

There should be nothing in the paragraph that does not deal directly with the focus of the paper. In addition, there should be nothing in the paragraph that does not deal with the aspect of the focus addressed in the paragraph, which is a subsection of the subject matter the focus encompasses. Writer 3, for example, when he is discussing the coaching function of his father in a paragraph, should not include material dealing with his father's teaching activities.

● **Coherence in Paragraphs**

Obviously there is no coherence without unity. Therefore, first select for unity, then write for coherence. To achieve coherence, keep in mind the basic structure of a paragraph—a series of related sentences that includes (1) a core sentence (often the first sentence) of greater generality than any other sentence in the group, and (2) a number of sentences of lesser generality supporting the core sentence.

Plan and edit your paragraphs to fit this structural definition, exempting only transitional paragraphs, short paragraphs whose purpose is to glue large sections of a long paper together by forecasting or summarizing. Then insert whatever additional transitions are necessary, as we discussed earlier.

Let's take as an example a paragraph from Writer 3's first version:

FIRST VERSION

[1] He taught this important lesson, as well as many others, in his Sunday school class. [2] As I entered junior high school, I was looking for direction in my life, and my father, as Sunday school teacher, provided me with guidance and leadership just as he had done as a coach. [3] He was not a preacher and never claimed to be, but what he said to the Sunday school class was more important than any sermon I heard as a youth. [4] He taught me that all the material things in the world meant nothing if I was not at peace with myself. [5] He taught me something more important than the basic, traditional church values. [6] To live my own life cleanly and uprightly was not enough. [7] He taught me a philosophy that has shaped my view of social issues and politics. [8] This philosophy is one of the main reasons I decided to study political science and become involved in politics and social matters. [9] He told me that "as long as somebody in the world is hungry, as long

as somebody in the world is homeless and as long as somebody in the world is oppressed, then we have failed our Christian duty of making a better life for all." [10] Going to church and praying at every meal was not enough. [11] He told me that we should try our hardest in everything that we did so that others could be as fortunate as we were.

---

1. Sentence 1 is a transitional sentence, meant to glue this paragraph to the preceding one.
2. Sentence 2 is the core sentence, the statement of broadest generality.
3. Sentence 3 is an editorial comment on sentence 2 that repeats part of the content of that sentence but also introduces the other major idea in the paragraph: that the father was superior to the church as a teacher and moralist and his values were preferable to those of the church. This dual core will almost certainly cause trouble.
4. Sentence 4 is a development of sentence 2.
5. Sentence 5 is either an evaluation of and therefore a development of sentence 4 or a development of sentence 3. It is not clear whether sentence 5 says that the statement in sentence 4 is more important than "basic, traditional church values" or that in a moment he will show us this more important thing.
6. Sentence 6 is a development of sentence 5, but only in the sense that it tells us what the thing referred to in sentence 5 is not. But at least we are now led to believe that the important thing is about to appear.
7. Sentence 7 does not produce the thing (and therefore develop sentence 5) but makes almost a core-level generalization.
8. Sentence 8 again does not produce the thing but cites another effect of the thing, this time at the level of generality of sentence 4.
9. Sentence 9 produces the thing, the philosophical statement, in a development of sentences 7 and 8.
10. Sentence 10 returns to developing the line established in sentence 3 and pursued in sentences 5 and 6 but absent in sentences 7, 8, and 9.
11. Sentence 11 returns to the concepts and the level of generality of sentences 4 and 9.

The paragraph lacks both unity and coherence, for the following reasons. First, the writer tries to develop two cores, one showing the father as a teacher, the other arguing that he was a better teacher and moralist than other members of the church. Sentences 2, 4, 7, 8, 9, and 11 deal with the first core, sentences 3, 5, 6, and 10 with the second. There can be no unity in a paragraph with two cores.

Furthermore, there can be little coherence in a paragraph where related ideas are separated. Had Writer 3 kept the related ideas together so that he had, say, a 1, 2, 3, 4, 5 sequence for the one core and a 6, 7, 8, 9, 10, 11 sequence for the other, at least the ideas would have stuck together—and the arrangement would have revealed that the writer needed a paragraph break after sentence 5. In addition, the levels of generality shift erratically. Paragraphs can be diagrammed by the level of generality of their sentences. The highest level of generality exists in the core sentence; no other sentence should rise to that level. Diagramming reveals the depth of development of an idea, as we shall see.

Here are three sample diagrams. In each, sentence 1 is presumed to be the core sentence and to appear first. A lower level of generality is indicated by a greater indentation.

```
1           1           1
  2           2           2
  3             3           3
  4           4             4
  5             5         5
                  6           6
                    7           7
                                  8
                                  9
```

In the first diagram, all four items that support the core are at the same level of generalization, one level more concrete than the core itself. In the second diagram, each item is given more development and that development appears to be equally apportioned. In the third diagram, we find fewer major items but deeper development; furthermore, the development is unequal, 5 and its developing sentences seemingly having more weight than 2 and its supports.

There is no ideal paragraph pattern that can be diagrammed, but if you cannot diagram your paragraph, it almost certainly has problems of unity or coherence or both. The sample paragraph of Writer 3 cannot be diagrammed with any assurance because of the competing cores and the ambiguous relationships between some sentences. Use paragraph diagramming, therefore, as a diagnostic device. Here is an additional example to help you understand the principle:

> Writers should give careful thought to the way they compose paragraphs. One sentence in the paragraph should be at a level of generality higher than that of any others. Every other sentence should be at a level of generality appropriate to its relationship to the sentence preceding it and, of course, to the core sentence. Most difficult is maintaining the level appropriate to the relationship with the preceding sentence.

Blocking the paragraph produces a pattern like this:

1 Writers should give careful thought to the way they compose paragraphs.
  2 One sentence in the paragraph should be at a level of generality higher than that of any other.
  2 Every other sentence should be at a level of generality appropriate to its relationship to the sentence preceding it and, of course, to the core sentence.
    3 Most difficult is maintaining the level appropriate to the relationship with the preceding sentence.

Finally, an effective paragraph appeals to a reader partly by offering textured information. *Texture* refers to the quality of a paragraph growing out of a proper mix of general and specific, abstract and concrete, broad statement and example, condensed statement and illustration. The term sometimes refers also to stylistic variation—for example, variation in sentence structure and length for emphasis and variety.

There is no rule for achieving effective texture. But normally neither details nor generalizations can comfortably stand alone. A series of concrete details usually requires a generalization to give them significance and coherence. A generalization requires details for support or for illustration. Unrelieved sameness of tone and unrelenting sameness of sentence structure bore the reader. The following paragraph, for example, is not adequately textured because the generalizations lack supporting detail, all the observations except the first are at roughly the same level of abstraction, and most of the sentences are structurally similar.

> Automotive workers are becoming increasingly interested in benefits other than financial. They are beginning to ask for additional fringe benefits rather than higher wages. The reasons for this shift are puzzling to management. The reasons will perhaps not be that obscure to workers in other fields. Certain trends in the economy tend to affect all people in the same socioeconomic class alike.

Here is an improved version:

> Automotive workers are increasingly interested in nonmonetary benefits. Even though these workers made sweeping wage concessions during the recession, economic recovery finds them negotiating contracts emphasizing job security, improved medical and dental coverage, firmer pension guarantees, and better quality-of-work provisions. Management, according to both of Detroit's metropolitan newspapers, finds this trend puzzling. But most blue-collar workers will probably understand and sympathize. Extensive layoffs taught the workers something about the difference between pay and no pay. In many cases, some of them tragic, it showed them

what sickness and injury—even simply age—bring when the insurance coverage is gone. The post-recession reasoning apparently runs something like this: It could happen again. Any job is better than none. Therefore, I want guarantees of employment and I want my family protected. And since I'm going to be at this job a long time, I'd like it to be as safe and satisfying as possible. As a Chrysler worker said last week to a *Time* reporter, "It isn't 'Get what you can while you can' anymore; it's 'Hang on to what you have.'"

FIRST VERSION

WRITER 5

TYRANT

We were in a peculiar state of shock that second day of classes, and for good reason. Mr. B. stood in front of us, drumming his broad fingers on the podium, beaming his sinister satisfied grin over our anxious faces. Just what he was up to no one knew, but he was up to something; he scraped his fingers through that full black beard of his to let you know that. All eyes were upon him, all ears attuned to his footsteps as slowly he began circling the room. Some pretended to be searching through their notes to avoid eye contact, just as I was when the footsteps came to a casual halt just behind my back.

A huge hand came over my shoulder and flipped through the pages of my homework. It traced certain words, paused over a few passages, rubbed the paper as if checking the thickness, and finally resumed the tedious drumming on the top of my desk. Except for the deadly looks I shot at those who saw humor in my situation I didn't move a muscle. I could feel him breathing on my back. The hand stopped drumming its fingers and picked up my notebook by the corner of one page of my homework. Holding it aloft long enough to build a suitable dramatic tension, in a deep voice that always had a hint of sarcasm in it, he spoke his first words to me, "What is this, Mr. Humbert?" I replied timidly that it was my homework assignment. "No, Mr. Humbert," (apparently I had misunderstood the question.) "This is chicken scratching, Mr. Humbert, chicken scratching." (He was talking about my handwriting.) After one last vain attempt to make out what I had written, he shook the page loose, sending my notebook flying across the room, crumpled it up, and casually tossed it in the other direction. He then informed me that I could retrieve my homework. I sat motionless trying to contain my anger. When he asked why I hadn't gone to get my notebook, I explained that he had indicated no specific time I should do so, and not wishing to appear presumptuous, I didn't. Having made my point I got up. To my surprise, nothing more was ever said about my handwriting.

The rest of the year continued in much the same manner, extended periods of silence just before the hammer fell on some unsuspecting victim, and abusive treatment for those who had committed some small indiscretion or who had the catastrophic misfortune of being caught. It wasn't long before the eighth grade, tired of this unwarranted persecution, turned its thoughts to revenge. We reasoned that the best way to shoot him down would be to catch him making mistakes in class. We'd hit him in his home territory; nobody got the best of the eighth grade.

So we all studied like hell and even assigned specialists to certain fields; dates to Mike, battles to Steve, opinion and press to Earl, and foreign policy to Pete. The moments we caught him were few and far between, but when we did everybody felt a great sense of satisfaction. Justice had been reckoned.

On the day of the Civil War debate class morale was low. We all had the third-quarter blues and as if that wasn't enough, Mr. B. was on a rampage. The day before, he had thrown Steve out of class for not doing his homework. (He had drop-kicked Steve's book out into the hall. When Steve went out to get it, Mr. B. closed the door behind him and locked it.) Now it was decided that Mr. B. would take a seat on the North side of the debate. He was killing us. Everything the South came up with he had a counter for. Just when it seemed all was lost, he made one little mistake. The debate was supposedly to take place in 1860, but Mr. B. quoted from Lincoln's Emancipation Proclamation (1863). Mike rose from his desk and remained standing until Mr. B. recognized him; then he pointed out the mistake. We were allowed to carry on the debate by ourselves from that point on. Mr. B. also began treating us a little more like human beings and student-teacher relations improved almost to normal.

We learned a lot from Mr. B.; a lot more than most of us were willing to give him credit for until the last day of class, when he actually apologized for any hard feelings his unorthodox methods of teaching may have caused. He went on to say he was proud of the way we refused to knuckle under to his tyranny and he regretted he wouldn't be back next year to have us as ninth graders. We weren't sorry to see him go then, but what a time we would have had in ninth grade.

CLASS EXERCISES

1. Examine Writer 5's first version (above) for unity and coherence.
   - What mode of organization is used? Has it been maintained? If not, how has the pattern been broken? How could it be restored?
   - What techniques has the writer used to maintain coherence? For example, show how full paragraphs and individual sentences are tied together by repetition. Where is coherence lacking?
   - How is the paragraphing structured? How many levels of generality has the writer used in his paragraphs?
   - How does the paper maintain unity? What sentences, if any, violate the commitment of the focus?
2. An early draft version of one of Writer 2's paragraphs follows. Rewrite it to make it more unified and coherent.

When tryouts for cheerleading came along, I decided to go out for them along with thirty-nine other girls, including Julia. I was so excited about tryouts because being a cheerleader was what I always dreamed of. When the day of tryouts arrived, I blew my chance of being a cheerleader by messing up my cheer in front of the entire gymnasium. Julia got up there and performed her cheer flawlessly. My stomach turned. She was perfect. I was positive at this point I didn't make it. I was right. Julia did make it, and this came as no surprise. I knew it from the beginning. It was inevitable. The same thing happened in the eighth grade, then again in the ninth grade. I was so jealous of Julia that I let it show. I'd catch myself watching her with envy; she'd turn and catch me looking. Julia felt uneasy around me. Her uneasiness and my jealousy continued practically throughout our school years together.

THE EXPRESSIVE STYLE

When we talk of constructing sentences and paragraphs, we are talking of *style*. Style is another name for the results of a series of choices you have made in selecting words and ways of arranging them in sentences and paragraphs. Many make those choices unconsciously; knowing aim and audience brings those choices to the surface, enabling the writer to make more and better choices.

Stylistic choices are an inescapable fact of language. If you choose to write *steal* instead of *rip off,* that's a stylistic choice; knowing your audience helps you to make the choice. If you choose to refer to the reader as *you,* instead of linking yourself with the reader and writing *we,* or impersonalizing your relationship and referring to the reader, yourself, and the world as *one* ("One should note that . . ."), those are stylistic choices that should have been determined by considerations of aim and audience. Each choice shapes in some way the voice you project. We will deal here with the stylistic characteristics of the expressive aim.

Expressive writing uses many first-person pronouns—*I, me, mine, us, our,* and so on. In harmony with this, the expressive writer often emphasizes his or her *idiolect,* a language unique to the writer. All of us have habits of speech that enable our friends to identify us; it is these habits that the expressive writer indulges. In addition, the expressive writer searches for figures of speech (see the Glossary), for imaginative comparisons; the writer is dealing with feelings, and feelings are difficult to convey adequately in literal statements. The expressive writer leans heavily on concrete diction, for reasons that follow.

If your aim in writing about a relationship is expressive, the voice you project must imply to the members of the audience that you and they share, have shared, or will share a common experience, and that you are about to outline that experience and share with them an insight that offers a point of view, a solution, or a consolidation. If you set out to do that, then you will write to the audience not as a superior or an inferior but as one who has been through a common experience. The danger here is "talking down" to your audience. Remember that your advantage is not one of greater wisdom or strength but of *time:* you have lived through what some of them are living through or will live through. And if part of your audience has already lived through the common experience, you haven't even that advantage.

● **Inflated Diction**

Talking down to an audience manifests itself as inflated diction. The writer falls into this trap by using words that are outside the vocabulary of the audience—not just "big" words but rare words.

The writer uses words that may seem common enough, but appear to have technical meanings when they occur in combination. For example, there's nothing wrong with the word *individual* by itself so long as it is used precisely. *Individual* is not a synonym for *person;* it means one person set off from all groups and considered as unique. If that's what you mean, use the word. But notice what happens when the word occurs in a combination such as "An individual raised in an environment that . . . ." If you write like that in an expressive paper, the voice you project is that of a sociologist; suddenly whatever contact you had with your audience may evaporate because you are implying a clinical, detached, superior, "scientific," perhaps even a statistical approach to a common human experience. You have, so to speak, gone expository.

The writer also chooses words that are too general, too abstract, or too grand for the idea or emotion they attempt to capture. Inflated diction makes the writer look foolish. For example, Writer 1's first version is afflicted with inflated diction:

> a sharing of grievous emotions
> anxieties were soon substantiated
> the crushing news engulfed us
> to eliminate a sense of disbelief and unreality
> to alleviate the progression
> a fresh effusion of tears
> a total realignment of my values and priorities

● **Clichés**

Clichés also mar any style but especially the expressive. Probably no one deliberately tries to sound like everyone else (and, therefore, like no one in particular), but many writers do so by using clichés, that is, trite, stale, overworked expressions:

> wise as an owl
> last but not least

> it was an experience I will never forget
> the passing scene

You can use these phrases without thinking—or, more exactly, when you use them you are *not* thinking. Clichés have usually been emptied of content by overuse, and their use has the fatal effect of making you sound like nobody. This is especially dangerous in the expressive aim, in which you must establish a believable and individual, if not unique, voice. The diction of the expressive aim in particular needs to be not only clear but vigorous and attractive. Trite expressions come up to none of these three standards. Writer 1's use of clichés in the first version that follows makes her sound like a stranger to her own experience:

impending death	meant the world to me
loved one	petty rivalries
hurting more than helping	wise counsel
sense of foreboding	broke my spirit
complete shock	burst of swelling pride
racking sobbing	the fate that had befallen us
stern facade	release of tension
torturing my mind	heavy burden
filled with panic	

FIRST VERSION

WRITER 1

LEARNING OF THE NATURE OF MY BROTHER'S ILLNESS

Every family, at one time or another, is confronted with the impending death of one of its members, and must learn to cope with the situation in their own way. Some families try to escape from the inevitable separation from their loved one by running from doctor to doctor in an effort to secure a favorable diagnosis. Others try to ignore the knowledge of the illness, and hope that it will "go away." These unrealistic approaches usually end up hurting more than helping. My family was faced with the imminent death of my seventeen-year-old brother, Paul, almost two years ago. Through a sharing of grievous emotions, we were gradually able to face the reality of his terminal illness, and come to an acceptance of it together.

For three years, my sister, Donna, and I had not been forced to deal with the exact nature of Paul's illness. He had been diagnosed with leukemia on June 30, 1970, but my parents simply told us that he had a "blood disorder." Outside of Paul's frequent hospital visits, our lives, from the time of the diagnosis, hadn't changed significantly. Occasionally, I experienced an unfounded sense of foreboding, but I wanted to remain ignorant of my qualms. These anxieties were soon substantiated. One evening about 5:30, my parents returned home with Paul from

Children's Hospital. Paul was not feeling well, and immediately went to bed. My parents explained that they had something very important to discuss with my sister and me. We gathered together at a table in the basement. We sat in silence for a moment as my mother hesitated to speak, and then, suddenly, her voice broke, and trembled that my older brother was fighting a losing battle with leukemia. The complete shock that was registered in my sister's face must have been echoed in my own. I was eating at the time, and was aware of a McDonald's hamburger turning to dust in my mouth. Looks of bewilderment passed between Donna and I as the crushing news engulfed us. We were spontaneously filled with racking sobbing, and desperately wished that someone would tell us the prognosis was wrong, that the whole thing was a terrible mistake. I couldn't seem to eliminate a sense of disbelief and unreality. My mother appeared exhausted and defeated after having made this revelation. The stern facade had melted from my father's face, and was replaced by a look of tenderness and vulnerability. We then began to question our parents. Did Paul know what he had? What were the doctors doing to alleviate the progression of the disease? I whispered the question that was torturing my mind, "Aren't they going to do *anything* to help him?" My father sighed as he explained that every available medication had been exhausted. His words brought a fresh effusion of tears as my sister and I were consumed with anger and overwhelming bitterness that my brother should have to suffer with this illness, and that we could do nothing to help him. I was filled with panic at the realization of the loss that was at stake. My close relationship with Paul meant the world to me. Being only a year apart, we enjoyed so many common interests—school, friends, experiences. We never engaged in the petty rivalries characteristic of many brothers and sisters. Instead, I would often seek him out for wise counsel, friendship, or just to pass the time of day. Our relationship was precious and rare. It broke my spirit to think that there would come a time when I could no longer feel that burst of swelling pride I had always felt in introducing him as my brother.

A moment of numbness preceded a communal effort to regain lost composure after the discovery. My mother's hands attempted to comfort our exhausted bodies, and to soothe our spent minds. We knew that we had no choice but to reluctantly accept the fate that had befallen us. A swelling of strength and determination emerged from each of us as a result of our commitment, and we could all sense the tremendous release of tension in the atmosphere now that things were out in the open. We had acquired a heavy burden, but the concerted family will to rise above it made the load seem lighter.

It was as though I was seeing the world with different eyes as a result of this revelation. My perspective on life around me had changed drastically. I experienced a total realignment of my values and priorities, and was stunned by the realization of how very precious my family was to me. Even though I would always be able to allot time to homework and friends, I realized that moments spent with my family created memories that were irretrievable. I cannot say that I didn't wish every day that we could revert back to the "way we were." We couldn't be carefree and lighthearted as we were before Paul was stricken with leukemia. We had a great concern to deal with, and it added a deeper, more compassionate aspect to our personalities. Paul taught us how to make the best of the situation, and never complained of his misfortune. Instead, he took pleasure in a sunny day, relished talking with his friends, and he continually worked to improve his mind and body. He was our constant source of strength, support, and comfort. He truly lived each day to the fullest, and left us a beautiful philosophy to live by.

The stages that our family passed through in learning to accept Paul's terminal illness were similar to those that Paul, himself, had to cope with. Shock and bewilderment are usually characteristic of both the patient's and the family's initial reaction to the revelation. The next stage seems to be denial, followed by anger and frustration, severe depression, and finally, when both parties realize there is no other choice, acceptance. Being able to talk and cry together at times will make the family much more comfortable about the impending separation. The more the grief can be expressed before death, the less unbearable it becomes afterward.

● Concrete Diction

Expressive writing usually depends on *concrete diction* for its effectiveness. When you select the most specific and evocative word or phrase from among your available choices, your diction is concrete. For example, in each of the following lists, the last item is the most concrete:

> vehicle, car, old car, old Oldsmobile, 1938 Oldsmobile, a 1938 Oldsmobile sedan with a broken right headlight
> light, dim light, glow

The two examples illustrate the two different ways of making a relatively abstract word or phrase more concrete:

1. Adding words to more sharply define the image or concept
2. Choosing a more specific word

Words that more sharply define the image are *evocative;* that is, they evoke things that simple specificity does not. It is possible to be specific without being concrete. Relentlessly specific prose by itself can produce endless inventories that only seem to convey ideas and images clearly to the reader: "I, John Jones, a white male, 20 years old, was walking down Euclid Avenue in Cleveland, Ohio, at 6:30 P.M., on August 15, 1978." Specific but not evocative. Here are concrete versions of that sentence:

> One steamy afternoon last summer I was sauntering down Euclid Avenue.
> I sloshed down Euclid Avenue late one rainy afternoon last summer.

On August 15, 1978, I was running down Euclid Avenue in Cleveland, frantic to reach home before dark.

There are dozens of other possibilities. Notice that in each version the concreteness issues from offering the reader a relatively exact notion of who was doing what, where, when, under what conditions, and in what manner—perhaps even for what reason. But not all parts of the sentences are equally concrete. The principle is that what the writer wishes to emphasize should be expressed as concretely as possible.

In the versions above, we arbitrarily assumed that the manner of walking was important; therefore, we selected more specific and evocative verbs: *sauntering, sloshed, running*. In the first two versions we assumed that the date and place were not important; in the last version we assumed it was. Making the date specific, you will notice, conveys to the reader that the date *is* important; the reader becomes curious about the date.

Specificity and evocativeness spring from careful attention to (1) concrete nouns and verbs and (2) modifiers that will make the nouns and verbs even more concrete. You choose the best noun or verb available for your purpose and then make it better by additions, if necessary:

I climbed over the fence into the alley.

There is nothing wrong with that sentence so long as all it is intended to do in the paper is indicate that you went from one place to another, over an obstacle. There is, however, very little for the readers to see exactly; the readers simply note that you say you went over a fence to get to an alley. If you want the readers to see and, therefore, become engaged in the experience, there are three units in that sentence that could be made more concrete: two nouns and a verb.

The verb *climbed* is very vague. Did you leap or scramble or claw or inch your way over? (Notice that the more exact verb helps define the following noun more clearly—a person cannot leap the fence that he must scramble over; the verb suggests the height of the fence.)

The first noun is *fence*. Was it tall or low, made of pickets, chain links, bricks, concrete blocks? The second noun is *alley*. Was it wide or narrow, light or dark, clean or littered? If littered, littered with what?

In a sentence in which the nouns and verbs are the most concrete available to you, increased concreteness can be achieved by adding words that do one of three things:

1. add a detail (fence ⟶ a picket fence)
2. add a quality (fence ⟶ a picket fence ⟶ a rotting picket fence)
3. add a comparison (fence ⟶ a picket fence ⟶ a rotting picket fence ⟶ a rotting picket fence leaning toward me at a drunken angle)

Using concrete diction can help solve one very troublesome problem that all writers face: adjusting their diction to the reader. If concreteness were simply a matter of selecting the absolutely specific word for an idea or concept, there would be no problem. Perfect writers would communicate perfectly with perfect readers. But neither writers nor readers are perfect. Concrete diction offers a solution to that dilemma.

For example, suppose you are trying to describe a roommate who is driving you crazy with constant compulsive neatness. You might do it with one word: *meticulous*. It's a "perfect" word: based on the Latin root *metus* (fear), it means a person who is compelled to be neat out of a fear of being found wanting. But suppose your audience doesn't know what *meticulous* means? Then it simply looks like a big word, perhaps an insult to the readers. You could, of course, try *neat,* but that isn't what you mean totally. The solution is to be concrete: Describe what it is your roommate *does*. Whatever your readers' vocabulary, they will understand the concrete details at their own level of diction.

● **Sentence Patterns**

Certain sentence patterns also weaken expressive writing. You talk down to the reader by using an order of words that is not above but *below* the reading capability of the audience. Unfortunately for the writer, most people are better readers than they are writers; that is, they can comprehend (and they *expect* to comprehend) more complex patterns than they can reproduce in their own writing.

The previous sentence, for example, could have been broken down into simpler units:

> Most people are better readers than they are writers.
> They can comprehend complex patterns.
> They can't write the same complex patterns.
> So the writer is in an unfortunate position.

Instead, as a combination of these short examples, the sentence came out "Unfortunately for the writer, most people are better readers than they are writers; that is, they can comprehend (and they *expect* to comprehend) more complex patterns than they can reproduce in their own writing." You, as reader, would have been insulted by the other sequence.

An overuse of the *passive voice* can also weaken the expressive paper. "Their grief was shared by me" (passive) instead of "I shared their grief" (active). Another example of Writer 1's use of the passive is "every family is confronted by."

Overuse of the passive voice can weaken any paper but is especially damaging to the expressive paper. "Their grief was shared by me" (passive) instead of "I shared their grief" (active) robs the statement of vigor and conviction; in fact, since the passive buries the actor or agent in the predicate position, it is a construction that seems to want to avoid responsibility. Strong, readable sentences put the actor in the subject position and use a vivid verb in the active voice. A preference for nouns when verbs are available can also rob the expressive paper of power. If Writer 3, for example, had to choose between "My father coached me" and "My father was my coach," he should choose the first version. It is stronger, more direct, and easier to read and understand.

CLASS EXERCISES

1. Examine Writer 1's first version on pages 105–107. Discuss ways in which the inflated phrases and clichés can be turned into concrete diction.
2. Improve the following passages by combining statements where appropriate and giving preference to strong verbs and the active voice.

> As the end of our sophomore year was finally arriving, I made a decision to try out for the swing choir. At my school, the swing choir is the top choir. My audition went very well. For the first time in a long while, I had a positive feeling about my performance. There had been good vibes. The small group watching had been responsive. After school, I ran down to the music hall. The list was to be posted there. I found the list. There was my name. I did it!

> My guess is that the key element in the rise in the cost of housing for college students is the fall in the rate of the beginning of new construction. Prices are allowed to rise because of the lack of competitive pressure. The same situation is observable in the prices books are assigned in the college bookstore. Now that the college has a monopoly on the selling of textbooks, prices are beginning to climb. And I say it stinks.

● ASSIGNMENT: The First Version

1. Write several drafts until you create a first version that communicates your focus to your audience.
2. Submit your paper for responses.

● **READER RESPONSES**

Responding to someone else's paper not only helps the other writer to see where the strengths and weakness are. It also helps you develop your own writing power. Why? Because it sharpens your ability to stand back and look at not only *what* has been said but also *how* it has been said. It develops in you the power of self-criticism that you will need after this class is over, when it will not be as easy to get advice on your work. You need, therefore, to develop your own responding skills. But being critical of your own work is hard because you are very close to it. Responding to the writing of others enables you to get enough distance to notice elements like focus, organization, and diction.

Responding gives you two kinds of sight. You learn to see and react to what is being communicated. But you also learn to see *writing as writing*. To your ability to respond instinctively as an intelligent reader, you will add the power to examine writing as an artist, as one who understands the principles and inner workings of the art of writing. Aristotle, in *Posterior Analytics,* called such a person a *master craftsman*—a person who not only could engage well in the craft but who also had the *art,* who understood what he was doing and could explain it to others. Responding gives you that kind of power. Use the reader guide outlined on p. 57 to organize your response.

INSTRUCTOR'S RESPONSE TO WRITER 1

You have written a promising paper in which some questionable choices have been made.

FOCUS

Your original focus was "My family's sharing of grief over my brother's death helped me to accept it and caused me to realign my values." But the paper does not maintain this concentration on you. You should not begin with generalizations about "every family" and then discuss other people's strategies. Your focus deals with you and your family; that's what your paper should deal with, too.

DEVELOPMENT

There is a curious difference between the focus statement and the development. The focus says that it was the family that helped you to change. Not only is there no sign of your family helping you to change, there is no sign that the family changed at all except for that one release of grief when all of you admitted Paul was mortally ill. Instead it is Paul who teaches you to deal with death. Did you by any chance stick too closely to your exploratory list and neglect your focus? If you will look over your list again, you will see that you seem to have begun at the top of your list and written your paper by turning fragments into sentences.

ORGANIZATION

The narrative mode is faithfully carried out through paragraphs 2 and 3. Then it disappears. You need to concentrate on chronological order. The narrative mode almost never requires an introductory paragraph that summarizes the chronology or the insights that arise from a series of events. You also need to try to recall more exact detail so that you can describe the events more concretely. If you concentrate on the scene you will be more likely to get a smooth flow of narrative. As it is, there are serious gaps between paragraphs 2 and 3, 3 and 4, and 4 and 5.

STYLE

It's hard to write exactly and efficiently about strong emotions. So you're not alone in your problems. First, your voice varies throughout the piece. "The more the grief can be expressed before death, the less unbearable it becomes afterward" is the voice of a clinical psychologist, a detached analyst. Compare that voice with this one: "I was eating at the time, and was aware of a McDonald's hamburger turning to dust in my mouth." Then compare that with this from the same paragraph: "His words brought a fresh effusion of tears as my sister and I were consumed with anger and overwhelming bitterness . . . ." One way to avoid those shifts in voice is to keep the role of your audience ever in mind. Another way is to be aware of the different effects growing out of general and specific terms. General terms like *confronted, impending, inevitable separation, imminent,* and *grievous emotion* are better suited to an expository aim. When you use them in an expressive paper, you establish an undesirable sense of detachment from the experience. When readers encounter formal, generalized terms such as "ignorant of my qualms" "anxieties substantiated," and "fresh effusion of tears," they cannot experience the narrative but only learn about it. Mixed in with these terms are clichés that violate the personal sense of grief you are trying to convey: "her voice broke," "crushing news," "filled with panic," "broke my spirit." The sentence patterns are for the most part varied and interesting. Occasionally you need to phase out a passive and tighten up loose structures. For example, in the sentence, "I was eating at the time, and was aware of a McDonald's hamburger turning to dust in my mouth," the coordinate structure with *and* suggests that both experiences are equally important.

CONVENTIONS

The grammar, spelling, and punctuation are adequate. The lapses include:

1. superfluous commas, as in the first paragraph ("illness, and come") and the second paragraph ("at the time, and was").
2. wrong case, as in the second paragraph: "between Donna and I."
3. wrong tense, as in the fourth paragraph: "Even though I would always be able."

STUDENT RESPONSE TO WRITER 1

FOCUS

The focus is very easy to find in the first paragraph at the end. Everything in the paper seems to deal with that focus.

DEVELOPMENT

There is something funny about the story. I couldn't find the change that you said happened. You just say that you changed. The details are mainly judgments and opinions, not descriptions.

ORGANIZATION

Primary mode is narrative. The first and last paragraphs, though, are descriptive. I couldn't follow the time sequence in part of the story. When did all this changing happen? The theme makes it sound like it happened all of a sudden. But the focus says something else.

STYLE

There is something old-fashioned and formal about the diction. It doesn't sound like a young person talking. So it doesn't sound sincere.

CONVENTIONS

OK.

CLASS EXERCISES

1. As a class, use the reader guide to give responses to Writers 3, 4, and 5.
2. Compare the instructor and student responses to Writer 1. Discuss what advice you would follow in revising the paper.

● **ASSIGNMENT: Reader Response**

1. Using the reader guide, give written responses to several of your classmates' first versions.
2. Discuss your responses with your classmates.

● **REVISING AND EDITING**

Recall that *revising* can entail major changes in your paper. Serious problems with focus necessitate a complete overhaul. Problems with organization can also require extensive rewriting. Inadequate development requires adding more detail, examples, or information. Development that is inappropriate for your audience requires complete rewriting. These problems must be solved before you attack problems of diction or sentence structure.

Editing requires correcting any mistakes in spelling, punctuation, and grammar.

REVISION

WRITER 1

PAUL

For three years I had lived with a lie or at best a half-truth. My parents had known that my seventeen-year-old brother Paul had leukemia since June, 1970. But, wanting to spare us, they had told my sister Donna and me only that he had a "blood disorder."

Over those three years, except for Paul's frequent visits to the hospital, our lives, and mine in particular, changed almost not at all. Occasionally I would feel a sense of foreboding and depression, but I pushed those feelings away. I did not want to know.

But one evening about two years ago the truth came home. My parents returned with Paul from Children's Hospital; Paul, who was not feeling well, went immediately to bed. Dad, Mom, Donna, and I trooped down to the basement where we gathered around a small table on which I had spread out a meal from McDonald's. Still acting as if this were a normal day, we began to eat. Suddenly Mom blurted out that Paul was fighting a losing battle with leukemia. I was aware of a hamburger turning to dust in my mouth. I began to cry. Inside I was whispering, "It's a mistake, it has to be a mistake," but the exhaustion I could see in my mother and the way my father's face seemed to have gone slack—he looked so vulnerable, my strong father—told me that there was no mistake. And the way Donna's eyes, smeary with tears, shifted away from mine told me something else: that we had known it all the time. Only now the fact was loose there in the room.

We talked and we wept through a series of necessary questions, necessary because I was still pretending that this new reality was new. "Aren't they going to do anything to help him?" I asked, and my father patiently explained that everything available had been tried.

Sitting there, alone among my family, I went through the normal feelings that are grief. Rage and bitterness at my brother's fate and also at my own helplessness. Panic because Paul had been my mainstay. We were only a year apart; he had been my friend and counselor and, I now realized, my bridge to people and things I valued, and I thought bleakly of the time when I would no longer feel that burst of swelling pride when someone said, "Paul's sister." Then came the guilt for the selfishness.

Those feelings stayed with me in the weeks that followed, but another, more positive feeling began to emerge, for all of us, I think. I began to realize how very precious to me were the days and hours I had with my family. As a hedge against the darkness, we began to spend more time together, and in that time we were more gentle with one another, as if we were storing up memories, not only of Paul but of the family.

I can't say that I didn't wish every day that we could revert to the "way we were." But we had gained something because of what we were about to lose. Paul, of course, went on being Paul. He laughed on good days, worked hard at being healthy, and never complained. And then he died.

CLASS EXERCISES

1. Compare Writer 1's first and revised versions.
   - Indicate which changes seem to have improved the paper.
   - What advice has been followed?
2. Analyze the sentence structures of your first version. How many types of patterns did you use? What sentence patterns from Chapter 10, "Sentence-Combining," were not represented? Practice one of the types you did not use.

3. Do the exercises in Chapter 9, "Editing," for any errors you had in your first version.
4. Revise the following two paragraphs from Writer 3's paper.

> As I entered high school I had an important decision to make, and I needed a good counselor. My high school guidance counselor gave me little direction in what I should pursue as far as career opportunities and my education were concerned. I expected that my father, the blue-collar worker, would be content if I graduated from high school and got any job that I could. That was not the case. My father insisted that I work hard at my studies and go on to college and make something of myself. He told me not to waste my brains or talent. He told me that things would be difficult no matter what route I chose, but that anything that is worthy in life is never too hard to reach. While my guidance counselor and teachers looked on from the sidelines, it was my father who helped me plan a curriculum in high school and it was my father who helped me decide where I should go to college and what I should pursue as a career.
>
> This wasn't the only time that he helped me as a counselor during my high school years. I decided to quit the basketball team in order to have more time to study and to take a part-time job in a grocery store. I thought that this might separate us because it looked as though I was giving up at sports and not giving it my best. It did just the opposite as it brought us closer together as my father respected my decision and respected my courage for making it while so many of my classmates were angered at me and resented what I did. Many of my high school relationships ended at this point, but my relationship with my father became stronger as he respected my intellect, my independence from conformity (the unwritten rule that no one is supposed to quit playing sports at my high school), and my decision to plan for my future education by getting a job on my own and not asking him for money all the time.

● ASSIGNMENT: Revising and Editing

1. Guided by the advice you received on your first version, rewrite your paper, revising its major problems and editing it for conventional correctness.
2. Submit your paper for evaluation.

A WRITER'S PROCESS

Below we present the sequence followed in Writer 4's writing process.

THE GUIDING QUESTION AND POTENTIAL SITUATIONS

Subject: My relationship with my grandmother

My Values and Expectations

—love and concern from my family

—never expected anyone close to me to die

My Subject

—my grandmother gave me a special love

—my grandmother's death but I didn't realize what had happened, or didn't want to

Question: Why was my grandmother so special to me, and why can't I accept her death?

Situations

—an essay for my girlfriend Lana, who would like to have known my grandmother
—a letter to my parents
—an essay for the class

EXPLORATION

STATIC VIEW

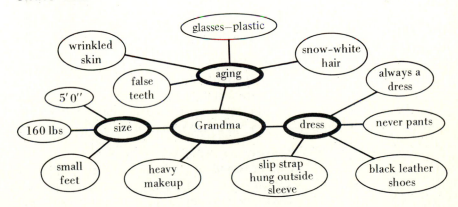

DYNAMIC VIEW

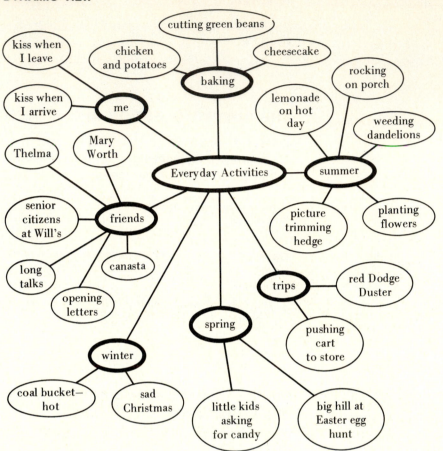

RELATIVE VIEW

Classification

—optimist, loving, low-tempered
—never flies off the handle about small things
—always feels I can accomplish anything (college)
—always has a kiss for me

Compare: to death of Grandpa

Death of Grandpa

—too young to realize
—wasn't close (love)
—in funeral home I didn't stay by
  him very much, I would talk to my
  friends

Death of Grandma

—old enough to realize
—very close (lot of love)
—was always by the casket

Analogy: My grandma was like a good song. During the prime of a good song, it is always good every time you listen to it. After the song is no longer a hit, one tends to listen to other songs. Just as people die, one tends to turn to other people. But every time you hear that song, you remember how good it was. The same is true with my grandma. Every time I see a picture of her I remember her.

FOCUS AND SITUATION

Subject   *Point of Significance*

My grandmother's relationship with ── ed me to realize what love was all
me and her death ──────────────────── about.

(*Question:* Why was my grandmother so special to me, and why can't I accept her death?)

Situation

I want to write an essay for my girlfriend Lana because I want her to know my grandma.

AUDIENCE AND MODES OF ORGANIZATION

AUDIENCE ANALYSIS

1. My Audience will be my girlfriend Lana.
2. Audience in itself:
   a. Background: Lana is my age and goes to college. Her background is similar to mine.
   b. Values: She is a good listener and very considerate of others. She is also an emotional person.
3. Audience in relation to the subject:
   a. Knowledge and opinion: She hasn't yet experienced the death of anyone close. She has had a close friend in the hospital. She can sympathize with me but can't tell me how she would feel if someone close to her were to die.
   b. Strength of opinion: She can postulate how she will feel, but something inside her tells her she just really doesn't ever want to experience it.
   c. Willingness to act: She's not very willing to act on her opinion because she's afraid if she did lose someone she loved she would probably not do as she thought she would.
4. Specific role: A grandchild who is fond of grandparents
5. Analysis of role:
   a. Background: A happy grandchild will know the special things a grandparent can do for you that a parent can't. She will know how the differences in age affect the relationship. She will know what grandparents can teach you about love and death.
   b. Values: She will value expressions of sympathy, respect, and love, espe-

cially since the relationship between grandparents and grandchildren is usually short.

    c. Attitude toward the subject: She will be prepared to like my grandma.

6. Relational role: She will be a peer.

MODE OF ORGANIZATION: NARRATIVE

¶ 1   Sundays at Grandma's when I was a child
¶ 2   Sunday dinner
¶ 3   Grandpa's death
¶ 4   Grandma's move
¶ 5   Grandma when I was in sixth grade
¶ 6   Grandma's stroke
¶ 7   Grandma in nursing home
¶ 8   Grandma's death
¶ 9   At the funeral
¶10   Now

FIRST VERSION

A LOVE UNMATCHED BY ANYONE ELSE

When I was a small child and Grandma and Grandpa Ambrose lived at Snake Run, my family tried to visit them every Sunday. Mom always made sure we looked our best. I always wore my black and gray suit, a skinny black tie, and a black felt hat which let my ears show. Whenever I'd open the front door of their house, grandma always gave me a big kiss and a hug which knocked my hat off. I didn't mind that she knocked the hat off because that always gave me a good reason to keep it off.

Grandma's Sunday meals were placed on a big table in the dining room, which seated eight people. There were corn, green beans, chicken gravy with hot homemade biscuits, and two platters overflowing with crispy fried chicken on the table. It looked like a bunch of fans clapping at a football game when we all started eating. All through the meal Grandma kept asking everyone if they had enough of this or that. She was always considerate of others. After supper I used to change into old clothes and take a walk with her. We'd walk down an old dusty road and talk about how things were done when she was a kid. She'd point out a patch of ground where there used to be a bunch of trees or tell how she used to swim in the "crick" on Sunday afternoons after church. No matter how many Sundays we took a walk, each one was a little different. One Sunday we'd turn down one road and the next Sunday we'd turn down a different one.

One Sunday when my family went over to Grandma and Grandpa's house, we didn't eat supper, and Grandma didn't take me for a walk—Grandpa had died. I was awfully young when Grandpa died. I didn't fully understand what had happened. I don't believe my mom and dad wanted me to understand at this stage in life. I can barely remember being at the funeral home. I was afraid to go up by the casket. Instead I played with the letters on the bulletin board which announced the hours of the funeral home. My family spent a few days at Grandma's house after the funeral. It didn't seem like a sad occasion to me. I couldn't understand why everyone was crying. All I thought about was eating all the good food and desserts that the neighbors brought over.

After a few weeks, Grandma had an auction, sold her house, and moved into a trailer across the street from us. This is when all the fun started for me. I figured since Grandma was so close I'd go over every night. During the school year I'd get her mail after school and take it to her. I'd always ask her if she needed anything at the store and sometimes I'd play canasta with her. That is, until Mom would call and tell me it was time to come home. This basic routine went on until I started middle school.

In middle school it seemed like I had more school functions to attend. Even though I had more things to do, I still managed to go to the store for her and on Saturdays I mowed her grass. She always had cold lemonade waiting for me after I mowed the grass. We would sit on the front porch and drink lemonade and talk about things. We used to talk about school or how the lawn looked. The thing I liked most about our talks was getting her to ask me to come over for supper on Sundays. I liked eating with Grandma because I got to help fix it. I enjoyed that because my mom was very particular about who got in her kitchen. Grandma and I used to make cheesecake on Sundays also.

When I was in the last part of my sixth grade year, Grandma seemed different. She didn't cook much anymore and she didn't care too much about Christmas anymore either. But she still loved to play canasta with me. Mom started sending a supper meal over with me when I took her mail over. I didn't think much of it. I thought Mom was just trying to be nice. I didn't know Grandma had been going to the doctor for high blood pressure.

My sixth grade summer, Grandma had a light stroke which put her in the hospital for quite some time. I remember the sense of loss I felt. I didn't have any little jobs to do for her. Dad and I spent many nights going down to the hospital. My dad, Grandma, and I got very close in the two weeks she was in the hospital. Gradually, after several visits, Grandma's sight became very bad. Dad said it was hardening of the arteries. I didn't know what he meant by this; all I knew was that Grandma couldn't make out my face.

Since Grandma's condition had gotten worse, we had to admit her to a nursing home. The help was coldhearted and didn't seem to care. I hated the nursing home. The food was chopped up like baby food so that swallowing was easier. Grandma was so unhappy. She would burst out crying when we came to see her on Sundays after church. Somehow, as soon as Dad walked in the room, she knew it was her son. The visits got more and more emotional as time went on. Dad and I would try little things to make her happy. When she said she wanted to go home, we'd walk her outside for a little bit, bring her back and tell her she was home. We also combed her hair a lot. She claimed it made her feel better. Every once in a while we brought fried chicken for her. She loved the fried chicken. Even though she was in a nursing home, couldn't see, and didn't like it, she still found enough love in her heart to ask us if we wanted some of her chicken. The visits to the nursing home got too emotional for me sometimes. After a while I couldn't handle the leaving part of the visit; so I would stay home and visit a friend or play the pinball at the drug store.

One Sunday when I was at Will's playing the pinball, my older sister came down and told me it was time to go home. Her eyes were bloodshot and her eyelids were red. I knew something was wrong. Just before we got home, she burst out crying and told me Grandma had died. I didn't cry. I don't know why. Then I looked at her and said, "You're not serious are you?" She said, "Yes, Mom and Dad are at the nursing home now." I guess she didn't know how long she had been crying because just as she finished talking, Mom and Dad drove up. As soon as Dad started hugging Deb and me and I heard him crying, I knew for sure that Grandma wasn't with us anymore.

Between the previous moment and the funeral home, I don't remember anything. I couldn't tell you what kinds of food all the neighbors sent over or anything. I was so stunned by her death that I stayed out of school for a couple of days. At the funeral, everyone sat in the church in sorrow. I was one of the pallbearers. I didn't know what was going on. I wasn't supposed to watch them close the casket, but I'll never forget the empty feeling inside when I saw the caretaker close the casket. I knew once he closed it, I'd never see my grandma's face again.

I still call the trailer across the street "Grandma's trailer," and I still wish I had her next door when things go bad. Most of all I wish my grandma could meet you, because she told me to "Get a good one"!

3

WRITING WITH A
PERSUASIVE AIM

In the Public World/Issues

The chapter will discuss persuasive writing, which concentrates on the audience, the reader. While persuasive writing certainly contains all the elements of discourse—a writer, a subject matter, and a language/form—it is persuasive because it emphasizes the *audience*. This chapter will move you from the private to the public world to give you an opportunity to write about matters that you share with others. In your private world, you are the authority on your own experience. In the public world, however, you are not the ultimate authority. The views that you hold can be challenged by others who also participate in and interact with the subjects that you find compelling.

Your experience in the public world influences you in profound ways. Your life is shaped by attitudes and events, policies and practices of the public world you inhabit. You hold memberships in many societies—some imposed on you by the neighborhood, the state, the country, and even the hemisphere in which you were born and brought up. Other societies you have joined by choice. You may have chosen to be a member of a certain school system, a political district, a church organization, or a political party. You may have joined a youth group, a sports team, a school club. These societies in which you have participated have changed your outlook and way of life. You do not have complete control over this public world. What others in these societies do, what they profess, what they argue over can determine to some extent the way your life develops.

But you are not entirely helpless in this public world. In this chapter you will learn ways in which you can influence these larger contexts through writing. In *expressive* writing you had a chance to see how writing could help you understand and share some insight into your private world. *Persuasive* writing enables you

1. to come to a better judgment on or insight into subjects in your public world, and
2. to influence your reader to accept your judgment—to understand, respect, perhaps share or act on it.

Persuasive writing is one of the most powerful types of writing. But it takes sophistication and skill to become an effective persuasive writer. This chapter will begin to examine the crucial powers and skills that this kind of discourse demands.

● THE GUIDING QUESTION AND POTENTIAL SITUATIONS

THE SUBJECT

The subject context for this writing experience is a broad one. In the societies that constitute your public world, there is inevitable disagreement about principles, policies, and practices. In short, the public world is cluttered with *issues*—different points of view on how things should be run, how resources should be allocated, how justice ought to be administered, and so on. Issues can be moral, economic, political, cultural, educational, or religious. They swirl around you. But only some at any given period in your life become compelling for you; only some touch your life. These compelling issues are the subjects for your next writing task.

An issue normally becomes compelling when its implications strike your life. Educational issues such as inadequate high school curricula, poor teaching, and student lack of ability to read, write, and think critically are national issues that may not have been or may not be compelling in your educational situation. Campus policies on housing, admissions, and grading may not be issues in your situation. Disagreement over gun control, abortion, crime prevention or punishment, environmental pollution, while important in themselves, may not compel you at this point if you have had little personal experience with them.

Selecting your subject entails choosing an issue that you find compelling because it has touched your life. You may wish to narrow this context to help you decide. You may wish to consider only educational or social or political contexts in which to determine an issue that genuinely puzzles and disturbs you. Use your strategy for posing questions to help you select the issue that is most compelling in your present life.

THE GUIDING QUESTION

Make a list of possible subjects that have aroused strong feelings in you in the last year—disagreements over beliefs, policies, or practices that have impinged on your way of life. If you want to use this paper as a genuine learning experience, a way of reaching new understanding, select a subject about which you can be open-minded even if you tend now to favor one side of the issue over another. The planning stages of writing can then help you analyze the issue in order to reach a more intelligent, balanced, and reasonable judgment about it.

To start your investigation, use the two-part strategy introduced in Chapter 1 to sort out your feelings of puzzlement, anger, or confusion:

1. Identify the expectations or values to which this issue pertains. What values does it challenge or embody? What expectations of yours does one or the other side of the issue call into question?
2. Formulate a question that asks what you need to learn to resolve the issue in your own mind.

Below are the guiding questions that five writers posed to themselves.

GUIDING QUESTIONS

WRITER 1   **Subject:** The interhall transfer system at Midwestern University

My Values and Expectations   **My Subject**
—easy interhall transfer system   —applications, deadlines, and interviews

—fair treatment on a "first-come,
first-served"

—transfers based on class rank and
requested roommate

Question: Why does the Quadrangle continue to use its present policy of interhall transfers?

WRITER 2

Subject: The issue that I will be discussing is national health insurance. I have a personal interest and a couple of personal experiences in this area as well as a somewhat informed view on the public debate.

My Values and Expectations

—the basic right to health care for all

—our health care system should not
put people into bankruptcy due to
health problems that they cannot
afford

—a country so prosperous as ours is
should have an affordable health
care system

—the richness of this nation and the
ability of our country to spend bil-
lions of dollars on national defense

My Subject

—our health care system has become a privilege for the rich

—many people are deep in debt in
medical payments that are caused
by illness that is no fault of theirs

—with the sole exception of South
Africa, we are the only industrialized nation without a national
health insurance plan

—the quality of health care available
to many people remains poor

Question: Despite the problems that may accompany a national health insurance plan, won't such a plan help solve many of the national health care problems that we have today?

WRITER 3

Subject: The women's movement

My Values and Expectations

—being a wife and mother
—developing my talents

My Subject

—looking down on housewives
—emphasis on job rights

Question: How has the women's movement affected housewives' attitudes toward themselves?

WRITER 4

Subject: I want to examine the conflict in Northern Ireland because I have relatives there and saw first-hand some of the problems.

My Values and Expectations

—peace and tolerance

My Subject

—attitude of the Irish people I met
—continuous violence

Question: What has caused the struggle in Northern Ireland to continue on and on?

WRITER 5

Subject: Drunk drivers, especially the penalties

My Values and Expectations

—the rights of a person

—one should stay within the bounds
of the law

My Subject

—many people are killed by drunk
drivers

—the justice system is clogged with
cases and many offenders of the
law are left off

—individuals are wrong when taking another's life

—law should be enforced when broken

—I don't drink but fully accept that others do and I respect their choice and their rights of what they want to do

—people enjoy driving

—people enjoy drinking

Question: What type of penalty should be given for drunk driving?

COMMENTARY

Writer 1 has chosen a good issue to pursue, one that is immediately affecting his life-style as a college resident. He does not probe his dissonance very deeply, however. Nor does he seem very open-minded about the problem. His question, suggesting that he wishes to understand the reasons for the policy, has two problems: (1) He will probably not be able to answer it, and (2) the only solution that can come from the question is a change in his own attitude, not a change in the situation. It would be better if his question allowed for both types of resolution. Writer 1 revised his question to read: "What are the advantages and disadvantages of the Quad's policy for interhall transfers?"

Writer 2 has enough personal experience to tackle his issue with more than generalizations and clichés. The statement of his values, however, suggests that he may be unwilling to investigate other sides of the issue. His question will also give him trouble because the way it is phrased can only lead to the answer yes or no rather than to a solution, a judgment. Writer 2 revised his work by adding to his statement of dissonance and by rewording his question:

My Values and Expectations

—low taxes

—individual rights to choose health care

My Subject

—health insurance would probably increase taxes

—might limit choices

Question: On what bases is a national health care program feasible and desirable? Do these bases outweigh the problems of such a system?

POTENTIAL SITUATIONS

Setting the writing situation for persuasive discourse is a crucial part of your planning, because this kind of writing emphasizes the audience.

Before you can make a list of feasible alternatives, however, you should consider the different kinds of changes that persuasion can bring about in a reader. Each kind entails a different level of difficulty.

1. If you choose an audience that is relatively uninformed about your subject, your first goal will be to persuade your readers of the reasonableness of your judgment.
2. If you choose an audience that agrees with you and is informed but is indifferent or unwilling to act, your task will be to strengthen the audience's commitment to your position and perhaps to mobilize it into action.
3. If you choose an audience that holds the opposite point of view, your job will be very challenging. You might try only to get the audience to respect your point of view, though not sharing it, or you might aim at something much more difficult—to change the audience's position in favor of yours.

When you analyze your audience later, you will have to make careful decisions along these lines. But keeping these goals in mind now will guide you in setting up the possible writing situations you envision for this paper. Here are the ones the student writers chose.

WRITER 1
—a letter to the director of the residence halls, who presumably thinks the system is a good one
—an essay that I will share with my next-door neighbor in the dorm who doesn't seem to have an opinion on the issue
—an article for the school paper

WRITER 2
—an article in my local newspaper to arouse the readers to the issue
—a letter to the local chapter of the American Medical Association, which is opposed to national health insurance
—an essay for my classmates who may be indifferent to the situation
—a letter to my local doctor, who shares the views of the AMA

WRITER 3
—an article for *Ms.* magazine, which has fostered the women's movement
—an essay for my classmates, especially the women in the class who are preparing for careers but who also want a family
—an article for the school newspaper

WRITER 4
—a letter to my relatives in Ireland who feel strongly about the the IRA
—an essay for my classmates who are indifferent to the problem and view it as something happening across the ocean
—a guest editorial for the city newspaper which has recently published a series of stories on the subject

WRITER 5 —a letter to the parents and friends of a girl I know who was killed—they are angry over the sentence given to the killer
—an article in our local paper about the subject
—an essay for my classmates who only have outside experience with the subject
—a letter to a friend of mine who drives when drunk

● **COMMENTARY**

Writer 1 has selected three different forms with three different audiences that pose three different challenges. If he writes for the director of residence halls, he will be working to change a fixed opinion of the reader, since it is obvious that he and the director are on opposite sides of the question. On the other hand, writing an essay for his next-door neighbor involves first interesting the reader, then informing him (neither necessary for the director), and finally persuading him. Since the next-door neighbor is presumably powerless to do anything about the policy even if he were interested, informed, and persuaded, this would seem a less desirable choice of writing situation. The third possibility is better than the second but less attractive than the first, because although it would be aimed at a large audience, some of whom could be assumed to be interested and informed, achieving any change would still require mobilizing this audience to approach the first audience, the director. Here the clear intent of the writer—a change in the rules—dictates choosing the first audience.

Writer 2, on the other hand, has one bad choice and three suitable ones. The first, an article in his local newspaper, is unappealing. Local newspapers generally don't print contentious political articles, especially from college students, particularly when they deal with topics not in the headlines. The second situation is more workable. The local chapter of the AMA is doubtless well informed on an issue so vital to their livelihood, but the writer may be able to gain a hearing for his point of view. An essay for his classmates, who will be vitally affected by this issue soon, would seem a reasonable choice. A letter to his local doctor is likewise a suitable choice; a personal contact between writer and reader is already there. A letter like that, however, coming out of the blue, might seem like a personal attack and should therefore be prefaced very carefully.

CLASS EXERCISES

1. Discuss the subjects, questions, and situations of Writers 3, 4, and 5. How carefully did they pinpoint the gap between their values and expectations and their subjects? Were their questions well stated?
2. Choose an issue with which the class is familiar. Identify the disso-

nances that exist for different individuals in the class. Formulate questions that arise from these puzzlements.

3. List the *types* of issues that could be used as subjects by individuals who had personal experiences with them. Discuss varieties of writing situations in which these issues could be addressed.

5. Examine the following case and state the various dissonances that Daniel experienced.

> Daniel, a freshman at State University, wanted to make friends and have some fun on the weekends. He found himself spending every weekend at beer parties because there was nothing else to do. Most people ended up with hangovers the next day. Although he liked drinking, he had previously been concerned about excesses at his high school where several of his classmates had had driving accidents and one or two had become alcoholics. He was frustrated.

● ASSIGNMENT: The Guiding Question and Potential Situations

1. Select an issue that you find compelling because it has touched your life.
2. Identify the values and expectations that are challenged by the issue.
3. Write a question to guide your search for a more balanced judgment on the issue.
4. List several actual situations in which you could write on the issue.
5. Seek advice on this phase of your planning before proceeding.

● EXPLORATION

In order to reach a balanced understanding of your issue, you need to engage in careful exploration, recalling as much as you know from your own experience and from your reading. You should also take into consideration as many sides of the issue as possible. The exploratory guide can help you remain open-minded so that you gain an informed, reasonable understanding of the issue. This distance is difficult to maintain because an issue that has touched your life will always generate strong feelings. Sometimes, however, those feelings produce more heat than light. Your exploration will enable you to stand back and view your subject more dispassionately.

Here is a restatement of the exploratory guide:

● **Static View**
  - Define your issue so that someone unfamiliar with it could understand its essential elements.
  - Make a list of the pros and cons or as many sides of the issue as you can.
  - Recall and record the details of your personal experiences with the issue.

● **Dynamic View**
  - Trace the history of the issue as far as you can, noting its causes and effects.
  - Identify the changes that have taken place in the issue both in your own experience and in the public world.
  - Speculate on the future of the issue.

● **Relative View**
  - Classify your issue, defining the larger groups into which it can be placed.
  - Compare and contrast your issue with other issues.
  - Create at least one analogy for your issue and explain its basis.

Below are two student explorations.

EXPLORATION

WRITER 2   NATIONAL HEALTH INSURANCE

STATIC VIEW

Arguments For NHI
—make the health care system equitable for all persons
—health problems, illnesses and hospital bills will not bankrupt families or cause severe financial burdens

Arguments Against NHI
—government intervention in the medical field
—government control of doctors and medical facilities

—need a preventive system and not a disease-curing system

—"socialized medicine"

—not really that expensive

—cut down on individual medical costs

—cost to the taxpayer

—right of individuals to choose by whom and where they want to have their medical problems treated

—people can still choose doctor and medical facility they want

—failure of the British system

—government's duty to assure that everyone gets the same health care

—success of the Canadian and Swedish systems

—decent care with tough controls

—people will come to the doctor before they get real sick and will not wait until it is too late as they no longer have to worry about the cost.

The national health insurance issue is currently one of America's most controversial domestic (social) issues. A national health insurance plan is currently in committee in both houses of Congress. It is one of the hottest political issues of our time. The Democrats have endorsed the slow adoption of a national health insurance program in their platform while the Republicans have denounced the program. Congress is currently working on a $25 billion plan which incorporates the plans of Senators Long and Kennedy and Carter's plan. The main argument for the plan is to curb rising medical costs and the main argument against it is its costs (both in implementing and maintaining).

Features of an NHI

—government program to pay for all medical costs (doctors, medicine, hospital, etc.) that are incurred by everyone—comprehensive plan pays for everyone and all their costs whereas some of the scaled-down plans pay only a part of the costs or pay up to a certain amount of the costs

—people (patients) choose their own doctors & hospitals & clinics

—government makes payments directly to doctors and hospitals

—sets medical costs and doctors' and hospital fees—uniform costs and limits— all fees are the same everywhere in the country for the same things

—covers surgical costs

—immunization program

My Personal Experience

—when my aunt got cancer and the financial burden which the family incurred then and which they still feel today 7 years after she died after a year of illness and the medical costs and hospital costs that go with it

—when my grandfather became ill and all of the costs which my grandmother incurred and which our family incurred and which are still affecting us a year and a half after he died

DYNAMIC VIEW

History of the Issue

—1930s: Introduction of Medicare, Medicaid, and many other government programs in these areas during the New Deal
—1940s: Rejected by conservatives
—1950s: Dead issue
—1960s: Issue was raised again by many liberals and was continually introduced in Congress
—1970s: Became a hot issue (especially as other nations started up national health programs); continually introduced in Congress; rising medical costs have made the issue hot again and the issue is right at the forefront of political, social issues

RELATIVE VIEW

It is classified in the broader category of social issues which are directly related to the area of government and human needs. It is very similar to issues such as social security, pensions, education, child care, and the ensuring of basic rights. It is different from these issues in that it is much more controversial (many more ideological divisions) and the sides are in sharp contrast with each other and the ideas cause deep divisions.

Classification (Social Issues)

—Health issues
—Politically relevant issue at this time
—Politically divisive issue

Analogy

—Being deprived of adequate health insurance is like signing your own death warrant.
—Having a catastrophic illness these days is the same as going into bankruptcy.

EXPLORATION

WRITER 4   NORTHERN IRELAND

STATIC VIEW

—essentially a working-class struggle between the Catholics & the Protestants, intensified by the involvement of different political factions
—groups in the war: IRA—Protestant Provisional Army—British government (British soldiers)—Northern Irish—Southern Irish—indirectly the British middle class
—the cities of the war: dreary, grimy, ugly Irish industrial towns contain the fighting—Londonderry, Belfast, Dublin, lately London

—fighting has been continuous for over 50 years

—N. Ireland torn with internal hatred   Southern Irish afraid fighting will spill over the border

—people: one reason they fight is because they do not have anything else to do; most Americans would reject this argument; however, the boredom of a city such as Belfast cannot be described

—often the average, middle-class Englishman really hates the Irish

—an economic-political-social-religious war

Economic

—for years the poor Catholic factory workers were prevented from working in Protestant factories; the same was true for the Protestant workers & Catholic factories

—the hate intensified so much that to both sides the only recourse was violence

—other economic situations affecting the struggle: England has always accepted Irish labor, supplied the jobs. Some English say: "They take our jobs & shoot our boys"

—the general economic situation of N. Ireland is very dismal

—the lower classes of Catholics & Protestants work in factories

—menial jobs, inflation is high & creeping higher

Political

—should N. Ireland be a separate country? Many N. Irish still dream of a united Ireland

—House of Commons—London—scene of the political debates

—Ian Paisley—hateful Protestant leader

—B. Devlin—Catholic Crusader. Both prejudiced due to their backgrounds

—should England have soldiers in N. Ireland or not?

—English soldiers get killed & it's an Irish war

—England's alternatives: withdraw, do not accept Irish immigrants, laborers or refugees, stop all trade with Ireland

—other alternatives: intensify military pressure. Harsh sentences for all people involved in any way with unlawful groups

Social

—the hatred in N. Ireland is a social disease, has infiltrated the schools, affected & finished old friendships between C & Protestants

—Military victory is not the solution because the problem is within the people

Religious

—religious leaders (Ian Paisley for example) have done nothing to help ease the problem. They do not preach love & reconciliation

—In Ireland you choose what you want to read in the Bible

—the church has a medieval stranglehold on the average N. Irish person

—the religious leaders of Ireland today are a disgrace to their religions

—the C & P are fanatics—many people go to church daily & at night are the hooded faces with the tar & feathers—N. Irish bigots

—the bombings: senseless, cruel, sickening—the people responsible should be punished without mercy

—the bombings have intensified over the past two years—both sides responsible

—the particular incident that stands out in my memory is the bomb that went off in downtown Dublin during rush hour—killed almost only women & children—small kids killed, maimed

—the children: famous picture of the children stoning the British soldiers—a war of children

—many kids have nervous breakdowns along with their mothers

—children are indoctrinated by their families to hate the opposite group

—the children of N. Ireland today will be the IRA members of tomorrow—they are brought up in hatred & cannot escape it

—I pity the children—those who have been disfigured & maimed and mentally warped by their parents

Personal Experience

—Went to S. Ireland (Cork) two years ago, during the time of the internment & supposed British tortures

—Saw no evidence of the war except an occasional IRA spray-painted on walls

—the people I stayed with were very old & super Catholic

—turned ferocious when you mentioned the fights in the North

—they hated the British & the Protestants

—I know the ugly cities the people of N. Ireland live in & I can understand what is happening & why, better than can a lot of people

—My uncle in London has a girlfriend from Belfast. Eileen told me a lot about how her life has changed in Belfast & how her family lives with the fighting

—Eileen's best girlfriend & this girl's boyfriend were murdered last Christmas—no reason—Her sister (12 yrs. old) has suffered one nervous breakdown & is on the verge of another. Her little brother can tell who is fighting (the IRA & the Protestants or the British & the IRA) by the sound of the gunfire. He can distinguish between the different sounds the automatic weapons make.

—On my second trip to England I really came face to face with the Irish bombings. My uncle & Eileen & Vito & I decided to visit the Visitors' Gallery in the House of Commons. We started out early in the morning & on the way Eileen said that she had seen a newspaper that said the House of Commons had been bombed. Didn't believe her but when we arrived in central London there really had been a bomb. Bobbies, fire & firemen all around. Scared me to think we could have all been hurt. I have slides of the scene & every time I see them I get upset.

—Many places in London that were not previously guarded were guarded the second time I went. Huge fences had been put up in places where people could possibly throw bombs.

DYNAMIC VIEW

—as the standard of living in N. Ireland has been raised, the fighting has increased

—the last two years have shown an increase in senseless killings, bombings, shooting & murders

—the P's & C's have completely separated themselves, barricaded themselves into their own ghettos

—political tension not quite as high. England still does not have a strong position

—buildings have been bombed & never rebuilt

—families have been bombed out. Some families have left, some have stayed.

—the hatred has increased over the years

—some women have united & formed political groups

—small children have lost legs, arms & eyes

Changing Attitudes Toward the Struggle

—the increase in bombings happened when the word "bomb" was everyday language in the newspapers, airport bombs, Vietnam bombs, Arab-Israeli bombs

—Americans do not pay much attention to the Ireland issue

—Ireland has always been torn with fighting

—the green grass has always been stained red

—Ireland is just a tiny isolated spot of hatred in a world today that is filled with hatred

—the fighting has always been more or less confined to the island itself, except recently with the London bombings

—Ireland's war is very small compared to the larger, more flammable situations like the Mideast

—the fighting in N. Ireland does not really affect the people of the U.S. except perhaps the old Irish immigrants & their children

Future

—the bloodshed could get worse, bombings could increase; considering the problem from a cynical point of view, hopefully they will all kill each other off; not realistic; the fighting will always be there in isolated areas, the P's & C's will completely segregate themselves from each other

—doubtful that England will ever instigate a major policy change, the fruitless debates in Parliament will continue

RELATIVE VIEW

Comparison/Contrast: strife in N. Ireland compared to the civil rights struggle of the 60s in the U.S.

—both issues involve senseless lynchings & bloodshed

—the two problems each took different courses. In the South the blacks & whites were originally separated & are now slowly moving together. In N. Ireland the P's & C's at one time coexisted together, now they are segregated.

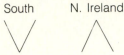

South   N. Ireland

—both struggles hurt the children, with the racial issue of the South, the scars are beginning to heal; in N. Ireland they are still being made
—both issues have (or had) political, social, & economic dimensions
—the third parties that were (& are) involved in both fights really got hurt, the social workers & civil rights people from the North & the British soldiers from England
—perhaps the reason why the fighting has continued in Northern Ireland for so long is because international pressure has never come down really hard; with the racial issue in the South, eventually the national outcry became strong & brought govt. pressure on the situation

Analogy
—the struggle in N. Ireland is like a hereditary disease
—the hatred in N. Ireland has been perpetuated because parents have transmitted their hatred to their children like a disease
—sometimes diseases become immune to the treatments that are given; perhaps the fighting in N. Ireland has reached that "immune stage" & new, harsher medicines must be discovered.
—the hatred has affected all levels of society in N. Ireland just like a diseased organ of the body can poison other organs & systems
—some hereditary diseases fade as the generations continue
—hopefully the fighting will fade as a new generation of children grows up & totally rejects the values of their parents

Classification
—areas of violence where the children have been seriously affected, both mentally & physically

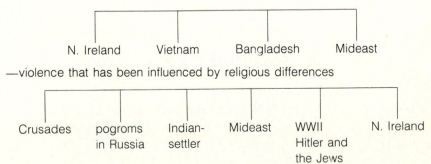

—countries that have been involved in wars with outside interference

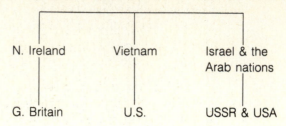

N. Ireland   Vietnam   Israel & the
                                     Arab nations

G. Britain   U.S.   USSR & USA

● **COMMENTARY**

Writer 2 has listed some major pros and cons of the issue and has demonstrated knowledge of the way a health care program would be set up. It would help his investigation to detail some of the reasons why the programs worked in Canada and Sweden and not in Great Britain. It would also be important for him to investigate the problems with the private health insurance programs of his grandfather and aunt. His dynamic and relative views will be useful to him, not only in formulating a judgment but also in writing the paper.

CLASS EXERCISES

1. Study the explorations of Writers 3 (pp. 170–171) and 4.
   • Have the writers adequately defined their issues, noting the pros and cons?
   • Have they cited their personal experience?
   • Is their historical exploration adequate?
   • What classifications, comparisons, contrasts, and analogies help them to better understand the issue and answer their questions?
   • What other classifications could they have made?
2. As a class, explore the issue you chose to investigate in your last class exercise.

● **ASSIGNMENT: Exploration**

1. Explore the question you formulated, discovering as many personal and public facets as you can.
2. Seek advice on your work.

FOCUS AND SITUATION

INCUBATION

Incubation occurs during all stages of composing, but its work before focusing remains crucial. Allow sufficient time after exploring for the ideas to settle, because a focus never arises directly from your exploration. Then review your guiding question and exploration to determine what answer, what better-qualified view of your issue seems to be emerging. Usually several possibilities suggest themselves. In order to determine which best represents your new conclusion, test them by formulating focus statements.

A PERSUASIVE FOCUS

Remember the distinction between *insight* and *focus*. Insights are the potential answers that the mind discovers during incubation. Some of these under scrutiny appear less useful responses to a writer's original question or inconsistent with a writer's sense of experience. They are discarded. The insights that seem most promising, however, have to be tested by putting them in words and eventually by shaping them into a whole discourse.

A persuasive focus is a *probable judgment* or a *claim*. Issues are subjects about which no absolute certainty can be gained. What you are striving for is the most balanced position, supported by good reasons (warrants), that you can come to at this point. Given time for further reflection and reading, you may conclude something else, but now you try to answer your question without prejudice, based on as thorough an examination of the subject as you can muster. If you have explored well, you may even end by taking a position opposite to that which you anticipated.

Because you will be writing with a persuasive aim, your focus should reflect the emphasis on the reader. You will not be using the first person pronoun this time, as you may have done when stating your expressive focus. Now you will be extending your judgment beyond your own experience. As you formulate various focus possibilities, try them out with the writing situations you have proposed, asking not only which focus best answers your question, but also which is best phrased for your audience.

As you formulate your focus, examine it in light of the potential writing situations you posed, asking which audience would best benefit from your judgment and what kind of persuasive task each situation would entail. When you have taken these matters into consideration, you will be able to decide on the situation you find most appropriate for your writing.

FOCUSES AND SITUATIONS

WRITER 1

Subject
The interhall transfer system at the Quadrangle

Point of Significance
is an overcomplicated, unfair tradition which discriminates against the underclassmen, the lower-ranked, and those without a roommate request.

(**Revised question:** What are the advantages and disadvantages of the Quadrangle's policy for interhall transfers?)
Situation: I want to write a letter to the director of the residence halls, who is the one that can do something about the situation.

WRITER 2

Subject
A national comprehensive health insurance program

Point of Significance
is either an extreme benefit or a costly, wasteful government program, depending on one's need, attitude, income, and place in the social structure.

(**Revised question:** On what bases is a national health care program feasible and desirable? Do these bases outweigh the problems of such a system?)
Situation: I will write a letter to the local chapter of the AMA because I want them to at least hear, and hopefully respect, a position different from their own. In my focus, though, I do want to recognize that the other position exists.

WRITER 3

Subject
The women's movement

Point of Significance
makes the role of housewife difficult to understand.

(**Question:** How has the women's movement affected housewives' attitudes toward themselves?)
Situation: My audience will be readers of *Ms.* magazine.

WRITER 4

Subject
The conflict in Northern Ireland

Point of Significance
is a social disease perpetuated by learned bigotry and ignorance.

(**Question:** What has caused the struggle in Ireland to continue on and on?)
Situation: I will write a guest editorial for the city newspaper.

WRITER 5

Subject
The penalty for killing while driving drunk

Point of Significance
should be looked at for every individual case.

(**Question:** What type of penalty should be given for killing while driving drunk?)
Situation: I think the best situation for this focus would be to write to the parents and friends of the girl who was killed, because they need to understand the justice of the sentence given their daughter's killer. I would like to center my paper around her case, but the penalty given her killer would not work for everyone. My

classmates will be a secondary audience. Because of these two audiences I'll write this in essay form—in fact it will be better to have the class as primary audience so I could explain the details and then send the essay to the girl's parents and friends, saying I thought they would be interested in this essay I wrote for my class.

● **COMMENTARY**

Writer 1's point of significance has forecast the burden of his argument: the present arrangement is overcomplicated and discriminatory. Unless he can assume that his reader, the director, accepts simplicity and equality as unquestioned values, he will have to argue for those principles in order to validate the policies that will lead to changed practices. In other words, the focus is already determining the major outlines of the discourse.

Writer 2's focus is well done in that it sets up four criteria by which the program is seen as desirable or undesirable. One possible weakness lies in the term attitude, *which seems ambiguous compared to the more easily measurable "need, income, and place."*

CLASS EXERCISES

1. Discuss the focuses of Writers 3, 4, and 5.
   • Examine the relationship that exists between the focus and the audience and medium.
   • Discuss the boundaries the focus places on the writing.
2. List possible focuses and writing situations for the issue you explored as a class.
3. Examine the following focuses and their relationship to the proposed situations.
   a. Focus: I don't like the Quadrangle's interhall transfer policy.
      Situation: letter to the President of Midwestern University
   b. Focus: The history of national health care insurance.
      Situation: paper for my history teacher
   c. Focus: The women's movement should be opposed by all housewives.
      Situation: letter to Congress
   d. Focus: The struggle in Northern Ireland has been going on for ten years.
      Situation: essay for class
   e. Focus: Drunk drivers have killed many people.
      Situation: letter to school newspaper

● ## ASSIGNMENT: Focus and Situation

1. Allow sufficient time for incubation.
2. Formulate a focus, expressing the judgment you have formed on the issue.
3. Try out the focus by relating it to your potential writing situations. Choose a situation you want to work with.
4. Get advice on your focus and choice of situation.

● ## AUDIENCE, APPEALS, AND MODES OF ORGANIZATION

SETTING THE ROLE FOR THE AUDIENCE

In order to set the role you want the audience to play, you need careful analysis. The audience guide below, repeated from Chapter 1 for those beginning their writing with the persuasive aim, will help you analyze your audience.

AUDIENCE GUIDE

1. State your audience and the reasons for choosing it.
2. Analyze the audience in itself.
   a. Identify the levels and types of experiences that your audience has had (cultural, recreational, educational, and so on).
      • What is the median level of education in your audience?
      • Are most of your audience males or females?
      • What is the median age of your audience?
      • Is there anything special about your audience that will affect their image of you and themselves (racial, cultural, recreational, occupational, etc.)?
   b. Identify the hierarchy of values that your audience holds (money, power, friendship, security, intellectual growth).
3. Analyze the audience in relation to the subject.
   a. Identify the knowledge and opinion your audience holds on the subject.

b. Determine how strongly your audience holds those views.

c. Assess how willing your audience is to act on its opinion—if acting is appropriate.

4. In light of the information you gained above, determine the specific role your audience will play.

5. Repeat steps 2 and 3, but this time analyze only the *specific* role you want the audience to play.

a. Determine what levels and types of experience fit the role your audience will play.

b. Identify the values that fit that role.

c. Determine what opinion you want your audience to hold in that role, how strongly you want the audience to hold it, and whether you want the audience to act on it.

6. Determine your voice and the *relational* role you want your audience to play. State why you have chosen that relationship.

AUDIENCE ANALYSIS

Below are the analyses of Writers 1 and 5.

WRITER 1

1. I have chosen to write to the residence hall director, who can do something about the situation.

2. a. Background: Older man, in his sixties, who graduated from Midwestern University years ago and became an officer in the armed forces. Now he manages the hall he used to live in. He is strong-willed.

b. Values: He apparently values upholding the old traditions. He probably wants things to be the same as when he was a student. He dislikes complainers.

3. a. Attitude toward the subject: He agrees with the present policy.

b. Strength of attitude: Very strong, since the system hasn't changed.

c. Willingness to act: He will not be easily moved to act on the subject, except perhaps to defend the present policy.

4. Specific role: A judge rather than a manager. He will judge policy on the merits of the case, not continue doing something just because it has always been done that way.

5. Analysis of the role:

a. Background: I am going to have to be very careful with his army background, because army officers are mainly managers, not judges. But he should be able to relate to stories, examples about students, since he was one once and now works among them.

b. Values: Fairness and disinterestedness are the marks of a judge.

    c. Attitude toward the subject: A judge will not deliver a decision until hearing the evidence, and will suspend judgment until the proof is in.

6. Relational role: I will try to project the voice of a subordinate who nevertheless on this one issue has some information that maybe the director hasn't heard or hasn't remembered.

WRITER 5

1. My main but indirect audience will be the parents and friends of the girl that was killed.

2. a. Background: Parents and friends of the victim
    b. Values:
      —love their children
      —want the best for the family
      —a just legal system
      —justice carried out when crime is committed
      —value family life
      —value the life of others
      —a law-abiding neighborhood
      —individual rights

3. a. Attitude toward the subject: They want as much penalty as possible for the person who killed their child. They want justice done to the offender.
    b. Strength of attitude: They feel strongly that if it wasn't for a person driving drunk their child would be alive today.

4. Specific role: As parents and friends who want to see a positive outcome from their daughter's/friend's death.

5. Analysis of the role:
    a. Background: Educated enough to be aware of society's and criminal points of view.
    b. Values: They will put a high value on a reasonable certainty of something good coming out of this tragedy and less value on revenge.
    c. Attitude toward the subject: I want them to accept the judge's sentence as proper.

6. Relational role: I feel for their loss but want to show them another view of sentencing an individual for a crime. I want to show them that a different type of sentencing may be (and is) much more beneficial to the community and the defendant—Instead of 3–5 years in prison where no good can be done. Sure, he will think of what he did, but a more productive sentence would be 1–2 years of constant public speaking. This is not easy plus it is a betterment to the community because when he speaks to high schools others will be influenced not to drink and drive because of his testimony. Also he would have to write a check to the parents of the person he killed every week for a dollar for the rest of his life. So he will have on his mind what he did forever. Plus a three-year probation. This is not the type of sentence for all people but in certain circumstances this is better. In other cases years in jail are better for the person and the community.

● **COMMENTARY**

Writer 5 has produced a good analysis up to a point—and that point is item 6, the relational aspect of voice. He has written in his answer to item 6 a summary of his proof without answering the tough question: How do you talk to parents to convince them that the killer of their child doesn't belong in jail, when you yourself are younger and less experienced than they and have lived through no comparable grief? A possible answer would be to project the voice of a friend of the dead daughter; of one, therefore, who is in some ways inferior to the parents, but who has strong feelings and a viewpoint similar to those of the victim.

CLASS EXERCISES

1. Discuss the audience analyses of Writers 1 and 3 (p. 172).
   • How good were their choices of specific and relational roles?
   • What will their analyses of these roles entail in writing their papers?
2. Select at least two audiences for the subject you have worked on as a class. Do an analysis of these audiences. Discuss the writing implications for each one.

PERSUASIVE APPEALS

Because persuasive writing emphasizes the audience, the effective writer plans to balance three kinds of appeals, all of which are important to a good piece of persuasion.

● **Credibility Appeals**

In order to persuade an audience effectively, you must convince them of your *credibility*. You establish credibility by showing that

1. you are knowledgeable about your subject,
2. you care about the audience's welfare,
3. you know and respect their point of view, and
4. you can argue fairly and intelligently about the subject.

In other words, you set up a positive image of yourself in the eyes of your reader. This appeal is extremely important because if your readers lack confidence in your knowledge, suspect that you are uninterested in them, or distrust your persuasive methods, they will pay little attention to you.

● **Rational Appeals**

The second appeal is to your audience's *reason*. The audience needs convincing arguments—good reasons, or warrants—in order to undergo the kind of change you intend—either to respect your judgment, to accept it as theirs, or to act on it. When you persuade, you discuss a subject about which no certainty exists. You need, therefore, to command a repertoire of informal logical skills, skills that deal with probabilities, not with the certainties of formal logic. Chapter 3 will present some of these skills. Chapter 4 will present others.

● **Affective Appeals**

The third appeal that must be integrated with the other two is the appeal to the *attitudes, values,* and *emotions* of your audience. No matter how cogent your argument may be, its power will be enhanced if you support it with appeals to the audience's affective side.

The master persuader controls all three of these appeals well in any piece of writing. Persuasion is in essence a discourse which combines the credibility, rational, and affective appeals.

MISUSE OF THE APPEALS

Each of these appeals, however, can be distorted—ruining the persuasive balance. When that happens, persuasion, instead of playing a powerful and healthy role with the audience, deceives or degrades them. For example, if the entire argument rests on the credibility appeal, the writer shows disrespect for the audience's reason and values. Many advertisements fall into this trap in their effort to establish images for their product at the expense of the knowledge, intelligence, and values of the audience. If writing overemphasizes or rests solely on the appeal to values and emotions, it often is a distorted piece of persuasion. Finally, some pieces of discourse fail persuasively because they consider their audiences to be walking intellects with no values or feelings. While any given piece of persuasion may have a slightly different proportion of the three appeals, the goal is to achieve a good integration or balance of the three.

But in addition to knowing the importance of the three appeals, you also need to understand *how* to incorporate them into your writing. Although your previous writing courses may have given you some help with the appeal to reason, most texts offer little guidance with the other two, which require sophisticated strategies and much practice to perfect. This chapter will discuss strategies for using all three appeals.

STRATEGIES FOR PERSUASIVE APPEALS

● **Credibility Appeals**

Here are some techniques, with examples, for establishing credibility.

1. Provide information to show that you have firsthand experience or some other kind of authority on the subject. Don't brag but simply establish your credentials for writing on the subject.

    Example: Writer 1 establishes in his first paragraph that he is one of the persons affected by the limitations on freshmen transferring.

2. Make some references to your audience's interests and point of view to indicate that you know and respect them.

   Example: Writer 3 refers in her first paragraph to the enduring achievements of her audience: "The women's liberation movement left behind changes so complete yet so subtle. . . ."

3. Identify yourself with your audience in some way. Play up your similarities with them and minimize your differences.

   Example: Writer 3 in her first paragraph unites herself with her audience in one major belief: "our belief that anything which frees people from rigid roles, stereotypes, and limited options is to be applauded."

4. Use examples and lines of reasoning that your audience can relate to. Choose your material, in other words, by reference to their interests and knowledge.

   Example: Writer 1 uses comparisons with army life; his audience is a retired army officer. Unfortunately, the comparisons are negative and will irritate the reader.

5. Use facts, ideas, and reasoning accurately. You will lose credibility if your audience concludes your thinking is careless or your information inaccurate.

   Example: Writer 3 in her third paragraph deftly inserts references to popular TV programs, books, magazines, and movies to support her point.

6. Provide specific support for your focus, and avoid generalizations which can cause your audience to suspect that you don't know what you are talking about or that you do not understand their need to have specifics to work with.

   Example: Writer 1 damages his argument with his statement in the second paragraph, "It's almost as if someone sits around all day thinking of new ways to torture freshmen." This is a fundamentally silly statement, referring to nothing real and conveying only ill will.

7. Use correct grammar, spelling, and punctuation. If you do not control the basics of the language, you throw the rest of your appeals into question.

In order to include any of these strategies in your persuasive plan, your audience analysis must be carefully done. The specific and relational roles your audience will play and your voice as a writer must be clear in your mind.

● **Rational Appeals**

There are many informal logical techniques that a persuasive writer can use. Here we present several techniques,* clustering them under the modes of organization you have been working with.

* Adapted from Chaim Perelman and L. Olbrechts-Tyleca, *The New Rhetoric* (Notre Dame: University of Notre Dame Press, 1969).

As part of your planning, decide which of these strategies you can use to argue your focus. The ones you choose will depend on several factors: the material in your exploration, your audience analysis, and your plan of organization. In a short paper, you will probably use only a few selected techniques or one fully developed line of reasoning. On pages 152 to 155, we discuss how these arguments can be organized.

DESCRIPTIVE TECHNIQUES

1. Use a compelling descriptive example from your own or another's experience to support your focus.

   Example: Writer 1 in his third paragraph has constructed a generalized example to show the futility of applying for transfer if you are a freshman.

2. Suggest possible specific applications or illustrations of a principle you hold or advocate.

   Example: Writer 1's second paragraph, for example, contains three illustrations, short descriptions that make an abstract principle (discriminating against freshmen) concrete. To support his focus, he cites the disappearance of the custom of wearing beanies and restrictions on who could wear yellow corduroy trousers; then he points to the retention of the freshman chant on the first day of classes.

3. Set up or refer to a model for an action or behavior you which to propose.

   Example: Writer 1 has suggested in his third paragraph that the model for interhall transfers should be that of renting an apartment.

4. Set up an ideal for an action or principle you wish to promote.

   Example: Writer 1 sets up the principle of "first-come, first-served" as the ideal.

NARRATIVE TECHNIQUES

1. Show that one event is the cause or the effect of another.

   Example: Writer 4 might argue that hereditary hatred and bigotry are the causes of violence in Northern Ireland.

2. Show that an act or event will have favorable or unfavorable consequences.

   Example: Writer 1 summarizes the consequences of the present transfer policy: "A freshman with a legitimate reason for transfer will usually be forced to stay in a miserable situation until most upperclassmen have had a chance to transfer."

3. Show that one thing is the means and the other the end.

   Example: Writer 1 argues that class rank is not the proper means to determine the end of eligibility for transfer; the proper means is simply applying early enough.

4. Argue that waste would occur if some action already begun is abandoned or if some talent or presence is lost.

Example: Writer 2 could perhaps argue that a comprehensive health insurance plan would be the next logical step in health coverage and therefore would prevent the loss of the progress achieved so far.

5. Show the direction of any stage in a long process.

Example: Writer 2 could break up into a series of stages the path to compulsory health insurance and argue for reaching one or two goals on the road to eventual comprehensive coverage.

6. Show the connection between persons and their actions or the lack of connection between them.

Example: Writer 4 might imply that the past actions of the people of Northern Ireland are a legitimate index to their future actions; she assumes a direct and abiding connection between qualities in their character ("bigotry and ignorance") and their actions ("violence").

7. Use the authority of a person, based on his or her creditable actions or experience.

Example: Writer 5 might introduce the opinion of a distinguished jurist on probationary sentences.

8. Use a narrative example to support your focus.

Example: Writer 2 might illustrate the dangers of skimpy health insurance coverage by telling the story of his aunt's illness.

CLASSIFICATION TECHNIQUES

1. Use an analogy, showing how a relationship in one sphere that resembles a relationship in another sphere supports your focus.

Example: Writer 1 constructs a closing analogy between living in the Quad and being in the army.

2. Classify someone in a group and show the implications of membership in that group.

Example: Writer 1's argument concentrates on the ill treatment that arises from belonging to one group, the freshman class.

3. Use a comparison or contrast to support your focus.

Example: Writer 1 compares early discrimination at Midwestern with present-day discrimination, college admission practices with hall managers' practices, buying basketball tickets and meals with hall transfers, and trying to transfer with interviewing for a job.

Affective Appeals

1. Determine what frame of mind, attitude, or emotional state you wish your audience to be in as a result of reading your paper. Use examples, analogies, or comparisons that will stimulate those attitudes and emotions.

Example: Writer 3, desiring a sympathetic and active audience, packs her middle paragraphs with examples that will abrade their sense of justice: the stereotypes of *Better Homes and Gardens,* Geritol commercials, TV situation comedies, and popular movies.

Example: Writer 3 ends with a striking, active analogy: "We feel like we are rolling logs in water, moving our feet as fast as we can to maintain our balance while the water and log move swiftly beneath us, constantly changing like the society in which we live."

2. Show that you are sensitive to certain values, attitudes, and feelings that are central to the role your audience will play.

Example: Writer 3 is careful in her first paragraph to set out an exact statement of the values that she and her readers share and that they must continue to share if they are to accept her point: "anything which frees people from rigid roles, stereotypes and limited options is to be applauded." On the other hand, Writer 1 needs to rewrite his introduction in order to touch on the feelings of his audience, the director. As it stands, the paper directs its attention only to the values, attitudes, and feelings of the freshmen. The value problem for the director, playing the role of judge, is that both precedents and present views of "fairness" have value.

3. Use specific and concrete language that is appropriate to your subject.

Example: Writer 3 evokes the anxieties of housewives with a concrete contrast: "While they described the Israeli kibbutzim, we pictured our children in Sugar and Spice or some other day-care center, herded about with 30 or 40 other kids by three or four adults who could not possibly spend enough time with them or give enough love to them."

CLASS EXERCISES

1. Examine each of the passages below. Identify the type of appeal(s) working there and discuss their merit in the light of their focus.

a. Focus: Everything in this world is transient, and the earlier we learn to accept that fact, the less hurt we will feel.

It was when my girlfriend died suddenly that I realized that it doesn't pay to cherish anything very much, because it hurts too much when they take it away from you. She and I were 16. She was driving (newly licensed) to the train station to pick me up. There was this truck. Seventy years of plans crashed.

b. Focus: Cable television stock is a bad investment at the moment because the industry is threatened by new technologies.

Two technologies in particular threaten cable television. Both are called "wireless cable." One, direct broadcast satellites, bounces a signal directly from a satellite to any home with a low-priced dish antenna and receiving equipment. The second, multipoint distribution services, takes the satellite signal and rebroadcasts it on a microwave frequency to homes with appropriate antennae. The unarguable advantage of the new systems is not only their simplicity but that they can be made available to rural areas where running a cable is prohibitively expensive. Moreover, whatever the liabilities of the new systems, looming over the cable TV investors is the grim fact that only a 5% change in subscription in a 200,000-home market results in a $63 million loss of revenue and a $13 million loss in book net income over the 15-year life of the franchise.

2. For the focuses and audiences of Writers 1, 2, and 5, discuss the appeals that could be used.

ORGANIZING A PERSUASIVE PAPER

Most persuasive writing includes

1. an introduction
2. a section of proof
3. a refutation (refutation can be interwoven with other parts of the paper or omitted)
4. a conclusion

Introduction

The introduction of a persuasive paper has three functions: (1) it establishes the credibility of the writer; (2) it begins the appeal to the audience's attitudes, values, and feelings; and (3) it announces the writer's focus. Most of the introduction should be devoted to establishing your credibility. Here you can introduce the appeals that you selected.

Normally the introduction is one paragraph that concludes with your focus. Remember that your task in the introduction is to bring the audience from its own preoccupations into your subject arena. You must make bridges, indicating why your readers should listen to you, why they should care about your subject and your focus. Think of the audience as needing answers to four questions:

1. Why should I be interested in this *subject*?
2. What are you going to tell me *about* this subject?
3. Why should I want to listen to *you*?
4. Why should I want to read this *now*?

Proof

Your proof is the longest section of your paper, usually several paragraphs in length. In this section you concentrate on interweaving your lines of reasoning, your appeal to attitudes, and your credibility appeal. At the core is your rational appeal. But this should be advanced with details, information, examples, and language that work to sustain your credibility and to stimulate the attitudes and feelings you want your audience to experience.

● **Refutation**

If you use a refutation, sometimes you may place it after the proof and sometimes you may introduce it at other places in the paper, wherever opposing points of view are advanced.

● **Conclusion**

The ending of a persuasive paper requires the writer to do two things: to summarize the proof and to restate the major conclusion. In a short paper, the summary and the major conclusion may be included in a single sentence. In a longer paper, the two may require a paragraph if they involve both changing the audience's mind and urging action. However, the ending should be as brief as possible, for several reasons. A long summary may irritate readers who have paid close attention to your proof. Furthermore, the ending does not lend itself to the introduction of new issues, new arguments, or new tasks; whatever needs to be argued should have been argued earlier. In addition, if you have arranged your argument properly in the body of the paper, the conclusions will have been explicit or self-evident. The purpose of the ending is simply to draw together what you have said so that the reader cannot mistake your intentions; the fact that your ending is no more than a neat condensation is a virtue in the persuasive aim.

PERSUASIVE PLANS

In what order should your arguments be presented? That depends on which ones you have chosen. If descriptive lines of reasoning predominate, then use the descriptive mode of organization and incorporate other lines of reasoning within that framework. If your major argument is an extended analogy, then you will want to use a classificatory framework. If your arguments are predominantly narrative, then the narrative mode will serve. Make a plan to help you organize your appeals. A plan can be extremely useful for drafting longer papers with complex appeals. But remember that a plan is only a guide, which can be changed as your writing progresses if new directions open up.

1. First make a list of the appeals you would like to use.
   a. List your credibility appeals.
   b. List your rational appeals.
   c. List your affective appeals.

2. Then create an organization plan for your paper, indicating where these appeals will be introduced.

Here are the plans created by our five writers.

WRITER 1

1. Appeals
   a. Show my own experience as a freshman
   b. Try to understand the audience's point of view; use comparisons and contrast; one analogy
   c. Appeal to audience's sense of fairness and efficiency
2. Organization Plan
   a. Introduction: Introduce subject & background; state focus
   b. Proof
      ¶ 1 Compare transfer policy with other unfair treatment of freshmen
      ¶ 2 Compare and contrast transfer policy with admissions policy and bases for getting basketball tickets and meals
      ¶ 3 Compare and contrast transfer policy with getting scholarship and going for job interview
      ¶ 4 Analogy of transfer with being in the army
   c. Conclusion: Summarize

WRITER 2

1. Appeals
   a. Show my knowledge of the issue—both from reading and from personal experience
      Show I know audience's point of view
   b. Use narrative examples, illustrations, comparisons, consequences for the poor
   c. Appeal to their compassion for the ill
   d. Appeal to their value of preventing illness
2. Organization Plan
   a. Introduction: Show that I know the audience's knowledge and point of view on this issue; state my focus
   b. Proof
      ¶ 1 Catastrophic illness: example of my aunt and other kinds of illnesses
      ¶ 2 Contrast rich and poor on what is catastrophic
      ¶ 3 Give illustration: the elderly
      ¶ 4 Discuss preventive medicine
   c. Conclusion: Use illustrations: Sweden & Canada

WRITER 3

1. Appeals
   a. Establish myself as a woman who grew up in the sixties
      Identify myself as a sympathizer with women's liberation but also with those confused about W.L.
   b. Use argument based on group membership
      Classification: supermom and supercareerwoman

        c. Set up a feeling of uneasiness

   2. Organization Plan

      a. Introduction: Establish myself as a sympathizer yet one confused; establish a feeling of uneasiness; set up my focus

      b. Proof

         ¶ 1 supermom

         ¶ 2 supercareerwoman: give specific examples in vivid language that people who grew up in the sixties can relate to

      c. Conclusion: Perhaps use analogy of rolling logs to help set feeling of confusion and uneasiness

WRITER 4   1. Appeals

      a. Show I have firsthand knowledge of the issue

      b. Use narrative example from my own experience

      c. Stir up the audience to anger over the situation

   2. Organization Plan

      a. Introduction: Introduce subject vividly; indicate my own connection with the issue

      b. Proof

         ¶ 1 My first trip to Southern Ireland: bigotry

         ¶ 2 My second trip, London: incidents in London, security measures

         ¶ 3 Bombing of the House of Commons

      c. Conclusion: Hearing back at home about Tower of London bombing

WRITER 5   1. Appeals

      a. Indicate that I have a friend who killed someone while driving drunk
Show that I also have close contact with the youth detention probation office, not as a criminal but by knowing the personnel and the way the system works
Show I am concerned for the well-being and sorrow of the victim's family and sympathize with their ordeal

      b. I will recreate the accident and then go on with a narrative example to show the actual good consequences of the sentence on my friend Kevin and the possible good consequences for society

      c. Even though they are angry and sad, I want them to channel their anger into helping both the offender and society

   2. Organization Plan

      a. Introduction: Get audience's attention; introduce subject; state my focus

      b. Proof

         ¶ 1 The accident

         ¶ 2 The trial and sentence

         ¶ 3 The consequence of the sentence on Kevin

         ¶ 4 The possible consequence of the sentence on others

      c. Conclusion: Restatement and emphasis

● **COMMENTARY**

Writer 3 has specifically planned to establish both her credibility and affective appeals at the beginning of her paper. She has, in the bargain, linked herself sympathetically with her audience. In her organization plan she has outlined a useful two-part classification that will probably allow for comparison and contrast, and she plans to cap this with another kind of comparison, an analogy. She is bringing together a great many effective devices to support her focus.

Writer 1, on the other hand, may be too narrow in his choices. Although the appeals list shows an awareness of the need for varied appeals, the organization list shows only a proof centered—quite properly, perhaps—on the rational appeal. Where will he "Try to understand the audience's point of view" and where will he "Appeal to audience's sense of fairness and efficiency"? The proof itself, as a series of comparisons and contrasts arranged on an ascending scale of importance, is well arranged; but something more may be needed to support the focus in the face of this hostile audience.

CLASS EXERCISES

1. Discuss the organization plans of Writers 2, 4, and 5.
   • Have they effectively interwoven their credibility, rational, and affective appeals?
   • Do their plans support their focuses?
   • What modes of organization does each writer use?
2. Using Writer 4's exploration and focus, set up alternative organization plans for her.

● **ASSIGNMENT: Audience, Appeals, and Modes of Organization**

1. Do an analysis of your audience, setting the specific and relational roles you want them to play.
2. Identify the credibility, rational, and affective appeals you plan to use.
3. Set up your organization plan.

THE FIRST VERSION

With your plans in mind, allow yourself time to write several drafts before you complete a first version that you will share with your instructor and classmates. Your plans should offer you valuable guidance, but if your drafting prompts you to reorganize or add sections that you had not anticipated, be flexible enough to do so. Your exploration should offer you rich material to use in developing your paragraphs. Remember that your audience needs sufficient information in order to accept your rational and affective appeals.

Styles vary according to aims. In Chapter 2 we described the style of the expressive aim. Now we will discuss the style of the persuasive aim.

DICTION

1. The language of persuasion contains an unusual amount of humor, wit, and satire, probably because humor pleases audiences and therefore makes them more receptive to the writer.
2. The language of persuasion is remarkably concrete. The concrete presents itself to readers as reality and fact, while the general and abstract convey something vague, someone's unsubstantiated opinion.
3. The language of persuasion contains a high proportion of figures of speech, probably because figures of speech are highly connotative. This point requires some discussion.

● Connotation

Words have two sides of meaning: denotation and connotation. The denotation of a word is the direct, specifying meaning of the word, without any of the additional suggestions, overtones, or affective colorings that the word may have taken on. *Slim,* for example, denotes slenderness, as does *skinny.* The two words point to approximately the same meaning. But they connote quite different attitudes: *Slim* suggests elegance, handsomeness; it is an approving word. *Skinny,* on the other hand, suggests gawkiness, awkwardness. In other words, denotation points to the object; connotation is a matter of what effect the word has on the readers, often because of their associations with the word or the thing it names.

Words rarely connote the same thing to everyone. The catchwords of our day—*high tech, punk, enhance*—provoke strong and opposite reactions in different audiences. Words strong in connotation should therefore be selected with specific audiences in mind, and all word choices should be reviewed for appropriate connotation. That is to say, connotation is a device for constructing the affective appeals necessary in persuasion. As you use the checklist of affective appeals, be aware of the potential of connotative diction.

The following is the next-to-last paragraph of Writer 1's first version:

> Being in the Quad is like being stuck in the army. You have to serve your time before you can get out. You are just another number. You have to share your quarters. You are issued equipment (furniture) to use. Privileges are granted to those who are ranked. There are a lot of strict rules and regulations. There is a lot of mindless yelling and screaming going on, and it gets very noisy.

The audience for this paragraph is the director of residence halls, a retired army officer, who, according to Writer 1's audience analysis, doesn't like complainers. It's hard to imagine a worse set of connotations for this audience:

being stuck in the army
have to serve your time (a prison metaphor)
just another number
Privileges . . . to those who are ranked
mindless yelling and screaming

The army could still be used as a basis for comparison, but the main idea would have to be something like "The transfer system is like the army's seniority system, without its benefits or its rationale." The writer could then redevelop the comparisons.

SENTENCE PATTERNS

A good persuasive writer commands a wide range of sentence patterns, possessing the ability to combine or expand them easily. If your repertoire of structures is limited, you can increase your fluency by studying and practicing different patterns. Only by effort and use can you incorporate them into your own style. If you need work with a particular combination, we include exercises in Chapter 10. If you discover when you try these imitating and generating exercises that you need even more practice, your teacher can suggest workbooks devoted to sentence-combining.

As in the expressive aim, there is no sentence pattern peculiar to the persuasive aim. Sentence length and complexity should, of course, be kept within the range of ability of the reader. But there are a few special considerations in persuasion that affect sentence patterns. One has to do with the relational aspect of voice.

We pointed out in Chapter 1 that the writer can relate to the reader as a superior, an inferior, or a peer (an equal). In a piece of persuasion, the best relationship depends on the actual writing situation (what is your relational role to the readers?) and your intention to keep readers comfortable in their role (most readers are more comfortable as equals than as inferiors). Generally speaking, no role you adopt should falsify the actual role you play in relation to the audience. Your father, for example, is your father whether he's sitting across from you at the table or reading a letter from you, and to pretend otherwise would be foolish. What is the actual relationship between you? The answer won't be the same for all fathers and children. Further, the role you adopt should reflect realistically the relationship you and the audience have to the subject matter. Suppose, for example, that you are an entry-level employee in an engineering consulting firm and you are asked because of some special training you have had to answer in writing a question put by the president of the firm. Realistically, you are the expert and he is something less. But notice that this is a temporary difference; when you give him his answer, he will know as much as he wants to know about your special field, for the time being. You would do well not to adopt a superior role. In other words, for you the roles in the company take precedence over the temporary reversal of roles in the technical field. But this does not mean that you proclaim yourself inferior in the technical field; you're not. The best approach would be one that conveys that you have taken up the task assigned you, that while you are no more intelligent than he is, you do have a piece of information that he needs, and you are furnishing it. That's more of a peer relationship than it is superior or inferior, and it works well not only where writer and reader are in fact peers socially and professionally, but also where the social and professional roles are radically different.

When you have chosen the relationship, you must translate it into language. One way we indicate relationships with others is by the pronouns we use to refer to them and ourselves. These pronouns enable us to distinguish the *speaker* (first person: *I, we*), the *person spoken to* (second person: *you*), and the *person or thing spoken of* (third person: *he, she, it, they*). Which person you choose heavily influences the relationship you signal to the reader. Examine the different persons of the following sentences:

1. First person plural: "We know how persons of high self-esteem close themselves off to persuasive messages that may diminish their self-images; it's a way some of us have of limiting the social reality we will expose ourselves to." That signals a peer relationship. The *we* and *us* offer equality to the reader; they imply that writer and reader have a common background of experience and a common ability to reflect on that background together. It's worth noting that this relationship will hold only when there is some basis for it in reality; the teacher who gushes, "We all love to write!" when writing is agony for some in the class is not establishing a peer relationship.

2. First person singular: "I know now how persons of high self-esteem close themselves off to persuasive messages that may diminish their self-images; I understand that they are limiting the social reality to which they expose themselves." That's a superior voice. It's autobiographical. The reader is being told to listen, but to take no part in the proceedings; the reader is put on the shelf. Notice that this personal voice is not interpersonal at all.

3. Third person plural: "Rhetoricians today know how persons of high self-esteem close themselves off to persuasive messages that may diminish their self-images; they limit the social reality they expose themselves to." That's a slightly superior voice, without the potential abrasiveness of the first person. It's an impersonal, reflective voice that maintains a certain distance from both the audience and the subject.

4. Second person: "You know today how persons of high self-esteem close themselves off to persuasive messages that may diminish their self-images; you limit the social reality to which you will expose yourself when you do that." The second person can create the most ambiguous relationship because the *you* can be taken to be the superior, dictatorial *you* or the vague, universalized *you*, everyone, common experience—a sort of weak *we*.

Here's how Writer 1 drafted the first version.

FIRST VERSION

February 9, 1984

Mr. Vincent Neumann
Director, Residence Halls
Midwestern University

Dear Mr. Neumann:

Did you know that eighty percent of the Quad population is made up of freshmen? That means the three upper classes combined only make up twenty percent of the total. Obviously the proportion of freshmen to upperclassmen is extremely unbalanced. The reason is due to the Quad's policy for interhall transfers. Many freshmen are trapped simply because of a priority system which favors the upperclassmen, the academically ranked, and those with a mutually requested roommate going to the desired hall. Even a freshman with a legitimate excuse for a transfer to another residence hall may be forced to stay in a place which can make life miserable until others have been transferred first. Interhall transfers are unfairly granted according to class, class rank, and whether you have a requested roommate available or not.

This policy persecutes freshmen just like all the others that have given upper-classmen higher-ranked privileges. Freshmen, for example, used to be forced to wear beanies at Midwestern. Only seniors were supposed to wear those glaring yellow cords with stupid grafitti all over them. Freshmen at the Quad are forced to get up at 5:30 in the morning on their first day of school and yell chants at the other residence halls on campus. It's almost as if someone sits around all day thinking of new ways to torture the freshmen. Why should you, then, be surprised to find that the interhall transfers are the same way? Fortunately, most of these other unfair traditions have died over the years. These other practices, however, are relatively trivial compared to the dwelling of a college student. Interhall transfers are still based on those worn-out traditions. Why hasn't the interhall priority system also changed over the years like most of those other unfair activities? What sound evidence has been given which states specific rationale for giving the upper classes and academically ranked an advantage?

It becomes apparent that both the college admission people and hall managers are using some of the same criteria for priority purposes. Although class rank does, in fact, show qualifications for admission to the college or university, it does not necessarily show a student's qualifications for the interhall transfer. Just like Midwestern basketball tickets, cafeteria meals, and most other things, interhall transfers should be on a strict "first-come, first-served" basis. Paying school housing fees is very similar to renting an apartment. When you rent an apartment, however, you are not asked your class (age), your grade point average, and your roommate. The apartment is rented to whoever gets there first. Why should the Quad's interhall transfers at Midwestern University be handled any differently?

Instead of using the simpler "first-come, first-served" method, the hall manager insists on applications, personal interviews, deadlines, notices, et cetera. In fact, my scholarship wasn't even as hard to get as a simple transfer. Going for a transfer is like going to a big job interview. There is a lot of nervousness and tension in anticipation of the questions that will be asked to determine whether you will get one of the limited transfers. Unlike a job interview, you know you are just wasting your time because you have no apparent qualifications. You may argue that almost continual rock and roll music tends to hinder your studies. You may argue that people are almost constantly barging into your room without knocking to ask questions about yesterday's homework assignment. You may argue that you would rather be heard and not seen when using the toilet since they have no doors on them in the Quad. But it will do no good. It is useless to argue when you are in the lowest class and have no class rank yet. Why do some people think that just because class (age) and academic rank are important factors to consider for things like jobs, college admissions, scholarships, etc., that it should also be used as criteria for housing?

Being in the Quad is like being stuck in the army. You have to serve your time before you can get out. You are just another number. You have to share your quarters. You are issued equipment (furniture) to use. Privileges are granted to those who are ranked. There are a lot of strict rules and regulations. There is a lot of mindless yelling and screaming going on, and it gets very noisy.

Overall, the interhall transfer system at the Quad is overcomplicated and unfair. Unlike other unfair and more trivial traditions of the past, it has not been recognized as discriminating against the lowerclassmen, those of lower or no academic rank, and those without an available roommate request. With its applications, deadlines, and interviews, it ignores the fairest and most accepted "first-come, first-served" way. Being in the Quad is like being in the army because you can't get out once you sign up.

Sincerely,
Writer 1

CLASS EXERCISES

1. The letter below was written for a dual audience, the press as primary audience and the newspaper reader as secondary audience. The purpose was to reform the press. Rewrite the letter as if you were to publish it in your campus newspaper.

   I'm happy to see in recent polls that a large segment of the responsible citizenry is beginning to recognize that Reaganomics isn't turning out to be the disaster that forecasters declared it would be. Could it be that the experts—the economists and the press—were wrong? Heaven forbid!

   The country made it clear the last time around that they were mainly worried about inflation and interest rates. President Reagan has responded to that concern and, contrary to the hand-wringing prophecies of doom, Reaganomics has steered us away from the disaster toward which the nation was plummeting.

   Maybe with some positive support from the press instead of its usual negativism, the president might be able to do something about unemployment also.

2. Select the word or phrase with the proper connotation in each choice below. The writer's audience is an English instructor who has inquired by mail about buying a home computer for word processing. The instructor knows very little about computers.

   Dear Prof. Hawthorn:

   Thanks for your (*inquiry, letter, questions*) about home computers. I'll keep my (*advice, recommendations, suggestions*) brief.

   First, the IBM Personal Computer is probably (*the best around for, best suited to, perfect for*) your purposes. But it's also the (*most expensive, highest-priced, one with the fanciest price tag*). The Apple IIe is (*less expensive, cheaper, a bargain by comparison*). It's technically not the machine that the IBM is, but there is (*mucho, a lot of, abundant*) software available for it.

However, the best (*choice, bet, alternative*) for you would probably be the KAYPRO III. It is (*cheaper, less expensive*) than the Apple IIe, has (*much greater, incredibly better, super*) word processing capability, and the necessary software (*is part of the package, comes with the computer, costs zilch*). Put the KAYPRO III together with a (*Smith-Corona TP-1 letter-quality, S-C TP-1*) printer and you will be (*ready to go, hot to trot, prepared for almost any writing task*).

3. Examine how Writer 1 developed his first version. What appeals were used? What kind of diction and syntax did he create?

● **ASSIGNMENT: The First Version**

> 1. Write a first version that communicates your focus to your audience.
> 2. Submit your writing for reader response.

● **READER RESPONSES**

In responding to persuasive writing, you will be giving the writer somewhat different advice from the kind you offered for expressive writing. Your best procedure is to read the paper completely as if you were the intended audience, without trying to be analytical. Then ask yourself the simple question: "Am I persuaded?" You can then go back and try to isolate the features that led to a yes or no answer.

Playing the roles the writer intended for the audience is crucial to giving good advice. If your classmates share their audience analyses as well as their papers with you, you can do a better job. If you do not know what the intended roles are, you can let the writer know what roles seem to be coming across in the paper. If you have no notion about audience roles, the writer has a serious problem.

Below are some questions to guide you in using the reader guide to assess persuasive writing.

READER GUIDE

● **Focus**
- What is the writer's focus?
- Is the point of significance a probable judgment?
- Are there any sections of the paper that seem to be out of focus? Which ones?
- Is the focus clearly stated in the introduction?

● **Development**
- What audience roles seem to be at work in the paper?
- What credibility appeals has the writer used? How effective were they for the audience?
- What rational appeals has the writer made? Were they persuasive for the audience?
- What appeals were made to the audience's attitudes, values, and feelings? Were they effective?

● **Organization**
- What mode of organization has the writer used? Has it been maintained?
- Are there sections that seem out of order? If so, what are they?
- What devices has the writer used to make transitions from one paragraph to the next? Are they effective?
- Are there places within the paragraphs where the writer moves without transition from one idea or example to another?
- Does the paper maintain a consistent person, number, and tense?

● **Style**
- Does the writer use words that help establish credibility and emotional appeal?
- Are there any sentences which need combining? If so, which?
- Has the writer used any figures of speech? Is the paper marred by clichés?
- Are there sentences which are too wordy? If so, which?

● **Conventions**
- Are there mistakes in grammar, spelling, and punctuation?

INSTRUCTOR'S RESPONSE TO WRITER 1

FOCUS

Your focus is clearly stated in the introductory paragraph, and it contains a probable judgment: "Interhall transfers are unfairly granted according to class, class rank, and whether you have a requested roommate available or not." The key word is "unfairly." As the first paragraph shows, your argument is that a "first-come, first-served" policy is fair, the present seniority system unfair. That focus is pursued throughout the paper.

DEVELOPMENT

The voice and audience role are disastrously out of harmony. You seem intent on insulting your audience by attacking his values. The first sentence assaults his intelligence; as director he is expected to know the facts you cite. Recall also that you want him to play the role of judge, not manager; avoid, then, insulting remarks like that in the second paragraph: "Why should you, then, be surprised to find that the interhall transfers are the same way?" Remember that you said he didn't like complainers; then avoid self-pitying remarks such as "It's almost as if someone sits around all day thinking of new ways to torture the freshmen." Recall also that he is a retired army officer; slurs on the army will only alienate him.

The rational appeals you have made in the second, third, and fourth paragraphs—arguing by comparison, by cause and effect, by waste, and by direction—would be strong and compelling if they were not undercut by your contemptuous attitude toward your reader.

ORGANIZATION

You have used the classification mode consistently so that the paper is coherent. You have lined up a series of comparisons that begins with an historical comparison and contrast and ends with an analogy. The order of the items is reasonable because it begins in the past, moves into the present, and ends with an analogy that is timeless. The similarity of means, along with very good transitions, makes the paper coherent.

STYLE

You use parallelism well in the fourth paragraph. The sentence structure throughout is pleasingly varied and neither too simple nor too complicated. Your diction is generally good, although you could improve your effect by not characterizing a former campus practice as "stupid." Remember to consider the connotations of your words. The final analogy is phrased in a fashion that will irritate your reader. Nobody, for example, likes to be told that a treasured institution is "mindless." You might also tighten the diction somewhat. For example, in the third sentence, you mean simply "The reason is . . . ," not "The reason is due to . . . ," and in the second paragraph, in "relatively trivial compared to the dwelling of a college student," "relatively" is redundant and "dwelling" is not the best word.

CONVENTIONS

You have a good command of the conventions of standard written English.

STUDENT RESPONSE TO WRITER 1

FOCUS

The focus is easy to locate: 'Interhall transfers are unfairly granted according to class, class rank, and whether you have a requested roommate or not.'

DEVELOPMENT

Tells a lot about interhall transfers. But seems biased. Why didn't you try to find out why they do transfers in this way?

ORGANIZATION

Classification mode.

STYLE

Seems to me to whine a lot. If you've got a strong argument, you ought to make it without crying.

CONVENTIONS

OK.

COMMENTARY

The student critique is not as helpful as it might be. The student isolates the focus, for example, but does not answer the important question of whether the focus is maintained consistently. Under "Development," it does little good to say that the paper "talks a lot about interhall transfers." Of course, it does; that's its topic. Simply identifying the organization as "classification mode" ignores the questions of the order of the items. The writer needs to know also whether he has handled each aspect adequately.

On the other hand, the critic makes two good points. The comment on style needs fleshing out, but it is perceptive. Writers often can't hear their own shifts of voice. The critic needs to cite a couple of examples. The reader also has a valid point when charging bias under "Development." The word bias *may be too strong, but it is noteworthy that Writer 1 seems not to have set out the administration's reasons for its course of action. He has therefore missed a chance to refute those reasons and also to indicate that he has taken the trouble to understand the director's view of the matter.*

CLASS EXERCISES

Read the first version of Writer 3. As a class, use the reader guide to assess the strengths and weaknesses of that essay.

● ASSIGNMENT: Reader Responses

1. Using the reader guide, give written responses to several of your classmates' first versions.
2. Share these responses in groups.

● REVISING AND EDITING

As you examine the responses to your work, be sure first to note any problems with focus, development, or organization. As we indicated earlier (pp. 62–63), these problems must be solved before you deal with difficulties of style or conventions.

GUIDE TO REVISING AND EDITING
● **Focus**
- Most problems of focus necessitate major revising.

● **Development**
- If your paper is not developed for the audience roles you intended, you have a major revising job.

- If you lack any of the three kinds of appeals, your revising task will be challenging.
- If you only need more development in one section or another, that task may be less complicated.

● **Organization**
  - If you have serious problems with organization, you have a major overhaul in store.
  - If you lack transitions, you can sometimes supply them without revising the entire paper.
  - If you have trouble with consistency, you can clean up that difficulty with minor effort.

● **Style**
  - If your diction is too general, ill-suited for the audience, or inaccurate, you can remedy it with serious effort without complete revision of the content.
  - You can also readily combine sentences by using any of the constructions available in the language (see Chapter 10).

● **Conventions**
  - If you have mistakes in conventions, check Chapter 9.

REVISED VERSION

WRITER 1   Mr. Vincent Neumann   February 29, 1984
            Director, Residence Halls
            Midwestern University

Dear Mr. Neumann:

Eighty percent of the Quadrangle population is, as you know, made up of freshmen. I am one of them. Like many of the others, I am in the Quad because I can't get out. Although I have tried twice to leave, I am stuck because of the Quad's policy on interhall transfers. Transfers are granted according to class, class rank, and whether you have a requested roommate available. Since freshmen by definition have no class ranking, are at the bottom of the four-class system, and have had less opportunity to find a roommate, the system discriminates against them, sometimes causing hardship and resentment. A freshman with a legitimate reason for transfer will usually be forced to stay in a miserable situation until most upperclassmen have had a chance to transfer. Interhall transfers are unfairly granted according to class, class rank, and whether you have a requested roommate or not.

This antiquated transfer policy is one of the last vestiges of upperclass privilege at Midwestern. Most of the other old inequities have been swept away. Freshmen, for example, used to be forced to wear beanies. At one time, only seniors were supposed to wear those glaring yellow cords with grafitti all over them. Freshmen at the Quad are still forced to get up at 5:30 a.m. on their first day of school to chant at the other residence halls, but this is the only other remaining discriminatory practice, and it is trivial and harmless compared to the transfer policy.

What rationale would justify giving upperclassmen preference in a matter like this? No other major university in the state has such a policy. It seems that transfer criteria are being confused with admissions criteria. Anyone would agree that class rank should qualify a person for admission to the college or university. But class rank has nothing to do with suitability for transfer. Just like Midwestern basketball tickets, cafeteria meals, and most other nonacademic things, interhall transfers should be on a "first-come, first-served" basis. Paying school housing fees is very similar to renting an apartment. When you rent an apartment, you are not asked your class, your grade point average, or your roommate. The apartment is rented to whoever gets their first. Why should the residence halls be handled any differently?

But instead of using the simpler "first-come, first-served" method, the hall manager insists on applications, personal interviews, deadlines, notices, et cetera. My scholarship wasn't as hard to get as a simple transfer. Going for a transfer is like going for a job interview. There is a lot of nervousness and tension in anticipation of the questions that will be asked to determine whether you will get one of the few available slots. Unlike a job interview, if you are a freshman you know you are probably wasting your time because you have no qualifications. You may argue that almost continual rock and roll music tends to hinder your studying. You may argue that people are almost continually barging into your room without knocking to ask questions about yesterday's homework assignment. You may argue that you would rather be heard and not seen when using the toilet, because the toilets in the Quad have no doors. But it will do no good. You are in the lowest class and you have no class rank yet.

Being in the Quad is like being in the army, but without the benefits and without the reasons for the restrictions. In the beginning you are just another number. You have to wait for promotion. You have to share your quarters. You are issued equipment and furniture. Those in the ranks above you are given greater freedom. There are a lot of strict rules and regulations. But all these things exist for a reason: military discipline and the chain of command require those conditions. But university life does not.

The interhall transfer system at the Quad is overcomplicated and unfair. Unlike other unfair but trivial traditions, it has hung on, unrecognized as discriminating against lowerclassmen, those of low or no academic rank, and those without an available roommate request. With its applications, deadlines, and interviews, it ignores the fair, acceptable way—first-come, first-served.

Sincerely,
Writer 1

● **COMMENTARY**

The revision is a great improvement. The army references that once worked against the writer now work for him. The introduction includes his qualifications to speak on the topic. He has edited out the slighting references to the audience. The whine in the second paragraph is gone, replaced by good solid reporting. And he has slipped in the fact about other universities' policies very neatly.

CLASS EXERCISES

1. Revise Writer 3's first version on the basis of the responses you gave in the previous class exercise.
2. The following is a letter written by a student to his state representative, a Democrat who had recently been voting against extension of welfare benefits in Illinois. Read the letter in order to discover what role is being forced upon the legislator. Then revise the letter to give it a better chance of being heard by the representative.

> It is going to come as a shock to you to find out that the infant mortality rate in parts of Chicago is 33 per 1000 live births—the worst in the U.S. and the same as the rate for Honduras, the poorest country in Central America. And it's not going to get any better as long as you go on voting against needed funds for dependent children. How does it feel to be a murderer?
>
> In your last newsletter, you blamed a lot of inner-city woes on the president's economic policies, the way he has cut back on child nutrition and day-care programs and on adult education and neighborhood support. So he's no angel either. But the inner-city problems were there a long time before he paraded into the White House; Chicago was in trouble ten years ago, like all heavy-machinery cities. And the problem was that a lot of shortsighted bureaucrats like you just let things slide. No planning, no new programs.
>
> Don't you realize that one in five kids in this country grows up in poverty, and that one in three does in Chicago? Don't you know that poor kids are more likely to be sick or abused and to be intellectually crippled because of their mothers' lousy nutrition? Don't you know that when they grow up they are more likely to be criminals, to be unemployed, to end up as patients in a state mental hospital? More than that—don't you *care*?
>
> Aren't you afraid of all those little faces that are going to come back to haunt you?

3. If you made mistakes in grammar, spelling, and punctuation, study the appropriate exercises in Chapter 9.
4. To improve your sentence patterns, ask your instructor for advice on the sentence-combining exercises suitable for you in Chapter 10.

ASSIGNMENT: Revising and Editing

> Guided by the advice you received on your first version, rewrite your paper, revising its major problems and editing for correctness of conventions.

A WRITER'S PROCESS

Below we present the sequence followed in Writer 3's writing process.

THE GUIDING QUESTION AND POTENTIAL SITUATIONS

1. **Subject:** The women's movement

2. **My Values and Expectations**
 —being a wife and mother
 —developing my talents

My Subject
 —looking down on housewives
 —emphasis on job rights

3. **Question:** How has the women's movement affected housewives' attitudes toward themselves?

4. **Potential Situations**
—an article for *Ms.* magazine, which has fostered the women's movement
—an essay for my classmates, especially the women in the class who are preparing for careers but who also want a family
—an article for the school newspaper

EXPLORATION

WRITER 3   WOMEN'S MOVEMENT

STATIC VIEW

—watching a countless stream of feminists on the *Phil Donahue Show* talk about options—and then say in a patronizing tone "Well if you know all your options and that's what you chose to be—a housewife. . . ."
—feminists talking about how boring and degrading housework is, how unfulfilling
—feminists talking about universal day care—picturing my daughter at Sugar and Spice or some other day-care center, herded about with 30 or 40 other kids by 2 or 3 or 4 adults who can't possibly spend enough time with her

—Congress passed initial tax deduction for child care expenses which excluded relatives from being eligible to babysit

—telling someone at a cocktail party what you do & watching their eyes glaze over at the word *housewife*

—feminists calling volunteerism a bad thing which allows society to take unfair advantage of women's labor

—feminists talking about shared parenting—watching the satisfaction and joy my husband has with Mary Sharon

DYNAMIC VIEW

—in the past—women lauded and praised for raising children, baking bread, being "supermom"

—today—emphasis on career women or the women who can do it all—house that looks like a picture in *Better Homes and Gardens,* well-behaved, beautiful, intelligent, planned-for children, and rising career (she takes Geritol to make it all possible)

—modern books & movies seldom show a mother with young children in a new role; no images except those of the past on television or in movies

—frequent movies and TV shows which picture women with older children, finding themselves often after a divorce precipitates things, e.g., *One Day At A Time, An Unmarried Woman, See How She Runs*

—future—some integration of new freedoms that will bring forth books, movies, TV shows which can show women with husband and babies coping with life, making choices in a more free way

—increased acceptance of woman who chooses to stay home

RELATIVE VIEW

Classification: women's movement is a social movement which had its greatest impact through changes in attitudes, values of society; is also political leading to changes in laws

Comparison/Contrast

—women's movement started in Friedan's book; media coverage & TV changed attitudes and gradually changed laws

—left housewives feeling disoriented, women with large families feeling undervalued

—black movement started in the main with changes in laws & then moved (or is moving) slowly toward changes in attitudes

—in some areas left the early blacks who'd had to adapt a certain way to survive feeling younger ones felt they were "Uncle Toms," a term of derision

Analogy: Being a housewife today is like rolling logs in water. You move your feet as fast as you can in order to maintain your balance while the water and the log move swiftly under your feet constantly changing like the society in which we live.

FOCUS AND SITUATION

Subject   **Point of Significance**
The women's movement ——————— makes the role of housewife difficult
to understand.

Situation: My audience will be readers of *Ms.* magazine

AUDIENCE, APPEALS, AND MODE OF ORGANIZATION

AUDIENCE ANALYSIS

1. My audience is active feminists and women who basically accept feminist views.
2. a. Background: They vary across all classes, income levels, and ages. The leadership is by and large middle-class working women, frequently college educated, rarely working as waitresses or at other dead-end jobs.
   b. Values: They believe in equal pay for equal work, equal opportunity. They value freedom, choice, power, intellectual growth; their stated emphasis usually begins with (1) ERA, (2) abortion, and (3) universal day care, and then varied other concerns, including increased part-time jobs, decrease in volunteerism, shared parenting, & housework in the family.
3. a. Attitude toward the subject: They are thoroughly knowledgeable about the issues of equality but blind to the effect on the segment of women I represent.
   b. Strength of attitude: They feel strongly that they are opening choices for all women. They often feel the lack of support from many housewives is the result of bad press and ignorance of housewives as to what the women's movement stands for.
   c. Willingness to act: They are very willing to act on what they learn, on their opinions.
4. Specific role: Leaders, representatives of all American women, with all that entails.
5. Analysis of the role:
   a. Background: They will have the requisite experience with feminist issues, but they must be brought to realize the *effects* of their work on people like me and therefore the real reasons for their relative failure. This should be valuable information for them.
   b. Values: They should particularly value representing all women in America, not just those most like themselves.
   c. Attitude toward the subject: Most people tend to defend themselves by insisting that the work they have done is right and adequate. The leaders will be no different. I want them to see the work that needs to be done for women like me and the necessity for this work if the movement is to succeed.
6. Relational role: Peers.

APPEALS AND MODE OF ORGANIZATION

1. Appeals
   a. Establish myself as a woman who grew up in the sixties;
      Identify myself as a sympathizer with women's liberation but also with those confused about W.L.
   b. Use argument based on group membership.
      Classification: supermom and supercareerwoman.
   c. Set up a feeling of uneasiness.
2. Organization
   a. Introduction: Establish myself as sympathizer yet one confused; establish a feeling of uneasiness; set up my focus.
   b. Proof
      ¶ 1 supermom
      ¶ 2 supercareerwoman: give specific examples in vivid language that people who grew up in the sixties can relate to
   c. Conclusion: Perhaps use analogy of rolling logs to help set feeling of confusion and uneasiness.

FIRST VERSION

WRITER 3

THE BALANCE POINT

The decade of the '60s is commonly referred to as a turbulent era in this country, gorged with social and political movements that sought to make radical changes in our laws, attitudes, values, and life-styles. While many of these movements were here and gone quickly, leaving in their wake only memories, others such as the women's liberation movement left behind changes so complete and yet so subtle that we are just beginning to be aware of what they mean to us. Perhaps the major residue of these movements of the '60s is our belief that anything which frees people from rigid roles, stereotypes, and limited options is to be applauded.

The women's liberation movement was intended to free women, to open up options for them, to give them more choices, yet for many housewives the result has been a lessening of choices. In trying to demolish the necessity for women to be "supermom," the woman who could raise perfect children, bake bread, cook gourmet meals, and sew all her own clothes in a spotless house, feminists unintentionally belittled the role of housewife and mother. A countless stream of feminists on *The Phil Donahue Show* spoke about how boring, degrading, and unfulfilling it is to be a housewife. Those of us who found satisfaction in this work felt defensive or wondered what was wrong with us. Feminists argued on behalf of universal day-care centers, adding that it's not the quantity but the quality of time that is important to children. While they described the Israeli kibbutzim, we pictured our children in Sugar and Spice or some other day-care center, herded about with 30 or 40 other kids by three or four adults who could not possibly spend enough time with them or give enough love to them. Feminists talked about mental stagnation that was inevitable with being home all the time but added that volunteerism, which for many of us was a way of getting out, was bad since it allowed society to unfairly exploit women's labor. At the end of these talk shows some woman would inevitably get up and explain that she freely chose to be a housewife and that she was very happy. The answer was always the same, the feminist would say in a patronizing tone, "Well if you knew all your options and that's what you chose to be—a housewife . . . OK." The message that came across to us was that we could not possibly have known all our options. Instead of enjoying the additional option of working outside the home we sensed that society now believed we *should* be working.

The supermom image became unfashionable, but was not really replaced. Instead, a new image was superimposed on it which required even more of women. The new heroine, the supercareerwoman, was the woman who could do it all. She had two intelligent planned-for children, lived in a *Better Homes and Gardens* house, was married to a loving, supportive man, and was a full-time worker with a rising career. If we took Geritol, the commercial said, then we could do it too. Modern books, movies, and magazine articles were filled with these new superwomen, but very few of them had preschool children. In fact, preschool children almost vanished from popular media, but when they were present mothers filled the same role they always had. Television series like *One Day At A Time* and movies like *See How She Runs* and *An Unmarried Woman* show a woman unable to break free from the restrictive, self-sacrificing, traditional role until a divorce precipitates things.

What all of this means to us is difficult to measure. Most of us approve of equal pay for equal work, welcome our husband's participation in parenting, encourage our daughters to build with erector sets, and allow our sons to play with dolls, but it is our own role that is most difficult to understand. There are few images on television or in movies and books that we can look to for advice. There are few women who have gone before us that we can emulate. We must integrate these new ideas with nothing to guide us but our own common sense. We feel like we are rolling logs in water, moving our feet as fast as we can to maintain our balance while the water and log move swiftly beneath us, constantly changing like the society in which we live.

WRITING WITH A PERSUASIVE AIM

In the Public World/The Media

● **THE GUIDING QUESTION AND POTENTIAL SITUATIONS**

THE SUBJECT CONTEXT

The subject context for your second writing experience with a persuasive aim will be another facet of your public world—the mass media that have surrounded your life. Have you ever taken the time to calculate the number of hours that you have devoted to television, radio, magazines, or newspapers? These hours have had a subtle influence on how you think and what you value, but you may be unaware of this influence because the media work hard at being unobtrusive, playing to the corners of your mind, costumed often as entertainment. Many television programs or magazines do not want to be caught off guard with their influences showing.

Chapter 4 offers you an opportunity to scrutinize one of the media to which you have devoted a lot of attention. You will learn how to conduct an evaluation of that medium, to assess its worth to you as a consumer, a viewer, listener, or reader, and ultimately as one influenced by its messages and values. If you make a list of those programs and publications with which you have had experience over an extended period of time, it will help you to select the medium you wish to investigate. Are any of these media controversial? Do they arouse mixed feelings in you? Do you feel addicted yet dislike some aspects of the program or publication? Do you like something that others whom you respect think is harmful or a waste of time? Do you hate commercials, for example, yet buy the products? Do you neglect responsibilities in order to watch certain programs? Are you irritated if some show is about to be cancelled? Do you dislike the new direction a program or magazine is taking? Are you worried about the negative impact of some media on someone close to you? Strong feelings are an indication that a particular medium is important to you. This writing experience will give you a chance to find out how important that medium is, to examine its worth and nature, and to assess its influence on you or those close to you.

Continuing to use the strategy for raising a compelling question will help you select a medium that bears close scrutiny. Here are five examples of media that the writers in this chapter selected to investigate.

QUESTIONS

WRITER 1

Subject: *Sports Now**

My Values and Expectations
—I wanted a good sports magazine
—I like factual sports reporting

—I like a well-written sports article that reports facts as well as the emotions involved

My Subject
—I subscribed to *SN* for eight years
—*SN* does not seem to be reporting as much factual information as it did
—*SN* seems to stress the emotional surroundings and aspects of sporting events

* Titles have been changed in Writer 1's process.

—I expect the print media to cover all aspects of an event—full coverage and complete review

—*SN* doesn't seem to give a full account of the events it covers
—roommate believes *SN* is God's gift to the world

Question: How adequate is *Sports Now* as a reporter of sports events?

WRITER 2

Subject: Fashion magazines

My Values and Expectations
—looking fashionable

—being economical

My Subject
—latest fashions but unreal look-alike models

—high prices of fashion clothes

Question: What real benefit do fashion magazines offer an average American girl?

WRITER 3

Subject: Comic books

My Values and Expectations
—the sophistication of the imagination

My Subject
—seem to parents a waste of time if not harmful

Question: What advantages can be gained from reading comics which seem to adults to be harmful wastes of time?

WRITER 4

Subject: *Monday Night Football*

My Values and Expectations
—two good teams playing each other
—good camera work

—accurate announcing
—truthful analysis, not cover-up or double-talk
—game to come before entertainment

—don't want to spend whole afternoon viewing game
—good halftime show

My Subject
—most games are between top teams
—camera angles and instant replays good
—semiaccurate announcing
—announcers who tell it like it is

—ABC guilty of occasionally putting show biz before game
—Monday night format ideal

—exciting halftime highlight

Question: Why do I enjoy watching ABC's *Monday Night Football* so much more than Sunday afternoon football on other networks?

WRITER 5

Subject: My campus newspaper

My Values and Expectations
—I expect to have campus news
—I expect the material I read to contain responsible and truthful material

My Subject
—I regularly read the *Campus News*
—several editorials and stories published recently in the *Campus News* have been irresponsible or contained total misrepresentations of facts

—I expect a newspaper to evaluate its reporters regularly and fire those whose work isn't fit to print

—the sports editor and two columnists have continuously published asinine and untrue material with no rebuke

Question: How responsible as a newspaper is the *Campus News*?

● **COMMENTARY**

Although Writer 2 has noted two aspects of fashion magazines, "high prices" and "unreal look-alike models," which conflict with her values, her question does not reflect that dissonance. Her revised question read: "What real benefit do fashion magazines, with their high prices and ideal models, offer an average American woman?" Notice also that she inadvertently uses the sexist term girl *to identify her audience. See the Glossary for a discussion of sexist language.*

Writer 4 has identified several values that seem to be either met or exceeded by his subject. His question, however, doesn't capture a real dissonance because he already seems to know the answer. His use of the first person in the question also suggests expressive discourse because it centers on his personal reactions. His revised question read: "What features of Monday Night Football *make it superior to other sports shows, especially for those not expert about football?"*

POTENTIAL SITUATIONS

Audiences for a subject like mass media can be simplified into two kinds: those people who, like you, view, read, or listen to the media (the consumers) and those people who create the material in the mass media (the producers). You cannot write for both simultaneously. The choice will depend on your focus. The writers identified several situations that seemed feasible for their questions.

WRITER 1
—a letter to the editor of *Sports Now*
—an essay that I would show to one of the guys who lives a couple of doors down the hall from me in the dorm and who believes *Sports Now* is God's gift to the world and that it covers sporting events so well that there is no need to read any other sports magazines. He does not understand why I do not like *Sports Now* and prefer other magazines
—an essay for the class—I can combine this situation with the one above

WRITER 2
—a letter to the publishers and editors of *Mademoiselle*
—an essay for two friends of mine who love to read fashion magazines
—an essay for the class

WRITER 3   —an article for *Parents* magazine for distressed parents of children who read comics
—a letter to my mother, who always hated my comic books
—a letter to the kid who lives next store and who loves comics

WRITER 4   —an article for *TV News*
—an essay for class
—a letter to my younger brother

WRITER 5   —a letter to the editor of the *Campus News*
—an essay for my cousin Nancy, who is a freshman
—an essay for class

● **COMMENTARY**

Writer 2 has covered most of the possible audiences in her list of possible situations: those who produce and sell the magazine, those who buy and read it, and the group interested in writing about media, the class. She will have to decide which group will profit most from her insight.

Writer 3 has chosen widely varying situations. An article for Parents *Magazine requires a good deal of factual background information and poses a formidable credibility problem, since Writer 3 is not a clinical psychologist or a parent. A letter to his mother would be much less challenging. It would also probably be oriented toward the past rather than the future, in that Writer 3 would probably be arguing that he turned out all right despite (or perhaps because of) reading comic books. The third possibility, the letter to the kid next door, would require a voice considerably different from the other two possibilities; and it would doubtless concentrate on reassuring the boy rather than changing his opinion, as in the other two cases. Writer 3 has an excellent range of possibilities.*

CLASS EXERCISES

1. Examine the questions and situations of Writers 1, 4, and 5.
   - Discuss as a class the kinds of investigations the questions will stimulate
   - Do the questions capture well the dissonances of the writers?
   - What other questions could be asked?
   - Which situations seem most promising? Why?
2. Select a medium with which the class has had experience.
   - Identify aspects of the medium that clash with or exceed your expectations.
   - Write several questions that could be investigated.
   - Suggest several writing situations for these questions.

3. Study the following case, identifying the values and expectations of Carol and the aspects of the program that seem to clash with her values. What questions could she ask?

Every day Carol set aside an hour from her housework to watch *Days of Our Lives*. On this particular afternoon, Marie had just been shot by her new husband's old girlfriend, Liz. Carol felt sorry for Marie but also sympathized with Liz, who loved Neil but had lost him to Marie through a long series of misfortunes. When Carol finished watching the program, she got a call from her sister-in-law, Sally, who sobbed that she had just learned of her husband Bill's weekend affair with an old girlfriend. Carol was immediately enraged at the news and condemned her brother, whose behavior was hard to understand in the light of his religious and family background. When Carol left the phone, she began to wonder about her own husband's recent late nights at the office.

● ASSIGNMENT: The Guiding Question and Potential Situations

1. Select a medium that you wish to assess.
2. Identify the expectations and values you hold for that kind of medium and the aspects of the medium that clash with or exceed those expectations.
3. Write a question to guide your search for a judgment.
4. List several writing situations that would fit with your subject.
5. Seek advice on this phase of your planning.

● EXPLORATION

You can use the exploratory guide provided in the preceding chapters or the ones described in the Appendix when you examine a medium. When you look at your subject from a *static view,* you will be searching for those recurrent features that characterize and distinguish your subject from others like it. A radio show or TV series, for example, will have a characteristic setting, theme, star characters, master of ceremonies, or announcer with identifiable personality and physical traits. Magazines will have recurrent special features, columns, types of stories, ads, and a characteristic layout. The same is true for newspapers.

The *dynamic view* will reveal something different about these media. Over a period of time, programs and magazines change. Features or characters are added or dropped. Physical appearances or themes may change. Your attitude toward the subject may undergo a transformation.

Finally, in assessing the value of a medium, the *relative view* is most important. When you classify, put your subject into the category in which it most appropriately belongs. If it is a TV series, can it be classified as a situation comedy, a murder mystery, a documentary, or an adventure series? If it fits in more than one category, decide on the best one.

EVALUATION

When a subject has been classified, criteria that mark a good example of that class can then be specified. As part of your exploration you can ask what constitutes a good situation comedy or a good murder mystery or a good documentary. Whatever your criteria are, they must be general enough to apply to *any good example in that category*. One writer who investigated the TV series *M*A*S*H* classified it as a situation comedy, for which she set the following criteria:

A good situation comedy must have

1. complex, consistent, human characters
2. a serious theme
3. a variety of wit and humor (slapstick, sarcasm, one-liners)
4. a range of emotion
5. a realistic treatment of subject (not fantasy)

She then judged *M*A*S*H* by these criteria and evaluated it as a good situation comedy. When you explore your subject, therefore, add to your relative perspective a list of criteria for the category in which you have classified your subject. Examine the explorations of Writers 1 and 3 to see how they have added this dimension to their explorations.

EXPLORATION

WRITER 1 SPORTS NOW

STATIC VIEW

—weekly magazine of sports articles and features
—large circulation throughout the United States

—usually around 120 pages
—usually has 5 feature articles, each about 10–15 pages
—has 10 departments that regularly appear and are reported on (departments change with the changes in sporting seasons)
—loaded with advertisements
—writers include B. O., M. M., S. W., R. F., P. P., and B. G.
—very colorful magazine—many excellent photographs, including the cover of the magazine
—sometimes they have editorials that report on some problem in the world of sports
—small section (1 page) in the back that gives a wrap-up of the week's sporting events—some scores

DYNAMIC VIEW

—The magazine has changed over the years as it has gone to more feature articles and has fewer regular departments, columns, or editorials than it once had.
—The magazine used to be about 90 pages long seven or eight years ago but has grown to 120 pages—mostly advertisements.
—When I first subscribed to it 7 or 8 years ago it was mostly articles and very few advertisements, but now it seems like every other page is an advertisement of some kind.
—I used to look forward to checking the mail box to see if *Sports Now* had come, but I no longer care whether it comes or not.
—The magazine used to give a full story (narrative) of a particular sporting event, but now gives a poor report of sporting events as they prefer to cover the emotional and similar aspects of sporting events.

RELATIVE VIEW

Classification
—*Sports Now* would fall into the category of sports magazines that are published weekly—it falls into the category of weekly sports magazines that cover the week's top sporting events and cover all the leagues of the sports in season.

Criteria that make for a good sports magazine
—objective reporting
—factual reporting and factual information
—limited coverage of the emotional aspects of the event—clutter up an article too much
—reporters who actually know a lot about the sport they are covering
—excellent pictures of the sporting event—ones that are relevant or particularly important
—narrative mode of writing
—good coverage of all sports—not just particular ones

Comparison/contrast

Sports Now	Sports Weekly
—weekly sports magazine—slick magazine paper	—weekly sports newspaper—newspaper material
—color pictures	—black-and-white pictures
—5 feature articles and some regular departments	—3 or 4 feature articles, but regular departments for all sports whether in season or not
—some factual reporting but not in great detail	—complete factual reporting of all sporting events—statistics of all events, weekly stats compiled for sports
—writers cover more than one sport	—writers usually only cover one sport
—lots of advertisements	—few advertisements

Analogy: Reading *Sports Now* is like reading a sales catalog because of all the advertisements that are in the magazine. Reading *Sports Now* is like reading an emotional book as all the emotion is spilled forth in the articles.

EXPLORATION

WRITER 3

FASHION MAGAZINES

STATIC VIEW

Pages and pages of ads
—makeup ads
—cigarette ads
—sterling silver ads
—shampoo ads
—perfume ads
—jewelry ads
—vacation ads
—toiletry ads for women

Beautiful models
—perfect figures
—straight teeth
—peaches 'n cream complexions
—long fingernails
—manageable hair that looks good in a variety of styles
—big, beautiful eyes
—little feet

Stylish clothes, meaning "faddish"
—styles are not lasting
—expensive outfits

Average outfit
—longer skirts
—woolen sweaters either short, long, slinky, or big (large knit)
—patterned shirts, full blouses
—scarf
—argyle knee socks
—platform shoes, spike heels
—head-hugging hats
—skinny belts

Accessories
—bangles
—earrings
—gold necklaces
—stickpins
—small leather bags
—mod watches
—sexy evening wear
—hair-coloring techniques

Various articles
—dieting tips
—travel tips
—exercise hints for a slim, trim figure
—marriage advice
—recipes for delicious snacks

Letters to the editor or to an expert
—beauty problems
—sexual problems
—boyfriend and girlfriend problems
—a horoscope section

"Shop by mail" sections
—rings, bracelets, earrings
—purses
—smock tops
—shoes
—body shapers

DYNAMIC VIEW

Process of production
—a lot of camera magic involved in photographing these models
—photographers only choose the best of their pictures
—girls are of a very highly select group, not your average girl
—fashion magazines save you a lot of time by giving you a preview of the
  clothes and accessories carried at the department stores

—sometimes articles are written by experts in a particular field, such as doctors, marriage counselors
—ads consume over half of the fashion magazine
—in special issues celebrities write articles on some crafts or hobbies that
they enjoy
—the average person can't trust this kind of information on handling life's
problems, college advice, etc.
—many fashion magazines show the person how to conform to their fashions
in clothes, their hairstyles and accessories, and their advice on how to act
and what to think on today's current problems
—sophisticated reader would not take everything at face value that is pictured or written about in these fashion magazines
—these styles pictured in fashion magazines are often impractical for the average person's budget, figure, and taste
—there doesn't seem to be any individuality in these fashion magazines;
everybody looks the same

RELATIVE VIEW

Comparison: Fashion magazines are a lot like college. Fashion magazines do
not pertain to, or cannot be of value to everyone. Unless the reader has a perfect
figure and a lot of money I don't believe the fashion magazines can be of any help.
Some of the articles are written for a very liberal audience and they can't relate to
the conservative reader who doesn't believe in premarital sex or some of the other
current topics. Since a reader may not be able to relate with these articles, she is
left without much of a variety in the fashion magazine world.

College doesn't apply to everyone. Only the select few who want to study and
learn some more in order to succeed in the profession of their choice go on to
college. For some, trade school or an early start in a job. But at least they do have
an alternate route.

Analogy: Fashion magazines are like fad diets. Fashion magazines do not pertain
to the average American girl. The girls chosen for these pictures are of a very
select group; they do not portray the average girl, because most average girls do
not have perfect figures, straight teeth, and cute smiles.

Fad diets such as grapefruit diets and water diets cannot hardly apply to the
average person who is working hard, either mentally or physically, for how can
anyone survive on such a small amount of calories all day. Maybe these diets
work wonders for celebrities or people who rest all day but not for the average
person who works hard.

Evaluation: Criteria for a good fashion magazine: it should offer practical advice
on fashions for average girls; it should advertise clothes that are affordable and
not too faddish. Most fashion magazines do not meet the criteria.

● **COMMENTARY**

Writer 3 has recorded under the static view a catalog of features common to most fashion magazines. But she has not selected very concrete language, using such phrases as "jewelry ads," "makeup ads," which present little that can be seen or felt or heard. Her exploration would improve if she added specific examples for each feature, as she does occasionally with "argyle knee socks" and "head-hugging hats." Most of the ideas under the dynamic view are actually static. Although this writer needs help using the dynamic perspective, more important is that she has discovered some useful ideas, even though misplaced. A dynamic exploration would have speculated on past fashion magazines, the changes the writer has noted since she began to read the magazines, and the typical way the contents are sequenced in a single issue. The connection made between colleges and fashion magazines is not a comparison but an analogy, because the two are of unlike order; however, her idea that fashion magazines are not for all may lead to an insight. The exploratory guide is a tool, not an end in itself.

CLASS EXERCISES

1. Examine the explorations of Writers 1 and 5 (pp. 217–219).
   - What distinctive descriptions do they give of their subjects? Could you identify the subjects from the features they record?
   - What parts of the subjects are explored? What kind of language is used to record the ideas?
   - What changes in the subject, sequences, or history have been analyzed?
   - What do the comparisons and contrasts or analogies reveal about the subject? About the attitude of the writer toward the subject?
   - What other aspects of the subject could be explored?
2. As a class, explore the subject you chose in the class exercises (see p. 179).
   - Record as many ideas under each perspective as the class can generate.

● **ASSIGNMENT: Exploration**

1. Explore the question you formulated, creating as many personal and public facets as you can. Be sure to include evaluative criteria under the relative perspective.
2. Seek advice on your work.

FOCUS AND SITUATION

INCUBATION

Even though you may feel as if you are in a pressure cooker, with assignments and exams piling up, allow your mind a rest so that the ideas can germinate and combine with one another. Usually a greater number of significant insights spring from a good night's sleep than from an all-night vigil.

FORMULATING A PERSUASIVE FOCUS

In order to answer your question assessing the merit of the medium you are investigating, go back to your exploration and especially to the relative perspective where you identified criteria for the category in which your medium was classified. Relate your subject to each criterion, deciding whether your medium meets, falls short, or exceeds the criterion. To make this assessment, examine all the facts you have compiled about your subject—all the static features and the dynamic changes it has undergone. Then formulate your judgment in the same two-part statement you have been using to clarify your insight. You will probably try several formulations before you arrive at the one that best expresses your evaluation.

CHOOSING AN AUDIENCE

When you have a working focus, decide which of your writing situations will provide the appropriate audience and means of sharing that new understanding. Choosing an audience for a paper dealing with mass media becomes easier if you keep in mind the principle that the best audience is the one that will profit most from sharing your insight. Specific audiences will vary from writer to writer, but generally two audiences may be selected from: the consumers and the producers. You should decide in the beginning which one of those audiences you will focus on, since you cannot write for both simultaneously.

Let's look at the principle in practice. Writer 3 has stated as her focus, "Some fashion magazines are not practical guides for the American girl." Writer 3 has two general audiences to choose from:

1. actual and potential readers of the magazines
2. publishers and editors of the magazines

Which should she choose? Let's apply the principle that the best audience is the one that will profit most.

If she chose the first, she would be writing for an audience that may or may not be aware of the impracticality of the magazines; hence, there is potential profit for that audience. If she chose the second, she would be writing for an audience whose members doubtless are fully aware of the nature of their publication. The publishers know quite well that they are not offering "practical guides for the American girl," and they are successful precisely because they are consciously selling something else—a romantic illusion.

Therefore, the logical choice should be the readers, not the publishers. But which readers? Not "the American girl" or even American girls who read fashion magazines, but American girls of limited means who think that they will find practical advice in fashion magazines applicable to their appearances, incomes, and life-styles.

Here are the focuses and situations of the five writers in this chapter.

WRITER 1 **Subject**   **Point of Significance**
Sports Now ————————————— lacks objectivity in its reporting of sports events.

(**Question:** How adequate is *Sports Now* as a reporter of sports events?)
Situation: I will write an essay for the guy down the hall who can't see any problems with the magazine.

WRITER 2 **Subject**   **Point of Significance**
Some fashion magazines——————— are not practical guides for the American woman.

(**Revised question:** What real benefit do fashion magazines, with their high prices and ideal models, offer an average American girl?)
Situation: I will write an essay for two friends of mine who love to read fashion magazines.

WRITER 3 **Subject**   **Point of Significance**
Comics———————————————— relax the reader, develop the imagination and reading skills, and provide hero models.

(**Question:** What advantages can be gained from reading comics, which seem to adults to be harmful wastes of time?)
Situation: I will write an article for *Parents Magazine* for distressed mothers of children who read comics.

WRITER 4 **Subject**   **Point of Significance**
Monday Night Football——————— is more enjoyable than Sunday afternoon football because of the quality of the action, the magnetism of the personalities, and the show-biz approach.

(**Revised question:** What features of *Monday Night Football* make it superior to other sports shows, especially for those not expert about football?)
Situation: I want to write an article for *TV News*, especially for those who don't have any extensive knowledge of football.

WRITER 5

Subject	Point of Significance
Many of the editorials, columns, and news stories of the *Campus News*	have been irresponsible and hence fostered growing feelings of distrust and disrespect on the campus.

(**Question:** How responsible a newspaper is the *Campus News*?)
Situation: I want to write an essay for my cousin Nancy, who is a freshman.

● **COMMENTARY**

Writer 2 has created an effective focus: the subject is carefully qualified ("some") as is the predicate ("for the American girl") and the single most important criterion ("practical") is clearly set out. The selection of audience is adequate. She has rejected as her audience her classmates and the publishers and editors of these magazines. She may have decided that the publisher and editors know what they are doing, that they deliberately do not offer practical advice, preferring to sell a profitable myth. In that case, changing their minds would be a formidable task. She may also have decided that her classmates are too mixed a group for the topic and that since she would be writing about the American girl reader, she might as well write for the American girl reader.

Writer 3 has made a questionable choice of audience. Parents Magazine prefers articles by authorities, and Writer 3 does not have the usual credentials. In addition, the magazine prefers factual articles incorporating up-to-date information. Much research has been done recently on Writer 3's topics, but his exploration list showed little knowledge of the results of that research. He has something valuable to say to someone with whom he has an established relationship—his mother or the neighbor boy—but he is out of his depth in choosing Parents Magazine.

CLASS EXERCISES

1. Discuss the focuses of Writers 1 and 5.
    • On the basis of their explorations on pp. 181–185 and 217–219, discuss whether their judgments are fair estimates of the media.
    • Are the situations selected appropriate for their focuses? Why or why not?
2. Formulate focuses for the medium you explored as a group.
3. Examine the following focuses and situations, judging their merit.
   a. Focus: *Sports Now* should be banned from the shelves.
      Situation: An editorial for the city newspaper

    b. Focus: The limitations of fashion magazines.
       Situation: An essay for class
    c. Focus: Comic books have changed over the years.
       Situation: A letter to the publisher of a leading comic book
    d. Focus: I love *Monday Night Football.*
       Situation: A letter to my Dad
    e. Focus: The editor of the campus newspaper ought to be fired.
       Situation: A letter to the Dean of Students

● ASSIGNMENT: Focus and Situation

1. Allow sufficient time for incubation.
2. Review your exploration, especially your criteria, and formulate a focus in two parts: subject and point of significance.
3. Identify the writing situation most appropriate for your focus.
4. Get advice on your work.

● AUDIENCE, APPEALS, AND MODES OF ORGANIZATION

SETTING THE ROLE FOR THE AUDIENCE

As you probably found out in the last chapter, setting a role for your audience is crucial in persuasion because your three appeals—credibility, rational, and affective—are actually made not to the audience itself, but to the *specific and relational roles* you have set. Using the audience guide on pp. 142–143 will help you set those roles.

    By concentrating heavily on the values the audience holds, the writer can define the audience's image of itself. Once the writer has defined that image, he or she can select the proper voice with which to address the reader. Knowing the values and, therefore, the self-image of the audience is so important because a persuasive writer tries to avoid attacking the audience head on. An audience is rarely persuaded to change its ways by a writer who attacks the image the audience holds of itself; the writer must find a role for the reader that does not threaten the audience's self-esteem. If, for example, you want to convince a winning Little League baseball coach that his methods are harmful to the children he coaches, you might try finding a role other than coach for him to play. Chances are that he is also a parent, a role he could play with pride. And you might choose then to project the voice of another parent, a concerned equal. Study the analyses of Writers 1 and 2 below.

AUDIENCE ANALYSIS

WRITER 1

1. My audience will be a guy that lives down the hall from me.
2. a. Background
   —20 yr. old college student
   —avid sports fan; has participated in many facets of competitive sports
   —member of the cross-country team on campus
   —keeps up on all types of sports
   b. Values
   —values complete coverage of sporting events
   —likes stories that report not only facts and figures but also the emotional aspects of sporting events
   —believes that color pictures make a magazine better than do black-and-white pictures
   —doesn't matter to him who the authors of an article are as long as the article is full of emotion and is supplemented with color pictures
3. Attitude toward the subject
   —has been reading *SN* for quite a few years
   —reads it every week from cover to cover—knows about all aspects of the magazine
4. Specific role: Up-to-date sports fan, someone who needs the latest accurate sports information
5. Analysis of the role
   a. Background: Role requires him to know up-to-date coverage when he sees it, and the opposite. He should also remember when *SN* was up to date and objective and accurate.
   b. Values: He will value comprehensiveness, objectivity, and up-to-the-minute coverage.
   c. Attitude toward the subject: He will need to act, to switch his preference from *SN* to *Sports Weekly*.
6. Relational role: We have a familiar relationship on the subject; we both know about *SN* and have equal knowledge of sports and sporting events. But in one way he is superior—he reads *SN every* week. So I shouldn't come on too strong.

WRITER 2 1. My audience will be two friends of mine, both of whom are very different, but who love to read fashion magazines.

2. a. Background
—both went to high school with me
—both live in the suburbs & come from middle- to upper-middle-class families
—both were fairly active in school activities
—both are attending Midwestern University as freshmen this fall and they are both in occupational therapy as their career
—both have volunteered in many hospitals and schools, where they have had an opportunity to get an idea of their future career
—one friend, Chris, worked this summer for 6 weeks in a car factory and as a waitress so she could pay for her room and board at college
—both of these girls would go into the library and before doing any studying would glance over the latest issue of *Seventeen* or *Glamour*.
—Chris is not quite as glamorous as my other friend; she wears jeans, overalls, smock tops, tennis shoes, little or no jewelry; her hair hangs straight and is rarely curled, which is certainly not the latest style, but just right for her
—Chris comes from a very religious family and so many of their current articles on living together, premarital sex, and abortion really don't interest her
—She is a little plump, so many of the fashions shown on the pencil-thin models aren't right for her
—My other friend, Karen, is more the glamorous type; she always wears fancy clothes & she loves jewelry. She is very thin & so many of the fashions in magazines don't flatter her either
—Even though she loves these things in the magazines she will not always pay their high prices and gets many of her clothes at budget stores
—Although not coming from such a deeply religious family as Chris, Karen still holds many of the values that her parents have, and she also finds many of the articles unhelpful, since she can't relate to marriage, etc., at this time in her life

b. Values
—both of these girls value their college life and try to do their best, since they have found the field that interests them
—they value the new friendships they have made at college and the old ones from the high school years
—they value a good career in which they are happy
—they value being an individual in their thoughts, actions, & clothes
—since they are away at college they value practical advice and information on all aspects of life to make their stay away from home as pleasant as possible

3. a. Attitude toward the subject: I think both of my friends like to read these magazines and maybe wish, as we all do, that we had that perfect figure or that much money so we could afford those things

       b. Strength of attitude: This is a very deeply established habit for them

       c. Willingness to act: I think if they examined themselves as I have, they would find that truly these magazines have been very impractical for them

4. Specific role: They will play the role of women who take charge of their own lives, in fashion as in other things

5. Analysis of the role

       a. Background: They are experienced enough to know that illusions are bad in all walks of life when they cut into your control and efficiency as a person.

       b. Values: They value their own independence and integrity and sense of reality.

       c. Attitude toward the subject: They must be willing to act on their reevaluation of the magazines.

6. Relational role

       —these girls are two of my best friends

       —we correspond to each other by letter

       —I am always interested in their life-styles at college & they enjoy hearing about my college

       —we respect each other's individualism in dress, mannerisms, & background, and because we are so different we have so much fun together

COMMENTARY

This is a shrewd assessment of two very different young women. They can be discussed as a single audience because they share a fascination with these magazines, because neither is the fashion model type, and because they are close friends of the writer. If Writer 2's estimate of their values is accurate, they should have no difficulty playing the role she intends for them because they already possess those values in general. If they "respect each other's individualism," they should listen readily to what Writer 2 has to say, because it is an attack on unrealistic stereotyping.

CREDIBILITY AND AFFECTIVE APPEALS

In Chapter 3 we discussed in detail the importance of achieving a *balance* of the three appeals: the credibility appeal, the rational appeal, and the affective appeal. We also identified some techniques for getting these appeals into your piece of writing. In the following, we repeat the techniques for establishing credibility and for appealing to the audience's attitudes and emotions. We illustrate each strategy with examples from the student writing in this chapter. For the rational appeal we introduce the deductive chain that you can use either alone or in conjunction with the other rational strategies listed in Chapter 3.

- **Strategies for Credibility Appeals**

  1. Provide information to show that you have firsthand experience or some other kind of authority on the subject.
      Example: Writer 1 points out in the first paragraph of his first version that he used to buy *Sports Now* regularly and that he has made a practice of reading other sports magazines.

  2. Make some references to your audience's interests and point of view to indicate that you know and respect them.
      Example: Writer 2 spends several sentences in the first paragraph of her first version describing the interests and anxieties of the average reader of teenage fashion magazines.

  3. Identify yourself with your audience in some way. Play up your similarities with them and minimize your differences.
      Example: Writer 5 uses his first paragraph to establish that he is one of the victimized readers of the *Campus News.*

  4. Use examples and lines of reasoning that your audience can relate to. In other words, choose your material, by reference to the interests and knowledge of the audience.
      Example: Writer 2 chooses her examples from magazines that she knows her two readers enjoy—*Glamour* and *Mademoiselle.*

  5. Use facts, ideas, and reasoning accurately. You will lose credibility if your audience concludes your thinking is careless or your information inaccurate.
      Example: Writer 1 methodically develops in four succeeding paragraphs the four criteria set out in the focus sentence in his first paragraph: "A good sports magazine is one that includes coverage of all sports, employs writers who are experts on the particular sport they cover, encourages objective reporting, and concentrates on factual accounts of sporting events."

  6. Provide specific support for your focus, and avoid generalizations that can cause your audience to suspect that you don't know what you're talking about or that you do not understand their need to have specifics to work with.
      Example: Writer 1 supports his point that *SN* does not cover all sports by a precise count of the number of pages given to Wimbledon and the U.S. Open.

  7. Use correct grammar, spelling, and punctuation. If you do not control the basics of your language, you throw the rest of your appeals into question.
      Example: Writer 1's paper has been carefully proofread.

- **Strategies for Affective Appeals**

  1. Determine what frame of mind, emotional state, or attitude you wish your audience to be in as a result of reading your paper. Select

examples, comparisons, or analogies that will stimulate those attitudes or feelings.

Example: Writer 2 illustrates the impracticality of fashion magazine advice and heightens the indignation of the reader by using an "average outfit" from *Glamour* that has four parts and eight accessories.

Example: Writer 5 ends his indictment of the *Campus News* with a stinging remark: "I am certainly not proud to admit that part of my fees has helped to support such a journalistic nightmare."

2. Show that you are sensitive to certain values that are central to the role your audience will play.

Example: Writer 2 prepares her audience for the role of women who must take control of their lives. She shows in her second paragraph that, in an age of inflation, both the career and college woman are forced into important choices and that fashion magazines tend to frustrate successful exercise of those choices.

3. Use specific and concrete language that is appropriate to your subject.

Example: Writer 2 makes a vivid case by use of exact descriptions: "The new, brightly colored ankle-to-thigh leg warmers, which are worn over jeans, must be the most unusual new fad pictured this year in *Mademoiselle* magazine."

RATIONAL APPEALS

In this chapter we introduce you to another type of rational argument, modeled on formal logical proof but still appropriate for the realm of probability in which you are writing. We refer here to *informal deductive proof*. Let us examine one form a deductive proof would take if a writer wanted to use it to evaluate something, in this case a particular medium. Suppose the writer who wanted to evaluate *M*A*S*H* arrived at the following focus:

*M*A*S*H* ——————————————— is a good situation comedy.

This focus is actually the *conclusion* of a deductive proof. But the writer has to do more than merely assert the conclusion. She has to prove it by giving reasons or criteria by which she came to that conclusion. Her criteria for a good situation comedy were:

1. complex, consistent, human characters
2. a serious theme
3. variety of wit and humor (slapstick, sarcasm, one-liners)
4. a range of emotion
5. a realistic treatment of subject (not fantasy)

But will these criteria hold up under the scrutiny of others? Will they be accepted by her audience? To test this, the writer casts these criteria or reasons into the form of a *principle:*

Any situation comedy that has complex, consistent human characters, a serious theme, a variety of wit and humor, a range of emotion, and a realistic treatment of a subject is a good situation comedy.

If the writer thinks that the audience will accept these criteria, she then has a solid basis for proceeding. If the audience will not accept them, then the writer has two alternatives: (1) to prove them to the audience (this doubles the persuasive task), or (2) to find other criteria the audience will accept.

● **The Deductive Chain**

Setting up a principle is only the beginning of the persuasive task. The main job of the writer in building the rational appeal is to prove that *M∗A∗S∗H* meets all these criteria. Her proof is expressed in a *joining statement:*

M∗A∗S∗H ——— has ——— complex, consistent, human characters, a serious theme, a variety of wit and humor, a range of emotions, and a realistic treatment of the subject of war.

If the writer puts these statements together, they form a deductive chain.

A principle (A + B):

(A) Any situation comedy that has complex, consistent, human characters, a serious theme, a variety of wit and humor, a range of emotion, and a realistic treatment of a subject—is—

(B) a good situation comedy.

A linking statement (C + A):

(C) M∗A∗S∗H—has—(A) complex, consistent, human characters, a serious theme, a variety of wit and humor, a range of emotion, and a realistic treatment of the subject of war.

A conclusion, the writer's original focus (C + B):

(C) M∗A∗S∗H—is—(B) a good situation comedy.

Notice some interesting features of this chain:

1. It has only three ideas—A, B, and C. Each is repeated twice. In fact, because A links B to C, the reasoning can work. If a chain were to have more than three ideas, it wouldn't work.

2. Ideas B and C are the two parts of the writer's focus.
3. Idea A came from the writer's criteria. The writer therefore had all the ingredients for such reasoning in her planning. What she did was put them in this logical format to see if her thinking was tight.
4. The linking statement is what the writer will have to develop in the paper, using whatever material is available—examples, details, facts, and so on. This linking statement becomes, in effect, the new focus of the paper. If the writer succeeds in proving the linking statement, then the original focus has been proved indirectly.

Here are the deductive chains planned by some of the writers in this chapter.

WRITER 2   **Principle:** Any fashion magazine that displays clothes that are unreasonably priced, faddish, and unsuited to the average figure does not offer practical advice to girls.
Linking statement: Most fashion magazines display these kinds of clothes.
Conclusion (focus): Therefore, most fashion magazines do not offer practical advice to girls.

WRITER 3   **Principle:** Any publication that relaxes the reader, develops imagination and reading skills, and provides hero models is a valuable publication for children.
Linking statement: Comic books do these things.
Conclusion: Comic books are valuable publications for children.

WRITER 4   **Principle:** Any TV sports show that has action, great personalities, and fast presentation is a good sports show.
Linking statement: *Monday Night Football* has these qualities.
Conclusion: *Monday Night Football* is a good sports show.

WRITER 5   **Principle:** Any newspaper that lacks honesty, responsibility, and common sense is not a good newspaper.
Linking statement: The *Campus News* lacks honesty, responsibility, and common sense.
Conclusion: The *Campus News* is not a good newspaper.

●   **Validity of Reasoning**

If you want to be convincing, you must be sure that your deductive chain is valid, i.e, that it has correct reasoning form. Here is a checklist by which you can test for validity.

1. *Does your chain have only* three *ideas, each repeated twice? Does each idea mean the same thing in both its statements?* Examples of lack of validity:
   a. Any radio station that insults listeners is a poor station.
      WXYZ has strange programs.
      WXYZ is a poor station.
   b. Any TV show that condones violence is a dangerous show.
      Hill Street Blues has a lot of violence.
      Hill Street Blues is a dangerous show.
2. *Have you extended the conclusion beyond the premises (principle and linking statement)?* Example of lack of validity:
   Any ads that degrade the body are in bad taste.
   Some deodorant ads degrade the body.
   All deodorant ads are in bad taste.
3. *Have you arrived at a positive conclusion when one of the premises is negative; have you concluded something from two negative premises?* Examples of lack of validity:
   a. Any game show that ridicules its contestants is a bad show.
      The Joker's Wild does not ridicule its contestants.
      The Joker's Wild is a bad show.
   b. Any newspaper that ruins the reputation of citizens does not deserve reading.
      The Mirror does not ruin the reputation of citizens.
      The Mirror deserves reading.

CLASS EXERCISES

Examine the following deductive chains for validity. If invalid, what kind of problem exists?

1. Any show that deprives its viewers of reality should not be shown.
   Love Boat puts its viewers in a trance of romance.
   Love Boat should not be shown.
2. TV shows falsely portray life.
   Family life that is shown without problems or crises is a superficial portrayal of life.
   The Brady Bunch falsely portrays family life as one in which all crises and problems are easily solved.
3. Any show that makes a comedy of war is unrealistic.
   *M*A*S*H* is a comedy about war.
   *M*A*S*H* is unrealistic.
4. Any news program that misrepresents issues should be avoided.
   Most newscasts do not represent issues.
   All news programs do not have to be avoided.
5. Any soap that glorifies infidelity is not a worthwhile program.
   Doctors Hospital does not glorify infidelity.
   Doctors Hospital is a worthwhile program.

ORGANIZATION

This paper will have the same framework as the one in the previous chapter:

1. Introduction
2. Proof
3. Refutation (optional)
4. Conclusion

● ### Introduction

Your introduction accomplishes several things. It sets up your credibility, using whatever appeals you have selected. Important for this paper will be the amount of experience you have had with the particular medium and the kind of criteria you select. When you plan to use a deductive chain as your rational appeal, you should state it in the introduction—not in the way you formulated it in your plan, but informally. For example, Writer 2 expressed her deductive chain in the following way in her introduction:

Everyone would agree that fashion magazines that display clothes that are unreasonably priced, faddish, and unsuited to the average woman doesn't offer very practical advice. But as the young reader anxiously looks through the latest monthly fashion magazine, hoping to find that one eye-catching outfit that would spark up her wardrobe and her season, she is frequently discouraged by the outrageous prices of the outfits and is doubtful as to whether she has that perfect figure needed to wear the latest fashions. For these reasons most fashion magazines do not offer practical fashion advice.

If you compare this expression of the deductive chain with its more formal version above, you will notice the difference between the more formal and informal statements of the chain. The joining statement, for example, has much more detail than in the original. Putting your deductive chain in the introduction allows your reader to see the shape of your argument, the reasons for your conclusion.

● ### Proof and the Evaluative Mode of Organization

A fourth way of organizing a persuasive paper is to use the evaluative mode. The evaluative mode of organization involves

1. setting standards or criteria by which something can be judged,
2. relating your subject to the criteria, and
3. drawing conclusions that follow.

This pattern is like that of the deductive chains previously illustrated. In those chains the principle contains evaluative criteria, the linking statement relates the subject to those criteria, and the conclusion makes an evaluative judgment.

Anything can be evaluated. You can evaluate a rock so long as you state a standard. A standard often is based on a purpose you have in mind: A small, flat rock is better than a large round one, if you want to skip a rock across the water; if you want to kill a snake with a rock, the large round one is better. The center of value rests in the use you propose for the subject. The correctness of your conclusion, furthermore, does not rest on your opinion. It is a fact that snakes are more easily killed with large rocks than with small ones; and it is a fact that large rocks do not skip well, especially if they are round.

Using the evaluative mode lays on you the absolute burden of making clear to the reader what the standard is. If the standard is acceptable to the audience, the conclusion will generally be acceptable, supposing that the account of the subject is clear and exact. For example, it is useless to argue to an audience of deer hunters that deer hunting is "bad" unless you have first convinced the hunters that the suffering of the deer outweighs the satisfaction of the hunter.

Hence, in the evaluative mode your business is to convince the audience of the correctness of your judgment by

1. persuading the audience of the reasonableness of the standard you have established, and
2. describing the subject faithfully and accurately, showing how it meets or doesn't meet the standard.

The evaluative mode, although it looks easy, has its peculiar dangers. You must distinguish standard from conclusions by being certain that the standard is not simply the conclusion in disguise. That is, if the underlying sequence is this:

> A thing is good if I like it, bad if I don't.
> I don't like this thing.
> Therefore, it is bad.

there is no standard apart from the conclusion. The task is to find a standard external to your likes and dislikes that the audience will accept as objective and fair.

The evaluative mode provides a clear way of organizing your proof. You take up each criterion, one by one, and discuss how your subject does or does not meet that criterion. Often a paragraph is devoted to each criterion. For example, the writer dealing with *M*∗*A*∗*S*∗*H* had established five criteria that *M*∗*A*∗*S*∗*H* met. She organized her proof around those five points:

¶ 1 *M*∗*A*∗*S*∗*H*'s complex, consistent, human characters
¶ 2 *M*∗*A*∗*S*∗*H*'s serious theme
¶ 3 *M*∗*A*∗*S*∗*H*'s variety of wit and humor
¶ 4 *M*∗*A*∗*S*∗*H*'s range of emotion
¶ 5 *M*∗*A*∗*S*∗*H*'s realistic treatment of situations

Writer 2's plan of proof looked like this:

¶ 1   Fashion magazines display clothes unreasonably priced.
¶ 2   Fashion magazines show faddish clothes.
¶ 3   Fashion magazines show clothes ill suited to the average figure.

It is important to note that the deductive chain can also be used with the descriptive, narrative, and classification modes of organization.

● **Conclusion**

In your conclusion, you need a final appeal to the attitudes, values, or emotions of your audience. A restatement of your conclusion also leaves the audience with the point you wish them to accept.

ORGANIZATION PLANS

Drawing up a persuasive plan is a useful way to ensure that you integrate your appeals. First list the appeals you plan to use. Then create a paragraph plan including your introduction, proof, and conclusion. Here is Writer 1's plan:

1. Appeals
   a. Credibility
      Show how long I took *Sports Now* and how much I liked it; show that I have good criteria—well thought out.
   b. Rational appeal—use deductive chain.
      Principle: Any sports magazine that includes all sports, whose reporters know a lot about the sport they are covering, and that is factual and objective is a good sports magazine.
      Linking statement: *Sports Now* does not have these qualities.
      Conclusion: *SN* is not a good sports magazine.
   c. Affective appeal: Appeal to my audience's value of fairness and objectivity. Appeal to pride in knowing a lot about sports—to passion for sports.
2. Organization Plan
   ¶ 1   Introduction: Show my knowledge of *SN*; state my deductive chain, which includes my criteria.
   ¶ 2   Show how *SN* doesn't deal with all sports.
   ¶ 3   Show how *SN* by contrast with other magazines has writers who cover too many sports—they are not expert in all.
   ¶ 4   Show *SN*'s lack of objectivity.
   ¶ 5   Show by contrast *SN*'s lack of stats and other facts.
   ¶ 6   Conclusion: Restate my original focus.

In order to see the relationship between an organization plan and the writer's paper, examine Writer 1's first version, relating it to his plan.

SPORTS NOW: THE NUMBER ONE SELLER BUT NOT THE BEST*

Not many people would dispute the fact that *Sports Now* is by far the number one selling sports magazine in America as far as quantity is concerned. I used to buy *SN* regularly when I was younger. I didn't care how well an article was written as long as the article dealt with sports. Now that I am older and have learned to appreciate well-written articles, I have become disgusted with the sports reporting that *SN* does. A good sports magazine is one that includes coverage of all sports, employs writers who are experts on the particular sport they cover, encourages objective reporting, and concentrates on factual accounts of sporting events. By these standards, *SN* is not a good sports magazine.

Unlike the other two top sports publications, *Modern Sports* and *Sports Weekly,* *SN* gives little coverage to all the different sports. One sport that gets relatively little attention is tennis, which has been featured only twice this summer despite the heaviest summer schedule in the sport's history. The magazine gave only six pages of coverage to the Wimbledon finals and only five pages to the U.S. Open. However, most of these pages were filled up with pictures. Although *SN* recently had their National Hockey League preview which I thought was an excellent article giving a rundown of all the hockey teams, coaches and biographies of the top players, hockey will not be covered thoroughly again until the playoffs start next April. Of all the sports publications, *SN* has the best preseason reports on hockey, but it fails to follow through like the other magazines which will give weekly reports on the division standings and a wrap-up of the top games of the week. Only occasionally will *SN* have a feature on a hockey player who may be having a spectacular season.

Another important aspect of a good sports magazine is that the writers know a good deal about the particular sport they are covering. The writers in most sports magazines become specialized in one sport and will only cover events in this particular area. A reader can count on seeing their column regularly and one can rely on what they say. No such thing occurs in *SN* because each writer covers more than one sport and only a couple of writers continually cover the same sport, jumping from sport to sport. For example, over the last two months, one reporter covered college football, the Ali-Holmes fight, the Hagler-Minter fight, a feature article about a boxing coach in Kansas City, the baseball pennant races, and the U.S. Open tennis tournament. I'm sure that this writer knows something about all of these particular events, but I question how knowledgeable and creditable he is. When I pick up *Sports Weekly* to read about the pennant races I do not question the credibility of Jack Gilroy, Phil Green, or Bob Chase, because I have been reading their baseball reports for years. If I want to read the latest report on Big Ten football, Jim Flaherty will be there with an article in *Sports Weekly,* but I do not know from week to week who will be covering college football in *SN.*

* Titles and names have been changed.

Another important thing that a good sports magazine must have in its reporting is objectivity. Sometimes *SN*'s articles contain subjective themes. Before the Holmes-Ali fight, Paul Pearson gave a prefight preview. Throughout the article he said that Holmes was in better shape and much younger, but kept saying that there was only one Muhammed Ali and the mystique that surrounded him was enough to give the old man an edge on Holmes. He gave Holmes much less respect than he deserved and implied that Holmes was never the true champion that Ali had been. He wrote that Holmes was mistaken in claiming that it would be a mismatch and refuted Holmes' belief that Ali could get hurt. He was clearly for Ali to pull it off. Two weeks later in his report of the fight he did not give Holmes much credit for his victory, implying in his article that Ali had lost, not that Holmes had won. He continually wrote about how Ali had slowed down and lost his punch, but said little about how strong and fast Holmes really was. *SN* has also had the tendency to pick other favorites such as Notre Dame in college football and the New York Yankees in baseball, and most of their articles about Bjorn Borg play him up while at the same time portraying Jimmy Connors and John McEnroe to be nothing but "American brats." That kind of coverage is comparable to the *New York Times* printing editorials on the front page.

Another important aspect of a good sports magazine is that it needs to be factual in its reporting and not just report on the emotional aspects of a sporting event. *SN* skimps on the facts and statistics of sporting events, but it lays the emotional aspects, such as the determination and courage that an athlete or a team shows in their performance, on quite heavy. Other sports magazines give detailed reports of sporting events by giving statistics on how well certain players did. *SN* leaves me with a vague notion of what occurred during a certain event. It occasionally will list statistics throughout an article, but most magazines list all the statistics in a compact form after giving a review of the sporting event. *SN* uses the themes of determination and effort and courage to describe sporting events, but I already know that most athletes have courage and determination and give it their best effort. I want to know how well their determination and effort paid off and how well they performed. Only a magazine with statistical reports can transfer this information and *SN* fails to do it.

I enjoy objective sports reporting of all sports by reporters who have a deep inside knowledge of these sports and are able to give me a report of the factual elements of sporting events as well as the emotional surroundings. *SN* fails to do this and that is why it no longer appeals to me as a sports magazine.

CLASS EXERCISES

1. Examine the organization plan of Writer 1 (p. 201).
   - Has the writer enough appeals? Are they well integrated throughout the paper?

- Are there other appeals that could be used?
- In the light of this plan, what material from his exploration (pp. 181–185) can be used?

2. Examine Writer 1's audience analysis (p. 191).
   - Was his choice of audience a good one?
   - What specific and relational roles has he chosen? Will they work well for his focus?

● **ASSIGNMENT: Audience, Appeals, and Mode of Organization**

1. Analyze your audience, setting the specific and relational roles you want them to play.
2. Identify the credibility and affective appeals you will use.
3. Create a deductive chain to use for your rational appeal.
4. Set up your organization plan.

● **THE FIRST VERSION**

Using your plan as a guide, write out several drafts of your paper until you have one that best carries out your plan. The material in your exploration should offer ideas and examples. But you will probably have to generate more material when drafting your paper. Compare Writer 2's first version with her organization plan and exploration.

FIRST VERSION

WRITER 2   FASHION MAGAZINES OFFER IMPRACTICAL FASHION ADVICE

Every young woman in today's American society cannot help but feel the pressures of having to be attractive, glamourous, and sexy. Many popular fashion magazines such as *Glamour*, *Seventeen*, *Mademoiselle*, *Teen*, *Vogue*, and *Harp-*

er's Bazaar portray how the ideal woman should look. Marlo Thomas, Cher, Ellen Burstyn, Cybill Shepherd, Princess Caroline of Monaco, and even Susan Ford are just a few of the many popular celebrities who often appear in these magazines to model the very stylish clothes. But can the average American girl really relate to and identify with these fashionable models? Although many girls are pretty, they never seem to think of themselves as being as perfect as they would like to be; either they are too tall, too short, too skinny, or too fat; their hair is unmanageable, or their complexion is blemished. Everyone would agree that fashion magazines displaying clothes that are unreasonably priced, faddish, and unsuited to the average girl don't offer very practical advice. But as the young reader anxiously looks through the latest monthly fashion magazine, hoping to find that one eye-catching outfit that would spark up her wardrobe and her season, she is frequently discouraged by the outrageous prices of the outfits and is doubtful as to whether she has that perfect figure needed to wear the latest fashions. For these reasons most fashion magazines do not offer practical fashion advice.

In today's age of inflation, the career girl and the college girl definitely need practical fashion advice. Both require a variety of clothes that are stylish and reasonably priced. While browsing through a popular fashion magazine, *Glamour,* one will notice that the average outfit consists of a midi skirt or pants, a woolen sweater, a patterned shirt, and crazy-colored argyle kneesocks. The outfits shown are never complete without such accessories as a head-hugging hat, scarves, skinny belts, bangles, earrings, gold necklaces, mod watches, and leather bags. Each outfit, excluding the accessories, comes to a staggering figure, considering that a variety of clothes is necessary for work or school. Evening dresses, also, come with a high price tag. The price of these formal dresses hardly seems worth it for one night.

Some of these expensive clothes tend to be very faddish. The most drastic change in fashions has occurred in the length of the woman's hemline, which has gone from one extreme, the mini, to the other extreme, the maxi, and all lengths in between, in a period of two or three years. Fashion changes, although not as apparent, have also occurred in the styles of shoes, sweaters, and makeup. In one college issue, *Mademoiselle* magazine says that yesterday's classic blazer is being replaced by big, bulky sweaters, and high-heeled platform shoes are giving way to the lower, more comfortable heels and fashionable cowboy boots. The new, brightly colored ankle-to-thigh leg warmers, which are worn over jeans, must be the most unusual new fad pictured this year in *Mademoiselle* magazine. Today, earth tones of browns and light oranges are common in lipstick and nail polish, instead of the pink pastels. That earthy fragrance is even present in many perfumes where the scent of roses or lily of the valley used to dominate. Some fashion changes are very impractical for everyday use, and some have even been surrounded by controversy. Experts argue about how unsafe platform shoes are for driving, and twisted ankles are not unheard of as a result of walking on these four-inch heels. Also, many of the clothes shown in these fashion magazines seem impractical both in price and texture, for anything but special occasions. Today's girl definitely needs reasonable, comfortable and good-looking clothes for relaxation and other activities, such as attending football games and going to school, to work, or shopping.

In addition to being expensive and faddish, a further limitation to the practicality of the fashion advice presented by these magazines is that the clothes are designed for the tall, pencil-thin girl. The models featured in these magazines are from a very highly select group, rather than an average girl. These beautiful models all appear to have perfect figures to complement all of these expensive clothes, as well as gleaming, straight teeth, clear complexions, long fingernails, big eyes, little feet, and manageable hair that looks attractive in a variety of styles. One cannot help but wonder how much camera magic is involved in these photographs, for it seems unrealistic that a person can ever be so perfect. It is widely known that many celebrities whose photos appear in fashion magazines have had different types of cosmetic surgery. Many celebrities admit to having facelifts, and rumor has it that some have even gone so far as to have their buttocks lifted. Clothes on a model whose appearance has been improved by plastic surgery and camera tricks may look very peculiar on a girl with an average face and figure. Unable to physically relate to these fashion models, the young woman feels bewildered about the kind of clothes that are flattering to her.

The average American girl avidly reads a variety of these popular fashion magazines, hoping to find information that will guide her to select clothes that are comfortable, flattering, and affordable. But most fail the girl miserably because their fashion advice is so impractical. Experience proves that the clothes they portray are expensive, faddish, and unbecoming to the average figure. Therefore, most fashion magazines are not helpful to the average American girl.

REFUTATION

An effective persuasive writer knows that the audience is not neutral on an issue it is interested in. Inevitably, the audience will object to some parts of a writer's argument; the wise writer anticipates these objections and brings them into the paper in order to answer them. Answering objections is called *refutation*.

In order to refute, you have to know what the objections are. Sometimes that is easy; your audience may have written something on the subject. But commonly you must construct those statements yourself by concentrating on what you know of your audience's values and opinions.

Drawing up such statements and using them in your paper can actually add to the persuasive force of your paper in several ways. First, you meet the very practical problem of not seeming to ignore opposing views; you enhance the plausibility of your argument. Second, if you state objections fairly and accurately, you add to your own credibility. Third, by acknowledging the audience's emotional involvement in the issue you will defuse some of the potential hostility.

How you refute statements of objection is obviously very important. Theories of formal argument teach that there are two means of refutation: direct and indirect. *Direct* means an attack on an audience's statements of fact or statements of proof. *Indirect* means an attack on the audience's character or method of reasoning.

There are three kinds of direct refutation:

1. *Denial:* You deny the audience's statement and maintain that something else, perhaps the opposite, is true, whether the statement is a matter of fact or a matter of proof. This becomes an important kind of refutation for writers using the evaluative mode. These generally are objections to the standard being employed, and that type of objection, because it is so basic, needs to be brought forward and dealt with. For example, in the statement "Philosophy isn't worth studying because it doesn't get you a job," the basic assumption is that one should only study what will produce a job. That's a probable judgment that can be denied. Of course, it's also possible to deny it as a statement of fact, since people who study philosophy do get jobs.

2. *Distinction:* You accept an audience's statement in one sense, but deny it in another, more important sense. Look, for example, at the very vulnerable statement "Poison should not be put into public water supplies, and fluoride is poison."

3. *Retort:* You use the audience's reasoning to draw a different conclusion. If, for example, a Republican argues that the Democrats risked higher inflation by selling gold internationally and raising the prime interest rate at home in November 1978, a Democrat might reply that both practices raised the exchange rate of the dollar and prevented a depression in the United States.

Indirect refutation is effective in persuasive writing only when the objections being refuted can be attributed to someone other than the audience. There are two kinds of indirect refutation:

1. *Attacking the objector's character.* This kind of refutation is useful only if the objector can be shown to be biased or ignorant. A writer who asks his or her audience to play either of those roles is in trouble. A writer who maliciously attacks a third person is likewise in trouble.

2. *Attacking the objector's reasoning.* Simply stated, you examine an objector's process of deduction or induction and point out flaws. This can amount to calling the objector stupid, a role the audience should never be asked to play, although it can be a suitable role for a third person.

The danger in using indirect refutation lies in the damage it can do to the credibility of the writer. It is better to accept and acknowledge a minor objection than to risk losing the sympathy and respect of the audience.

Below is Writer 3's first version, which uses refutation.

FIRST VERSION

WRITER 3

THE COMICS: NOT FUNNY

Johnny is not your average sixth grader. Although only eleven years of age, he has a list of accomplishments that range from breaking up infamous diamond smuggling rings to rescuing astronauts stranded on the moon, not to mention saving the world from certain destruction many times over. Widely admired and recognized as a citizen of all nations, he is somewhat of a recluse, spending many hours a day shut away in his room. Some speculate he is deeply involved with critical research on some new device or some special power to add to his already vast repertoire, but Johnny's mother has put an end to the controversy with her single explanation: "Johnny spends one hundred and ten percent of his allowance on comic books." Tell the truth now. How many of you have ever seriously considered that comics might have some value other than as an alternative to juvenile delinquency?

Some of you with little Johnnys of your own at home know what a peculiar feeling it is when the words your child speaks to you most often are not "Can I go out to play" nor "But I don't wanna go to bed" nor even (though wouldn't it be nice) "I love you," but rather the singularly disgusting phrase, "Ma, can I have some money for comic books?" Of course, the more industrious of you have turned this to your advantage by using it to get Johnny to take out the garbage or even, under unusual circumstances, to take his little sisters to the Saturday matinee. For those of you who still have your doubts, consider that while your child is eagerly engaged in the fight of right against wrong he is not sliding through your neighbor's rose garden, not throwing a baseball through the basement window, not trying to light kitty-cat's tail on fire, and most important of all, not trampling about underfoot.

How many of you have even stopped to think that while your child is wasting his time reading those dumb comic books that he is in fact reading, a skill once almost universally possessed before the advent of that most nonparticipatory medium, television. What is more, your impressionable youngster isn't reading some seedy rag that will age him too quickly. No, he reads how Dr. Doom, caught up in his plan of world conquest, flees from capture by the Fantastic Four. He reads of the Black Panther, an American superhero who rules a prosperous and peaceful nation in Africa. Kids form hero images of characters like Black Panther or the Fantastic Four. These hero images are a convenient place for a child to place his values of right and wrong, both to work with those values and to have a place to store them intact when the more personal issues of adolescence begin to occupy his mind.

While it is true that a comic book habit does involve a certain cost, there are other hobbies that are equally expensive and much less advantageous. The notorious chemistry set is one. In addition, if your child didn't spend so much money on comics, he might spend it on candy. You can buy a lot of comics with the money it takes to pay one dentist bill. Anybody still not convinced can just turn their backs on the situation in hope that maybe some day their little Johnny will grow out of it. Maybe. However, the really shrewd parent knows how to get even. They save all those old comics that their children have so carelessly tossed under the bed and take good care of them because one day when little Johnny becomes big Johnny those old comics are going to be worth some good money. The first issue of Batman sold for ten cents and is now worth four hundred dollars.

● **COMMENTARY**

Writer 3 in paragraphs 3 and 4 sets out to refute what he assumes will be the two strongest objections to his position: first, that reading comic books is a waste of time, and, second, that comic books are costly. To the first he replies that reading comic books teaches reading, furnishes rich material for the child's fantasy life at a time when that is important for development, and nurtures proper values. To the second he replies that comics are cheap by comparison with other diversions and that spending on comics prevents spending on candy, which rots the teeth. Whatever the quality of the proof, the refutation is well constructed.

THE PERSUASIVE STYLE

Recall the advice you were given in Chapter 3 about the style of the persuasive aim:

1. Root your diction deeply in concrete details.
2. Pay close attention to the connotation of your words.
3. Choose the proper person in which to address your reader; let it grow out of the relational role you have selected.
4. Make sure the relationship of your ideas is clearly signaled by transitions.
5. Plan each paragraph first for unity and second for coherence.

CLASS EXERCISES

1. Read the following two paragraphs from a paper on advertising:

   What would you say if I were to tell you that you are emitting foul odors from a hundred forty-seven different parts of your body, your teeth are yellow and scummy, your hair is snowing dandruff (that is the dandruff that survives growing in the oil), your face is a scabby prune, and your brain is plugged up because you don't use Q-tips? Hopefully, unless you are the latest creature feature, you would tell me to get lost, go fly a kite, or go suck an egg. Why, then, are the men and women on body product commercials allowed to bombard us each T.V. evening with advertising pitches designed to make us feel inferior, unattractive, and undesirable unless we use what they are selling? When we are able to recognize and understand these manipulative psychological techniques used by advertisers, we will have the power to defy Madison Avenue's subliminal seduction. Otherwise, we will remain computers, involuntarily fed data that programs us to obediently pay top dollar for preselected products.

Advertising today, as a result of much research, practice, and money, has developed precise and effective ways to suck our subconscious through a tunnel of garbage that we, in turn, pave with our hard-earned paychecks. Close-Up toothpaste is one of the top five sellers on the market today because when that toothy girl tells us to put our money where our mouth is, we do it. Close-Up guarantees that whiter teeth and fresher breath will turn Billy on, implying that using a gooey red gel on our teeth will remarkably improve our love life. So rather than buying a product that might be advantageous to the health of our teeth, we are sold on the sex appeal image. Love's Baby Soft products say, "You can try hard or you can try soft. Soft'll get 'em every time." The ads show before-and-after sequences. First the girls are aggressive and get no response from the guys. Then they are passive and saccharine sweet, which results in instant dates. This ad also follows the "product—man" routine, but implies that using X product will get the woman a man by changing her personality. Hmmm—simply a variation on a theme, but still a psychological trap that is very carefully set for us.

- For what audience are these paragraphs written?
- What kinds of appeals are present?
- What kinds of connotations do the paragraphs contain?
- Rewrite the paragraphs for a different audience.

2. Using Writer 4's deductive chain (p. 197), compose an introduction for a paper intended for a specific audience that you select.
3. Classify and evaluate the following as refutations of parts of the arguments of Writers 1 and 2.
   a. Somebody who doesn't read *SN* all the time—and the writer admits he doesn't—isn't an authority on the magazine.
   b. The writer has put *SN* in the wrong category. It isn't a news magazine like *Sports Weekly* or *Modern Sports,* but a feature magazine. So his criteria are wrong.

c. Writer 2 asks fashion magazines to perform the wrong function. They deal, after all, with *fashion,* which by definition is faddish and expensive. They aren't consumer magazines, dedicated to telling you how to get the most out of a buck. So her criticism is irrelevant.

d. Writer 2's argument is probably sour grapes. She's probably one of those dumpy women who can't wear fashionable clothes, so she's ticked off at the fashion mags.

● ASSIGNMENT: The First Version

1. Write a first version of your paper that communicates your focus to your audience.
2. Submit your paper for responses.

● READER RESPONSES

Responding to a persuasive piece of writing involves playing the role of the intended audience in order to tell the writer whether the focus is clear and maintained, whether the appeals work, and whether the organization and style blend to assist the writer in effecting the desired change in the audience. This time be sure to look for the writer's deductive chain. Ask whether the criteria or principles are ones that the audience will accept. Check to see if the writer has developed the linking statement sufficiently. Below is a restatement of the reader guide for persuasive writing.

READER GUIDE

● **Focus**
- What is the writer's focus?
- Is the point of significance a probable judgment?
- Are there any sections of the paper that seem to be out of focus? Which ones?
- Is the focus clearly stated in the introduction?

- **Development**
  - What voice and audience role seem to be at work in the paper?
  - What credibility appeals has the writer used? How effective were they for the audience?
  - What rational appeals has the writer made? Were they persuasive for the audience?
  - What is the writer's deductive chain? Is it valid? Are the criteria acceptable to the audience?
  - How has the writer proved the linking statement?
  - What appeals were made to the audience's attitudes, values, and feelings? Were they effective?

- **Organization**
  - What mode of organization has the writer used? Has it been maintained?
  - Are there sections that seem out of order? If so, what are they?
  - What devices has the writer used to make transitions from one paragraph to the next? Are they effective?
  - Are there places within the paragraphs where the writer moves without transition from one idea or example to another?
  - Does the paper maintain a consistent person, number, and tense?

- **Style**
  - Does the writer use words that help establish credibility and affective appeals?
  - Are there any sentences which need combining? If so, which?
  - Has the writer used any figures of speech? Is the paper marred by clichés?
  - Are there sentences which are too wordy? If so, which?

- **Conventions**
  - Are there mistakes in grammar, spelling, and punctuation?

INSTRUCTOR'S RESPONSE TO WRITER 2

FOCUS

Your focus is announced in the first paragraph and is strictly adhered to in the remainder of the paper. The focus is set up in a deductive chain in paragraph 2, and it serves also as the conclusion of your paper.

DEVELOPMENT

Your paper is well tailored to its audience, your fashion-conscious friends. Especially impressive is your regard for the intelligence of your audience; every generalization is illustrated (and therefore supported) by a series of concrete examples that are stated exactly, without exaggeration.

Those generalizations are subdivisions of the linking statement; the body of the paper consists of a series of criteria developed by illustrative details that violate the criteria, therefore proving that fashion magazines that put a premium on expense, faddishness, and an atypical figure are not practical.

By doing these things, you have satisfied the requirements of the persuasive aim. You have established your credibility by showing your detailed knowledge of the problem, by your concern for the good of the audience, and by your lack of deception. You have, furthermore, established the plausibility of your argument by, as noted, your profuse use of illustrations and by the reasonable standard of judgment that you set up. You have also taken into account the emotional state of your audience by sympathizing with the doubt and discouragement the advice in fashion magazines may engender in the reader.

ORGANIZATION

You have used the evaluative mode for your proof, within the larger persuasive framework, and you have been faithful to your deductive chain throughout; the plan works well. In addition, you have eased the reader from paragraph to paragraph with careful transitions. In the first sentence of paragraph 2, "the career woman and the college woman" echoes the "average American woman" of the preceding sentence. In the first sentence of paragraph 3, "some of these expensive clothes" grows out of the phrase "the price of these formal dresses" in the preceding sentence. Paragraph 4 begins with a phrase summarizing the two preceding paragraphs: "In addition to being faddish and expensive. . . ."

STYLE

The style is adequate but could be improved. You have maintained the third-person point of view throughout the paper. Your diction in the descriptive passage is vivid and accurate. You have wisely stayed away from sarcasm, establishing instead a reasonable, informal tone by choosing words with the proper connotation.

The diction could be improved. You should avoid the sexist term *girl*. The paper is also a bit wordy. Take the first paragraph as an example. The opening phrase, "Every young woman in today's American society," could become "Young American women." In the third sentence, the phrase ". . . are just a few of the many popular celebrities who often appear" is largely unnecessary. Consider the logic of the statement: If you give a list of famous people, then obviously they are "celebrities," and celebrities are by definition popular; and if they represent a "few," then obviously there must be "many." In the fifth sentence, "being as perfect as they would like to be" can be whittled down to one word, "perfect."

CONVENTIONS

You have a good command of the conventions of standard written English. Occasionally your grasp of punctuation slips: "Many popular fashion magazines such as, . . ." ("Many popular fashion magazines, such as. . . ."). But there is no serious problem here.

CLASS EXERCISE

Read the first version of Writer 5, at the end of this chapter. As a class, use the reader guide to respond to the paper.

● ASSIGNMENT

1. Using the reader guide, give a written response to several of your classmates' papers.
2. Share these responses with your classmates.

● REVISING AND EDITING

As we said in Chapter 1, when you have accumulated useful responses, you are ready to rewrite. That involves two kinds of work—revising: improving focus, development, organization, or style; and editing: cleaning up mistakes in grammar, spelling, and punctuation, and making final changes in diction and sentence structure. Below is Writer 2's revised paper.

LET THE READER BEWARE

Young American women cannot help feeling pressed to be attractive, glamorous, and sexy. Many popular fashion magazines such as *Glamour, Seventeen,*

Mademoiselle, Teen, Vogue, and *Harper's Bazaar* portray how the ideal woman should look. Marlo Thomas, Cher, Ellen Burstyn, Cybill Shepherd, Princess Caroline of Monaco, and even Susan Ford model in these magazines.

But can the average American woman really profit by identifying with these people? Fashion magazines that display clothes that are unreasonably priced, faddish, and unsuited to the average woman don't offer very practical advice. The young reader anxiously scanning the latest monthly fashion magazine is frequently discouraged by the outrageous prices of the outfits and is doubtful whether she has the perfect figure needed to wear the latest fashions. Most fashion magazines do not offer practical fashion advice.

With today's inflation, the career woman and the college woman need very practical fashion advice. Both require a variety of clothes that are stylish and reasonably priced. The most recent issue of *Glamour* features outfits consisting of midi skirts or pants, woolen sweaters, patterned shirts, and crazy-colored argyle kneesocks. These outfits are incomplete without such accessories as head-hugging hats, scarves, skinny belts, bangles, earrings, gold necklaces, mod watches, and leather bags. Each outfit, excluding the accessories, costs a staggering figure, considering the variety of clothes necessary for work or school. Evening dresses also come with a high price tag. One issue of *Seventeen* features Susan Ford in formal dresses, the latest spring prom look. What those dresses cost hardly seems worth it for one night.

Some of the expensive clothes are faddish. In two years the hemline has gone from mini to maxi. *Mademoiselle* says that yesterday's classic blazer is being replaced by big bulky sweaters, and platform shoes are giving way to cowboy boots. Some outfits are appropriate for special occasions only—like the bizarre outfit *Seventeen* advised for a wine-tasting party. Today's girl needs reasonable, comfortable, attractive clothing for school, work, and recreation, and these are scarce in the popular fashion magazines.

In addition, the clothes shown are designed for a tall, pencil-thin figure. When one considers how unaverage that kind of figure is, then adds in the fact of plastic surgery—as when a celebrity has her breasts redesigned and her buttocks lifted—and compounds all of that with the magic a camera can perform, one has to wonder what she has to be to wear these clothes well.

The American woman needs advice on how to select clothes that are comfortable, flattering, and affordable. In the popular fashion magazines, she is instead advised to buy clothes that are expensive, faddish, and unbecoming to the average figure. Let the reader—and the buyer—beware.

COMMENTARY

The changes Writer 2 made go beyond the suggestions of the instructor.
The deductive chain remains as the focus, but it has been stripped down to

absolute essentials. In addition, it has been separated from the illustrative material now in the first paragraph to make it stand out. The paper again stays with the deductive chain throughout.

The most obvious change is the removal of any descriptive and illustrative material that does not bear directly on the criteria. The material dealing with the risks of platform shoes, for example, is gone, because "dangerous" is not a criterion in this paper.

The basic organization pattern has not been disturbed: the evaluative mode remains with the deductive chain as the backbone. But the long paragraphs have been broken up to make the organization clearer to the reader. The first paragraph, for example, is there to introduce the topic, establish a connection with the reader, and create interest—but the focus is held back for the second paragraph where it gains prominence.

The style is remarkably improved. The introductory sentences of the developmental paragraphs have been shortened to allow the main idea of the paragraph to emerge easily. A striking concluding statement has been added. The wordiness that characterized the first version is gone.

This version has been carefully edited. The few slips that remain are trivial.

CLASS EXERCISES

1. Revise Writer 5's first version on the basis of the responses you gave in the last exercise.
2. Revise the following sentences in light of the audience and roles indicated.
   a. Student to teacher as teacher: "There are three things wrong with your crummy grading policy."
   b. Student to classmate as viewer of campus movies: "The paucity of aesthetic values in the selections of films for projection in the Union this term are remarkably horrendous."
   c. Businessman to housewife as potential buyer: "Buying that brand of dishwasher was your first mistake."
   d. Assistant professor to dean as judge of promotion: "The accompanying dossier will demonstrate that I am as professionally adept as anything this college has to offer."
3. Make an assessment of the consistent errors of convention (grammar, spelling, or punctuation) that have appeared in your last papers. Then study the sections of Chapter 9 that pertain to those errors.
4. In order to gain more syntactic fluency, ask your instructor to recommend the sentence-combining exercises in Chapter 10 that are most suitable for you.

● ASSIGNMENT: Revising and Editing

1. Guided by the advice you received on the first version, rewrite your paper, revising its major problems and editing for problems of convention.
2. Submit your revision for evaluation.

A WRITER'S PROCESS

Below we present the sequence followed in Writer 5's writing process.

THE GUIDING QUESTION AND POTENTIAL SITUATIONS

My Subject: The *Campus News*

My Values and Expectations
—I expect to have campus news
—I expect the material I read to contain responsible and truthful material

—I expect a newspaper to evaluate its reporters regularly and fire those whose work isn't fit to print

My Subject
—I regularly read the *Campus News*
—several editorials and stories published recently in the *Campus News* have been irresponsible or contained total misrepresentations of facts
—the sports editor and two columnists have continuously published asinine and untrue material with no rebuke

Question: How responsible a newspaper is the *Campus News*?

Potential Situations
—a letter to the editor of the *Campus News*
—an essay for my cousin Nancy, who is a freshman
—an essay for class

EXPLORATION

STATIC VIEW

—the *Campus News* is a college newspaper run by college students
—all reporters and workers are paid

—7 full-time nonstudent staff members
—half-size page
—approx. 18–20 pages every issue
—issued daily
—contains general articles, international, national, state, city, campus news
—editorial page, sports, comics, classified ads, personals, lots of ads, many columnists
—mechanics of the printing are well done
—Editor: Edith Cole
—Some columnists—Ned Brown, Michael Mace, Tom Morton

DYNAMIC VIEW

—The writers and reporters change very rapidly due to promotions and graduation.
—Due to the rapid turnover of personnel the philosophy undergoes minor changes every year.
—From 1983 to 1984 they went from a more citywide emphasis, slighting campus activities, back to more emphasis on student concerns.
—When I first read the paper, I was very impressed that a bunch of college kids could put together such an interesting paper.
—The more I read the paper, the less thrilled I became with it.
—After working with them as director of the campus car race, I lost all respect I had for them.
—My attitude changed to one of almost disgust and anger with the material they print.
—Most of my classmates feel the same way.

RELATIVE VIEW

A Good Newspaper
—emphasizes professionalism in all actions
—prints responsible editorials and focuses on what the audience is interested in

The Campus News
—is at the bottom of the ladder of professional publications
—needs to focus on honesty—no yellow journalism
—needs competent staff that doesn't resort to plagiarism to fill columns
—prints useless garbage that serves to disgust the readers

Contrast/Comparison: Comparing the *Campus News* to the *City Star* is like comparing a quack to a doctor. Not only does the quack look, talk, and act dumber, the quack *is* dumber. And only years of dedication to a high set of goals will ever let the quack begin to approach the same level as the doctor.

Analogy: Reading the *Campus News* every morning before class is like visiting a mental hospital. When you finish with either one or the other, you are filled with pity, a little disgust, and a definite sense of relief that you aren't associated with either.

FOCUS

Subject   **Point of Significance**

Many of the editorials, columns, and news stories of the *Campus News* ——— have been irresponsible and hence fostered growing feelings of distrust and disrespect on the campus.

Situation: I want to write an essay for my cousin Nancy, who is a freshman.

AUDIENCE ANALYSIS

1. Audience: my cousin Nancy—currently a freshman
2. a. Background: Grew up on a farm. Very religious. Active in high school: yearbook, newspaper staff. Very capable and talented at relating to people. Fun-loving; somewhat irresponsible when it comes to things she doesn't enjoy doing. Enjoys physical activity. Diver in high school, gymnast. Very good sense of humor. Enjoys life all the time.
   b. Values: (1) God, (2) friendships, (3) honesty, (4) personal acceptance, (5) high morals, (6) companionship, (7) security, (8) money.
3. Attitude toward the subject: Being on the newspaper staff in high school, she is aware of the problems associated with running a newspaper and the goals the paper must have to maintain its image. She is a very impressionable young woman, and is therefore very open to others' opinions. She reads the *Campus News* but doesn't really understand the other sides of the issues the *Campus News* covers.
4. Specific role: Aspiring journalist hoping to join the staff of the *Campus News*.
5. Analysis of the role
   a. Background: She will know how responsibility and objectivity emerge in journalistic prose, what they look like in print.
   b. Values: She already has the necessary professional values: objectivity, fairness, honesty.
   c. Attitude toward the subject: She will be highly motivated to act on whatever opinion she forms, since she wants to work on the paper.
6. Relational role: Nancy has always been slightly under me. I believe she respects my opinions highly and really tries to do what she thinks I would like her to do. This has become more apparent since she came to college. We have a good family relationship—love, small disagreements, and respect for each other's talents.

ORGANIZATION PLAN

1. Appeals
   a. Credibility: I will show my concern over someone who reads the *Campus News*.

      b. Rational appeal: Deductive chain.
         Principle: Any newspaper that lacks honesty, responsibility, and common sense is not a good newspaper.
         Linking statement: The *Campus News* lacks honesty, responsibility, and common sense.
         Conclusion: The *Campus News* is not a good newspaper.
      c. Affective appeal—Use a lot of connotative language to show disgust over the practices of the *Campus News*.
  2. Organization Plan
    ¶ 1   Introduction: Set vivid scene of someone reading the paper; show my concern; express deductive chain
    ¶ 2   The irresponsible editorials
    ¶ 3   The inflammatory nature of the columns
    ¶ 4   The incompetence of the editor and my conclusion

FIRST VERSION

WRITER 5

THE NEW, NEW JOURNALISM

The muted rustle of turning pages, heard above the whir of the air conditioner and the drone of the lecturer, struck a dissonant chord in my mind. My concentration disrupted, I searched for the source of the disturbance. After several minutes of searching, the flash of a turning white page and the rustle which followed answered my question. A young woman three seats to my left and one row down was reading the day's edition of the *Campus News*. Obviously a freshman, with her bright white topsiders and notebook totally devoid of any stickers, she was enthusiastically scanning Midwestern's simpleminded version of a newspaper. I wasn't sure how many weeks of exposure to the *Campus News* it would take before this young coed would begin to realize just how much of a waste of time it was to read the *Campus News,* but I knew from sharing that attitude with most of my upperclass friends that she would eventually come to her senses. Many of the editorials, columns, and news stories of the *Campus News* have been irresponsible and hence fostered growing feelings of distrust and disrespect on the campus. The *Campus News* is a sad excuse for competent, professional journalism and has been a continued source of embarrassment to the students it supposedly represents.

One of the best ways for a newspaper's readers to discern the values and viewpoints of the paper is for them to read the editorial page. A successful, professional newspaper is one which gains respect through its editorials. Controversial or not, if the readers can rely on the accuracy and honesty of a paper's editorials, they will keep on reading. The obvious bias and manipulation of information which the *Campus News* exhibited in their coverage of the 1980 all-campus elections is just one of the many examples of their ineptness. Their elation over the prospects of a joke student government caused them to totally abuse their power as a medium at Midwestern. Without thought to the widespread ramifications both to current and future students, the *Campus News* editors jubilantly flaunted the names of Ted Vincent and company all over three weeks' worth of newspapers, while almost ignoring the other candidates completely. I only hope that these editors are happy with their fun-loving student body president, for I know of very few others who are willing to claim him as their representative.

The attitudes and opinions of a newspaper can also be viewed through its columns. The ability of a newspaper's columnists to acquire interested daily readers is a major factor in that paper's success. A column attracts attention by either exposing to its readers some insight which inspires or rejuvenates them or by presenting an opinion which is considered controversial but not outlandish. Any column which incites the wrath of a majority of its readers is excessively inflammatory and is a detriment to the paper. Countless times over the past three years, the columnists of the *Campus News* have exceeded these limits of controversy. Most recently this was the case with the David Cordell column concerning the homecoming queen contest. The phrasing and vocabulary used in this column so incited the fury of the students that the paper could focus on little else for the next two weeks. This example is bad enough but the most flagrant abuse of this basic rule of responsible journalism occurred last spring, exactly four days before the running of the Midwestern Grand Prix race. With total disregard for the purpose and importance of the Grand Prix, George Barry, now head sports editor, printed a column in which he stated that due to the lack of competitiveness of the Grand Prix, he would be spending the weekend at Oakwood University watching a truly great sports event, the Tiny 500 bike race. The unbelievable gall and ignorance shown by this columnist in calling an event which raises 40,000 dollars annually for scholarships a worthless waste of time and money and announcing his preference for an event at a rival university which loses 7,000 dollars every year was reason enough for most of the students I know to want to abandon the letter-to-the-editor rebuttal method and simply form a lynch mob. The writings of this columnist were simply inexcusable, but a tremendous amount of the responsibility for this column ever appearing should be placed on the shoulders of the head editor.

The head editor of any newspaper should be the one with the ultimate goals and best interests of the paper in mind. The appearance of and resulting bad feelings from several of the columns and editorials which have appeared in the *Campus News* over the past three years could not possibly have been in the best interests of the paper. Not only the incompetence displayed by the editor in allowing these stories to be printed, but also the failure of the staff to learn from their blatant mistakes is proof enough to me that the paper as a whole has lost sight of its goals. The editors must strive to regain the lost confidence and trust of the students. These people are paid to present a professional, interesting, newsworthy paper to the students of Midwestern. I am certainly not proud to admit that part of my fees has helped to support such a journalistic nightmare.

STUDENT RESPONSE TO WRITER 5

FOCUS

"Many of the editorials, columns, and news stories of the *Campus News* have been irresponsible and hence fostered growing feelings of distrust and disrespect on the campus." Very well maintained throughout.

DEVELOPMENT

Very creative introduction. Excellent, well thought out examples. You can tell that you really know the issue. Good appeal to audience's rationality and need for credibility, but is emotional appeal there? (Maybe in last paragraph—conclusion.) Fits your audience well.

ORGANIZATION

Good, well-developed criteria for a professional newspaper. You used the evaluative mode well. Coherence, person, and tense good.

STYLE

No problems. Very inflammatory writing yourself!

CONVENTIONS

Check the use of commas throughout.

5

WRITING WITH AN EXPOSITORY AIM

In the College World/ Research Papers

In the past chapters, you have searched for meaning in your private world of persons and places and in the public world of the media and issues. Research writing extends your exploration beyond your own experience to the experience of the culture, collected in the library. This treasure is rich with data, experiments, arguments, philosophies, and information, but you need training to locate these valuable resources.

AIMS FOR RESEARCH WRITING

Your aim will direct the kind of research you do, indicating the amount of material you need and even specifying your method of data gathering. Because you usually do research for class at this stage of your career, the instructor often specifies your aim. What are the aims of research writing in the college world?

Some instructors, especially in writing classes, require that you do research to support a *persuasive aim*. Each focus in Chapter 3 could have been further developed by gathering data beyond the writer's personal experience and general reading knowledge. If you do research for a persuasive aim, the amount you need is limited to whatever will convince the audience. You then use these data in conjunction with credibility and emotional appeals to persuade the audience (see pp. 145–150). Emphasis is on the *audience*, not the subject matter.

Research writing sometimes assumes a *pseudopersuasive aim*, when the minimum expectations of the professors are that you will retrieve information familiar to them and organize it in a familiar pattern so that you will persuade them that you understand the subject as they and others like them understand it. Another type of pseudopersuasive aim exists when instructors assign research so that you will persuade them that you know how to do research: that you know how to retrieve the appropriate material, organize it well, and come to known conclusions; that you know your way around the library and can construct formally adequate footnotes and a bibliography. Pseudopersuasive papers approach the status of examinations. Even if your professor has only this minimal expectation, you can plan a more meaningful aim. Because research consumes so much time, why not use the opportunity to discover something more valuable for you and your readers than that you know the research process?

This chapter will demonstrate the use of the *expository aim*, one of the most common for research. The expository aim emphasizes the *subject* rather than the audience. One kind of expository aim is the *informative expository aim*.

● ## The Informative Expository Aim

The informative expository aim relays information *new to the audience*. With an informative aim, you convey information to readers who lack that information. That statement may seem embarrassingly obvious, but the real embarrassment comes when you labor to tell an audience what it already knows. The informative aim is carried out only when you tell the audience something it does not already know. Even in the hothouse atmosphere of college writing, the principle applies. The student writer who cries out in despair, "What can I possibly tell my history professors about the Civil War that they don't already know?" is giving up too soon. Consider two answers to the question. Unless you have an almost supernaturally well-informed instructor, if you had the time and energy you could probably unearth a lot he or she doesn't know about the Civil War, such as (1) the name of the Treasurer of the Confederacy's horse or (2) what it cost in dollars for the Union to take Richmond. The name of the Treasurer's horse is trivia. What it cost the Union to take Richmond, on the other hand, might have had serious effects on the course of the war and its aftermath. You might find time and energy to research that. You generally find time and energy to discover things that you regard as important or know, in the bargain, are important to others you write for. If you have formulated a significant starting question, you will know what to investigate.

● **The Scientific Expository Aim**

The *scientific expository aim* proposes a new hypothesis about a subject, a hypothesis unknown even to those knowledgeable about the subject. This type of expository aim is more challenging for the inexperienced writer because it demands extensive background and research on the subject. Writers of dissertations pursue this aim. It may not be beyond you if you write about a subject on which you are an acknowledged expert. If you wish to use this aim, you must be able to advance and prove a hypothesis that, in addition to acquainting your audience with new information, is, as far as you and your audience know, new to the field. If you think you can manage a scientific aim, confer with your instructor, who will give you special guidance. The rest of this chapter addresses the informative expository aim.

● THE GUIDING QUESTION AND POTENTIAL SITUATIONS

THE SUBJECT

Often topics are assigned for research. In classes in which instructors suggest topics, ask yourself the following question: Do I know enough about any of these topics to prefer one over another? If not, you should do some background reading so that you can decide if a topic is worthy of your scrutiny.

If your instructor does not suggest topics, you may profit from selecting an issue that intrigues you, perhaps the one you wrote about in Chapter 3. Or choose a subject from your intended field of study. Doing research on ideas, theories, movements, or major figures in that field will acquaint you with reference materials in that discipline. You must know enough about a subject to formulate a useful question. No matter how you select your subject, unless you make a personal commitment to it, motivated by your intellectual curiosity, the research writing will not be worthy of your time or attention. Until you can ask a question expressing your awareness of dissonance about the subject, you lack a genuine starting point. Writer 1's first choice of subject was quasars, a topic suggested by the instructor that sounded interesting. But because he knew nothing about the subject, he was unable to formulate a starting question. He instead turned to genetic engineering, a subject that had disturbed him since he saw *The Boys from Brazil.* For his second choice he could articulate his question.

THE GUIDING QUESTION

If you sail into the library with an open-ended topic, you could drift for hours without the compass of a guiding question. A question helps to chart your search for sources, narrowing your selection. The guiding question arises from your dissonance about the subject.

Here are four topics about which writers were able to ask questions.

WRITER 1   **Subject:** Genetic engineering, one of several current research topics suggested in my biology course

My Values and the Subject: In particular, I'm very curious about cloning since I saw *The Boys from Brazil* and saw David Rorvik interviewed on *Today.* He claims his book, *In His Image,* documents how the first human clone was produced. My interest leans toward the current gene transplantation experiments rather than toward research into chromosome structure, though I know the one depends on the other. I'm not sure how cloning fits with my value of not messing with nature.
—treatment of hereditary diseases may become possible through genetic engineering
—could human beings actually control their own evolution?
—patenting of higher life forms because they are genetically engineered for a certain purpose—how far up could this go?
—designing drugs and antibodies to be produced by recombinant bacteria—new hope in cancer treatment

Question: Why is genetic engineering, esp. gene transplantation, so controversial? Can this research interfere with nature?

WRITER 2   **Subject:** Coaching baseball—baseball is my favorite sport. I've coached baseball for seven years at the 9- & 10-year-old level.

My Values and the Subject: Next year I'll be coaching the 11 & 12 year olds and it will be a much different situation. First of all, this is the first level where the kids pitch instead of using a pitching machine, so I'll have to teach pitching for the first time. I'll also have more kids on my team and I may not have an assistant coach, so I'll have to learn how to better organize practices and how to keep the kids from getting bored. Pitching also introduces many to how to play other positions and different strategies (both offensive and defensive).

Questions: What are some different drills, etc., to keep players interested and organized? What different strategies can be used when you use a pitcher (especially defensive, e.g., pickoff plays)? What are some good ways to teach pitching to beginning players?

WRITER 3 **Subject:** Physical therapy and especially the quadriplegic and other spinal injuries

My Values and the Subject: I have always been interested in majoring in physical therapy. I enjoy working with others, esp. handicapped. After reading several articles on new advanced technology in regenerating the nervous system so people with paralysis can some day walk again, I want to look in more depth into this subject:

Question: What new techniques have scientists come up with in the rehabilitation of a paraplegic?

WRITER 4 **Subject:** Breast cancer

My Values and the Subject:

—Most importantly, I am interested in this subject because my own mother has breast cancer. She had a mastectomy at Christmastime and is now receiving chemotherapy treatments.

—I am taking Med Chem this semester, which is a cancer course in which a variety of speakers and doctors on cancer come in each week to speak about everything related to cancer.

—I am also curious about this disease since I am a woman with an increased chance of having breast cancer because my mother has it. Also breast cancer is one of the leading causes of death in women.

—What really interests me is how diet is related to breast cancer—this subject is very much involved in my own career of nutrition, medicine, and biology.

Question: What are the dietary causes of breast cancer? Is sugar a leading initiator of breast cancer?

● **COMMENTARY**

Writer 1 chooses a topic about which he already knows enough to be familiar with some issues. His question will direct his research to the controversial nature of genetic engineering. This topic is very broad but he narrows it to gene transplants, an aspect that will provide more guidance for his research. The second question does not fully articulate his dissonance. Does he mean to indicate that interference with nature is a problem? Or does he simply wish to know whether such interference exists? The question is not clear and will not be helpful in directing his investigation.

Writer 2 chooses a good subject for research because he needs the information for his summer job. He values good instruction and anticipates the difficulties his new job will bring. His questions will narrow his research to a manageable task.

POTENTIAL SITUATIONS

Writing a research paper for a college class sets the type of discourse you will be using—a formal research format, which is explained on pp. 270–272. At the beginning, however, you need to identify the audience for your paper.

THE AUDIENCE

Because your research papers currently are academic, one audience will inevitably be your teachers, but they are not necessarily the primary audience. You may choose to make your classmates or a public group your primary audience. Such a choice, of course, will affect your selection of material, since what will be new information to your classmates may not be new to your teacher.

The primary audience determines the primary characteristics of the paper, and never so clearly as in the academic research paper. If your primary audience is a classmate and your secondary audience your teacher, the teacher will be watching you address the primary audience and will judge you on how well you address the classmates, not the teacher.

Below are the audiences chosen by the four writers.

WRITER 1   —Primary: Biology teacher
—Secondary: Writing instructor

WRITER 2   —Primary: Parents of Little League players and pitching coaches of youth leagues
—Secondary: Writing class

WRITER 3   —Primary: A friend who is paralyzed from the waist down
—Secondary: Writing instructor and class

WRITER 4   —Primary: Kristin, a premed student who will attend med school in the fall
—Secondary: Writing teacher

● **COMMENTARY**

Writer 1 has picked a challenging primary audience in that a college biology teacher can generally be presumed to be well informed on a topic such as genetic engineering. The writer will therefore have to make sure that the information he offers has escaped the teacher. Writer 2 has made his task unnecessarily difficult by choosing two primary audiences instead of one and then selecting very different primary audiences. The knowledge and values of youth league parents are quite different from those of pitching coaches.

CLASS EXERCISES

1. Discuss the subjects, questions, and audiences posed by Writers 3 and 4.
   - Do the writers know enough about the subjects to ask good questions?
   - Do the writers' values and interests warrant choosing these topics?
   - To what kinds of investigations will their questions lead?
   - Are their audience choices good ones?
2. As a class, make a list of subjects that come to your mind as potential topics. Discuss the kinds of things you would need to know to be able to ask good guiding questions. Suggest audiences for these topics.
3. Consider the following cases:

   John heard about germ warfare in his political science class. The subject sounded interesting. Although he was planning a career in dentistry, John thought that the topic of germ warfare might sustain his interest for this paper.

   Erica wrote a term paper in high school on an assigned topic—the causes of the French Revolution. She thought it would make a good choice for her composition class.

   - Discuss whether these topics are good ones for John and Erica.

● ASSIGNMENT: The Guiding Question and Potential Situations

1. Select a topic about which you already have enough interest and knowledge to ask a good question or set of questions.
2. Identify the values and interest you have in the subject.
3. Pose the question(s) you wish to investigate.
4. Identify the audience or audiences for this topic.
5. Submit your work for guidance.

EXPLORATION

Library research extends your exploration beyond the search into your own memory and imagination. Because this work is lengthy and complex, you will profit by following four steps: (1) exploring your own mind, (2) compiling a bibliography, (3) annotating, and (4) notetaking.

EXPLORATORY GUIDE

● **Static View**
- What definitions, ideas, theories, and information on my topic do I already know from experience, class lectures, and reading?
- What subtopics are part of my subject?
- What attitudes do I possess about the subject?
- What information do my audience and I need?

● **Dynamic View**
- What do I know about the history of my subject?
- What causes or effects am I aware of?
- What do I need to trace?

● **Relative View**
- How can I classify my subject now?
- What comparisons can I now make in order to further understand my subject?

EXPLORATION

WRITER 1   GENETIC ENGINEERING

STATIC VIEW

Cloning
—genetic engineering involves replacing one gene by another
—cloning is the production of whole organisms from a single body cell
—Ira Levin's book *The Boys from Brazil* is about a Nazi scientist's plan to clone Hitler
—David Rorvik says his book *In His Image* is about how the first human clone, now a fifteen-month-old boy, was produced

—James Watson, the geneticist, said in a newspaper interview that in no way is Rorvik's claim true
—what other controversy exists about genetic engineering?
—what techniques and processes are involved?

DYNAMIC VIEW

—genetic engineering is a recent development, hardly covered in biology textbooks

Need to Trace:
—when did gene transplants begin?
—who did them?
—what kinds have been done?
—how do they work?
—what do they mean for us?

RELATIVE VIEW

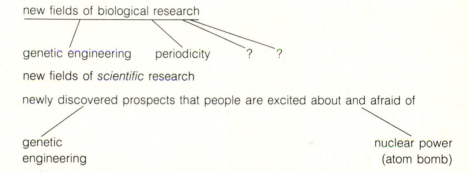

new fields of biological research

genetic engineering   periodicity   ?   ?

new fields of *scientific* research

newly discovered prospects that people are excited about and afraid of

genetic
engineering

nuclear power
(atom bomb)

EXPLORATION

WRITER 3   ### SPINAL INJURIES: STATIC VIEW

—the new technology deals with using a computer-based locomotive system
—one girl has tried this and it kind of worked—but more work needs to be done

Need to Know
—techniques & processes involved
—numbers of victims involved
—has advance on my subject been slow, fast
—number of victims who have tried new technology
—exactly who is involved in finding and experimenting with this new technology
—cost

DYNAMIC VIEW

—spinal cord injuries have been around forever
—have been trying to come up with answers for years

Need to Trace

—how the doctors, biologists, scientists have progressed in this area—what have they found?

RELATIVE VIEW

Classification

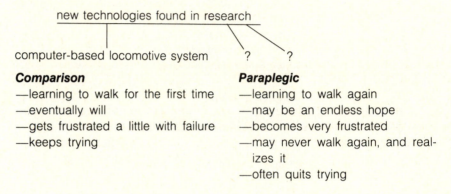

new technologies found in research

computer-based locomotive system   ?   ?

Comparison

—learning to walk for the first time
—eventually will
—gets frustrated a little with failure
—keeps trying

Paraplegic

—learning to walk again
—may be an endless hope
—becomes very frustrated
—may never walk again, and realizes it
—often quits trying

COMPILING A WORKING BIBLIOGRAPHY

After you have recorded your current knowledge, you need a working bibliography (a list of books, journal and newspaper articles, and other sources) to extend your inquiry. Its length should be in proportion to the number of references you need for your paper, because this research process is like an inverted pyramid:

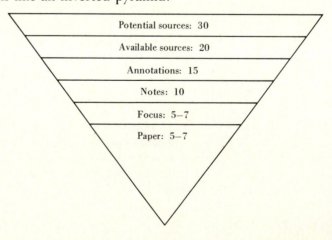

Potential sources: 30

Available sources: 20

Annotations: 15

Notes: 10

Focus: 5–7

Paper: 5–7

In each phase of the process, some sources will be eliminated; therefore, the broader the start (in proportion to the desired length of the research paper), the better. If you gather a substantial working bibliography, you will not have to retrace steps unnecessarily. Because research is so time-consuming, efficiency is important.

Below is a selected list of reference tools that will point you toward the titles for your bibliography.

REFERENCE TOOLS FOR BOOKS

	SOURCES INDEXED
Card Catalog	Books available in the library (see sample card, p. 235)
Cumulative Book Index	New books published each month in English around the world
Essay and General Literature Index	Chapters or sections of books from 1900, especially on social sciences and humanities
National Union Catalogue	Works cataloged by the Library of Congress and contributing libraries

REFERENCE TOOLS FOR PERIODICALS

	SOURCES INDEXED
Readers' Guide to Periodical Literature	Over 160 widely read magazines (see sample entries, p. 236)
International Index 1907–1965; Social Sciences and Humanities Index 1965–1974; Social Science Index 1974–; Humanities Index 1974–	Journals in anthropology, archaeology, art, economics, geography, history, law, literature, music, philosophy, political science, psychology, religion, sociology, theater
Art Index	Journals and museum bulletins on archaeology, architecture, art history, fine arts, industrial design, interior decorating, photography, landscaping
Biology and Agricultural Index	Journals, pamphlets, bulletins in agriculture, geology, ecology, conservation
Catholic Periodical Index	Catholic journals published around the world
Consumers' Index	Journals about consumer interests
Education Index	Periodicals, books, monographs, bulletins, and reports on education: administration, preschool, elementary, exceptional children
Industrial Arts 1913–1957; Applied Science and Technology Index 1958–; Business Periodicals Index 1958–	Journals in accounting, advertising, chemistry, economics, electronics, engineering, management, math, physics, etc.
Music Index	Journals in music and related fields
PMLA Supplement	Journals and books on the major western and some eastern European languages and literatures

REFERENCE TOOLS	
FOR NEWSPAPERS	**SOURCES INDEXED**
New York Times Index	Copy from *The New York Times*
Times Official Index	Copy from *The London Times*
ABSTRACTS	**ITEMS INDEXED**
Abstracts of English Studies	Summaries of articles from English and American journals on literature
Historical Abstracts	Summaries of articles on cultural, economic, intellectual, political, and social history
Sociological Abstracts	Summaries of articles on sociology
Psychological Abstracts	Summaries of articles, books, and dissertations on psychology
DICTIONARIES	**ITEMS INDEXED**
Oxford English Dictionary 1884–1928; Supplements, 1933, 1972 (A–G), 1976 (H–N)	Variant spellings, etymologies, pronunciations, meanings, quotations from English works
Dictionary of American English on Historical Principles	Words originating in America or relating to American history, etymologies, quotations
Dictionary of Americanisms on Historical Principles	Words or expressions originating in the United States, etymologies, quotations
BIOGRAPHIES	**ITEMS INDEXED**
Dictionary of National Biography	Biographies of prominent English people
Dictionary of American Biography	Biographies of prominent Americans
Who's Who	Biographies of prominent living English people
Who's Who in America	Biographies of prominent living Americans
International Who's Who	Brief biographies of prominent people throughout the world
Current Biography	Biographies of living international people
Contemporary Authors	Biographies of novelists, poets, playwrights, etc.
OTHER SOURCES	**ITEMS INDEXED**
Almanacs and Handbooks of Facts	Data, facts, names, dates
Atlases and Gazetteers	Maps, names of towns, cities, mountains, and rivers
Bibliographies	Lists of books on subjects or authors
Concordances and Books of Quotations	Sources and wordings of quotations
Encyclopedias	Introductory and summary articles on topics
Yearbooks	Articles and bibliographies on major topics of that year

Card catalog

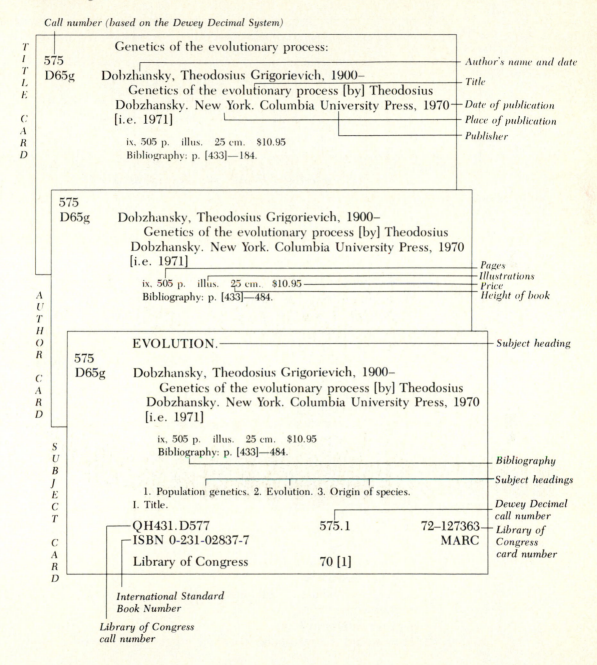

Call number (based on the Dewey Decimal System)

T I T L E C A R D

A U T H O R C A R D

S U B J E C T C A R D

575
D65g
Genetics of the evolutionary process:

Dobzhansky, Theodosius Grigorievich, 1900–
    Genetics of the evolutionary process [by] Theodosius
Dobzhansky. New York. Columbia University Press, 1970
[i.e. 1971]

    ix, 505 p.   illus.   25 cm. $10.95
    Bibliography: p. [433]—184.

Author's name and date
Title
Date of publication
Place of publication
Publisher

575
D65g   Dobzhansky, Theodosius Grigorievich, 1900–
    Genetics of the evolutionary process [by] Theodosius
Dobzhansky. New York. Columbia University Press, 1970
[i.e. 1971]

    ix, 505 p.   illus.   25 cm. $10.95
    Bibliography: p. [433]—484.

Pages
Illustrations
Price
Height of book

EVOLUTION.

575
D65g   Dobzhansky, Theodosius Grigorievich, 1900–
    Genetics of the evolutionary process [by] Theodosius
Dobzhansky. New York. Columbia University Press, 1970
[i.e. 1971]

    ix, 505 p.   illus.   25 cm. $10.95
    Bibliography: p. [433]—484.

    1. Population genetics. 2. Evolution. 3. Origin of species.
I. Title.

QH431.D577   575.1   72–127363
ISBN 0-231-02837-7   MARC

Library of Congress   70 [1]

Subject heading

Bibliography
Subject headings
Dewey Decimal
call number
Library of
Congress
card number

International Standard
Book Number

Library of Congress
call number

Readers' Guide to Periodical Literature

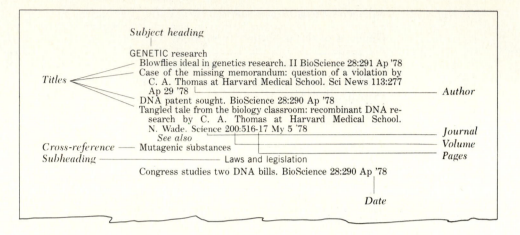

● **Using the Reference Tools**

For the most efficient use of these reference tools,

1. Determine the guides that will be most useful by checking the list cited earlier, which indicates the kinds of subjects indexed.
2. Start with current volumes and move backward as far as time permits.
3. Record promising titles on separate slips (see sample bibliography cards, pp. 237–239).
4. After using *all* the guides time permits, arrange slips by journal (e.g., all *Time* articles together).
5. Check your library's list of journals or the card catalog.
    a. Record the call numbers of those in the library.
    b. Set aside the journal or book titles *not* in the library.

CLASS EXERCISES

1. What reference tools would you consult for a bibliography on the five subjects below?
   • Arab-Israeli conflict
   • open classrooms
   • themes in William Faulkner's novels
   • white-collar crime
   • preservatives in food
2. How would the reference tools you suggested be useful?

ANNOTATING

After you have determined which titles are available in the library, you need to sort out the sources that deserve close reading and notetaking.

Because time is a determining factor in your research, a careful skimming of the available sources will help you to identify those most valuable for data and ideas. If you, instead, start taking notes on the first article you have struggled to locate on the shelves, you may waste your efforts taking notes on what turns out later to be the least useful title. As a consequence, time may run out for the best ones.

Annotating involves:

1. grouping titles from the same journals together so that you may locate them more quickly.
2. skimming the articles or books to determine
   a. aspects of topics.
   b. depth of treatment and amount of documentation.
   c. authority of the author.
   d. focus of the writer.
3. recording impressions on bibliography slips.

Step 1 saves needless wandering in the stacks. Step 2 can be done quickly by reading the first and last paragraphs and skimming the subtitles and footnotes. Step 3 aids your memory after you have canvassed the entire list. Below are Writer 1's annotated bibliography cards, on which he intends to take notes as a basis for his paper. He has selected these cards from a potential pool of twenty-eight titles by eliminating some that were not available in the library and rejecting others he deemed superficial or irrelevant.

● **Bibliography Cards**

Writer 1's working bibliography cards are illustrated below.

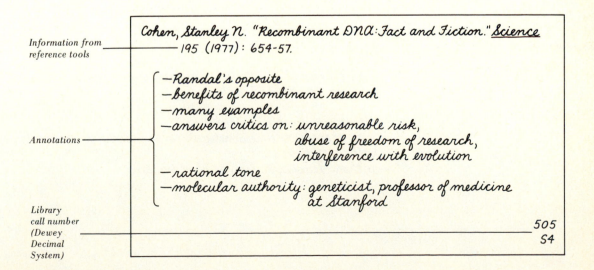

Information from reference tools — Cohen, Stanley N. "Recombinant DNA: Fact and Fiction." *Science* 195 (1977): 654-57.

Annotations —
—Randal's opposite
—benefits of recombinant research
—many examples
—answers critics on: unreasonable risk,
          abuse of freedom of research,
          interference with evolution
—rational tone
—molecular authority: geneticist, professor of medicine
        at Stanford

Library call number (Dewey Decimal System) — 505 S4

Galston, Arthur W. "Here Come the Clones." <u>Natural History</u>, Feb. 1975, 72-75.

    new genetic engineering techniques:
        cloning, nuclear transplantation, chromosomal
        insertion, single-gene insertion
    detailed example of gene insertion to cure genetic disease
    fairly technical
    author: teaches biology at Yale

                                               570.5
                                             N213

Grobstein, Clifford. "The Recombinant-DNA Debate." <u>Scientific American</u>, July 1977, 22-33.

    policy change we face with recomb. research:
    —need for—research to determine risks;
            —central research facilities;
            — policies for commercial use, international
                research and application
    —careful discussion
    —author: credentials unknown

                                               605
                                             S3

McDougall, Kenneth J. "Genetic Engineering: Hazard or Blessing?" <u>Intellect</u> 104 (1976): 528-30.

    —definition, genetic engineering
    —gene therapy to cure genetic diseases—state of research
    —rather technical
    —author: teaches biology at U. of Dayton

                                             370.5
                                         S4

McWethy, Jack. "Science's Newest 'Magic'— A Blessing or a Curse?"
U.S. News and World Report, 12 July 1976, 34-35.

—overview article
—debate over the safety and value of recomb. research
—some possible benefits and risks
—author: assoc. editor for *U.S.N. + W.R.*

320.5
Un3

Randal, Judith. "Life from the Labs." *The Progressive*, March 1977,
16-20.

Risks
       —within the research
       —external from: —universities
                        —government
                        —private industry
                        —private individuals
       —many examples
       —some ideas for reducing the dangers
       —loss of info.
       —author: covers health and science for *N.Y. Daily
           News*, nat. syndicated

051
C93

Rivers, Caryl. "Cloning: A Generation Made to Order." *Ms.*, June
1976, 51.

—1st clonal frog, 1968
—human cloning:
       —state of research,
       —consequences of it
—author: cred. unknown

1161101
M55

CLASS EXERCISES

1. Study the annotated working bibliography cards of Writer 1.
   - Which articles promise to be most useful? Why?
   - What kinds of annotations has he made?
   - What bibliographic information was recorded?
2. Annotate the following article from page 65 of the November 15, 1982 issue of *Time*.

ARTIFICIAL GENES: BIOTECH COMES TO THE DRUGSTORE

Skeptics have wondered whether genetically engineered drugs might become the synfuels of the 1980s, crippled by uneconomical costs and uncertain usefulness. Now there is early evidence that the skeptics may be wrong. Genentech, an industry leader, licensed for sale a gene-spliced substance that has just become the first such medicine ever approved for human use by the U.S. Food and Drug Administration. Says Dr. John Potts, professor at Harvard Medical School and chief of medical services at Massachusetts General Hospital: "This is really a landmark because it is the first practical development of a useful medicine by new techniques."

What Genentech has done is to develop the first insulin drug that is made with a synthetic duplicate of human genes. Called Humulin, it differs from insulin products now on the market, all of which are made from cells extracted from animals, particularly cattle. Humulin can be used to treat the approximately 8% of the world's 70 million diabetics (including 10.3 million in the U.S.) who are allergic to the animal product and have previously had to seek more complex treatments with other drugs like steroids.

Yet Humulin represents only a small advance for an American industry that has produced scant profits for its backers and worldwide sales of just $25 million. Another form of human insulin, made conventionally through chemical processes by Denmark's Novo Industri, has been on the market in Great Britain since June. Though Humulin's cost will decline as production runs increase, it will initially be twice as expensive as animal-based insulin and its eventual market is limited, no more than $20 million.

Since Humulin has been licensed to giant Eli Lilly & Co. for production and sale as a nonprescription drug, Genentech stands to make at most 10% of any profits. Says Analyst Marilyn Hill of Arthur D. Little in Cambridge, Mass.: "Royalties and fees are not going to make these companies a big success. Genentech still has to show that it can develop its marketing clout with its own products." Investors apparently agree. Although Genentech's stock ran up from $33 a share to $46 in the weeks preceding the announcement, it is well below the fantastic $89 it briefly hit when shares were first issued in October 1980. Last week Genentech reported a loss of $1.2 million during the third quarter, on sales of just $7.2 million.

Genetic engineering is still undergoing the shakeout that afflicts any young industry, especially one that has attracted some 300 new entrants in the past two years. Bethesda Research Laboratories of Maryland had to narrow its focus last year after trying too many research efforts at once. To conserve $130 million in capital, Cetus Corp. of Berkeley, Calif., one of the industry's largest firms, shut down five of 13 major projects this past summer and ended probes into several other costly areas. A number of companies have failed only a year or two after their start-up. Southern Biotech of Tampa filed for bankruptcy in June, after issuing $5.5 million in stock, because of "an unsuccessful research project."

Questions also remain about the miracle drug interferon. Genentech and Biogen of Switzerland have each developed a multipurpose form of the drug that is now being tested on humans and could be on the market by late 1984. So far, interferon is showing good results against a variety of noncancerous tumors but less promise against cancer. Says Biogen Chairman Dr. Walter Gilbert, a Nobel prizewinner: "The industry has proved it can make these drugs in commercial amounts. Whether they are useful against diseases like cancer and herpes, or even the common cold, depends on these medical tests."

Still, gene splicing shows promise of living up to most of the extravagant claims made by its supporters, who expect it to reap sales of $25 billion by the year 2000. One of the most encouraging signs is the quick action by the FDA, which licensed Humulin after just five months of testing, one of the quickest approvals in the agency's history. Genentech President Robert Swanson said last week that his company expects to market a number of other new products in the next few years, including an agent that dissolves blood clots and could be useful in treating heart patients, and a human growth hormone that has successfully been tested for more than a year and could be available within twelve months to treat children afflicted with dwarfism.

NOTETAKING

Notetaking begins with the close reading of the articles you have selected as important. The ultimate quality of your research paper is often determined at this stage in which you record ideas and information. Several powers are important here:

1. understanding and interpreting the source accurately
2. passing the information through the sieve of your own mind to isolate the relevant material
3. recording the material
    a. without distorting it
    b. without "lifting" the syntax and diction of the writer

Taking notes on cards will help you to develop these powers, allowing you to put similar information together on the same card, a later help in organizing. Notice important features of the notetaking process:

1. The information should be sorted out and organized according to *key words* chosen by you.
2. The information should be recorded in your own words, unless put in quotation marks.
3. The data should be recorded economically.
4. The arrangement should allow you to review the ideas quickly.

● **Sample Notecards**

Writer 1's sample notecards are shown below.

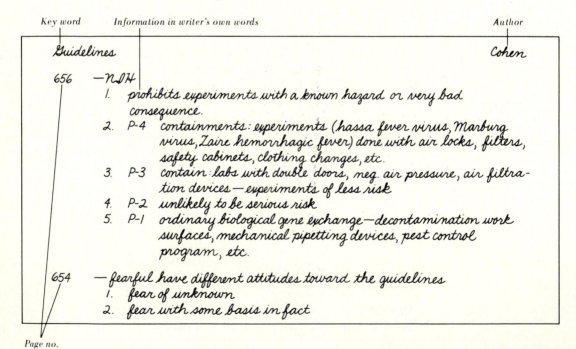

Key word   Information in writer's own words   Author

Guidelines   Cohen

656   —NIH
         1. prohibits experiments with a known hazard or very bad consequence.
         2. P-4   containments: experiments (hassa fever virus, Marburg virus, Zaire hemorrhagic fever) done with air locks, filters, safety cabinets, clothing changes, etc.
         3. P-3   contain: labs with double doors, neg. air pressure, air filtration devices—experiments of less risk
         4. P-2   unlikely to be serious risk
         5. P-1   ordinary biological gene exchange—decontamination work surfaces, mechanical pipetting devices, pest control program, etc.

654   —fearful have different attitudes toward the guidelines
         1. fear of unknown
         2. fear with some basis in fact

Page no.

Advantages   *Cohen*

655   1. advance of fundamental scientific and medical knowledge (structure and function of genes, plasmids)
      2. practical applications (nearer)
        — construction of bacterial strains that can produce antibodies and hormones

656   — new types of vaccines – not disease-carrying *E. coli*
        — grain without nitrogen fertilizer
        — pollution-free energy from water

657   "We must then examine the 'benefit' side of the picture and weigh the already realized benefits and the reasonable expectation of additional benefits, against the vague fear of the unknown that has in my opinion been the focal point of this controversy."

Direct quotation taken because it sums up author's position.

● **COMMENTARY**

The key words fit the information collected on each card. The writer has recorded the material concisely, using only necessary words of his own. He has also been careful to note the pages from which the information was taken.

CLASS EXERCISES

1. Read the following article from the March 1977 issue of *The Progressive*—one of Writer 1's sources.
2. Compare the sample notecards on pp. 252–254 with the article.
   - How accurately has the writer recorded the information?
   - What key words have been used? Why?
   - What other facts or ideas could have been taken?
   - How concisely has the material been recorded?

LIFE FROM THE LABS: WHO WILL CONTROL THE NEW TECHNOLOGY?

by Judith Randal

As recently as five years ago, almost anyone who suggested that the species barrier could be broken much more easily and at far less cost than it took to split the atom would probably have been regarded as a science fiction buff at best, and more probably as a nut.

Today this is no longer fantasy. At the very time, ironically, when thousands of species are threatened by man or already extinct, the tools that will cause entirely unrelated species to exchange hereditary material have become a reality. What now confronts us is the problem of weighing the potential benefits of this new technology against the potential risks—without sacrificing the freedom of scientific inquiry or endangering the world on a previously unimagined scale.

Interspecies hybrids are nothing new, but the issue of such unions—the mule is an example—have always been distinguished by an inability to reproduce. Moreover, those forms of life—bacteria and blue-green algae—which do not have distinct cell nuclei and those which do, have always been autonomous biological kingdoms whose boundaries could not be crossed. With the discovery of enzymes that will fit ordinary bacteria with the genes of any plant, animal, insect, or virus a scientist may choose, and with the evidence that generation after generation of germs will then continue to express the characteristics conveyed by the transplants, such distinctions are fading fast.

As they fade, we suddenly face the prospect that man will be moving genes back and forth across boundaries that many millions of years of evolution have set in place. That prospect now engages the scientific community in a furious debate—one of which most Americans are still unaware, while the rest wonder which biologists to believe.

The dilemma of balancing scientific risks and benefits is, of course, a familiar one. In the case of nuclear energy, both the risks and the benefits are at least familiar and more or less quantifiable. And when physicists have created new elements, they have done so with the knowledge that their behavior will be highly predictable. By contrast, even the experts can only guess what will happen when germs are provided with exotic genetic material and what trade-off this new technology will require. And whereas radiation generally decays, novel microbes might multiply indefinitely in a hospitable environment.

Last June, the National Institutes of Health (NIH) published voluntary guidelines which, in effect, sort proposed genetic experiments according to their estimated risk and then define those which are potentially so hazardous that they should be deferred pending further developments, or completely avoided.

Some biologists, including Nobel laureates David Baltimore and James Dewey Watson of the Massachusetts Institute of Technology and the Cold Spring Harbor Laboratory on Long Island, respectively, are satisfied that the NIH guidelines provide adequate safeguards against the escape into our midst of bacteria that might prove to be drug-resistant. There are others, within and without the Nobel ranks, who think such an "Andromeda Strain" scenario is overblown, and who protest that the NIH has imposed needless limitations on scientific inquiry.

But there are still others—and they, too, include a Nobelist, Professor George Wald of Harvard—who are not at all convinced. They point out that accidents have happened under the best-regulated scientific circumstances, and they would, therefore, have the work go forward only in highly secure facilities and sparsely populated places—if at all.

The bacteria that receive gene transplants are called DNA recombinants. DNA, or deoxyribonucleic acid, is the molecule of heredity (except for some viruses). In the course of the experiments, segments of the DNA of two or more species are annealed. The novel micro-organisms created in this process offer insights into biological mechanisms that are not otherwise easily obtained, thus arousing the scientific curiosity of those who long to unravel the mysteries of cancer and other forms of serious disease. If, indeed, these organisms could be counted on to remain laboratory curiosities—and if reputations and money were not riding on them—there would be little reason to give gene-juggled microbes a second thought.

But this is not the case. In at least one university biology department, opposition to the experiments is already construed as an attempt to block scientific progress. Graduate students who balk at using the technique may find it hard to earn a degree or to find a post at the laboratory of their choice. At the same time, both academia and industry have correctly perceived that programming bacteria to turn out quantities of valuable chemicals and drugs is the stuff of which fortunes may soon be made. Today's fairly modest research project could be the basis of tomorrow's big business deal.

Last October, for example, Dr. Herbert Boyer of the University of California, San Francisco, was a leader of two research groups that reported they had successfully used recombinant technology to induce the production of beta galactosidase, a milk-digesting protein, in *Escherichia coli,* a species of bacteria whose usual habitat is the human or animal intestine. In this case, the protein was one that *E. coli* are capable of producing anyway. But Boyer was quick to point out that "we've gone out of the area of basic science into the area of practical application" and to predict that bacteria could be induced to become factories for the manufacture of insulin and other medications and chemicals.

What is important here is that the University of California [and the California] Institute of Technology, which was also represented on the Boyer team, lost no time in applying for patents on the technique. This means that, while the work was done with NIH funding and therefore adhered to the NIH guidelines, the income generated by it in the future could free both institutions—or for that matter any institution in a like position—from such constraint.

Scientists and the NIH Guidelines. Universities, it is true, might be reluctant to incur the displeasure of the NIH. And an NIH regulation (which has never been used) would permit the agency to withhold funding from other projects should a grantee or contractor defy the recombinant guidelines. Nonetheless, the NIH might well be reluctant to discipline the research community. And as universities become more pressed for funds, they are being driven to engage in projects that may become ethically dubious, though financially rewarding.

To be fair, there probably would have been no safety guidelines had it not been for the scientists themselves. In mid-1974, eleven prominent molecular biologists—Baltimore and Watson among them—called for and obtained a two-year moratorium on what seemed to be the riskiest gene grafts. It would seem, then, that since scientists initiated and designed the guidelines, they would also have a strong stake in complying with them.

But moral considerations do not necessarily prevail—especially when a recent Federation of American Scientists survey disclosed that 10 percent of those responding thought the guidelines needlessly strict, and when compliance is entirely voluntary.

Under the NIH guidelines, laboratories engaged in the least potentially dangerous studies are designated P-1 (P standing for precautionary). Those somewhat up the line of potential risk are called P-2, and so on. P-4 laboratories have the most elaborate precautions to prevent the contamination of personnel or the escape of bacteria into the environment, and are the only facilities where the potentially most hazardous experiments are sanctioned.

Laboratories at Fort Detrick, Maryland, built for the Pentagon's now-abandoned germ warfare program and now used by the National Cancer Institute, house a P-4 facility. And the multimillion dollar lunar-receiving laboratory at the Johnson Space Center in Houston, designed for the isolation and containment of those "moon germs" that never materialized, would also qualify as P-4. So does the laboratory on Plum Island, off the eastern tip of Long Island, which the Department of Agriculture maintains for the study of hoof-and-mouth disease.

E. coli bacteria are the focus of most of the experiments conducted to date because this species of germ is the most thoroughly studied, and therefore the best understood. Many scientists would feel more comfortable working with a species that does not infect man, though considerable steps have been taken to disarm *E. coli*.

A special strain, K-12, is used; as far as is known, K-12 will not take up residence in people. And enfeebled substrains of K-12 have been developed that are dependent on an array of special requirements—the presence of certain nutrients, ultraviolet light, and extreme temperatures, for instance—in order to survive or reproduce. The theory is that the needs of such enfeebled strains can be supplied only in the laboratory. One scientist has aptly described the weaknesses that have been bred into the K-12 substrains as "messiah genes."

All this sounds reassuring—more than the facts may warrant. The behavior of bacteria is unpredictable, and the estimates of risk are necessarily crude. And the enzymes that permit scientists to transplant genes from one species to another do not act directly on the bacterial recipients, but on go-betweens. This multiplies the possibilities that something may go wrong.

These go-betweens are viruses known as phages, which naturally infect germs, or tiny, free-floating circles of hereditary material called plasmids, which do the same. Some scientists worry about what might happen if gene-shuffled phages or plasmids came into contact with bacteria that—unlike the enfeebled K-12 substrains—had not been designed to commit suicide in the event of their escape to the outside world.

Exchanges of plasmids, in particular, are known to occur in nature between strains and even between species of bacteria. Proponents of genetic research generally argue that if it happens in nature, there is probably nothing to fear. Critics are not so sure; their concern is that if sufficiently large numbers of these deviants were rapidly introduced, the situation could get out of hand.

Dr. Stanley Falkow, a microbiologist at the University of Washington in Seattle and an expert on *E. coli*, has questioned the wisdom of introducing certain plasmids even into enfeebled strains of K-12. On the basis of studies he has conducted on calves, he has advised the NIH recombinant DNA Advisory Committee that "it may not be too farfetched to suggest that some DNA recombinant molecules could profoundly affect the ability of this *E. coli* strain to survive and multiply in the gastrointestinal tract." Another of Falkow's worries is that a recombinant might somehow acquire the ability to reproduce in water, and so pose a massive environmental threat. Whatever the present hazards of *E. coli*—and it already causes most urinary tract infections and is dangerous to many who are chronically ill—it cannot ordinarily multiply in the presence of oxygen.

These concerns aside, the chemicals that form the basis of the new technology are, in principle, precision instruments that cut specific segments of DNA from one type of cell to be transplanted into others. When they are prepared by sophisticated scientists experienced in recombinant experimentation, restriction enzymes may or may not behave predictably. Such variability contributes to the inherent risk.

The Dangers That Amateurs Could Pose. At present, anyone can buy restriction enzymes off the shelf or by mail from such suppliers as Miles Laboratories, and there is nothing to prevent the amateur from dabbling in the technology, nor is there any point in licensing the production of restriction enzymes, since anyone who knows anything about biochemistry can concoct his own from readily available ingredients.

A few years ago, a Massachusetts Institute of Technology undergraduate, having read published reports, demonstrated on paper that he knew how to build an atom bomb. Since DNA recombinant work requires only a meager investment in equipment and can be carried out in limited space, a similarly resourceful high school student could conceivably collect the necessary materials and then simply turn the experimental brew loose on the general environment.

DNA recombinants, like radiation, would not make their presence quickly known to the senses should they escape. They might well prove impossible to trace. Geiger counters will detect radiation; an equivalent device for detecting bacteria has not been invented yet.

Other possible hazards in the process are even more troubling. A Government interagency committee formed by White House directive "to review Federal policy on the conduct of research involving new forms of life" reports that the National Science Foundation, the Energy Research and Development Administration, and the Department of Defense have agreed to observe the NIH guidelines and that the Agriculture Department has indicated its probable willingness to go along. But neither the Occupational Health and Safety Administration, the Center for Disease Control, nor the Environmental Protection Agency—all of which might logically be involved—has assumed any oversight responsibilities for recipients of research grants or contracts, and the NIH, too, has demurred. Such loopholes raise the possibility of reckless mischief.

Furthermore, no one knows how much research is in progress. There is reason to wonder whether the Central Intelligence Agency or its equivalents abroad might not secretly carry out experiments their governments officially decried. And there is, as in nuclear science, the possibility of exploitation by lunatics or terrorists.

There is also the inevitability of exploitation by U.S. private industry. The Pharmaceutical Manufacturers Association, the trade group to which the largest drug firms belong, for example, has told the Senate health subcommittee that it generally agrees with the NIH guidelines, but that its members will want to make larger quantities of DNA recombinants than is permitted under the rules that apply to academic researchers.

Meanwhile, seven of these firms—Miles Laboratories, Eli Lilly, Hoffmann-LaRoche, Merck Sharpe and Dohme, Abbott Laboratories, Upjohn, and Pfizer—are already at work with recombinants or are gearing up. There are other such firms that do not belong to the PMA; because they are generally smaller and less visible, they are perhaps even more likely to cut corners in striking out on their own.

What Role for Private Enterprise? The drug industry is only one of many that has sniffed potential profits in this new technology. While the public interest may dictate full disclosure about recombinant research, private enterprise operates on the principle that if the costs of bringing experimental findings to commercial realization are to justify the investment, trade secrets must be kept.

Thus, at a Commerce Department meeting last November at which several large firms were represented, the consensus was that the private sector should publicly register its projects, but let it go at that. While nuclear reactors must be licensed before they are built, any corporation wishing to build a containment facility for microbes can simply go ahead with no questions asked. In fact, should it decide to perform recombinant experiments at even the P-3 or P-4 level without proper safeguards, it could do that, too.

Dr. Ronald Cape, who heads a biologically oriented California firm called Cetus and who attended the Commerce Department meeting, said later that there was agreement that "the registry would discourage undergound or fly-by-night operations because anybody who decided to go into this field would have to stand up and be identified." But Cape obviously had some misgivings, since he also wondered aloud whether this type of enterprise should be in the profit-making sector at all.

Cetus is now doing nothing with recombinants and, according to Cape, is not in a rush to enter the field: "If we go into the business at all, we'll start off with the safe biological containment kinds of things." But the company numbers among its senior consultants molecular biologist Joshua Lederberg, a Stanford University Nobel Prize winner, who is on record as believing the NIH guidelines are too strict.

Lederberg is not the only academic to find himself in a somewhat ambiguous position. One of the most eloquent critics of the entire recombinant movement is Professor Robert Sinsheimer, chairman of the biology division at the California Institute of Technology, who regards the NIH guidelines as "sorely inadequate." Yet people at Caltech are engaged in this work, and the institution, which already has a P-2 laboratory, is building a P-3 facility. Sinsheimer says he would not want to be associated with an institution where a department chairman had veto power over his subordinates. And he doubts the public would benefit if the experiments were halted at Caltech while they proliferated elsewhere. As he sees it, this would be as meaningless as having a nation unilaterally disarm.

Even if we were to ignore or resolve the danger of catastrophic accident, the emerging genetic technology would raise formidable and frightening problems—many of them similar to, but much more acute than, those already posed by other scientific developments. The production and promotion of antibiotics, and their consequent overuse, has already led to the existence of drug-resistant germs. Now it is being suggested that bacteria can be programmed to manufacture antimicrobials more cheaply. It is not difficult to envision a new surge of highly promoted drugs—and a new health hazard.

General Electric has applied for patents on a technique which will use plasmids to confer on one strain of pseudomonas bacteria some genes endowing it with the capacity to digest more, if not all, of the various hydrocarbons that constitute crude oil. The new species could obviously prove a godsend for cleaning up oil spills. But what would happen if it found its ways into petroleum storage tanks, pipelines, or the wing tanks of a commercial jet aircraft in flight? And what will be the impact on the ocean environment itself? No one knows.

After our experience with antibiotics, pesticides, and many other scientific and technological "advances," we have surely learned that the remedies we devise often create new and acute ailments. An urgent question must, therefore, be asked: Can't at least some of what seems attainable through DNA recombinants be achieved by other, safer means? Perhaps the short-run cost of such alternatives might be higher, but the long-run savings might be immense.

Few people, unfortunately, are even aware that such questions must be raised. But some rearguard actions are being fought. Harvard University, for example, is eager to remodel a floor of its 40-year-old biology building into a P-3 (moderate risk) recombinant research facility, and it has received the approval of the NIH and the promise of some $285,000 of the agency's money. Work has already begun. But some members of Harvard's biology department—notably George Wald and Ruth Hubbard—are convinced that the insect-ridden structure, which by the University's own admission is also subject to floods, is no place for such an endeavor.

When their objections caught the ear of Cambridge's mayor, Albert E. Velluci, and the Cambridge City Council, a classic town-and-gown dispute ensured. Hearings were held, and last July a three-month "good faith" moratorium (which has since been extended) was imposed on P-3 and P-4 experiments at both Harvard and the Massachusetts Institute of Technology.

A citizens' review board appointed at the time has been looking into the situation. Chaired by a former mayor who owns a heating oil firm, the four men and four women—whose occupations range from nurse, social worker, physician, and structural engineer to professor of urban policy and community activists—recommended in January that the experimentation be permitted to resume. But in the belief that "a predominantly lay citizen group can face a technical scientific matter of general and deep public concern, educate itself appropriately to the task, and reach a fair decision," the panel also agreed that the NIH guidelines do not go far enough, and made further safety recommendations of its own. Among these is a proposed city ordinance that would automatically declare any research not in strict conformity to safety requirements to be a public health hazard.

The Cambridge Compromise.   The Cambridge review board obviously arrived at a political compromise. But its report made an essential point: "Knowledge, whether for its own sake or for its potential benefits to humankind, cannot serve as a justification for introducing risks to the public unless an informed citizenry is willing to accept those risks."

But not every town can be expected to react like Cambridge, and there are limitations to the local-option approach. Scientists, like industries, can readily move on if they don't like what they find in one place. Having already complied with a self-imposed moratorium, recombinant proponents are not likely to stand still indefinitely for what they regard as undue interference. They are, in general, an impatient lot, further pressed by what they feel is a need to make up for lost time in the face of competition from abroad.

Scientists of many nations are eager to participate in recombinant research, and some are already doing so with far less disclosure than there has been here. Britain's Official Secrets Act means, for example, that we may know less about what has been going on in British labs than we do about what has been happening in ours. Further, if U.S. firms cannot experiment at home, nothing can stop them from going abroad.

The new genetic technology is seductive—not only because it is cheap, fast, easy, and potentially lucrative, but also because it is intellectually appealing and holds out the promise of impressive benefits in spite of the admitted risks. The opportunity has probably passed, if it ever existed, to impose a total ban on the work—and any such ban would be breached. If there is one nightmare that biologists on all sides of the issue share, it is that Federal legislation might be drawn so inflexibly that it would impede both the progress and the safety of the research.

How, then, will the inevitable compromises be drawn? By making the research unpatentable? By insisting that all experiments be conducted in regional Federal facilities which industry would have to support in order to qualify for profits from the discoveries? By establishing an intricate system of licensure and environmental monitoring?

It is difficult to make even an educated guess. But it is clear that whatever is to be done must have the careful and immediate attention of scientists, and of the rest of us. A population explosion among microbes can occur in a matter of days, or even hours.

Definitions   *Randal*

17—DNA recombinants: bacteria that receive gene transplants

 —DNA: deoxyribonucleic acid: molecule of heredity

 —E. coli: bacteria whose habitat is in human or animal intestines

18—K-12: strain of E. coli not in humans

18—phages: viruses that infect germs called plasmids (free-floating circles of hereditary material)

Controversy   *Randal*

16—David Baltimore and James Dewey Watson
      (MIT Nobel Laureates)—adequate guidelines

 —George Wald (Harvard)—guidelines not a safeguard

20—Joshua Lederberg (Stanford, Nobel Prize)—guidelines
                                                    too strict

 —Robert Singheimer (Cal. Inst. of Tech.)—guidelines sorely
                                                    inadequate

 —George Wald and Ruth Hubbard—against Harvard's renovation
      of 40-yr.-old P-4 facility

 —Cambridge City Council: moratorium on P-3 and P-4 at Harvard and MIT

Guidelines (NIH)   Randal

18 — 1974: eleven molecular biologists (incl. Baltimore + Watson) made two-
              year moratorium on risky gene grafts

18 — survey of Fed. of Amer'. Scientists: 10% — guidelines were too strict

  — NIH   — levels of danger: P-1 to P-4 (precautionary)
              — P-4 must take precautions of contamination
              — P-4 places: — Fort Detrick (Pentagon's germ warfare);
                              — Johnson Space Center, Houston (moon germs);
                              — Plum Island, Long Island (Hoof + mouth)
18 — profits could cause university to defy NIH guidelines

19 — no agency will oversee use — not
              — Occupational Health + Safety Admin.,
              — Environmental Protection Agency
              — Center for Disease Control

Dangers/Private Enterprise   Randal

19 — Pharmaceutical Manufacturers Assoc.: wants to make larger quantities
              than NIH guidelines (Miles Lab, Eli Lilly, Abbot Labs, Upjohn)

   — smaller companies are greater threat: "cut corners"

   — trade secrets — against the public right to know

   — bacteria to manufacture antimicrobials might lead to drug overuse

   — GE plasmids (to clean oil spills) might get into petroleum storage
        tanks, pipelines, wing tanks of jets; threat also to ocean
        environment

Dangers/Academic   *Randal*

17 —*graduate students who fear techniques risk diploma and lose lab positions, jobs*
—*scientists may take risks to improve their reputations*

18 —*milk-digesting protein* ⟶ *into E. coli* ⟶ *manufacture of insulin* ⟶ *patent* ⟶ *threat to general research*

18 —*behavior of bacteria unpredictable; deviants in nature but if too many too fast* ⟶ *they may get out of control*

—*enzymes act on go-betweens (phages); if phages contact bacteria, E. coli may survive and multiply in intestines (Dr. Stanley Falkow, microbiologist, U. of Wash.)*

18 —*if recombinants multiply in water* ⟶ *environmental threat*

● ### Notetaking and Plagiarism

Good notetaking also helps the writer later to avoid *plagiarizing*, the undocumented use of a source's ideas or style. Several forms of plagiarism are illustrated below, demonstrating *unacceptable* ways of incorporating ideas from a source into a paper.

The original passage from Randal's article:

> The dilemma of balancing scientific risks and benefits is, of course, a familiar one. In the case of nuclear energy, both the risks and benefits are at least familiar and more or less quantifiable. And when physicists have created new elements, they have done so with the knowledge that their behavior will be highly predictable. By contrast, even the experts can only guess what will happen when germs are provided with exotic genetic material and what trade-off this new technology will require. And whereas radiation generally decays, novel microbes might multiply indefinitely in a hospitable environment.

1. *Paraphrasing*, substituting other words, but retaining the ideas and general word order without documenting:

> The difficulty of keeping equal scientific hazards and helps is a normal one. In the instance of nuclear energy, both the disadvantages and the benefits are at least known and more or less measurable.

When scientists have found new discoveries, they have done so with the understanding that their actions will be very normal. In opposition, even the authorities can only speculate on what will occur when germs are given unusual genetic substance and what exchanges this innovative technology will demand. While radiation usually diminishes and dies, new microbes might increase continuously in a favorable environment.

2. *Stealing key phrases,* without quoting them:

Genetic engineering is a fascinating new scientific endeavor. Germs are provided with exotic genetic material to discover what the new combinations will produce. Such experiments are different from the work in nuclear energy where the behavior is highly predictable. Radiation generally decays but novel microbes might multiply indefinitely. This potential hazard raises the old dilemma of balancing scientific risks and benefits.

3. *Stealing an entire sentence or section,* without quoting it:

There are many questions raised about new work in genetic engineering. What will happen when germs are provided with exotic genetic material and what trade-off will this new technology require? And whereas radiation generally decays, novel microbes might multiply indefinitely in a hospitable environment.

- ## Proper Incorporation of the Source

Below is one way of properly incorporating the ideas from the source:

Writer's own words

Another potential disadvantage of genetic engineering is described *Author's name* by Randal, who suggests that, unlike the radiation produced through nuclear energy, which tends to decay, the microbes made through combining new genes may continue to increase in the right atmosphere (34).

Page in source

Notice several features of the above incorporation:

1. It inserts the author's name into the paper at the beginning to signal that the writer is moving from his or her own ideas to a source.
2. It uses the ideas but not the vocabulary and word order of the source.
3. It places the page in the source at the end of the source material.

If you work from carefully taken notes, the danger of plagiarizing diminishes, because the notes separate you from the source so that you cannot, even unintentionally, copy the source. Another advantage of good notetaking is that it frees you from being dominated by the *styles* of different sources.

CLASS EXERCISES

1. As a class, take your own set of notes from the Randal article.
   - Create your own key words.
   - Record the information accurately, but in your own words.
   - If you use a quote, identify it by quotation marks.
   - Be sure to include your page numbers.

2. Check for inaccuracy and plagiarism in the following notes taken on the *Time* article "Artificial Genes":
   a. "According to *Time,* 'Genentech licensed for sale the first such medicine ever approved for human use.'"
   b. "Since 1980, 300 new firms dealing in genetic engineering have sprung up."
   c. "Forecasting 'sales of $25 billion by the year 2000,' investors in genetic engineering firms are encouraged by the quick action of the FDA in licensing Humulin after only five months of testing."

● ASSIGNMENT: Exploration

1. Using the exploratory guide, examine your prior knowledge about your topic and list questions that you need to answer.
2. Using the reference tools, compile a working bibliography of potential sources.
3. Annotate the most promising titles.
4. Take notes on the best.
5. Seek advice on your work.

● FOCUS AND SITUATION

INCUBATION

Because research yields such extensive information, you need time to mull over the collected material. Some writers sort through their notes to organize them, laying them out on tables or transferring key ideas to large "think sheets." Whatever the method, you need to assimilate the material during incubation or you may fall into the trap of some amateur writers who mistakenly assume that the insight is *in* the data. This false assumption ends in the "regurgitation" paper.

Avoiding these traps is not easy, however, because the weight of the material tends to dominate you. If you want to exert control over your paper, your focus must become the key. Without a focus your paper would probably be a patchwork of materials that could be read better in the sources. Unless you are able to shape the data to accomplish your aim, you have wasted your time and your reader's. But discovering the insight depends on incubation time.

THE INFORMATIVE FOCUS

After trying out several potential answers to your original or revised question, formulate the one that best accounts for the material you have unearthed in your investigation. A good focus expresses your unique understanding of the material without distorting or repeating the material. Do not regret spending time at this stage because a good focus is the key to a good paper. If you miscalculate here, your revision will be extensive because organizing and incorporating research into a paper is very time-consuming.

Each half of your focus makes a commitment to your audience and controls your material. The first half indicates the scope of your paper—the aspect of the subject to which you will devote your attention. The second half puts your imprint, your thinking, on the data. It communicates the conclusion you have come to about the material you have gathered. It controls what data you will include and what you will put aside. Remember that an informative focus must convey something new to some audience. As you formulate your focus, try out different audiences with it, asking whether it is offering them new information. There are at least three kinds of pitfalls to avoid when deciding on a focus.

1. *A factual idea which conveys no new information:* "Genetic engineering is being done in many universities."
2. *An idea that violates the integrity of the data, by denying a large number of sources or otherwise violating factuality:* "Genetic engineering is accomplishing nothing."
3. *An idea that goes too far beyond your research:* "Genetic engineering is being done in many countries."

Here are the focuses and audiences of the four writers.

WRITER 1	Subject	Point of Significance
	Genetic engineering————————	is a complex proposition.

(*Questions:* Why is genetic engineering, esp. gene transplantation, so controversial? Can this research interfere with nature?)

Audience
—Primary: Biology teacher
—Secondary: Writing instructor

WRITER 2

Subject	**Point of Significance**
A successful pitching coach———————	must know the many different aspects of pitching.

(*Questions:* What different strategies can be used when you use a pitcher? What are some good ways to teach pitching to beginning players?)

Audience
—Primary: Parents of Little League players
—Secondary: Writing class

WRITER 3

Subject	**Point of Significance**
The use of drugs and newly developed techniques———————	has had notable results in the rehabilitation of spinal cord injury victims.

(*Question:* What new techniques have scientists come up with in the rehabilitation of a paraplegic?)

Audience
—Primary: A friend who is paralyzed from the waist down
—Secondary: Writing instructor and class

WRITER 4

Revised Subject	**Point of Significance**
The characteristics and causes of bulimia and anorexia———————	are diversified and not very well understood.

(*Revised questions:* What are the causes of anorexia nervosa? How do family interactions play a part in the development of anorexia nervosa? What are the characteristics of this illness and related disorders?)

Audience
—Primary: Adolescent girls who have a personal interest in the subject
—Secondary: Writing teacher

⬤ **COMMENTARY**

Two major problems exist for Writer 1's focus. The first half commits him to dealing with the entire subject, an unmanageable task. The second half does not convey new information to either his biology teacher or anyone else. He has not, therefore, controlled the data with any idea of his own.

CLASS EXERCISES

1. Evaluate the following focuses:
   a. "Genetic engineering started in the U.S."

    b. "The history of genetic engineering."

    c. "I don't agree with genetic engineering."

    d. "Genetic engineering will never succeed in cloning humans."

    e. "Genetic engineering ought to be stopped."

    f. "The changing guidelines of genetic engineering show it lacks adequate control."

- What focuses are workable? Why?
- To what kind of development does each focus commit the writer?
- What kind of aim does each focus invoke?

2. Discuss the focuses and audiences of Writers 2, 3, and 4.

- Do they convey new information and imprint the writers' thinking on the material?
- Are the audiences good choices?
- To what does each focus commit the writer?

● ASSIGNMENT: Focus and Situation

1. After allowing the time for incubation, review the material you have gathered during your research.
2. Formulate several focuses until you find one that best conveys the important point you wish to make about your subject.
3. Determine the audience(s) to whom this focus will convey new information.
4. Get advice before proceeding.

● AUDIENCE AND MODES OF ORGANIZATION

The expository aim necessitates taking a certain stance toward your audience that reflects a series of assumptions you make about your relationship with them.

1. You assume *one* dissimilarity: You will know more than they do about the focus you will develop. You are not superior to them in intelligence, character, status, or even general knowledge of the subject.

2. You assume *two* similarities:
   a. You and they are both interested in the subject.
   b. You and they are equally intelligent. You do not tell the audience what to think about the information or how to respond to it.
3. You assume that the audience understands the role you are playing—a relayer of information, not an advocate.

This last assumption puts on you the burden of factuality and comprehensiveness, the burden of not "shaving," exaggerating, or omitting significant facts. The audience guide will help you determine what your audience already knows about the subject.

The specific role of the audience for the research paper depends on your reason for offering the information. Are you updating the information of an expert? Introducing a novice to an unfamiliar branch of knowledge? Surveying recent developments for someone who simply likes to keep up a general knowledge of the field? These three possible roles—expert, novice, generalist—require different background information from you and varying depths of development.

AUDIENCE GUIDE

1. State your audience and the reasons for choosing it.
2. Analyze the audience in itself.
   a. Identify the levels and types of experiences that your audience has had (cultural, recreational, educational, and so on).
      • What is the median level of education in your audience?
      • Are most of your audience males or females?
      • Is there anything special about your audience that will affect their image of you and themselves (racial, cultural, recreational, occupational, etc.)?
   b. Identify the hierarchy of values that your audience holds (money, power, friendship, security, intellectual growth).
3. Analyze the audience in relation to the subject.
   a. Identify the knowledge and opinion your audience holds of the subject.
   b. Determine how strongly your audience holds those views.
   c. Assess how willing your audience is to act on its opinion—if acting is appropriate.
4. In light of the information you gained above, determine the specific role your audience will play.
5. Repeat steps 2 and 3, but this time analyze only the *specific* role you want the audience to play.
   a. Determine what levels and types of experience fit the role your audience will play.

b. Identify the values that fit that role.

c. Determine what opinion you want your audience to hold in that role, how strongly you want the audience to hold it, whether you want the audience to act on it.

6. Determine your voice and the *relational* role you want your audience to play. State why you have chosen that relationship.

AUDIENCE ANALYSIS

WRITER 1

1. I have changed my mind. My primary audience will be my writing instructor, my secondary audience my biology teacher.

2. a. Background: She is about 40, a Ph.D. in English, interested in a wide variety of things.

   b. Values: She has a very "liberal" view of things—talks a lot about values and the freedom to "do and be."

3. a. Attitude toward the subject: I don't think she knows much about gene manipulation—probably has an "educated woman in the street" knowledge, the kind you get from reading *Time* or *Newsweek*. But she certainly will view with suspicion anything called "manipulation" and she will view with alarm any unexplored dangers.

   b. Strength of attitude: She will not hold the attitude strongly because it rests right now on little information.

   c. Willingness to act: She won't act on any attitude based on as little information as hers is now.

4. Specific role: a concerned, educated, adult U.S. citizen.

5. Analysis of the role

   a. Background: She will remember something about elementary biology, but to be safe I will supply most of what's needed. She will have in the back of her mind other "experimental" programs that went wrong, like Three Mile Island.

   b. Values: Her primary values will be the health and safety of citizens, herself among them.

   c. Attitude toward the subject: I want her to believe that there is the possibility of great harm in the present experiments. She will be predisposed to this point of view by her concern.

6. Relational role: I want to write as one informed, concerned citizen speaking to another concerned citizen.

WRITER 3

1. My audience is a friend who is paralyzed from the waist down.

2. a. Background: She is a 22-year-old paraplegic whose future was changed by an auto accident.

   b. Values: She still values life, even though hers has changed a lot.

3. a. Attitude toward the subject: She knows a lot from personal experience. She thinks the public tends to ignore cord injury victims because they don't understand how things are. Most important, she still hopes to walk again.
   b. Strength of attitude: She holds these views very strongly.
   c. Willingness to act: She would do almost anything to find a way to walk again.
4. Specific role: Victim looking for a solution.
5. Analysis of the role
   a. Background: She will know that research goes on. She may not know the most recent developments.
   b. Values: She will value hope for recovery over everything else.
   c. Attitude toward the subject: She will be a little skeptical about the possibility of a cure but a reasonable change will be very attractive to her.
6. Relational role: My voice should say to her that she knows more about the subject through experience than I do, but I have the latest information for her and in it may be some hope for her.

COMMENTARY

Writer 1 has very wisely switched primary and secondary audiences. The writing instructor will be much easier to write for in the informative aim. The analysis has also led the writer to a narrowing of his emphasis ("great harm") that was not there in the focus.

Writer 3 has analyzed the motives of her audience well. But she must avoid the voice of a savior. That is, she will have to be careful not to promise the audience too much—not to suggest she knows a cure when she doesn't.

ORGANIZING A RESEARCH PAPER

In a good research paper, the facts *as assembled* speak for themselves—which is not the same thing as "the facts speak for themselves." They don't, of course, unless put in some kind of order. In research writing, the order the facts are put in should be clear to the reader.

Introductions and Conclusions

In research writing, the introduction is the place to state the topic, interest the audience, review for the reader the background information needed to understand your discussion, and state the focus. This review often becomes a "review of the literature," a summary of the most relevant research writing on the topic.

In the conclusion of a research paper, the writer usually summarizes the findings and restates the focus. Occasionally the conclusion points to future research that needs to be done in the area, but that approach is more appropriate to the scientific expository aim than to the informative.

● Organization Plans

The nature of the subject material and the focus often dictate the organizational structure, following one of three modes: description, classification, or narration. Organizing according to these modes will help you to control your material. A sentence plan, moreover, keeps your focus alive throughout a long paper, each sentence acting as a minor focus for a section or paragraph. Below are sample plans for the three modes:

DESCRIPTIVE MODE

Subject	*Point of Significance*
Genetic engineering———————	has physical dangers.

Organization

¶ 1 Introduction.
¶ 2 The lack of predictability of ⌐poses a physical danger.
    the genetic material——
¶ 3 *E. coli* itself——————— is harmful to animals and possibly
    to humans.
¶ 4 The limitations of the experi- ⌐pose possible threats.
    menters——
¶ 5 The shortsightedness of the ⌐is a potential danger.
    developers——
      Private industry——————— is not careful about guidelines.
      Universities——————— are going beyond restrictions.
¶ 6 The long-range effects——— could be physically dangerous.
¶ 7 Conclusion.

Notice that this organization plan divides the first half of the focus into parts and then shows how each part can be dangerous.

NARRATIVE MODE

Subject	*Point of Significance*
The attitudes toward regulation of	⌐have been in conflict since its
genetic engineering——	beginning.

Organization

¶ 1 Introduction.
¶ 2 In 1974, eleven scientists——— self-imposed a moratorium.
¶ 3 In 1975, the Asimolar Confer- ⌐urged stricter guidelines.
    ence——

¶ 4 In 1976, the NIH guidelines——— were considered too strict by some and inadequate by others.

¶ 5 In 1977, a survey of scientists——— showed different ways of adhering to the guidelines.

¶ 6 Conclusion.

CLASSIFICATION MODE

Subject

The dangers and advantages of genetic engineering

Point of Significance

pose a dilemma for scientists and the general public.

Organization

¶ 1 Introduction.
¶ 2 Several dangers——————————— exist for scientists.
¶ 3 Other dangers————————————— threaten the general public.
¶ 4 Some advantages————————————— are gained by science.
¶ 5 Other advantages———————————— accrue to the general public.
¶ 6 Conclusion: the dilemma.

Variations on this plan can be devised. Notice that the plan sustains the two parts of the focus throughout, preventing the writer from first speaking of genetic engineering and then later discussing its impact on scientists and the public.

Here are the organization plans of Writers 1 and 3.

WRITER 1

Focus

Subject

Genetic engineering————————————— is a complex proposition.

Point of Significance

Organization: Descriptive mode

¶ 1 Introduction: Background.
¶ 2 Doing genetic engineering research——— poses dangers and controversy.
¶ 3 The results of genetic engineering——— are complex to control.
¶ 4 The prestige and profits—————— pose risks to researchers.
¶ 5 Private enterprise's research——— has other complex dangers.
¶ 6 Amateurs————————————————— pose other difficulties.
¶ 7 Need for regulation————————— raises political problems.
¶ 8 The research——————————————— poses moral problems.
¶ 9 Conclusion.

WRITER 3

Focus

Subject

The use of drugs and newly developed techniques ⌐has had notable results in the rehabilitation of spinal cord injury victims.

Point of Significance

Organization: Descriptive mode

¶ 1   Introduction.
¶ 2   Naloxone —————————— lessens paralysis right after injury.
¶ 3   TRH ————————————— lessens paralysis with less pain.
¶ 4   Clonidine ————————— lessens paralysis without having to be given immediately after injury.
¶ 5   Health care ——————— is being upgraded.
¶ 6   Electrical stimulation——— uses EMG biofeedback, computerized systems, and electrical stimulation.
¶ 7   Regeneration and nerve plasticity ⌐are still being worked with but have a long way to go.
¶ 8   Conclusion.

● **COMMENTARY**

Paragraphs 2, 3, and 4 work well in Writer 3's plan to implement and advance her focus. But her plans for paragraphs 5, 6, and 7 do not advance her focus. The second half of each statement does not specify any rehabilitative effect. They need to be revised to read:

¶ 5   Upgraded health care——— has some rehabilitative effect.
¶ 6   Electric stimulation using computers and biofeedback ⌐has some rehabilitative effect.
¶ 7   Regeneration and nerve plasticity ⌐have minimal effect but promise for rehabilitation.

CLASS EXERCISES

1. Examine the organization plans of Writers 1 (p. 264) and 4 (at the end of the chapter).
    • Does each part of them support the focus?
    • Do the plans follow one of the modes of organization?
2. Below are three focuses that call for different modes of organization. Beneath them are paragraph plans. For each focus, select and order the paragraphs that seem appropriate.
    a. "The progress being made in genetic engineering has continued to offer benefits to society."

b. "As a new type of scientific discovery, genetic engineering offers many advantages with some inherent dangers."

c. "Many aspects of genetic engineering hold great promise for society."

¶a. As scientific research, genetic engineering uses new methods and insights.

¶b. The earliest work established new scientific possibilities and guidelines.

¶c. The safeguards provide models for careful experimentation.

¶d. Recent developments of new companies have brought medical and economic benefits.

¶e. Genetic engineering techniques have revolutionized scientific methodology.

¶f. Like nuclear experimentation, genetic engineering poses severe dangers.

¶g. Materials used in genetic engineering build on natural resources.

¶h. Work in the late seventies produced several scientific breakthroughs.

¶i. Like a new medicine, genetic engineering has benefits and unwanted side effects.

● ASSIGNMENT: Audience and Modes of Organization

1. Using the audience guide, analyze your audience in order to set the specific and relational roles you want them to play.
2. Using your focus as a guide, create an organization plan that supports that focus and uses your data well.
3. Get advice on this important planning work before proceeding.

● THE FIRST VERSION

Effective informative research should possess:

1. *Surprise:* You must give your audience information that is new to it. If you are writing for your instructor, you must write for a role that

allows you to give new information or a new shape or conclusion to the information.

2. *Factuality:* You must make sure that your data can be verified. When you read your sources, therefore, check the credentials of the author and the basis for the information (experiments, surveys, and so on). Transfer the information accurately to your notes and then to your paper. The more familiar you are with the subject, the more discerning you can be about the factuality of your information.

3. *Comprehensiveness:* The scope of your guiding question and eventually your focus will determine the amount of evidence needed to reasonably inform your audience without distorting your audience's understanding. Your audience's knowledge and expectations will also affect comprehensiveness. Most instructors do not expect an exhaustive account, given time limitations and your background. You can gain valuable guidance by asking your instructor for comments on your guiding question before you begin exploring and then on your focus before you write the paper.

Drafting the research paper entails using the data you have collected and information from your own experience to develop each section of your plan. In order to interweave this material successfully you must let the audience know which material is from your sources and which is from your own ideas and information. You have two ways of presenting material from your sources: citation and quotation.

CITATION

When you *cite* a source, you summarize its ideas, information, or facts in your own words, and you identify the source by two important means:

1. by indicating in the text that the forthcoming material is from a certain source, and
2. by identifying the page reference at the end of the material, in parentheses.

If you do *not* include an author reference in your paragraph, you must mention it, along with the page number, in the parentheses.*

Here are examples of citations from the writers in this chapter:

> Dr. Casper notes that bulimics are generally more sensitive and experience greater depression, food obsession, bodily discomfort, anxiety, guilt, and insomnia. She adds that bulimics generally prefer not to cook since the temptation to binge is so great (1031–33).

> According to an article by Joan Arehart-Treichel in *Science News,* a new seven-year study was started in 1975 to see if upgraded care of

---

* Citation style in this chapter is based on the new official documentation style of the Modern Language Association (MLA).

spinal cord patients would improve their condition. Fourteen of the nation's top spinal cord centers are participating (9, 12).

Notice some features of these citations:

1. They show the reader where the writer's text leaves off and the material from a source begins. If the writer did not introduce the material with a reference to the source ("Dr. Casper notes"), the reader would not know how far back the source extends.
2. Citations *do not* use the words of the original; they use only the *substance,* the information.
3. They *do not* use quotation marks, but *do* identify the source by introducing it at the beginning and closing it with the page number.

Citations give the paper credibility because research focuses are not supposed to be supported entirely from your own previous knowledge. Most of the material in your paper should be citations that supplement your own knowledge. If you have taken notes properly, most of the cited material should already be in your own words.

QUOTATION

When you *quote* an authority, you give the exact words of the authority within quotation marks. You also supply the page number for a quotation. Here is an example of a quotation:

> As Randal says, this would be a "godsend for cleaning up oil spills. But what would happen if [the bacteria] found its way into petroleum storage tanks, pipelines, or the wing tanks of a commercial jet aircraft in flight?" (18).

(Note that brackets enclose material that was not in the original.)

When should you use quotations? Seldom. The best guide is to ask yourself whether this material is so eloquently said that you want to use both the substance and the style of the original. If not, it would be better to put the information into a citation. Why? For several reasons:

1. The paper belongs to you; its center is your focus. You introduce authorities only as illustration or evidence. Your style must, therefore, dominate. Quotation introduces conflicting styles.
2. In exploring others' writing, you are looking for concepts, ideas, and information that can be phrased in different ways, depending on your exact focus and what you find useful.
3. You can convince the reader that you command your material only if you have assimilated that material for your own purposes. Summary and citation suggest assimilation. Quotation suggests raw data, unassimilated. If you cannot say in your own words, appropriate to your purpose, what the source has said in his or her words, it's a pretty good guess that you do not control the material in the source.

If you have a quotation of more than four typescript lines, you set it off from the text by triple-spacing, indenting, and typing the extract single-spaced and without quotation marks. For example:

> Emotionally it's a new world and it's been the most vital and most difficult task to learn how to live with it, to feel comfortable owning my emotions, allowing them to identify me. I am still feeling vulnerable and fragile, especially confused about my womanhood—easily influenced by others' expectations, frightened of losing control, losing people, losing my place (Combs 16).

If you wish to leave out material in the middle of the quotation, you use three ellipses separated by spaces to indicate that material is missing.

> Emotionally . . . it's been the most vital and most difficult task to learn how to live with it, to feel comfortable owning my emotions, allowing them to identify me.

Another important distinction will help you in developing your paper—the distinction between *fact* and *inference*.

THE INFORMATIVE AIM

Information and evidence consist of:

1. fact—what is commonly known, or what is not commonly known but can be quickly verified by referring to an authority both the reader and writer all accept
2. inference—what results when the writer connects one fact with another

A critical difference between the two is that a fact is held to be true, an inference only conditionally true. For example:

1. It is a fact that Henry Ford said, "All history, as written, is bunk." For most literate audiences that statement is a fact so widely known that it does not require documentation (i.e., an endnote).
2. It is not a fact that "all history, as written, is bunk." The fact is that Henry Ford said it. Ford's saying it does not, of course, make the content of his statement a fact; it remains an inference of Ford's. You cannot count on finding an audience that would accept Henry Ford as an acceptable authority on all history, as written.

Another example:

1. It is a fact that in World War II, American armies halted at the Rhine River in the invasion of Germany. That is commonly known.
2. It is a fact that the American armies halted at the Rhine River by order of General Dwight D. Eisenhower. That is probably not uni-

versally known; in a paper designed for some audiences, establishing it as a fact would require an endnote.

3. It is a fact that Dwight D. Eisenhower blamed the partition of Berlin and of Germany on the occupation of Berlin by the Russians, and on the fact that the American armies halted at the Rhine and did not press on when they could themselves have easily occupied the capital city of Germany. Again, these are widely known facts, but for some audiences they would require documentation. The concept contains an inference made by Eisenhower which is not universally accepted.

4. It is a fact that after the war Eisenhower blamed the halting of the American armies at the Rhine on orders he received from President Roosevelt, dead when Eisenhower blamed him. That fact would require documentation for most audiences other than historians. And the documentation would still prove only that Eisenhower said that Roosevelt had issued such orders, not that Roosevelt had.

5. It is a fact, in need of documentation for almost any audience, that a respected historian has recently published a book informing the public that he can find no record of any such orders from Roosevelt and that Eisenhower issued the order on his own authority. The only fact here is that the historian said what he said.

The point of these examples is that, given the unspoken agreement between writers and readers of research writing, you will be able to hold and convince the reader only so long as you carefully sort out fact and inference in your sources and in what you yourself are asserting. That sorting out convinces the reader not only of your impartiality and objectivity but also of your command of the material.

As you draft your paragraphs, be sure that when taking material from your notecard, you insert the source in order to avoid the enormous task of matching material to notecards when you are ready to type your bibliography. To keep track of your sources in your draft, place the author and page number in parentheses after your citations or quotations. For example:

> Dr. Casper notes that bulimics are generally more sensitive and experience greater depression, food obsession, body discomfort, anxiety, guilt, and insomnia. She adds that bulimics generally prefer not to cook since the temptation to binge is so great (Casper, 1031–33).

CONVENTIONS IN RESEARCH PAPERS

Like formal reports (discussed in Chapter 8), research papers often have a cover page that contains essential identifying information, centered neatly on the sheet:

- the title or number of the course
- your name

- the title of the paper
- the date
- the instructor's name

To the usual conventions of grammar, spelling, and punctuation, the research paper adds the mechanics of sources in parentheses within the text and a bibliography. These additional conventions exist mainly to ensure that the reader understands who is responsible for every piece of information in the paper and can, if he or she wishes, consult the sources.

● **Works Cited**

A bibliography records the sources that form a basis for the paper. The form for the bibliography differs from one academic field to the other. Below is the MLA bibliographic form.

1. Books

   Dobzhansky, Theodosius. *Genetics of the Evolutionary Process.* New York: Columbia University Press, 1970.

2. Periodicals
   a. Without continuous pagination

   Grobstein, Clifford. "The Recombinant-DNA Debate." *Scientific American,* July 1977, 22–33.

   b. With volume numbers

   Cohen, Stanley N. "Recombinant DNA: Fact and Fiction." *Science* 195 (1977): 654–57.

Notice that in the bibliography:

1. The sources are alphabetized, with the last name of the writer appearing first.
2. The second line is indented.
3. Inclusive pagination is given for articles; no pagination is given for books.

See the student examples on pp. 276, 283–284, and 296–297 for the format.

● **Variations**

Different fields of knowledge and sometimes different publications in the same field use types of documentation other than the one this book illustrates. Here are two common bibliographic variations.

1. Variation 1 numbers the items in the bibliography so that the information in the text consists of the item number and the page number. Assume, for example, that an item is number 5 because of its alpha-

    betical place in the bibliography. The reference in the text would then be (5, 12).

2. Variation 2 puts the name of the author and the date of publication—for example, (Tenbrunsel, 1982)—in the text so that the reader can immediately see the currency of the source. But if a precise page reference is desired, the writer will have to include a footnote or endnote in addition to the parenthetical reference.

Whatever system is used should, of course, be used consistently.

THE EXPOSITORY STYLE

The style of a research paper should suggest the objectivity and impartiality of your investigation. That is to say, the voice projected should be that of a disinterested (not the same as an uninterested) observer—one vitally concerned with the subject matter, but unbiased—a researcher so interested as to have investigated all of the available literature on the subject (given limitations of time) and so interested in arriving at the truth of the matter that he or she has set aside all personal interests, even though personal interests may explain why the researcher is so vitally interested. Precision, exactness, honesty are necessary. Disinterestedness is established by being open with the audience—no disguises, no trimming of facts, little humor, few flourishes of style, as little metaphor as possible. The first person pronoun tends to disappear. The writer uses the most concrete diction possible; if a high level of abstraction or technical language is necessary, the writer provides whatever definitions and examples are required by the audience. Sentences tend to be declarative, and the reader is not addressed directly. Rhetorical questions disappear.

The style of research writing strives for authenticity, to gain the conviction on the part of the reader that the researcher is telling the truth as far as he or she knows it. Authenticity, as we illustrated earlier, is established by conveying to the reader that researcher and reader have the same purpose: to discover the truth. And earlier we discussed the implications of that purpose as they affected development and organization. At the stylistic level, authenticity manifests itself in what may be called the *gesture of honesty* and the *gesture of knowledge*.

The gesture of honesty requires that you reveal the sources of all information or inferences that you did not arrive at independently. The gesture of knowledge requires that, in addition to revealing all sources that support your position, you list the sources that you read that did *not* agree with you.

"Works Cited" documents what you used in the presentation. These sources are encompassed in the note and bibliography cards you took in the exploratory stage; there should be no problem in recording either.

FIRST VERSION

WRITER 1

ENGINEERING OUR OWN EVOLUTION: COMPLEXITIES IN AN UNCHARTED FIELD

It has been called "one of the most promising—and at the same time most hazardous—new fields since creation of the atom bomb" (McWethy 34). It has been hailed as "science's newest 'magic,'" (McWethy 34), and its technology has been labelled "a sorcerer's apprentice" (Grobstein 30). This science is genetic engineering, "the directed intervention in the genetic material of an organism for the purpose of changing inherited characteristics" (McDougall 529). Such intervention, which has been going on for years in plants and animals, is called hybridization. But between 1971 and 1973, molecular biologists, particularly Paul Berg and Stanley Cohen at Stanford University and Herbert Boyer of U. of C., developed means of putting *any* two kinds of DNA together in order to cross the species barrier.

The kind of research called recombinant DNA "is not a single entity, but rather . . . a group of techniques that can be used for a wide variety of experiments" (Cohen 654). One technique of cloning, for example, is used to create a number of genetically identical individuals. Yale biologist Arthur Galston explains that individual cells that are not differentiated are separated by chemical and mechanical techniques from the blastula of a developing fertilized egg. They will be able to produce whole new organisms when they are cultivated in the right medium (for lower animals) or are implanted in a substitute mother (for mammals). With the technique of nuclear transplantation, just the nucleus of either a fertilized egg or just an ordinary body cell is destroyed mechanically or by radiation. Then the nucleus from another body cell is injected, and the receptor cell develops into a normal embryo that will be a carbon copy in one generation. The complicated techniques of inserting chromosomes and single genes involve going into cells on even smaller levels (72–73).

Recognizing the implications of recombination, scientists imposed a temporary ban on certain experiments considered the most dangerous until they met in February 1975 at the Asimolar Conference to urge the National Institutes of Health to write research guidelines. In June 1976 the NIH upheld the ban on hazardous experiments and ordered four levels of containment (lab facilities of varying requirements—air locks, filters, etc.) for experiments ranging from lowest (P-1) to highest (P-4) categories of possible risks (Cohen 656).

Ordinarily, news of scientific developments reaches the public slowly through science magazines and science columns in newspapers. But the fantastic potential of these recombination techniques was quickly learned. People wanted to know, especially in places like Cambridge where Harvard was conducting P-3 and P-4 experiments in a questionable place, if the research was safe (Randal 16–20). What would genetic engineering mean for our futures—a cure for genetic diseases like diabetes and sickle cell anemia? A worldwide epidemic owing to some laboratory mistake? A society of clones?

This possibility of engineering our own evolution—of actually controlling and/or creating plant, animal, and human life on this planet—is a complex proposition.

The complexities are not merely technical. There are dangers in doing the research itself. According to scientists, says *New York Daily News* science writer Judith Randal, the behavior of bacteria itself is unpredictable. Add to this the fact that the chances of error increase because the enzymes involved in gene transplants act on virus go-betweens called phages, rather than directly on the bacteria. Although genetic deviations occur in nature, too, some scientists fear that if too many of them are introduced too fast, the changes could get out of control (18). The enzymes themselves may or may not act predictably. Moreover, most experiments use the popular *E. coli* bacteria, which can infect animal and human intestines, even though a special strain of *E. coli* called K-12 has been developed which will not infect humans. But Dr. Stanley Falkow, a microbiologist expert on *E. coli,* fears that DNA recombinant molecules even in weakened strains of K-12 could increase the ability of this *E. coli* strain to survive and multiply (Randal 18), causing chronic diarrhea and bladder infections in livestock or humans (McWethy 34). Dr. Falkow also fears that if the strain reproduces in water, it could be an environmental threat (Randal 18).

The results of genetic engineering become so entangled that it is practically impossible to separate and group them. For instance, if by some laboratory accident or mistake a dangerous bacterium escaped and infected people outside, there is both a medical problem and a legal one. Or consider this. According to Kenneth McDougall, a biology professor at the University of Dayton, recombinant techniques hold hope for correcting genetic diseases—especially those caused by single-gene defects, like diabetes, PKU, gout. Rather than treatment by diet or drugs, which some genetic diseases don't even respond to, it will be better just to replace the defective gene. Laboratories have already been able to isolate certain genes related to specific diseases and to produce them in bulk. Then the genes must be put into the right cells of the organism. Two processes for doing this, called *transformation* and *transduction,* have been perfected in bacteria but have not been proved in mammals. Another problem is gene regulation—getting a gene to produce the right amount of a substance at the right time (13). Once these obstacles are overcome, the practice of this genetic therapy could be open to malpractice suits like any other medical procedure—perhaps more so, as long as it is new and controversial.

There are also safety and social problems. Randal suggests that prestige and profit from the new research might bring outside dangers: daring scientists may take greater risks to improve their reputations; biology students who question the techniques might risk their degrees or be kept out of certain professional labs, as supposedly has already happened in at least one university (17).

Unbelievably, the NIH guidelines for experiments are still voluntary. The penalty for breaking a rule is having your NIH research funding reduced or cut off. Randal wonders whether general research will be prevented if techniques such as the production of insulin from bacteria are patented. Will enough profits be made so as to take all the power out of the NIH sanction (18)?

Thus, the economics of private enterprise further complicate the picture. Pharmaceutical companies have been quick to produce cheaper and better drugs. Companies including Miles Laboratories, Eli Lilly, Abbott Laboratories, and Upjohn have already told a Senate health subcommittee that they want to make greater quantities of DNA recombinants than NIH rules now permit for academic research. And, as Randal points out, smaller firms may actually be a bigger threat because they may "cut corners" and not take the right precautions (19).

Randal sees other difficulties with private enterprise: (1) the emphasis on trade secrets goes against what many consider the public's right to know about such controversial research; (2) once bacteria can be created to produce antimicrobials cheaply, there might be an overuse of drugs. GE is trying to patent a procedure for cleaning up oil spills. But what would happen if the bacteria found their way into petroleum storage tanks, pipelines, or the wing tanks of a commercial jet? There might even be an impact on the ocean environment itself (20).

Amateurs pose still more complexities. Right now, anybody can order the enzymes through the mail. Once harmful recombinants got loose, we would probably not find out about it until they showed up in some negative way. They would also be practically impossible to track (Randal 18).

These kinds of possibilities bring genetic engineering into the political arena. As all writers covering the field seem to agree, some agency must have charge of regulating research done in universities, by industry, and by government, and also the application of that research, commercial or otherwise.

But maybe the greatest complexities in genetic engineering are moral. Cloning of amphibians has been an accomplished fact since 1968 (Rivers 51). Now, human cell nuclei have swollen in size "as much as a hundredfold" in experiments by J. B. Gurdon at Oxford where they were inserted into frog eggs (Rivers 51). Rivers estimates that human cloning will be achieved inside ten years and says:

> The consequences of human cloning are almost impossible to imagine. Widespread human cloning would alter human society beyond recognition. The family would no longer exist, sexuality would have no connection with reproduction. The idea of parenthood would be completely changed. The diversity of human beings provided by sexual reproduction would vanish. One could imagine entire communities of people who looked exactly the same, whose range of potential was identical. Some scientists have suggested that "clones and clonishness" could replace our present patterns of nation and race.

The misuses of cloning are not hard to predict. . . . Would women and men project their egos into the future by producing their own "carbon copies"? Would society choose to clone our most valued citizens (51)?

Thus, the new capabilities that the field of genetic engineering gives to us obviously involve considerations beyond science alone. The complexities are not merely technical. They are legal and medical, economic and political. They have to do with ecology; they are concerned with personal safety and national security. They are, above all, social and moral on an international scale. When we assume the responsibility for the direction of life on our planet, we must determine priorities and make value judgments about the quality of life in our futures.

WORKS CITED

Cohen, Stanley N. "Recombinant DNA: Fact and Fiction." *Science* 195 (1977): 654–57.
Galston, Arthur W. "Here Come the Clones." *Natural History,* Feb. 1975, 72–75.
Grobstein, Clifford. "The Recombinant-DNA Debate." *Scientific American,* July 1977, 22–33.
McDougall, Kenneth J. "Genetic Engineering: Hazard or Blessing?" *Intellect* 104 (1976): 528–530.
McWethy, Jack. "Science's Newest 'Magic'—A Blessing or a Curse?" *U.S. News and World Report,* 12 July 1976, 34–35.
Randal, Judith. "Life from the Labs." *The Progressive,* March 1977, 16–20.
Rivers, Caryl. "Cloning: A Generation Made to Order." *Ms.,* June 1976, 51.

CLASS EXERCISES

1. Identify the following statements as either facts or inference. Refer to the first two pages of Judith Randal's "Life from the Labs: Who Will Control the New Technology?," pp. 243–245.
   a. "Randal says that most Americans are still unaware of the debate among serious scientists about gene transplants."
   b. "People will be moving genes back and forth across boundaries that many million years of evolution have set in place."
   c. "The mule cannot reproduce."
   d. "Judith Randal is a woman."
2. You are writing a paper on the relative worth for the home gardener of three kinds of cucumber: the Spartan Green, the Ohio, and the Straight-8. Turn the quotations below into citations.

   The most important consideration for the home gardener is the maturation rate of the fruit. If all the fruits ripen at the same time, the gardener lives in feast or famine; he will have too much at one time and none at all at others. For some fruits, of course, taste is also a prime consideration. It is a reasonable rule of thumb that the most popular commercial variety usually has the least flavor." (From Terry Leonard's book, *Home Gardening*, page 25. The book was published in 1980 by Universal Press, whose home office is in Los Angeles.)

"The Straight-8 cucumber is the obvious first choice of commercial growers. It is resistant to insects and disease. It is uniform: it grows to a length of eight inches without noticeable curving, and there it stops. It matures simultaneously. One picking, or two at the most, will clear a field." (From page 8 of an article by John Bruce, "New Commercial Choices: Cukes." Published in *The Grower's Guide*, volume four, 1979, covering pages 7 through 9.)

"Investing in the Straight-8 cucumber, the darling of the commercial grower because it leaves no waste space in the box and rarely bruises, is like buying a tank to use as a station wagon. The seeds are expensive. The cuke has a rind like leather. It's too big to pickle. And it tastes like damp sawdust." (From page 26 of a book by Brenda Mayday, *The Lazy Person's Guide to Gardening*. Published in New York in 1981 by T. M. Press.)

3. From the notes you took on the Randal article, write a paragraph that includes citations and at least one quotation. Include a reference to your source and avoid the forms of plagiarism.
4. Seek responses on your incorporations from your instructor and classmates.
5. Study the material used by Writer 1 for support.
   • What sections of information lack documentation?
   • What purpose do the direct quotations serve? Should the material have been put into citations instead?
6. Study the "Works Cited" of Writer 1. What errors, if any, in form are present?
7. Make bibliography entries for the three sources you worked with in Exercise 2.

● ASSIGNMENT: The First Version

1. Using your organization plan and your notes, write a first version of your paper.
2. Document your citations and quotations.
3. Supply a bibliography for your paper.
4. Submit your paper for advice.

● **READER RESPONSES**

The central question in reading a research paper is "Who is in control?" The sign of the good paper is that the authority of the writer comes through clearly. The writer's voice dominates. The writer controls the material; the material does not control (and thus defeat) the purposes of the writer. That control will be most clearly evidenced in

1. *the proportion of citation to quotation:* Too many quotes means too little control.
2. *the organization:* Does the paper fit together in an easily discernible order?
3. *the transitions:* Does the writer move easily from one event to another, from one category to another? Does the writer move easily out of his or her own ideas into borrowed material and back again?

The following reader guide will help you respond to the research paper.

READER GUIDE

● **Focus**
- What is the writer's focus?
- Does each section begin with a sentence that supports some aspect of the focus? If not, where are the problems?
- Does any section introduce material unrelated to the focus?

● **Development**
- Has the writer written an introduction that interests the audience in the subject?
- What material—facts, inferences, ideas—works well to support the focus?
- Does it give new information to the audience?
- Has the writer properly incorporated data into the paper?
- Has the writer used enough citations to explain the focus?
- What sections need more development?
- Does the paper have too many quotations?
- Are the sources credible?
- Does the conclusion help the reader to see the paper's main points?

● **Organization**
- What mode of organization has the writer used?
- Has it been followed? If not, where has the paper gone astray?
- Are there adequate transitions between paragraphs?
- Is coherence maintained within paragraphs?
- Does the paper have consistent tense and voice?

- **Style**
  - Has the writer kept to an expository style?
  - What kind of diction is used?
  - Is there too much jargon for the audience?
  - What sentences need combining?
  - Are there any sections which use diction and syntax too controlled by the language of the sources?

- **Conventions**
  - Where has the writer made mistakes in grammar, spelling, and punctuation?
  - Has the writer used proper and accurate bibliography form?

INSTRUCTOR'S RESPONSE TO WRITER 1

FOCUS

Your focus appears as the fifth paragraph: "This possibility of engineering our own evolution . . . is a complex proposition." It is, first of all, metaphorical and therefore not as precise as it might be. What is the complexity? Great rewards wrapped in great dangers? You seem to be attempting a summary of the rewards and dangers, but it is not done systematically. Paragraph 2, for example, describes a technical procedure, paragraph 3 reports a political decision, and paragraph 4 notes a public reaction to the general topic. It doesn't appear that a strong focus is holding your paper together.

DEVELOPMENT

You have not taken adequate care with quotation and citation. In paragraph 7, for example, only one citation appears. But surely the material in the first two sentences didn't come from the *Intellect* source. And where did the idea in the last sentence come from? Is all of paragraphs 8, 9, 10, 11, and 12 from Randal? Lumping together that much material from any one source inevitably affects the shape of your paper (see comments under "Organization"). Strangely enough, the most important data-related statement in the paper is undeveloped and undocumented: "As all writers covering the field seem to agree, some agency must have charge of regulating research done in universities, by industry, and by government, and also the application of that research, commercial or otherwise."

ORGANIZATION

The paper is basically disorganized because you have not used a mode of organization consistently. If you will look back at your organization plan, you may see that the subjects of the topic sentences are not mutually exclusive and don't proceed from a single basis of division or classification. As a result, your organization is not set firmly in either the descriptive or classification mode. For example, paragraph 1 is a subdivision of paragraph 7, and paragraph 12 is a subdivision of both. Paragraph 13 isn't a part of the subject but an inference drawn from an inspection of the parts.

You might have been able to organize according to the kinds of problems: "legal and medical, economic and political . . . social and moral . . . ." The distinctions between them have been unnecessarily blurred in the paper. Paragraph 6, for example, begins with "The complexities are not merely technical," but the problem that the paragraph develops is a technical one. Paragraph 7 begins by asserting that "The results of genetic engineering become so entangled that it is practically impossible to separate and group them." But the moral and legal aspects of the cases then discussed can very easily be separated—and you have done it. Deciding to devote five consecutive paragraphs to a single source may have skewed your organization because you adopted the organization of your source, and it did not fit yours.

STYLE

You are obviously at home with the language. Only infrequently does the style of the sources clash with your somewhat more sensational style: "fantastic potential," "unbelievably, the NIH guidelines. . . ."

CONVENTIONS

Mechanically, more than competent. But see the comment under "Development" for citation problems.

CLASS EXERCISES

1. Read the first versions of Writers 3 (below) and 4 (at the end of the chapter). Using the reader guide, respond to the papers.
2. Identify any mistakes in the form of the bibliography.

FIRST VERSION

WRITER 3

NEW HOPE FOR VICTIMS OF SPINAL INJURY

In the United States alone, there are more than 200,000 Americans who are paraplegic because of spinal cord injuries. About half of the new cases each year are a result of motor vehicle accidents; most of the rest involve accidents from sporting events. The average age of spinal injury victims is 19 yrs. old (Clark 102). Within the past 3 years, researchers have been developing drugs that prevent damage to the spinal cord and testing electronic devices to help restore movement in paralyzed limbs. There is also hope that someday damaged nerves will be regenerated. As of right now, drugs and electrical stimulation are more promising; but work on regeneration will still continue.

Following an accident, there is swelling and hemorrhaging of the spinal cord, and eventually scar tissue forms. Endorphins (pain-relieving proteins naturally present in the body) reduce the flow of blood to the spinal cord after the injury ("A Treatment for Spinal Cord Injury" 293). Researchers have found a drug called naloxone that can improve blood flow to the cord and stop the action of endorphins. Cats have been used in experiments to test the drug. In one experiment, nine cats were injected with naloxone forty-five minutes after their injury. The results showed that three weeks later, two had died, three were normal, and four were spastic ("Naloxone: Reducing Shock Trauma" 260). Many experiments, including this one, show that cats have far less paralysis when given naloxone immediately after the injury. In humans, this drug is being used mainly to see if there are any side effects from it. If the drug seems to be safe, then doctors will start using it to lessen paralysis (Clark 102). The problem with naloxone is that it inhibits the actions of endorphins; therefore, it increases the pain of the spinal cord injury patient ("A Treatment for Spinal Cord Injury" 293). Overall, naloxone is a promising drug for the future of paraplegics, but it must be given immediately after the injury.

Experts have come to believe that steroid hormones may be more effective than naloxone. The most promising hormone is one called thyrotrophin releasing hormone (TRH). It helps control matter released from the thyroid gland and activates blood flow (Clark 102). Alan I. Faden, Thomas P. Jacobs, and John W. Holaday found that TRH blocks the action of endorphins without blocking the pain-relieving ability. In an experiment, they gave twenty-six cats drug treatments for four consecutive hours, starting an hour after the injury. Six of the cats were given TRH, and the other twenty were given different hormones. The researchers' report in the *New England Journal of Medicine* basically stated that in TRH treatment there was normal neurological function in the six cats. Therefore, Faden, Jacobs, and Holaday concluded that TRH may be an effective way to treat spinal cord injury patients. Clinical trials are being planned in the U.S., and European colleagues say that Europeans will be looking into TRH in the near future ("A Treatment . . ." 293).

Clonidine is a drug that has been found to help bring back normalization of the sensory–motor system. N. Eric Naftchi, a professor of rehabilitation medicine at New York University, did a complex experiment to test the use of clonidine in forty-seven mongrel cats. Thirty cats were not treated, and the remaining seventeen were treated at different time intervals. Naftchi measured a stimulated nerve response, called a somatosensory evoked potential (SEP), to seek the level of the injury (1042). Before the treatment of clonidine, cats showed no SEP, which means spinal cord nerves were completely made nonfunctional (Fackelmann

166). Clonidine therefore, was given orally until SEPs returned. The big advantage clonidine has over naloxone and TRH is that it doesn't have to be given immediately after the injury. Research has shown that better results occur the sooner the patient is treated. Clonidine can wait until vital signs have stabilized. Clinical trials are promising because patients feel heat and pain sensation after being given the drug (Naftchi 1043). Naftchi states, "Clonidine might cause severed nerve fibers to grow through scar tissues that block nerve regrowth" (Fackelmann 166). Other scientists say that Naftchi's statement needs to be confirmed.

In 1966, Robert Hiest, a graduate of Juffs University, was left paralyzed from the neck down, due to a motorboat accident. One year later, he was able to drive himself to work, bowl, and handle a motorboat again. Robert's progress was successful because of the health care advances between 1940 and 1960 which consist of: antibiotics to cure bladder infections, the recognition of rehabilitation as a medical specialty, and the establishment of rehabilitation centers for the spinal cord patient. According to an article in *Science News,* a new seven-year study was started in 1975 to see if upgraded care of spinal cord patients would improve their condition. Fourteen of the nation's top spinal cord centers are participating. Some of the care the patients are receiving is as follows: they receive quick emergency care shortly after the accident, they do demanding exercises to help build damaged muscles and limbs, they learn to control bladder function, and they also receive sex counseling to help adjust psychologically to their handicap. Reports have shown that upgraded health care in the fourteen spinal cord centers has helped tremendously in the rehabilitation of these patients. Another health care aid comes from neurosurgeon Jewell Osterholm at Jefferson Medical College in Philadelphia, who is attempting to bathe the damaged spinal cords in ice solution to reduce swelling. Researchers have found this approach to be promising (Arehart-Treichel 9, 12).

Researchers have been working on the use of electrical stimulation, which substitutes for the loss of impulse activity in a spinal cord patient. Clinical reports for the human being state that electrical stimulation increases the size of atrophied muscles and has a physiological effect on denervated muscles. Electrical stimulation programs have been organized to strengthen and increase the "joint range" of muscles, improve voluntary movement, and eliminate spasticity (Craik 1456–7). An effective approach in the field of electrical stimulation is the use of electromyographic (EMG) biofeedback. EMG feedback is used during the acute stage since the patient is not ready for physical therapy. The following report examines the progress of a twenty-two year old male, who suffered a spinal cord injury in an automobile accident in June 1979. There are basically three reasons why EMG biofeedback treatment was chosen: (1) it could be easily fitted into the exercise program, (2) it could provide immediate information on voluntary activity of damaged muscles, and (3) it could work with any electrode used for EMG feedback. When positive EMG responses were shown, a specific electrode placement was recorded; but, when there was no EMG response, an alternative placement was chosen. The training begins three times a week for twenty minutes, and consists of gluteal muscle settings with EMG biofeedback. Only voluntary, stationary exercises were permitted because of instability of the spinal cord. There were eight sessions in total, with the patient having the use of a wheelchair in the last session, and also an addition of manual exercises to the gluteus and hamstring muscles. No EMG activity was shown in the calf muscles. When the patient returned for a checkup visit eight months later, they found an increase in EMG activity in all muscle groups. However, both calf muscle groups remained inactive (Coogler, Nacht, and Wolf 290–923). Another device used is the electrical stimulator. It gives off an electrical signal which causes the quadriceps to contract. The knee joints extend and standing occurs. Standing improves the function of the bladder and provides better blood flow to paralyzed parts of the body (Bajo 256).

Better than any drug or computer device would be the regeneration of nerves in a damaged spinal cord. Some researchers say that regeneration is impossible since there are no Schwann cells (non-nerve cells) present in the spinal cord (Clark 102). In 1976, Leon Matyinian and A. S. Andreasian cut the spinal cords of 350 rats to see if the spinal cord could be cured by injecting a specific enzyme into the body. Results showed that forty percent of the rats recovered. Three years later, Lloyd Guth found that the enzyme therapy did not work. The reason was because of incomplete transection of the spinal cord. Guth used a "probing device" to make sure the cord was completely transected and found that out of ninety-two rats tested, all remained paralyzed. ("Nerve Regeneration Not Duplicated" 326–7). There is an assumption that the central nervous system (CNS) can retain its plastic property after a CNS injury; however, there is evidence that the spinal cord cannot remake nerve connections. There are many theories about the return of function after a spinal cord injury, but there is no evidence to tell what is responsible for recovery (Craik 1458). Regeneration is still a question mark in the minds of researchers today.

Research to help rehabilitate spinal cord patients has progressed drastically in the past few years. With the finding of new drugs and the use of electrical stimulation, a paraplegic has a much more promising outlook for the future. Although regeneration has a long way to go, scientists are not giving up on the idea. Hopefully, someday spinal cord patients will be able to walk again and lead a normal life.

WORKS CITED

"A Treatment for Spinal Cord Injury," *Science News,* 7 Nov. 1981, 293.

Arehart-Treichel, J. "Spinal Cord Injuries." *Science News,* 5 July 1980, 118–119.

Bajd, Tadej, et al. "Use of Two-Channel Functional Electrical Stimulator to Stand Paraplegic Patients." *Journal of the American Physical Therapy Association* 61 (1981): 526–527.

Clark, M. "The Fight Against Paralysis." *Newsweek,* 18 Oct. 1982, 102.

Coogler, Carole E., Marilyn B. Nacht, and Steven L. Wolf. "Use of Electromyographic Biofeedback during the Acute Phase of Spinal Cord Injury: A Case Report." *Journal of the American Physical Therapy Association* 62 (1982): 290–293.

Craik, Rebecca L. "Clinical Correlates of Neural Plasticity." *Journal of the American Physical Therapy Association* 62 (1982): 1456–1461.

Fackelmann, K. A. "Progress in Paralysis Treatment." *Science News*, 11 Sept. 1982, 166.

Naftchi, N. E. "Functional Restoration of the Traumatically Injured Spinal Cord in Cats by Clonidine." *Science*, 10 Sept. 1982, 1042–1044.

"Naloxone: Reducing Shock Trauma." *Science News*, 26 April 1980, 260.

"Nerve Regeneration Not Duplicated." *Science News*, 19 May 1979, 326–327.

● **ASSIGNMENT: Reader Responses**

1. Give a written response to one or two of your classmates' papers.
2. Share your comments in a workshop.

● **REVISING AND EDITING**

When you revise a research paper, it is essential that you attend to the major problems first—problems of focus, organization, and development. For a specific discussion of the kind of revision each of these elements entails, consult Chapter 1. If you have any of these major problems, you will be wasting your time working on refining your diction or sentence structure before you have tackled these severe flaws.

Writer 1's revision required a considerable investment of time because the paper needed:

1. a narrower focus more in harmony with the scope of his material.
2. a clear and consistent pattern of organization.

REVISION

WRITER 1   ENGINEERING OUR OWN EVOLUTION: THE RISKS

Genetic engineering, or GE, is the popular term for recombinant DNA research, "the directed intervention in the genetic material for the purpose of changing inherited characteristics" (McDougall 529). Such research ranges from long-established and relatively innocent experiments in producing hybrid varieties of plants and animals to cloning, the creation of a number of genetically identical individuals. Experiments in cloning have brought GE into the public eye recently and have created a storm of controversy. The controversy tends to center on the moral and social aspects of GE, often overlooking the actual physical dangers that lurk in the experiments.

Scientists recognize the dangers. Those engaged in the research imposed a temporary ban on certain experiments considered the most dangerous until they met in February 1975 at the Asimolar Conference to urge the National Institutes of Health to write research guidelines (Cohen 656). In June, 1976, the NIH upheld the ban on hazardous experiments and ordered four levels of containment (lab facilities of varying requirements—air locks, filters, etc.) for experiments ranging from lowest (P-1) to highest (P-4) categories of risk (Cohen 656).

What are those risks?

First, there is the lack of predictability of the genetic material itself. Most recombinant research utilizes bacteria. The behavior of bacteria is itself unpredictable. The enzymes used in gene transplants act on virus go-betweens called phages rather than directly on the bacteria. Since the action of the enzymes and the behavior of the phages is unpredictable at present, the chances of error increase (Randal 18).

Second, the bacterium commonly used—*Escherischia coli*—is harmful to humans and animals. Even though a special strain of *E. coli* called K-12 has been developed which will not infect humans, one microbiologist, Dr. Stanley Falkow, an expert on *E. coli,* fears that recombinant DNA molecules even in weakened strains of K-12 could "profoundly [increase] the ability of this *E. coli* strain to survive and multiply in the gastrointestinal tract" (Randal 18), causing chronic diarrhea and bladder infections in livestock or humans. Since *E. coli* is also common in fish, insects, and plants, Dr. Falkow worries "that a recombinant might somehow acquire the ability to reproduce in water, and so pose a massive environmental threat" (Randal 18).

Third, there is always the possibility of human error. Suppose that in advanced research a scientist were attempting to correct a genetic disease—like diabetes, sickle cell anemia, or gout—by replacing the defective gene. Laboratories have been able to isolate certain genes related to specific diseases and to synthesize them in bulk. Then the genes must be inserted into the right cells of the host organism. Two processes for doing this, called *transformation* and *transduction,* have been perfected in bacteria (McDougall 529–530).

Gene transplanting obviously involves a series of complicated tasks in which, to put it simply, the right material must be inserted at the right time into the right cell. Suppose someone made a mistake and dangerous DNA were inserted. Nobody knows what would be created. The threat has been present since 1973, when molecular biologists developed means of putting *any* two kinds of DNA together, crossing the species barrier.

Fourth, there is the danger posed by human shortsightedness, ambition, and greed. Pharmaceutical companies have been quick to pick up on "bacterifacture" to produce cheaper and better drugs; it is entirely possible, for example, that we will soon have insulin-producing bacteria because of GE (Randal 18). Companies including Miles Laboratories, Eli Lilly, Abbott Laboratories, and Upjohn have already told a Senate health subcommittee that they want to make greater quantities of DNA recombinants than NIH rules now permit for academic researchers (Randal 19). Judith Randal, science writer for the *New York Daily News,* points out that smaller firms may pose an even larger threat, since they may "cut corners" and not take proper precautions (Randal 19). Even if such firms were to take adequate precautions—and no one knows what "adequate precautions" are—much more recombinant material would be in circulation, available to the research amateur. Right now, anybody can order the enzymes used in recombinant research through the mail (Rivers 51).

Even the pursuit of seemingly noble ends by private enterprise poses dangers. General Electric, for example, is trying to patent a procedure for creating a strain of bacteria that can break up the hydrocarbons composing crude oil. As Randal says, this would be a "godsend for cleaning up oil spills. But what would happen if [the bacterium] found its way into petroleum storage tanks, pipelines, or the wing tanks of a commercial jet aircraft in flight?" (18). And what will the bacteria do to the ocean environment?

Fifth, there is the danger of the absolute unknown, the long-range effect of stepped-up evolution. Genetic deviations, of course, occur in nature. GE allows human beings not only to engineer their own evolution but to speed up the process a thousand, even a millionfold. What impact that will have on the earth, nobody knows.

At present, the only control over genetic engineering is a set of NIH guidelines. Compliance with those guidelines is voluntary. A policy of continued vigilance is in order.

INSTRUCTOR RESPONSE TO WRITER 1

FOCUS

The focus is clearly stated at the end of the first paragraph: "That controversy tends to center on the moral and social aspects of GE, often overlooking the actual physical dangers that lurk in the experiments." And each section begins with a sentence that supports some aspect of the focus: "Scientists recognize the dangers"; "First, there is the lack of predictability . . ."; "Second, the bacterium commonly used . . . ," etc.

DEVELOPMENT

The paper leans heavily on citation rather than quotation; control is clearly in the hand of the writer, not the sources. Each introductory generalization is explained and illustrated, as is proper in the informative aim for a general readership. Each, with one exception, is supported by at least one source, guiding the general reader or novice audience to further reading. The exception is paragraph 6. Some indication in the text of sources would be helpful to the reader. In addition, the last sentence of paragraph 7 requires a note. Overall, however, the comprehensiveness of the treatment, given the new, restricted focus, and the factuality of the approach guarantee that the writer will surprise the reader with new information.

ORGANIZATION

The systematic division of the topic, "physical dangers," into five parts allows tight, easy-to-follow organization. This descriptive organization is followed throughout.

STYLE

The style has been toned down somewhat in the revision. The language tends to be informative, not inflammatory. Most notable is the complexity of the sentence structure, indicating the writer's awareness of an educated, actively engaged reader. Since the primary audience is the writing instructor, this is an appropriate choice of level.

CLASS EXERCISES

1. Using your responses to Writers 3 and 4 as a basis, revise the necessary sections of their first versions.
2. In a workshop, exchange papers and revise at least one paragraph by one of your classmates.

● ASSIGNMENT: Revising and Editing

1. Applying the criticism you received, revise your paper.
2. Edit your paper, making sure your bibliography is correct.

A WRITER'S PROCESS

Below we present the sequence followed in Writer 4's writing process.

THE GUIDING QUESTION AND POTENTIAL SITUATIONS

WRITER 4

Subject: Breast cancer

My Values and the Subject
—Most importantly, I am interested in this subject because my own mother has breast cancer. She had a mastectomy at Christmastime and is now receiving chemotherapy treatments.
—I am taking Med Chem this semester, which is a cancer course in which a variety of speakers and doctors on cancer come in each week to speak about everything related to cancer.
—I am also curious about this disease since I am a woman with an increased chance of having breast cancer because my mother has it. Also breast cancer is one of the leading causes of death in women.
—What really interests me is how diet is related to breast cancer—this subject is very much involved in my own career of nutrition, medicine, and biology.

Question: What are the dietary causes of breast cancer? Is sugar a leading initiator of breast cancer?

Audience
—Primary: Kristin, a premed student who will attend med school in the fall
—Secondary: Writing teacher

EXPLORATION

STATIC VIEW

—I already know that breast cancer is a metastasizing tumor located in the breast and is therefore malignant. It must be treated by surgery, radiation, or chemotherapy.
—I know that diet is partly a cause of cancer yet I'm not exactly sure why.
—I know that breast cancer is the leading cause of death among women.
—subtopics include causes, treatments, future improvements, population statistics, process of, prevention, etc.
—I'm very interested in this topic and concerned as to how diet might lead to breast cancer.

Info Needed:
—background on breast cancer—definition & development
—other causes
—what foods prevent or develop it

DYNAMIC VIEW

—breast cancer is a widely known area of research with new advances and a few breakthroughs. However, no miracle cures or definite causes have been pinpointed

Causes
—diet (high fat, low carbohydrate)
—smoking
—occupational hazard
—environmental factors

Effects
—lump
—possible mastectomy
—radiation
—effects of treatment

Need to Trace
—history of breast cancer
—how is diet a cause of cancer
—studies on this—proof
—what factors do cancer-causing foods have in common?
—how can these factors in foods be prevented from causing cancer?

RELATIVE VIEW

Classification

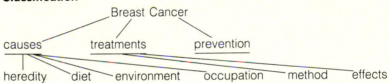

Comparison/Contrast
—compare cancer-causing foods to non–cancer-causing foods
—compare breast cancer diet to normal diet
—compare breast to lung cancer (leading killer in men)

GUIDING QUESTION AND POTENTIAL SITUATIONS, REVISED

Revised Subject: Anorexia nervosa. I was forced to change my topic because there was very little information on dietary influences on cancer. What there was appeared in hard-to-locate, highly specialized journals, written in language too technical for me to understand.

My Values and the Subject
—personal interest
—Karen Carpenter, Cherry Boone
—some of my friends
—family life—misunderstanding—confusion

Questions: What are the causes of anorexia nervosa? How do family interactions play a part in the development of anorexia nervosa? What are the characteristics of this illness and related disorders?

Audience:
—Primary: Adolescent girls who have personal interest in the subject
—Secondary: Writing instructor and class

Exploration: The exploration of my own personal experience with anorexia I did on my own because the subject is too personal for me to share with anyone—it is something I don't even understand, and maybe the true purpose of this paper is to help me discover something about myself.

FOCUS

Revised Subject
The characteristics and causes of bulimia and anorexia

Point of Significance
are diversified and not very well understood.

AUDIENCE ANALYSIS

1. My audience is adolescent girls who have a personal interest in the subject.
2. a. Background: They are young and fearful of unknown diseases, especially those featured in the media these days.
   b. Values: They value their own lives as well as the lives of their friends and families. They also value happiness and security along with personal growth.
3. a. Attitude toward the subject: These people have probably been confronted with this disorder through personal experience or the media. Yet they don't understand exactly what it is or the causes of it. They only know what they have seen and heard—some probably have facts distorted and don't know anything about it.
   b. Strength of attitude: They fear this subject and are most likely embarrassed and frightened to express interest in it. They hold their opinions strongly since anorexia is a very serious disorder which is becoming increasingly infamous.
   c. Willingess to act: They will be very willing to accept my information and use it in their best interest.
4. Specific role: Possible victims of the disease.
5. Analysis of role
   a. Background: I will assume that they know nothing for certain about the disease.
   b. Values: I will assume that they value their lives and are frightened of the disease.

c. Attitude toward the subject: I want them to believe strongly that the best way to cope with the disease is to understand it.

6. Relational role: Peers—familiar, informal voice.

ORGANIZATION

CLASSIFICATION MODE

¶ 1 Introduction.
¶ 2 Definition of anorexia and personality characteristics of anorectics are not fully understood.
¶ 3 The causes of anorexia are complex.
¶ 4 The definition of bulimia is complicated.
¶ 5 Bulimia has some characteristics like anorexia.
¶ 6 Bulimia has causes similar to those of anorexia.
¶ 7 Conclusion.

FIRST VERSION

A SILENT CRY FOR HELP

My weight has been my major concern for most of my life. I was a "plump" newborn, a "chubby" child, and a "stocky" adolescent who had yet to lose her baby fat. Being teased by peers, looked upon by unknown degrading eyes, and feeling frustration and anger when clothes-shopping are just a few of my undesirable memories. I guess inside I felt totally out of control of my life, of my body, of me. Toward the end of my adolescence I finally hit my frustrational climax and discovered a diet, after the infinite number I failed at, that made me lose my unwanted weight. My diet was simple: Don't eat. Thus, I lost the weight as well as my health, a strong body, shiny hair, and my emotional stability. You see, I wasn't fat to begin with, just plump, but I still imagined myself to be horribly overweight and a disgusting sight. After my big weight loss I finally felt in control of me by doing the only thing that no one else could—controlling my body weight. I'm sure that you, as young women of today, can understand my feelings and problems. Our society, friends, and family all want us to be healthy and happy while conforming to their rules and living our lives as they choose so in a sense they each have a small bit of control over us. But we each need our own space to live and grow as we choose, yet this space is often consumed unknowingly by those who affect and care for us the most. To understand my own eating/weight problem, I have researched the topic of common eating disorders, directing my words at you as young female adolescents who may be experiencing a problem similar to mine. Take heed of the facts I present and consider carefully what you are really doing to yourselves. You aren't actually controlling your body through these eating disorders—you are killing it.

On February 4, 1983, Karen Carpenter's heart failed, resulting in her death at the young age of 32. The news of her heart failure wasn't nearly as disturbing as the true cause of her death—anorexia nervosa. Anorexia nervosa is a severely destructive eating disorder with several distinctive characteristics and many uncertain causes. There is no known medical illness to account for anorexia (Winokur 1031); instead this illness may be caused by multiple factors, including individual, family, and cultural factors (Garner 648). Karen's death made many ignorant people realize that an uncountable number of victims are fighting the hardest battle of their lives against some kind of eating disorder, and sadly enough, most are losing these secret battles. It is thought that anorexia afflicts a known 1/200 women and this factor is increasing with amazing speed (Knickerbocker 130). Anorexia nervosa and a related disorder, bulimia, are probably the two best-known eating disorders out of the many that exist. Because these disorders are becoming more widely recognized in addition to increasing in number (Graner 647), it is time that you learn their characteristics and causes to better understand them and perhaps to begin identifying and coping with the real underlying problems before the effects of these disorders take control and destroy you.

By definition, anorexia nervosa is a syndrome characterized by extreme weight loss due to loss of appetite, with numerous classifying symptoms. Commonly found in female adolescents, it is a neurotic or psychosomatic disorder (Morgan 356). It occurs most often in the female population since less than 7% of known anorectics are male (Knickerbocker 130). Its general symptoms include a 25% body weight loss, hyperactivity, an abnormal eating attitude and behavior, a delusion of fatness, lack of menstruation, and disturbed body functions (Casper 1031). Michael Strober, an expert on eating disorders, comments: "Disturbance of body image has been regarded as one of its [anorexia nervosa's] cardinal features" (695). Body size overestimation by anorectics has been shown to correlate positively with denial of illness, psychosexual immaturity, disturbed appetite, and the hopeless belief that one can't control one's own fate (Strober 700). Anorectics greatly fear getting fat and are therefore preoccupied with food and weight since management of their eating impulse is seen as the key to control and well-being (Palmer 188). In fact, some anorectics don't even sense hunger, while others suppress it or cope with it by eating and then vomiting (the binge-purge syndrome), or bulimia, which we shall discuss later (Casper 1030). Anorectics also tend to disregard their own bodies since avoidance of coping with their body and its shape causes them less pain and frustration (Strober 695). Nevertheless, their body-size perception is more fixed than normal as well as overestimated (Garfinkel 707). Thus anorectics perceive themselves as being fat without accepting the reality of their thin body shape. In essence then, anorexia nervosa is a complex eating disorder characterized by major weight reduction, great body-size overestimation, and odd eating behaviors.

Anorexia nervosa victims themselves have distinct traits and personality features correlating to the illness itself. They display obsessional traits and are self-denying, quite overcompliant, and overly formalistic and maintain extreme self-control (Strober 358). These victims also hold high expectations of achievement in academics due to their high levels of intelligence and conformity (Morgan 368). As extreme introverts, anorectics are socially withdrawn while feeling very insecure during social activities and are therefore sexually inexperienced (Beumont 620). Their failure to associate with the opposite sex stems from the fact that by losing so much body weight and developing amenorrhea, they are shedding their female image to be neither masculine nor feminine, but instead at a less dangerous position in between the two (Combs 13). Furthermore, by minimizing their sexuality, many anorectics are actually denying sexual maturity in order to control their physical developments due to puberty and aging (Combs 17). Besides being high achievers and sexuality dismissers, anorectics are also usually the youngest children in their families and once had normal appetites as youngsters (Crisp 183). The majority are also from upper social class families (Kalucy 381) due to the fact that our culture directs its preference for skinniness especially at upper social class women (Garner 648). In general, anorexia victims are perfectionists, introverts, and upper-class society members who strongly fear puberty. Of course, not all skinny girls are victims of this illness.

A variety of agents are involved in the development of anorexia nervosa. David Garner and Paul Garfinkel, noted research experts on anorexia, distinguish three classes of factors in anorexia development: predisposing, precipitating, and perpetuation factors. The predisposing factors, such as personal traits, perception disturbances, family relationships, personalities, and attitudes toward weight, are those that initiate the development of the disorder itself. Precipitating factors include interpersonal separation, sexual development and conflicts, increased pressure to achieve, and some event or comment that magnifies feelings of inadequacy. These actually develop the disorder from its beginning stage and reinforce the desire to lose weight. Weight loss feedback, increased anxiety and social withdrawal, and environmental reinforcement are perpetuating factors that preserve the disorder itself (654). H. G. Morgan, another eating disorder researcher, studied patients in whom possible precipitating factors such as physical illness, teasing, school worries, and disturbed family interactions were found to have occurred a year prior to the onset of anorexia (362).

Nevertheless, of all of these possible causes of anorexia, family and cultural factors are probably the most prominent ones (Garner 648). Garner and Garfinkel find that our culture considers slender females attractive, independent, and in control. Their studies also show that this preference for skinniness is seen in beauty contest data and in an increased number of magazine diet ads that have shown a definite emphasis towards a thinner body standard for females over the past 20 years. Presently, increased demands have appeared just when women have greater difficulty adjusting since they feel they must be perfect while still filling the ideal feminine role. Consequently, these difficulties are often expressed through anorexia. Careers like modeling and dancing also cause increased concern for body slimness, leading to a greater risk for anorexia (648–653).

The family is also a primary cause of anorexia. Although the typical anorectic's family is seemingly very close, there are actually severe underlying problems within the family relationship structure (Knickerbocker 136). The parents are often overly concerned and protective as well as resistant to change, which results in a strong, controlling, and guilt-instilling relationship with the victim (Piazza 182–183). Psychiatrists have found that the anorectic's entire family is often overly concerned with weight, food, and activity; therefore, when problems arise, the child copes by changing her body shape since this is the only way her family has ever dealt with any major issues (Kalucy 381). Moreover, rewards and punishments are often equated with allowance and denial of certain foods, so the child forms harmful images about eating specific foods (Kalucy 389). Furthermore, maternal dominance of the child suppresses the child's need for individuality, independence, and experiences, thus leaving the child poorly prepared for adolescence (Kalucy 389). A final surprising note on familial causes of anorexia is that the anorectic is actually convinced that she is attractive, admired, and accepted in her ill state because her family and friends tend to give her consistent reinforcement (Branch 631). Overall, the causes of anorexia are multiple and not very well understood. As one recovered anorectic asks, "What causes anorexia? A little bit of everything—sexual fears, heredity, behavioristic reinforcements—as well as a bad family situation" (Knickerbocker 138).

Often referred to as the binge-purge syndrome, bulimia is a subgroup of anorexia nervosa (Palmer 188). Bulimia, although not a distinct syndrome, resembles anorexia nervosa and may be considered a result or a phase of anorexia (Russell 429–444). However, it is also possible that bulimia may develop without any earlier bouts with anorexia (Russell 445); hence, it is uncertain whether bulimia and anorexia are definitely separate or are connected eating disorders. Regina C. Casper, M.D., an expert on eating disorders, describes bulimia as a complex disorder which begins when the victim, unable to overcome hunger impulses, learns instead to binge—that is, to eat enormous quantities of food. After binging, she then purges herself by vomiting in order to not only relieve the tension and distressing emotions caused by her binging but also her initial hunger. The greatest danger found in bulimia is that the deliberate vomiting that occurs after overeating has been found to lead to severe physical difficulties, such as cell electrolyte and metabolic imbalance, heart trouble, and esophagus impairment, to name a few (Beumont 617). Thus, bulimia is a common illness that may stem from anorexia and is identified by the victim's tendency to overeat and then vomit in order to lose weight or to stay slender.

Though bulimia is quite similar to anorexia in the nature of the illness itself, bulimia victims display many differences in personality when compared with anorectics. For instance, while anorectics are described as introverted, sexually inexperienced, and very self-controlled, as well as ordinarily already slender prior to the illness, bulimics tend to be extroverts with sexual experience who have great difficulty abstaining from food and who were originally obese or overweight preceding their illness (Beumont 620). Furthermore, Dr. Casper notes that bulimics are generally more sensitive and experience greater depression, food obsession, bodily discomfort, anxiety, guilt, and insomnia. She adds that bulimics generally prefer not to cook since the temptation to binge is so great (1031–1033). Margaret Ray Combs, a researcher of eating habits, found most bulimics to be perfectionists who set high goals and felt great emotional pressure, repressed anger, and a strong sense of loneliness (17). The bulimia victim may also display hysterical bouts because she carries the awful secret of her vomiting as a safeguard against food, a secret which hides her embarrassment of a disgusting habit that soon becomes uncontrollable (Russell 441). Hence, as extroverts who are usually of normal weight and who feel much anger and loneliness in response to their surroundings, bulimics are distinguishable from anorectics.

Bulimics and anorectics also share some similarities in that both often experience amenorrhea and have a constant fear of becoming fat (Russell 432). Anorectics also vomit although less frequently and not as habitually as bulimics (Russell 432). Both are also high achievers who are overly dependent on their parents even though they often feel extensive conflicts in personal relationships with their family (Russell 442). Thus, bulimia and anorexia are both distinct and similar eating disorders that may or may not develop from each other.

Margaret Ray Combs has found that identifying the causes of bulimia is a very difficult feat due to the secretive habits of its victims. Combs explains that bulimia's causes are similar to those of anorexia in that stress and emotional strain from family conflicts, increased career pressure, and greater competition in sports are all responsible for the onset of both illnesses. Bulimics often lose control since society emphasizes thinness, thus causing most females to spend the majority of their lives denying themselves tempting foods (13–16). As a result of the increased stress and pressure on career women, partly because of competition, bulimia is becoming more common and is even thought to be present in 20 to 30% of college females (Combs 16). The effects and causes of eating disorders such as bulimia and anorexia are best seen in Combs' study of one anorexic woman who, after increasing her weight from 74 to 95 pounds on her 5′5″ frame, describes her eating disorder:

> Emotionally it's a new world and it's been the most vital and most difficult task to learn how to live within it, to feel comfortable owning my emotions, allowing them to identify me. I am still feeling vulnerable and fragile, and especially confused about my womanhood—easily influenced by others' expectations, frightened of losing control, losing people, losing my place. I need to continually test my strength by wielding an iron hand over the thing which is nearest and dearest to me, my own body. . . . Personally, I feel that my illness was/is a product of the conflicts all women have to deal with being a female in our society today. There is such a gross contradiction in the emphasis on being skinny, tiny, angular, fragile, and young-looking. How ironic that feminism is running side by side with a school of thought that haunts our every waking hour with visual and mental images of fraility, denial, and unimportance (16).

Overall, the causes of bulimia are uncertain yet quite similar to those of anorexia: family conflicts, academic and career pressures, and cultural influences.

Eating disorders are complex illnesses that develop in and affect both the victim's mind and body; their characteristics are numerous and varied, and the multitude of causes are as yet even more elusive. In this study, I have tried to emphasize the causes and characteristics of anorexia nervosa and a related disorder, bulimia. As for myself, I have discovered facts and important information about eating disorders that will help me to cope with and control my own illness even better as well as to possibly help another victim in the future. I'm sure that you can see, just as I saw, the relationships between the societal and familial causes and the illnesses' characteristics, relationships that will help you to identify for yourself those factors that cause and perpetuate such illnesses as anorexia and bulimia. One who has never experienced such battles as we have with eating will never fully understand just what anorexia and bulimia are; but surprisingly and sadly enough, those of us who have experienced these disorders will never understand them either. Perhaps this is why we must always be armed to face the battle of who shall be in control: us or the agonizing illness.

WORKS CITED

Bakan, R. "The Role of Zinc in Anorexia Nervosa: Etiology and Treatment." *Medical Hypothesis,* July 1979, 731–736.

Beumont, P. J. "'Dieters' and 'Vomiters and Purgers' in Anorexia Nervosa." *Psychological Medicine* 6 (1976): 617–622.

Beumont, P. J. "The Psychosexual Histories of Adolescent Girls and Young Women with Anorexia Nervosa." *Psychological Medicine,* Feb. 1981, 131–140.

Beumont, P. J. et al. "The Onset of Anorexia Nervosa." *Australian and New Zealand Journal of Psychiatry,* Sept. 1978, 145–149.

"Body Image." *Current Health,* 5 Jan. 1979, 22.

Branch, Hardin and Linda J. Eurman. "Social Attitudes Toward Patients with Anorexia Nervosa." *American Journal of Psychiatry* 137 (1980): 631–632.

Bruch, Hilde. "Developmental Deviations in Anorexia Nervosa." *Israel Annals of Psychiatry and Related Disciplines,* Sept. 1979, 255–261.

Buddelberg, Barbara and Claus. "Family Therapy of Anorexia Nervosa." *Praxis der Kinderpsychologie and Kinderpsychiatric,* Feb.–Mar. 1979, 37–43.

Buvat, J. and M. Buvat-Hervaut. "Misperception of Body and Concept and Dysmorphophobias in Mental Anorexia: 115 Cases of Both Sexes. 1. The Deterioration of Perceptive Mechanisms." *Annales Medico-Psychologiques,* April 1978, 547–592.

Casper, Regina C. et al. "Bulimia: Its Incidence and Clinical Importance in Patients with Anorexia Nervosa." *Archives of General Psychiatry* 37 (1980), 1030–1035.

Combs, Margaret Ray. "By Food Possessed: Some Binge and Purge, Others Starve Themselves All for the Sake of an Image." *Women's Sports,* 4 Feb. 1982, 12–16.

Crisp, A. H. "Clinical Features of Anorexia Nervosa: A Study of a Consecutive Series of 102 Female Patients." *Journal of Psychosomatic Research* 1980, 179–191.

Dubois, J. C. "Anorexia Nervosa in Men: Obsession with 'Weight Identity.' Some Nosological and Therapeutic Considerations." *Annales Medico-Psychologiques,* April 1978, 619–624.

Garfinkel, Paul E. "The Stability of Perceptual Disturbances in Anorexia Nervosa." *Psychological Medicine,* Nov. 1979, 703–708.

Garner, David M. "Cultural Expectations of Thinness in Women." *Psychological Reports* 47 (Oct. 1980): 483–491.

Garner, David M. "Perceptual Experiences in Anorexia Nervosa and Obesity." *Canadian Psychiatric Association Journal,* June 1978, 249–263.

Garner, David M. and Paul E. Garfinkel. "Sociocultural Factors in the Development of Anorexia Nervosa." *Psychological Medicine,* Nov. 1980, 647–656.

Genisicke, Peter. "Anorexia Nervosa: A Deficiency of Family Socialization?" *Zeitschrift fur Psychosomatische Medizin and Psychoanalyse,* July–Sept. 1979, 201–215.

Kalucy, R. S. "A Study of 56 Families with Anorexia Nervosa." *British Journal of Medical Psychology* 50 (1979): 381–395.

Knickerbocker, Laura and Alan J. Bankman. "Anorexia Nervosa: More Than Just a Teenager's Disease." *Cosmopolitan* 190 (1981): 130.

Loro, Albert D. and Carole S. Orleans. "Eating Disorders: A Bibliography of Recent Chemical and Research Reports." *Professional Psychology,* Dec. 1980, 946–948.

Morgan, H. G. and G. F. M. Russell. "Value of Family Background and Clinical Features as Predictors of Long-term Outcome in Anorexia Nervosa: Four-year Follow-up Study of 41 Patients." *Psychological Medicine* 5 (1975): 355–371.

Palmer, Robert L. "The Dietary Chaos Syndrome: A Useful New Term?" *British Journal of Medical Psychology,* June 1979, 187–190.

Piazza, Eugene. "Anorexia Nervosa: Controversial Aspects of Therapy." *Comprehensive Psychiatry,* May–June 1980, 177–189.

Russell, Gerald. "Bulimia Nervosa: An Ominous Variant of Anorexia Nervosa." *Psychological Medicine* 9 (1979): 429–448.

Russell, Gerald, "The Current Treatment of Anorexia Nervosa." *British Journal of Psychiatry,* Feb. 1981, 164–166.

Schwartz, Donald M. "Do Anorexics Get Well? Current Research and Future Needs." *American Journal of Psychiatry,* March 1981, 319–323.

Strober, Michael. "Body Image Disturbance in Anorexia Nervosa During the Acute and Recuperative Phases." *Psychological Medicine,* Nov. 1979, 695–701.

Strober, Michael. "Personality and Symptomatological Features in Young, Nonchronic Anorexia Nervosa Patients." *Journal of Psychosomatic Research,* 1980, 253–259.

Winokur, Andrew. "Primary Affective Disorder in Relatives of Patients with Anorexia Nervosa." *American Journal of Psychiatry,* June 1980, 695–698.

STUDENT RESPONSE TO WRITER 4

FOCUS

Focus is at end of introductory paragraph, but a bit unclear. Focus is maintained throughout paper. Topic sentences do reflect the main idea of the paper.

DEVELOPMENT

Information is supportive. Informative sources have been used well. Sufficient amount of data. Evidence worked in well. Citations used properly.

ORGANIZATION

Well-organized. Transitions seem all right. Coherence could be improved with more clarity in sentences.

STYLE

Appropriate formal style. Some sentences long and confusing. I had to read some two or three times in order to understand them the way they were meant. It would be more clear if a few shorter sentences were used. Easier to understand and more interesting when not trying to figure out what a sentence is saying.

CONVENTIONS

I would like to see a few more commas. Commas don't always have to be used, but it seems some sentences run on forever without a break. Overuse of "thus."

6

WRITING WITH AN EXPOSITORY AIM

In the College World/ Essay Examinations

Essay examinations test not only your ideas and information but also your writing skills because exams speed up the composing process. Exam week is not the time to acquire writing skills but rather the time to display them. Is there any purpose, then, in devoting a chapter to essay exam writing? Perhaps, depending on your type of problem with exams. If you find a discrepancy between the quality of your writing in composition courses and your writing on exams for other courses, you might have one of three types of problems: (1) You may believe that other instructors expect only a demonstration of mastery of content; (2) you may not know how to transfer your skills to a pressure situation; (3) you may lack experience in exam writing. This chapter will help you improve your performance on essay exams by demonstrating how a writer functions during exam-taking and by providing practice and giving criticism not only on content but also on writing skills.

THE EXPOSITORY AIM

In essay examinations, almost always your primary aim is expository, your secondary aim persuasive. You attempt to persuade your examiners that you have mastered the material by, first of all, demonstrating your mastery of the material—and that should be done by concentrating on the subject matter, not the audience. That is, you will try to inform the examiner of two things:

1. that you have learned the material
2. that you have learned from the examiner

It's possible to oversimplify this second principle dangerously. Demonstrating that you have learned from the examiner does not imply that you must *agree* with the examiner, and it certainly does not mean that you should only put into an answer what the examiner said about the topic in lecture or discussion. (You may disagree with the examiner, putting contrary information into the answer.) Simply regurgitating what the examiner has said may demonstrate that you have listened to the examiner but not that you have mastered the material, since in any course the material available on any topic exceeds what the examiner has said.

● GUIDING QUESTIONS

Two kinds of questions guide the writing of essay exams: questions you raise during the course for which you will write an essay examination, and questions posed at the time of the examination. The first, a long-range questioning attitude, is important preparation for an essay exam. As you attend lectures and analyze readings, you should continually ask:

1. How does this new material fit into my previous learning?
2. Are there any conflicting viewpoints among the readings or between the readings and the lectures?
3. What seems significant in this material to my instructor, the future reader of my essay exam?

Keeping track of important questions not only helps you prepare for eventual exams but also aids you in learning itself.

● **AUDIENCE**

The audience for an essay examination is obviously the examiner. You have had an opportunity to analyze this audience throughout the course. As with exploration, analysis of the audience should take place *before* the time of examination; you should go into examinations sure of the role you are to play and of the role the examiner will play. In order to do that, you can use the same audience guide you have used through five chapters of this book—and use it with great profit, since you should by the time of the examination have a rather full dossier on the examiner's attitudes, not only toward the subject matter but toward the students.

In most cases, the specific and relational roles of the audience for essay examinations are simple to spell out. The examiner specifically reads as a professional in the field of examination, that is, as a professional sociologist, psychologist, historian, and so on. Your relation to the examiner is as a subordinate, generally as a younger and less experienced professional. You use the audience guide to confirm those roles and to determine the examiner's opinions and attitudes within that framework.

AUDIENCE ANALYSIS

WRITER 1

1. My audience is my criminal justice teacher.
2. a. Background: He is a black ex-policeman who supported himself through graduate school by working as a cop. He knows street crime from experience and probably white-collar crime from books.
   b. Values: Justice seems a passion with him; equal justice. He respects the law, although he is sarcastic about the way it's applied in the courts.
3. a. Attitude toward the subject: He thinks most white-collar crime goes unpunished.
   b. Strength of opinion: He holds that opinion doggedly.
   c. Willingness to act: I think maybe the reason he's teaching the course is that he holds that opinion so strongly.
4. Specific role: I want him to act as what he is, a teacher of criminal justice.
5. Analysis of the role
   a. Background: He will know that there is an awful lot of material to be mastered for this exam, and he will remember, along with all the facts, the pressure I'm working under.
   b. Values: He will value justice and order and clarity and knowledge, and he should value my valuing those things.

c. Willingness to act: He will act, I hope, by giving me a good grade.

6. Relational role: I can't compete with him in his knowledge of crime, street or white collar, so I had better just try to speak as a subordinate—which is what I think a student is anyway—and show him that I understand where he's coming from and that I agree with him. I do anyway.

● **COMMENTARY**

Writer 1's analysis above is very good; the writer knows the audience well. The decision in 6, however, suggests that he is intimidated by the examiner and will simply try to agree with the examiner's opinion. It is never a good idea to try to give back exactly what the examiner gave to you. In the first place, it's impossible. In the second, it says little to the examiner about your command of the subject matter.

It would probably simplify Writer 1's task if he stopped viewing his reader as both a criminal justice professional and a teacher; notice that duality in his answer to 5b. The answer to 5a shows that the student is viewing the reader less as a scholar than as an examiner. If that's the aspect of "teacher" that the writer chooses to isolate for the reader, then he should emphasize the aspects of that role that will affect his answers. For instance, the teacher as examiner will be less interested in an exhaustive treatment of a subject than in an orderly presentation of the major points, with representative illustrations; he will be less interested in seeing all the details than in finding that all parts of the major outline are there.

● **EXPLORATION: PREPARING FOR THE EXAMINATION**

For an essay exam, you do two kinds of exploring: (1) while studying for an exam, and (2) during the examination itself. The exploratory guide you have been using works well to help you review your readings and lectures. If you study the material, organizing it under the three views, you will more easily perform the kinds of thinking required on tests:

1. recalling known material
2. discovering new relationships, required for the comparison and evaluation questions

The following exploratory guide will help you direct your studying.

EXPLORATORY GUIDE

- **Static View**
  - What are the key terms, ideas, theories, persons, dates, or events studied?
  - How would I define or identify them?
  - If asked to explain any of them, what important information and understanding do I need?
  - What examples or instances of them can I recall?

- **Dynamic View**
  - Did any of the above change, develop, or go through stages? If so, what, how, why?
  - What causes or effects do I know about these changes or movements?

- **Relative View**
  - How would I classify any of the above?
  - Are there obvious comparisons or contrasts between ideas, movements, theories, procedures?
  - Are there contrasting viewpoints in the readings? Between the readings and the lectures?

We will present the exploration of Writer 1 on white-collar crime, a subject on which he was to be examined. The content is taken from a cluster of articles he was assigned. After reading these articles, he organized the information using the three views of the exploratory guide. We include his full set of notes in the exploration below so that you can compare them with his later essay answers.*

EXPLORATION

WRITER 1

STATIC VIEW

Terms and Definitions
—white-collar crime (Edwin Sutherland, 1939): "a crime committed by a person of respectability and high social status in the course of his occupation"

* Articles used by Writer 1: Tom Alexander, "Waiting for the Great Computer Rip-off," *Fortune*, 90 (July, 1974), 142–146, 148, 150; "A $40-Billion Crime Wave Swamps American Business," *U.S. News & World Report*, 21 February 1977, pp. 47–48; J. Taylor De Weese, "The Trojan Horse Caper—and Assorted Other Computer Crimes," *Saturday Review*, 15 November 1975, pp. 10, 58–60; Harry E. Graves, "White Collar Crime: Are New Laws Necessary?" *Vital Speeches*, 15 June 1977, pp. 525–527; "New Style in Public Enemies—the White Collar Criminal," *U.S. News & World Report*, 12 March 1973, pp. 53–55; Gerald D. Robin, "White-Collar Crime and Employee Theft," *Crime and Delinquency*, 20 (July, 1974), 251–262.

(popular—Webster): "a crime . . . committed by a person in business, government, or a profession in the course of his occupational activities"

Types of White-Collar Crime
—insurance fraud
—check & credit card fraud
—land sales fraud
—investment fraud—Ponzi game (see notes)
—tax fraud
—shell corporation (see notes)
    —mail fraud—"scam" operation: take over long est'd business, order big on credit, sell mdse fast, abandon business before paying supplier
    —bankruptcy fraud
    —housing fraud—FHA officials plotted with accountants/appraisers to falsify buyers' $ status and inflate home values
    —embezzlement
    —bribery
    —kickbacks, payoffs
    —computer theft
    —counterfeiting

Stock Fraud—Examples
—mutual fund mgr. buys heavily from Broker X, who repays favor by tipping mgr. on "hot" issues for mgr.'s personal purchase
—accountants & execs falsify earnings potential in reports ⟶ raises stock prices ⟶ participants sell at big personal profit
—execs learn of development that will raise/lower value of their co.'s stock, then buy/sell before public knows
—employee theft (Robin): middle-class theft within "large businesses and industrial complexes: supermarkets, department stores, factories, and manufacturing plants"
—occupational crimes (Robin): "all violations that occur during the course of occupational activity and are related to employment"

Computer Crime (Robert Courtney, IBM comp. safety)
—clerical errors, employee dishonesty, fires, employee sabotage, water damage, outside ("remote") manipulation
—losing the "paper trial"—Equity Funding swindle
—accidental nature of detecting computer crime
—Donn Parker (Stanford computer researcher)

Examples of Computer Crime
—program bank computer to ignore overdrafts
—teller pockets most deposit $ then later types false info into computer or transfers $ into customers' accts. from any long-inactive accts.
—bank customer replaces blank deposit slips with encoded slips for personal account

—burglar checks computer credit reports to locate rich victims
—Jerry Schneider, Pacific T&T scandal (see notes)
—"Trojan horse" caper: fraud is programmed into memory of computer, left dormant for a time, then triggered; or second dormant program covers tracks of first
—"tiger teams" test computer safeguards by attacking "on-line" computer system—central computer that stores & processes data is connected directly to remote terminals by telephone lines
—"spoofing"—mimicking a legit. terminal, for eavesdropping
—"piggybacking"—intercepting and *changing* computer messages tapped, e.g., insert additional credit transfers to accts.

DYNAMIC VIEW

Change in Sutherland Definition Needed (Robin)
—classify white-collar crime and employee theft in separate categories
—current definition does not include persons in lower classes: underestimates amount of crime, distorts frequency of types of crime, gives wrong impression of character of criminals

White-collar Crime Growing Rapidly
—fraud-embezzlement arrests up 86% 1960–71; up 70% 1971–76
—forgery & counterfeiting arrests up 50% 1960–71
—1972 SEC found 1000+ violations in 900 inspections
—1972 HUD land deal complaint up from 50/wk to 300/wk in 8 mos.
—crackdown on tax cheaters: 1971, 35% of guilty imprisoned; 1972, 44% of guilty imprisoned
—crimes against business up 10%/yr
—1973–77, white-collar conviction up 100%

Causes
—unsuspecting management
—careless security (e.g., honor obvious forgery)
—risk of getting caught slight
—victims embarrassed at being "taken" & don't prosecute
—society's attitude (white-collar crime as normal business practice) dictates token punishment, if prosecuted at all
—decline in ties with family, church
—our hedonistic life-styles

Social Effects
—public cynicism—double standard in courts, token punishment for stock manipulators

Costs
—in higher prices to consumers
—in lost tax revenues
—to investors, who rely on possibly falsified reports

—to citizens—credit info invasion of privacy

—no letup in growing white-collar crime wave and crime costs foreseen

—total cost for crimes against business up 75% (to $21.7 billion from $12.4 billion) from 1971–77

Changes Needed to Halt White-Collar Crime

—computer manufacturers continue work to make systems more secure (e.g., use separate minicomputers to control access and manage user ID); a losing battle

—educate users to understand computer capabilities and limits

—reform not laws themselves but administration of them by judges & juries

—need specific criteria for sentencing

—change social attitude that white-collar criminal is too good to go to prison

RELATIVE VIEW

Robin's Characteristics of White-Collar Crime/Criminals	& Employee Theft/Thieves
—violations of industrial laws	—not violations of industrial laws
—violations of regulatory laws (criminality debatable)	—violations of criminal laws
—committed by upper-class persons	—committed mostly by middle-class persons
—misdemeanors	—felonies
—relatively recent origin	—not recent in origin
—persistent & deliberate	—no comparative statistics available
—wide range of sanctions, criminal/civil, harsh/mild	—no such range of sanctions
—relative immunity from prosecution	
—few previous criminal records	
—lenient treatment by courts	
—involves a violation of trust	
—victim is diffuse	
—corporations and executive management seen as one and the same, i.e., corporations seen as individuals	—not seen as one
—crimes as highly skilled & technically complex acts	—generally not skilled
—criminal does not lose status among business associates	—generally does lose status
—criminal contemptuous of law & government	—criminal supports conventional legal structures
—criminals don't see themselves as criminals	—criminals don't see themselves as criminals

—criminals learn from others practicing such crime, in relative isolation from those opposed to it

—crimes probably not committed due to this "differential association"

—significance—requires changes in theories of criminal behavior

—does not require changes in theories

—traditional occupational white-collar crime: employee theft (not personal violence)

—noncomputer crime: average take per hit = $100,000

—computer crime: average take per hit = $1,000,000

INCUBATION

One period of incubation occurs between your study period and the exam. Allow enough time for ideas and information to settle. If you "cram" until the second before the test starts, you will never be as successful as you could have been with a good night's sleep.

CLASS EXERCISES

1. Study the exploration of Writers 1 and 2 (at the end of the chapter).
   - What key ideas have they summarized under each view?
   - In what ways will the visual organization of this material aid them in remembering it?
2. As a sample subject, use the information in this text on the writing process.
   - Make a list of questions that you raised as the course progressed.
   - Make a list of questions that you think your instructor would find important about this subject.
   - Explore this topic using the exploratory guide.

● ASSIGNMENT: Preparing for the Examination

1. Take notes on the readings and lectures on the subject assigned by your instructor for your essay examination.
2. List important questions that arise about the material.
3. Study the material, exploring it with the exploratory guide.
4. Allow yourself incubation time.

● PLANNING DURING THE EXAMINATION

Understanding the types of questions asked on an essay examination is one of the keys to good performance.

Below are four general types of questions often asked on essay exams. Notice their implications for your thinking and writing:

1. Questions that ask you to *define* or *identify:* Such questions demand concise and accurate answers. Long, padded paragraphs not only reveal fuzzy thinking but also waste valuable test time.
2. Questions that ask you to *explain:* These questions expect you to expand an answer, giving a full account, examples, important background material. Short answers here are not sufficient. To handle such questions well, you need to have a thorough understanding of the subject.
3. Questions that ask you to *compare* and *contrast:* Such questions are more demanding because they require not only a good understanding of two or more subjects but also the ability to detect points of likeness or difference quickly and to infer generalizations.
4. Questions that ask you to *evaluate:* Evaluating is often the most difficult task demanded by an essay question. Even though such a question expects you to know only one subject well, you must quickly isolate significant criteria against which to measure the subject. Sometimes the instructor has given these criteria during the course. Other times you must look for them in your own experience.

TIME PLANS

In addition to identifying the types of questions being asked, another task at the beginning of the examination is to plan *timing,* because one of the pitfalls of essay examinations is uneven time distribution. The type of question usually suggests the percentage of time you should allow for it. Lists, definitions, and identifications require succinct, accurate answers, not lengthy, meandering development. Explanations and descriptions entail fuller expansion, with examples and specific information. Comparisons take much longer because they require you to discuss two subjects. Finally, evaluations, too, are time-consuming because they demand that you either supply or apply criteria and relate your subject to them.

Many instructors guide your time planning by weighting the questions with points. If your instructor doesn't give such guidance, ask for it. A minute's foresight can prevent you from running out of time before you get to the most challenging (and often most heavily weighted) question.

● FOCUSES

Focused answers are the delight of instructors because they signal that you have control and direction in your answer. Here are some sample focuses for different types of questions:

1. "EXPLAIN" QUESTIONS

Subject	*Point of Significance*
World War II———————————	had five main causes.
Wallace Stevens' poetry———————	deals with three major themes.

2. "COMPARE/CONTRAST" QUESTIONS

Subject	*Point of Significance*
Desdemona and Ophelia—————	are alike in three ways, but have one significant difference.
Women's liberation and the black civil rights movemen———————	share five important characteristics.

3. "EVALUATE" QUESTIONS

Subject	*Point of Significance*
The Panama Canal Treaty—————	is an unsuccessful compromise for two reasons.

In order to write from such focuses you need to pause, quickly explore, and incubate for a moment. If you plunge into the answers with handfuls of information, you will likely waste time and leave the reader in doubt as to the precise answer.

● ORGANIZATION

The inescapable fact about any answer to a question on an essay examination is that you never have time to write the answer you really want to develop. Hence, brevity and precision are all-important. Brevity and precision are achieved by selecting a mode of organization before writing. The organization of an answer is usually determined by the question, almost always by the verb in the question: *define, explain, compare and contrast, evaluate, agree or disagree.*

DEFINE

All definition questions are classification questions. Definition is a matter of

1. stating the term to be defined.
2. putting the term into a class (e.g., a pencil belongs to the class of writing instruments).
3. distinguishing the term from all other members of the class—hence, creating a subclass.

For example, define a pencil:

A pencil is a writing instrument made of a wooden cylinder with a graphite core.

When Writer 1 encountered his first question, "Define white-collar crime and briefly identify several practices," he needed to know how to organize a classification:

1. Definition: "White-collar crime is . . ."
2. Identification (i.e., accounts of classes or subclasses)
   a. Class I
   b. Class II
   c. Class III

Notice that items a, b, and c are not *examples;* they are generalized classes.

EXPLAIN

Questions that demand explanations as answers are generally organized by description or narration, signaled by the words in the question itself. Fortunately, questions that begin with "Discuss" usually go on to suggest a mode of organization, almost always by means of a noun: "Discuss several factors contributing to the difficulty of combatting white-collar crime" invites a descriptive organization with the word *factors.* "Discuss the history of . . ." calls for the narrative mode. "Account for" questions generally require the narrative mode, whether the question asks for a simple chronological sequence or a cause-and-effect relationship. The alert writer, unless there is good evidence to the contrary, always assumes that "Account for" means "Show me cause and effect"; the writer, therefore, constructs a narrative account showing that not only did one event follow another but it occurred *because* the other had happened.

COMPARE AND CONTRAST

Comparing and contrasting are complementary activities; they rest on discovering similarities and differences between two (or three, four, or more) items or concepts. A list of similarities and differences, located in the exploratory stage, can be organized in several ways. Suppose, as with Writer 1, the two things to be compared and contrasted are white-collar crime and street crime. You could say everything you had to say about white-collar crime and then everything you had to say about street crime. But no comparison or contrast has happened; the reader is left to make the comparisons. You could, after isolating the similarities and differences, organize the paper by pointing out first all the similarities and then all the differences—or vice versa.

Or you could organize the paper on the basis of similarities alone— that is, compare the elements the two have in common. If, for example, you were comparing and contrasting two automobiles, you might well organize your paper by writing about the initial price of one and then of the other, the styling of one and then of the other, the frequency-of-re-pair record of one and then of the other, the mileage of one and then of the other, and so on.

Generally, when two things must be compared and contrasted in an essay exam, the best organization is to write an account of the similarities first and an account of the differences second. This simple two-part organization requires a good deal of forethought in order to generate the similarities and differences.

EVALUATE

In order to evaluate, you must set criteria, give an account of the actual-ity, and then reach a judgment by measuring the actuality against the criteria. If Writer 1 were asked, for example, to evaluate whether white-collar crime could produce more social damage than street crime and traditional offenses, he would have to set up criteria for measuring "so-cial damage."

 # THE EXAMINATION

Writer 1, faced with the questions that follow, first determined the na-ture of the questions: question 1 asked for a precise definition with some identification; questions 2 and 3 called for more developed answers; question 4 involved contrasting; and question 5 required evaluating. These determinations helped him to plan his time. With an hour for the test, he allocated the following time: question 1, 5 minutes; questions 2 and 3, 10 minutes each; question 4, 15 minutes; and question 5, 15 minutes. Writer 1 assessed wisely both the types of answers required and the timing. His plan indicates that he is prepared for each question. If, however, he feels less able to answer certain questions, he should plan to proceed first to those he can handle.

EXAM QUESTIONS

Here are the questions asked in Writer 1's exam:

1. Define white-collar crime and briefly identify several practices.
2. From both a technical and a nontechnical viewpoint, account for the vulnerability of computer systems to criminal penetration.
3. Discuss several factors contributing to the difficulty of combating white-collar crime.
4. How may white-collar crime and employee theft be contrasted as subcategories of occupational crime?
5. Evaluate whether white-collar crime can produce more social damage than street crimes and traditional offenses.

EXAM ANSWERS

WRITER 1

1. White-collar crime can be defined in two ways: popular—crime committed by workers in their occupations; and academic—crime committed by upper-class people, according to Sutherland.

    The following are some examples of white-collar crime:
    a. Stock fraud, like when company management gets inside dope about something that will lower the price of their stock and so these insiders dump their personal stocks before the price falls;
    b. The "scam" operation, like when some unscrupulous outfit takes over a reputable business, orders big on credit (the creditors don't realize the business has changed hands), then quickly sells the goods at a discount and disappears before paying the creditors;
    c. Embezzlement by computer, like when employees program a bank's computers to ignore their overdrafts;
    d. Theft by computer, like when Jerry Schneider tapped into Pacific Bell's supply computer, ordered equipment, and had it delivered to places where he picked it up, and then later sold it right back to PBT to fill the shortages he himself had created. Also included would be things like tax evasions, bribery, kickbacks, and even counterfeiting.

2. From a technical viewpoint, five factors make computer crime possible. The "timesharing" setup allows a lot of different people at a lot of different places to

use the same computer data banks at the same time by just identifying themselves to the machine. This makes impersonating a user possible if you can find out the right password.

Since computer communication is by telephone lines, wiretapping is possible to eavesdrop on your competitors, and "piggybacking" is possible—eavesdropping and then impersonating users to sabotage their operations.

The fact that computers have memories makes the Trojan horse trick possible. The fact that equipment and programs and codes are all pretty standard makes all these crimes easier. Also, there is the fact that computers work with electronic speed and can be programmed to neatly erase the dirty business they were first programmed to do.

From a nontechnical viewpoint computers are vulnerable mainly because of poor security. Companies don't guard their terminals and office people give out passwords or leave important printouts lying around in garbage cans.

3. Combating crime is difficult for three reasons.

White-collar crime in general is hard to fight mainly because of society's attitude toward it. A lot of businessmen consider bribes and payoffs expected practice. Likewise, taking advantage of inside info to buy or sell your stocks isn't criminal to a lot of people.

Judges and juries share this attitude. They just can't get used to the idea of an upper-class criminal. They think this person is too good to go to jail and just made a mistake. So white-collar criminals only get token punishment, which doesn't deter them much.

Another reason is that the victims are too embarrassed at being "had" to even admit they have been, or they don't want to lose the public's confidence or tarnish their image by publicizing a crime. The thing is, officials can't fight crime they don't know about.

Computer crime is a special case. Because electronic records can be erased instantaneously, there's no paperwork, say, for suspicious auditors to go over. Experts estimate only 1 in 100 computer crimes will be found out. Because of the nature of computers, it's practically all chance.

4. Though they share some characteristics, white-collar crime and employee theft can be distinguished on several counts. The most obvious difference is that white-collar crime is committed by members of the middle class. White-collar crime usually involves a lot of technical know-how, whereas simple employee theft doesn't. White-collar crime is thus fairly new on the scene; employee theft has probably been around as long as capitalism itself.

While white-collar crimes, like collusion and stock fraud and computer cheating, are usually only misdemeanors, employee theft is generally a felony. If alleged white-collar criminals are convicted, they could get anything from a slap on the wrist to a few years in jail, but they are more likely to get the light sentence because of society's attitudes that favor this class and are down on giant corporations and take business cheating for granted. And they aren't likely to lose much status with their peers. On the other hand, if alleged employee thieves are convicted, they face harsher, more consistent and prescribed punishment, and they do lose face with their fellow workers.

5. Whether I agree or disagree depends on what is meant by "social damage." If "social damage" means injury to or loss of property or life, then I disagree. Murder, rape, even muggings and robberies do the worst damage. There is no physical harm involved with fraud or embezzlement (unless you're dealing with the Mafia). But if "social damage" means damage to the moral fiber of society, then I will agree, because white-collar crime *can* corrupt extensively in the long run, more so than isolated street crimes can. White-collar crimes are sneaky and greedy. White-collar criminals want their piece of the action in ripping off the system. If Nixon, if politicians, if businesspeople can play dirty games, so can they. This leads to a general mood of distrust and crafty competition where everyone is out to take advantage of the next guy in secret. And if good people continue to see white-collar criminals getting off so lightly in the courts, they will get more and more disgusted. White-collar crimes can contribute much more to creating cynicism in society than even murder or rape can.

CLASS EXERCISES

1. Read the following sample essay examinations.
   - Determine the kinds of answers that the questions require.
   - Plan the time you would allow for each question within a 50-minute period.
2. Formulate focuses for answers to questions b, c, and d in each examination.

Essay Examination 1:
a. Define expository, expressive, and persuasive aims.
b. Distinguish writing in the private, the public, and the college worlds.
c. Discuss the strategies of the writing process.
d. Determine the value of the audience guide or of the reader guide.

Essay Examination 2:
a. Some urban scholars have pointed out that "cities stand at the center of the currents and crosscurrents of broad-scale change that alter and reconstitute societies." Discuss this idea as it applies to any three of the following:
   1. Ancient Rome
   2. Renaissance cities
   3. London or Paris in the industrial era
   4. The Middle Ages
   5. Egypt and Mesopotamia
b. Repeatedly in this course we have stressed that urbanization must be studied from a variety of perspectives or, in other words, by

examining a number of interrelated variables. By using at least four specific examples of cities, urban civilizations, or eras (such as the Middle Ages or Renaissance), explain why this approach is so important.

Note: Only one of your examples may be from the period before the Middle Ages.

    c. In depth and detail, compare and contrast any two of the following:
1. Urban life in the Middle Ages
2. Urban life in the Renaissance
3. Urban life in the industrial age

3. Read Writer 1's answer to question 2 of his essay examination (pp. 312–313).
   - What is the focus?
   - What mode of organization is used?
   - How much from Writer 1's exploration (pp. 303–307) has he managed to use?
   - How well does he answer the question?
4. For practice, answer the questions for the first essay examination in Exercise 1 above.

● ASSIGNMENT: The Examination

> 1. Read carefully the questions your instructor provides for your essay examination.
> 2. Determine the kinds of questions asked.
> 3. Make a time plan.
> 4. Focus, develop, and organize your answers.

● READER RESPONSES

Essay examinations do not generally produce deathless prose, because the answers are written under the pressure of time and usually in a physical setting that inhibits concentration. Even the advice intended to offset atrocities in answers—"Save the last ten minutes to reread and edit"—has a drawback: anyone who has ever tried to read an "edited" essay answer with its crossings-out and writings-over, its carets and arrows pointing to afterthoughts in the margins, and its despairing postscript—"Ran out of time!"—knows what a bad impression editing can sometimes leave.

An essay answer should be read with major criteria in mind. An adequate answer requires

1. a clear focus.
2. a development of that focus by generalizations, supported by representative facts.
3. a recognizable pattern of organization.
4. a style appropriate to the examiner's attitude toward the subject matter.

INSTRUCTOR'S RESPONSE TO WRITER 1 (ANSWER 1)

FOCUS

The focus is clear: "White-collar crime can be defined in two ways. . . ." Since the two definitions are complementary, you need not choose between them.

DEVELOPMENT

The focus is developed well—four generalizations, each accompanied by an illustration. You have chosen to use only four items for illustration, but you have indicated that you are aware of others: "Also included would be. . . ."

STYLE

The style wavers. The answer begins in standard written English but lapses into "like when" as a connective in all four examples, and such phrases as "inside dope," "big on credit."

INSTRUCTOR'S RESPONSE TO WRITER 1 (ANSWER 4)

FOCUS

The focus is clearly announced in the first sentence. You have understood the question, which asked only for contrast; the focus statement refers to similarities, but puts the emphasis on differences.

DEVELOPMENT

The focus is set up for good development. The differences between white-collar crime and employee theft emerge through a series of categories based on common elements:

1. which social classes commit crime
2. what technical knowledge is necessary
3. which is the newer type of crime
4. what the legal categories are
5. what the legal penalties are
6. what the social penalties are

But the development could be improved. The first comparison and contrast is incomplete: "White-collar crime is committed by members of the middle class." What class commits employee theft?

STYLE

As in the first answer, the style is uneven, perhaps as a result of the writer losing sight of his audience. The answer begins in relatively formal standard written English but then shifts to phrases such as "a lot of technical know-how," "new on the scene," and "are down on."

CLASS EXERCISES

1. Read Writer 1's answers to questions 3 and 5 of his essay examination (pp. 313–314).
   - What are the focuses?
   - What information has the writer used? Is it accurate (see the writer's notes, pp. 303–307) and adequate? Why or why not?
   - What mode of organization is used?
   - What style is used?
2. Read and respond to Writer 2's essay examination on pp. 323–324.

ASSIGNMENT: Reader Responses

Working in groups, respond to each other's answers on the essay examination you did in the last assignment.

REVISING AND EDITING

Although essay examinations are not normally revised, it may be useful for you to do so in your writing class in order to understand better the types of problems you exhibited on the exam. First, consider some features of the expository style that should characterize exams.

THE EXPOSITORY STYLE

The style of an essay answer is determined by the style of the examiner. Most examiners take their subjects seriously; a few do not. For the first audience, a breezy, informal style replete with large generalizations is wrong. Most examiners see their subjects as disciplines, that is, areas of subject matter approached systematically and logically. A style that leans heavily on impressions or personal estimates (as evidenced in phrases such as "I feel" or "I believe") is wrong for that audience; most essay examinations do not call for expressions of feeling or belief but for a logical synthesis of material. Most examiners see their function as teachers (as opposed to their function as repositories of fact) to be that of showing students how to *relate* bits of factual material—to get from A to B by seeing a chronological sequence, a cause-and-effect relationship, a contradiction, and so on. For that audience, transitions become very important: *because, since, therefore, on the other hand;* transitions show the direction in which a mind is moving.

Finally, most examiners realize that no one can set down in a brief examination time all the facts that lie behind a generalization. But they expect to see both a generalization and the *representative* facts that validate the generalization. Given a large question and short time, the best stylistic practice is to make heavy use of conventional qualifiers (*for example, for instance, such as, like*) and follow the qualifier with one or two representative items. Because you do not have time to revise your sentences, you must rely on your acquired syntactic fluency and your command of conventions. If possible, allow a little time for rereading your answers.

It is reasonable to suppose that an examiner does not require absolute accuracy in the fine points of standard written English. On the other hand, the examiner is going to be disappointed by a student who, while writing on the causes of the Civil War, cannot spell "Lincoln" or "Confederacy," or who cannot, by the proper use of subordinating conjunctions, relate a cause to an effect. In other words, conventions do matter in an essay exam. Remember that ordinarily the specific role of the audience is that of a professional in the field, a role in which standard written

English is the standard dialect. It is therefore worth saving five minutes at the end of an hour examination to proofread for errors of convention.

CLASS EXERCISES

1. Revise Writer 1's essay examination on the basis of your response and the response in the text.
2. If you had errors of convention in your answers, study the appropriate sections on grammar, spelling, and punctuation in Chapter 9.

ASSIGNMENT: Revising and Editing

Revise your own answers in your examination.

A WRITER'S PROCESS

Below we present the sequence followed in Writer 2's writing process.*

EXPLORATION

SUBJECT: CREATIVE THINKING

STATIC VIEW

Curiosity

Keys: Ideas and theories; definitions; important information

1. Curiosity is lost because questions are discouraged by parents and teachers. We lose the questioning habit.
2. In order to regain your curiosity, six techniques can be put into use:
   a. Be observant—look at and listen more closely to people, places, and things; pay attention to details and behaviors; and observe yourself.

* Articles used by Writer 2: Vincent Ruggiero, *The Art of Thinking: A Guide to Critical and Creative Thought* (New York: Harper & Row, 1984); Alvin L. Simberg, "Obstacles to Creative Thinking," in *Training Creative Thinking,* Gary A. Davis and Joseph A. Scott, eds. (New York: Holt, Rinehart and Winston, 1971).

b. Look for imperfections—realize where improvements can be made and recognize that things are inventions. Everything is open to improvement; and especially look at manufactured objects.

c. See dissatisfaction as a challenge—capitalize on disappointments and frustrations. Get beyond negative reactions by putting ingenuity to work. Ask yourself what the problem is and set about finding a solution.

d. Search for causes—be alert to any significant solution or event you cannot explain satisfactorily. Wonder and practice.

e. Be sensitive to implications—every discovery, invention, or new perspective makes an impact whose extent is seldom fully realized at first.

f. Recognize the opportunity in controversy—start without assumptions about exactly how much truth is on each side. Reconsider any issue from a more balanced perspective. Do not take sides—fit parts together in proper places. Record evidence for both sides; this helps you to be more objective and leads to a more enlightened position.

Examples

a. Be observant—watch people's actions in a cafeteria and compare them. Note mannerisms in group discussions. Look for clues from passersby.

b. Look for imperfections—look at manufactured objects such as blackboards, desks, clothes, cars. Evolution or developments.

c. See dissatisfaction as a challenge—roommate noisy when sleeping; pop quizzes; car refusing to start.

d. Search for causes—anthrax; diabetes. Good practices—reading or watching news.

e. Be sensitive to implications—study of homosexuality; shyness caused by genetic predisposition; committing crimes caused by genetic predisposition; convicted murderer engaging in a hunger strike while in prison had a legal right to starve himself to death.

f. Recognize the opportunity in controversy—abortion.

Making Important Distinctions

Avoid lumping all considerations together indiscriminately. Keep distinctions:

1. Between persons and ideas. Be aware of your reactions to people and try compensating for them. Judge ideas on merit. *Examples:* Winston Churchill; Joseph Stalin.

2. Between matters of taste and matters of judgment. For matters of taste—express our personal preferences without defending them. For matters of judgment—obligation to provide evidence; obligation to judge view by evidence presented. Express judgments on controversial issues as if they were matters of taste rather than matters of judgment.

3. Between fact and interpretation. For matters of fact—know with certainty, objectively verified or demonstrable. For matters of interpretation—explanation of meaning or significance. *Danger:* You will regard assumptions that ought to be questioned and contrasted with other views as unquestionable.

4. Between literal and ironic statements. Writers make points by saying the exact opposite of what they mean, using irony or satire. Be alert to subtlety and do not misread it or the message you receive will be much different from the writer's intention.

5. Between an idea's validity and quality of its expression. A thought's expression can deceive us about its validity. Separate the form from the content before judging. *Examples: impassioned, eloquent* → favorable; *lifeless, inarticulate, error-filled* → negative.

Obstacles to Creative Thinking

1. Perceptual blocks
   a. Difficulty in isolating the problem
      i. Know what you want to deal with
      ii. Things that are relevant
   b. Difficulty caused by narrowing problem too much; makes problem smaller than it is; ignores environment
   c. Inability to define terms (must define things specifically—then can stay on point more)
   d. Failure to use all of your senses when observing
   e. Difficulty in seeing remote relationships; look at similarities
   f. Difficulty in investigating the obvious
   g. Failure to distinguish between cause and effect; conclusion basis justifies your conclusion

2. Cultural blocks
   a. Desire to conform to an adopted pattern
   b. Thinking that it is not polite to be too inquisitive or doubt what you're told
   c. Overemphasis on competition or cooperation
   d. Too much faith in statistics
      i. Can be worded deceptively
      ii. Who says it? Need to be credible
   e. Difficulties arising from overgeneralizations
   f. Too much faith in reason and logic
   g. Tendency to follow an all-or-nothing attitude
   h. Too much or too little knowledge about the field in which you are working
   i. Belief that indulging in fantasy or daydreaming is worthless

3. Emotional blocks
   a. Fear of making a mistake or making a fool of yourself
   b. Grabbing the first idea that comes along
   c. Rigidity of thinking
   d. Overmotivation to succeed quickly
   e. Pathological desire for security; feel like you need it to exist
   f. Fear of teacher or audience and distrust of them
   g. Lack of drive in carrying something through to completion
   h. Lack of drive in putting a solution to work

Aspect—how to overcome these blocks
Be aware of blocks—specify them and think of ways to counteract them

DYNAMIC VIEW

To be successful in revealing challenges and meeting opportunities around you, you need lively curiosity and analytical skills. The skills help you to understand and evaluate any ideas encountered. Analysis is not taught systematically in American education so many learned it haphazardly and use it in a sporadic, unconscious, and inefficient manner.

I think we need to have classes beginning in grade school on analysis. These classes would help us to deal with problems in a more logical way and would provide challenges to think through situations. Analytical skills do need to be taught.

Children ask many questions because they are curious. Parents tire of answering and teachers do not have time to answer. The children soon lose the habit of questioning and even of thinking of questions. Curiosity withers because it is not practiced and thinking loses its dynamics.

This is true because if you look around at many people, they merely exist. People have become so lazy. They don't want to ask questions and they don't want to think.

RELATIVE VIEW

Classification: These readings give instructions on how to go about sharpening analytical skills. There are no contrasting viewpoints present.

Reading
—Reading is reasoning. What is seen on the page sets your mind at work, collating, criticizing, interpreting, questioning, comprehending, and comparing.
—Reading is an active, dynamic process.

Evaluating an Argument
1. Steps
   a. Summarize essential argument and evidence presented in support of argument.
   b. Evaluate the essential argument and evidence.
   c. Draw conclusion about the validity of the argument.
2. Terms
   —*Essential argument*—The central or controlling idea which is expressed directly and given prominence.
   —*Evidence*—The material used to support the essential argument; it demonstrates the validity of the writer's judgment. Four categories:
   　　　　—confirmed details or statistics
   　　　　—writer's own experience and observation
   　　　　—judgment of authorities
   　　　　—other people's evidence and observation
   —*Summarizing*
   —subheadings

—underline key sentences or paragraphs
—write out essential argument in complete sentences
—briefly list the kind and the amount of evidence
—write a brief version
—*Evaluating*—Reading essential argument and asking:
   —How clear?
   —What challenges?
   —What evidence?
   —Is all relevant?
   —Current sources?
   —Reliable and authoritative sources?
   —Examples typical and comprehensive?
   —Any omissions?
—*Judging*—Deciding whether author's view is more reasonable than any other, in light of evidence presented.
3. Conclusions
   a. If you agree/disagree in parts—explain and support position
   b. If you note vagueness/ambiguity—don't attempt to answer—use if/then approach
   c. If you deal with conflicting testimony—identify conflict and explain uncertainty

EXAM QUESTIONS

1. Identify the six techniques suggested for rekindling one's curiosity.
2. Contrast the processes of passive reading and analytical reading.
3. Discuss, with as much detail as you have time for, the three types of obstacles to creative thinking.
4. Judge the value of critical (not creative) thinking as a research skill.

EXAM ANSWERS

1. The six techniques suggested for rekindling one's curiosity are:
   a. be observant
   b. look for imperfections
   c. regard dissatisfaction as a challenge
   d. search for causes
   e. be sensitive to implications
   f. recognize controversy as a challenge
2. The processes of passive reading and analytical reading are quite different. In passive reading, the reader reads for pleasure or to learn about a subject. However, in analytical reading, evaluation must take place. When reading analytically, three steps can be taken to make the task of analyzing easier. These three steps are summarizing, evaluating, and judging. After the article is read,

summarize the essential argument and the evidence. This provides a miniature that can be easily evaluated, which is the next step. The reader needs to ask various questions in evaluating so that a judgment or conclusion can be made. Some of the questions asked are: Is the evidence relevant, has it been cited in a credible manner, has any been left out, and is it feasible? After evaluating, a judgment can be made relatively easily because the reader can agree or disagree with the writer on the basis of the evaluation.

Whereas passive reading is a pleasurable task and relatively simple and easy, analytical reading involves three steps that cause the reader to think. Analytical reading takes up a great deal of time and passive reading usually takes up less time. Furthermore, passive reading does not require as much thought or concentration as does analytical reading.

3. The three types of obstacles to creative thinking are perceptual blocks, cultural blocks, and emotional blocks. People perceive differently and are sometimes wrong in their perceptions. Some perceptual blocks include limiting the topic too much, difficulty in narrowing a broad topic, and difficulty in defining terms. Perceptual blocks cause us to focus on the wrong things or ideas.

Cultural blocks are those things that have been instilled in us from society. Some cultural blocks include believing fantasy or daydreaming is useless, believing that it is not polite to question authorities or wonder about certain things, overemphasizing competition cooperation, and wanting to succeed too quickly.

Emotional blocks include such items as fear of making a mistake or making a fool out of yourself, fear of your audience or teacher, thus causing distrust, the desire or need for security, rigidity of thinking, grabbing onto the first idea that comes to you, and the lack of drive or carrying out a solution.

All of these blocks cause problems in creative thinking. The important thing to remember is to just be aware of the ones that cause problems for you. After you have identified your blocks, try to counteract them and this will lead to more creativity in your thinking.

4. Critical thinking requires analytical skills and evaluative processes. In terms of a research skill, critical thinking is of utmost importance. In researching a particular subject, a researcher must be able to utilize the three steps in analytical or critical thinking. Because a great deal of information must be acquired, summarizing essential arguments and evidence is a key element. By summarizing information, the researcher will save time and effort.

Researchers must also evaluate the information they have compiled in order to form a conclusion or judgment. Evaluation is the second process of critical thinking, so it ties into researching skills directly.

Lastly, researchers must judge or make conclusions about large amounts of information. By being able to analyze through critical thinking, this task is handled quite easily.

Critical thinking does play the most dominant role as a research skill and by using analysis when we do our research paper, our task should become somewhat easier to achieve or accomplish.

WRITING WITH AN EXPOSITORY AIM

In the College World/ Critical Papers

Critical writing has an expository aim: it attempts to share a reader's meaning of a poem, play, short story, or essay. It attempts, in other words, to enable the audience to see in what has been read something not seen before. If the meaning is new to the audience, the aim leans toward the informative. If the interpretation is new to scholarship itself, the discourse leans toward the scientific. (If you need a refresher on the difference between informative and scientific expository aims, see Chapter 5.)

After reading a novel or a poem, have you ever asked, "What was the writer getting at?" Have you and friends ever argued over a play or a movie? These attempts to understand the creations of others, to find more satisfying interpretations, are critical acts. Writing is one of the best ways to penetrate the complexity of novels, poems, plays, and essays. This chapter will show you how to use your writing powers to interpret poetry and essays.

THE GUIDING QUESTION

Whenever you read a poem or essay, you have some kind of overall reaction. You may be puzzled, irritated, bored, stirred, or confused. A good way to begin critical writing is to select a poem, essay, or story that arouses some kind of strong reaction and then identify the values or expectations that this piece exceeds or falls short of. If you must write on an assigned piece, identify the strongest reactions you have to it and then question what you need to discover about the poem or prose piece in order to explain your reaction and to understand the piece better.

A good way to begin is with your initial raw response to an essay or poem—"Wow" or "Ugh" or "So?" Look beneath this reaction to identify some general feature of the essay or poem that may have provoked your reaction. Examine how these features relate to your expectations of a good essay or poem or how they jar some of your values. State this dissonance and formulate a question.

Your question should express not only your own personal dissonance but also something you want to understand about the piece of writing. Because your paper will be expository, it will emphasize the *subject,* providing a better explanation of it to an audience that lacks such understanding.

AUDIENCE AND SITUATION

Critical writing is writing about writing. In the beginning you assume that the audience has read the essay, poem, play, or whatever you are discussing. You and the reader share common *knowledge* of the essay or poem and presumably a common interest in it. Your choice of audience is, therefore, narrow in the beginning: the audience must be one that was interested enough to read the original work. Your task is not to cajole an audience into reading it.

Who might that audience be? There are three possibilities:

1. Your audience might be anyone attracted to the essay or poem by the name of the author, the topic, or the form: Some people like to read, for example, E. B. White's work, no matter what he writes about. Some like to read essays, no matter what essayist. Some like to read about death or sex or butterfly collecting. Other people like to read the poetry of Galway Kinnell. Still others enjoy reading poetry, no matter who wrote it.
2. Your audience might be anyone who read the essay or poem out of an interest external to personal preference—as when a student is assigned the reading of a poem, essay, short story, and so on. The interest in the audience in that case may not be so much in the essay or poem as in meeting a class assignment.
3. Your audience might be a teacher or some superior who has assigned the material.

The writing situation for critical papers done for classes usually entails an essay format and an audience of instructor, classmates, or both. We will first examine critical writing on poetry and then turn to writing about prose.

POETRY

Below is the poem "Wires," by Philip Larkin, on which Writers 1 and 2 wrote critical papers.

WIRES

The widest prairies have electric fences,
For though old cattle know they must not stray
Young steers are always scenting purer water
Not here but anywhere. Beyond the wires

Leads them to blunder up against the wires
Whose muscle-shredding violence gives no quarter.
Young steers become old cattle from the day,
Electric limits to their widest senses.[1]

THE GUIDING QUESTION AND SITUATION

WRITER 1

Subject: "Wires"

My Values and Expectations
—I feel that free spirits are beautiful

My Subject
—the reduction of energetic young steers to docile beasts by means of electric wires

—I hate total confinement

—It's a painful way for an animal to learn it can never venture beyond

—fencing in of steers

—the steers are unable to detect the electric wires until they actually feel the shock

Questions: Why does the fate of the young steers make me so angry? What do the steers and wires stand for?

Audience

—Primary: Mrs. Smith, my 12th grade literature teacher

—Secondary: Composition instructor

WRITER 2

My Subject: "Wires"

My Values and Expectations	**My Subject**
—young men becoming old men through their experiences	—young steers becoming old through experience with fence
—young person wanting to do new things	—young steers' impatience to explore
—old peoples' lack of movement	—old age's reluctance to disobey
—society's fence against people	—steers' violence against the wire

Questions: Why does this poem cause me to have feelings of anger against society? What deeper human truth seems to be expressed here?

Audience

—Primary: Ms. Brown and Mrs. Jones, my literature instructor and my roommate's

—Secondary: My composition class

● **COMMENTARY**

Writer 1 has done valuable beginning work. She shows in comparing her subject with her values that she is reacting to something ugly and unfair in the poem. Her two questions are closely related: if she can say what the steers and wires stand for, then she will be able to say why the poem makes her angry. In addition, she has chosen an audience, her twelfth-grade literature teacher, who presumably is interested both in verse and in her former student's ability to interpret.

ESSAYS

Writer 3 wrote a critical paper on a persuasive essay by one of his classmates. Here is the persuasive essay:

THERE'S NO PLACE LIKE HOME

The last years—they should be spent in happiness and serenity. Does a nursing home provide the happiness and peacefulness that a mobile, self-reliant, and competent elderly person deserves, or is institutional living depressing and saddening to older people? My grandmother's house makes me realize that elderly people should spend their declining years in their own homes as long as possible.

When I visit my grandma, the smile on her face and the sparkling gleam in her eyes are a sight to behold. As she welcomes me in, the charm and elegance of her little old house overwhelms me. The old, faded picture portraits hanging on the wall speak to me, telling me all about my grandmother's family, and her worn, but beautifully carved antique furniture relates to me a unique part of her personality. She serves me tea from her brass teakettle, which is a cherished family heirloom, as we talk to each other about the happenings in our daily lives. In the background the grandfather clock ticks loudly as Grandma's toy French poodle plays happily with his squeaky toys. The whole atmosphere is one of peacefulness. I ask a lot of questions because I find myself so fascinated with her stories. She brings out a dusty box filled with old electric trains, books, and "ancient" science experiment kits that belonged to her son—my dad—and reveals aspects of his youth that I'd never known before. My eyes roam around some more, admiring the delicately embroidered afghan on the old Victorian loveseat and wondering whether that old cathedral radio on the shelf still works, as my grandma busies herself in the kitchen.

The aroma of her own homemade hot vegetable soup, prepared from a recipe that she says has been in the family for years, and freshly baked bread fill the house, and suddenly I'm very hungry. Spicy pumpkin pie and beautifully decorated sugar cookies for dessert top off a delicious lunch.

After lunch I find I don't have to go far before I am surrounded by beauty again. Her backyard is filled with many varieties of trees and multicolored blossoms, obviously very carefully tended. Her hybrid tea roses are very fragrant, and she bids me goodbye after giving me a beautiful bouquet to enjoy at home. As I am leaving I notice the peacefulness and serenity that settle over her house at dusk. She says she spends her nights quietly reading a book or a magazine or watching T.V., but mostly anticipating a call or the next visit from her relatives. She seems so happy and content with her life that I could never imagine her living in a nursing home.

My experience with nursing homes includes several visits to a great-aunt whose family put her there a few years ago. I find myself so depressed in the atmosphere of a nursing home. The sterile, germicidal smell hits me almost immediately, and the monotonous, dull, pale green walls seem endless. The cheap, styleless furniture in the patients' rooms and the lack of personal pictures on the walls give me no inkling of the occupants' personalities. As I pass the huge, impersonal sitting room, the patients just stare blankly at me, giving me a cold, uneasy feeling. One elderly lady sits rocking back and forth, holding a stuffed baby doll tightly in her arms. Some old people can be heard whining and crying during the day. When I leave the nursing home I feel that the elderly lack privacy here; their care is impersonal, the food is bland, and the activity is limited.

I am convinced that young adults who truly love their parents and grandparents should make every effort to let them stay in their own homes by lending a hand with the more strenuous housework. The older persons' own possessions in their homes define and maintain their personalities, and the light housework that they do keeps them active and healthy. The reward is twofold—happiness for the elderly person and that unexplainable feeling that a young person has inside when helping to bring some joy to another.

GUIDING QUESTION AND SITUATION

WRITER 3

My Subject: "There's No Place Like Home"

My Values and Expectations	**My Subject**
—good reasons and examples	—good focus
—use of appeals	—a good example of grandmother's house
—writer's credibility	—didn't persuade me

Question: Why wasn't the essay persuasive despite the fact that the focus was good?
Audience: Teacher of the writing class

CLASS EXERCISES

1. Discuss the guiding questions of Writers 2 and 3.
   - What dissonances do they express?
   - To what kinds of interpretations or evaluations of the poem and essay will the questions lead?
   - In what better ways could the questions have been formulated?
2. Read the following poem by W. S. Merwin:

FINDING A TEACHER

In the woods I came on an old friend fishing
and I asked him a question
and he said Wait
fish were rising in the deep stream
but his line was not stirring
but I waited
it was a question about the sun
about my two eyes
my ears my mouth
my heart the earth with its four seasons
my feet where I was standing
where I was going
it slipped through my hands
as though it were water
into the river

it flowed under the trees
it sank under hulls far away
and was gone without me
then where I stood night fell

I no longer knew what to ask
I could tell that his line had no hook
I understood that I was to stay and eat with him[2]

3. As a class, discuss your initial feelings about the poem.
4. Identify the aspects that puzzle or delight you or conflict with your expectations about poetry.
5. Make a list of questions you would like to answer about the poem.

⬤ **ASSIGNMENT: The Guiding Question and Situation**

1. Select the piece of writing on which you will write a critical paper.
2. Identify the values and expectations that the piece either exceeds or does not meet.
3. Formulate a question about the work.
4. Identify you audience(s).

⬤ **EXPLORATION**

In order to explore an essay or poem, you have to know something about its form. You should have no trouble with the essay because by now you have a strong background in what constitutes a good essay, whether expressive, persuasive, or expository. You may, however, require help exploring a poem.

EXPLORING A POEM

To illustrate some of the terms you will need for the analysis of a poem, we will explore the following poem by William Stafford:

BESS

Ours are the streets where Bess first met her
cancer. She went to work every day past the
secure houses. At her job in the library
she arranged better and better flowers, and when
students asked for books her hand went out
to help. In the last year of her life
she had to keep her friends from knowing
how happy they were. She listened while they
complained about food or work or the weather.
And the great national events danced
their grotesque, fake importance. Always

Pain moved where she moved. She walked
ahead; it came. She hid; it found her.
No one ever served another so truly;
no enemy ever meant so strong a hate.
It was almost as if there was no room
left for her on earth. But she remembered
where joy used to live. She straightened its flowers;
she did not weep when she passed its houses;
and when finally she pulled into a tiny corner
and slipped from pain, her hand opened
again, and the streets opened, and she wished all well.[3]

Certain terms are useful to know when discussing poetry.

● **Imagery**

One of the primary functions of language is to convey *images*. An image
is an imitation in the mind of something that exists outside us, and the
kind of language that performs that function has come to have the name
of *imagery*. Imagery has several varieties:

1. *Direct imagery* consists of references to things that can be directly
    encountered by our senses:
    a. sight—streets, Bess, library, students, flowers, books, hands,
        friends
    b. sounds—"complained about food or work or the weather"
2. *Indirect imagery* consists of figures of speech (a fuller list of these
    appears in the Glossary). These are ways of using language that
    convert things that cannot be directly encountered by our senses
    into things that can be sensed or that convert things that can be
    directly encountered into concepts. Here are some of those ways:
    a. *Personification*—turning abstractions into persons:

        met her cancer
        Pain moved where she moved

> The great national events danced
> where joy used to live

    b.   *Metonymy*—using one term for another it suggests. The word *hand,* for example, recurs in Stafford's poem, but it stands for more than a physical hand. In "her hand went out to help" more than Bess's hand was used to help, and in "her hand opened again," more than her hand relaxed in death.

    c.   *Symbolism*—using an object or action that can be directly encountered by our senses to represent something more abstract:

> pulled into a tiny corner
> The streets opened,
> no room left for her on earth
> secure houses

Diction

The poet also pays close attention to diction, the choice of words. Stafford's poem is composed almost entirely of simple, ordinary words, appropriate to the simple, ordinary person he is describing (who did something complex and extraordinary). The exception occurs in one statement in the first stanza: "And the great national events *danced their grotesque, fake importance.*" The contrast between the importance of what Bess achieved and the relative insignificance of national events is made plain by this single act of language.

Persona

Acts of language are created by writers. And this leads us to one more term that the critical writer dealing with poetry should command: *persona.* By this time, the concept of a writer choosing a role to play in relation to the audience should be well established. In critical writing, which is writing about writing, the writer is first of all a reader; as a reader, the writer must bear in mind always that the author of the poem has created a voice and is, therefore, not necessarily identical with the voice that speaks in the poem. The created voice that speaks in the poem is called the *persona,* and the characteristics of the persona are discovered from the poem, not from the biography of the author.

Technical Language

Poets also pay closer attention than most prose writers to the *technical* resources of the language.

All writing has divisions of thought. The paragraph of prose becomes the *stanza* of poetry, the physical division on the page of units of thought. Stafford's poem contains two stanzas. The first centers on Bess's relationships with others, neighborhood and national. The second centers on her relationship with her own problem—which she treated in the same fashion as all else.

Within the stanzas, the poet arranges his words with extreme care. Notice these features:

1. *Rhythm* is the pace and pattern of movement in a statement. The first stanza contains longer lines and fewer pauses than the second, causing the reader's pace to slow in the second stanza. The two stanzas are quite different in several technical respects, most notably in the kinds of *repetition* the writer has used.

2. *Sounds.* The poet in the first stanza makes heavy use of repetition of consonants. Notice the repetition of the *s* sound in "Ours are the streets where Bess first met her cancer," and again (with the repetition of *w* added) in "She went to work every day past the secure houses." The pattern does not appear strongly again until the concluding clause of the poem: "and she wished all well."

3. *Rhyme* is, of course, a repetition of sounds—usually at the end of lines. Not all poems rhyme: "Wires" does: "Bess" does not. The reasons for using rhyme in a poem may vary, from providing the simple musical pleasure of a recurrent sound to suggesting a pattern of thought in the poem. Repetition, after all, both connects and emphasizes. An examination of the rhyme scheme of "Wires," for example, will suggest to the reader a connection between the stanzas that might otherwise be missed.

4. *Sentence structures.* The first stanza contains almost no repetitive structures. But the second stanza is built on them:

> Pain moved where she moved
> She walked ahead; it came.
> She hid; it found her.
> No one ever . . . no enemy ever. . .
> her hand opened again, and the streets opened. . . .

Exploring a poem means, then, first identifying its distinctive features and structural pattern and then determining what each of these elements *means* in the poem. In addition, you can compare the poem to other poems, classify the poem as to type—sonnet, lyric, ballad, and so on—and even create analogies for the poem.

This brief survey of terms does not attempt to deal in any depth with *prosody,* the science of sound in poetry. Your instructor may wish to go further into the study of sound effects—meter, types of rhyme, stanza forms, assonance, consonance, and so on. Certainly if your previous study has equipped you to analyze the technical design of a poem, you should put that knowledge to use. Only one of the writers in this chapter used such knowledge.

EXPLORATORY GUIDE FOR A POEM

- **Static View**
  - What are the major images (direct and indirect) in the poem? What do they mean?
  - Who is the persona in the poem? How does this choice of persona affect the poem?
  - What kind of diction is used? Why?

- **Dynamic View**
  - What kind of stanzaic structure is used? Why?
  - What kind of rhythm does the poem have? Why?
  - Word and sound lengths?
  - Line length?
  - Sound repetitions, echoes?
  - Pauses?

- **Relative View**
  - How can the poem be classified? What more does this classification tell about the poem?
  - With what other literature can this poem be compared?
  - What analogies can be created for the poem?
  - What is the central meaning of the whole poem? How do the parts relate to this meaning?

EXPLORATION

WRITER 1   "WIRES"

STATIC VIEW

Images (Direct)	**Meaning**
—wide prairies	—freedom of the young
—old "tamed" cattle	—people who have learned from experience
—young adventurous steer	—young people
—stretches of electric wires	—controls of society
—physical effects of electric shock	—punishments for going against society
—torn flesh muscles	—lures of adventure
—smell—fresh water	

Figures of Speech
—wires whose violence gives no quarter ⟶ personification

—young steers become old cattle ⟶ metaphor not old in years but in behavior

Persona ⟶ speaker—possibly author

—animals are silent/noncommunicative

Diction

—quarter ⟶ mercy
—widest ⟶ expands—wires
—electric ⟶ connotative—confining
—young steers ⟶ old cattle (not steer)
—cattle ⟶ grouping of blindly following creatures
—steer ⟶ carries with it strength, grace, spirit, variety or individuality

DYNAMIC VIEW

Rhythm

—1st stanza: 1st & 3rd lines—11 syllables
                2nd & 4th lines—10 syllables
—2nd stanza: 1st & 3rd lines—10 syllables
                2nd & 4th lines—11 syllables
—not a smoothly flowing poem

Sounds

—widest (long ī) electric (long ē) are the two strong contrasting sounds
—though, old, know (assonance)—draggy feeling of old cattle
—electric limits—harsh sound

Stanzas

—two stanzas—two worlds, inside fence & outside
—first stanza paints a sort of still life of prairie
—second presents a picture in motion of the violent encounter with electric
  wires and eventual taming/killing of the young steer's spirit
—the second stanza is sort of a mirror reflection or reversal of the first stanza
    line 4—11 syllables; "senses" rhymes with "fences" (1st stanza, line 1)
    line 3—10 syllables; "day" rhymes with "stray" (1st stanza, line 2)
    line 2—11 syllables; "quarter" rhymes with "water" (1st stanza, line 3)
    line 1—10 syllables; "wires" rhymes with "wires" (1st stanza, line 4)
    line 4(2)   ideas are contrasting
    with 1(1) (1)—from wide prairies (physical) with electrical fenced confine-
                      ment to vast thoughts, desires (mental) stifled by electric
                      shock (memory of)

—line 3(2)   (2) line two gives an early description of the tamed "old cattle"
  with 2(1)   and in line three the young steers become the nonstraying "old cattle"

—line 2(2)   The rather pastoral picture of "young steers" "scenting purer
  with 3(1)   water beyond" is in sharp contrast with the "muscle-shredding violence" of the fence

—line 4(1)   What is "anywhere" "Beyond the wires" leads the steer to ven-
  with 1(2)   ture toward the wires

—one encounter with the wire made a memory strong enough to tame an adventurous young steer

RELATIVE VIEW

Compare/Contrast

"Wires" by Larkin
—feeling: anger
—relatively short
—young steers' attempt to do something different
—animals become docile

—poem makes you feel as though you should take some action

—poem makes me think of humans but uses only cattle

"The Calf Path" by Foss
—feeling: helpless
—5 or 6 stanzas
—creatures simply follow blindly

—creatures have never thought to stray from the crooked path—docile by their own choice

—after reading poem you just sort of nod and say "Yeah. That's how it is."

—poem starts with calf and actually moves to modern-day humans on expressways

Classification

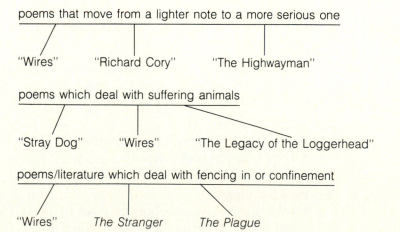

poems that move from a lighter note to a more serious one

"Wires"   "Richard Cory"   "The Highwayman"

poems which deal with suffering animals

"Stray Dog"   "Wires"   "The Legacy of the Loggerhead"

poems/literature which deal with fencing in or confinement

"Wires"   *The Stranger*   *The Plague*

literature in which something or someone had to suffer for going against society

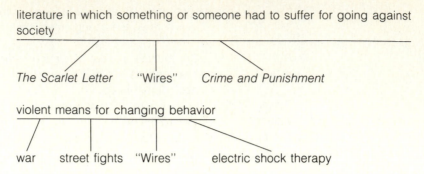

The Scarlet Letter   "Wires"   *Crime and Punishment*

violent means for changing behavior

war   street fights   "Wires"   electric shock therapy

Analogy: "Wires" is like the student government in my high school.
—you couldn't go beyond the boundaries set by the administration
—new, enthusiastic people would try to do something different only to come up against numerous spirit-weakening barriers
—the easiest way to get along was by not making waves

"Wires" is like a nightmare mental hospital.

This idea popped into my head this morning & I would really like to explore it further.

—people who don't conform to the rules are given shock treatment/or lobotomies till they no longer possess different, aggressive personalities
—society groups "insane" people together much like cattle
—two worlds—much like the inside & outside of mental hospital
—looking glass

Central Meaning: Bitter confrontations sometimes result from originally positive, well-meaning, adventurous objectives.

The exploratory guide below will guide your analysis of a prose essay.

EXPLORATORY GUIDE FOR AN ESSAY

- **Static View**
  - What are the focus, aim, and audience of this essay?
  - What kind of diction does the writer use?
  - What sentence patterns are used?

- **Dynamic View**
  - In what mode is the essay organized?
  - How is the essay developed?
  - Is the essay coherent?

- **Relative View**
  - What are the characteristics (criteria) of a good essay that has the aim and mode of the one you are reading?

- How does this essay relate to those characteristics?
- What analogy captures your reaction to the essay?

EXPLORATION

WRITER 3   "THERE'S NO PLACE LIKE HOME"

STATIC VIEW

Focus: The writer says that older people should be kept home and not put in nursing homes.

Aim: To persuade the reader of this and to provoke action.

Audience: Peers like me because we will understand best the writer's experience and be able to do something

Persuasive Appeals: The writer appeals to emotion by using a lot of sensory words about the grandmother's house. He appeals to reason with two examples from his own life. He shows his own credibility by presenting himself as one who has firsthand knowledge of the issue and who is sensitive and considerate of his grandmother.

Diction: Good sense words
—sight: "brass teakettle," "toy French poodle," "delicately embroidered afghan"
—taste: "spicy pumpkin pie"
—smell: "aroma of hot homemade vegetable soup," "hybrid tea roses"
—sound: "grandfather's clock ticks"
—some clichés: "sparkling clean," "sight to behold," "little old house," "eyes roam around," "stare blankly," "there's no place like home"

Syntax: Majority of the sentences are varied; most are complex

DYNAMIC VIEW

Mode: Narrative except in the first and last paragraphs

Order
—First paragraph—question/answer
—Paragraphs 2–4—narrative of grandmother's house
—Paragraph 5—narrative about nursing home
—Last paragraph—generalizations

Coherence: Maintains tense but account of visit to grandmother's is a single time while the visit to the nursing home seems over a period of years

Transitions: Mainly repetitive words

RELATIVE VIEW

Requirements for a Persuasive Essay
—keep audience foremost
—appeal to reason, personality, emotions
—language: concrete, connotations
—refute if necessary

Requirements for the Narrative Mode
—chronological order
—coherence: same person and number, transitions

EVALUATION OF THIS ESSAY

Aim
—last paragraph irritates audience

Appeals
—good example in the grandmother account
—nursing home account sounds impersonal
—good emotional and personality appeals
—concrete diction in account of grandmother's but not in nursing home account (the first and the last paragraphs)

Mode
—good narrative of grandmother's house
—first, last, and nursing home paragraphs break the chronology

Coherence: Transitions needed between first paragraph and grandmother's, between grandmother's and nursing homes, and before the last paragraph.
Person and Number: Ok
Focus: Maintained but not developed well
Analogy: Reading the essay is like coming out of a disappointing Academy Award–winning film

CLASS EXERCISES

1. Study the explorations of Writer 1 (pp. 335–338) and 3 (pp. 339–340). How complete is the list of the distinctive features of the poem (images, persona, diction) or of the essay (focus, aim, audience)? What could have been added?
2. For those doing a critical paper on poetry:
   a. Read the following poem by William Stafford:

A SOUND FROM THE EARTH

Somewhere, I think in Dakota,
they found the leg bones—just the
big leg bones—of several hundred
buffalo, in a gravel pit.

Near there a hole in a cliff
has been hollowed so that
the prevailing wind
thrums a note so low and persistent
that bowls of water placed in that
cave will tremble to foam.

The grandfather of Crazy Horse
lived there, they say, at the last,
and his voice like the thrum of the hills
made winter come as he sang, "Boy,
where was your buffalo medicine?
I say you were not brave enough, Boy.
I say Crazy Horse was too cautious."

Then the sound he cried out for his grandson
made that thin Agency soup that they
put before him tremble. The whole
earthen bowl churned into foam.[4]

    b. Using the exploratory guide for a poem, do a class analysis of the poem.
3. For further practice in exploring poetry, do an exploration of "Bess" (p. 332).
4. For those doing a critical paper on an essay, use the exploratory guide for an essay to examine any student paper in this book (or an essay provided by your instructor).

● **ASSIGNMENT: Exploration**

1. Explore the poem or essay you will write on.
2. Seek comments on your exploration.

FOCUS

After allowing incubation time for your exploration, examine the ideas that you have gathered about your poem or essay. Reread the questions you have asked about it and try out several answers. A critical focus will either interpret or evaluate the poem or essay.

THE CRITICAL FOCUS

A critical focus for an expository paper creates a synthesis of your mind with the work. The point of significance states your insight, your interpretation of the work or the aspect of the work named in the subject. The focus does not paraphrase the work, nor does it project the work into your private world. A critical essay on *The Scarlet Letter*, for example, does not recount the plot or relate the events to cases of adultery you have encountered. The purpose of the focus is to state an insight that will clarify and enrich the work for the reader.

FOCUSES

WRITER 1

Subject
All of the elements of "Wires ———

Point of Significance
contribute to a looking-glass image for society.

WRITER 2

Subject
"Wires' ————————

Point of Significance
grieves over the frustration experienced by the young attempting to develop their human capabilities

WRITER 3

Subject
"There's No Place Like Home"———

Point of Significance
is a good attempt to persuade, with disappointing flaws in mode.

● **COMMENTARY**

Writer 3 avoids the pitfalls of paraphrasing and projecting. The subject commits him to discussing the whole essay; this is not dangerous here because the essay is relatively short. The point of significance promises an evaluation of the aim and mode. His exploration supports the focus.

CLASS EXERCISES

1. Discuss the focuses of Writers 1 and 2.
   - What new interpretations of the poem do the focuses propose?
   - Which focus promises to be the more workable one?
   - What pitfalls (paraphrasing or projecting into their personal world) do the focuses avoid or fall into?
2. Discuss the following alternative focuses for Writer 3.
   a. "The essay is against nursing homes."
   b. "The essay compares nursing homes to staying at home."
   c. "The essay reminds me of my grandfather's situation."
   d. "A critique of 'There's No Place Like Home.'"
   e. "The essay is a satire on life in outer space."
   f. "The structure of the essay reveals that it is a modern fairy tale."
   - Which will lead to expository papers?
   - Which are weak? Why?

● ASSIGNMENT: Focus

1. After incubating, state your focus in two parts.
2. Make sure it avoids the pitfalls of paraphrasing or projecting.
3. Seek comments on your focus from your instructor.

● AUDIENCE AND MODES OF ORGANIZATION

ANALYZING THE AUDIENCE

The audience for an expository critical paper usually plays the specific role of an interested reader or viewer receptive to information and insight that will prove his or her understanding of the work. But the practical difference for student writers usually comes down to choosing to write for either your teacher or your classmates. When the option is present, it would be better to choose as a primary audience your classmates—either one or two individuals or the class as a whole—because writing for the teacher poses serious role problems. When you write for your classmates, the role of the teacher (as the secondary audience) becomes clearer and more definite as he or she judges your address to your peers.

AUDIENCE ANALYSES

WRITER 2
1. My audience will be Ms. Brown and Mrs. Jones, my literature instructor and my roommate's literature instructor.
2. a. Background: College literature teachers.
   b. Values: They value knowledge; they will welcome signs of good understanding of literature.
3. a. Attitude toward the subject: They know a lot about poetry, and one even knows this poem because it's in the textbook she uses. They will probably have an opinion on the poem, but I don't know what it is.
   b. Strength of attitude: They will be open-minded about my reading.
   c. Willingness to act: They will be fair in judging my reading.
4. Specific role: Interested readers.
5. Analysis of the role
   a. Background: They know more about this kind of thing than I do so I will not have to define technical terms.
   b. Values: They will value clarity and care in reading.
   c. Attitude toward the subject: I want them to discover something new about the poem.
6. Relational role: Peer relationship; my voice will be an equal's.

WRITER 3
1. My audience will be the teacher of the writing class.
2. a. Background: With essay she has had wide experience. She has a deep interest in writing and in teaching her students to write.
   b. Values: She seems to believe that the ability to write essays well is a key to success.
3. a. Attitude toward the subject: Her mother is dead—she has mentioned that in class. She has never mentioned nursing homes.
   b. Strength of attitude: I doubt she is interested in the subject.
   c. Willingness to act: I doubt she would do anything about nursing homes.
4. Specific role: She will be the teacher, I the student. I must show her that I understand the construction of the essay and its strengths and weaknesses. She is not interested in the subject or even in the essay, but in my showing that I can write a good critical paper on that essay.

5. Analysis of the Role
   a. Background: Hers is superior to mine.
   b. Values: She will value a good technical performance.
   c. Attitude toward the subject: I want her to accept my performance as outstanding.
6. Relational role: Voice of inexperienced but willing beginner writing for an expert.

● **COMMENTARY**

Writer 3's audience analysis is shrewd and exact. He knows exactly what the reader expects, even to emphasizing that it is the writer's understanding of the form, not the content of the essay, that the reader is interested in. He seems to see his audience more as an examiner than as an interested reader, and he elects a relational role that fits that specific role.

MODES OF ORGANIZATION

Since you assume that the audience has already read the poem or essay, a narrative organization tends to rehash the surface of the original—and that is knowledge the audience already possesses. That leaves the descriptive, classification, and evaluative modes. Critical papers using the *descriptive mode* will outline the major parts by breaking down the work into its components:

ESSAY	POEM
focus	images
development of the aim	persona
organization by mode	stanza structure
audience	diction
diction	rhythm
syntax	

Papers using the classification mode will organize by

• classifying the work
• defining the class or genre or type of writing
• demonstrating how the essay or poem has the characteristics of the class

Papers using the evaluative mode will include the following parts:

• criteria for a good essay or poem
• judgment about the essay or poem in question

- information from the essay or poem demonstrating how they meet or do not meet the criteria

● **Introduction and Conclusion**

The introduction to a critical paper usually identifies the work by title, author, and form and states the writer's focus. (For example, "The poem, 'Wires,' by Philip Larkin contributes to a 'looking glass' image for society.") Your introduction may also include references to other works of literature or subjects with which your audience is familiar and to which the poem or essay contributes a new dimension of meaning, a qualification, or a disagreement. (For example, "'Wires' seems to express the same kind of attitude toward life that can be found in the poems of Robert Frost.") The conclusion at the very least summarizes the main points developed and restates your focus. Many writers, however, find restatement somewhat mechanical and tedious unless it is phrased in a striking manner or includes some memorable detail. That is to say, the paper should end strongly.

● **Organization Plans**

To help you organize the information about the poem that you will use to support your focus, an organization plan is helpful. We discourage the use of the narrative mode because it often leads the writer into simply retelling the plot of a piece of fiction or the order of the contents of a poem. If a writer is familiar enough with criteria for good poetry, fiction, or essays, then the evaluative mode can be helpful. Below are the plans of Writers 1, 2, and 3, which illustrate the use of the descriptive mode (whole to parts: the focus and the parts of the poem that support the focus).

WRITER 1   **Focus:** All of the elements of "Wires" contribute to a looking-glass image for society.
Organization: Descriptive mode

    ¶ 1   Introduction: Focus.
    ¶ 2   The use of two stanzas is like a mirror.
    ¶ 3   The rhyme scheme supports the mirror idea.
    ¶ 4   The images of animals reflect human beings.
         Concluding sentence or two.

WRITER 2   **Focus:** "Wires" grieves over the frustration experienced by the young attempting to develop their human capabilities.
Organization: Descriptive-narrative mode

    ¶ 1   Introduction: Focus.
    ¶ 2   The 1st stanza relates to freedoms in the U.S.

¶ 3 The last stanza shows the results of freedom and answers the question.
¶ 4 The poem ends with the fate of the steers.
¶ 5 Conclusion.

WRITER 3   **Focus:** "There's No Place Like Home" is a good attempt to persuade, with disappointing flaws in mode.
Organization: Descriptive mode

¶ 1 Introduction: Focus and criteria.
¶ 2 The account of the visit to grandmother's is convincing.
¶ 3 The first paragraph mars the persuasion.
¶ 4 The account of the nursing home is unconvincing.
¶ 5 Conclusion.

If Writer 3 had used the *evaluative mode,* the plan would look like this:

¶ 1 Introduction: Focus and criteria.
¶ 2 The essay meets criterion 1.
¶ 3 The essay fails to meet criterion 2.
¶ 4 The essay partially meets criterion 3.

An organization plan using the *classification mode* would look like this:

Focus: "Wires" is a satire on society.

¶ 1 Introduction: Focus and definition of satire.
¶ 2 The poem has the first feature of the definition of satire.
¶ 3 The poem has the second feature of the definition.
¶ 4 The poem has the third feature of the definition.

To ensure that you continue to develop your focus in each paragraph, you can use the sentences of your organization plan as topic sentences for each of your paragraphs.

CLASS EXERCISES

1. Study the audience analysis of Writer 2.
   • How successful is his choice of audience?
   • What uses can the writer make of his analysis?
   • What voice will the writer assume?
2. Choose a high school literature teacher as an audience.
   • Using the audience guide, analyze your audience.
   • Share your analysis with the class.
3. Discuss the organization plan of Writer 1.
   • Will this plan support her focus?
   • Will it allow her to use well the material in her exploration?

● **ASSIGNMENT: Audience and Modes of Organization**

1. Using the audience guide, analyze your audience to set the specific and relational roles you wish them to play.
2. Set up your organization plan.
3. Get advice on your work before writing your first version.

● **THE FIRST VERSION**

Critical papers with an expository aim refer to the work, using examples from the essay or poem to support the focus. Here is an example from a student paper on John Donne's Holy Sonnet X, "Batter My Heart":

> The opening lines of the sonnet personify God as a metalsmith; that is an appropriate metaphor, since the theme of the poem deals with the need for reshaping, even remaking the sinful speaker.

The sentence itself has two components:

1. *a reference to the work:* "The opening lines of the sonnet personify God as a metalsmith"
2. *a statement relating a detail of the work to the focus of the work:* "That is an appropriate metaphor, since the theme of the poem deals with the need for reshaping, even remaking the sinful speaker."

Notice that these two components can appear in any order, with a little rewording. Below is a sentence from Writer 3's paper, illustrating how he refers to the work in the first half of the sentence and then relates that information to his focus ("'No Place Like Home' is a good attempt at persuading . . .") in the second half:

> The afghan, the homemade food, and the flowers speak with sensitivity of the active life she still leads at home.

Not every sentence of a critical paper, of course, must contain both components. But no topic sentence of a paragraph should lack both and most sentences should contain one or the other. The expository aim demands relentless concentration on the subject matter.

REFINING THE EXPOSITORY STYLE

● **Diction**

Since in a critical paper you assume your audience has some knowledge and interest in the work, you must project a voice that gives serious attention to the work. That voice generally expresses itself in relatively formal diction. Since you are writing about writing and are posing as a judge of writing, you must pay particular attention to the technical quality of your own prose. Critical papers begin with dissonance; the finished paper deals with the poem or essay. Hence, the first person pronoun tends to fade, and statements of feeling and belief disappear. The writer concentrates increasingly not on what is happening inside himself or herself but what has happened in the work. In order to concentrate in that fashion, the writer must use the appropriate terms for aspects of the work.

● **Sentence Patterns**

Many of the sentences in a critical paper include both a statement by the writer and a reference to or quotation from the poem or essay. Quotations especially need to be integrated as smoothly as possible into your sentences. Here are some suggestions for getting the two voices—yours and the author's—together.

1.   Whenever possible, construct the sentence so that the quotation becomes part of the natural syntax of the sentence; then you need no punctuation and there is no hitch in the flow of thought:

     Agee argues at length that "the movies handle fantasy best."

2.   When you can't get the blend recommended above, use a comma between the voices when the quotation is short and introduced by an attribution (he said, she answered, etc.):

     Faulkner replies, "Plot disappears in character."

3.   When you use a quotation to illustrate a statement of your own, or when a quotation is longer than a sentence, introduce it with a colon:

     St. Paul acknowledges that sin preceded attempts to govern it, but he also argued that it could not logically be recognized until the law defined it:

     Therefore as sin came into the world through one man and death through sin, and so death spread to all men because all men sinned— sin indeed was in the world before the law was given, but sin is not counted when there is no law.

     Note that because this quotation exceeds four lines it is indented and single-spaced and bears no quotation marks. Quotations from poetry are generally inset and single-spaced if they exceed two lines:

Steadfast of thought
Well made, well wrought,
Far may be sought
Ere that ye can find
So courteous, so kind
  As merry Margaret,
This midsummer flower,
  Gentle as a falcon
  Or hawk of the tower.

4. Verse quotations of two lines can be run in and treated formally as prose if a slash (/) is used to indicate breaks between the lines:

   As Donne says, "And to 'scape stormy days, I choose / An everlasting night."

FIRST VERSION

WRITER 2

FREEDOM AND FRUSTRATION

The poem "Wires" is symbolic of the "electric fences" or restrictions in society. The young steers would be the youth, maybe the hippies of the sixties, who are trying to go past society's boundaries, but eventually "blunder up against the wires," a confrontation with the law, and then become old from that day. The old cattle are the complacent elders of society who have become wary through their experiences and therefore live within the restrictions. The eight lines are very compact and get the main point across well. "Wires" is a poem that grieves over the frustration experienced by the young attempting to develop their human capabilities.

In line one the "widest prairies" are freedoms, possibly the large freedoms U.S. citizens enjoy, but the line also warns that even with all these freedoms there are restrictions, like laws in the U.S. Lines two through four set up the situation that will be resolved in the last stanza. The old cattle or people have learned through their encounter with the electric fence not to make waves, but the youth are impatient and aggressive and want to explore new life-styles beyond the wires or laws, similar to pot-smoking or other activities frowned on by authorities.

In the final stanza, the question of what will happen to these restless youngsters, posed in stanza one, is answered. Their quest to try new things leads them into a confrontation with the law. The "muscle-shredding violence" could be likened to the teenager getting busted for marijuana possession, a drug whose harmful effects are still debated, being thrown in jail and given a stiff sentence. The poem then goes on to say that this violence "gives no quarter." My understanding of this phrase would be no mercy is given to anyone going beyond society's restrictions. So saying this violence gives no quarter seems absurd because given the present condition of our judicial system, a rich white kid caught with drugs would probably get a lesser electric limit than a poor black kid brought before the bench on the same charges.

The above complaint aside, the poem finishes up by saying that after the offenders' confrontation with the electric wires, they change from young to old from that day on. This is true in a way because once experiencing the brutality of a jail sentence, for example, one is less likely to want to explore beyond the wires again and therefore becomes more complacent. These lines seem overly general, though, because many who are "shocked" once return to their old vices, as evidenced by the number of repeat offenders in jail.

This critic finds the poem "Wires" to contain several flaws but in the end it still creates a strong impression of frustration experienced by the youth in their struggle to try new things. The questions raised about the poem in the above paragraphs may not be so to another reader, as of course poetry is very personal, but, to the author's credit, the main theme of youth attempting to develop their human capabilities probably shines through to most readers.

FIRST VERSION

WRITER 3

FLAWS PERSUASION

Finishing the essay, "There's No Place Like Home," is like coming out of a disappointing Academy Award-winning film. There were plenty of good parts and some flaws. Even though the writer strengthened my conviction that keeping older people at home is better than putting them in nursing homes, I was irritated by some parts of the essay.

The account of the visit to Grandmother's was the most convincing. The faded picture portraits, antique furniture, grandfather clock, and dusty box of trains impress the reader with the personal tradition that surrounds the grandmother. The afghan, the homemade food, and the flowers speak with sensitivity of the active life she still leads at home. The diction gives the reader a full participation in the visit, engaging the senses: sight—"brass teakettle" and "toy French poodle," sound—"grandfather clock ticks," taste—"spicy pumpkin pie," and smell— "aroma of homemade vegetable soup." Even the few clichés, like "sparkling clean," "little old house," and especially the title, are forgotten in the vividness of the other details. Although it is unclear why the account is divided into three relatively short paragraphs, the organization supports the focus, taking the reader chronologically from the grandmother's welcome through the meal to the bouquet at the departure. All of these features combine to make the writer's point about the healthiness of remaining at home.

The persuasiveness of the writer's paper, however, is marred by the first paragraph, which explains too much, not allowing the reader to discover the conclusion through the narrative. The last paragraph also irritates because it again translates what the reader has already discovered and goes on to state directives about the reader's responsibility, oversimplified into "lending a hand with the more strenuous housework."

The most flawed aspect of the essay is the account of the nursing home visit. Although the writer starts with sight and smell impressions—"pale green walls" and "germicidal smell"—the majority of the details seem taken from stereotypical descriptions, not from the writer's visit. No mention is made of the aunt who was visited. The patients are generalized. The "whining and crying" comment seems to go beyond the time of the visit itself. The last sentence summarizes aspects which could have been persuasively developed—"impersonal care, bland food, and limited activity."

Perhaps the expectations set up by the grandmother narrative cause the nursing home account to contrast more negatively. In any case, this essay is partially convincing, winning me to feel more strongly about the writer's focus, but disappointing and irritating me because the writer failed to maintain the vivid narrative mode.

CLASS EXERCISES

1. Comment on the diction in the following:
   a. "Writer 3's story about her grandma doesn't excite me at all."
   b. "I believe that Writer 2 is about as wrong about 'Wires' as he can be."
2. Improve the syntax and diction of the following: "In line one the 'widest prairies' are freedoms, possibly the large freedoms U.S. citizens enjoy, but the line also warns that even with all these freedoms there are restrictions, like laws in the U.S."
3. Construct a single sentence from each of the following cases.
   a. You want to say that Joseph Addison, writing in 1711, showed signs of a feminist bent. Your proof is an issue of *The Spectator* that contains this statement by Addison: "I have often thought there have not been sufficient pains taken in finding out proper employments and diversions for the fair ones. Their amusements seem contrived for them, rather as they are women, than as they are reasonable creatures; and are more adapted to the sex than to the species."
   b. You wish to state that rhymes are determined by changing conventions and habits of pronunciation. Your example is a four-line passage from Alexander Pope:

   Benighted wanderers, the forest o'er,
   Curse the saved candle and unopening door;
   While the gaunt mastiff growling at the gate,
   Affrights the beggar whom he longs to eat.

● ASSIGNMENT: The First Version

1. Using your organization plan, write a first version of your paper.
2. Submit your paper for response.

● READER RESPONSES

A critical paper is, as we have noted, writing about a piece of writing to which the writer and reader have equal access. The reader will hold the writer responsible for certain things that would not apply if this were a paper dealing with a person, place, or thing known only to the writer.

1. The reader expects the writer to use the proper technical terms for components of the work, whether those terms are *image, metaphor,* and *stanza* or *focus, aim,* and *mode.*
2. The reader expects the writer to illustrate the analysis by referring to the work, pointing to the details being discussed.
3. The reader expects the writer to avoid the two pitfalls of critical writing: paraphrasing and projecting.
4. The reader expects the writer who evaluates a piece of writing to state clearly a set of acceptable criteria on which the evaluation will be based.
5. The reader expects the writer to show in the development of the paper an acceptable understanding of the work—not just a reaction but a total grasp of the work.

The following reader guide will help you in evaluating critical papers.

READER GUIDE

● Focus
- What is the writer's focus?
- Does each section of the paper begin with some aspect of the poem, story, or essay that supports the focus?
- Does any section merely discuss the piece without relation to the point of significance?

- **Development**
  - Does the writer use representative facts from the piece to support the focus, citing or quoting accurately?
  - Does the writer take into consideration whether the audience has or has not read the piece being judged?
  - Does the writer *refer* to elements in the material and relate them to the focus rather than *tell* the reader that they exist?
  - Does the writer show a grasp of the whole work to which the parts being discussed contribute?

- **Organization**
  - What mode of organization has the writer used?
  - Has it been followed? If not, where has the writer strayed?
  - Is coherence maintained between and within paragraphs?
  - Does the paper have a consistent tense and voice?

- **Style**
  - Has the writer used the proper technical terms for components of the work being discussed?
  - Has the writer maintained an expository style?
  - What sentences need combining?

- **Conventions**
  - Where has the writer made mistakes in grammar, spelling, and punctuation?
  - Has the writer incorporated quotes from the work in correct form?

INSTRUCTOR'S RESPONSE TO WRITER 2

FOCUS

The focus is not clear. The clause "The poem 'Wires' is symbolic of the 'electric fences' or restrictions in society" indicates that you are not in control of the terminology you need to discuss the poem. Language in a poem may symbolize various abstractions; but a poem can't symbolize anything. Possibly what you meant was "In the poem 'Wires,' the electric fences symbolize restrictions in society." But even that would be a focus dealing only with a portion of the poem. The real focus is the last sentence of the first paragraph, but it is not developed.

DEVELOPMENT

There is no consistent development of a focus. You have apparently started with a pseudomathematical equation ("electric fences" = restrictions in society) and have then attempted to give phrases in the poem exact restrictive equivalents, larger or narrower than the original, according to the feeling of the writer.

The paper does not deal with the poem but lands in one of the pitfalls we mentioned earlier. It speaks of your opinions about equal justice under the law, pot smoking, and the effects of incarceration. Nowhere does the paper try to deal with the poem. The emphasis falls on you, not on the subject matter, as you confess: "The questions raised about the poem in the above paragraphs may not be so to another reader, as of course poetry is very personal . . . ."

ORGANIZATION

Through the first three paragraphs of this five-paragraph paper, the mode is descriptive, a movement from the whole to the parts. The first paragraph is a summary interpretation. Paragraphs 2 and 3 approach the poem as if it had three parts: "In line one . . . . Lines two through four . . . . In the final stanza . . . ." But the last sentence of the third paragraph shifts into evaluation. The first sentence of the fourth paragraph shifts back to description ("the poem finishes up by saying") and then shifts again to evaluation. The fifth paragraph begins with evaluation and ends with a puzzling sentence: its first half seems to be a possible focus for another, different paper; its second half is a broad evaluation supported by nothing in the paper.

STYLE

Since the paper is radically defective, a discussion of its style would be inappropriate.

CONVENTIONS

The hard truth is that an audience will not take seriously a paper on a literary topic from a writer who cannot demonstrate conventional literacy. The errors of convention that litter this paper would destroy its credibility even if it had a clear focus, a logical development, and so on. Consider the first paragraph. In the second sentence either the punctuation or the diction is faulty. What may be intended there is "the youths of the sixties, perhaps the hippies," but then the tense sequence would break down: "are trying" would have to become "were trying." Even that correction would blunder up against the tense of the quotation, "blunder up against the wires."

INSTRUCTOR'S RESPONSE TO WRITER 3

FOCUS

The focus is maintained throughout the paper.

DEVELOPMENT

You use many examples from the essay. You speak of "aims," "modes," "diction," "clichés," and "organization" in order to speak the language of your audience, the teacher. Your major problem with development lies not in the sufficiency of the support but in the accuracy of the analysis. In paragraph 3, you claim that "the first paragraph, which explains too much, not allowing the reader to discover the conclusion through the narrative" is a flaw in the persuasive aim. The flaw is in the narrative mode.

Because you are evaluating the paper for its persuasiveness, you should also have commented on its appeals to emotion, reason, and personality.

ORGANIZATION

You have committed yourself to the evaluative mode. Unfortunately, you never make the transition from your initial reaction to a set of criteria by which the essay can be evaluated. The criteria here seem to be personal and secret. We know that you were either "irritated" or "convinced" by parts of the work; but the reader wants to know what prompted and therefore justified the irritation or conviction. Since the criteria are not set forth clearly in the beginning, no "convincing" pattern of organizing emerges.

STYLE

The style needs some repair. In the second sentence, for example, the diction fluctuates: "plenty of good parts" is down-home, chatty conversation; "some flaws" is more sophisticated, less personal, more objective. Yet both phrases occur in the same sentence. In the fourth paragraph, the second sentence is sophisticated except for the phrase "the majority of the details." You mean "most." "Majority" means at least one more than half; impressions should not be disguised as statistics.

The syntax is sound, except in a few places such as the first sentence of the second paragraph. "The account . . . was the most convincing"—as opposed to what? If the reference is to the account of the nursing home, then the account of the visit to grandmother's is *more* convincing than the other. But it's not clear that you intend that meaning only.

CLASS EXERCISES

Study Writer 1's first version (at the end of the chapter), giving responses as a group.

1. What sections both refer to the work and support the focus?
2. What mode of organization is used?
3. What elements of style support the expository aim?
4. Notice how the writer has enclosed exact references to the poem in quotation marks.

● **ASSIGNMENT: Reader Response**

> 1. Using the reader guide, respond in writing to some of your classmates' critical papers.
> 2. Share your responses in a workshop.

● **REVISING AND EDITING**

Since the core of a critical paper is, as we said in the reader guide, an interpretation supported by representative facts, you should inspect with great care these two facets of your paper. You can check the way your interpretations and facts interlock by asking yourself these questions:

1. Is every aspect of my interpretation supported by a fact—a citation or quotation?
2. Are there facts in the poem or essay that work against my interpretation? Have I taken them into account in the paper?
3. Are there important facts in the work that my interpretation does not take into account? If they had to be incorporated, would they change my interpretation?

REVISED VERSION

WRITER 2

FREEDOM AND FRUSTRATION

The poem "Wires" by Larkin is symbolic of the electric fences or restrictions in society. The young steers are the youth, maybe the hippies of the sixties, who are trying to go past society's boundaries, but eventually "blunder up against the wires," a confrontation with the law, and then become old from that day. The old cattle are the complacent elders of society who have become wary through their experiences and therefore live within the restrictions. The eight lines are very compact and get the main point across well. "Wires" is a poem that grieves over the frustration experienced by the young attempting to develop their human capabilities.

In line one of the poem the "widest prairies" are freedoms, possibly the large freedoms U.S. citizens enjoy, but the line also warns that even with all these freedoms there are restrictions, laws. Lines two through four then proceed to set up the situation that will be resolved in the second stanza, namely, the inevitable fate of the young steers. The old cattle have learned through their encounter with the electric fence not to make waves, but the youth, though, are impatient and aggressive and want to explore new life-styles beyond the wires or laws, similar to teens' pot-smoking or other activities frowned on by authorities.

In the final stanza the question of what will happen to these restless youngsters, posed in stanza one, is answered. Their quest to try new things leads them into a confrontation with the law. The "muscle-shredding violence" could be likened to the teenager getting busted for marijuana possession, thrown in jail, and given a stiff sentence. The poet appears to be grieving over the constant cycle of generations blundering up against the fence. After the electric limit people keep quiet and become indifferent. They follow the accepted ways without questioning.

"Wires" creates a strong impression of frustration experienced by the youth who struggle to live differently. The new generation doesn't seem to be given the freedom to develop their human capabilities. The boundaries which are imposed upon the young would limit their sensory development and in turn their imagination and as a result their creativity.

REVISED VERSION

WRITER 3

FLAWED PERSUASION

Finishing "There's No Place Like Home" was like coming out of a disappointing Academy Award film. The aim and the execution were laudable, but something was lacking in consistency and completeness.

The account of the visit to Grandmother's is consistent and complete. The faded picture portraits, antique furniture, grandfather clock, and dusty box of trains suggest the personal tradition that surrounds the grandmother. The afghan, the homemade food, and the flowers speak with sensitivity of the active life she still leads at home. The diction gives the reader full participation in the visit by engaging the senses: sight—"brass teakettle" and "toy French poodle"; sound—"grandfather clock ticks"; taste—"spicy pumpkin pie"; smell—"aroma of homemade vegetable soup." Even the few clichés, like "sparkling clean," "little old house," and especially the title, are forgotten in the vividness of the other details. Although it is unclear why the account is divided into three relatively short paragraphs, the organization supports the focus, taking the reader chronologically from the grandmother's welcome through the meal to the bouquet at the departure. All of these features combine to make the writer's point about the healthiness of remaining at home.

The first half of the paper is marred only by the first paragraph—which explains too much, not allowing the reader to discover the conclusion through the narrative—and by the last paragraph—which translates what the reader has already discovered and goes on to state the reader's responsibilities, oversimplified into "lending a hand with the more strenuous housework."

The account of the nursing home visit, however, which should balance the account of Grandmother's house, is incomplete and therefore inconsistent with the method of the earlier description and narration. Although the writer starts with sight and smell impressions, "pale green walls" and "germicidal smell," most of the details are stereotypical, not taken from the writer's visit. No mention is made of the aunt who was visited. The comment on whining and crying goes beyond the time of the visit itself. The last sentence summarizes aspects which could have been persuasively developed: "impersonal care, bland food, and limited activity."

By not maintaining the vivid narrative mode established in the second paragraph, the writer has failed to carry out completely his persuasive aim.

COMMENTARY

Writer 3 has improved his essay by announcing early his criteria ("consistency and completeness") and thereby setting up a clear organization pattern. There is throughout a good matchup of interpretation and fact. The style has also been improved, although there is still a problem with complicated syntax. The third paragraph—all one sentence—is very hard to follow. It should be broken up into at least two sentences.

Writer 1 has improved her essay by removing the distracting asides, such as that on the habits of "repeat offenders." The confusing last paragraph of the first version has been replaced by a strong summary paragraph. On the other hand, the second sentence, although changed, still suffers from the original problem— misstatement. And the interpretation itself is still hampered by its narrowness, by treating the poem as a simple allegory in which the wires "are" laws. As a result, parts of the poem are not used as fact to support interpretation. Rather, parts are extracted and values are assigned to them. In other words, Writer 2's basic difficulty is in her reading.

CLASS EXERCISES

1. On the basis of your class response to Writer 1, revise her paper.
2. Revise and edit the following:

> W. S. Merwin in Finding a Teacher tries to say what a teacher really teaches and how he teaches you. Its told as a meeting between the speaker and the old friend who is the teacher and who says only one word in the whole poem, Wait. That's one thing a teacher teaches you to do, wait. Not jump to conclusions.

The old friend who is also the teacher is also a fisherman or at least he is fishing when the speaker meets him. But the speaker finds out (or he later realizes) that there is no hook on the line so the teacher couldn't really be fishing. So there must be something else going on. So the teacher is really using fishing as a cover-up for something else he's doing. What he's doing is observing the world around him or more exactly he's really becoming aware of the world around him, "it was a question about the sun about my two eyes," etc.

It looks like the fisherman is really unsuccessful because he doesn't catch anything but then you realize that he really never meant to catch anything. So what was he up to?

He gave one piece of very general advice, Wait. Then he wanted the student to expose himself to his environment. So he offered himself as a model for that. But the student really learned something by himself. While he was waiting he came to understand the whole situation with the teacher and also to really understand what questions were important.

● ASSIGNMENT: Revising and Editing

1. On the basis of the responses you have received, revise and edit your paper.
2. Submit your work for evaluation.
3. Consult Chapters 9 and 10 for work on sentence structure and conventions.

A WRITER'S PROCESS

Below we present the sequence followed in Writer 1's writing process.

THE GUIDING QUESTION AND SITUATION

Subject: "Wires"

My Values and Expectations
—I feel that free spirits are beautiful

My Subject
—the reduction of energetic young steers to docile beasts by means of electric wires

—I hate total confinement

—It's a painful way for an animal to learn he can never venture beyond

—fencing in of steers

—the steers are unable to detect the electric wires until they actually feel the shock

Questions: Why does the fate of the young steers make me so angry? What do the steers and wires stand for?

Audience

—Primary: Mrs. Smith, my 12th grade literature teacher

—Secondary: Composition instructor

EXPLORATION

WRITER 1   "WIRES"

STATIC VIEW

Images (Direct)
—wide prairies

—old "tamed" cattle

—young adventurous steer

—stretches of electric wires

—physical effects of electric shock

—torn flesh muscles

—smell—fresh water

Meaning
—freedom of the young

—people who have learned from experience

—young people

—controls of society

—punishments for going against society

—lures of adventure

Figures of Speech
—wires whose violence gives no quarter ⟶ personification

—young steers become old cattle ⟶ metaphor not old in years but in behavior

Persona ⟶ speaker—possibly author
—animals are silent/noncommunicative

Diction
—quarter ⟶ mercy

—widest ⟶ expands—wires

—electric ⟶ connotative—confining

—young steers ⟶ old cattle (not steer)

—cattle ⟶ grouping of blindly following creatures

—steer ⟶ carries with it strength, grace, spirit, variety or individuality

DYNAMIC VIEW

Rhythm
—1st stanza: 1st & 3rd lines—11 syllables

                2nd & 4th lines—10 syllables

—2nd stanza: 1st & 3rd lines—10 syllables

2nd & 4th lines—11 syllables

—not a smoothly flowing poem

Sounds

—widest (long ī) electric (long ē) are the two strong contrasting sounds

—though, old, know (assonance)—draggy feeling of old cattle

—electric limits—harsh sound

Stanzas

—two stanzas—two worlds, inside fence & outside

—first stanza paints a sort of still life of prairie

—second presents a picture in motion of the violent encounter with electric wires and eventual taming/killing of the young steer's spirit

—the second stanza is sort of a mirror reflection or reversal of the first stanza

—line 4—11 syllables; "senses" rhymes with "fences" (1st stanza, line 1)

line 3—10 syllables; "day" rhymes with "stray" (1st stanza, line 2)

line 2—11 syllables; "quarter" rhymes with "water" (1st stanza, line 3)

line 1—10 syllables; "wires" rhymes with "wires" (1st stanza, line 4)

—line 4(2) ideas are contrasting

with 1(1)   (1)-from wide prairies (physical) with electrical fenced confinement to vast thoughts, desires (mental) stifled by electric shock (memory of)

—line 3(2) line two gives an early description of the tamed "old cattle" and

with 2(1)   in line three the young steers become the nonstraying "old cattle"

—line 2(2) The rather pastoral picture of "young steers" "scenting purer

with 3(1)   water beyond" is in sharp contrast to the "muscle-shredding violence" of the fence

—line 4(1) What is "anywhere" "Beyond the wires" leads the steer to ven-

with 1(2)   ture toward the wires

—one encounter with the wire made a memory strong enough to tame an adventurous young steer

RELATIVE VIEW

Compare/Contrast

"Wires" by Larkin	**"The Calf Path" by Foss**
—feeling: anger	—feeling: helpless
—relatively short	—5 or 6 stanzas

—young steers' attempt to do something different

—animals become docile

—poem makes you feel as though you should take some action

—poem makes me think of humans but uses only cattle

—creatures simply follow blindly

—creatures have never thought to stray from the crooked path—docile by their own choice

—after reading poem you just sort of nod and say "Yeah. That's how it is."

—poem starts with calf and actually moves to modern-day humans on expressways

Classification

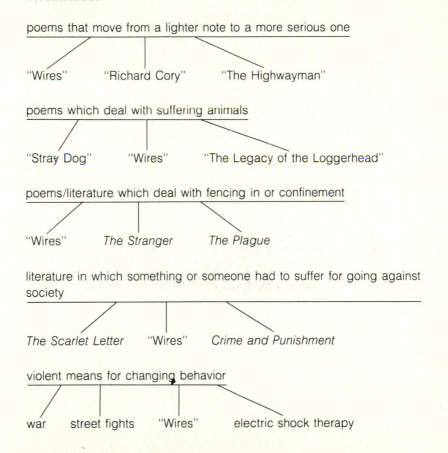

poems that move from a lighter note to a more serious one

"Wires"   "Richard Cory"   "The Highwayman"

poems which deal with suffering animals

"Stray Dog"   "Wires"   "The Legacy of the Loggerhead"

poems/literature which deal with fencing in or confinement

"Wires"   *The Stranger*   *The Plague*

literature in which something or someone had to suffer for going against society

The Scarlet Letter   "Wires"   *Crime and Punishment*

violent means for changing behavior

war   street fights   "Wires"   electric shock therapy

Analogy: "Wires" is like the student government in my high school.

—you couldn't go beyond the boundaries set by the administration

—new, enthusiastic people would try to do something different only to come up against numerous spirit-weakening barriers

—the easiest way to get along was by not making waves

This idea popped into my head this morning & I would really like to explore it further.

"Wires" is like a nightmare mental hospital.

—people who don't conform to the rules are given shock treatment or lobotomies till they no longer possess different, aggressive personalities

—society groups "insane" people together much like cattle

—two worlds—much like the inside & outside of mental hospital looking glass

Central Meaning: Bitter confrontations sometimes result from originally positive, well-meaning, adventurous objectives.

FOCUS

Subject	Point of Significance
All of the elements of "Wires"———	contribute to a looking-glass image for society.

AUDIENCE ANALYSIS

1. My audience is Ms. Smith, my 12th grade lit teacher.
2. a. Background: High school English teacher, master's degree, Advanced Placement English instructor, single.
   b. Values: Education/learning, individuality, maturity.
3. Audience in relation to the subject: Appreciates literature, feels it is important to pass this appreciation on to students.
4. Specific role: Teacher and literary critic.
5. Analysis of the role
   a. Background: She will need to know about metrics and appreciate their significance.
   b. Values: She will need to recognize the importance of technical expertise. She will need to value a work that harmonizes a great many technical elements.
   c. Attitude toward the subject: I want her to see that the poem is an organic whole.
6. Relational role: Equals; I will write as a literary critic.

Focus: All of the elements of "Wires" contribute to a looking-glass image for society.

Organization: Descriptive mode

¶ 1 Introduction: Focus.
¶ 2 The use of two stanzas is like a mirror.
¶ 3 The rhyme scheme supports the mirror idea.
¶ 4 The images of animals reflect human beings. Concluding sentence or two.

FIRST VERSION

WRITER 1

"WIRES"

While not everyone has the time to mentally reflect upon life, practically everyone has seen a carbon copy of himself or herself in a mirror, making it a universal image. In Philip Larkin's poem, "Wires," all of the elements contribute to a "looking-glass" image for society.

The two stanzas which make up the poem are like the outside and inside of the mirror. The first stanza deals with the pastoral dream-world of the young steer. The land of "purer water" is much like the wonderland world inside the mirror, a world that can only be dreamt of. The second stanza is the painfully real world, accurately reflected by the mirror with the impact of "muscle-shredding violence." The difference between the two stanzas is the difference between realities and dreams, between what people wish they looked like and what they see in the mirror. The young steer, desiring and attempting to enter the freer, more beautiful world inside the mirror, encounters an electric barrier like the glass that separates the two worlds of the mirror. Defeated, the young steer becomes one of the "old cattle," his dreams shattered.

The rhyme scheme and syllabication between the two stanzas give the effect that one stanza is a 180-degree mirror reflection of the other. Thus, line one of the first stanza rhymes with line four of the second—"fences, senses"; and line four of stanza one is coupled with line one of stanza two—"wires, wires"; the pattern is continued throughout the entire poem. The ideas of the paired rhyming lines are inverse in meaning much like the reverse reflection given by the looking glass. The poem moves from physical limits, "fences," for the steer's movement to psychological "electric limits," the memory of electric shock. The physical difference between the "old cattle" and the "young steers" becomes secondary to the psychological unity created by their common memory of the electric shock. The steer's dream for "purer water" is killed by the physically merciless wires. The thought of what lay "beyond the wires" prompted the steers to action, "to blunder up against the wires." Each psychological idea in stanza one is reversed to something physical in stanza two, and a physical idea in one becomes psychological in two.

The images in the poem are a reflection in the likeness of animals, steers of a human experience: dreaming and seeking a better existence only to be chastized by society for not conforming to norms. Much like the electric fence in "Wires," electric shock has been used on "insane" people to alter behavior. Nursing homes are filled with many old people who, like the "old cattle," no longer possess dreams for the future. The young steers enclosed by "wire" are like the thousands of "radical" youth behind bars. Each time a formerly free spirit has been battered to the point of defeat, one more person joins the "crowd" and becomes one of the "old cattle." "Wires" is Larkin's illustration of the two-sided world. Reality, the reflection in the mirrors, and dreams, that exist inside the mirror, can never cross each other, and those seeking to reach their dreams will encounter barrier after wearisome barrier.

NOTES

1. Philip Larkin, "Wires," *Today's Poets*, ed. Chad Walsh (New York: Scribner's, 1964), p. 284.
2. W. S. Merwin, "Finding a Teacher," *The New Naked Poetry*, eds. Stephen Berg and Robert Mezey (Indianapolis: Bobbs-Merrill, 1976), p. 266.
3. William Stafford, "Bess," *The New Naked Poetry*, eds. Stephen Berg and Robert Mezey (Indianapolis: Bobbs-Merrill,1976), p. 445.
4. William Stafford, "A Sound from the Earth," *The New Naked Poetry*, eds. Stephen Berg and Robert Mezey (Indianapolis: Bobbs-Merrill, 1976), p. 447.

8

WRITING WITH DUAL AIMS: EXPOSITORY AND PERSUASIVE AIMS

In the World of Work/Reports

We include a chapter on report writing to give you an opportunity to use the same composing processes when you write in the world of work as you do in the other worlds. Therefore, you can readily transfer the power you have developed to this kind of writing.

You may tend to view reports as impersonal, purely technical. But why is one report more successful than another? If a computer could write them, they would be equally effective. Each writer, however, handcrafts a good report, leaving a signature. This chapter will demonstrate one kind of report which recommends a solution for a problem.

We have deliberately limited ourselves to the evaluation report because it occurs in almost all fields of work in essentially the same form. Letters, résumés, and the host of other types of business and technical writing we have left to the separate courses in which these specialized forms are taught.

A brief treatment such as this cannot begin to represent the great variety and scope of communications that come under the head of "report"; it cannot convey the challenge that faces a working writer who must deal with the same subject matter in separate reports to superiors and co-workers and subordinates; it cannot hope to deal even with the frequent practice of collaborative writing, in which the writer becomes the voice of a group. We have chosen a common report form, embodying a common rhetorical stance.

EXPOSITORY AND PERSUASIVE AIMS

Reports tend to put emphasis both on giving information and on changing the mind of the reader. Hence, they have a dual aim, expository and persuasive, although often one aim is more prominent than the other. The duality occurs because in, for example, an evaluative report, the reader expects not only information but also a judgment on the information, a choice among alternatives. And such a choice must be supported by appeals, especially by credibility and rational appeals. In report writing situations, the reader is not automatically assumed to be hostile or apathetic, but it is assumed that the writer must persuade the reader to accept the position recommended.

● THE GUIDING QUESTION AND SITUATION

In the world of work, you are usually assigned your subject for a report. In a composition class, you usually have a choice. In order to set a situation in which you can write a report that addresses an actual problem you have faced, choose an employment experience or an organization in which you hold a responsible position. An evaluation report in such circumstances can be a powerful tool for effecting change and for demonstrating your initiative and capability as a person interested in the best functioning of the place of business or organization. This subject context includes many types of organizations or work situations: places where you hold part-time or summer work; churches in which you play an active role; organizations like the Girl Scouts or Little League in which you hold some position. Even neighborhood clubs or political organizations offer circumstances in which reports can be written. You write reports as an insider, examining the working or operating conditions and making suggestions for improvement. An outsider does not write reports, but rather letters of complaint.

To select a pressing problem that needs attention, make a list of the jobs or organizations in which you play an active role. As a help in making that choice, adapt the strategy used for identifying dissonance and asking a guiding question. For each possible subject, identify the values of the institution or organization and the aspects of your work that clash with these values. Then frame a question to point your investigation toward finding a solution to the problem you identify. Select one of these subjects to submit for advice.

Here are the five situations selected by the student writers in this chapter.

WRITER 1   **Situation:** My job as a nursing assistant

Values of the Institution	**Aspects of My Job**
—effective care of patients	—inability of nursing assistants to perform adequately certain responsibilities
—efficiency regulation that NAs work alone	

Question: What method could be devised so that the nursing assistant could have the help needed for heavy work, yet still remain independent for individual duties?

WRITER 2   **Situation:** Gunther's Restaurant—family style

Values of the Institution	**Aspects of My Job**
—high quality	—lack of pride in work
—good reputation	—high turnover
—sanitary facilities	—high accident rate
—good product—meals	—low-quality food
—good manager/employee relationship	—high absenteeism, tardiness, fatigue, and bickering among employees

Question: What can be done to improve the morale of the workers?

WRITER 3   **Situation:** My high school job at a computer company

Values of the Institution	**Aspects of My Job**
—efficiency, speed, good quality	—inefficient, slow
	—low-quality printout

Question: How could computer printout turnaround time be sped up?

WRITER 4   **Situation:** My job as a waitress at Village retirement home

Values of the Institution	**Aspects of My Job**
—complete consideration of the residents	—serving the residents of the Village is a ratrace
—courtesy and efficiency	—discourtesy to residents

Question: What method of waitressing could be devised to both be efficient and provide the most considerate service to the residents of the Village?

WRITER 5   **Situation:** My father's farm, on which I work

Our Values	**Aspects of the Farm**
—profitable position in the overall cattle industry for our farm	—losing money on the purebreed herd
—a herd of high-quality Angus cattle	—the quality of our herd is not deep enough; still a few toads left

Question: How can we, as a cattle farm, improve our profits and raise the quality of our stock above industry standards?

● **COMMENTARY**

Writer 1 identifies some important values of the hospital and those aspects of her job that clash with those values. Her question incorporates that dissonance and points her investigation toward finding a new work method for nursing assistants.

Although Writer 2 identifies many values and problems, she concentrates her question on lack of morale. This narrowing may exclude the best solution to her problem. The question also only minimally reflects the values of the institution.

CLASS EXERCISES

1. Discuss the guiding questions and potential situations of Writers 3, 4 and 5.
   • Have they clearly identified work problems that clash with the values of the institutions?
   • To what kinds of solutions will their questions direct them?
2. Select a problem that the class, as insiders, is familiar with.
   • Identify the aspects of the situation that clash with the values of the institution.
   • Pose questions that will lead to different solutions. Decide which solution is best.
3. Consider the following case:

   Bradley has a summer job in a factory that has been plagued by defective products. Many buyers have rejected the lots shipped to them. Bradley has seen the low morale, lack of pride in their work, and carelessness of his fellow workers. He also understands the heavy production schedule set four years ago by the company which in the past had a reputation for 100% acceptance of its lots by buyers.

- What dissonances exist here?
- What kinds of questions could be asked?

● ASSIGNMENT: The Guiding Question and Situation

1. Select a job or organization in which you hold a position.
2. Identify the values of the institution or organization that clash with aspects of your work.
3. Pose a question to direct your inquiry for a solution.
4. Seek advice on your planning.

● EXPLORATION

STATIC VIEW

In your search for a feasible solution, you need to examine the situation as carefully as possible, recalling every aspect of the working conditions and the precise nature of the problem, especially those features that make it unique to the institution. You must also thoroughly examine the structure and values of the institution. Gather as much data (statistics, information, related reports) as possible that bear on the subject. If necessary, consult whatever sources beyond your own memory you need to complete a full picture of the situation.

DYNAMIC VIEW

Also important is an investigation of the history of the problem. Try to determine its causes and its future outcome if a solution is not found.

RELATIVE VIEW

Finally, classify your problem and compare it to other problems; relate your situation to others in which similar difficulties were solved. Create an analogy for your problem. To generate creative solutions, first determine the criteria that the institution would insist on for *any good solution.* If your solution is ultimately to be considered feasible, you must think ahead: What important considerations will the institution apply to any proposed change? Would cost be one? Would maintenance of certain existing structures be another? Whatever those criteria, be sure to identify them. Then list as many solutions as come to your mind, even if some are unusual. Identifying a large number of possible solutions suggests that you have given the problem thorough consideration and have not simply pounced on the first.

EXPLORATORY GUIDE

- **Static View**
  - What are the significant features of the problem?
  - What data (statistics, information, related reports) bear on the subject?
  - Who is involved?

- **Dynamic View**
  - When and how did the problem begin?
  - What changes have occurred?
  - What are the causes of the problem?
  - What will happen if no solution is found?

- **Relative View**
  - How would I classify the problem?
  - How does this problem compare with other problems I have met?
  - What analogy can be discovered for my problem?
  - What criteria should an adequate solution meet (e.g., efficiency, inexpensiveness, fairness)?
  - What alternative solutions can I formulate?
  - How do these solutions meet the criteria I have posed?

EXPLORATION

WRITER 1

NURSING ASSISTANTS

STATIC VIEW

—It is very difficult to readjust an uncomfortable patient by yourself. It takes at least two to help pull someone up in the bed.

—It is safer to get a patient who has just been operated on up with two people. Often they are dizzy and weak, which is too much for a single assistant to handle.

—In order to give good back care to bed-ridden patients, it is necessary to roll them over. This is very difficult to do with only one person.

—Often patients who find it difficult to walk will feel insecure if there is only one person available to help them.

—It is more difficult to make a good tight bed by yourself than if there is another person available to assist.

—It is nearly impossible to make an occupied bed well with only one person.

—Comatose patients need a lot of care and attention, often more than one person can give.

—Although almost all functions of a nursing assistant are made easier if two are working together, there is no reason two assistants should take temperatures, pulses, respirations, and blood pressures. It also only takes one assistant to run sugar and acetone tests, collect intake and outputs, and chart.

—Isolation setup breakdown, and many functions carried out in isolation are nearly impossible for one person to do.

—It is difficult to get help from other people if they have an equally heavy load and do not feel they have time to offer you help.

—Sometimes two patients of the same assistant will be having a difficult time. This requires the assistant to run all evening while other assistants may have no one in distress.

DYNAMIC VIEW

—Before nursing assistants were so common in City Hospital there would be 1 assistant per twenty patients but the LPN's and RN's would also be available to help for heavy duties.

—There are many more nursing assistants, about 1 per 8 people. Now, however, the nurses are not required to help. So, although there are more assistants there are fewer nurses and very little joint effort.

—Often, two assistants would try to help one another in order to make the job easier and to offer the patient the best, most secure methods available. This was looked down upon by the supervisors and regarded as just an excuse to socialize.

—The idea of teamwork was almost instituted but it was defeated by Ms. Bratteng because she felt it would allow the assistants to fool around.

RELATIVE VIEW

Classification

—This problem is an administrative problem because they are the ones who determine hospital policies.

—It is also a problem for the assistants. The work is more difficult and much more demanding if done separately.

—It is a problem for the patients because they do not receive the best possible care.

Criteria for a Good Solution
—allow for efficient individual duties
—allow for teamwork

Solutions
—Team: Both assistants do work that requires 2 people.

> Marcy's assignment: Rm 319–323. Marcy does individual duties for these rooms.
>
> Erica's assignment: Rm 324–328. Erica does duties for these rooms.

Working Separately (present structure)	**Working in Teams**
—Rooms, patients assigned separately	—Two people, duties combined
—eliminates socializing among workers	—promotes socializing among workers
—difficult to treat total-care (comatose) patients	—much easier to care for comatose patients
—harder to reassure insecure patient	—easier to help unsteady patient to walk
—if there are two problems at one time, one has to wait	—two problems can be handled at once
—individual work is handled well by one person	—either individual work is divided or one person does more than the other
—each assistant is responsible for own duties	—both assistants are responsible for all duties; if one is lazy, the other must make up for it
—hard to help O.R. patient	—easy to help O.R. patient
—difficult to give good back care	—much easier to give good back treatment
—because it is so difficult to turn patients by oneself, individual assignments promote bedsores	—it is much easier to frequently position people with 2 assistants; discourages bedsores

WRITER 3   COMPUTER PRINTOUTS

STATIC VIEW

Features of the Problem
—old printers: DATA 100 and DOCUMATION
—proposed new printer: Xerox 5100

	DATA 100	DOC	X5100
Speed	800–1000 1/m (1/m: lines per minute)	1600–1800 1/m	5000–5400 1/m
Size (H × W × L)	4′ × 3′ × 6′	5½′ × 3′ × 6′	5′ × 5′ × 7′
Carriage control	Paper tape	Disk pack	EPROM
No. of carriage controls	1	48	00
Special forms	No	Yes	Yes
No. of printing cards	1	2	1
Lowercase	No	Yes (with extra printing band)	Yes
Special characters	No	Yes (with extra printing band)	Yes
Paper stacker	Drop (inefficient)	Feed (very efficient)	Chute (efficient)
Reconstruction of FCB	Not available	45 minutes	5 minutes
Air Cond. Reg.	Yes ↓ 70°F	Yes ↓ 75°F	Yes 75°F
Cost	$15,000	$50,000 + disk pack	$100,000
Extra disk pack	Not needed	$15,000	Not needed
Extra paper tapes	$500–$1000	N/A	N/A
Total	$15,000–$16,000	$65,000	$100,000
Cost per 1/m	$16.00	$36.11	$18.51
No. of employees to run	2	3	4
No. of printers for stand. jobs	7	4	3
Total employees	14	12	12

DYNAMIC VIEW

Causes and Effects of Problem
—long hours: turnaround time has been slow & quality of work has been poor on NYC, WASA, & SYS OUT A projects
—additional pay: programmers have been required to stay overtime to get work done
—additional personnel: more employees required to run DATA 100's than DOC's and X 5100's
—poor atmosphere: programmers have been hostile to operators, who have no control over slow speed

Future Solution
—cut time: turnaround time increased 300–400% on big projects
—cut in programmers time: programmers work standard hours

—cut in pay & personnel: just a few operators needed on X 5100; no operators needed after 8:00 p.m.

—good atmosphere: programmers will pipe down

RELATIVE VIEW

Classification: Problem is social and management problem

Social

—programmers mad at operators

—operators mad at system because they have to work longer

—steam constantly being let off, causing little work to be done

Management

—company could make more money with better printers

—quality can be increased, drawing more clients

—no. of employees can be cut or dispursed into other areas of research, where they would do more good

Criteria: Speed, cost, accuracy

Alternative Solutions

—phase out DATA 100s and keep DOCs

—phase out all DOCs and DATA 100s and get new X 5100s

—replace DATA 100s and DOCs with any other, more efficient printer

—continue as is, and lose money

● **COMMENTARY**

Writer 1's exploration shows a careful consideration of the problem from many angles. The features and criteria provide a good basis for a solution. Her investigation of previous attempts at teamwork should help her avoid unworkable or unacceptable solutions. Her proposed solution seems feasible. But she has not explicitly related it to the criteria, a necessary task before arriving at a conclusion. Her exploration and her eventual report will be stronger if she explores at least one other alternative solution.

CLASS EXERCISES

1. Compare the explorations of Writer 3 (above) and Writer 5 (at the end of the chapter).
   • Which exploration best assesses the problem? Why?
2. Explore the problem the class selected as a subject for a report.
   • Note down the features of the problem.
   • Trace its history and causes.

- Classify the problem.
- List criteria for a good solution.
- Describe at least two alternative solutions.
- Relate these to the criteria.

3. Examine the following items that Writer 2 listed as criteria for a solution to the restaurant problem:

   a. be speedy
   b. set up an employee benefit program
   c. maintain accuracy
   d. keep costs down
   e. reduce hours for employees
      - Are all of these criteria for *any good solution*?
      - Which are likely to be supplied by the institution?
      - Are any of these in fact solutions instead of criteria?

● **ASSIGNMENT: Exploration**

> 1. Using the exploratory guide, gather as much information as you can about your problem.
> 2. Seek advice on your exploration

● **FOCUS AND SITUATION**

INCUBATION

Allow your ideas to jell before deciding which solution best meets your criteria. Then go back to your exploration and examine the "Relative View" where you listed your solutions and criteria. Determine which solution best meets most of the criteria. That solution becomes the first part of your focus, which will be proposed in the form of a recommendation.

RECOMMENDATIONS (FOCUSES)

Don't assume that report writing is simply a matter of organizing material and transferring it to paper; consider the conclusions of a workshop held by the management of a leading automotive company. The purpose of the workshop was to determine the cause of communication problems that had been plaguing the company. They concluded that their major problem was a lack of focus in reports: their writers had been sending on information, but no significant recommendations.

But such recommendations do not leap from information. They come after careful exploring and incubating. A good recommendation for a report includes (1) a solution, and (2) advice on implementation. The solution is the alternative that best meets your criteria. The advice on implementation is the action that you propose should be taken on the solution. A formulation of a focus would look like this:

(Solution)	(Implementation)
X5100 ———————————	ought to be purchased.
(Solution)	(Implementation)
X5100———————————	ought to be further tested.

A solution springs from the data available to you. Implementation looks beyond the data. If you were trying to choose between two kinds of radio receivers, A and B, you might conclude from the data that A is cheaper initially, more reliable, equally versatile, and equally expensive in repair costs, and then move to the general conclusion that A is a better receiver than B. But you don't necessarily recommend the purchase of A, because you may have any of a series of misgivings:

1. The data were faulty or incomplete; you might recommend more testing.
2. The data were restrictive. You may know of another kind of receiver, C, that wasn't included in the data and that you haven't been able to investigate. You might recommend looking further.

Below are the recommendations (focuses) of the five writers.

RECOMMENDATIONS (FOCUSES)

WRITER 1

| **Solution** | **Implementation** |
| Teams of nursing assistants ——————— | should be organized immediately. |

(**Question:** What method could be devised so that the nursing assistant could have the help needed for heavy work, yet still remain independent for individual duties?)

WRITER 2

| **Solution** | **Implementation** |
| Gunther's Restaurant's motivation problem——————— | can be solved with accuracy and efficiency. |

(**Question:** What can be done to improve the morale of the workers?)

WRITER 3   **Solution**   **Implementation**
Three X5100 printers———————should be examined and possibly
                                       purchased in the near future.

(**Question:** How could computer printout turnaround time be sped up?)

WRITER 4   **Solution**   **Implementation**
A buffet system————————should be organized by the manager
                                       and used within a week's time, after
                                       informing residents, on a trial basis.

(**Question:** What method of food service could be devised to both be efficient and
provide the most considerate service to the residents of the Village?)

WRITER 5   **Solution**   **Implementation**
The sale of 38 head of Angus cows   ┌should occur immediately on our
and the embryo transplant of the   │farm.
remaining two————————┘
(**Question:** How can we, as a cattle farm, improve our profits and raise the quality
of our stock above industry standards?)

● **COMMENTARY**

*Writer 1 has a specific solution in the first part of the focus and a plan of
implementation in the second half. Although at first glance the implementation
does not specify who should be responsible, the writer knew that the audience
would be her superintendent, who would not appreciate being told of her responsibility.*

*Writer 2, however, does not yet have an adequate focus. The first part reiterates
the problem but does not offer a solution. The second half states the criteria, not the
implementation of the solution. This writer needs to return to the exploration,
examine the alternative solutions indicated there, and decide which best meets the
criteria. She then must determine how that solution will be implemented.*

CLASS EXERCISES

1. Compare the alternative focuses below with the focuses of Writers 1
   and 3 above. Determine which versions make the more effective recommendations for the audience.
   A. 1. "A new system for nursing assistants ought to be developed."
      2. "The present nursing assistant system has problems."
      3. "Nursing assistants working in teams ought to be organized
         immediately by the supervisor."
   B. 1. "Management should purchase a more efficient printer."

2. "Some X5100 printers ought to be studied."
3. "DATA 100s ought to be junked."
2. Formulate focuses for the problem the class explored.

● ASSIGNMENT: A Recommendation (Focus)

1. After allowing sufficient time for incubation, review your exploration, especially your criteria and alternative solutions.
2. Decide on the best solution and use it as the first part of your focus.
3. As the second part of the focus, state the kind of implementation that your solution should receive.

● AUDIENCE, APPEALS, AND MODE OF ORGANIZATION

AUDIENCE

In report writing, your audience is given, not chosen. A report often will be read by a superior who can act on the substance of the report. This fact makes audience choice irrelevant and audience analysis easy. You usually write *up*—that is, you write as subordinate to superior. Furthermore, you write for a busy, impatient audience. Part of the subordinate-superior relationship is that the subordinate always assumes (the truth of the matter is another thing) that the superior is busier than the subordinate. This has obvious stylistic implications: reports are written as concisely and exactly as possible. The first commandment of professional writing is that the reader's time is valuable.

In this instance, then, you will not choose your audience but identify him or her. And in the bargain, in using the audience guide you will see the audience not as an individual human being but as a link in a chain of command, a box in an organization chart. The audience is composed not so much of persons as of representatives of an institution (a company, a board of directors, a government) who qualify as an audience by being able to think corporately, not individually. Their criteria will not be personal preferences but what is useful to the institution. There is, in a very basic sense, nothing personal in professional readers. The editor of a magazine, for example, does not accept or reject your manuscript because of personal likes or dislikes, but because he or she sees the readership as liking or not liking it.

The difference between an individual audience (like the student on your left) and a corporate audience (like a management superior) is that the corporate audience responds to trends and directives that are easily discoverable. If, for example, you are reporting on the state of equal opportunity at some division of IT&T, you know that IT&T is under federal judgment to hire more minority personnel. This is a *value* they hold by default, and your writing should reflect that imposed value.

Below are the audiences to whom the writers in this chapter will address their solutions.

WRITER 1   **Audience:** Afternoon nursing supervisor

WRITER 2   **Audience:** Restaurant manager

WRITER 3   **Audience:** Vice-President of CAS

WRITER 4   **Audience:** Kitchen manager of Oxford Village Retirement Home

WRITER 5   **Audience:** My father, who owns the farm

AUDIENCE ANALYSIS

The specific role of the audience for an evaluation report is to make a decision with the help of the information in the report. Therefore, the specific role of the audience is that of decision-maker.

The relational role is generally defined by the distance between the positions of the reader and writer. Thus the chances of a peer relationship are greater when the reader is your immediate superior than when the reader is five steps up on the corporate or organization ladder. Using the audience guide will help you set this role.

The audience analyses of Writers 1, 2, and 4 follow.

AUDIENCE ANALYSES

WRITER 1   1. My audience is Ms. Bratteng, R.N., the afternoon nursing supervisor.

2. a. Background: Ms. Bratteng has a Bachelor of Science degree in Nursing,

was supervisor before she came to City Hospital from County Hospital. (She was fired from County's staff.)

  b. Value: My audience believes that rules should not be bent, twisted, or changed. She believes that hospitals set down rules which are perfect and should be followed to the letter. Ms. Bratteng is a very private person, so it is difficult to determine what her values are.

3. a. Attitude toward the subject: She knows the problem. She believes that nursing assistants should work individually.

  b. Strength of opinion: She holds this opinion very strongly.

  c. Willingness to act: She will defend this position vigorously.

4. Specific role: She will be the decision-maker who will also have to carry out and supervise the results of her decision.

5. Analysis of the role

  a. Background: She should know that there are serious problems in the wards. I will have to explain the alternatives carefully, without seeming to instruct her in things she ought to know. Actually, she probably knows these things anyway.

  b. Values: She should value the *best* way to do the job, not just the traditional way.

  c. Attitude toward the subject: I want her at least to begin thinking seriously about changing the system.

6. Relational role: My superior. My voice will be as a concerned employee who knows the system well.

WRITER 2   1. My audience is Mr. Ross Jackson, Restaurant Manager for Gunther's Restaurant.

2. a. Background: Mr. Jackson graduated from Midwestern University with a bachelor's degree in Restaurant, Hotel, & Institutional Management with a business option. He has free-rein control over his employees in the area of managerial supervision.

  b. Values: My audience is an understanding man. He believes that his employees are very important to his type of industry and therefore is willing to listen and to compromise with his employees.

3. a. Attitude toward the subject: Mr. Jackson is worried about the lack of motivation of his employees.

  b. Strength of opinion: He has been trying to find incentive programs which will help to solve this problem.

  c. Willingness to act: If I can help find solutions to the motivation problem, it may make his job easier.

4. Specific role: My manager, supervisor.

5. Analysis of the role

  a. Background: He knows that improved service will reflect to his credit and will produce a happier staff.

  b. Values: He will value harmony and productivity.

  c. Attitude toward the subject: He has not yet chosen a solution. He will try to act in the best interest of the employees because happy employees will provide more efficient service and produce greater profits.

6. My voice: A concerned employee who realizes that there is a problem with lack of motivation and wants to help find a solution.

WRITER 4

1. My audience is Nils Bostich, kitchen manager of Oxford Village Retirement Home.

2. a. Background: Nils is not much older than I; he graduated from the same high school that I did. He was recently promoted to manager from assistant manager.
   b. Values: Nils values friendship, security, doing the best job that can be done.

3. a. Attitude toward the subject: He wants residents to be happy and get the best service since they are paying for it.
   b. Strength of opinion: He holds this opinion very strongly; if the residents are dissatisfied, he hears about it first.
   c. Willingness to act: He will act immediately if he sees good reason.

4. Specific role: Decision-maker, in a very bad situation.

5. Analysis of role
   a. Background: He knows that the satisfaction of the customer comes first.
   b. Values: He will value keeping people happy.
   c. Attitude toward the subject: He will act if the solution is reasonable.

6. Relational role: Because I know Nils pretty well, I could talk to him in a familiar way. I have been employed there longer than he has and I know all the issues and problems. He would listen if I talked to him as someone concerned and making a suggestion.

● **COMMENTARY**

Writer 1 has used the audience guide well, bringing to the surface the hostility of the audience, along with steps to counteract it: "I will have to explain the alternatives carefully, without seeming to instruct her in things she ought to know." In addition, the writer helps to fix her own attention on a central arguing point by imputing a value position to her audience: "She should value the best way to do the job, not just the traditional way."

Writer 2's analysis, while it produced useful material, may not be so helpful. In item 5, for example, the writer says that Mr. Jackson "knows that improved service will reflect to his credit and will produce a happier staff." But up to this point the analysis has not revealed a man of strong self-interest; why would that trait be central to his managerial role? The real question is: What steps has Mr. Jackson already considered? Knowing that would help the writer select material.

CLASS EXERCISES

1. Examine the audience analysis of Writer 5 (at the end of the chapter).
   - What background information and values will the writer be able to employ in the reports?
   - What use can the writer make of this knowledge?
   - What other aspects of the audiences could have been noted?
   - How will the audience's role and the writer's voice work for the reports?
2. Identify the appropriate audience for the subject the class chose in the first exercise.
   - Analyze the audience.
   - Choose a role and voice.

MODE OF ORGANIZATION: THE FORMAT OF A REPORT

Different kinds of reports use different types of organization. Inside most institutions, standardized formats are used for some kinds of reports; large organizations generally circulate to their employees a manual that outlines the formats of different kinds of reports. Reports can use various patterns of organization. We will illustrate the evaluation report, which includes the following:

1. A title page, a table of contents, and a list of illustrations (if needed). These parts are guides for the busy reader who may not want to read the entire report. In short reports—those under 750 words—the title page, table of contents, and list of illustrations are usually dispensed with and the report is cast in the form of a memorandum, with an appropriate heading, such as this:

   Date: (fill in the date here)
   To: (fill in the recipient's name and title here)
   From: (fill in your name and job title or position here)
   Subject: (state the general topic of the report)

2. A concise introduction which contains
   a. A brief statement of the problem.
   b. A recommended solution.   } Focus (pp. 378–379)
   c. A method of implementation.
   The introduction is a summary of the most important sections of the report; it is for those busy readers, usually several job levels above the writer, who need to know only the most important parts of the communication. Notice that what you think of as the "meat" of the paper—the procedures, the evidence, the reasoning—doesn't appear here.

3. An overview which describes
   a. the purposes of the report.

    b. the problem to be examined.

    c. the scope of the report—an enumeration of the alternative solutions to be discussed later.

The overview can run to several paragraphs or pages, since it expands on material outlined in the introduction.

4. The criteria—a statement of the standards used to evaluate the alternatives. The reader needs to know the grounds on which you will choose your solution. Criteria for the purchase of a radio receiver, for example, might be initial cost, reliability, versatility, and repair costs. Or you might set up the appearance of the receiver as a criterion. The reader has a right to know. A statement of criteria is usually short; the actual application of the criteria occurs in the following section.

5. Discussion of alternative solutions in relation to the criteria. This is the lengthiest, most technical part of the report, an account of whatever research went into selecting the solution judged best. Each alternative is judged in light of the criteria.

6. A reiteration of the solution and the implementation.

APPEALS

● The Credibility Appeal

Establishing your credibility is important if you wish your report to be taken seriously. Recall that the report has persuasive elements in it. You establish credibility by showing that you share concern over the organization's interests and values, that you have analyzed the situation thoroughly, and that you are proposing responsible solutions. You also demonstrate credibility through the carefully chosen details you describe about the problem, the criteria you select, and the language in which you couch the report.

● The Rational Appeal

A report essentially uses deductive proof, because it *evaluates* several solutions in light of the criteria established. It is important, therefore, to select criteria that your audience will accept. If the audience will not accept your criteria, your case will be weak; or you must take space to explain and justify the criteria—space which a tight report cannot allow.

● The Affective Appeal

Although the appeal to the audience's attitudes and emotions is downplayed in a report which concentrates on facts, you still appeal to the audience's values through the criteria you perceive the audience to require.

● **ASSIGNMENT: Audience, Appeals, and Mode of Organization**

1. Identify and analyze your appropriate audience.
2. Make an organization plan that indicates in what sections of the report you will include your information and your appeals.

● **THE FIRST VERSION**

With the help of your planning, you should have the organization and material you need to write the report. But it will probably take more than one draft to create a first version that satisfies you.

EXPOSITORY STYLE

● **Diction**

The diction of reports tends to be relatively formal, although we hasten to add that *formal* does not mean stuffy or inflated. If you mean to say "Receiver A costs $4 less per set than receiver B," say so, instead of "Data acquired by this office indicate that, by comparative analysis, there is a differential of $4 in the purchase price of receivers A and B in favor of the former." Slang and colloquialisms have no place in report writing, but neither does difficult jargon. The style of report writing aims at conciseness, ease of reading, and precision. The good report is unambiguous, easy to read, and specific in detail.

The style of reports plays down the *I* in an effort to put the emphasis on the *subject*. There is a difference between "I have discovered that the Xerox 5100 has a printing speed of 5400 lines per minute" and "The Xerox 5100 has a printing speed of 5400 lines per minute." The second sentence removes the emphasis from the writer's discovery of the fact and places the emphasis on the fact.

The distinction between the *I* construction and alternatives becomes very important when you have to draw conclusions and make recommendations. The speed with which the Xerox 5100 prints lines is not a recommendation. It's either a fact or it isn't. But suppose that you have to recommend whether your company should buy the Xerox 5100; that recommendation will spring from a consideration of a great many facts other than its speed—such as its initial cost, its frequency of repair, its size, and so on. It is in this stage of the report that the removal of the *I* in any form should be complete—not in order to remove responsibility but in order to indicate that the responsibility rests squarely on your powers of research and reasoning.

Consider these three statements:

"I think the 5100 printer should be purchased."

"There is reason to believe that the 5100 printer should be purchased."

"It is clear that the 5100 printer should be purchased."

All three are the same statement because they are personal (two of them in a disguised fashion), and all three direct attention away from the conclusion itself. The proper statement is clear, unambiguous, and focused on the problem:

"The 5100 printer should be purchased."

The first statement is clearly personal because of the "I think." (The question is: What do you know and what have you concluded, and what, therefore, are you recommending?) In the second statement, "There is reason to believe" is a grammatical trick that cannot really hide the statement behind it, "I believe." (Again, the question is not one of belief but of knowledge and judgment.) "It is clear" means "It is clear to me." (Again, the question is: Why is it clear to you?) The statement that needs to be made is simply "The 5100 printer should be purchased."

● **Sentence Patterns**

There is nothing special about the sentence patterns of reports except that they tend to be shorter than they would be in more relaxed prose. The reason for that is simply that shorter sentences are easier for people in a hurry to read. The shorter sentence also tends to give the impression of concise, clear statement.

The syntax does tend to be more formal than in prose in the expressive aim, and that formality is expressed in several ways. Embedded clauses tend to come before the sentences to which they are attached: "Although receiver A has a better appearance, it does not operate as well. . . ." Prepositions tend to lead, not follow, their nouns: "The men with whom I worked," not "The men I worked with." What this formality expresses, of course, is the roles you and the reader play: subordinate and superior. The prose reflects the same protocol that you would observe if you were being introduced to a person of higher authority. Finally, professional writing demands standard written English, typed on a good-quality paper with few or no erasures, and no mistakes in grammar or spelling. Since style is the major means by which you project a personality to the audience, it is imperative that the personality projected be professional: competent, efficient, educated to the level of the position. The first versions of Writers 3 and 4 follow.

FIRST VERSION

WRITER 3

Date: December 8, 1979
To: Joseph Deacon, Director of Computer Services, CAS
From: (Writer 3)
Subject: Replacement Hardware

INTRODUCTION

The long turnaround time has decreased the quality of work being produced in the computer division of CAS. Replacing old DATA 100 and DOCUMATION printers with more efficient printers would totally eliminate the problem of turnaround time. It is recommended that CAS examine and test new and more efficient printers for possible replacement.

OVERVIEW

Since the addition of the Washington project, the turnaround time at CAS has been increased. Because of this increase in turnaround time they have had to hire new operators to get all of the backed-up jobs out. They have also had to increase the number of hours the programmers have to work, causing an unnecessary increase in overtime pay. These long hours have made the programmers very tired and cranky, making the work atmosphere hostile. CAS should look at the possibility of replacing their old printers with either the Xerox 5100 or the IBM 1354.

CRITERIA

The most important criterion for the printer to meet is that it must be faster than their present printers. It must be under $150,000, as the company could only afford two such printers. Lastly, the printer must be very efficient, with few errors per printout. It would also be helpful if the printer could be obtained relatively soon.

DISCUSSION OF ALTERNATIVES

Replacing Old Printers with X5100

The Xerox 5100 printer has a printing speed of approximately 5400 lines per minute, making it three to seven times as fast as CAS's DATA 100 and DOCUMATION printers. The X5100 is slightly more expensive than their existing printers, making up for these losses with its phenomenal speed and efficiency. Unlike the DOC printers the X5100 requires no diskpack for carriage control, storing them in

EPROM. This elimination of the diskpack also eliminates expenses in maintenance, room, and hardware. The reconstruction of the FCB, on the X5100, takes only five minutes, nine times as fast as the DOC reconstruction. The X5100 also has lowercase and special characters on the same standard band, eliminating the purchase of an extra band. The chute-type paper stacker on the X5100 is not quite as good as the DOC's feed stacker.

In the long run the staffing would be less. The DOC printer requires only three employees to run it, as compared to the four needed to run the X5100. CAS will, however, need only three X5100s running from 8:00 am to 4:00 pm, as compared to the four DOC printers presently needed to run 24 hours a day. CAS would need only one shift of twelve people a day to run the X5100s, eliminating the extra two shifts of twelve needed now to run the DOCs. CAS would be able to send their programmers home one or two hours earlier every day, because of the increase in efficiency. This cut in pay and personnel will give the company more profit.

The X5100 printers cost $100,000 each (as shown in Table 1), making the total for the three needed $300,000. The printers would more than pay for themselves in one year. Cutting programming time will, in one year, save CAS $104,000. The operation cut will give the company $280,320 in just one year. The cut in the cost of maintenance will average $129,540. Totaling the cuts in personnel and payroll will earn CAS a minimum of $513,860 in one year, showing a profit of $213,860 the first year and over half a million each successive year. (Further information on personnel cost and profit can be seen in Tables 2 and 4).

Replacing Old Printers with IBM 1354

The IBM 1354, although it is not quite as impressive as the X5100, should also be considered as an alternative to the problem of turnaround time. Printing at a speed of 3200 lines a minute, the IBM 1354 is two to four times as fast as CAS' present printers. It, like the DOC, will require a diskpack to control carriage, representing additional expenses in hardware, room, and maintenance. The additional expenses will be cheaper than those of the DOC printers. Reconstruction of the FCB on the IBM printer takes 10 minutes, four and a half times as fast as the reconstruction procedures for the DOC printers. The IBM 1354 is very much similar to the X5100 in most aspects; except for speed, it has most of the other qualities.

As with the X5100, staffing would also be cut with the IBM 1354. The three IBM 1354 printers would require a staff of 24 operators working in two shifts to get the work done. The programmers would be able to go home an hour earlier almost every day. This cut in pay and personnel is slight, but would still be beneficial to CAS.

Purchasing the IBM 1354 printers will represent an initial cost of $255,000. These printers will, in one year, pay for themselves, just as the X5100 printers will. They will show a profit of not quite $2,000 the first year, but over a quarter of a million each successive year. (Refer to Tables 2 and 4 for more information.)

RECOMMENDED SOLUTION

CAS should examine and test the X5100 printer and look at the possibility of purchasing three in the near future. The purchase of three of these printers would increase the quality of work at CAS. The programmers and operators would, once again, be at peace. Most importantly, the company will profit in dollars and cents from not only cuts in staffing but from new clients impressed with CAS' work and efficiency.

Table 1 Printer Specifications

	DOC	*X5100*	*IBM 1354*
Speed	1600–1800 1/m	5000–5400 1/m	3000–3200 1/m
Size (H × W × L)	$5\frac{1}{2}' \times 3' \times 6'$	$5' \times 5' \times 7'$	$5' \times 5' \times 6\frac{1}{2}'$
Carriage control	Diskpack	EPROM	Diskpack
No. of carriage controls	63	0	255
No. of print bands	2	1	2
Paper stacker	Feed	Chute	Chute
Reconstruction of FCB	45 min	5 min	10 min
Special forms	Yes	Yes	Yes
Lowercase	Yes*	Yes	Yes*
Special characters	Yes*	Yes	Yes*
Air condition	Yes 75°F	Yes 75°	Yes 70°F
Printer cost	$50,000	$100,000	$70,000
Diskpack cost	$15,000	Not needed	$15,000
Total cost	$65,000	$100,000	$85,000

Table 2 Personnel Cost

	DOC	*X5100*	*IBM 1354*
Operation†	$420,480 (3)	$140,160 (3)	$280,320 (2)
Programming‡	$520,000 (2)	$416,000 (0)	$468,000 (1)
Maintenance§	$518,160	$388,620	$453,390
Total	$1,458,640	$944,780	$1,201,710

Table 3 Printer Cost

	DOC	*X5100*	*IBM 1354*
No. needed	4	3	3
Price each	$65,000	$100,000	$85,000
Total	$260,000	$300,000	$255,000

Table 4 Profit

	DOC	*X5100*	*IBM 1354*
First year	$0	$213,860	$1,930
Each successive year	$0	$513,860	$256,930

*On separate printing band.
†Figures represent average pay scale; numbers in parentheses are no. of shifts.
‡Figures represent averages; numbers in parentheses are no. of hours of overtime expected daily from each programmer (also averages).
§Figures represent averages.

FIRST VERSION

WRITER 4   ***Date:*** February 17, 1983
To: Nils Bostich, Manager, Oxford Village Retirement Home
From: (Writer 4)
Subject: Food Service System

INTRODUCTION

The present system of food service at Oxford Village does not provide the residents with efficient, courteous service. To solve this problem, the kitchen manager should organize a buffet line within a week's time to be used on a trial basis.

OVERVIEW

The purpose of this report is to examine the possibility of organizing a buffet serving line to solve the problem of inefficiency in the system used at present. Three factors relate to this issue. First, the workers are all striving to get the job done faster than each other instead of working to give quality service. Because they hurry, there are often accidents due to carelessness, and this cuts down on efficiency. Lastly, these two problems affect the residents who often don't receive the courtesy or service they expect and are paying for. There are three possible solutions to the serving system: expanding time of service, organizing a cafeteria line, or organizing a buffet line.

CRITERIA

An effective solution to meet the service problem at Oxford Village should be inexpensive and efficient, provide residents with courteous service, and emphasize quality work on the part of the personnel.

DISCUSSION OF ALTERNATIVES

1. Expanding service time would involve having only one large meal serving instead of two smaller separate dining times. While this would eliminate pressure the workers experience when hurrying to serve at four o'clock to be ready for the six o'clock meal, this system would still be inefficient. Workers would be dealing with a greatly increased number of residents needing to be served. Possibly, more workers would be needed to get the job done quickly, which could mean added expense for Oxford Village. Also, offering a meal at only one time is unfair to the residents because it may not be convenient for them to eat at that specified time.
2. Organizing a cafeteria line would be too expensive because the whole kitchen would have to be remodeled. It would be impractical to spend money on a new system, because it might prove inefficient or be disliked by the residents.

3. If a buffet system was organized on a trial basis, the service problem could possibly be solved. The organization of a buffet line would cost nothing because Sunday dinner is served buffet style and Oxford Village already owns all the needed equipment. Also, since the workers are all knowledgeable about the buffet line, it wouldn't be necessary to spend time and money training them.

This proposed system is efficient and well liked by the people living at Oxford Village. Instead of filling out menu cards and waiting to be served, the residents can go directly to the food table and choose what they want. They also enjoy seeing the food before they get it, picking their own portion sizes, and not having to wait for help when orders get mixed up.

RECOMMENDED SOLUTION

The buffet system should be implemented within a week's time on a trial basis to observe if it is efficient and beneficial to the residents and the workers.

CLASS EXERCISES

Read the first versions of Writers 3 and 4.
- Have they organized their reports according to the format for the evaluation report? If not, where is material misplaced?
- What credibility appeals did they use?
- What criteria did they employ? Were these successfully related to their institutions' values?
- What features of the expository style do you find in the reports?

● ASSIGNMENT: The First Version

1. Using the format of the evaluation report, write several drafts of your report until you have a first version you wish to submit for reader response.
2. Submit your report for responses.

● **READER RESPONSES**

The unique property of report writing is that an ultimate and unassailable judge exists. If you submit a report to a superior, you get a simple, definitive answer. The recommendation of the report either will or will not be followed.

In responding, therefore, the reader should try to play the role of the intended audience as thoroughly as possible. And what the audience is looking for is an organization, developed adequately in its parts, that follows this pattern:

1. Title page or heading
2. Introduction
3. Overview
4. Criteria
5. Discussion of alternatives
6. Recommended solution

Here is a version of the reader guide to use when responding to reports.

READER GUIDE

● **Focus**

1. Has the writer expressed the solution and implementation in the last sentence of the introduction?
2. Has the focus been repeated in the last section of the report?

● **Development**

1. Introduction
   • Has the writer given a brief statement of the problem (a sentence or two) in the introduction?
2. Overview
   • Has the writer discussed the problem more fully in the overview, making sure that the audience is not told what it already knows? Is the discussion convincing? What works and what doesn't?
   • Has the writer clearly *enumerated*, not explained, the alternative solutions? Are they feasible solutions? Which do you think are best?
3. Criteria
   • Has the writer clearly stated the criteria? Are they good ones for the audience? Which are best?

4. Alternative Solutions
  • Has the writer fully discussed all solutions mentioned, relating them to the criteria?
  • Has the writer established credibility throughout the report?
  • Organization
  • Has the writer followed the format for the evaluation report?
  • If not, what sections need work?
  • Has the writer maintained coherence, person, and tense?
  • Style
  • Does the writer use the expository style for reports? What diction seems especially well chosen? Why? What words seem inappropriate?
  • Conventions
  • Does the report contain any mistakes in grammar, spelling, or punctuation?
  • Is the appearance of the report professional?

The first version of Writer 1 follows.

FIRST VERSION

WRITER 1

Date: November 12, 1979
To: Betsy Bratteng, R.N., Supervisor of Nursing
From: (Writer 1) Nursing Assistant
Subject: Assignment of Nursing Assistants

INTRODUCTION

The current method of assigning individual duties to nursing assistants on the medical-surgical units at City Hospital does not allow the aides to deliver the best care possible to total-care patients. This problem could be remedied by assigning workers in teams rather than singly.

OVERVIEW

It is very difficult for a single person to give good care to a patient who requires a lot of attention. It is impossible for a worker to individually turn comatose patients as frequently as necessary, give them adequate decubitus care, and align them properly. These duties require two people joining energy, perhaps working as a team sharing all duties or as two workers with individual duties working together on their most difficult patients. These are the solutions to be discussed in this report.

CRITERIA

In order for a system of assigning duties to nursing assistants successfully to fill the needs of all patients it must

1. allow the assistant to carry out specific duties, including taking blood pressures, temperatures, and pulse rates; charting; and other individual jobs efficiently, and
2. make it possible for the workers to join efforts in the care of total-care patients, O.R. patients, and comatose patients.

DISCUSSION OF ALTERNATIVES

There are two teamwork alternatives to review. The first involves two nursing assistants being assigned one set of patients. This method would allow the two assistants together to help those patients who need more help than one worker alone can provide. This solution requires that the individual duties be shared among the workers rather than having these jobs evenly divided between workers or having one worker carrying the load of another. For example, the taking and charting of vital signs is an individual job which has to be divided, as do sugar and acetone tests, ambulation of patients, blood pressures, and cleaning duties. Leaving the division of these duties to the workers themselves would lead to arguments concerning who does what and as a result would not allow the assistant to carry out individual tasks efficiently.

The second teamwork approach is the better combination of strict individual duties and the teamwork method previously mentioned. Individual duties for specific patients would be assigned to each assistant. Along with these assignments, each worker would be a part of a two-worker team who would combine efforts to care for patients of either assistant who require more care than one person can give. Using this format, a nursing assistant would be able to perform his/her specific individual duties (vital signs, charting) efficiently and would receive assistance to give the best possible care to comatose patients, O.R. patients and other total-care patients.

RECOMMENDED SOLUTION

The combination teamwork–individual duty method of assignment of nursing assistant duties should be initiated into the procedures at City Hospital.

INSTRUCTOR'S RESPONSE TO WRITER 1

FOCUS

You have expressed the solution and implementation in the last sentence of the introduction and the combination is repeated at the end of the report.

DEVELOPMENT

Introduction: The introduction is concise and exact.

Overview: You have dropped something in the overview and the omission will work against you. Remember that you have said that the problem to be addressed is not the present system, but "to deliver the best care possible to total-care patients." There are then not "two teamwork alternatives" to be considered, because that excludes the present system, but three:

1. individual assignments
2. teamwork assignments—model 1
3. teamwork assignments—model 2

Psychologically, this division is preferable; your present version ignores the fact that the present system is a possibility, thereby running the risk of making your supervisor even more hostile.

Wouldn't you say that the central issue is that it takes two people to lift, shift, and reposition one person who is almost inert? That issue should be prominent.

Criteria: You have clearly stated two criteria.

Alternative Solutions: You run into trouble here. The third alternative is missing, as I said above. In addition, the present system when it appears as a contrast appears as two systems: "This solution requires that the individual duties be shared among the workers rather than having these jobs evenly divided between workers or having one worker carrying the load of another." That sentence implies that under the present system two contradictory situations exist:

1. jobs divided equally between workers
2. jobs divided unequally between workers

If that is so, then you have a strong argument that you are not using. Or is it that the system does in theory divide jobs equally between workers, but in practice one worker has to carry the load of another? Clarify.

Furthermore, there is a hidden principle of division of duties that doesn't surface here. The problem is not so much that some patients require "a lot of attention" and others do not, but that some patients require a kind of care that others do not. Two different kinds of care appear in the report:

1. light, technical duty that ranges from taking blood pressures to cleaning
2. heavy physical duty involving lifting, shifting, and positioning of patients

The first can be done by an individual; the second requires a team. Yet that crucial point is never stated.

ORGANIZATION

You have followed the format of the evaluation report.

STYLE

You have tried to be concise, but the desire for brevity has occasionally garbled the style: "For example, the taking and charting of vital signs is an individual job which has to be divided, as do sugar and acetone tests, ambulation of patients, blood pressures, and cleaning duties."

1. How can an "individual job" be divided? Does that mean that the two tasks have to be assigned to one person? Or that one task has to be assigned to two persons? Or that, as in some hospitals, nursing assistants take the "vital signs" but may not chart the results, that task being reserved to the nurses?
2. What does "as do sugar and acetone tests" mean? Nursing assistants do not do sugar or acetone tests, although in some hospitals presumably they can draw the samples for the lab, while in other hospitals only nurses can. More exactly, why is this duty to be divided?
3. What does it mean to say that "blood pressures" have to be divided? The taking of blood pressures? Why?

CONVENTIONS

The conventions are generally observed.

CLASS EXERCISES

1. Read the first version of Writer 5 (at the end of the chapter).
2. As a class, give responses to Writer 5.

ASSIGNMENT: Reader Responses

1. Write responses to several of your classmates' first versions.
2. Share these responses in a workshop.

REVISING AND EDITING

Professional reports are often revised and edited by several hands. Sometimes reports are cooperatively written and then cooperatively revised. Most professional reports are typed (and sometimes typeset) by someone other than the writer. And sometimes professional reports go through another full stage—rewriting by a technical writer or editor. In any event, most professional reports are revised and edited in accordance with a checklist. Your reader guide is a checklist serving the same purpose. Most checklists begin with large considerations (clarity of purpose, organization, accuracy of data) and end with a request for a final reading to pick up typographical errors. Your reader guide moves in the same progression. Invest enough time to take seriously the responses you have available.

Below is Writer 1's revised version.

WRITER 1

Date: November 17, 1979
To: Betsy Bratteng, R.N., Supervisor of Nursing
From: (Writer 1) Nursing Assistant
Subject: Assignment of Nursing Assistants

INTRODUCTION

The current method of assigning duties to nursing assistants on the medical-surgical units at City Hospital does not allow the assistants to help deliver the best care possible to total-care patients because assistants are assigned as individuals to individual tasks. This problem could be remedied by assigning workers in teams rather than singly.

OVERVIEW

It is very difficult for one assistant to give adequate care to a patient who requires frequent attention, especially when that attention requires frequent lifting and turning of the patient. It is impossible for one assistant to turn comatose patients as frequently as is necessary. A duty such as this requires two assistants, working as a team in all their duties or as two workers with individual duties that can be performed singly and joint duties that can only be performed by the team.

CRITERIA

In order for a system of assigning duties to nursing assistants to meet the needs of all patients, it must

1. allow the assistant to carry out individual duties efficiently: taking blood pressures, temperatures, and pulse rates and charting them; obtaining samples for sugar and acetone tests; ambulation of patients; cleaning; and changing linen;
2. permit assistants to join efforts in duties beyond the strength of one individual: turning and positioning total-care, O.R., and comatose patients; and
3. avoid waste of time.

DISCUSSION OF ALTERNATIVES

There are three alternatives:

1. Assigning individual assistants to individual patients. This is the present system. It has the advantage of being easy to schedule and it meets the first

criterion, since any of the tasks listed can be performed by a single assistant. It does not, however, meet the second or third criteria. Few assistants possess the strength to lift, turn, and position unconscious or otherwise helpless patients. The assistant struggles to do the work properly, not only wasting time but endangering the condition of the patient.

2. Assigning two nursing assistants as a total team. All work would be shared by a team of two assistants, rather than having the work evenly divided between assistants. This method would meet the first and second criteria, but not the third. There is no need for two people to take blood pressures, temperatures, etc.; that would waste time. Supposing the aides attempted to divide those duties on their own, there is the possibility of argument and ill will and consequent further waste of time.

3. Assigning nursing assistants on a modified team system. Individual duties for specific patients would be assigned to each assistant. But each aide would also be a part of a team of two who would combine efforts to care for patients who require more care than one person can give. This method would satisfy all three criteria. It has the slight disadvantage of requiring the supervisor to draw up a slightly more complex schedule.

RECOMMENDATION

The modified team system of assigning nursing assistants should be initiated at City Hospital.

COMMENTARY

This is now an excellent report, outstanding for its conciseness. The overview has been changed to highlight the central problem, the reasons for it, and the kind of solution required. The criteria are now distinct and complete. The alternatives are likewise complete, and in this version both advantages and disadvantages have been noted.

CLASS EXERCISES

1. Suppose you are responding to a report intended to solve the problem of allowing hospital assistants on the evening shift to reach their cars safely without high cost to the hospital. What suggestions would you make if these were the alternative solutions listed?

   a. Let only the evening shift workers park in the front rows of the parking lot.

   b. Take a vote of the nursing assistants.

   c. Coordinate the shift change so that all assistants leave together.

       d. Assign a security guard to escort assistants to their cars as they finish work.

       e. Canvass other hospitals in the area to discover their practices.

2. Writer 2, who was trying to solve the problem of employee motivation for his manager, proposed the following criteria. What would you suggest?

- Performance evaluation
- Security motives: Promotion from within; seniority-based personnel system
- Employee-of-the-month award
- Attendance award
- Raise in pay for a well-done job
- Profit to company
- Responsibility
- Advancement

3. Following is the complete introduction to a report by a student employee. What suggestions for revision would you make?

> The quality of work being displayed at the American Motel on 111 E. Jackson Road is inferior by not measuring up to the standards of other American motels I have seen around the country (examples include Independence, Missouri; Dayton, Ohio; and Alexandria, Virginia). American usually sets a good standard of having an efficient, reliable staff to manage its hotels; however, since the introduction of a new manager last year at this motel, the changes in employees' attitudes have switched from efficient to lazy. Obviously, the instatement of the new management has not been in the company's best interest.

4. If the syntax of your first version was criticized, do some sentence-combining exercises in Chapter 10 to gain more syntactic fluency.

5. Consult the editing guide in Chapter 9 about any mistakes you have made in grammar, spelling, and punctuation.

● **ASSIGNMENT: Revising and Editing**

1. In light of the responses you received, revise your first version, dealing first with major problems and then eliminating any errors of convention.

2. Submit your revised version for evaluation.

A WRITER'S PROCESS

Below we present the sequence followed in Writer 5's writing process.

THE GUIDING QUESTION AND SITUATION

Situation: My father's farm, on which I work

Our Values	***Aspects of the Farm***
—profitable position in the overall cattle industry for our farm	—losing money on the purebreed herd
—a herd of high-quality Angus cattle	—the quality of our herd is not deep enough; still a few toads left

Question: How can we, as a cattle farm, improve our profits and raise the quality of our stock above industry standards?

Situation: A report to my father

EXPLORATION

STATIC VIEW

—too many cows for Dad to handle
—40 head of cows; 10 real good, 2 super cows
—1 cow was 1979 National Champion—other is probably next year's champ
—both worth over $100,000
—embryo-transplanting a cow's embryo into other donor cows—a single outstanding cow can produce 20—30 calves per year
—not cheap
—$5,000 each flush—8–10 eggs—may not all be fertile
—plus expenses for donor cows
—extremely high-quality calves though
—already use artificial insemination a little bit
—very erratic—but has improved herd somewhat
—could involve Dad's labor

DYNAMIC VIEW

—problem has been developing a long time
—paid a lot of money for a lot of these calves
—we don't have the market to sell their calves for large sums of money
—Dad has been forced to spend 4–6 hrs daily just taking care of the cattle—too much time
—he is neglecting some of the show calves because he is too busy

—Our A1 problems are a result of erratic checking procedures and some bad semen we got hold of

—The herd keeps growing but we just keep sinking bucks in without any return

RELATIVE VIEW

Criteria

—solution must increase overall quality

—solution must reduce Dad's labor

Comparison: The problem is a lot like the practice profit problems we had in several classes at school. Simple to cure if Dad will agree with solution.

Analogy: Our situation in the cattle industry could be compared to a king with a lopsided crown. The crown contains two of the world's finest jewels, but the weight of the other stones in the crown is hiding the beauty of the two and almost causing the entire crown to topple.

Alternative Solutions

—One solution is to sell all the cows but these two super cows and embryo-transplant them.

—Another possible solution is to intensify and shape up our A1 program to improve quality quicker.

—Another might be to go to a commercial herd (no purebreed).

Recommendation

—The first solution is the only one which meets the criteria.

—A1 doesn't because of its costs and increased labor.

—Commercial doesn't improve quality or labor.

Solution

The sale of 38 head of Angus cows
and the embryo transplant of the
remaining two ─────────────

Recommendation

── should occur immediately on our
farm.

(**Question:** How can we, as a cattle farm, improve our profits and raise the quality of our stock above industry standards?)

AUDIENCE ANALYSIS

1. My audience is my father, who owns the farm.
2. a. Background: Owner of the farm.
   b. Values: Very profit-conscious.
3. Attitude toward the subject: Senses the problem.
4. Specific role: The farm manager—the decision-maker. He needs to make a decision, but he seems to hold back.
5. Analysis of the role
   a. Background: He needs to know that we are in a bad situation that can only

get worse if we don't stop it. We cannot stand the constant financial drain; a decision for change must be made.

    b. Values: He is concerned about a good herd, but he needs also to be concerned for himself more than he is. The welfare of the manager has something to do with the health of the business.

    c. Attitude toward the subject: He needs to be motivated to act.

6. Relational role: He respects my opinion very much and I feel he just needs a logical push in the right direction, because he is ready for a change.

FIRST VERSION

INTRODUCTION

The quality of our herd of Angus cattle has long been a source of pride to our farm corporation. However, it is time to examine our cattle division in terms of not only quality, but also the amount of overall labor involved as well as the profitability. To adequately ensure continued high quality, reduce labor, and at the same time guarantee profitability, it is necessary that we liquidate our present herd of cattle except for the tag 2 and tag 15 cows, and enroll these two outstanding individuals in an intensive embryo transplant program as soon as possible.

OVERVIEW

Over the last 5 years the cattle division of our farm corporation has become an ever-increasing burden on our overall profitability. We have spent over $120,000 yearly on the management and upgrading of our purebred Angus herd, compared with annual dollar returns of approximately $75,000. To meet our goal of owning an extremely high-quality herd of cattle we have sacrificed any semblance of profit. Given the current and future economic situations, it is time to add profitability to our list of goals for the cattle division. Another factor of the problem is the amount of labor involved in caring for the 40 cows we currently own. Since I am in school, the brunt of the work has fallen on your shoulders. By drastically reducing the size of the herd, you would be free to pursue your highly profitable farm development interests, while still maintaining your contacts within the cattle industry. It is possible to meet all of these goals in a very positive way by following my recommended solution to our problem.

CRITERIA

Any viable solution to the deficiencies of our cattle division must at the very least maintain the quality of our herd, increase our profits, and reduce the amount of labor required to maintain the herd.

DISCUSSION OF ALTERNATIVES

1. Maintain current system: This alternative is definitely unworkable in light of our future goals. It maintains our herd quality, but is highly unprofitable to the tune

of losing over $55,000 annually and provides no relief to our current labor crunch.

2. Upgrade and revitalize our artificial insemination program: This alternative shows a bit of promise in that it would over time increase our overall quality. The current high quality of our herd is mainly due to our implementation 5 years ago of a partial A1 program. We can upgrade this program to include all the cows and revitalize it by increasing the efficiency of our heat detection methods to call all the cows on the first cycle; we could thereby make a definite upward step in herd quality. However, any adjustment in the A1 program would necessitate a tremendous increase in labor. It would take time, more of your time, to adequately observe and work with the cows to detect their heat cycles. It also would take more labor to corral, catch, and inseminate the entire herd instead of the 15 head we currently handle. The profitability question remains unanswered by this alternative. Expense would increase due to the cost of the semen and the fees of a competent A1 technician. Returns from the sale of higher-quality calves would be slightly increased, but these increases would not even begin to cover our yearly deficits in this enterprise.

3. Sell out except for the tag 2 and tag 15 cows and enroll them in an embryo transplant program: Herein lies the future of our cattle herd. Embryo transplant is the most exciting technological advancement in the history of the cattle industry. This process, which allows extremely high-quality cows to produce 20 to 30 calves a year, is one which we definitely need to get involved with. The increase in quality of our herd would be tremendous and would occur virtually overnight. The tag 2 and tag 15 cows are two of the top ten cows in America. A herd built around the traits and characteristics of these two cows would have to be one of the highest-quality herds in the entire world. Obviously, by enrolling these two cows in an intensive embryo transplant program we would tremendously increase our overall herd quality. The sale of the remaining 38 cows would cut our labor requirements to almost nothing for the first year. The herd numbers could gradually be built back up with the embryo transplant calves, but by the time the labor had increased to our present level, I would be home from college and able to help out. Our profitability picture would be completely turned around by this changeover. To start with, the initial cash which would be raised by the sale of the 38 cows (approx. $150,000) could be the answer to our short-term cash problems and could also be used to finance the initial expenses of the embryo transplant program. At $5,000 a flush and figuring four flushes per cow, we will need $40,000 the first year to fund this venture. This yearly expense will more than likely increase slightly over the next 5 years, but the needed capital will be more than matched by the returns from the sale of a few of the transplant calves. The only calf we have ever sold from either of these two cows brought $28,000 in last year's sale. With a minimum of promotional expense, we should be able to sell several of the transplant calves for around $20–25,000 apiece. At this price it would only take the sale of three of these calves to cover the total yearly expenses of the entire cattle division. The disposition of the remaining 30 to 40 calves would be totally up to us. The most

outstanding calves could be kept to begin building the herd numbers back up, and any calves we wished to sell would bring straight profit, pure and simple.

RECOMMENDED SOLUTION

To meet our goals of a profitable, high-quality, purebred Angus herd that is highly capital-intensive in nature, I recommend that the entire herd except the tag 2 and tag 15 cows be liquidated and that these two super cows be enrolled in an intensive embryo transplant program.

TWO

Guide to Editing and Sentence-Combining

9

EDITING

Most of the writing we do is meant to be shared, to be presented or published. Once we mail a letter or send a piece of writing off to a journal or submit it to a professor, we are usually unable to make further changes; the piece of writing, for better or worse, represents us. As editors of our own work, therefore, we examine every word, every sentence, with a "fine-tooth eye," assuring ourselves that what we have written will be accurate and worthy. This chapter will help you refine your editing skills through a series of checklists you use for reference as you edit your work. Each checklist treats a particular grammatical, punctuation, spelling, or mechanical *convention*—a widely accepted and established practice. Such conventions, of course, are not carved in stone; they shift according to historical and social contexts. Educated people in the Renaissance accepted great latitude in spelling (Shakespeare's name was spelled in a number of different ways in the seventeenth century, for example). The rapid advances in printing, the increased availability of printed texts and particularly dictionaries, however, led to standardized spellings, and today we are generally intolerant of "misspelled" words. Yet even today, "correct" spelling sometimes depends on where you live: In the United States, *check* is correct; in Canada and Britain the word is correctly spelled *cheque*. In the same way, comma conventions differ between English-speaking countries: in England, some sentences that North American teachers would label "comma splices"—and hence errors—are considered perfectly correct.

Editing a paper for grammatical, punctuation, spelling, or mechanical conventions is one of the last stages in the process of writing. As such, it comes at a time when you are ready to turn your attention from the major substance of a paper to its conventional or surface features. You probably know from experience that most of your audiences (professors, employers, business associates) expect adherence to the conventions of edited North American English, and that you are often judged by your ability to produce writing that meets such standards.

Conscientious use of the following editing checklists can help you to achieve correctness of conventions. But we do not mean to suggest that you should work through the entire set of checklists for every paper you write. Different writers have different editing problems, and by now, with the help of your instructor and classmates, you should have discovered your own major editing problems. We suggest, then, that you concentrate on those checklists that apply to your particular editing difficulties, reading through your essay at least several times with those checklists in hand. The first time through, read slowly and look for the errors you most frequently make. On the second (or perhaps the third) slow reading, check specifically for sentence errors (fragments or comma splices) and for subject-verb agreement and pronoun reference, especially if the subject is separated from the verb by one or more phrases or the pronoun is separated from its referent. Next, take a tip from professional proofreaders and read word for word to check spelling. To do this, you may want to read backwards or to move a piece of blank paper down the page, revealing only one line at a time. (If you are using a word processor, of course, you may be able to employ one of the spelling programs that will point out major errors for you.) And if your essay is typed in final draft, check the end of each line very carefully; errors often occur there, particularly if a word is hyphenated. Finally, never hesitate to ask your instructor if you are unsure about a particular convention. And as you strive to create conventionally correct pieces of writing, remember that *all* writers make errors. Inexperienced writers often view errors as failures, as dead ends. Experienced writers, on the other hand, are able to keep a sharp eye out for their errors and to view errors as practice in learning how not to make the same mistakes again!

● GRAMMATICAL CONVENTIONS

A. NUMBER

CHECKLIST

✔ Does the word in question refer to one *(singular)* or more than one *(plural)*?

✔ If the word is plural, is its ending correct?
- Add *s* if the word ends in a vowel plus *y*. (boys; keys)
- Change *y* to *i* and add *es* if the word ends in a consonant plus *y*. (dictionaries)
- Add *es* if the word ends in a consonant and the plural ending is pronounced as a separate syllable (sandwiches)
- Add *s* if the plural ending is *not* pronounced as a separate syllable. (books; papers)
- Add *s* if the word is a proper name and ends in *y*. (Careys)
- If the word ends in *o*, check your dictionary.

✔ If the word is a number or letter, is the plural formed by adding *'s*? (straight A's; a pair of 4's)

✔ Can you detect any unnecessary shifts in number?

UNEDITED	EDITED
1. Rest <u>home's</u> are seldom restful.	1. Rest <u>homes</u> are seldom restful.
2. Newton, Locke, and Leibniz were famous <u>contemporarys</u>.	2. Newton, Locke, and Leibniz were famous <u>contemporaries</u>.
3. Most students are unhappy when they receive <u>Ds</u>.	3. Most students are unhappy when they receive <u>D's</u>.
4. The <u>banjoes</u> seemed almost alive in the skilled hands of Roy Clark and Buck Trent.	4. The <u>banjos</u> seemed almost alive in the skilled hands of Roy Clark and Buck Trent.
5. How many <u>lunchs</u> have you missed lately?	5. How many <u>lunches</u> have you missed lately?
6. The <u>Henries</u> have asked me to join them at the concert.	6. The <u>Henrys</u> have asked me to join them at the concert.

B. TENSE

✔ Is the tense of each verb accurate?
  • If the tense is *present,* the action is happening now. (People talk.)
  • If the tense is *past,* the action happened before now and is completed. (People talked.)
  • If the tense is *future,* the action will happen later. (People will talk.)
  • If the tense is *present perfect,* the action began in the past and may continue into the present. (People have talked.)
  • If the tense is *past perfect,* the action happened in the past before another past time or event. (People had talked.)
  • If the tense is *future perfect,* the action will be completed in the future before another time or event in the future. (People will have talked.)
✔ If the verb is in one of the three perfect tenses, is it formed by using the auxiliary verb *has, had,* or *will have* with the past participle?
✔ Are unnecessary or confusing shifts in tense avoided?
✔ If direct discourse is used, are the verbs in the tense that the speaker used?

UNEDITED

1. A suburban homestead that was solar-powered and produced food all year long in both an outside garden and a solar greenhouse begins to make self-sufficiency possible.

2. The great Russian weightlifter has broke seven records this year.

3. The frightened child asked, "Who was it?"

4. Jody has studied so many hours that he forgot what sleep is like.

5. In the latest incoherent thriller flick, long passages of cinematic exposition alternate with gory bits, which were frequently presented in slow motion to extend the violence.

EDITED

1. A suburban homestead that is solar-powered and produces food all year long in both an outside garden and a solar greenhouse begins to make self-sufficiency possible.

2. The great Russian weightlifter has broken seven records this year.

3. The frightened child asked, "Who is it?"

4. Jody has studied so many hours that he has forgotten what sleep is like.

5. In the latest incoherent thriller flick, long passages of cinematic exposition alternate with gory bits, which are frequently presented in slow motion to extend the violence.

C. AGREEMENT BETWEEN SUBJECTS AND VERBS

✔ If the subject is singular, is its verb also singular?
✔ If the subject is plural, is its verb also plural?

✔ If the subject is third person and singular (<u>he</u>, <u>she</u>, <u>it</u> or a noun that <u>he</u>, <u>she</u>, or <u>it</u> can be substituted for, as in <u>Janet</u>, <u>Gordon</u>, or <u>the game</u>), does the form of the present tense verb end in *s*? (She runs.)

✔ If the verb is a form of *to be*, does its form agree with the subject? (I <u>am</u>; you <u>are</u>; he, she, or it <u>is</u>; we <u>are</u>; you <u>are</u>; they <u>are</u>.)

✔ If two singular subjects are joined by *or* or *nor*, is the verb singular? (Either Dave or Cathy <u>is</u> willing to pick you up.)

✔ If two plural subjects are joined by *or* or *nor*, is the verb plural? (Either first-year or second-year students <u>are</u> <u>enrolled</u> in this course.)

✔ If one singular and one plural subject are joined by *or* or *nor*, does the verb agree with the nearer form? (Neither Ruth nor her classmates <u>want</u> to do the assignment.)

UNEDITED	EDITED
1. The dolphin brain resemble the human brain in being very large and very wrinkled.	1. The dolphin brain resembles the human brain in being very large and very wrinkled.
2. Carrie Chapman Catt and Elizabeth Cady Stanton was women's rights leaders.	2. Carrie Chapman Catt and Elizabeth Cady Stanton were women's rights leaders.
3. Dr. Powell be my best instructor this term.	3. Dr. Powell is my best instructor this term.
4. Each of the boys tend to imitate his hero.	4. Each of the boys tends to imitate his hero.
5. Neither a biographical section nor a gazetteer section appear in *Webster's Third New International Dictionary.*	5. Neither a biographical section nor a gazetteer section appears in *Webster's Third New International Dictionary.*
6. The name *opossum*, along with *moose, terrapin,* and *caribou,* are of Indian origin.	6. The name *opossum*, along with *moose, terrapin,* and *caribou,* is of Indian origin.
7. A bird or a bee or a crab communicate information, emotions, and warnings.	7. A bird or a bee or a crab communicates information, emotions, and warnings.
8. Neither he nor his roommates eats in the cafeteria.	8. Neither he nor his roommates eat in the cafeteria.

D. AGREEMENT BETWEEN PRONOUNS AND THEIR ANTECEDENTS

CHECKLIST

✔ If the antecedent is singular, is the pronoun singular?

✔ If the antecedent is plural, is the pronoun plural?

✔ If the antecedent is first person, is the pronoun first person?

✔ If the antecedent is second person, is the pronoun second person?

✔ If the antecedent is third person, is the pronoun third person?

✔ If the antecedent is *everyone, everybody, each, either, neither, nobody, one,* or *anyone,* is the pronoun singular?

✔ If the antecedent is two nouns joined by *and,* is the pronoun plural?

✔ If the antecedent is two singular nouns joined by *or* or *nor,* is the pronoun singular?

✔ If the antecedent is two plural nouns joined by *or* or *nor,* is the pronoun plural?

UNEDITED

1. Nuclear reactors create the potential for disasters so severe that it could change the whole course of human history.

2. Each student should bring their book to class.

3. Although the members complained, the president ignored him.

4. When a student begins to write an essay, you need to have a clear focus.

5. William Aide and Robert Aitken will perform his arrangement of Mozart's "Flute Quartet."

6. Either Groucho or Harpo loses their pants in the final battle scene of the Marx Brothers' *Duck Soup.*

EDITED

1. Nuclear reactors create the potential for disasters so severe that they could change the whole course of human history.

2. Students should bring their books to class.

3. Although the members complained, the president ignored them.

4. When a student begins to write an essay, he or she needs to have a clear focus.

5. William Aide and Robert Aitken will perform their arrangement of Mozart's "Flute Quartet."

6. Either Groucho or Harpo loses his pants in the final battle scene of the Marx Brothers' *Duck Soup.*

E. PRONOUN REFERENCE

CHECKLIST

✔ Is the referent or antecedent for every pronoun present in the sentence?

✔ Is the referent or antecedent for each pronoun clear?

✔ If the pronoun is *this,* as in "this perplexed me," is the word *this* followed by a specifying noun? (This stubbornness perplexed me.)

✔ If the pronoun *this, that, such,* or *which* stands for a preceding statement, is the relationship between the pronoun and the preceding statement absolutely clear? (Sara missed all her classes today, which shocked me should be edited to read I was shocked that Sara missed all her classes today.)

UNEDITED	EDITED
1. Both his father and mother are in the hospital, and his sister is home alone. <u>This</u> caused Jim to withdraw from school.	1. Both his father and mother are in the hospital, and his sister is home alone. <u>This unexpected emergency</u> caused Jim to withdraw from school.
2. Since the strike ended at midnight, <u>they</u> say production should resume within twenty-four hours.	2. Since the strike ended at midnight, <u>union spokesmen</u> say production should resume within twenty-four hours.
3. Barbara shouted to Sue while <u>she</u> waited in line.	3. While Barbara waited in line, <u>she</u> shouted to Sue.
4. <u>It</u> says in the paper to expect the first snowfall before Thanksgiving.	4. <u>The paper</u> says to expect the first snowfall before Thanksgiving.
5. After Carlos attended Dr. Smith's class and Dr. Freeman's class, he decided to enroll in <u>it</u>.	5. Carlos attended both Dr. Smith's and Dr. Freeman's lectures before he decided to enroll in Dr. Smith's class.
6. Helen's voice was low and mellifluous, <u>which</u> pleased her.	6. Helen's low and mellifluous voice pleased her.

F. CASE (SUBJECTIVE, OBJECTIVE, POSSESSIVE)

CHECKLIST

✔ If a pronoun is the subject of a verb, is the pronoun in the subjective case? (*I; we; he; she; they; who*)

✔ If a pronoun is the object of a verb, is it in the objective case? (*me; us; him; her; them; whom*)

✔ If a pronoun is the object of a preposition, is the pronoun in the objective case? (Give the book to me.)

✔ If the pronoun is the subject *or* the object of an infinitive, is the pronoun in the objective case? (I expect her to attend.)

✔ If the pronoun is part of a compound, is it in the case that it would be in if it stood alone? (She and I will be late.)

✔ If the pronoun or noun comes before and modifies a gerund (an *ing* word used as a noun), is the pronoun or noun in the possessive case? (Joe's leaving disappointed him.)

✔ Are singular possessive nouns formed with *'s*? (Mary's coat is here. The Jones's house was sold today.)

✔ Are plural possessive nouns formed by adding *s'* or *es'*? (The boys' coats are over there. The Joneses' houses were sold today.)

UNEDITED	EDITED

UNEDITED

1. <u>Nelson and him</u> were going over some difficult technical problems when they arrived.

2. The snowballs hit <u>he and I</u> squarely between our shoulders.

3. The responsibility must rest on <u>she and I.</u>

4. Professor Foster asked <u>he and I</u> to lead the class discussion.

5. <u>Him</u> and the umpire debated the call until the ump threw him out of the game.

6. <u>Sheila</u> asking the question surprised all of us.

7. <u>Ramonas</u> sister called to say that Ramona will be home tonight.

8. I wish the professor had chosen someone <u>elses</u> paper to discuss in class.

9. The <u>womens'</u> room and the <u>mens'</u> room in the old railway station have been closed for repairs.

10. The two <u>violinist's</u> performance was well received by the audience.

11. The victory is <u>theirs</u>, not <u>your's.</u>

EDITED

1. <u>Nelson and he</u> were going over some difficult technical problems when they arrived.

2. The snowballs hit <u>him and me</u> squarely between our shoulders.

3. The responsibility must rest on <u>her and me.</u>

4. Professor Foster asked <u>him and me</u> to lead the class discussion.

5. <u>He</u> and the umpire debated the call until the ump threw him out of the game.

6. <u>Sheila's</u> asking the question surprised all of us.

7. <u>Ramona's</u> sister called to say that Ramona will be home tonight.

8. I wish the professor had chosen someone <u>else's</u> paper to discuss in class.

9. The <u>women's</u> room and the <u>men's</u> room in the old railway station have been closed for repairs.

10. The two <u>violinists'</u> performance was well received by the audience.

11. The victory is <u>theirs</u>, not <u>yours</u>.

CUMULATIVE EDITING EXERCISES

The following passages contain errors in *number, tense, agreement between subjects and verbs, agreement between pronouns and antecedents, pronoun reference,* and *case.* Edit each passage carefully, correcting every error you can find.

[A] The student's I usually encounter on campus have graduated from high school recently and were attempting to cope with the new experience of going to a large university. Many of these are confused and frustrated by the impersonal treatment he or she received in classes of 100 or more and by the sometimes apparently backward educational system with which they must deal. Consequently, its easy for those in his or her first year to find fault with almost everything, from poor food service and high prices to incompetent professor's, in order to release some of their frustrations'. But this was as far as most bothers to go, and only those students who chooses to be involved with council and committees for change seems to have ideas for solutions to them.

[B] "We have nothing to fear but fear itself," a famous national leader said to encourage his men to fight for their country. But the saying has many other applications. Fear is something every human has experienced sometime in their life. Fear generally come without reason and had a great effect on the recipient. Fear has also caused more mistakes than almost anything else.

Fear is something you feel the first time you stand in front of an audience of two hundred and has to give a speech. Fear is something you feel as your hard lines in the play you are in comes up and there's no one to help you out. Fear is taking your drivers test after you told everyone you're definitely getting your license. Fear is taking a final examination when you have earned only Ds in the course. In all these situations, the mistake happens most often after FEAR comes. My friends and me have been in most of these situations, and we believe fear makes us do things we wouldn't otherwise do. This makes fear my enemy and not speeches; fear and not acting; fear and not drivers examinations. Fear.

[C]   To keep a students interest, the subjects has to be presented to her in an interesting way. A student who hates a certain subject probably will not learn anything. Only if it is presented to them in a unique way will he or she learn. For example, one day me and a buddy was observing a classroom and I notice how enthusiastic the children was to go to math class. So out of curiosity I sat in on it. To my surprise the teacher was explaining how to subtract by using really interesting example of the childrens' favorite foods. The childrens reactions were great. Everyone was involved and at the same time were learning subtraction. So to keep the students interest you have to make the subject interesting!

G. 1. SENTENCE FAULTS: FRAGMENTS

CHECKLIST
- ✔ Does the sentence have both a subject and a verb that can change tense? If not, the sentence is a fragment.
- ✔ Is an *-ing* word used as the only verb? If so, the sentence is a fragment.
- ✔ If the subject is *who, which, whose,* or *whom,* is the sentence a question? If not, the sentence is a fragment.

✔ If the subject and verb are introduced by a subordinating word such as *although, since, when, after, because,* or *while,* is this clause connected to a main clause? If not, the sentence is a fragment.

✔ Can the sentence be turned into a question without omitting any words? If it cannot be, then the sentence is a fragment.

✔ If a fragment appears in your finished essay, is it used purposely to achieve emphasis?

UNEDITED

1. Sidney recently saw the revue *Ain't Misbehavin'.* <u>Which is a delightful tribute to Fats Waller.</u>

2. Mozart's *Mitridate Re di Ponto* is a tremendous achievement. <u>Showing Mozart's uncanny gift for characterization through music and his incredible understanding of what the human voice can actually do.</u>

3. The convicted murderer recanted his confession as soon as the sentence was passed. <u>Although he originally pleaded guilty.</u>

4. Thirty-five million Americans have high blood pressure. <u>Including one out of four persons over age 18 and growing numbers of children.</u>

5. Your muffler emits nerve-jarring, scraping sounds as it drags down the road. <u>Because the exhaust system has suffered a breakdown.</u>

6. Coleus, impatiens, and geraniums are the easiest plants to grow from cuttings. <u>Especially if the stems are dipped in a rooting hormone.</u>

7. How can we become better writers? Only by immersing ourselves in the entire writing process.

EDITED

1. Sidney recently saw the revue *Ain't Misbehavin',* <u>which is a delightful tribute to Fats Waller.</u>

2. Mozart's *Mitridate Re di Ponto* is a tremendous achievement, <u>showing Mozart's uncanny gift for characterization through music and his incredible understanding of what the human voice can actually do.</u>

3. <u>Although the convicted murderer originally pleaded guilty,</u> he recanted his confession as soon as the sentence was passed.

4. Thirty-five million Americans, <u>including one out of four persons over age 18 and growing numbers of children,</u> have high blood pressure.

5. <u>Because the exhaust system has suffered a breakdown,</u> your muffler emits nerve-jarring, scraping sounds as it drags down the road.

6. Coleus, impatiens, and geraniums are the easiest plants to grow from cuttings, <u>especially if the stems are dipped in a rooting hormone.</u>

7. (Intentional fragment. Leave as is.)

G. 2. SENTENCE FAULTS: FUSED SENTENCES

CHECKLIST ✔ If the sentence contains two or more main clauses, are they joined by *and, but, or, nor, for, yet, so,* or by a semicolon? If not, the main clauses are fused sentences. See page 427 for more examples of such words.

UNEDITED	EDITED
1. Everything on the Mediterranean has been strained beyond limit by the hoards of sunworshippers as a result, the pollution of the sea is worse than ever.	1. Everything on the Mediterranean has been strained beyond limit by the hoards of sunworshippers; as a result, the pollution of tne sea is worse than ever.
2. Start with this 10¢ coupon then get details at your store on how to save $1.00.	2. Start with this 10¢ coupon, and then get details at your store on how to save $1.00.
3. Wine industry people tend to rate a winery's size by annual production in cases storage capacity in gallons can also indicate physical size.	3. Wine industry people tend to rate a winery's size by annual production in cases, but storage capacity in gallons can also indicate physical size.
4. John left for classes Tim went to work.	4. Tom left for classes, and Tim went to work.
5. I might stay I might go I'll have to wait and see.	5. I might stay, or I might go; I'll have to wait and see.

G. 3. SENTENCE FAULTS: COMMA SPLICES

CHECKLIST ✔ If the sentence contains more than one main clause, are the clauses joined by only a comma? If so, the sentence is a comma splice.
✔ Are the main clauses joined by a comma plus a word such as *therefore, however,* or *moreover*? If so, the sentence is a comma splice.

UNEDITED	EDITED
1. To test a turkey for doneness, make a small cut in the thickest part, no pink should show.	1. To test a turkey for doneness, make a small cut in the thickest part; no pink should show.
2. We had a Dante's *Inferno* among my father's books, such books were common in rural districts at the time.	2. We had a Dante's *Inferno* among my father's books. Such books were common in rural districts at the time.
3. The long, white beaches on Barbados are warm year round, therefore tourists flock there in every season.	3. The long, white beaches on Barbados are warm year-round, so tourists flock there in every season.

4. The quarterback held onto the ball, however he was sacked by two blitzing linebackers.

4. The quarterback held onto the ball, but he was sacked by two blitzing linebackers.

or

Although the quarterback held onto the ball, he was sacked by two blitzing linebackers.

or

The quarterback held onto the ball; however, he was sacked by two blitzing linebackers.

H. DANGLING AND MISPLACED MODIFIERS

CHECKLIST

✔ Does each modifier in the sentence *clearly* refer to the word(s) it describes?

✔ Could the modifier possibly describe *either* the word before it or the word after it? If so, the modifier is *squinting* (it looks both ways at once).

✔ If the modifier is an introductory phrase such as "Walking down the road," does it modify the subject of the main clause? If not, the modifier is *dangling*.

✔ Is each modifier placed as closely as possible to the word(s) it modifies? If not, the modifier is *misplaced*.

UNEDITED

1. Properly pickled, no one can resist a mushroom.

EDITED

1. Properly pickled, a mushroom is irresistible.

or

No one can resist a properly pickled mushroom.

2. Students who practice writing often will begin to improve their styles.

2. Students who often practice writing will begin to improve their styles.

or

Students who practice writing will often begin to improve their styles.

3. Riding my bike peaceably, the gas-guzzling Chrysler almost ran me down.

3. Riding my bike peaceably, I was almost run down by a gas-guzzling Chrysler.

4. New sports medicine clinics have sprung up to care for people all over the nation wounded in the pursuit of physical fitness.

4. New sports medicine clinics have sprung up all over the nation to care for people wounded in the pursuit of physical fitness.

5. The beloved maestro waved to the audience with his baton filled with expectancy.

5. The beloved maestro waved with his baton to the audience filled with expectancy.

6. The man with the dog who was asking questions startled us.

6. The man, who had a dog, startled us with his questions.

I. PARALLEL OR GRAMMATICALLY EQUAL STRUCTURES

CHECKLIST

✔ In a series of words, does each item in the series have the same form—a noun followed by a noun, a gerund by a gerund, a participle by a participle, and so on? (The garden was filled with rhododendrons, azaleas, and hydrangeas; My favorite sports are swimming, hiking, and bicycling; Gasping and coughing, the diver emerged from the water.)

✔ In a series of phrases, does each item in the series have the same form—a prepositional phrase followed by a prepositional phrase, an infinitive phrase followed by an infinitive phrase, and so on? (The true gourmand delights not in the cooking but in the eating; Sylvia's coach wants her to work out, to diet, and to sleep nine hours a night for the next two months.)

✔ In a series of clauses, does each item in the series have the same form—a relative clause followed by a relative clause, a noun clause followed by a noun clause, and so on? (What we aim for and what we achieve coincide more often than not.)

UNEDITED

1. During preregistration week, we are usually concerned with choosing good courses and that we can find an inexpensive place to live.

EDITED

1. During preregistration week, we are usually concerned with choosing good courses and finding an inexpensive place to live.

2. The architectural features responsible for most accidents in buildings are stairs, running into doors, and windows.

2. The architectural features responsible for most accidents in buildings are stairs, doors, and windows.

3. Unscrupulous landlords often force tenants to move out on short notice or make them pay exorbitant rents.

3. Unscrupulous landlords often force tenants to move out on short notice or to pay exorbitant rents.

4. Most men now know <u>that their skin is vulnerable to the elements</u> and <u>taking special care of it</u>.

5. Dr. Land's 1947 development of Polaroid's instant photography was <u>for children</u>, <u>for adults</u>, and <u>not fiddling with the details of camera use</u>.

4. Most men now know <u>that their skin is vulnerable to the elements</u> and <u>that it requires special care</u>.

5. Dr. Land's 1947 development of Polaroid's instant photography was <u>for children</u>, <u>for adults</u>, and <u>for anyone who didn't want to fiddle with the details of camera use</u>.

CUMULATIVE EDITING EXERCISES

The following passages contain errors in sentence structure: *fragments, fused sentences, comma splices, dangling and misplaced modifiers,* and *nonparallel structures.* Edit each passage carefully, correcting every error you can find.

[A]   As an upper-middle-class citizen, it is difficult to imagine the hardships others, such as the characters in *The Grapes of Wrath,* have had to endure. Not until I read that novel did I experience what I would consider the worst situations anyone could live through. Outcasts from their own land, forced from the family home, starving, penniless, and with little hope. The novel shows a family illtreated by those they turned to for help. We all hope such circumstances will never recur in the United States, they should not be forgotten for that reason. A work such as Steinbeck's ensures that life in the late 1920's was not the cozy, being comfortable existence most of us now enjoy. Were it not for such pieces of literature which enable us to see not only the very best of life, whether luxury or loving, along with the opposite extreme of squalor and degradation, we would be much shallower people. Thus Steinbeck enriches us as we experience his words the readers can adapt them to their own lives.

[B]   The language of modern advertising is, in my view, misleading at best, dishonest at worst. I have little respect for the persons responsible for most ads, in fact, in most cases the opposite effect to that which was intended is created in me. That is, I will remember to *not* purchase a product because it either offended, was misleading, or embarrassed me.

Phrases like "We're bigger because we're better." Bigger than what? Better than what? Blades are "sharper," cars are "tougher" or "more economical," "stronger" mouthwashes do the job "better," and soaps are "more effective." Now all these phrases or words are comparison words, the trouble is they aren't being compared to anything.

Regarding supermarkets, a pet peeve I have is about the little "Special Today" signs often displayed under certain products. This proclamation would lead one to believe there was a special price for today. Not so, in fact, the sign simply means that the store is "featuring" that particular product for the day. Quite legal. But definitely misleading.

[C]   He gave homework assignments every night, five days a week, that's the best thing my old high school math teacher ever did for me. Mr. William King gave me so much math homework in my four years at high school I had math formulas

coming out my ears! Every day Mr. King would take the last five minutes in class

to assign homework. That we had to turn in the next day. In this way, my math

teacher made me learn responsibility for doing my work, develop good study

habits, and also trying always to learn more. Liking Mr. King and then liking math

class even more, the subject really intrigued me. Since that time, however, I have

found that courses *other* than math assign homework and also demand a lot of my

attention.

● PUNCTUATION CONVENTIONS

A. PERIODS, QUESTION MARKS, AND EXCLAMATION POINTS

CHECKLIST
- ✔ If the sentence is a statement, does it end with a period?
- ✔ If the sentence poses an indirect question, does it end with a period? (She wondered if I would pick up her papers.)
- ✔ If the sentence poses a direct question, does it end with a question mark? (Will you pick up my papers?)
- ✔ If the sentence makes an especially emphatic command or statement, does it end with an exclamation point? (Keep away from the fire!)
- ✔ If a term is an abbreviation, month, title, or degree, is a period used appropriately (Sept., Dr., M.D., etc.)? If in doubt, check the dictionary. See pages 444–445 for abbreviations without periods.
- ✔ If part of a quotation is omitted, does an ellipsis (three periods in a row) take the place of the omitted passage? (The visiting ambassador said: "I will meet with the press . . . at 4:00.")
- ✔ If the omission of part of a quotation occurs at the end of a sentence, do four periods mark the omission as well as the end of the sentence? (The visiting ambassador said: "I will expect newsmen to refrain from harassing me. . . .")

UNEDITED

1. Could an increasing accumulation of carbon dioxide in the atmosphere significantly raise global temperatures by early in the next century or even alter our way of life.

2. The critic asked whether the film was in any way fresh or innovative?

3. According to Lance Morrow, "After centuries of racks, gougings, hangmen, and unspeakably inventive tortures, much of mankind adopted the lockup as its principal instrument of punishment . . ."

4. "Save my baby" screamed the woman as she leaped from the burning balcony.

5. Rachel's sister recently received an MS degree.

EDITED

1. Could an increasing accumulation of carbon dioxide in the atmosphere significantly raise global temperatures by early in the next century or even alter our way of life?

2. The critic asked whether the film was in any way fresh or innovative.

3. According to Lance Morrow, "After centuries of racks, gougings, hangmen, and unspeakably inventive tortures, much of mankind adopted the lockup as its principal instrument of punishment. . . ."

4. "Save my baby!" screamed the woman as she leaped from the burning balcony.

5. Rachel's sister recently received an M.S. degree.

B. COMMAS

CHECKLIST

- If the sentence contains two main clauses, are they joined by a semicolon or a comma followed by *and, but, or, nor, for, so,* or *yet?* (It's summertime, and the livin' is easy.)
- If the sentence opens with an introductory word, phrase, or clause, does a comma follow the introductory element? (The preceding sentence offers an example of an introductory clause followed by a comma.)
- Are words, phrases, or clauses in a series separated by commas? (Deliver us from goblins, ghosts, long-legged beasts, and things that go "bump" in the night.)
- Are commas used to set off the name of a person spoken to? (Dr. Jones, would you step this way?)
- Are commas used to set off dates, addresses, and places? (Vladimir Nabokov died in early July, 1977, at his home in Montreux, Switzerland.)
- Are interrupting expressions set off by commas? (The assignment, he argued forcefully, was too time-consuming.)
- If a modifier follows the word(s) described and is *not* essential to the

meaning of the sentence but rather supplies *extra* information, is that modifier set off by commas? (Willie Nelson, who wrote "Red Headed Stranger," has three hot-selling albums; The steelworkers, who accepted the arbitrator's ruling, returned to work today; Julia Child, TV's culinary star, launched a new series last year.)

✔ If a modifier follows the word or words described and *is* essential to the meaning of the sentence, is that modifier *not* set off by commas? (The man who first walked on the moon recorded his sensations in detail; Salmon smoked over an open alder fire has a unique flavor; He who laughs last laughs best.)

UNEDITED

1. Subscribers will have no minimum number of books to buy and they may cancel subscriptions at any time.

2. Of course I have always been a football fanatic.

3. Historian Barbara Tuchman's description of the fourteenth century is exciting artistic and scholarly.

4. Larry will you give me a hand?

5. April 1 1978 was a day I will never forget.

6. The composing process is as we noted earlier a complex one.

7. The court's statement was as we expected inconclusive.

8. Boccaccio's Doctor Simon who was a proctologist had a chamber pot painted over his door.

9. People, who have very poor eyesight, should not qualify as aircraft pilots.

EDITED

1. Subscribers will have no minimum number of books to buy, and they may cancel subscriptions at any time.

2. Of course, I have always been a football fanatic.

3. Historian Barbara Tuchman's description of the fourteenth century is exciting, artistic, and scholarly.

4. Larry, will you give me a hand?

5. April 1, 1978, was a day I will never forget.

6. The composing process is, as we noted earlier, a complex one.

7. The court's statement was, as we expected, inconclusive.

8. Boccaccio's Doctor Simon, who was a proctologist, had a chamber pot painted over his door.

9. People who have very poor eyesight should not qualify as aircraft pilots.

C. SEMICOLONS

CHECKLIST ✔ If two main clauses have *not* been joined by a coordinating conjunction (*and, but, or, nor, for, so, yet*), have they been joined by a semicolon? (We arrived on campus today; tomorrow we face the long lines of registration.)

✔ If two main clauses are linked by a term in the following list, is that word *preceded* by a semicolon?

accordingly	*furthermore*	*meanwhile*	*similarly*
also	*hence*	*moreover*	*still*
anyway	*however*	*nevertheless*	*that is*
as a result	*in addition*	*nonetheless*	*that is to say*
besides	*indeed*	*on the contrary*	*then*
consequently	*in fact*	*on the other hand*	*therefore*
for example	*likewise*	*otherwise*	*thus*
for instance			

(The rain seeped slowly through the soles of my shoes; consequently, I caught my first cold of the season.)

✔ If a sentence contains a semicolon, does the semicolon have a main clause before it and a main clause after it (except in the following ✔)?

✔ If a sentence contains a series which contains commas, are the items in the series separated by semicolons instead of by additional commas? (The crowd in Tehran included angry students in jeans; women in the black *chador*, the traditional veil; peasants and merchants, whose clothing marked them immediately; and the black-robed mullahs, the leaders of the Shi'ite branch of Islam.)

UNEDITED

1. The last known case of smallpox occurred recently in London, hence the disease has not yet died out.

2. Socrates taught by asking questions, Plato apparently could answer many of them well.

3. Mary's courses included English 402, History of the English Language, Psychology 204, Introduction to Cognitive Psychology, and Philosophy 210, Logic for Nonmajors.

4. Conference participants attended large morning lectures, then they formed small discussion groups every afternoon.

EDITED

1. The last known case of smallpox occurred recently in London; hence the disease has not yet died out.

2. Socrates taught by asking questions; Plato apparently could answer many of them well.

3. Mary's courses included English 402, History of the English Language; Psychology 204, Introduction to Cognitive Psychology; and Philosophy 210, Logic for Nonmajors.

4. Conference participants attended large morning lectures; then they formed small discussion groups every afternoon.

5. Smokers should be more considerate of nonsmokers, for instance, they should never smoke in elevators.

5. Smokers should be more considerate of nonsmokers; for instance, they should never smoke in elevators.

D. COLONS

CHECKLIST
✔ If a sentence introduces a list, a series of explanations or illustrations, or other specifying material, does a colon precede this material? (Lynda's writing is characterized by three elements: sound logic, careful attention to detail, and wry humor.)
✔ If a sentence contains a colon, is the colon *preceded* by a main clause?
✔ If a sentence introduces a quotation, is the quotation preceded by a colon?

UNEDITED

1. As the experienced climber attempted to climb Everest, she said "I may indeed reach the summit, but I will never conquer this mountain."

2. During the first cooking class, we practiced using these tools, a paring knife, a butcher knife, a cleaver, a wire whisk, and a mortar and pestle.

3. Dawn's preferred class hours are: eight-thirty, nine-thirty, and ten-thirty.

4. Ainsley has recently developed a new interest, collecting rare treatises on magic.

5. Everyone who owns a McDonald's restaurant attends "Hamburger U" and receives a degree in QSC, quality, service, and cleanliness.

EDITED

1. As the experienced climber attempted to climb Everest, she said: "I may indeed reach the summit, but I will never conquer this mountain."

2. During the first cooking class, we practiced using these tools: a paring knife, a butcher knife, a cleaver, a wire whisk, and a mortar and pestle.

3. Dawn's preferred class hours are eight-thirty, nine-thirty, and ten-thirty.

4. Ainsley has recently developed a new interest: collecting rare treatises on magic.

5. Everyone who owns a McDonald's restaurant attends "Hamburger U" and receives a degree in QSC: quality, service, and cleanliness.

E. DASHES

CHECKLIST
✔ Are all dashes made with two unspaced hyphens with no space either before or after them? (Walk—don't run—to the nearest exit.)
✔ Is the dash used to emphasize an unexpected element, or to mark off

a summary word, phrase, or clause at the end of a sentence? (When Ivan wants to be alone, he whistles nervously to himself—a habit his friends have come to recognize and respect.)

✔ Are pairs of dashes used within the sentence to mark an abrupt parenthetical element or interruption in thought? (Often a favorite children's story—like *Goodnight Moon*—contains no obvious moral or lesson at all.)

✔ Are commas omitted before and after dashes?

UNEDITED

1. Some psychologists believe that in our society the biggest thrill and sense of power comes from our biggest killer the automobile.

2. The poet William Blake was a complex combination of innocence and experience, fantasy and practicality, a man behind a mask.

3. Some Western medical practitioners have always believed,— without knowing why,—that they achieved spectacular successes with acupuncture.

EDITED

1. Some psychologists believe that in our society the biggest thrill and sense of power comes from our biggest killer—the automobile.

2. The poet William Blake was a complex combination of innocence and experience, fantasy and practicality—a man behind a mask.

3. Some Western medical practitioners have always believed— without knowing why—that they achieved spectacular successes with acupuncture.

F. PARENTHESES AND BRACKETS

CHECKLIST

✔ Are parts of sentences that add incidental explanatory, illustrative, or specifying information enclosed in parentheses?

✔ Are any special directions to the reader enclosed in parentheses?

✔ When parentheses fall within other parentheses, are brackets used for the "inner" parentheses? *For example:* But others oppose the plan (see Hugh Jones, *The Weight of Power* [Princeton, 1968], pp. 72–84).

UNEDITED

1. Light beer contains less than half the calories, 68, and half the alcohol, 2.5 percent, of regular beer.

2. The word *hypnosis*, from the Greek, meaning "put to sleep," was coined in the nineteenth century by Scottish physician James Braid.

EDITED

1. Light beer contains less than half the calories (68) and half the alcohol (2.5 percent) of regular beer.

2. The word *hypnosis* (from the Greek, meaning "put to sleep") was coined in the nineteenth century by Scottish physician James Braid.

3. Six companies are currently competing for the right to sell fighter aircraft, see illustration on opposite page.

3. Six companies are currently competing for the right to sell fighter aircraft (see illustration on opposite page).

4. Please note the exceptions to this rule (see page 42 of *A Guide to Writing,* New York, 1975).

4. Please note the exceptions to this rule (see page 42 of *A Guide to Writing* [New York, 1975]).

G. APOSTROPHES

CHECKLIST

✔ Is the apostrophe plus *s* used to mark possessive nouns which do not end in *s*? (boy's; girl's)

✔ Is the apostrophe used alone to mark possessive nouns that do end in *s*? (boys'; girls')

✔ In a contraction, does the apostrophe appear in the space of the omitted letter(s) or number(s)? (don't; we'd; it's)

✔ Does the possessive pronoun *its* omit the apostrophe? (The boat lost its anchor.)

UNEDITED

1. The rampaging rhino trapped it's prey.

2. The evening paper advertised ladie's coats at half price.

3. Jack doesn't mind cleaning up after the store closes; its all in a days work.

4. If you were'nt there to hear him tell the story, then you probably wont think its funny.

5. An excellent article on ways to prevent high blood pressure appeared in the October 78 issue of *Health*.

EDITED

1. The rampaging rhino trapped its prey.

2. The evening paper advertised ladies' coats at half price.

3. Jack doesn't mind cleaning up after the store closes; it's all in a day's work.

4. If you weren't there to hear him tell the story, then you probably won't think it's funny.

5. An excellent article on ways to prevent high blood pressure appeared in the October '78 issue of *Health*.

CUMULATIVE EDITING EXERCISES

The following passages contain errors in the *conventions of punctuation*. Edit each passage carefully, correcting every error you can find.

[A]   I was rummaging in my purse for a pen when he took the chair next to mine

tossing a confident "Hi" in my vicinity. Most of the students in my psychology class know Mike by sight now. He's an extrovert; the kind of person who likes to draw attention to himself; to be noticed by others. Its important to him that strangers know he is sports-minded or "very athletic" as he thinks of himself. Education, is not as important to Mike as are the social benefits school offers. He thinks no party is complete or successful unless he is on the guest list. A self-centered person Mike has numerous but, not close, friends. He tends to use rather than to enjoy his buddies?

While others arrive on time for class, Mike is invariably late. He begins conversing with a friend over other student's heads (we all learn that he scored three goals in last nights' game. Later the professor asks a question which requires a vote, then Mike raises his hand for both enjoying the snickers his action receives. Unselfconsciously he sneaks sips from a can of Old Fashioned Lemonade which the friend naturally fetched for him. We have been told that Mike the athlete does'nt smoke but he does enjoy other habits, cracking his knuckles frequently is the most annoying of them.

[B]   Some people feel that capital punishment should be brought back into practice everywhere in order to create a healthy society. There are many reasons why this murderous deed—should not be practiced!

In a truly healthy society all person's would be able to work in unison (helping each other). Such a society would not have to resort to just having the "problem cases" eliminated because its impossible to know exactly where to draw the line. People, who like to have a sense of power, would probably keep sentencing people to be killed until only they were left.

Now the committee or jury responsible for sentencing these people; how can one know for sure that these are fair, just people. What gives this jury the right to say what is wrong and what is right. These people are human and humans are greatly influenced by irrational motives. This will affect their conclusions and therefore their verdict.

Although capital punishment, might set a good example for some is it really fair to those who are the examples. Is it fair for them to be murdered just so no one else does what they did.

[C]   Every decade is remembered for some specific reason. The reason may be a simple change in music or may be as major as a war. The 50's are remembered because they gave us "Rock 'n Roll," plus the threat of the "H" bomb! When recalling the 60's, one remembers the Beatle's hippies and Vietnam. Now that the 70's are over we are asking ourselves what major events stand out vividly in our minds?

Here is what stands out most vividly to me, the 70's allowed women to play a major role in society. Certainly the women's liberation movement blossomed in the

70's. The world became aware, of the fact, that women had brains, and planned

to use them. Women got together as a group and fought for what they believed

in. No more were they going to stand in the background. Many argued that they

have the right to choose what they will do with their life, and are choosing it.

Equal job opportunities and pay was a major battle for women, and now as

we are approaching the mid 80's it seems as though women have won the

battle. Its made one thing very clear, it doesn't matter whether you choose to

stay at home or go out into the work force, the decision is the woman's. We see

more women in top executive jobs, as well as political positions than ever before.

Flora MacDonald who is in the Canadian government is an example of a

woman who made her mark in the political world. In other parts of the world,

Margaret Thatcher and Indira Gandhi, both proved that they were capable of

running a country. Women still have a long way to come but it was the 70's that

began their ascent.

● SPELLING CONVENTIONS

A. *IE/EI*

CHECKLIST

✔ Does *i* come before *e*
except after *c*

or when sounded like *a* as in *neighbor* or *weigh*
or in exceptions like *weird* and *efficient?**

UNEDITED	EDITED
1. Being <u>decieved</u> was not the worst of it, since his neighbor was also a <u>theif.</u>	1. Being <u>deceived</u> was not the worst of it, since his neighbor was also a <u>thief.</u>
2. The <u>peir</u> <u>wieghed</u> nearly <u>ieght</u> tons, but the hoist <u>wielded</u> it like a toy in its <u>feirce</u> grip.	2. The <u>pier</u> <u>weighed</u> nearly <u>eight</u> tons, but the hoist <u>wielded</u> it like a toy in its <u>fierce</u> grip.
3. <u>Sieze</u> the day, and <u>forfiet</u> your <u>consceince.</u>	3. <u>Seize</u> the day, and <u>forfeit</u> your <u>conscience.</u>
4. Although he had <u>niether</u> his opponent's <u>hieght</u> nor his <u>wieght</u>, Mike's skill at karate ensured his victory.	4. Although he had <u>neither</u> his opponent's <u>height</u> nor his <u>weight</u>, Mike's skill at karate ensured his victory.

B. UNPRONOUNCED *E*

CHECKLIST

✔ 1. Does the word end in an unpronounced *e*?
✔   Does the suffix you are adding begin with a consonant?
    • If the answer to each question is yes, *keep* the *e*. (direful; discouragement)
✔ 2. Does the word end in an unpronounced *e*?
✔   Does the suffix you are adding begin with a vowel or a *y*?
    • If the answer to each question is yes, *drop* the *e*. (writing; lovable; hazy)
✔ 3. Does the word end in a soft *ce* or *ge*?
✔   Is the word followed by any suffix except *ing*?
    • If the answer to each question is yes, *keep* the *e*. (manageable; disadvantageous; pronounceable)

UNEDITED	EDITED
1. The <u>carless</u> driver is often <u>completly</u> responsible for an automobile accident.	1. The <u>careless</u> driver is often <u>completely</u> responsible for an automobile accident.
2. The gifts were <u>gratfully</u> accepted.	2. The gifts were <u>gratefully</u> accepted.
3. We were <u>hopeing</u> for sound <u>guideance</u>, but we actually got less-than-<u>desireable</u> advice.	3. We were <u>hoping</u> for sound <u>guidance</u>, but we actually got less-than-<u>desirable</u> advice.

*Other common exceptions: *counterfeit, either, neither, height, weight, seize, forfeit, foreign, leisure.*

4. Continueal encouragment
kept them from getting shakey.

4. Continual encouragement
kept them from getting shaky.

5. His resourcfulness in studying
for examinations was immediatly
noticable to his classmates.

5. His resourcefulness in studying for examinations was immediately noticeable to his classmates.

C. DOUBLING CONSONANTS

CHECKLIST
✔ 1. Is the final vowel in the word a *long* vowel?
  • If so, *don't* double the consonant. (sleeping; biting)
✔ 2. Does the word contain only one syllable?
✔   Does the word end in one consonant preceded by a single vowel?
✔   Does the suffix you are adding begin with a vowel?
  • If the answer to each question is yes, *double* the consonant. (throbbed)
  • If the answer to any question is no, *don't* double the consonant. (raining)
✔ 3. Does the word have more than one syllable?
✔   Does the word end in one consonant preceded by a single vowel?
✔   Is the last syllable in the word accented?
✔   Does the suffix you are adding begin with a vowel?
  • If the answer to each question is yes, *double* the consonant. (occurrence)
  • If the answer to any question is no, *don't* double the consonant. (listening)
✔ 4. Is the last syllable of the word accented?
✔   If you add a suffix, does the accent shift to the *first* syllable of the word?
  • If so, *don't* double the consonant. (infér; ínference)

UNEDITED

1. The traveller, given her preference, would have gone to Italy.

2. The growlling continued through the night, permiting no one to sleep.

3. Sailing can be fun, even for the beginer.

4. She spent most of the morning rolling out dough and bakking bread.

EDITED

1. The traveler, given her preference, would have gone to Italy.

2. The growling continued through the night, permitting no one to sleep.

3. Sailing can be fun, even for the beginner.

4. She spent most of the morning rolling out dough and baking bread.

D. *SEDE, CEED, CEDE*

CHECKLIST   ✔ If the spelling is *sede*, is the word *supersede*?
✔ If the spelling is *ceed*, is the word *exceed, proceed,* or *succeed*?
✔ Are all the other words ending with that syllable spelled *cede*? *(precede)*

UNEDITED

1. In order to <u>succede</u> at her job, the president of the company refused to allow any authority to <u>superceed</u> hers.

2. Those who <u>procede</u> with care will never <u>exsede</u> the speed limit.

3. The rock star was <u>preceeded</u> by a second-rate local group.

EDITED

1. In order to <u>succeed</u> at her job, the president of the company refused to allow any authority to <u>supersede</u> hers.

2. Those who <u>proceed</u> with care will never <u>exceed</u> the speed limit.

3. The rock star was <u>preceded</u> by a second-rate local group.

E. WORDS THAT SOUND ALIKE BUT HAVE DIFFERENT SPELLINGS

CHECKLIST   ✔ Have you checked each use of the following pairs of words to make sure you have made the correct choice?

1. accept (I will be happy to <u>accept</u> your invitation.)
   except (My niece will eat anything <u>except</u> spinach.)
2. affect (usually a verb: Her resignation <u>affects</u> all of us.)
   effect (usually a noun: The movie won an Academy Award for special <u>effects.</u>)
3. already (The meeting was <u>already</u> over when I arrived.)
   all ready (It isn't often that we are <u>all ready</u> on time.)
4. choose (present tense: I <u>choose</u> you.)
   chose (past tense: I <u>chose</u> you yesterday.)
5. cite (verb: Always <u>cite</u> your references.)
   site (noun: The homes were built on the <u>site</u> of an old churchyard.)
6. its (possessive: The dog hid <u>its</u> bone.)
   it's (contraction of *it is*: <u>It's</u> snowing heavily today.)
7. lead (adjective: He uses a <u>lead</u> pencil.)
   led (verb: He <u>led</u> his horse across the river.)
8. lose (verb: We must be careful not to <u>lose</u> our tickets.)
   loose (adjective: These slacks are too <u>loose</u>; they will have to be altered.)
9. principal (main: Her <u>principal</u> objection was to the high price of the stereo.)
   principle (basic truth, rule, or standard: Sir Thomas More was a man of <u>principle</u>.)
10. their (possessive: The children lost <u>their</u> mittens.)

there (like *here*: Put the paper over <u>there</u>.)
they're (contraction of *they are:* <u>They're</u> joining us for dinner.)

11. to (preposition: I went <u>to</u> the movie.)
    too (adverb: The oven is <u>too</u> hot for baking bread.)

12. weather (Our <u>weather</u> has been unusually cool this year.)
    whether (like *where, when, why:* <u>Whether</u> or not she gets to the
    party on time depends on the number of friends she picks up.)

13. who's (contraction of *who is:* <u>Who's</u> sorry now?)
    whose (possessive: <u>Whose</u> coat is on the floor?)

14. you're (contraction of *you are*: <u>You're</u> next.)
    your (possessive: May I borrow <u>your</u> pen?)

F. MISCELLANEOUS SUFFIX AND PREFIX PATTERNS

CHECKLIST

✔ 1. Does the word end in *c*?
✔   Does the suffix you are adding begin with *e, i,* or *y*?
   • If the answer to both questions is yes, *add k* before the suffix.
     (panicky; frolicking)

✔ 2. Are the last letters of the stem word and the first letter of the
      suffix the same?
   • If the answer is yes, *keep both letters.* (fatally; rottenness; room-
     mate; cannot)

✔ 3. Are the last letter of the prefix and the first letter of the stem word
      the same?
   • If the answer is yes, *keep both letters.* (disservice; dissection; ir-
     removable; misstep; overrate)

UNEDITED	EDITED
1. Opening leaf buds are per-fectly <u>mimiced</u> by the caterpillar's green-and-yellow markings.	1. Opening leaf buds are per-fectly <u>mimicked</u> by the caterpil-lar's green-and-yellow markings.
2. The <u>suddeness</u> with which the death scene ended startled even the most <u>imovable</u> members of the audience.	2. The <u>suddenness</u> with which the death scene ended startled even the most <u>immovable</u> mem-bers of the audience.
3. My <u>roomate</u> and I are both <u>disatisfied</u> with our landlord.	3. My <u>roommate</u> and I are both <u>dissatisfied</u> with our landlord.

G. SPELLING INVENTORY

CHECKLIST

✔ Have you made a spelling inventory sheet on which you list all words
  which you have misspelled?
✔ Have you grouped your misspellings into the following categories?
  • *ie/ei*
  • long vowel sound

- short vowel sound
- unpronounced *e*
- last-letter consonant
- double consonant
- sound-alike words
- prefix
- suffix
- letter reversals
- omitted letters
- words whose spelling differs markedly from your pronunciation of them

✔ Have you studied the checklists on the preceding pages that apply to the categories your misspellings fall into?

✔ Have you thought of special ways to remember the spellings of words you pronounce differently from their spelling? For example, do you remember that there is a *cog* in *recognize,* even though you pronounce it *reckanize?* Or a *govern* in *government* even though you don't pronounce the *n?*

✔ Do you practice pronouncing syllable by syllable the words you misspell?

✔ Do you correctly copy words you have misspelled so that your hand will get a "feeling" for the correct spelling?

✔ Do you note words you have misspelled so that your eyes will get accustomed to seeing those words spelled correctly?

✔ Have you studied your dictionary so that you know how to find the pronunciation, syllabification, grammatical classes, and usage of words?

✔ If you have trouble spelling the first part of a word or if you can't find a word in the dictionary, have you asked someone to help you spell it?

CUMULATIVE EDITING EXERCISES

The following passages contain errors in the conventions of spelling. Edit each passage carefully, correcting every error you can find.

[A]   The five-year periode between 1930 and 1935 marked some of the roughest

yeares of the Depression, provideing the best exampals of posative and negative

human behavior in times of crisus and uncertanty. During the "Dirty Thirties,"

newspapers presented glosy views of life, while minoraty groups were blammed for causing all the hardships faced by everyone else. But the survivers of the Depresion were those who made do with what little they had.

North American newspapers choose too present completely unrealistic pictures of life durning the thirties. My reading of microfilm from the period revealled full-page storys of the World Seres or the Stanley Cup instead of reports on the bredlines or recipes for "depression stew." Human interest storys like those about the Dionne Quintuplets made headlines. The newspapers resolutly avoided the grim starvation of jobbless people. Newspappers painted a rosie picture and stayed clear of the harsh realty. Shirley Temple's movies were very popular during the Depression ara. Perhaps it was somehow desireable for the average person to avoid realty and excape to the foreign land of "The Good Ship Lollipop," while impoverrished people on street corners asked, "Brother can you spar a dime?"

[B]   Teechers all have there own unique characterestices, but the one I wish they all sharred was patients. I beleive that studants enjoy learning more if they know the teacher will be patient with each and every one. Learning new subjects is always difficult, and if the teacher isn't patient, he or she could turn them away from learning alltogether. I have seen this hapen often sinse I am in the freashman early field expereince program. I found out through observing, that if teachers are patient with they're students and try to keep them from giving up, those

studants will finish what is due and will be prowd of their work.

[C]   Unfortunately, modern advertizing has becom a modern necesity, a way of

showing or prooving who has the better or better-priced product. But adver-

tizements do more: they lead kids to ask for things just because they saw them

advertized. They lead parants to buy things just because they seem glamorus. I

think most advertisements rip us off and that, iroincaly, we are realy paying for

only the expense of the advertissement itself. I once bought a certin shampo, and

the advertisements promised that it did not give the greecies. Well, after a few

times of washing my hair with it my hair *turned greesy*. I belive you could call that

false advertizement. At any rate, that ad surely didn't help me chose the best

product for my hair!

MECHANICAL CONVENTIONS

A. PREPARING FINAL COPY

CHECKLIST   ✔ If the essay is typed, have you used unlined white bond paper?
   ✔ If the essay is handwritten, have you used white, lined loose-leaf paper?
   ✔ Have you allowed one-inch margins at the top, bottom, and both sides of the paper?
   ✔ Is the essay double-spaced throughout, including footnotes and quotations?
   ✔ Is each new paragraph indented five spaces from the left margin?

✔ Is each extended quotation (more than four lines) set off from the body of the paper by an extra line space, and is it indented ten spaces from the left margin?

✔ Is the title of the essay centered on the first page of the essay?

✔ Is the title written *without* quotation marks or underlining?

✔ Do your name, your instructor's name, the course number (if appropriate), and the date appear at the upper right-hand corner of the first page?

✔ Except for the first page, which is unnumbered but which counts as page one, are all pages numbered consecutively in the upper right-hand corner?

B. CAPITALIZING

CHECKLIST ✔ Have you capitalized the following items?

• The first letter of the first, last, and all other words in a title except articles, conjunctions, and prepositions?

• The first letter of all proper names?

• The first letter of the first word in every line of verse (unless intentionally lowercase, as in some modern poetry)?

• The first letter of the first word in a sentence?

• The first letter of a title or abbreviation of a title that comes before a proper name? (Prime Minister; Ms.)

• The pronoun *I*.

• The first letter of a month, day of the week, or holiday?

• The first letter of the title of a historical event? (Battle of Cutting Knife Creek)

• The first letter of the name of a language, people, religion, city, county, country, province, body of water, mountain, desert, specific location, or division of government? (English; Rocky Mountains; Third Street; Parliament)

UNEDITED

1. Over 150 million cars are now on the roads in north america.

2. Derived from the greek words for house and management, our word *economy* meant simply household management.

3. In tokyo during january, may, and september, japanese wrestlers perform ritual fights in the kuramae kokugikan stadium.

EDITED

1. Over 150 million cars are now on the roads in North America.

2. Derived from the Greek words for house and management, our word *economy* meant simply household management.

3. In Tokyo during January, May, and September, Japanese wrestlers perform ritual fights in the Kuramae Kokugikan Stadium.

4. Edgar allan Poe's "Murders In The Rue Morgue" was made into an excellent movie.

5. Prime minister Begin spoke to the assembled Senators.

6. The united states independence day and the canadian confederation day both fall in early july.

7. In the nineteenth century, dr. Livingstone first conquered the nile.

4. Edgar Allan Poe's "Murders in the Rue Morgue" was made into an excellent movie.

5. Prime Minister Begin spoke to the assembled senators.

6. The United States Independence Day and the Canadian Confederation Day both fall in early July.

7. In the nineteenth century, Dr. Livingstone first conquered the Nile.

C. QUOTING

CHECKLIST
- Are all quoted words enclosed in double quotation marks?
- Is the quotation within a quotation enclosed in single quotation marks?
- Are titles of articles, book chapters, essays, lectures and speeches, poems, short stories, songs, and individual episodes of radio and television programs enclosed in double quotation marks?
- Are periods and commas placed *inside* the closing quotation mark?
- Are colons and semicolons placed *outside* the closing quotation mark?
- When an entire sentence, rather than the part in quotation marks, is a question or an exclamation, is the question mark or exclamation mark outside the closing quotation mark?
- When the quoted part of a sentence is a question or an exclamation, is the question mark or exclamation point inside the closing quotation mark?

UNEDITED

1. French novelist Gustave Flaubert once said: He who plants a vine becomes entangled in its branches.

2. Aristotle defined rhetoric as the faculty of discovering all the available means of persuasion.

3. The chairman of our Energy Conservation Commission recently remarked: "People ask themselves, "How little insulation

EDITED

1. French novelist Gustave Flaubert once said: "He who plants a vine becomes entangled in its branches."

2. Aristotle defined rhetoric as "the faculty of discovering all the available means of persuasion."

3. The chairman of our Energy Conservation Commission recently remarked: "People ask themselves, 'How little insulation

can I get away with"? when they should be asking "How much insulation should I install to get the most efficient use of energy"? Such attitudes must change."

can I get away with?' when they should be asking 'How much insulation should I install to get the most efficient use of energy?' Such attitudes must change."

4. My first boss used to greet us every morning by shouting "Au boulot!;" loosely translated, his greeting meant "To the grindstone"!

4. My first boss used to greet us every morning by shouting "Au boulot!"; loosely translated, his greeting meant "To the grindstone!"

D. ITALICIZING (UNDERLINING)

- ✔ Are words that are referred to as words italicized?
- ✔ Are foreign words italicized?
- ✔ Are titles of ballets, books, operas, paintings, pamphlets, periodicals and newspapers, plays, films, radio and television programs, sculptures, and names of ships, trains, or aircraft all italicized?
- ✔ Have you avoided the unwarranted use of italics for emphasis?

UNEDITED

1. Marni is characterized by exuberant joie de vivre and by the ability to empathize with others.

2. Tonight, the Metropolitan Opera Company will present Verdi's Otello.

3. *Wherever* he goes, the popular rock idol is *adored* by throngs of fans.

4. The word doubt comes from a Latin word which meant "to waver."

EDITED

1. Marni is characterized by exuberant *joie de vivre* and by the ability to empathize with others.

2. Tonight, the Metropolitan Opera Company will present Verdi's *Otello*.

3. Wherever he goes, the popular rock idol is adored by throngs of fans.

4. The word *doubt* comes from a Latin word which meant "to waver."

E. NUMBERING

- ✔ As a general rule, are the numbers one through ten spelled out?
- ✔ If a series contains numbers both under ten and over ten, are numerals used throughout for consistency?
- ✔ Are arabic numerals used to express dates, page numbers, addresses, identification numbers, and hours of the day when used with A.M. or P.M. (September 23, 1980; 3721 Princess Avenue; P.O. Box 86773; page 27; Channel 9; 1:00 P.M.)?

✔ If a number is the first word in a sentence, is the number spelled out? (Seventy-six trombones led the big parade.)

✔ In technical or statistical writing, are numerals used consistently to save space?

UNEDITED

1. Tokyo's 775-square-mile metropolitan area, with its <u>twelve</u> million people, contains <u>twenty-six</u> cities, <u>five</u> towns, <u>one</u> village, and the <u>seven</u> islands south of Tokyo Bay.

2. At precisely <u>ten</u> A.M. on <u>September seventh</u>, <u>nineteen twenty-eight</u>, the Chief of Scotland Yard presented himself at <u>ten</u> Downing Street.

3. Channel <u>Nine</u>, a Public Broadcasting Station, reports that <u>seventy-two-and-one-half</u> percent of its budget comes from contributions.

4. The greenhouse, which costs $2,500 to build, is placed on and attached to leveled <u>four-inch by four-inch</u> rough cedar foundation supported by concrete piers; the floor consists of 12″ × 12″ pavers placed on a <u>two-inch</u>-thick sand bed.

5. A bill passed last year lifts the minimum wage from $2.65 an hour to $2.90 this year, to $3.10 next year, and to $3.35 the following year; but some top officials feel that eliminating the increases might open up as many as <u>four hundred and fifty thousand</u> jobs.

EDITED

1. Tokyo's 775-square-mile metropolitan area, with its <u>12</u> million people, contains <u>26</u> cities, <u>5</u> towns, <u>1</u> village, and the <u>7</u> islands south of Tokyo Bay.

2. At precisely <u>10:00</u> A.M. on September <u>7</u>, <u>1928</u>, the Chief of Scotland Yard presented himself at <u>10</u> Downing Street.

3. Channel <u>9</u>, a Public Broadcasting Station, reports that <u>72½</u> percent of its budget comes from contributions.

4. The greenhouse, which costs $2,500 to build, is placed on and attached to leveled <u>4″ × 4″</u> rough cedar foundation supported by concrete piers; the floor consists of 12″ × 12″ pavers placed on a <u>2″</u>-inch-thick sand bed.

5. A bill passed last year lifts the minimum wage from $2.65 an hour to $2.90 this year, to $3.10 next year, and to $3.35 the following year; but some top officials feel that eliminating the increases might open up as many as <u>450,000</u> jobs.

F. ABBREVIATING

✔ As a general rule, are abbreviations avoided in formal prose?

✔ Are abbreviations used for the following titles and degrees: Mr.; Mrs.; Ms.; Jr.; Sr.; Dr.; M.D.; M.A.; Ph.D.; L.L.D.?

✔ Does the abbreviation B.C. *follow* the date and the abbreviation A.D. *precede* the date?

✔ If you have used the capitalized initials of a place, organization, or agency (CBS, FBI), will the meaning of those initials be known to your readers?

✔ In footnotes or bibliographical citations, are the following standard abbreviations used?

cf.	(compare)	i.e.	(that is)	rev.	(revised)
ed.	(edition or editor)	no(s).	(number[s])	trans.	(translated by)
eds.	(editions or editors)	p.	(page)	vol.	(volume)
e.g.	(for example)	pp.	(pages)	vols.	(volumes)

UNEDITED

1. Dr. Horowitz said he would have our psych. exam. graded by next Fri.

2. The chief spokesman for the PQ recently held a press conference.

3. The years between 55 B.C. and 200 A.D. saw the apogee of the Roman Empire.

4. The SCA is currently recruiting students with an interest in the medieval period to join in their first festival here.

EDITED

1. Dr. Horowitz said he would have our psychology examination graded by next Friday.

2. The chief spokesman for the Parti Québecois recently held a press conference.

3. The years between 55 B.C. and A.D. 200 saw the apogee of the Roman Empire.

4. The Society for Creative Anachronism is currently recruiting students with an interest in the medieval period to join in their first festival here.

G. HYPHENATING

CHECKLIST

✔ As a general rule, if you are at all uncertain about how to hyphenate a compound word, have you checked your dictionary?

✔ Have you hyphenated two words which are working as one unit? (yellow-green shirt; ninth-century England)

✔ Are two-word numbers hyphenated? (twenty-eight pages)

✔ Is a hyphen used to link numbers which indicate a range? (pp. 253–297)

✔ If fractions are written out, are they hyphenated? (one-half cup milk)

✔ Are hyphens used to link words you have compounded or coined for a special purpose? (My roommate shot me an I-told-you-so look.)

✔ Are words that begin with the prefixes *ex* or *self* hyphenated? (ex-student; self-appointed critic)

✔ Is a hyphen used to link prefixes to proper nouns or numbers? (pro-Egyptian; anti-British; pre-1900)

✔ If a word has two or more prefixes before it, is each prefix followed by a hyphen? (Our instructor has given us one-, two-, and three-hour examinations.)

✔ Are words that might be confused with other words hyphenated? (He needed time to re-create.)

✔ Is a word that must be divided at the end of a line hyphenated *between syllables?* When in doubt, check the dictionary.

UNEDITED	EDITED
1. By the time you leave, you will have acquired a taste, perhaps a passion, for the <u>delicacies</u> of smoked fish.	1. By the time you leave, you will have acquired a taste, perhaps a passion, for the <u>delicacies</u> of smoked fish.
2. <u>Old fashioned</u> glasses are making a comeback.	2. <u>Old-fashioned</u> glasses are making a comeback.
3. The detective slipped into a <u>bullet proof steel gray vest.</u>	3. The detective slipped into a <u>bullet-proof steel-gray</u> vest.
4. Luke's <u>brother in law</u> recently bought an expensive <u>self winding</u> watch and a <u>red and white</u> Audi.	4. Luke's <u>brother-in-law</u> recently bought an expensive <u>self-winding</u> watch and a <u>red-and-white</u> Audi.
5. What has brought on such a <u>down at the mouth</u> expression?	5. What has brought on such a <u>down-at-the-mouth</u> expression?
6. The <u>pre Columbian</u> pottery exhibit contained <u>800 to 900 year old</u> items.	6. The <u>pre-Columbian</u> pottery exhibit contained <u>800-</u> to <u>900-year-old</u> items.
7. This reading course offers a number of <u>pre</u> and <u>post tests.</u>	7. This reading course offers a number of <u>pre-</u> and <u>post-tests.</u>
8. Her boss asked that she <u>recount</u> her expenditures.	8. Her boss asked that she <u>re-count</u> her expenditures.

CUMULATIVE EDITING EXERCISES

The following passages contain errors in *mechanical conventions.* Edit each passage carefully, correcting every error you can find.

[A]   On december second, nineteen hundred and seventy one, a new country,

the union of Arab Emirates, was formed. Later named the United Arab Emirates

(U.A.E.), the small country lies on the persian gulf, in the strategic position between the East and the West. The events leading up to, and resulting from, its formation show the Emirates' importance in world affairs.

In the 18th-century, france, Britain, and holland were looking for trading centers. The area which is now the U.A.E. was ideal in view of their furtherance of trade with India. By the early nineteenth century, all but the british were gone, but powerful local arab "pirate boats" attacked all trade vessels in the Gulf. The East india company of Eng. retaliated in eighteen twenty and, in economist K. G. Fenelon's words: forced the seven sheikdoms in the 19th-century to end piracy and protect trade routes to India by under-taking defense of that area." The truce thus established led to the country's original name of the Trucial States. Local matters were still the individual rulers' concerns, but all Foreign and navigational policies were controlled by britain.

[B]   My grandfather was born may 12 nineteen twenty one, in a small city outside calgary Alberta. He lived on a very small farm. His parents didn't have much money and so my grandfather *never had any extras*. In fact, because his parents had to work so hard, my grandfather was largely neglected when he was a child. Maybe that's why he first began to care about other people more than himself.

Through-out the years, people would come to my grandfather with their problems. He would sit down and listen intently to what they had to say. Many times he listened like that to my troubles, gave me one of his I can help you looks, and then he almost always could help me find a way to solve my problems. He loved being useful and he loved making people happy and satisfied. More than Anyone Else, he taught me how to help and love other people.

[C] I believe twentieth century advertising, which some say is dishonest, is actually a good example of effective persuasion that can help consumers. Without advertising, for example, many products would cost us more $$s than they do now. When Safeway or some other big grocery chain has a sale, their advertising enables them to get the attention of many, many people. Because these firms can buy large quantities, they are able to sell the goods to us at reduced prices. In this way, advertising saves us 100's of dollars. Another way ads save us money is by forcing companies to try to *stay ahead of their competition.* As my Dad, who is a salesperson says, if I know what the competition is offering from studying their ads, I can almost always offer my customers some better deal. So advertising is beneficial to us because it saves us money and helps consumers make wise choices.

10

SENTENCE-COMBINING: IMITATING AND GENERATING SENTENCES

Whether you are writing for the academic world or for the private world, whether your aim is expressive or persuasive, whether your mode is narration or classification—as you write to explore and create your own particular meanings, you will be doing so with sentences. Because sentences are crucial in helping you to achieve meaning, we have included sentence exercises in this text. This portion of the text provides much practice in crafting effective sentences.

Learning to expand and combine sentences allows you to bring ideas together in new ways, creating a variety of relationships, conjunctions, and emphases. As your stock of sentence options grows, your writing will become more mature, more varied and interesting. But how can you best increase the number and variety of your sentence options? You can best do so not by memorizing rules or by studying grammar, but by imitating and practicing sentence patterns and by trying your hand at combining the sets of sentences provided in this chapter in as many effective ways as possible. Even more important than imitating sentence patterns and combining sets of sentences in various ways, however, is generating new sentences yourself and assimilating them into your own writing. Creating and internalizing new sentence options for use in your own writing is your goal.

The patterns that follow generally increase in complexity, but the basic features of each set remain constant. You are asked (1) to study a sentence pattern, (2) to combine sets of sentences in imitation of the pattern, (3) to combine the sets of sentences in several other possible ways, (4) to generate your own sentences and combine them, and (5) to decide which combination is most effective.

● I. SIMPLE EXPANSION COMBINATIONS

In Combination A, which follows below, the pattern sentence contains the following shorter sentences:

1. The stunt man approached the precipice.
2. The stunt man was lean.
3. He was muscular.
4. The precipice was narrow.
5. It was icy.

These short sentences, when combined, can yield "The lean, muscular stunt man approached the narrow, icy precipice." (Note that the words lean, muscular and narrow, icy are highlighted in Combination A to call your attention to their important positions in the sentence.) Can you think of different ways to combine these five sentences? Combine the sentences in as many ways as you and your classmates can think of. Then compare the results. Which combination seems best?

Combination A: The lean, muscular stunt man approached the narrow, icy precipice.

1. After studying Combination A, combine each of the following sets of sentences into a sentence that imitates that combination. Then combine them in any other ways you can.

1. Men marched through the city.
2. They were haggard.
3. They were hollow-cheeked.
4. The city was silent.
5. The city was hungry.

. . . .

1. Alice met the Queen.
2. Alice was little.
3. She was timid.
4. The Queen was furious.
5. The Queen was crimson-faced.
6. She was the Queen of Hearts.

. . . .

1. The clothing is designed.
2. The clothing is expensive.
3. The clothing is faddish.
4. The clothing is presented by magazines.
5. They are fashion magazines.
6. The designing is for the girl.
7. The girl is tall.
8. The girl is pencil-thin.

Note: You may want to compare your combination of the set of sentences above with the original sentence in a student essay on page 207.

. . . .

1. Businessmen admire.
2. There are many such businessmen.
3. They admire the way the Cowboys play.
4. They play football.
5. The way they play is cold.
6. It is precise.
7. It is reliable.
8. It is dependable.
9. It is predictable.
10. It is efficient.
11. It is businesslike.

. . . .

1. The student just passed the test.
2. The student was relaxed.
3. The student was carefree.

4. The test lasted three hours.
5. The test was in physics.

. . . .

1. The chimp demanded a candy bar.
2. The chimp was playful.
3. The chimp was aggressive.
4. The candy bar was chocolate nut.

. . . .

1. The coach whipped his team into shape.
2. The coach was tough.
3. He was an ex-professional.
4. He coached football.
5. The team was from a small college.

2. Now write a series of at least five short sentences and then combine them into one sentence that imitates Combination A. Then combine them in at least two other ways and choose the one that is most effective.

1. The line grinds out cars.
2. It is the General Motors line.
3. It is an assembly line.
4. The grinding out is swift.
5. The grinding out is smooth.
6. The grinding out is effortless.

Combination B: The General Motors assembly line grinds out cars swiftly, smoothly, and effortlessly.

Another possible combination:
Swiftly, smoothly, and effortlessly, the General Motors assembly line grinds out cars.

Add any other combinations you can think of.

A Note on Punctuation: The words *swiftly, smoothly,* and *effortlessly* are separated by commas. See pages 425–426 for further examples of the use of commas to separate words or items in a series.

1. After studying Combination B, combine each of the following sets of sentences into a sentence that imitates that combination. Then combine them in other ways that are equally effective.

1. The mass of ice marched.
2. The ice was moving.
3. The marching was down a valley.
4. The marching was slow.
5. The marching was quiet.
6. The marching was inexorable.

. . . .

1. We tend to use technologies.
2. The technologies are new.
3. Our use is profuse.
4. Our use is unwise.
5. Our use is even harmful.

. . . .

1. H. L. Mencken criticized foibles.
2. The foibles belonged to society.
3. The society was American.
4. The criticism was witty.
5. It was sarcastic.
6. It was unmerciful.
7. The unmercifulness occurred often.

. . . .

1. The lecturer droned.
2. The lecturer was nondescript.
3. The lecturer was bespectacled.
4. The droning went on and on.
5. The droning was mechanical.
6. The droning was monotonous.
7. The droning was interminable.

. . . .

1. The cat eyed its prey.
2. The cat was scruffy.
3. The cat was yellow.
4. The prey was imaginary.
5. The cat eyed it craftily.
6. It eyed it tauntingly.
7. It even eyed it murderously.

. . . .

1. Oil massages you.
2. The oil is bath oil.
3. It is Beauty's oil.
4. The massaging is gentle.
5. The massaging is soothing.
6. The massaging is almost loving.

. . . .

1. She studied diligently.
2. She studied so that she could answer the questions.
3. They were the examiner's questions.

4. Her answering was very quick.

5. Her answering was very accurate.

Combination B1: She studied <u>diligently</u> so that she could answer the examiner's questions very <u>quickly</u> and very <u>accurately</u>.

Add any other combinations you can think of.

1. After studying Combination B1, combine each of the following sets of sentences into a sentence that imitates that combination. Then combine them in several other ways that are equally effective.

1. The aircraft landed.
2. The aircraft was malfunctioning.
3. The landing was immediate.
4. The landing was so that it could unload the passengers.
5. The passengers were worried.
6. The unloading was quick.
7. The unloading was safe.

. . . .

1. The packhorses were loaded.
2. They were gold rush packhorses.
3. The loading was very careful.
4. The loading was so that the packhorses could negotiate the trails.
5. The trails were steep.
6. The trails were treacherous.
7. The negotiating was confident.
8. The negotiating was sure-footed.

. . . .

1. The boys argued.
2. The arguing was loud.
3. The arguing was so that they could avoid the call.
4. The call came from their mother.
5. Their avoiding was very efficient.
6. Their avoiding was very effective.

. . . .

1. Geoff played the game.
2. His playing was cautious.
3. He played so that he might meet the challenge.
4. The challenge was his opponent's.
5. His meeting of the challenge would be convincing.
6. It would be overwhelming.

2. Now write a series of sentences and then combine them into one sentence that imitates Combination B1. Then combine them in at least two other ways. Choose the one you find most effective.

II. CLAUSAL EXPANSION COMBINATIONS

1. Alfred the Great reigned.
2. He was the king of the West Saxons.
3. He was their most famous king.
4. His reign was in the ninth century.
5. It was the second half of that century.

Combination A: Alfred the Great, who was the most famous king of the West Saxons, reigned in the second half of the ninth century.

Add any other combinations you can think of.

A Note on Punctuation: The words "who was the most famous king of the West Saxons" form a clause which provides *extra information* for the sentence, information that is not essential to its meaning. Such clauses are set off by commas. See pages 425–426 for additional examples of clauses punctuated in this way, and note the difference in meaning which would occur if the commas were removed.

1. After studying Combination A, combine each of the following sets of sentences into a sentence that imitates that combination. Then combine them in other ways that are equally effective.

1. Joe Morgan was named to the All-Star team.
2. He played second base for the Reds.
3. He was often named to the All-Star team.

. . . .

1. The !Kung survive.
2. They live in the desert.
3. The desert is the Kalahari.
4. The Kalahari is harsh.
5. It is unyielding.
6. They survive by joining groups.
7. The groups are for protection.
8. The groups are also for shelter.

. . . .

1. Nicholas Reynolds has discovered the remains.
2. He is an archaeologist working in Scotland.
3. The remains are of the structure.
4. The structure is the oldest one yet found in the British Isles.

. . . .

1. Roger Shuy has written articles.
2. There are many such articles.
3. Shuy is professor of linguistics.
4. The articles are on differences.
5. The differences are in dialects.
6. These dialects are regional.

. . . .

1. The Inuit can teach us.
2. The Inuit are the native people of Alaska.
3. They can teach us the following.
4. We can adapt to climates.
5. The climates are harsh.

2. Now write a series of sentences and combine them into one sentence that imitates Combination A. Then combine your sentences in at least two other ways. Choose the one that is most effective.

1. The screens give the most complete visual account.
2. The screens are large, folding ones.
3. The screens once decorated the houses.
4. The houses were in Kyoto and Edo.
5. The visual account is of everyday life.
6. It is life in old Japan.
7. The account has come down to us.

Combination A1: The large folding screens, <u>which once decorated the houses in Kyoto and Edo</u>, give the most complete visual account of everyday life in old Japan that has come down to us.

Add any other combinations you can think of.

A Note on Punctuation: Like the previous combination, this one contains a clause ("which once decorated the houses in Kyoto and Edo") which adds *extra information* to the sentence and hence is set off by commas. What difference in meaning would occur if the commas were omitted?

1. After studying Combination A1, combine each of the following sets of sentences into a sentence that imitates that combination. Then combine them in other ways that are equally effective.

1. Horse Creek flows.
2. Horse Creek is a stream.
3. The stream is small.
4. It is unnavigable.
5. It is 25 miles long.
6. It is in the Oregon Cascades.
7. It flows through mountains.
8. The mountains are timbered.

9. The timber is dense.
10. The mountains are protected.
11. The protection is from loggers.

. . . .

1. The beer provided a reward.
2. The beer was frosty.
3. The beer had been lovingly protected.
4. The protection was from the sun.
5. The sun was hot.
6. The reward was instant.
7. The reward was for the members of a group.
8. The group was a hiking group.
9. The group had finally arrived.
10. The arrival was at the campsite.

. . . .

1. The house had a stairway.
2. It was a traditional house.
3. The house was simple.
4. The house was infinitely appealing.
5. The stairway was open.
6. The stairway was a symbol.
7. The symbol was one of welcome.

. . . .

1. The language resists the controls.
2. The language is English.
3. The language is growing.
4. The language is also changing.
5. The growing and changing happen constantly.
6. The controls are those of the standardizers.
7. The standardizers are among us.
8. They try to regulate the language.

. . . .

1. *Return of the Jedi* replaces the complexity.
2. *Return of the Jedi* is a movie.
3. It uses simple names.
4. It uses simple plots.
5. The complexity is of everyday life.
6. The complexity is replaced with polarization.
7. The polarization is sharp.
8. The polarization differentiates good from bad.
9. It does this rigidly.

2. Now write a series of sentences and then combine them into one sentence that imitates Combination A1. Then combine them in several other ways that are equally effective.

1. The man made us an offer.
2. We feared the man.
3. The offer was one that we couldn't refuse.

Combination A2: The man <u>whom we feared</u> made us an offer that we couldn't refuse.

Add any other combinations you can think of.

A Note on Punctuation: In Combination A2, "whom we feared" forms a clause which adds *essential* rather than extra information to the sentence. Such clauses are not set off by commas, in contrast to clauses which provide extra information—like the ones you have experimented with in Combinations A and A1. Again note the difference in meaning which would occur if "whom we feared" were set off by commas. And see pages 425–426 for examples of additional sentences punctuated in this way.

1. After studying Combination A2, combine each of the following sets of sentences into a sentence that imitates that combination. Then combine them in other ways that are equally effective.

1. The chef created a menu.
2. We hoped to emulate the chef.
3. The menu was innovative.
4. The innovation was from beginning to end.

. . . .

1. The crowds heard a speaker.
2. They were fortunate crowds.
3. Martin Luther King addressed the crowds.
4. The speaker was one that they won't forget.

. . . .

1. The umpire gave them a warning.
2. The players taunted the umpire.
3. The warning was stern.
4. The warning silenced them.
5. It did this immediately.

. . . .

1. The executive gave him a look.
2. He admired the executive.
3. The look was sharp.
4. The look was full of contempt.

. . . .

1. The child splashed us.
2. We teased the child.
3. The splashing was with water.
4. The water was in his bucket.

2. Now write a series of sentences and then combine them into one sentence that imitates Combination A2. Then combine them in as many other effective ways as you can.

1. Officials beheaded Mary.
2. Mary was Queen of Scots.
3. This happened after Queen Elizabeth's spy did the following.
4. The spy intercepted and decoded letters.
5. It was Queen Elizabeth's chief spy who did this.
6. The letters were Mary's.

Combination B: Officials beheaded Mary Queen of Scots after Queen Elizabeth's chief spy intercepted and decoded Mary's letters.

Add any other combinations you can think of.

1. After studying Combination B, combine each of the following sets of sentences into a sentence which imitates that combination. Then combine them in several other effective ways.

1. The students ordered pizza.
2. The students were weary.
3. There were three pizzas.
4. The pizzas were extra-large.
5. The pizzas were deluxe.
6. This happened after the students had completed their assignment.
7. The assignment was their last one.
8. It was a lab assignment.

. . . .

1. Stephanie savored her cup of coffee.
2. It was her second cup.
3. She also read the paper.
4. It was the student newspaper.
5. She then went to class.

. . . .

1. Mark returned to the town.
2. The town was rural.
3. It was the town where his ancestors had lived.
4. His ancestors had worked there.
5. They had done so for centuries.

. . . .

1. Rhonda and I attended school.
2. It was a high school.
3. It was an all-girls school.
4. At this school we met guys.
5. We met them at dances.
6. The dances were held only on weekends.

. . . .

1. The audience stomped.
2. The audience clapped.
3. The audience whistled.
4. They did this until the players reappeared.
5. They were bluegrass players.
6. Their reappearance was for an encore.

. . . .

1. Jonathan Swift usually published his works.
2. Swift was an eighteenth-century satirist.
3. The publishing was anonymous.
4. He did this although his authorship was known to many.

2. Now write a series of sentences and then combine them into one sentence that imitates Combination B. Then combine them in several other ways. Choose the one that is most effective.

1. His friend sunbathed on a rock.
2. The rock was flat.
3. The puppy slept.
4. It slept beneath the alders.
5. Gene baited a wriggler.
6. It was a red wriggler.
7. He baited it on a number 8 hook.
8. He waded into the water.
9. The water was icy.

Combination B1: <u>While his friend sunbathed on a flat rock and the puppy slept beneath the alders</u>, Gene baited a red wriggler on a number 8 hook and waded into the icy water.

Add any other combinations you can think of.

A Note on Punctuation: The words "While his friend sunbathed on a flat rock and the puppy slept beneath the alders" form an introductory dependent clause (see the Glossary). Such clauses are followed by a comma. See page 425 for another example of an introductory clause punctuated in this way. Also note that we have added the word *while* in order to form an introductory dependent clause.

1. After studying Combination B1, combine each of the following sets of sentences into a sentence that imitates that combination. Then combine them in other effective ways.

1. Cities have a surplus of physicians.
2. Rural areas need physicians.
3. Their need is desperate.
4. We should follow the lead.
5. The lead is that of other countries.
6. We should send every medical school graduate.
7. We should send them to rural areas.
8. The sending would be for two years.

. . . .

1. Energy boils.
2. The mood intensifies.
3. It is the mood of the dancers.
4. The dancers sweat.
5. Their sweating is profuse.
6. Their muscles quiver.
7. The muscles are tired.
8. The quivering is from exhaustion.

. . . .

1. The sky was blue.
2. The blue was brilliant.
3. The sun warmed the grass.
4. The grass was beneath her feet.
5. The freshman picked up her chemistry books.
6. She headed for the library.
7. The library was uninviting.

. . . .

1. I was eating.
2. I became aware of the following.
3. The hamburger was turning to dust.
4. It was a McDonald's hamburger.
5. The turning to dust was in my mouth.

Note: You may wish to compare your combination of the set of sentences above with the original sentence in a student essay on page 106.

. . . .

2. Now write a series of sentences and then combine them into one sentence that imitates Combination B1. Then combine them in other possible ways. Choose the one that is most effective.

1. The atmosphere grows steadily.
2. It is an atmosphere of desperate failure.
3. The growing makes the men and women old.
4. The men are worn out.

5. The women are nervous and overworked.
6. It makes them old before their time.

Combination C: <u>That the atmosphere of desperate failure grows steadily</u> makes the worn-out men and nervous, overworked women old before their time.

Add any other combinations you can think of.

Note: We added a word *(that)* in combining all of these sentences. The result is a sentence which opens with a noun clause: "That the atmosphere of desperate failure grows steadily." See the Glossary for other examples of noun clauses.

1. After studying Combination C, combine each of the following sets of sentences into a sentence that imitates that combination. Then combine them in other effective ways.

1. Our stereo stays on.
2. It does so all night.
3. It does so all day.
4. This may cause friction.
5. The friction will be with our neighbors.
6. They are new neighbors.

. . . .

1. The pilot landed.
2. The piloting was of an aircraft.
3. The aircraft was crippled.
4. The landing was safe.
5. This left the passengers full.
6. They were full of gratitude.

. . . .

1. The discoverer would speak.
2. The discoverer was well known.
3. He discovered the structure of DNA.
4. He would speak soon.
5. This filled the audience with expectation.
6. The audience was impatient.

. . . .

1. Computer equipment is fairly standardized.
2. Computer programs are also fairly standardized.
3. Computer codes are also fairly standardized.
4. This standardization makes crimes easier to commit.
5. This standardization makes crimes easier to cover up.

. . . .

Note: You may wish to compare your combination of the previous set of sentences with the original sentence in a student essay on page 313.

1. The team would lose.
2. This would happen eventually.
3. This left the players despondent.
4. It also left the coaches despondent.
5. Their despondency was about their record.
6. The record was of the season.

. . . .

1. The vegetables of Anjou are probably the best in France.
2. The fruit of Anjou is also probably the best in France.
3. This made our mouths water.
4. The watering was in anticipation.
5. The anticipation was of our meal.
6. The meal would be our first in France.

2. Now write a series of sentences and then combine them into one sentence that imitates Combination C. Then combine them in several other ways. Choose the one that is most effective.

1. The following happens at bedtime.
2. We crawl into our sleeping bags.
3. We hope the following.
4. The hike will be an easy one.
5. It is tomorrow's hike.

Combination C1: At bedtime, we crawl into our sleeping bags and hope that tomorrow's hike will be an easy one.

Add any other combinations you can think of.

1. After studying Combination C1, combine each of the following sets of sentences into a sentence that imitates that combination. Then combine them in several other effective ways.

1. The following has happened for centuries.
2. People throughout the world have looked.
3. Their looking was at the heavens.
4. The people believed the following.
5. The stars controlled their lives.

. . . .

1. The following will happen in the future.
2. We may leave home.
3. We may leave at 9:00 A.M.
4. We may know the following.
5. Our computer will do the wash.
6. It is a household computer.

7. It will also clean the house.
8. It will also cook dinner.

. . . .

1. The following happened in junior high.
2. Films and film strips stated the following.
3. Drinking causes brain damage.
4. Drinking causes cirrhosis.
5. Drinking causes eventual alcoholism.
6. The films and film strips were on the evils of drinking.

. . . .

1. The following happened in ancient Greece.
2. Citizens appeared.
3. The citizens were ordinary.
4. The appearance was in courts.
5. The courts were law courts.
6. The citizens appeared on their own behalf.
7. They argued the following.
8. They wanted the lands to be returned to them.
9. The lands were confiscated ones.

. . . .

1. The following happened during lectures.
2. The lectures are three hours long.
3. We sit in seats.
4. The seats are ours.
5. We imagine the following.
6. The bell will never ring.

2. Now compose a series of sentences and then combine them into one sentence that imitates Combination C1. Then combine them in several additional ways. Choose the one that is most effective.

1. One of the functions of the wilderness is to teach us the following.
2. Constant activity is not the only way of life.

Combination C2: One of the functions of the wilderness is to teach us that constant activity is not the only way of life.

Add any other combinations 'you can think of.

1. After studying Combination C2, combine each of the following sets of sentences into one sentence that imitates that combination. Then combine them in several other effective ways.

1. Thousands failed.
2. The thousands were movie lovers throughout the city.
3. Their failure was to believe the following.

4. The board would be successful.
5. It was a new censorship board.
6. Their successfulness would be in the ban.
7. The ban was of an old favorite.

. . . .

1. A majority decided.
2. The majority was of workers.
3. The workers were beer workers.
4. They were on strike.
5. Their decision was to agree to the following.
6. They would accept the offer of management.
7. The offer was for a raise.
8. The raise was for five percent.

. . . .

1. The following happens at the end of the day.
2. Their bodies ached.
3. Their aching was to discover the following.
4. A still pool waited.
5. The pool was beyond the next rapids.

. . . .

1. The visitors need.
2. They are visitors at the city zoo.
3. Their need is to remember the following.
4. They should not give food.
5. The food is junk.
6. Their giving is to the animals.

2. Now complete the following sentences. Check to see whether they imitate Combination C2:

    a. After a tough exam, we all hope . . .
    b. Professors should always realize that . . .

3. Now compose a series of sentences. Combine them into one sentence that imitates Combination C2. Then combine them in several other ways. Choose the one that is most effective.

III. PHRASAL EXPANSION COMBINATIONS

1. The following has happened along the creek.
2. The following has also happened in logged areas.

3. Trees leaf out.
4. They are deciduous trees.
5. The leafing out is in late spring.
6. The leafing out is to create the shade of summer.
7. The shade is green.
8. The leafing out is also to create the brilliance of autumn.
9. The brilliance is fiery.
10. The leafing out is also to create the desolation of winter.

Combination A: Along the creek and in logged areas, deciduous trees leaf out in late spring to create the green shade of summer, the fiery brilliance of autumn, the desolation of winter.

Add any other combinations you can think of.

1. After studying Combination A and noting the way in which prepositional phrases are used in it (see the Glossary), combine each of the following sets of sentences into one sentence that imitates that combination. Then combine them in several other effective ways.

1. The following has happened throughout the country.
2. It has happened in spite of opposition.
3. The opposition has been vocal.
4. Recycling centers have sprung up.
5. They have sprung up in the last decade.
6. The springing up has been to combat habits.
7. The habits are wasteful.
8. The habits are those of individuals.
9. The springing up has also been to combat ways.
10. The ways are spendthrift.
11. The ways are of big business.
12. The springing up has also been to combat spending.
13. The spending is extravagant.
14. The spending is by government.

. . . .

1. The following has happened from 1950 onward.
2. It has happened in every nation.
3. The nations are industrialized.
4. Televison has tended to become a baby-sitter.
5. The baby-sitter is for children.
6. The children are mesmerized.
7. The tendency is also to become a means of escape.
8. The escape is for adults.
9. The adults are bored.
10. The tendency has also been to become a friend.
11. The friend is electronic.
12. The friend is one to people.

13. The people are lonely.
14. The people are old.

. . . .

1. The following happens in his albums.
2. It happens in his performances.
3. The performances are public ones.
4. Ry Cooder's sound has continued to reveal his respect.
5. Cooder is a guitarist.
6. The sound is jazz-folk.
7. The respect is for the musical past.
8. The continuing has also been to reveal his joy.
9. The joy is infectious.
10. The joy is in the present.
11. The continuing has also been to reveal his hope.
12. The hope is abiding.
13. The hope is for the future of music.
14. The music is North American.

. . . .

1. The following happens during the summer.
2. It also happens in the early fall.
3. Advertisements leap out.
4. The advertisements are for new cars.
6. The leaping out is from pages of magazines.
7. The leaping out is to announce features.
8. The features are the newest ones in design.
9. The leaping out is also to announce advances.
10. The advances are the latest.
11. They are engineering advances.
12. The leaping out is also to announce rises in costs.
13. The rises are inevitable.

. . . .

1. The following happens on every campus.
2. The following also happens in surrounding areas.
3. Students arrive.
4. They are university students.
5. They arrive in early fall.
6. They experience reunions.
7. The reunions are with their old friends.
8. The arrival is also to experience long lines.
9. The long lines are of registration.
10. Their arrival is also to experience challenge.
11. The challenge is of new classes.

. . . .

1. The following happens throughout the delta.
2. The following also happens in irrigated places.
3. Sweet corn and beans burgeon.
4. The burgeoning is in the hot summer sun.
5. The burgeoning is to yield work for farmers.
6. The work is backbreaking.
7. The burgeoning is also to yield a movable feast.
8. The feast is for insects.
9. The burgeoning is also to yield meals.
10. The meals are flavorful.
11. The meals are for consumers.
12. The consumers are fortunate.

2. Now write a series of sentences and then combine them into one sentence that imitates Combination A. Then combine them in several other ways. Choose the one that is most effective.

1. The jets broke the barrier.
2. The jets were low-flying.
3. It was the sound barrier they broke.
4. The jets shattered windows.
5. The jets created panic.

Combination B: The low-flying jets broke the sound barrier, shattering windows and creating panic.

Add any other combinations you can think of.

A Note on Punctuation: We have chosen to combine these sentences by turning the last two ("The jets shattered windows" and "The jets created panic") into *participial phrases* that end the sentence. Such phrases are preceded by a comma, as in the example of Combination B. See the Glossary for a definition of the participial phrase and for other examples of phrases punctuated in this way.

1. After studying Combination B, combine each of the following sets of sentences into a sentence that imitates that combination. Then combine them in other effective ways.

1. REM (rapid eye movement) sleep occurs.
2. It occurs roughly every 90 minutes.
3. REM sleep relaxes muscles.
4. REM sleep triggers dreams.

. . . .

1. The Norse traveled far.
2. The Norse were ninth- and tenth-century people.
3. The Norse ravaged Italy.
4. They ravaged Greece.

5. They colonized Greenland.
6. They colonized Iceland.
7. They discovered America.

. . . .

1. The Norse invaded England.
2. They were adventuring.
3. The Norse injected words into the language.
4. The words were Norse.
5. The language was English
6. The Norse influenced the sound structure.
7. The structure was of English.

. . . .

1. Her final service ace won.
2. The winning was of the tennis match.
3. The ace defeated her opponent.
4. The opponent was exhausted.
5. The ace thrilled the fans.

. . . .

1. The monster attacked.
2. The monster was frighteningly real.
3. The attack was on the city.
4. The monster pulverized buildings.
5. The monster snapped railway cars in two.
6. The monster did this easily.

2. Now write a series of sentences and then combine them into one sentence that imitates Combination B. Then combine them in several other ways. Choose the one that is most effective.

1. The following is held every four years.
2. The following is held in Moscow.
3. The International Tchaikovsky Competition is among the world's tests.
4. These are the world's most demanding and prestigious tests.
5. They are tests of talent.
6. The talent is musical.

Combination B1: Held every four years in Moscow, the International Tchaikovsky Competition is among the world's most demanding and prestigious tests of musical talents.

Add any other combinations you can think of.

A Note on Punctuation: Whereas we used a participial phrase in Combination B to close the sentence, in Combination B1 we have used a participial phrase ("Held every four years in Moscow") to open the sentence. Introductory participial phrases are followed by a comma, as in the example in Combination B1. See pages 425–426 for additional examples of sentences punctuated in this way.

1. After studying Combination B1, combine each of the following sets of sentences into a sentence that imitates that combination. Then combine them in other effective ways.

1. The following is characterized by Picasso's use of nightmare sequences.
2. *Guernica* remains a depiction.
3. The depiction is timely.
4. The depiction is vivid.
5. The depiction is of war.

. . . .

1. The following is covered with strawberries and whipped cream.
2. A sundae provides relief.
3. The relief is refreshing.
4. The relief is from the day.
5. The day is hot.
6. The day is humid.

. . . .

1. The following was partially destroyed by years of neglect.
2. The house presented challenges.
3. The house was centuries old.
4. The challenges were frustrating.
5. The house also presented headaches.
6. The challenges and headaches belonged to the new owners.

. . . .

1. The following was torn by division.
2. The division was ideological.
3. The women's liberation movement proliferated.
4. The proliferating was into groups.
5. There were dozens of these groups.
6. They were splinter groups.
7. They were competing groups.

. . . .

1. The pinch hitter was grazed.
2. The grazing was by a ball.
3. The ball was wild.
4. It was fast.
5. The pinch hitter flung a curse.
6. The curse was sizzling.
7. The flinging was toward the mound.

2. Now write a series of sentences and then combine them into a sentence that imitates Combination B1. Then combine them in several other ways. Choose the one that is most effective.

1. The alligator attacked.
2. The attacking was of his prey.
3. The alligator stunned the prey.
4. The alligator carried the prey into the water.

Combination B2: The alligator attacked his prey, stunning it, and carried it into the water.

Add any other combinations you can think of.

A Note on Punctuation: We have chosen to combine these sentences by turning the third one ("The alligator stunned the prey") into a participial phrase. When such a phrase occurs in midsentence, as it does in Combination B2, it is set off by commas. See the Glossary for another example of a participial phrase punctuated in this way.

1. After studying Combination B2, combine each of the following sets of sentences into a sentence that imitates that combination. Then combine them in other effective ways.

1. Jan picked up her notes.
2. The notes were psychology ones.
3. She clutched the notes.
4. She carried them out of the room.

. . . .

1. The white water caught the canoe.
2. The water swamped it.
3. The water pulled the canoe.
4. The pulling was into the rapids.
5. The rapids were ahead.

. . . .

1. The train lumbered.
2. The lumbering was into the station.
3. The train filled the station with smoke and noise.
4. The train disgorged the passengers.
5. They were disgorged onto the platform.
6. The platform was icy.

· ·

1. The fans mobbed the superstar.
2. The fans were frantic.
3. The fans terrified the superstar.
4. They tried to grab pieces.
5. The pieces were of the superstar's clothes.

· ·

1. The man uncrossed his legs.
2. The man was stricken.
3. The man pulled his legs under him.
4. He lunged out of his seat.
5. He lunged into the aisle.

2. Now write a series of sentences and then combine them into one sentence that imitates Combination B2. Then combine them in several other ways. Choose the one that is most effective.

1. They move delicately through the patterns.
2. The patterns are changing.
3. The patterns are of their strands of silk.
4. The strands are long.
5. The strands are scarlet.
6. The dancers glide.
7. The gliding is across the stage.
8. The dancers are costumed as flowers.
9. They are lotus flowers.

Combination B3: Moving delicately through the changing patterns of their long scarlet strands of silk, the dancers glide across the stage, costumed as lotus flowers.

Add any other combinations you can think of.

A Note on Punctuation: We have chosen to combine the sentences above by taking "the dancers glide across the stage" as the main clause of our sentence and modifying it with an opening participial phrase ("Moving delicately through the changing patterns of their long scarlet strands of silk") and a closing participial phrase ("costumed as lotus flowers"). As we noted earlier, introductory participial phrases are followed by a comma, while those which close a sentence are preceded by a comma. See page 425 for other examples of phrases punctuated in this way.

1. After studying Combination B3, combine each of the following sets of sentences into a sentence that imitates that combination. Then combine them in other effective ways.

1. He combed his memory.
2. He did so for syllogisms.
3. The syllogisms were half-remembered.
4. The student settles into his desk.
5. The student is prepared for the exam.
6. The exam is a midterm.
7. It is in logic.

. . . .

1. They are spurred by the craze for fitness.
2. They are fired up as a result of the feminist movement.
3. They are buttressed by court rulings.
4. They are also buttressed by legislative mandates.
5. Women have been moving from cheerleading.
6. The cheerleading is miniskirted.
7. Their moving has been to playing hard.
8. The play is for themselves.
9. They are convinced of their final victory.

. . . .

1. He slipped into the phone booth.
2. The slipping was quiet.
3. The booth was nearby.
4. Clark Kent trades his business suit.
5. It is traded for the cape.
6. The cape is familiar.
7. The cape is red and blue.
8. Clark Kent is prepared.
9. His preparation is for his ongoing battle with evil.

. . . .

1. One searches.
2. This was through layers.
3. The layers were of artifacts.
4. The artifacts were ancient.
5. The archaeologist studies every fragment.
6. The archaeologist is convinced of the significance of the site.

. . . .

1. It lounged in the waters.
2. The waters were deep.
3. The waters were green.

4. The salmon ignored the baited hook.
5. The salmon is sated.
6. The sating is from her meal.
7. The meal was of small fry.

2. Now write a series of sentences and then combine them into one sentence that imitates Combination B3. Then combine them in several other ways. Choose the one that is most effective.

1. One goes on diets.
2. They are fad diets.
3. Doing so lures many.
4. The many want a solution.
5. They want an easy solution.
6. It is a solution to weight problems.

Combination C: Going on fad diets lures many who want an easy solution to weight problems.

Add any other combinations you can think of.

A Note on Punctuation: We have chosen to combine the sentences above by turning the first two ("One goes on diets" and "They are fad diets") into a gerund phrase ("Going on fad diets") which opens the sentence. Such a phrase is *not* followed by a comma. In addition, we turned sentences 4, 5, and 6 into a clause which provides information essential to the sentence. As we noted on pages 425–426, such a clause is *not* set off by commas. See the Glossary for examples of other clauses of this type.

1. After studying Combination C, combine each of the following sets of sentences into a sentence that imitates that combination. Then combine them in other effective ways.

1. One converts to the system.
2. The system is metric.
3. This causes difficulty.
4. The difficulty is for government.
5. The difficulty is for businesses.
6. The difficulty is for citizens.
7. They don't want to give up their ways.
8. Their ways are old.

. . . .

1. One makes paper.
2. One does so by hand.
3. This has become an art.
4. The art has been lost.
5. The losing has been in this century.

. . . .

1. One remembers points.
2. The points are major.
3. The points are from lectures.
4. This presents a task.
5. The task is formidable.
6. The task is necessary.
7. The task is for students.
8. The students want to perform well.
9. Their performing is in this course.

. . . .

1. One invests in stocks.
2. Doing so can lead to pleasure.
3. It can lead to profit.
4. We all dream of this profit.

. . . .

1. One watches TV.
2. Doing so can take up time.
3. It can do so often.
4. The time is valuable.
5. The time cannot be recaptured.

2. Now write a series of sentences and then combine them into one sentence that imitates Combination C. Then combine them in several other ways. Choose the one that is most effective.

1. The beginning must surely have coincided.
2. The beginning was of consciousness.
3. The consciousness was reflexive.
4. The consciousness was in the brain.
5. It was the brain of our remotest ancestor.
6. The coinciding was with the dawning.
7. The dawning was of the sense of time.

Combination C1: The beginning of reflexive consciousness in the brain of our remotest ancestor must surely have coincided with the dawning of the sense of time.

Add any other combinations you can think of.

1. After studying Combination C1, combine each of the following sets of sentences into one sentence that imitates that combination. Then combine them in other effective ways.

1. The reading is of printed works.
2. This reading is by men and women.
3. The men and women are ordinary.
4. Their reading can be traced in general.

5. The tracing is to the inventing.
6. The inventing is of the printing press,

· ·

1. The advertising is for cereals.
2. The cereals are sugar-filled.
3. The advertising is also for junk foods.
4. The advertising is on TV shows.
5. The shows are for children.
6. This advertising should be banned.
7. The banning should happen at the beginning of the coming season.

· ·

1. Embarking lures.
2. The embarking is on a round.
3. The round is of adventures.
4. The adventures are gastronomic ones.
5. The luring is of many North Americans.
6. The luring is to the island.
7. The island is Maui.

· ·

1. Creating was one of the plans.
2. The creating was of the Bois de Boulogne.
3. The Bois de Boulogne is in the wooded land.
4. The land is west of Paris.
5. The plans were Napoleon III's.
6. The plans were great.

· ·

1. Our understanding is of the following.
2. It is of the parts.
3. It is also of the functions.
4. The parts and functions are of our bodies.
5. This will result in the following.
6. We will take care of ourselves.
7. The care will be better.

2. Now write a series of sentences and then combine them into one sentence that imitates Combination C1. Then combine them in several other ways. Choose the one that is most effective.

1. People might try joining clubs.
2. The people are shy.
3. They might also try participating.

4. The participating is in activities.
5. These are small group activities.

Combination C2: Shy people might try <u>joining clubs and participating in small group activities</u>.

Add any other combinations you can think of.

1. After studying Combination C2, combine each of the following sets of sentences into a sentence that imitates that combination. Then combine them in several other effective ways.

1. Dissatisfied nonvoters should stop.
2. They should stop complaining.
3. They should also stop shouting.
4. The shouting is at leaders.
5. The leaders are elected.
6. The leaders are political.

. . . .

1. We enjoy walking.
2. The walking is brisk.
3. We also enjoy exercising.
4. We do these things at every opportunity.

. . . .

1. The surfers began practicing.
2. They were novices.
3. They also began training.
4. They did so with balance exercises.

. . . .

1. The cryptographers continued decoding.
2. The decoding went into the night.
3. It went far into the night.
4. They also continued searching.
5. The searching was for the message.

. . . .

1. The Green Knight kept doing the following.
2. He laughed.
3. He also challenged everyone in the hall.
4. The hall was King Arthur's.

2. Now write a series of at least four sentences and then combine them into a sentence that imitates Combination B2. Then combine them in several other ways and choose the one you find most effective.

1. The following happens in backgammon.
2. The player throws the dice.

3. The player then studies her position.
4. The player plans her strategy.
5. The player anticipates the probabilities of her next throw.
6. The player makes her move.

Combination C3: In backgammon, the player throws the dice and, after studying her position, planning her strategy, and anticipating the probabilities of her next throw, she makes her move.

Add any other combinations you can think of.

A Note on Punctuation: The introductory prepositional phrase ("In backgammon") is followed by a comma. In addition, the three parallel phrases which follow the word *after* ("studying her position, planning her strategy, and anticipating the probabilities of her next throw") are, like other items in a series, separated by commas (see p. 425.)

1. After studying Combination C3, combine each of the following sets of sentences into a sentence that imitates that combination. Then combine them in several other effective ways.

1. The following happens at Sun Valley.
2. The skier takes the lift.
3. The skier is a novice.
4. The skier then checks his skis.
5. The skier crosses his fingers.
6. The skier holds his breath.
7. The skier heads down the mountain.
8. It is a "baby" mountain.
9. The mountain is for beginners.

. . . .

1. The following happened when I was a guest in China.
2. I was taken to a restaurant.
3. The restaurant was spacious.
4. I then met relatives and close friends.
5. I toasted each person in turn.
6. I ate four courses.
7. The courses were of hors d'oeuvres.
8. I began the serious eating.

. . . .

1. The following happens during spring break.
2. The group heads.
3. Their heading is for the beach.
4. They then swim all morning.
5. They sunbathe all afternoon.
6. They dance at parties.

7. The parties last all night.
8. They exhaust themselves.

. . . .

1. The following happens at Disneyland.
2. A vacationer enters the gates.
3. She then buys her tickets.
4. She stands in lines.
5. She jostles.
6. The jostling is for a seat.
7. The seat is in the auditorium.
8. The auditorium is crowded.
9. She settles down to enjoy the show.

. . . .

1. This happens during the show.
2. The interviewer introduces her guest.
3. She then breaks the ice.
4. She elicits funny stories.
5. She baits the guest.
6. The baiting is with questions.
7. The questions are leading.
8. The questions are calculated to get a laugh.
9. She captivates the audience.
10. The captivating is with her own charm.

. . . .

1. One ignores warnings.
2. The warnings are those of air traffic controllers.
3. The warnings are that their equipment is inadequate.
4. Ignoring the warnings endangers the lives.
5. The lives are of passengers.
6. There are millions of such passengers.

Combination D: To ignore the warnings of air traffic controllers that their equipment is inadequate is to endanger the lives of millions of passengers.

Add any other combinations you can think of.

Note: We have chosen to combine the six sentences above by using a parallel pattern: "To X . . . is to X," as in the words of the song "To know you is to love you." "To ignore the warnings of air traffic controllers" and "to endanger the lives of millions of passengers" are called *infinitive phrases.* See the Glossary for examples of other infinitive phrases.

1. After studying Combination D, combine each of the following sets of sentences into a sentence that imitates that combination. Then combine them in other effective ways.

1. One discontinues negotiations.
2. The negotiations are deadlocked.
3. This destroys the hopes.
4. The hopes belong to the employees.
5. The hopes are for a settlement.
6. The settlement is an eventual one.

. . . .

1. One dismisses the complaints.
2. The complaints belong to the farmers.
3. The complaint is the following.
4. Their profits are too low.
5. This dismissing bites the hand.
6. The hand is of our feeder.

. . . .

1. One eats the food.
2. The food is full of preservatives.
3. The preservatives are unnecessary.
4. They are chemical preservatives.
5. One eats in vain.

. . . .

1. One argues the following.
2. History reflects only the story of the mighty.
3. This ignores the record.
4. The record belongs to people.
5. The people are countless.
6. The people are ordinary.
7. The record is in shaping the course.
8. The course is of events.

. . . .

1. One sits.
2. The sitting is among the monoliths.
3. The monoliths make up Stonehenge.
4. This recaptures the sense.
5. The sense is of the past.
6. The past is distant

2. Now write a series of sentences and then combine them into one sentence that imitates Combination D. Then combine them in several other ways. Choose the one that is most effective.

1. The quarterback searched for his receivers.
2. He was a scrambling quarterback.
3. The quarterback then knifed back to the line.

4. It was the line of scrimmage.
5. He fell on the ball.
6. The falling was to avoid being tackled.
7. The tackling was by two oncoming linebackers.

Combination D1: The scrambling quarterback searched for his receivers, knifed back to the line of scrimmage, and fell on the ball <u>to avoid being tackled by two oncoming linebackers</u>.

Add any other combinations you can think of.

A Note on Punctuation: In our combination, we have used three parallel verbs (*searched, knifed,* and *fell*) which all belong to the compound verb of the sentence. The phrases that go with each of these verbs form a parallel series and, as such, they are separated by commas.

1. After studying Combination D1, combine each of the following sets of sentences into a sentence that imitates that combination. Then combine them in other effective ways.

1. B. B. King cradled his guitar.
2. B. B. King tilted his head back.
3. B. B. King closed his eyes.
4. He did so to set the mood.
5. The mood was for his tunes.
6. The tunes were soulful.
7. The tunes were blues tunes.

. . . .

1. Navratilova matched shot for brilliant shot.
2. The matching was throughout the volley.
3. The volley was long.
4. Navratilova went to the net.
5. She powered the ball.
6. The ball went past her opponent.
7. She won the match.
8. The winning was in sets.
9. The sets were straight.

. . . .

1. Paul Kane left his eastern home.
2. He was a nineteenth-century artist.
3. Paul Kane traveled.
4. The traveling was over the prairies.
5. He lived among the Indians.
6. He did so to record the life-styles.
7. The life-styles are unspoiled.
8. The life-styles were of Native Americans.

. . . .

1. The river meanders.
2. The river is mighty.
3. The meandering is through the valley.
4. The river swells.
5. It does so as it enters the gorge.
6. The gorge is narrow.
7. The river rushes.
8. The rushing is to cascade.
9. The cascading is over a spectacular 80-foot falls.

. . . .

1. The comedian muffed his opening.
2. He was young.
3. He lost his composure.
4. The loss was momentary.
5. He went on.
6. His going on was to win the audience.
7. He won them with his subtle humor.

2. Now write a series of sentences and then combine them into one sentence that imitates Combination D1. Then combine them in several other ways. Choose the one that is most effective.

1. The office tries.
2. It is the student employment office.
3. The trying is to help students find jobs.
4. It does so by introducing them to employers.
5. The employers are prospective ones.

Combination D2: The student employment office tries to help students find jobs by introducing them to prospective employers.

Add any other combinations you can think of.

1. After studying Combination D2, combine each of the following sets of sentences into a sentence that imitates that combination. Then combine them in other effective ways.

1. Moses tried.
2. The trying was to help his people.
3. He did so by leading them to the land.
4. The land was promised.

. . . .

1. Juanita's roommate promises.
2. The promise is to help her.
3. She does so by giving her a course.
4. The course is a crash course.
5. The course is in calculus.

. . . .

1. Copernicus wanted.
2. The wanting was to revolutionize astronomy.
3. He did so by proving his theory.
4. The proving was to his fellow scientists.

. . . .

1. Cicero managed.
2. The managing was to regain his inheritance.
3. He did so by outwitting his guardian.
4. The guardian was deceitful.
5. The outwitting took place at a trial.

. . . .

1. Muhammad Ali hoped.
2. His hoping was to cap his career by the following.
3. He wins the title.
4. The title is the heavyweight one.
5. The winning would be for an unprecedented third time.

2. Now write a series of sentences and then combine them into one sentence that imitates Combination D2. Then combine them in several other ways. Choose the one that is most effective.

1. Black authors have used autobiography.
2. They are authors such as W. E. B. DuBois, Eldridge Cleaver, Frederick Douglass, and Booker T. Washington.
3. They have used autobiography for the following reasons.
4. They examine their lives.
5. They examine their cultures.

Combination D3: Black authors such as W. E. B. DuBois, Eldridge Cleaver, Frederick Douglass, and Booker T. Washington have used autobiography to examine their lives and cultures.

Add any other combinations you can think of.

1. After studying Combination D3, combine each of the following sets of sentences into a sentence that imitates that combination. Then combine them in other effective ways.

1. The firefighters demanded.
2. The demand was for an engine.
3. The engine was additional.
4. The engine was to back up their old one.
5. The old one was outdated.

. . . .

1. Men stole a car.
2. The men were armed.

   3. There were two men.
   4. The car was abandoned.
   5. They stole the car to escape.
   6. The escape was with $8 million.
   7. The $8 million is in securities.
   8. The securities are negotiable.

   1. The band carved.
   2. It was an Indian band.
   3. The Indians were Nootka Indians.
   4. They carved out an area for the following reason.
   5. They called it their own.

   1. Many gardeners store vegetables and fruit.
   2. They are home gardeners.
   3. The vegetables and fruits are to enjoy in the winter months.

2. Now write a series of sentences and then combine them into a sentence that imitates Combination D3. Then combine them in other ways. Choose the one that is most effective.

   1. The following is an accomplished guitarist.
   2. The following is also an accomplished banjo player.
   3. Roy Clark can also play other instruments.
   4. There are eight of these other instruments.
   5. He can play them with ease.

Combination E: An accomplished guitarist and banjo player, Roy Clark can also play eight other instruments with ease.

Add any other combinations you can think of.

A Note on Punctuation: The introductory phrase ("An accomplished guitarist and banjo player"), which is called an *appositive phrase,* is properly followed by a comma.

1. After studying Combination E, combine each of the following sentences into a sentence that imitates that combination. Then combine them in other effective ways.

   1. The following was a $1 million project.
   2. The following was a ten-year project.
   3. The Kinsey Report is based.
   4. The report is the latest.
   5. The basing is on interviews.
   6. The interviews were with homosexuals.
   7. There were 979 interviews.

1. The following is a delicate, winey liquid.
2. *Cidre* adds piquancy.
3. The piquancy is special.
4. The adding is to dishes.
5. The dishes are French Canadian.

. . . .

1. The following is a steamy, 2226-square-mile sultanate on the north coast of Borneo.
2. Brunei sits on petroleum.
3. The petroleum is estimated.
4. The estimation is at 1.6 billion barrels.

. . . .

1. The following was winner of the Kentucky Derby and the Preakness.
2. Affirmed went on to capture the crown.
3. The crown was the Triple Crown.
4. The crown is coveted.
5. The capturing was in the Belmont Stakes.

. . . .

1. The following was a consummate wordsmith.
2. Vladimir Nabokov was one of the authors.
3. The authors are great.
4. The authors are of the twentieth century.

2. Now write a series of sentences and then combine them into a sentence that imitates Combination E. Then combine them in other ways. Choose the one that is most effective.

1. Noam Chomsky believes.
2. Chomsky is the MIT linguist.
3. He is an influential linguist.
4. He believes the following.
5. Children are born with knowledge.
6. It is a potential knowledge.
7. It is a knowledge of grammar.

Combination E1: Noam Chomsky, the influential MIT linguist, believes that children are born with a potential knowledge of grammar.

Add any other combinations you can think of.

A Note on Punctuation: In this combination, we have used an appositive ("the influential MIT linguist") not as an introductory phrase but as one which interrupts the subject ("Noam Chomsky") and the verb ("believes"). Appositives which interrupt the subject and verb in this way are set off by commas. See the Glossary for additional examples of sentences punctuated in this way.

1. After studying Combination E1, combine each of the following sets of sentences into a sentence that imitates that combination. Then combine them in other effective ways.

1. Bede wrote.
2. He was an eighth-century historian.
3. The writing was the following.
4. The Jutes came to England.
5. Their coming was in response to a plea.
6. The plea was from the king.
7. The king was Celtic.
8. The king was named Vortigern.

. . . .

1. Ngo Dinh Diem was overthrown.
2. He was the South Vietnamese president.
3. The overthrowing was by a military coup.
4. The overthrowing was in November 1963.

. . . .

1. Samuel Johnson lent.
2. He was the compiler.
3. The compiling was of the 1755 *Dictionary of the English Language.*
4. He lent the touch.
5. It was the first touch.
6. The touch was of genius.
7. The lending was to lexicography.
8. The lexicography is English.

. . . .

1. *Juke* had a meaning.
2. *Juke* is a word of African origin.
3. The meaning originally denoted "disorderliness."

. . . .

1. Jose Ortega y Gassett described.
2. He was a philosopher.
3. He was Spanish.
4. The describing was of "the look."
5. "The look" comes.
6. The coming is direct.
7. The coming is from some people.
8. The people are charismatic.

. . . .

1. Jacques Tati walks.
2. He is French.

3. He is a movie actor.
4. He walks loosely.
5. He walks as though the parts of his body were somehow discon-
nected.

2. Now write a series of at least six sentences and then combine them into one sentence that imitates Combination E1. Then combine them in several other ways. Choose the one that is most effective.

1. The following happened in the earth seventeenth century.
2. Sir Robert Bruce Cotton collected.
3. The collecting was of relics.
4. They were relics of Britain.
5. It was ancient, pre-Christian Britain.
6. Some relics collected were coins.
7. Some were medals.
8. Some were inscribed stones.
9. Some were manuscripts.

Combination E2: In the early seventeenth century, Sir Robert Bruce Cotton collected the relics of ancient pre-Christian Britain—<u>coins, medals, inscribed stones, and manuscripts</u>.

Add any other combinations you can think of.

A Note on Punctuation: In this combination, a dash is used to mark off the series of items at the end of the sentence (see pp. 428–429 for other uses for dashes). A colon could be used equally effectively in this sentence (see p. 428). Note also that the items in the series ("coins, medals, inscribed stones, and manuscripts") are separated by commas.

1. After studying Combination E2, combine each of the following sets of sentences into a sentence that imitates that combination. Then combine them in other effective ways.

1. The following has happened since its invention.
2. The laser has been applied.
3. The application has been to many fields.
4. The fields are diverse.
5. One field is engineering.
6. One field is medicine.
7. One field is communications.
8. One field is defense.

. . . .

1. The following is as a dancer.
2. Mikhail Baryshnikov has it all.
3. Baryshnikov is Russian.
4. He has strength.
5. The strength is superior.
6. He also has grace.

7. The grace is fluid.
8. He also has dramatic ability.
9. The ability is powerful.
10. He also has good looks.
11. The looks are boyish.

. . . .

1. The following happened in the early twentieth century.
2. Summer W. Matteson photographed the richness.
3. The richness was of tribes.
4. The tribes were North American Indian tribes.
5. One tribe was Hopi.
6. One tribe was Gros Ventre.
7. One tribe was Sechelt.
8. One tribe was Cree.

. . . .

1. The following happened at 9:00 A.M.
2. My brother began his day.
3. The beginning was with his favorite breakfast.
4. It included Big Macs.
5. There were three of them.
6. It also included fries.
7. There was a double order of them.
8. It also included Coke.
9. There was a half-gallon of this.

. . . .

1. The following happened in a dash.
2. The dash was to the North Pole.
3. Robert Peary faced hardships.
4. His companions also faced hardships.
5. The hardships were excruciating.
6. One hardship was cold.
7. The cold was extreme.
8. One hardship was frostbite.
9. One hardship was hunger.

2. Now write a series of sentences and then combine them into one sentence that imitates Combination E2. Then combine them in several other ways. Choose the one that is most effective.

1. The film presents an image.
2. The image is of women.
3. There are three women.
4. They are peasant women.

5. Their faces are stolid.
6. Their hands are spread open.
7. The hands are on their knees.

Combination F: The film presents an image of three peasant women, their faces stolid, their hands spread open on their knees.

Add any other combinations you can think of.

A Note on Punctuation: The phrases with which we have chosen to close this sentence ("their faces stolid, their hands spread open on their knees") are set off by a comma preceding them and are themselves separated by a comma. See the Glossary for a definition of such *absolute phrases* and for other sentences containing such phrases.

1. After studying Combination F, combine each of the following sets of sentences into a sentence that imitates that combination. Then combine them in other effective ways.

1. The twins dressed.
2. The dressing was identical.
3. They were at a disco party.
4. Their short-sleeved plaid shirts were crisp with newness.
5. Their pants were bloused at the boot.
6. The pants were olive green.
7. They were Army pants.

. . . .

1. The couple sat in folding lawn chairs.
2. The couple was elderly.
3. The sitting was at an open-air concert.
4. The couple's shoulders moved jauntily.
5. The movement was with the beat of the music.
6. The music was lighthearted.
7. The couple's feet tapped in unison.

. . . .

1. The architect's house created.
2. The creation was of a sense of openness.
3. The house's spaces were framed with smoky glass.
4. The spaces were large.
5. The spaces were white.
6. The house's stairway was ascending.
7. The stairway was railless.
8. The stairway ascended to a balcony.
9. The balcony was immense.
10. The balcony was brightly lit.

. . . .

1. The precocious dancers evoke the themes.
2. A theme is of courtship.
3. A theme is of etiquette.
4. The girls are casting glances.
5. The glances are intriguing.
6. The glances are over the shoulder.
7. The boys are doing grand jetés.
8. They also do pirouettes.
9. They do them a little numbly.

. . . .

1. Her sister waved.
2. The sister is Dawn.
3. The waving is to her.
4. One hand made an arc.
5. The arc was slow.
6. Her voice faded.
7. The fading was quick.

. . . .

1. Mick Jagger suddenly appeared.
2. The appearing was onstage.
3. His suit was trimmed.
4. The suit was tight.
5. The suit was white.
6. The trimming was with a sash.
7. The sash was red.
8. His sandals were studded.
9. The studding was with rhinestones.

2. Now write a series of sentences and then combine them into a sentence that imitates Combination F. Then combine them in several other ways. Choose the one that is most effective.

1. Parking areas were clogged.
2. Loading zones were also clogged.
3. The clogging was with cars.
4. Terminals were besieged.
5. The besieging was by passengers.
6. The passengers were distraught.
7. The airport was hit.
8. It was a major airport.
9. The hitting was by snafus and snarls.
10. There were unprecedented numbers of these snafus and snarls.

Combination F1: Parking areas and loading zones clogged with cars, terminals besieged by distraught passengers, the major airport was hit by unprecedented numbers of snafus and snarls.

Other Combinations:

A Note on Punctuation: As in Combination F, commas are used to set off the absolute phrases ("Parking areas and loading zones clogged with cars" and "terminals besieged by distraught passengers") from the main clause.

1. After studying Combination F1, combine each of the following sets of sentences into a sentence that imitates that combination. Then combine them in other effective ways.

1. Her hair was neatly coifed.
2. Her dress was crisp.
3. Her dress was also starched.
4. The dress was a shirtwaist.
5. It was red, white, and blue.
6. The ERA opponent distributed bread.
7. The bread was home-baked.
8. The bread was apricot.
9. The distributing was to the assembled legislators.

. . . .

1. His arteries were free of obstruction.
2. His angina was gone.
3. Robert left the hospital.
4. He returned to work.
5. The work was at his old job.
6. The job was at the bank.

. . . .

1. His timing was considerably improved.
2. His fast ball was perfection.
3. The perfection was absolute.
4. Don Gullet fired his shutout.
5. The shutout was his second.
6. The shutout was of this season.

. . . .

1. Its rooms were infested with roaches.
2. Its toilets were clogged.
3. Its showers were out of order.
4. The ship ran into a sea of troubles.
5. It was a cruise ship.
6. It was newly refurbished.

. . . .

1. Its windows are bricked against bombs.
2. The windows are shop windows.

3. Its streets are barricaded.
4. Its thoroughfares are patrolled.
5. The patrolling is by soldiers.
6. The soldiers are British.
7. Belfast is gripped with fear.

. . . .

1. Their profits were dwindling.
2. Their costs were soaring.
3. The soaring was steady.
4. The cattlemen cut their herds.
5. The cutting was by thirty percent.

. . . .

1. Its mood turned suddenly surly.
2. The legislature voted.
3. The voting was against cloture.

2. Now write a series of sentences and then combine them into one sentence that imitates Combination F1. Then combine them in several other ways. Choose the one that is most effective.

● **IV. COMBINED PATTERNS**

---

1. All the newspapers seem to be running columns these days.
2. They are running wine columns.
3. More and more people are going in for wine tasting.
4. These people are also going in for wine one-upmanship.
5. They are also going in for other forms of recreation.
6. The forms of recreation are connected with the juice.
7. It is the juice of the grape.
8. The grape is noble.

Combination A: All the newspapers seem to be running wine columns these days, and more and more people are going in for wine tasting, wine one-upmanship, and other forms of recreation that are connected with the juice of the noble grape.

Add any other combinations you can think of.

A Note on Punctuation: In Combination A, we have chosen to use two main clauses in our sentence ("All the newspapers seem to be running wine columns these days" and "More and more people are going in for wine tasting, wine one-upmanship, and other forms of recreation"). A sentence which contains two main clauses *must* use either a semicolon or a comma followed by a coordinating conjunction to separate the two clauses. In Combination A, we have used a comma followed by the coordinating conjunction *and*. See pages 425–426 for examples of other sentences containing two main clauses.

1. After studying Combination A, combine each of the following sets of sentences into a sentence that imitates that combination. Then combine them in other effective ways.

1. Students are working their ways.
2. There are more and more such students than ever before.
3. Their ways are through college.
4. Their employers find them bright.
5. The brightness is remarkable.
6. The employers find them responsible.
7. The responsibility is consistent.
8. The employers find them aggressive.
9. The aggression is confident.

. . . .

1. Convertibles have always been popular.
2. The popularity has been with the rich.
3. Rolls Royce produces one.
4. It has a roof.
5. The roof is cloth lined.
6. The roof is snugly tailored.
7. It has an interior.
8. The interior is luxurious.
9. The interior is leather.
10. It also has a body.
11. The body could be described.
12. The description would be as "art on wheels."

. . . .

1. The place is Old Town's Bazaar.
2. It is famous.
3. The fame is for its musicians.
4. The musicians are strolling.
5. The fame is for margaritas.
6. The margaritas are giant-sized.
7. The fame is for *enchiladas rancheras*.
8. These are special.
9. They are made with tortillas.
10. The tortillas are dipped in tomatillo sauce.
11. They are stuffed with chicken.

12. They are topped with sauce and melted cheese.
13. They are garnished with refried beans and sour cream.

. . . .

1. All of Britain bubbled with celebration.
2. The jubilee was commemorated.
3. The jubilee was marking the 25-year reign.
4. The reign is of Elizabeth.
5. The commemoration was by a carriage procession.
6. The procession was dazzling.
7. The commemoration was also by a Royal Progress.
8. The progress took place on the Thames.
9. The commemoration was also by bonfires.
10. There were hundreds of these.
11. The bonfires were on beacon hills.
12. The hills are all over the United Kingdom.

. . . .

1. The war hit even harder.
2. It was the Second World War.
3. Tennis courts were torn up.
4. The tearing was to make way for patches.
5. The patches were vegetable patches.
6. Eggs seemed to disappear.
7. The disappearing was by magic.
8. Our leaders encouraged us.
9. The encouragement was to eat pemmican.

2. Now write a series of sentences and then combine them into one sentence that imitates Combination A. Then combine them in several other ways. Choose the one that is most effective.

1. We checked into a hotel.
2. It had no log fires.
3. It had no bar.
4. It had central heating.
5. The heating was effective.
6. It had hot-water bottles.
7. The hot-water bottles were unnecessary.
8. They were in the cupboard.
9. It also had a bath as big as a boat.
10. It also had a welcome.
11. The welcome was affable.

Combination A1: We checked into a hotel which had neither log fires nor a bar, but which did have effective central heating, unnecessary hot-water bottles in the cupboards, a bath as big as a boat, and an affable welcome.

Add any other combinations you can think of.

1. After studying Combination A1, combine each of the following sets of sentences into a sentence that imitates that combination. Then combine them in other effective ways.

1. The workers agreed.
2. The agreement was to a new contract.
3. The contract did not provide for increased benefits.
4. The contract did not provide for shorter hours.
5. The contract provided a raise.
6. It was an across-the-board raise.
7. The contract also provided a clause.
8. It was a cost of living clause.
9. The contract also provided a bonus.
10. The bonus was semiannual.

. . . .

1. Barbara ordered a banana split.
2. It did not have whipped cream.
3. It did not have maraschino cherries.
4. The split had ice cream.
5. There were six flavors.
6. The split also had three bananas.
7. The split also had fruit toppings.
8. There were four of them.

. . . .

1. The doctor recommended an exercise.
2. The exercise would not harm him.
3. The exercise would not tire him.
4. The exercise would strengthen his muscles.
5. The exercise would also increase his lung power.
6. The exercise would also stimulate his heart.
7. The exercise would also improve his circulation.

. . . .

1. Kerry decided.
2. The decision was for the time being.
3. The decision was on an essay.
4. The essay would not challenge her.
5. It would not teach her anything.
6. The essay would satisfy the instructor.
7. The essay would also be painless to write.
8. It would also get a sure C.

. . . .

1. We made an offer on the island property.
2. The property did not have electrical power.
3. The property did not have a water pump.
4. The property did have a tiny cabin.
5. It was made of logs.
6. The property also had a 60-foot waterfall.
7. The property also had a stand of towering hemlocks.
8. The property also had a view.
9. The view was of Howe Sound.

2. Now write a series of sentences and then combine them into one sentence that imitates Combination A1. Then combine them in several other ways. Choose the one that is most effective.

1. The following happens on any weekend.
2. Jack can quite easily sleep.
3. His sleeping is all day.
4. The following happens if he is particularly energetic.
5. He arises before noon.

Combination A2: On any weekend, Jack can quite easily sleep all day or, if he is particularly energetic, arise before noon.

Add any other combinations you can think of.

A Note on Punctuation: In Combination A2, we have chosen to use a coordinating conjunction ("or") to join the verb phrases "sleep all day" and "arise before noon." In addition, we chose to interrupt the two verbs ("sleep" and "arise") with a dependent clause ("if he is particularly energetic"). A clause which interrupts verbs in this way is set off by commas.

1. After studying Combination A2, combine each of the following sets of sentences into a sentence that imitates that combination. Then combine them in other effective ways.

1. The budding gourmet may buy a blender.
2. The following happens if the gourmet's budget is not limited.
3. The gourmet may splurge on a food processor.
4. The processor is a Bosch.
5. It is German-made.
6. It is high-powered.
7. It is expensive.

. . . .

1. Early mapmakers would label uncharted areas.
2. The labeling would be "Terra Incognita."
3. The following happened when the mapmakers wanted to be more decorative.
4. They would fill in the areas.

5. The filling in would be with beasts.
6. The beasts were fanciful.
7. The filling in would also be with monsters.

· ·

1. This happens during good weather.
2. The hang glider can enjoy a glide.
3. The glide is simple.
4. The glide is easy.
5. The following happens as she becomes more experienced.
6. The hang glider can execute maneuvers.
7. The maneuvers are fancy.
8. The maneuvers are technical.

· ·

1. The following takes place in the wild.
2. Caribou may pose.
3. They may pose endlessly.
4. The posing is for the camera.
5. The caribou may streak away quickly.
6. The streaking happens if the caribou sense nervousness.
7. The streaking also happens if they sense fear.

· ·

1. The following happens at the planetarium.
2. Visitors can enjoy the displays.
3. The displays are weekly.
4. The following happens when atmospheric conditions are favorable.
5. Visitors can view the planets.
6. They can also view the stars.
7. The viewing is through a mounted refracting telescope.

2. Now write a series of sentences and then combine them into a sentence that imitates Combination A2. Then combine them in several other ways. Choose the one that is most effective.

1. The SALT talks began.
2. The beginning was two days early.
3. The beginning caught the negotiators off guard.
4. They are chief negotiators.
5. The SALT talks moved to a stalemate.
6. The moving was quick.
7. The stalemate quashes hopes for a settlement.
8. It also leaves participants stunned.
9. It leaves observers stunned as well.

Combination B: The SALT talks began two days early, catching the chief negotiators off guard, and moved quickly to a stalemate, quashing hopes for a settlement and leaving both participants and observers stunned.

Add any other combinations you can think of.

A Note on Punctuation: In Combination B, we have chosen to use two *participial phrases* ("catching the chief negotiators off guard" and "quashing hopes for a settlement and leaving both participants and observers stunned"). Such phrases are set off by commas.)

1. After studying Combination B, combine each of the following sets of sentences into a sentence that imitates that combination. Then combine them in other effective ways.

1. The government has not curbed inflation.
2. That leaves most voters unhappy.
3. The unhappiness is increasing.
4. The government has, in fact, fueled fires.
5. The fires are of inflation.
6. The government backs an increase.
7. The increase is huge.
8. The increase is in the minimum wage.
9. The government promotes increases.
10. They are tax increases.
11. They are Social Security taxes.
12. The government forces a settlement.
13. The settlement is expensive.
14. The settlement is of the strike.
15. It is a coal strike.

. . . .

1. Donald surveyed his batch.
2. It was his latest.
3. The batch was of beer.
4. The beer was homemade.
5. He arranged the bottles.
6. The arranging was lovingly.
7. He arranged them on the shelves.
8. He began to label each one.
9. The labeling was careful.
10. He hummed to himself.
11. He calculated how much money he had saved.

. . . .

1. The following happened in the first decades of our century.
2. George S. Curtis traveled.

3. The traveling was extensive.
4. The traveling was throughout the West.
5. The traveling was throughout the Northwest.
6. Curtis carried equipment.
7. The equipment was complicated.
8. The equipment was carried on the backs of mules.
9. Curtis photographed American Indians.
10. The photographing was in their habitat.
11. The habitat was natural.
12. Curtis captured the flavor.
13. The flavor was extraordinary.
14. The flavor was of their lives.
15. Curtis preserved images.
16. The images are of our native culture.
17. The preserving is for generations.
18. The generations are future ones.

. . . .

1. The four-wheeler sped.
2. It was tough.
3. It was a Cherokee.
4. The speeding was up the road.
5. The road was abandoned.
6. It was a logging road.
7. The four-wheeler kicked up dust.
8. There were clouds of dust.
9. The four-wheeler turned off.
10. It went into open country.
11. It negotiated the terrain.
12. The terrain was rocky.
13. The negotiation was with ease.
14. The four-wheeler headed toward the summit.
15. The summit was round.
16. It was the summit of the hill.

. . . .

1. Bird watchers usually keep lists.
2. The bird watchers are amateur.
3. The lists are species lists.
4. Bird watchers note as many details as possible.
5. The details are specific.
6. Bird watchers become more and more curious.
7. This happens gradually.
8. The curiosity is about their data.
9. Bird watchers conjure up hypotheses.
10. The hypotheses are provocative.

11. Bird watchers plan for more observations.
12. The observations are extensive.

2. Now write a series of sentences and then combine them into one sentence that imitates Combination B. Then combine them in several other ways. Choose the one that is most effective.

1. Professor Williams calls writing "textured."
2. This is the kind of writing that he advocates.
3. The advocating is in his lectures.
4. It is a kind of writing that goes beyond communication.
5. It is the simplest communication.
6. It is the communication of the simplest ideas.
7. It is the kind of writing that goes beyond the plainest of the plain styles.

Combination C: Professor Williams calls the kind of writing that he advocates in his lectures "textured," writing that goes beyond the simplest communication of the simplest ideas, beyond the plainest of the plain styles.

Add any other combinations you can think of.

A Note on Punctuation: The kind of sentence used in Combination C is recommended in Joseph Williams's *Style: Ten Lessons in Clarity and Grace* as being especially effective in that it repeats a term used early in the sentence (in Combination C that word is *writing*) and amplifies on the term in succeeding phrases or clauses. Note that in Combination C we have amplified the term *writing* by saying that it is writing "that goes beyond the simplest communication of the simplest ideas, beyond the plainest of the plain styles" and that we have used repetition of the words *simplest* and *plain* as well. Also note the ways in which commas are used to punctuate this kind of sentence.

1. After studying Combination C, combine each of the following sets of sentences into a sentence that imitates that combination. Then combine them in several other ways.

1. Highly paid network anchors often possess credentials.
2. The credentials are only skin deep.
3. The credentials are based on the look.
4. The look is handsome.
5. The look is blow-dried.
6. The look is of dolls.
7. The dolls are Ken and Barbie.
8. The credentials are based on the sonorous tones.
9. The tones are of Ted Baxter.
10. Ted Baxter is on the *Mary Tyler Moore Show.*

. . . .

1. Aristotle fathered a type of philosophy.
2. We call the philosophy "empirical."
3. The philosophy bases knowledge on observation.
4. The philosophy bases truth on knowledge.

. . . .

1. A Soviet war veteran told.
2. The telling was to a camera crew.
3. They were a visiting crew.
4. They were a *National Geographic* crew.
5. The veteran told them the following.
6. He hoped Russia would protect the peace.
7. He also hoped America would protect the peace.
8. This peace is bread and life.
9. This peace is blood and family to those who have been to war.

. . . .

1. Artists created forms.
2. The artists were black.
3. The artists were jazz artists.
4. The artists were such as Charlie Parker, Eubie Blake, and Duke Ellington.
5. The forms were musical.
6. They were forms that were new.
7. The newness was dynamic.
8. These forms established them as masters of their craft.
9. These forms also established them as legends in their own times.

. . . .

1. The introduction of DDT led to consequences.
2. These consequences touch on the preservation.
3. The preservation is of wildlife.
4. The preservation is also of humanity itself.

2. Now write a series of eleven or twelve sentences and then combine them into one sentence that imitates Combination C. Then combine them in several other ways. Choose the one that is most effective.

3. Here are some free exercises in combined patterns. Combine the following sets of sentences in as many effective ways as you can think of. Then compare them and choose the one(s) you find most effective.

1. A hill was nearby.
2. The hill was steep.
3. We swung off the hill.
4. We did so sometimes.
5. We swung from ropes.

6. The swinging was like Tarzan.
7. The ropes were tied.
8. The tying was to branches.
9. They were tree branches.

. . . .

1. The following is on television.
2. The walls are painted.
3. The walls are in a cell.
4. It is a jail cell.
5. The paint is white.
6. The white is brilliant.
7. The white is glowing.
8. These walls are in a real jail cell.
9. These walls are filthy.

. . . .

1. He made one last attempt.
2. The attempt was vain.
3. The attempt was to make out what I had written.
4. He shook the page loose.
5. He crumpled the page up.
6. He tossed the page.
7. The tossing was in the other direction.
8. The tossing was casual.

● V. FREE PARAGRAPH COMBINATIONS

1. Combine each of the following sets of sentences into one sentence. When you have all the sets combined, you will have written a paragraph on the topic of literacy. Compare your combinations with those of others in the class and decide which are most effective.

1. Congratulations.

. . . .

1. The following happens because you can read this sentence.
2. The following happens because you can transcribe this sentence.
3. You are considered to be literate.

4. The considering is by every country.
5. The countries are in the United Nations.

. . . .

1. The following happens in some countries.
2. This ability to read and transcribe would place you.
3. The placing would be in a minority.
4. It would be a decided minority.
5. The following happens in Afghanistan, for instance.
6. You would be among 12 percent.
7. It is an elite 12 percent.
8. The 12 percent is of the population.

. . . .

1. The following happens in the United States, however.
2. Your literacy consigns you.
3. The consigning is to the majority.

. . . .

1. The following is according to government figures.
2. The figures are the latest figures on literacy.
3. Only one percent of the public is incapable.
4. It is the American public.
5. The one percent is incapable of reading.
6. The one percent is incapable of writing.
7. This small fraction largely consists of farmworkers.
8. They are elderly farmworkers.
9. They are black farmworkers.*

2. Here is another paragraph broken into short sentences:

1. Students should be encouraged.
2. The encouraging should be to think.
3. The encouraging should be to speak.
4. The encouraging should be to write.
5. The thinking, speaking, and writing should be according to their own conceptions.
6. These conceptions are of literacy.

. . . .

1. Teachers should permit freedom.
2. It should be the greatest possible freedom.
3. The freedom is in writing.
4. The writing is students' personal writing.

*Adapted from Robert Pattison, *On Literacy* (London and New York: Oxford University Press, 1982), pp. 3–168.

5. Teachers should do so with these understandings.
6. One understanding is that society at large will not accept ideas.
7. The ideas are ones written in this completely free form.
8. Another understanding is that the speech and writing must be clear.
9. The speech and writing must also be comprehensible.
10. Another understanding is that the students should develop an awareness.
11. The awareness is of the uses of language.
12. The developing is as a result of their own writing.*

● **VI. RECOMBINING AND REVISING EXERCISES**

Most of the following paragraphs appear in student essays in this book. All of them can be improved by revising the sentence structure. Revise the paragraphs, attempting particularly to achieve better sentence variety and coherence through combining or recombining parts of the sentences. Don't hesitate to delete or add words if you want to. Finally, compare your revision to those of others in your class, discuss the relative merits of each, and decide which one(s) are most effective.

[A]   Genetic engineering, or GE, is the popular term for recombinant DNA research, "the directed intervention in the genetic material for the purpose of changing inherited characteristics." Such research ranges from long-established and relatively innocent experiments in producing hybrid varieties of plants and animals to cloning, the creation of a number of genetically identical individuals. Experiments in cloning have brought GE into the public eye recently and have created a storm of controversy. That controversy tends to center on the moral and

*Paragraphs one and two are adapted from Robert Pattison, *On Literacy* (London and New York: Oxford University Press, 1982), pp. 3–168.

social aspects of GE, often overlooking the actual physical dangers that lurk in the experiments.

[B]   In junior high, we saw films and filmstrips on the evils of drinking and taking drugs. These films stated that drinking caused brain damage and cirrhosis and that the person who drank heavily was doomed to become an alcoholic. The description of these films may seem a little dramatic but in essence this is the message that came across to us, the students. Unfortunately, what these films didn't convey was that students who drank were denying themselves the education that could help them in the future. Many of you would dispute that fact very strongly but it may be because you haven't stopped and thought about it. We are aware of the health problems involved, such as brain damage, cirrhosis, alcoholism, and severe depression. But do you realize the effect drinking has on a student and that student's performance in school?

[C]   In the United States alone, there are more than 200,000 Americans who are paraplegic because of spinal cord injuries. About half of the new cases each year are a result of motor vehicle accidents; most of the rest involve accidents from sporting events. The average age of spinal injury victims is 19 yrs. old. Within the past 3 years, researchers have been developing drugs that prevent damage to the spinal cord and testing electronic devices to help restore movement in paralyzed limbs. There is also hope that someday damaged nerves will be regenerated. As of right now, drugs and electrical stimulation are more promising; but work on regeneration will still continue.

Following an accident, there is swelling and hemorrhaging of the spinal cord, and eventually scar tissue forms. Endorphins (pain-relieving proteins naturally present in the body) reduce the flow of blood to the spinal cord after the injury. Researchers have found a drug called naloxone that can improve blood flow to the cord and stop the action of endorphins. Cats have been used in experiments to test the drug. In one experiment, nine cats were injected with naloxone forty-five minutes after their injury. The results showed that three weeks later, two had died, three were normal, and four were spastic. Many experiments, including this one, show that cats have far less paralysis when given naloxone immediately after the injury. In humans, this drug is being used mainly to see if there are any side effects from it. If the drug seems to be safe, then doctors will start using it to lessen paralysis. The problem with naloxone is that it inhibits the actions of endorphins; therefore, it increases the pain of the spinal cord injury patient. Overall, naloxone is a promising drug for the future of paraplegics, but it must be given immediately after the injury.

[D]   Being in the Quad is like being stuck in the army. You have to serve your time before you can get out. You are just another number. You have to share your quarters. You are issued equipment (furniture) to use. Privileges are granted to those who are ranked. There are a lot of strict rules and regulations. There is a lot of mindless yelling and screaming going on. It gets very noisy.

[E]   One Sunday when my family went over to Grandma and Grandpa's house, we didn't eat supper, and Grandma didn't take me for a walk—Grandpa had died. I was awfully young when Grandpa died. I didn't fully understand what had happened. I don't believe my mom and dad wanted me to understand at this stage in life. I can barely remember being at the funeral home. I was afraid to go up by the casket. Instead I played with the letters on the bulletin board which announced the hours of the funeral home. My family spent a few days at Grandma's house after the funeral. It didn't seem like a sad occasion to me. I couldn't understand why everyone was crying. All I thought about was eating all the good food and desserts that the neighbors brought over.

[F]   The attitudes and opinions of a newspaper can also be viewed through its columns. The ability of a newspaper's columnists to acquire interested daily readers is a major factor in that paper's success. A column attracts attention either by exposing to its readers some insight which inspires or rejuvenates them, or by presenting an opinion which is considered controversial but not outlandish. Any column which incites the wrath of a majority of its readers is excessively inflamma-

tory and is a detriment to the paper. Countless times over the past three years, the

columnists of the *Campus News* have exceeded these limits of controversy. Most

recently this was the case with the David Cordell column concerning the home-

coming queen contest. The phrasing and vocabulary used in this column so in-

cited the fury of the students that the paper could focus on little else for the next

two weeks. This example is bad enough but the most flagrant abuse of this basic

rule of responsible journalism occurred last spring, exactly four days before the

running of the Midwestern Grand Prix race. With total disregard for the purpose

and importance of the Grand Prix, George Barry, now head sports editor, printed

a column in which he stated that due to the lack of competitiveness of the Grand

Prix, he would be spending the weekend at Oakwood University watching a truly

great sports event, the Tiny 500 bike race. The unbelievable gall and ignorance

shown by this columnist in calling an event which raises 40,000 dollars annually

for scholarships a worthless waste of time and money and announcing his prefer-

ence for an event at a rival university which loses 7,000 dollars every year was

reason enough for most of the students I know to want to abandon the letter-to-

the-editor rebuttal method and simply form a lynch mob. The writings of this col-

umnist were simply inexcusable, but a tremendous amount of the responsibility for this column ever appearing should be placed on the shoulders of the head editor.

[G]   Not many people would dispute the fact that *Sports Now* is by far the number one selling sports magazine in America as far as quantity is concerned. I used to buy *SN* regularly when I was younger. I didn't care how well an article was written as long as the article dealt with sports. Now that I am older and have learned to appreciate well-written articles. I have become disgusted with the sports reporting that *SN* does. A good sports magazine is one that includes coverage of all sports, employs writers who are experts on the particular sport they cover, encourages objective reporting, and concentrates on factual accounts of sporting events. By these standards, *SN* is not a good sports magazine.

APPENDIX: EXPLORATORY GUIDES

In this text, we have presented detailed discussion and examples of an exploratory guide which leads you to view a subject from three different perspectives—the static, dynamic, and relative perspectives—and hence to both broaden and deepen your understanding of the subject. Page 31 contains the first major discussion of this exploratory guide. You may want to use any or all of the following guides, however, in exploring your subject.

INFORMAL EXPLORATORY GUIDES

A. BRAINSTORMING

This technique, often used in business and particularly in advertising, involves listing any ideas that occur to you about your subject in the order in which the ideas occur and as fast as you can. Brainstorming often works particularly well in small groups. You may ask several friends or classmates to spend thirty minutes with you talking about your subject and brainstorming together, with one person acting as secretary and noting down all the ideas you and your friends come up with. Brainstorming can thus be a good means of generating spontaneous ideas that provide raw material for a paper.

B. SPEEDWRITING

This technique might be called "brainstorming in writing." Simply sit in a quiet place and write your guiding question at the top of a sheet of paper. Set an alarm for the length of time you want to speed write (15 minutes is a good length of time) or have someone agree to call you after the time has elapsed. Then, concentrating on your question, write down everything that comes into your mind, and *do not stop* writing until the time is up. Like brainstorming, this technique will produce irrelevant material, but it may also lead you to a new and surprising insight.

C. LOOPING

This technique is a form of directed speedwriting. It assumes that you have a topic at hand but that you need help getting good ideas about the topic. Professor Peter Elbow, whose book *Writing With Power* describes this technique most fully, uses the metaphors of a "voyage out" and a "voyage home" to describe the process of looping. In the "voyage out" you focus on first thoughts or prejudices about your topic, although you are free to stray as far away from your topic as you want. The aim of the "voyage out" is to lose direct sight of the topic in order to follow the creative flow of your thoughts. The second part of the loop, the "voyage home," asks you to sort through all the new ideas and examples you have generated, select those that give you a new insight into or are particularly applicable to your topic, and use those to produce a new revision that you can eventually use as part of your essay. As with speed writing, looping will provide you with a mass of raw material, and much will have to be thrown away. More importantly, however, the looping process may lead you to a new insight about your topic or your relationship to that topic.

D. MEDITATING

This technique involves thinking in a concentrated yet relaxed way about your subject. You may not think of yourself as using this technique, but most of us do meditate or "think hard" about major problems in our lives, although this activity is seldom visible to other people. When researchers at Harvard's Pre-School Project found that the brightest children spent more time "staring" than they did anything else, the researchers concluded that the children were thinking hard or meditating on some object and that this activity was closely related to how well they learned. If you want to meditate on your guiding question, find an absolutely quiet spot, sit in the position you find most comfortable, and focus your inner attention on your subject until you are lost in thought. This technique may be especially helpful for *incubating* ideas.

● FORMAL EXPLORATORY GUIDES

A. THE JOURNALISTIC FORMULA: WHO, WHAT, WHEN, WHERE, WHY, HOW?

This is probably the simplest and most widely used means of gathering information about a subject, and it has long been used by members of the news media. Although it can be used with all four aims of discourse, it is particularly useful with the expository aim. If you are to write an article for your student newspaper, for example, on a strike that is affecting your campus, the journalistic formula could guide your earliest efforts at gathering information:

1. Who is on strike (what specific groups?)
2. What are the terms of the strike?
3. When did the strike begin and how long is it expected to last?
4. Where are the strikers? Are there picket lines? Where is strike headquarters? Where are negotiations taking place?
5. Why did the strike occur? What issues, demands, or pressures brought it on?
6. How is the strike being conducted? Picket lines? Publicity campaign? Demonstrations?

Answering these questions may not provide the detailed, in-depth information that using the four exploratory views outlined on pages 511–512 may yield, but it may well open doors to your subject and help you gather necessary basic information.

B. KENNETH BURKE'S PENTAD: ACTION, AGENT, MEANS, PURPOSE, SCENE

Burke, a modern philosopher, rhetorician, and literary critic, developed the pentad (which is closely related to the questions asked in the journalistic formula) as a tool for analyzing dramatic events, and it can be particularly useful in writing about literary works. Using the pentad involves answering the following questions and then examining the relationships among various elements in the pentad (which Burke calls the ratios):

1. What is the action? (What is happening?)
2. Who is the agent? (Who is doing the action?)
3. What is the means? (How is the agent doing the action?)
4. What is the purpose? (Why is the action being done?)
5. What is the scene? (Where and when is the action occurring?)

If you use these questions to analyze the poem "Wires," printed on page 327, you will find that (1) the cattle, both young and old, are the Agents; (2) their staying behind the wires is the Act; (3) their blundering into the wires is the Means of their staying; (4) keeping the cattle contained and thus making them old is the Purpose; and (5) the prairie, with its electric fences and wires, is the Scene.

Answering these questions thus helps you begin to understand the poem, but the pentad can do more for you if you look at the possible relationships among the elements of the pentad. In this instance, the relationship between agent and scene seems particularly important, and in fact, it is the contrast between the promise of freedom suggested by the "wide prairies" and the cattle's realization that they "must not stray" which creates the conflict of the poem and generates the ironic tone. By concentrating on the relationship between agent and scene in this poem, you could evolve a focus and gather details from the poem to support that focus.

C. THE CLASSICAL TOPICS OR "PLACES"

This technique, which was first developed by Aristotle, involves asking another set of questions about your subject:

1. What is it? (Calls for *definition*.) If you are writing about a campus strike, for instance, definition will probably play an important role in your investigation: What constitutes a strike in this situation? How

could the terms and issues of this strike be defined? What are the elements of the strike?

2. What caused it? (Calls for establishing *causal relationships.*) Answering this question will also yield important information for an article on a campus strike and would probably reveal a complex web of causes that may lead to any number of hard-to-identify effects.
3. What is it like? (Calls for *comparison and contrast.*) The treatment of *analogy* in this text (see the Glossary) provides a good example of how to use the topic of comparison. In addition to using analogies to point up likenesses, however, this topic asks you to tell what your subject is *unlike,* and doing so may spark a new insight for you.
4. What do people say about it? (Calls for *testimony.*) Gathering testimony, especially by authorities, experts, or other highly respected persons, can often help you investigate a topic. If you choose to use this topic in a paper, however, the testimony you gather must be appropriate to your subject *and* to your audience.

D. LARSON'S TOPIC QUESTIONS

This exploratory guide, developed by Professor Richard Larson, includes 116 questions for a writer to answer. Here we present a shortened version of his guide:

Questions about objects:

1. What are its dimensions?
2. What is it made of?
3. What is its structure?
4. What is it like or unlike?
5. Where does it come from?
6. How does it work?
7. What is it used for?

Questions about happenings:

1. Exactly what happened?
2. How is it like similar happenings?
3. What were its causes?
4. What were or are its effects?
5. What are the implications of these effects?
6. How is it related to other happenings?
7. How might the happening have been changed?

Questions about concepts (abstract terms like love *or* freedom*):*

1. How is the concept defined? By others? By me?
2. How is it related to other concepts?
3. How is it related to my values and the values of others?

4. How does the concept affect me or affect others?
5. What are the characteristics or features of the concept?

Questions about propositions (statements to be proved or disproved):

1. How are key words in the proposition defined?
2. What reasons or proof will I have to offer for the audience to accept the proposition?
3. What are the effects, consequences, or implications of the proposition?
4. What reasons can be brought against the proposition?
5. What other propositions does it take for granted?

E. TOULMIN'S SYSTEM OF ANALYSIS

This final exploratory guide was developed by Stephen Toulmin, a modern philosopher, and presented in his book *The Uses of Argument* and in his textbook *An Introduction to Argument.* His system is particularly helpful in analyzing arguments or in examining your own arguments. We offer here a simplified form of the Toulmin system, which asks that you answer the following questions:

1. What is the CLAIM being made?
2. What are the GROUNDS or GOOD REASONS that support the claim?
3. What UNDERLYING ASSUMPTIONS support the grounds?
4. What BACKUP EVIDENCE exists to add further support?
5. What REFUTATIONS can be made against the claim?
6. In what way(s) is the claim QUALIFIED?

As an example, let us assume you have been asked to examine a brief prepared by a striking union on your campus. You could gather information for your analysis by asking and answering Toulmin's questions: (1) What claim do the strikers make? The claim may well be that the employer should provide increased health benefits, so let's take that as our example. (2) What are the grounds for this claim? After interviewing union officials, you find that health care is inadequate and that a disproportionate amount of the workers' salaries must go to providing health care; they feel these grounds justify their claim. (3) This claim and grounds suggest a number of underlying assumptions which you could examine, the most obvious one being that workers at the college have a right to adequate health care. The underlying assumptions are often omitted from an argument because the writer assumes agreement on them, but it is important in an analysis to uncover and evaluate these assumptions. (4) What backup support could the union offer to support the assumption that they have a right to adequate health care? A clause in their contract, perhaps, or a legal precedent established by other groups in their position? Can you think of any other means of backup support? (5) If the union's brief is effective, it will no doubt have considered possible refutations to its claim and offered answers to these refutations. Your job is to analyze these answers. (6) Finally, you should determine whether the claim is qualified in any way. Are there, for instance, any conditions under which the union would *not* press its claim? If so, these are the qualifications.

Answering Toulmin's questions in the way demonstrated here can thus help you gather information necessary to analyze any argument, whether or not it is your own.

GLOSSARY

absolute phrase   See *Parts of sentences.*

abstract diction   Words or phrases that *do not* refer to things that can be sensed. Usually opposed to *concrete diction.*

EXAMPLES   goodness; sentimentality; justice; complexity; success; immaturity.

adjective   See *Parts of speech.*

adjective clause   See *Parts of sentences.*

adverb   See *Parts of speech.*

adverb clause   See *Parts of sentences.*

affective appeals Appeals to the basic values, attitudes, and emotions of an audience. Use of vivid sense imagery and concrete examples usually makes powerful emotional appeals. See pp. 149–150 for a full discussion of such appeals.

agreement Subjects and verbs are said to *agree* or to be *in agreement* when they are identical in number (either singular or plural) and person (first, second, or third).

EXAMPLES He studies every night. (Both He and studies are singular and third person).

Long plane trips leave me exhausted. (Both trips and leave are plural and third person.)

aim The major goal or purpose of a piece of discourse. In this text, we identify four basic, large-scale aims: the *expressive aim,* which puts major emphasis on the writer; the *persuasive aim,* which puts major emphasis on the audience; the *expository aim,* which puts major emphasis on the subject matter; and the *literary aim,* which puts major emphasis on the language and formal properties of the discourse itself. While any piece of writing may contain all four aims, only one will be dominant (see pp. 20–21 for further discussion of aim.)

alliteration In a phrase or sentence, the recurrence of words that emphasize the same initial sound.

EXAMPLES Prisoners Make Palace-to-Plane Escape.

The prime, proper, private parlors . . .

Colt Defense Clouts the Cowboys.

Drowsy and drugged on honey and happiness . . .

allusion A reference to a person, place, event, or work; usually drawn from history, literature, or mythology.

EXAMPLES His boss was a perfect Scrooge. (The allusion is to the miserly and bitter old man in Dickens's *A Christmas Carol.*)

The old general had finally met his Waterloo. (The allusion is to the battle at which Napoleon was defeated in 1815.)

Since his appointment, the ambassador has revealed a number of Machiavellian tendencies. (The allusion is to the fifteenth-century political theorist Machiavelli, who held that, for a ruler, any means are justified if they attain the end of political power.)

ambiguity Uncertainty of interpretation, usually because the phrase or passage in question could have two or more meanings.

EXAMPLES How did you find your sister? (How did you locate her, or what condition was she in?)

When the Dodgers met the Expos, they emerged triumphant. (Who won?)

No one builds cars like our company builds cars. (Do they build them better or worse than others?)

analogy   An extended comparison between two seemingly dissimilar things. In this text, used especially in the planning stages to help a writer gain a new or enlarged perspective on a subject (see pp. 31–32).

EXAMPLES   Our streams and rivers and lakes are the circulatory system of our nation's body. Their health is intricately linked to our nation's health.

The sixteenth-century English public schools were prisons in which barbarous headmaster/wardens drilled lessons by rote into cold, hungry, stupefied children.

The script for a new movie on the Second World War provides only a comic-strip version of history in which characters are reduced to flat stereotypes with unbelievable dialogue which would easily fit into a bubble.

antecedent   The word for which a pronoun stands.

EXAMPLES
antecedent   pronoun
Elizabeth, who is Jim's youngest sister, arrived at noon today.

antecedent   pronoun
Colleen was in class yesterday, but today she is ill.

antonym   A word having the opposite sense of another word.

EXAMPLES   Evil is an antonym for good; light, for dark; innocent, for guilty; easy, for difficult; hate, for love; bravery, for cowardice; and so on.

appositive   A word or phrase that identifies or extends the meaning of a word that immediately precedes it.

EXAMPLES
appositive
Bill Reid, Northwest Coast Indian artist and author, will speak at our university this week.

appositive
The famous line "Play it, Sam" occurs in *Casablanca*.

case   The form of nouns or pronouns that shows whether they are *actors* (subjective case: I, we, he, she, they), the *receivers of action* (objective case: me, him, her, us, them), or the *possessors of something* (possessive case: my book; his or her coat; their car; Steve's catalog).

clause   See *Parts of sentences*.

cliché   A word or phrase that has been used so often that it has become dull, stale, or stereotyped.

EXAMPLES   The comedian had them rolling in the aisles.

This product is tried and true.

Let's put our cards on the table.

In big business, power is the name of the game.

Divers who raced against time to free the trapped submarine crew later received a heroes' welcome from thankful family and friends.

concrete diction Words or phrases referring to specific things that can be sensed. Usually opposed to *abstract diction*.

EXAMPLES Peanut butter and strawberry jam sandwiches; honk; scratchy; red; fractured ankle; damp and moldy.

conjunction See *Parts of speech*.

connotation The suggested or associated meanings that surround a word; opposed to or in addition to the literal or *denotative* meaning of the word.

EXAMPLES The word welfare denotes health, happiness, general well-being, or public relief. But the same word often connotes a handout or something for nothing.

Odor denotes only a scent or smell, but it usually connotes an unpleasant or bad smell.

The contractors who say, "We don't build houses; we build homes" are counting on the favorable connotations of the word home to help them sell their product.

credibility appeals Sometimes called ethical appeals, these are appeals designed to prove the good will, good sense, and good character of the writer. See pp. 146–147 for a full discussion of such appeals.

declarative statement One which announces or states, as opposed to one which asks a question (*hypothetical statement*) or gives a command (*imperative statement*).

EXAMPLES The ability to use language is the most distinctive characteristic of human beings.

Bob had a Big Mac Attack last night.

This month's rate of inflation was 15 percent.

denotation The explicit or literal meaning of a word; see *Connotation*.

dependent clause See *Parts of sentences*.

editing Usually the final stage in the writing process, *editing* is the final polishing of a piece of writing: checking the format conventions (margins, titles, pagination, spacing, footnotes or bibliography, etc.); and proofreading for errors in spelling, grammatical, or punctuation conventions. See pp. 61–62 and the introduction to Chapter 9 for further discussion of editing.

euphemism An agreeable or inoffensive term that makes an idea or thing more attractive or acceptable to us.

EXAMPLES	A chubby (instead of a <u>fat</u>) child
	The rest room (instead of <u>toilet</u>)
	No credit (instead of <u>failure</u>)
	A tipsy person (instead of a <u>drunk</u>)
	Retrenched teachers (instead of <u>fired</u>)
	Blown away (not <u>murdered</u>) opponent

figures of speech   Expressions that create forceful, emphatic images or descriptions. See *Metaphor, Simile, Hyperbole, Understatement, Personification.*

focus   As we use the term in this text, *focus* refers to a two-part statement which answers your guiding question and hence expresses a basic insight into the topic you are exploring. The focus contains a *subject*, which specifies your topic, and a *point of significance*, which presents your best answer to your guiding question and thus brings new meaning to the subject. See pp. 41–45 for further discussion of *focus, subject,* and *point of significance.*

gerund   An *-ing* form of the verb that is used primarily as a noun. May be active or passive (*driving; being driven*).

EXAMPLES

gerund
<u>Curling</u> is a popular sport in cold, icy climates.

gerund
Vic and Stan enjoy <u>dining</u> in gourmet restaurants.

gerund phrase   See *Parts of sentences.*

guiding question   A question which expresses your puzzlement over a situation, topic, person, or concept, and which will guide your exploration of that topic as you prepare for writing. See pp. 24–28 for a full discussion of this term.

hyperbole   A phrase or statement that is exaggerated or extravagant.

EXAMPLES	Wild horses couldn't keep me away.
	My brother will buy anything as long as it is on sale.
	The long-distance runner's aching feet were on fire.
	The first sip of Martini and Rossi is sheer surprise and every sip after is simply beautiful. A taste like no other on earth.
	His cough was tremendous, vibrant, utterly explosive.

imagistic language (imagery)   Language characterized by the use of figures of speech and vivid descriptions which create pictures in the reader's mind.

EXAMPLES   Straw-hatted and garden-gloved, she was squatting on her hams in front of a flower bed and pruning or tying something up.

Only the eerie green glow of the Cyalume cylinders marked the swordfish 100 yards to starboard, as he began tearing across the inky water and encircling the boat with line.

He had café-au-lait eyes.

The overalls of the workers were white, their hands gloved with a pale corpse-colored rubber.

independent or main clause See *Parts of sentences.*

infinitive The *to* form of the verb, as in *to eat, to sleep, to wake.* May be active or passive *(to know; to be known).* May be used in a sentence as noun, adjective, or adverb.

infinitive as noun

EXAMPLES To graduate with honors is Marni's immediate goal.

infinitive as adverb

He was too frightened to protest.

infinitive as adjective

The union leaders gave the order to strike.

infinitive phrase See *Parts of sentences.*

irony The effect created by a deliberate contrast between a literal statement and its often entirely opposite meaning.

EXAMPLES To do your best writing, simply write down random thoughts on a scrap of paper as they occur to you; then turn it in as soon as you have filled up one side of the page.

The instructions that come with the build-your-own computer are so simple that a child of 35 or 40 can easily follow them.

Tonight's cafeteria specialty, Mystery Meat, is sure to delight your taste buds.

jargon The special technical language of a group.

EXAMPLES While the base line of the trace is an accurate (0.2° per 1000 cy/sec of audio output) and reproducible (± 0.5 percent) measure of the core temperature of the animal, a transistor alone will not detect rapid change of temperature. (from an experimental psychology report)

In Richard Whately's system, all propositions were considered to be subject-copula-predicate in form. All arguments were held to be reducible to syllogisms and syllogisms to be based on the *dictum de omni et nullo.* (from logic)

The director of instructional resources ordered 20 new self-instructional viewing modules. (from education)

metaphor An implicit comparison.

EXAMPLES Let your brush be a dancer, twirling lightly on the palette, leaping deftly to the canvas, and there gliding without a falter or a jerk.

Our life is a candy store, and we are its self-indulgent owners.

Television has become a vast electronic desert dotted only by a tiny, occasional oasis.

mode   A pattern of organization. In this text, we identify four large organization patterns—*description, narration, classification,* and *evaluation*—and provide examples of each mode. See pp. 50–52 for further discussion of mode.

modifier   A word, phrase, or clause that describes or in some way limits another part of a sentence.

EXAMPLES
modifiers   word modified
Her gold earrings glinted in the sun.

modifier   word modified   modifiers   word modified
Working hurriedly, the cook assembled an elegant chocolate mousse.

words modified   modifier
I will meet you after you finish the physics exam.

Free modifiers are those that can occur at the beginning, middle, or end of a sentence, as in the following example: *Clutching his chest,* the stricken man lurched through the door; *or* The stricken man, *clutching his chest,* lurched through the door; *or* The stricken man lurched through the door, *clutching his chest.*

mood   The property of verbs that expresses inquiry or fact *(indicative mood),* condition or possibility *(subjunctive mood),* or command or request *(imperative mood).*

EXAMPLES   I finished the assignment. Did you finish the assignment? (Both verbs are indicative.)

Finish the assignment! (Verb is imperative.)

If I were to finish the assignment, I could go to bed. (Verb is subjunctive.)

noun   See *Parts of speech.*

noun clause   See *Parts of sentences.*

number   The concept of singularity and plurality.

EXAMPLES   Boat: the number is singular, that is, one boat; boats: the number is plural, that is, more than one boat.

object   A noun or noun substitute that is affected by the action of a verb. Often described as answering the questions "What?" or "Whom?" In the sentence "Sam hit the ball," the word *ball* (the object) answers the question "*What* did Sam hit?"

DIRECT OBJECT   The direct receiver of the action of a verb.

EXAMPLE   Mary asked Jim.

INDIRECT OBJECT	The indirect receiver of the action of a verb.

EXAMPLES

indirect object   direct object

Jack gave <u>him</u> the <u>notes</u>.

OBJECT OF PREPOSITION	The noun or noun substitute that follows a preposition.

EXAMPLE

object of preposition

We went to the <u>movie</u>.

OBJECT OF INFINITIVES, PARTICIPLES, AND GERUNDS	The noun or noun substitute that follows an infinitive, participle, or gerund.

EXAMPLES

object of infinitive

The author asked him to read her <u>novel</u>.

object of participle

Adding the <u>eggs</u> carefully, the baker assembled his famous gateau.

object of gerund

Smelling fresh-baked <u>bread</u> is one of the joys of Christmas.

paradox   An apparently contradictory statement that may, after closer inspection, be at least partially true.

EXAMPLES   As Saint Augustine might have said, To know God is to know what He is not.

To be free is to know the limits of constraint.

The truly wise man, said Socrates, knows that he does not know.

parallelism   Repetition of the same structure within a sentence.

EXAMPLES   Unjustly accused, hurriedly tried, and falsely condemned, he became the first political prisoner of the revolution.

The perfect wine is neither too dry nor too sweet, too fruity nor too acid, too mellow nor too bold, but a subtle interplay of all these.

The town, like a dream, had faded, and most of its inhabitants, like chaff, had scattered far and wide.

participial phrase   See *Parts of sentences*.

participle   A form derived from the verb that functions primarily as an adjective. Participles can be present (*-ing* forms: driving; equating) or past (driven; equated). May be active or passive (coaxing; being coaxed).

EXAMPLES

present participle

The <u>driving</u> rain forced her off the road.

past participle

The path was blocked by a <u>fallen</u> branch.

PARTS OF SENTENCES	Although a sentence can consist of only one word (as in *Help!*), most written sentences contain at least one subject-verb unit. This basic unit, however, may be expanded by adding other subject-verb units (called *clauses*) or groups of words (called *phrases*).
subject	A noun, or any word, phrase, or clause that can stand in its place, and including all its modifiers. Usually acts as the topic of the verb.
predicate	A verb and all its modifiers. Acts as a *comment* on the subject.
clause	A group of words containing a subject and a predicate.
MAIN OR INDEPENDENT CLAUSE	Contains a subject and a predicate and can stand alone as a sentence.

subject   *predicate*

EXAMPLE   The batter swung at the ball.

SUBORDINATE OR DEPENDENT CLAUSE	Contains a subject and a predicate but cannot stand alone as a sentence. Subordinate clauses can function in a sentence as nouns, adjectives, or adverbs.

noun clause as subject

EXAMPLES   That we are on vacation no doubt means we will have bad weather all week.

adverb clause (modifies will have won)

If Josh takes first place in the skating championship tomorrow, he will have won three years in a row.

adjective clause (modifies book)

The book that I ordered was out of print.

adjective clause (modifies skater)

The skater, who had pirouetted beautifully, suddenly fell.

phrase	A group of words that functions as a single part of speech but does *not* contain both a subject and a predicate. The most frequently used phrases include:
NOUN PHRASE	A noun and all its modifiers.

noun phrase subject

EXAMPLE   The red fire engine roared down the street.

VERB PHRASE	A verb form that consists of more than one word.

verb phrase

EXAMPLE   The tourists are seeing the sights.

PREPOSITIONAL PHRASE	A preposition, its object, and any modifiers—usually functions as an adjective or an adverb.

prepositional phrase adverb

EXAMPLES   We went to the store.

prepositional phrase adverb

He swam <u>across the river</u>.

prepositional phrase adjective

He bought a car <u>with a convertible top</u>.

prepositional phrase adverb

He bought a car <u>with his savings</u>.

PARTICIPIAL PHRASE   A participle, either present or past, and its object and/or modifiers. Functions as an adjective.

present participial phrase   *prepositional phrase*

EXAMPLES   <u>Tossing their hats</u> <u>in the air</u>, the band members saluted the victorious team.

past participle phrase   *prepositional phrase*

<u>Tossed relentlessly</u> <u>by the waves</u>, the small canoe began to give way.

A participial phrase that occurs in midsentence is set off by commas, as in "The band members, <u>tossing their hats in the air</u>, saluted the victorious team."

INFINITIVE PHRASE   An infinitive (*to go; to do;* and so on) and its subject, object, and modifiers. Functions as a noun, adjective, or adverb.

infinitive phrase as noun

EXAMPLES   <u>To hear Isaac Stern</u> is a rare privilege.

infinitive phrase as adjective

Yesterday was a day <u>to remember forever</u>.

infinitive phrase as adverb

Jenny played the song <u>to make him sad</u>.

GERUND PHRASE   An *-ing* form of the verb, its object, subject, or modifiers. Functions as a noun.

gerund phrase as noun subject of verb

EXAMPLES   <u>Teasing Ian and Kristy</u> is Lance's favorite sport.

gerund phrase as object of verb

Greg enjoyed <u>painting landscapes and still lifes</u>.

gerund phrase as object of preposition

Before <u>ordering the pizza</u>, Gary played the guitar for us.

ABSOLUTE PHRASE   A noun and part of a predicate, most often a participle. Functions independently in that it does not modify a particular word in the sentence.

absolute phrase

EXAMPLES   <u>All differences resolved</u>, the two brothers shook hands.

absolute phrase

The dancers leapt onto stage, <u>faces flushed and expectant</u>.

PARTS OF SPEECH   Traditionally categorized as *nouns, pronouns, verbs, adjectives, adverbs, conjunctions, prepositions,* and *interjections.* In addition, words can be categorized according to their *function* in a sentence (*subject; modifier; object of preposition;* and so on) or their *form* (the *-ed* of most past tense verbs or the *-s* of most plural nouns). One difficulty with systems of classification is that many English words can belong to more than one part of speech and can serve various functions in a sentence. Note the differing uses of *arm,* for example, in the sentences below:

EXAMPLES

subject/noun

Her <u>arm</u> was broken at the elbow.

verb

<u>Arm</u> yourself for a tough debate.

modifier/adjective

<u>Arm</u> wrestling requires great strength.

noun   A word, like *cabbage* or *hat,* that can be made plural (*hats; cabbages*) and possessive (*the hat's owner*).

pronoun   A word that "acts for" a noun. Pronouns include the following categories:

PERSONAL PRONOUNS

Subjective	Objective	Possessive
I	*me*	*my, mine*
you	*you*	*your, yours*
he; she; it	*him; her; it*	*his; her; hers; its*
we	*us*	*our; ours*
you	*you*	*your; yours*
they	*them*	*their; theirs*

REFLEXIVE PRONOUNS   *Myself; ourselves; yourself; yourselves; himself; herself; itself; themselves.*

INDEFINITE PRONOUNS   *All; another; any; anybody; anything; anyone; both; each; each one; either; everybody; everyone; everything; few; many· most; much; neither; nobody; none; no one; one; other; several; some; somebody; someone; something.*

DEMONSTRATIVE PRONOUNS   *This; that; these; those.*

INTERROGATIVE PRONOUNS   Pronouns used to ask direct questions: *who; which; what; whose;* and their combinations with *ever.*

RELATIVE PRONOUNS   Pronouns that introduce noun or adjective clauses: *who; whom; whose; which; that;* sometimes *what;* and their combinations with *ever.* See *Relative clause* under *Parts of sentences.*

verb   A word, like *sing* or *see,* that shows the difference between present (*she sings; he sees*) and past (*she sang; he saw*). If a *verb* can take an object, it is called a *transitive verb.* In "They ate the pizza," *ate* is followed by the direct object *pizza;* hence *ate* is transitive. Some verbs do not take objects, and are called *intransitive verbs.* In the sentence,

"She seemed happy," the verb *seemed* could not be followed by an object and is hence intransitive.

adverb　A word, like *quickly* or *intensely*, that is often compared by using *more* and *most* (*more quickly; most quickly*) and that is often marked by the suffix *-ly*. May modify verbs, adjectives, or other adverbs. This category includes adverbs that answer the questions "When?" (*again; now; soon; immediately; yesterday*); "Where?" (*here; there; everywhere; up; down; inside*); "To what degree?" (*never; only; maybe; possibly; not*); and adverbs that intensify the words they modify (*very; too; quite; extremely; rather; somewhat*).

adjective　A word, like *small* or *happy*, that can be compared (*small, smaller, smallest; happy, happier, happiest*) and that can modify nouns or pronouns. This category also includes words that limit rather than describe nouns, such as the articles *a, an,* and *the,* the *ordinal* and *cardinal numbers*, such as *first* and *second* or *one* and *two*. Note that demonstrative, indefinite, and interrogative pronouns may *function* as adjectives within a sentence.

conjunctions　Words that serve to connect words, phrases, or clauses.

COORDINATING CONJUNCTIONS　*And; but; or; nor; for; so; yet.* The coordinating conjunctions are the only words with which two main clauses can be joined; see *Fused sentence.*

CORRELATIVE CONJUNCTIONS　*Both-and; either-or; neither-nor.*

SUBORDINATING CONJUNCTIONS　*When; since; because; if; although; unless; after; before; while; as; until;* and so on. See *Subordinate clause* and *Sentence fragment.*

preposition　A word, like *to* or *with*, that introduces a prepositional phrase. Most frequently used prepositions include *above; across; after; against; around; at; before; behind; below; beneath; beside; between; beyond; by; down; during; except; for; from; in; near; off; out; over; through; toward; under; until; with; without.* See also *Prepositional phrase* under *Parts of sentences.*

interjection　Words like *Oh!; Ouch!; Ah!; No!;* and so on.

---

personification　A figure of speech that gives human qualities to abstractions or to inanimate or nonhuman objects.

EXAMPLES　Hunger sat shivering on the road.

Tenderly, the night lay its gentle covers over the tired, sleepy earth.

What stunning conjuring tricks our magical mechanical age plays with old mother space and old father time.

phrase   See *Parts of sentences*.

point of view   The position in space and time from which the writer, while consistently maintaining first, second, *or* third person stance, views or considers the topic.

EXAMPLES   Efficient use of time is important for you as a college student. You must arrange class and work schedules so that you have time left over for both study and relaxation. (The use of second person is consistent, as is the present time frame.)

As I walked down the corridor, past closed doors on either side, the point of light at the end became larger and brighter, always brighter. (The use of first person is consistent, as are the past time frame and the spatial relationships.)

predicate   See *Parts of sentences*.

preposition   See *Parts of speech*.

prepositional phrase   See *Parts of sentences*.

pronoun   See *Parts of speech*.

rational appeals   Those which appeal to the reason of the audience by using valid examples, informal reasoning, or deductive chains to support an argument. See pp. 147–149 for a full discussion of such appeals.

reader response   Providing detailed constructive responses to a piece of writing. In this text, we provide a *reader's guide* to help you prepare good responses to your classmates' papers. See pp. 56–61 for further discussion of responding and for the full reader's guide.

relative clause   Adjective clause introduced by a relative pronoun.

revising   Reworking major aspects of focus, development, organization, or style. See pp. 61–64 for a full discussion of revising.

satire   The use of irony, derision, sarcasm, and wit to expose foolishness or evil.

EXAMPLES   In *Babbitt*, Sinclair Lewis satirizes Middle America as he depicts an annual convention of realtors: "In the midst of these more diffident invitations, the golden doors of the ballroom opened with a blatting of trumpets, and a circus parade rolled in. It was composed of the Zenith brokers, dressed as cowpunchers, bareback riders, Japanese jugglers. As a clown, beating a bass drum, extraordinarily happy and noisy, was Babbitt . . . . Their coats were off, their vests were open, their faces red, their voices emphatic. They were finishing a bottle of corrosive bootlegged whiskey and imploring the bellboy, 'Say, son, can you get us some more of this embalming fluid?'"

Woody Allen's "The Whore of Mensa," from which the following excerpt is taken, opens with a "private investigator" listening to his "client": "Well, I heard of this young girl. Eighteen years old. A Vassar student. For a price, she'll come over and discuss any subject—Proust, Yeats, anthropology. Exchange of ideas . . . . I mean, my wife is great, don't get me wrong. But she won't discuss Pound with me. Or Eliot. I didn't know that when I married her . . . . Whenever I have that craving, I call Flossie. She's . . . . a master's in comparative lit."

sexist language   Terms or phrases which discriminate in favor of members of one sex. Some terms, such as *chairmen, postmen,* or the salutation *Dear Sirs* used to address people whose names are unknown, imply that only *men* hold such positions. Other terms, such as *lady doctor, poetess,* or *male nurse,* call unnecessary attention to gender and are hence sexist. Sexism is also evident when a speaker or writer fails to use the same kind of terminology in referring to men and women, as when an office worker refers to male workers as *colleagues* but to female workers as *the girls* or when a professor refers to the poets Longfellow and *Miss* Dickinson. Such sexist language—or the stereotyping of terms such as *broad, chick,* or *babe*—can be fairly easy to recognize and control. More troublesome for writers are decisions they must make about the use of the pronouns *he, his,* and *him.* Until recently, the sentence "Each student must bring his books to class" was commonly used to refer to both male and female students. Today, however, we are more aware of the sexist implications of the habitual use of *his* in such expressions. The simplest way to avoid this form of sexist language is to use the plural whenever possible ("Students must bring *their* books to class"). If you cannot use the plural, then omit all unnecessary pronouns (replace "Each student must bring his books to class" with "Books must be brought to class") or use the more awkward *he or she* or *his or her* ("Each student must bring his or her books to class").

simile   An explicit comparison between two things typically considered unlike.

EXAMPLES   Like ancient trees, we die from the top.

Phantomlike, she slipped past the waiting soldiers.

He had chirped, like an irate bird, in my ear all day long.

He was as bold as a buck in springtime.

subordinate or dependent clause   See *Parts of sentences.*

symbol   The representation of a concept, usually by association, and especially with a material object. For most people, the dove symbolizes peace; the river, time; the sun, life.

EXAMPLES   During our recent family crisis, my mother was a veritable Rock of Gibraltar. (symbol of permanence)

To many North Americans, the golden arches of McDonald's restaurants symbolize one thing: a fast, reasonably priced meal.

synonym   A word that has the same, or almost the same, meaning as another.

EXAMPLES   Fiery is a synonym for <u>burning</u>; damp, for <u>moist</u>; <u>incredible</u>, for <u>unbelieva-</u><u>ble</u>; peak, for <u>pinnacle</u>; <u>start</u>, for <u>originate</u>; <u>book</u>, for <u>tome</u>.

syntax   The pattern of word order in phrases and sentences. A *subordinate clause* is one syntactic pattern; a *main* or *independent clause* is another.

tense   Although *tense* is a technical term, we will use it loosely here to refer to that property of verbs that allows them to express time (see p. 411).

EXAMPLES

Present:	She talks.
Past:	She talked.
Future:	She will talk.
Present perfect:	She has talked.
Past perfect:	She had talked.
Future perfect:	She will have talked.

understatement   The deliberate representation of something as of much less magnitude than it really is. Understatement and its counterpart, *hyperbole*, are generally regarded as types of *irony*.

EXAMPLES   After hurling a million profanities at his opponent, Jack ran mad with spleen, spite, and hatred; in short, here began a breach between the two (from Jonathan Swift: The first part of the sentence exemplifies *hyperbole*; the second part exemplifies *understatement*).

In defusing the live bomb, the squad handled a rather delicate situation efficiently.

It isn't very serious. I have this tiny little tumor on the brain (from J. D. Salinger).

verb   See *Parts of speech*.

verbal   *Participles, gerunds,* and *infinitives*, the three verbal forms, resemble verbs but do not function as verbs.

voice   The property of verbs that indicates whether the subject of the verb is an *actor* (active voice) or *acted upon* (passive voice).

EXAMPLES

	Active voice	Passive voice
Present:	He asks.	He is asked.
Past:	He asked.	He was asked.
Future:	He will ask.	He will be asked.
Present perfect:	He has asked.	He has been asked.
Past perfect:	He had asked.	He had been asked.
Future perfect:	He will have asked.	He will have been asked.

INDEX

Abbreviating, 444–445
Abstracts, 234
Affective appeals, 146, 149–
    150, 193–195, 385
Agreement
    pronoun and antecedent,
        412–413
    subject and verb, 411–412
Aim. *See also* Expository aim;
    Expressive aim;

Informative expository
    aim; Literary aim;
    Persuasive aim; Scientific
    expository aim
definition, 21
dual, 367–368
informative, 269–270
in research writing, 223–225
Analogy, 90
Analogizing. *See* Exploration

Annotating, 236–237
Antecedent, 412–413
Apostrophes, 430
Appeals, 368
    affective, 146, 149–150,
        193–195, 385
    classification techniques, 149
    descriptive techniques, 148
    narrative techniques, 148–
        149

Appeals *(Continued)*
    in persuasive writing, 145–
        150, 190–191
    in reports, 385–386
Audience
    in critical papers, 326–327
    in essay examinations, 301
    in expository writing, 228,
        343–344
    in expressive writing, 45–48,
        53, 86–88
    in persuasive writing, 142–
        143
    primary, 228
    in reports, 380–381
    in research papers, 228, 259–
        260
    role, 46, 86–87, 142, 157–
        159, 190–191, 301, 380–
        381
    voice, 46–47, 87, 301, 381
Audience guide
    in expressive writing, 47–48
    in persuasive writing, 142–
        143
    in research papers, 260–261

Bibliography
    cards, 237–239
    in research papers, 232, 271–
        272
Biographies, 234
Brackets, 429–430
Brainstorming, 511
Burke's Pentad, 513

Capitalizing, 441–442
Card catalog, 233
Case, 414–415
Citation
    in research papers, 267–268
Citizen writing, 9
Colon, 428
Classical topics, 513–514
Classification mode
    in critical papers, 347
    in persuasive writing, 89–91
    in research papers, 264

Classification techniques, 149
Classifying. *See* Exploration
Clichés, 104–105
Clustering, 82
Coherence, 94–101
    in paragraphs, 97
Commas, 425–426
Comma splices, 419–420
Comparing. *See* Exploration
Comparison and contrast, 90
Conclusions
    in critical papers, 346
    in persuasive writing, 201
    in research papers, 262–263
Concrete diction, 107–109
Connotation, 156–157
Consumer writing, 8–9
Contrasting. *See* Exploration
Conventions. *See also*
        Grammatical conventions;
        Mechanical conventions;
        Punctuation conventions;
        Spelling conventions
    defined, 408–409
    in expressive writing, 63
    in research papers, 270–271
Core sentence, 97–99
Credibility appeals, 145, 193–
        194, 385
    strategies for, 146–147
Critical papers
    audience, 326–327
    focus, 342
    guiding question, 326
    modes, 345–346
    reader guide, 353–354
    reader responses, 353
    situation, 326–327

Dangling and misplaced
        modifiers, 420–421
Dashes, 428–429
Deductive chain, 196–197
Defining, in essay
        examinations, 310
Denial, 207
Denotation, 156–157
Descriptive mode
    in critical papers, 347

in expressive writing, 50–51
    in research papers, 263
Descriptive techniques, 148
Development
    in expressive writing, 53–55,
        57, 62–63
    in persuasive writing, 145–
        150, 166–167, 194–197
Dewey decimal system, 235
Diagramming the paragraph,
        99
Diction, 333. *See also* Style
    concrete, 54, 107–109
    in expository writing, 349
    in expressive writing, 103
    inflated, 104
    in persuasive writing, 156
    in reports, 386–387
Dictionaries, 234
Distinction, 207
Documentation forms. *See*
        Bibliography
Dual aims, 367–368
Dynamic view. *See* Exploration

Editing, 408–410. *See also*
        Grammatical conventions;
        Mechanical conventions;
        Punctuation conventions;
        Revising and editing;
        Spelling conventions
Essay examinations, 299–324
    audience, 301
    exploration, 302–303
    expository aim, 300
    focus, 309
    guiding questions, 300
    incubation, 307
    organization, 309–311
    problems, 299–300
    reader responses, 315–316
    style, 318–319
Ethnograph, 11
Evaluative mode
    in critical papers, 347
    in essay examinations, 311
    in persuasive writing, 181,
        199–201
    in reports, 384–385

Explaining, in essay
    examinations, 310–311
Exploration
    in critical papers, 331–332
    in essay examinations, 302–303
    in expository writing, 230
    in expressive writing, 30–32, 78–79
    in persuasive writing, 130–131
    in reports, 371–372
    in research papers, 230
Exploratory guides, 511–516
    alternative, 81–82
    brainstorming, 511
    classical topics, 513–514
    in critical papers, 335, 338–339
    in essay examinations, 302–303
    in expository writing, 335
    in expressive writing, 78–79
    free writing, 511
    journalistic, 512–513
    Kenneth Burke's Pentad, 513
    Larson's topic questions, 514–515
    looping, 511–512
    meditating, 512
    in reports, 372
    Toulmin's system of analysis, 515–516
Expository aim
    audience, 259–260, 301–302, 343–344
    diction, 333, 349
    in critical papers, 325
    in essay examinations, 300
    exploration, 302–303
    first version, 348–350
    focus, 309
    guiding question, 225–226, 300, 326
    incubation, 307
    informative expository aim, 224–225, 269–270
    modes, 345–346
    organization, 309–311, 345–346

reader guide, 353–354
reader responses, 353
revising and editing, 357
scientific expository aim, 225
sentence patterns, 349–350
sentence structure, 334
situations, 225–226, 228, 326–327
style, 272–273, 318–319, 333–334, 348–350, 386–388
Expressive aim
    audience, 45–47, 86–87
    audience guide, 47–48
    classification mode, 89–91
    defined, 21
    development of, 62–63
    exploration, 30, 78–79
    first version, 53, 94–97
    focus, 41–43, 62, 84
    guiding question, 23–24, 74–75
    incubation, 41
    modes, 50
    organizational plans, 89–90
    reader guide, 57–58
    reader responses, 56, 111
    revising and editing, 61–67, 114
    situations, 27, 41–44, 74, 76, 84
    starting guide, 24
    style, 53–54, 103–105

Fact, in research papers, 269–270
Figures of speech, in
    expressive style, 103
First version
    of critical papers, 348
    of expository writing, 348–350
    of expressive writing, 53, 94–101
    of persuasive writing, 156–159, 204
    of reports, 386–388
    of research papers, 266–267, 273

Focus, 62
    in critical papers, 342
    in essay examinations, 309
    in expository writing, 256–257, 342
    in expressive writing, 41–43, 53, 62, 84
    in persuasive writing, 139
    in reports, 377–378
Format
    for final paper, 440–441
    for report, 384–385
Free writing, 511
Fused sentences, 419

Grammatical conventions
    agreement between pronoun and antecedent, 412–413
    agreement between subject and verb, 411–412
    case, 414–415
    comma splices, 419–420
    dangling and misplaced modifiers, 420–421
    fragments, 417–418
    fused sentences, 419
    number, 410
    parallelism, 421–422
    pronoun reference, 413
    sentence faults, 417–419
    tense, 411–412
Guiding question
    in critical papers, 326
    in essay examinations, 300
    in expository writing, 225–226, 326
    in expressive writing, 23–24, 25–26, 74–75
    in persuasive writing, 124–125, 175–176
    in reports, 368–369

Hyphenating, 445–446

Idiolect, 103
Imagery, 332
Incorporating a source, 255
Incubation
    in essay examinations, 307

Incubation (*Continued*)
  in expository writing, 256–257
  in expressive writing, 41
  in persuasive writing, 139
  in reports, 377
Inference, in research papers, 269–270
Informative expository aim, 224–225, 269–270
Informative focus, 257
Insight
  in expressive writing, 42
  in persuasive writing, 139
Introduction
  in critical papers, 346
  in persuasive writing, 199
  in research papers, 262–263
Italicizing, 443

Journalistic formula, 512

Larson's topic questions, 514–515
Library of Congress system, 235
Literary aim, 21
Looping, 511–512

Mechanical conventions, 440–446
  abbreviating, 444–445
  capitalizing, 441–442
  hyphenating, 445–446
  italicizing, 443
  numbering, 443–444
  preparing final copy, 440–441
  quoting, 442–443
Meditating, 512
Modes as content, 51–52
Modes of organization, 50. *See also* Classification mode; Descriptive mode; Evaluative mode; Narrative mode
Modifiers, 420–421

Narrative mode
  in expressive writing, 51
  in persuasive writing, 199–201
  in research papers, 263
Narrative techniques, 148–149
Newspapers, researching, 234
Note cards, 252–254
Notetaking, 241–243
Number, 95–96, 410
Numbering, 443–444

Organization. *See also* Classification mode; Descriptive mode; Evaluative mode; Narrative mode
  in expressive writing, 50–52, 63, 89–91
  in persuasive writing, 151–152, 199–201
Organizational plans, 263–264
  in critical papers, 346
  in essay examinations, 309–311
  in persuasive writing, 201

Paragraphs, 96–101, 333
Parallelism, 421–422
Paraphrasing, 254–255
Parentheses, 429–430
Passive voice, 107–108
Pentad, 513
Periodicals, researching, 233
Periods, 424–425
Person, 95–96
Persona, 333
Persuasive aim
  affective appeals, 194–195
  appeals, 145–150, 190–191
  audience, 178, 187–188
  deductive chain, 196–197
  definition, 123
  diction, 156–157
  evaluative mode, 181
  exploration, 180–181
  focus, 187
  guiding question, 175–176

  incubation, 139
  modes, 190–191
  situations, 175–176
  style, 209
Persuasive appeals, 145–150
Persuasive plans, 152–153
Plagiarism, 241–242, 254–255
Poetry, 331–335, 345
Pronoun reference, 413
Proof, 151–152
  in persuasive writing, 199–201
Punctuation conventions, 424–430
  apostrophes, 430
  brackets, 429–430
  colons, 428
  commas, 425–426
  dashes, 428–429
  parentheses, 429–430
  periods, 424–425
  semicolons, 426–428

Quotations
  in expository writing, 349–350
  in research papers, 268–269
Quoting, 442–443

Rational appeals, 145–146, 147–148, 195–196, 385
Reader guide
  in critical papers, 353–354
  in expressive writing, 57–58
  in persuasive writing, 163, 211–212
  in reports, 393–394
  in research papers, 278–279
Reader responses
  in critical papers, 353
  in essay examinations, 315–316
  in expressive writing, 56, 111
  in persuasive writing, 162–163, 211–212
  in reports, 393
  in research papers, 278

Recommendations, in reports, 377–378
Reference tools, 233–234
Refutation, 152, 206–207
Relative view. *See* Exploration
Reports
    appeals, 385–386
    audience, 380–381
    exploration, 371–372
    first version, 386–388
    focus, 377–378
    guiding question, 368–369
    incubation, 377
    modes, 384–385
    reader guide, 393–394
    reader responses, 393
    recommendations, 377–378
    revising and editing, 397–398
    situation, 368–369, 377–378
Research papers
    annotating, 236–237
    audience, 259–260
    bibliography, 232
    bibliography cards, 237–239
    citation, 267–268
    first version, 266–267
    focus, 256–257
    modes, 262–265
    notetaking, 241–243, 254–255
    organizing, 262–264
    plagiarism, 254–255
    quotation, 268–269
    reader responses, 278
    reference tools, 233–234
    revising and editing, 284
    style, 272–273
Retort, 207
Revising and editing
    critical papers, 357
    essay exams, 318–319
    expressive writing, 61–63, 61–67, 114
    persuasive writing, 166–167, 214
    reports, 397–398

research papers, 284
Rhyme, 334
Rhythm, 334
Role. *See* Audience

Scientific expository aim, 225
Semicolons, 426–428
Sentence-combining, 449–509
    clausal expansion, 455–465
    combined patterns, 492–502
    free paragraph combinations, 502–504
    phrasal expansion, 465–492
    recombining and revising, 504–509
    simple expansion, 450–454
Sentence faults, 417–419
Sentence patterns
    in expository writing, 349–350
    in persuasive writing, 157–158
    in reports, 387–388
Sentence structure, 334. *See also* Sentence-combining; Sentence patterns
Situations and potential situations
    expository writing, 225–226, 228
    expressive writing, 23–24, 27–28, 41–44, 74, 76, 84
    persuasive writing, 127–128, 175–176, 178
    primary and secondary, 28
    reports, 368–369
Spelling conventions, 433–438
    doubling consonants, 435–436
    ie/ei, 433–434
    inventory, 437–438
    prefixes, 437
    -sede, -ceed, -cede, 436
    sound alike, 436–437
    suffixes, 437
    unpronounced *e,* 434–435
Stanza, 333

Starting guide, in expressive writing, 24–25
Static view. *See* Exploration
Style, 386–388. See also Grammatical conventions; Mechanical conventions; Punctuation conventions; Spelling conventions; Sentence-combining
    coherence, 94–95
    in expository writing, 272–273, 318–319
    in expressive writing, 53–55, 63, 103–105
    imagery, 332
    in persuasive writing, 209
    sentence patterns, 157–158, 349–350
    transitions, 95–96
    unity, 94–95

Tense, 96, 411–412
Texture, 100
Toulmin's system of analysis, 515–516
Transitions, 95–96

Underlining. *See* Italicizing
Unity, 94–101
    of paragraphs, 97

Validity of reasoning, 197
Voice. *See* Audience

Worlds of writing, 5
    college, 9–11
    private, 6–8
    public, 8–9
    working, 11–12
Writing
    as learning, 12–13
    as process, 21–22
    as a record of meaning, 13–15
    as a whole-brained activity, 15–16

Editing Symbols